Princess Jellyfish 05

Akiko Higashimura

D0534197

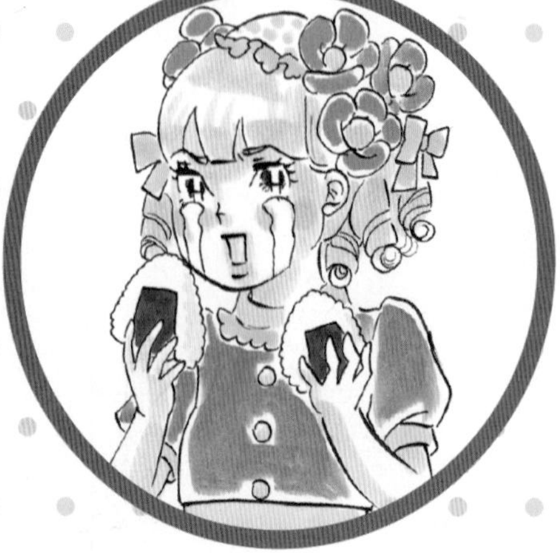

DEAREST READERS!

IT'S SUPER EASY FOR AN AMARS TO GET BY IN THIS DAY AND AGE BECAUSE NOW, YOU CAN BUY ***ANYTHING*** ONLINE! SO BEGINS THE DOWNWARD SPIRAL! EVERY DAY, IN THE DEAD OF NIGHT, I ADD TONS OF DVDS OF MORNING DRAMAS TO MY SHOPPING CART. I'VE OFFICIALLY REACHED OVER 50,000 POINTS ON RAKUTEN, AN ONLINE STORE! ***SOMEONE PLEASE STOP ME!***

–AKIKO HIGASHIMURA

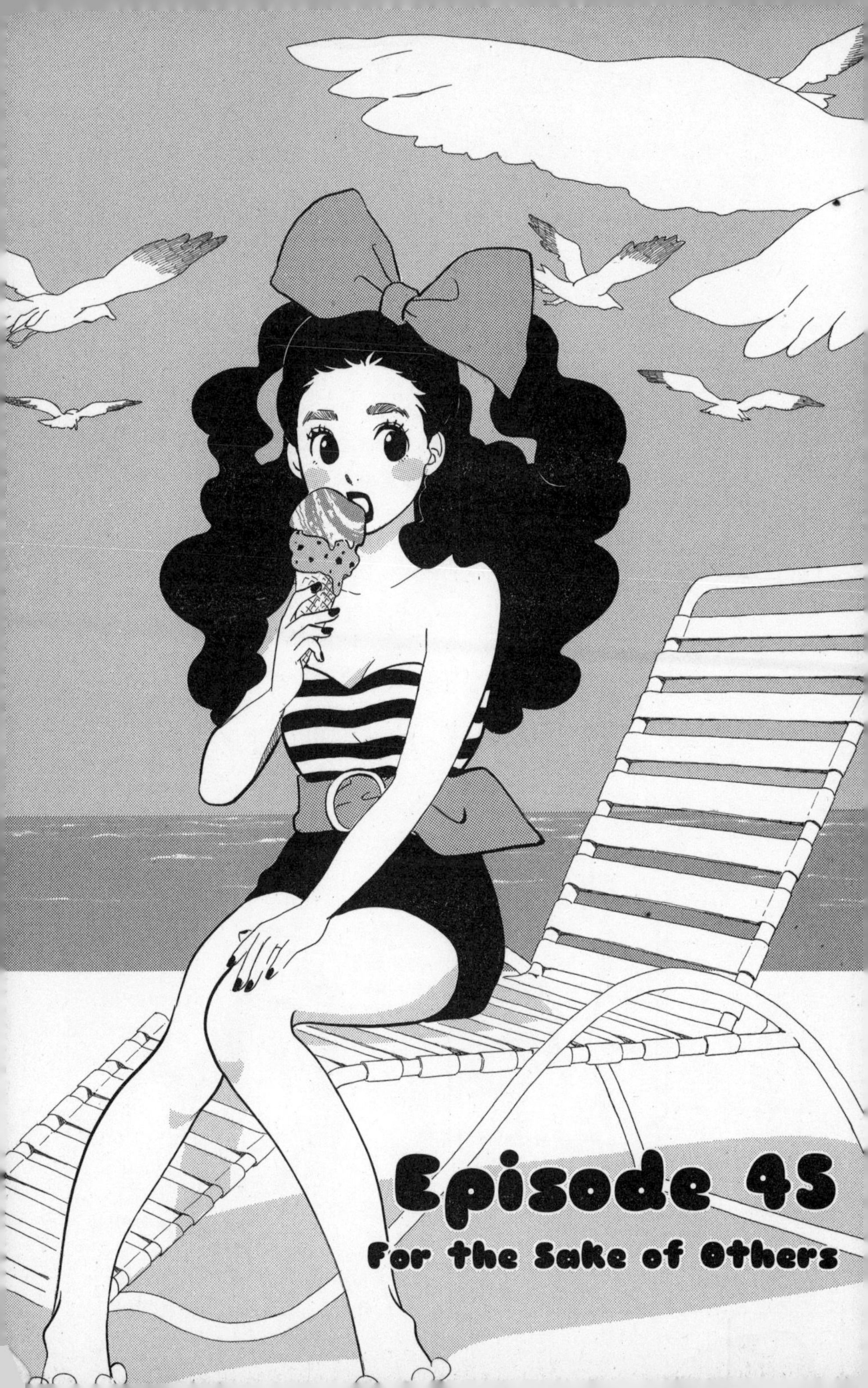
Episode 45
For the Sake of Others

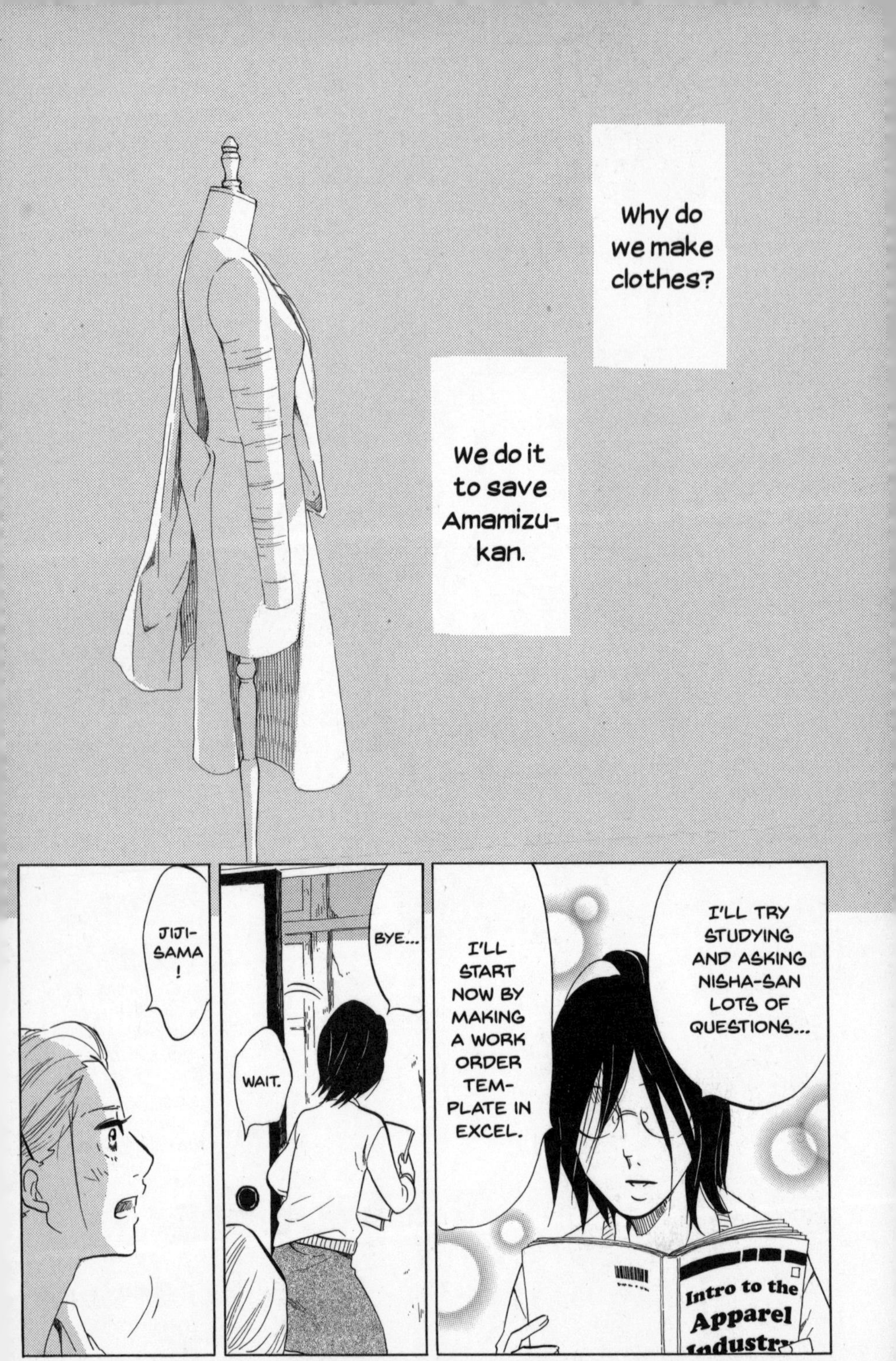
Why do we make clothes?
We do it to save Amamizukan.
I'LL TRY STUDYING AND ASKING NISHA-SAN LOTS OF QUESTIONS...
I'LL START NOW BY MAKING A WORK ORDER TEMPLATE IN EXCEL.
Intro to the Apparel Industr
BYE...
WAIT.
JIJI-SAMA!

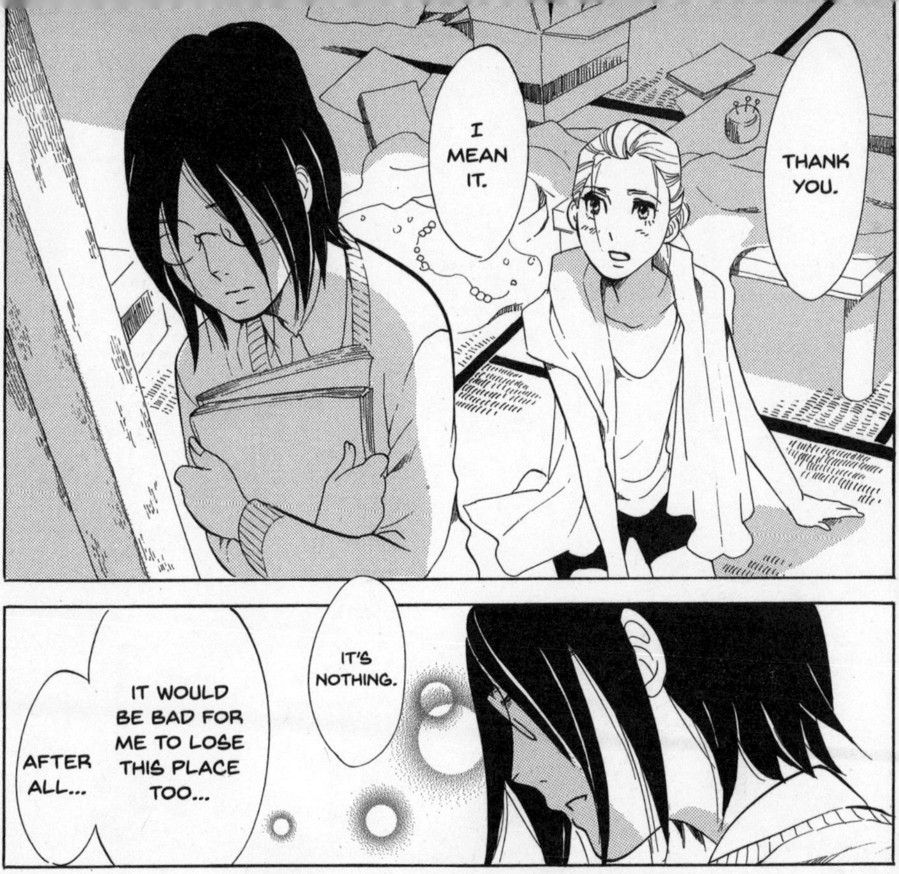
THANK YOU.
I MEAN IT.
IT'S NOTHING.
IT WOULD BE BAD FOR ME TO LOSE THIS PLACE TOO...
AFTER ALL...

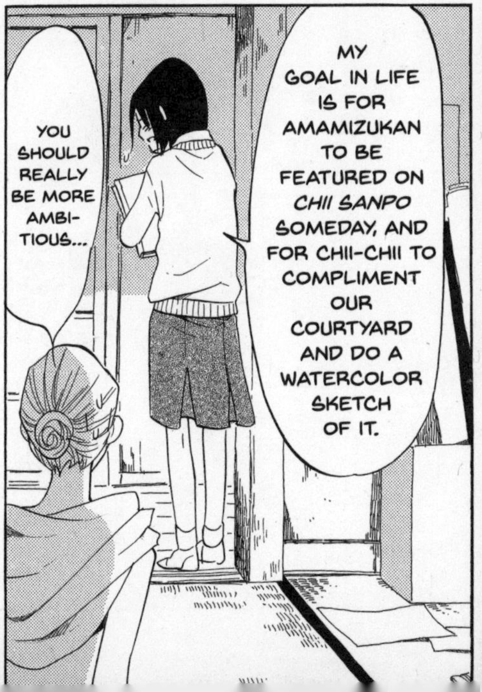
MY GOAL IN LIFE IS FOR AMAMIZUKAN TO BE FEATURED ON *CHII SANPO* SOMEDAY, AND FOR CHII-CHII TO COMPLIMENT OUR COURTYARD AND DO A WATERCOLOR SKETCH OF IT.
YOU SHOULD REALLY BE MORE AMBI-TIOUS...

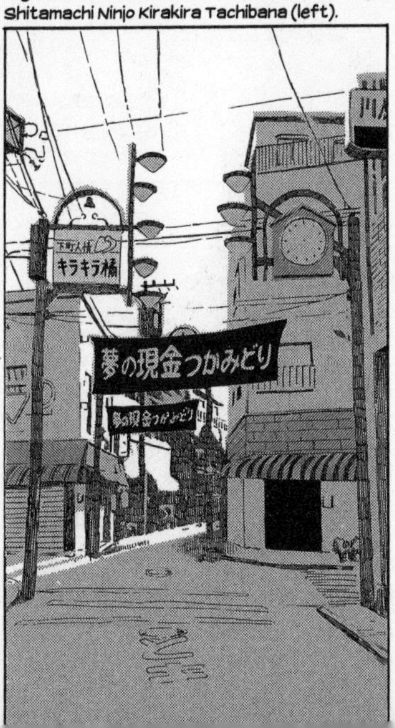
キラキラ橘
夢の現金つかみどり

Signs: "Grab the Cash of Your Dreams" Game (center). Shitamachi Ninjo Kirakira Tachibana (left).

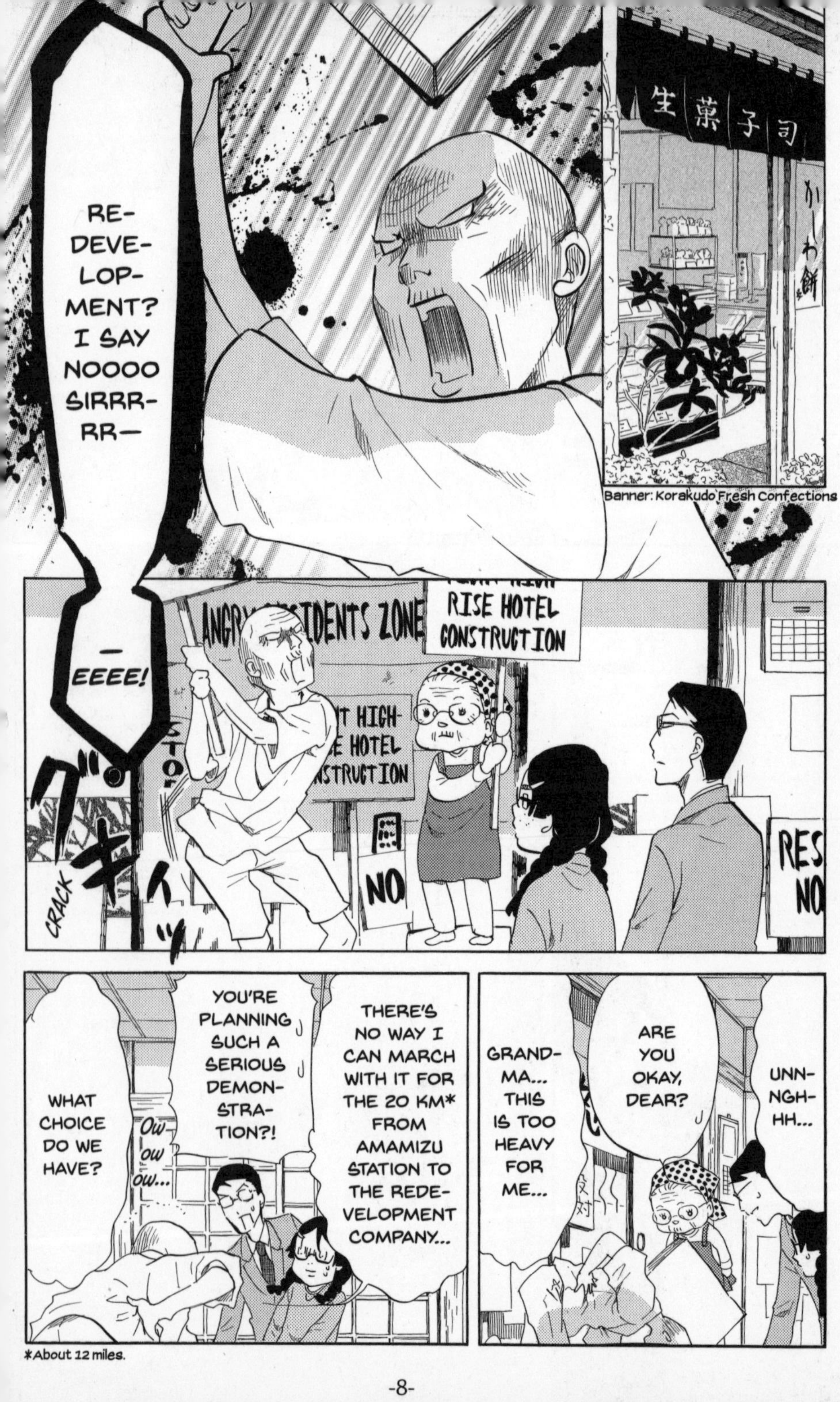
生菓子司
Banner: Korakudo Fresh Confections
RE-DEVELOPMENT? I SAY NOOOO SIRRRRR—
—EEEE!
RISE HOTEL CONSTRUCTION
ANGRY RESIDENTS ZONE
HIGH-RISE HOTEL CONSTRUCTION
NO
RES NO
CRACK
UNN-NGH-HH...
ARE YOU OKAY, DEAR?
GRAND-MA... THIS IS TOO HEAVY FOR ME...
THERE'S NO WAY I CAN MARCH WITH IT FOR THE 20 KM* FROM AMAMIZU STATION TO THE REDEVELOPMENT COMPANY...
YOU'RE PLANNING SUCH A SERIOUS DEMONSTRATION?!
OW OW OW...
WHAT CHOICE DO WE HAVE?

*About 12 miles.

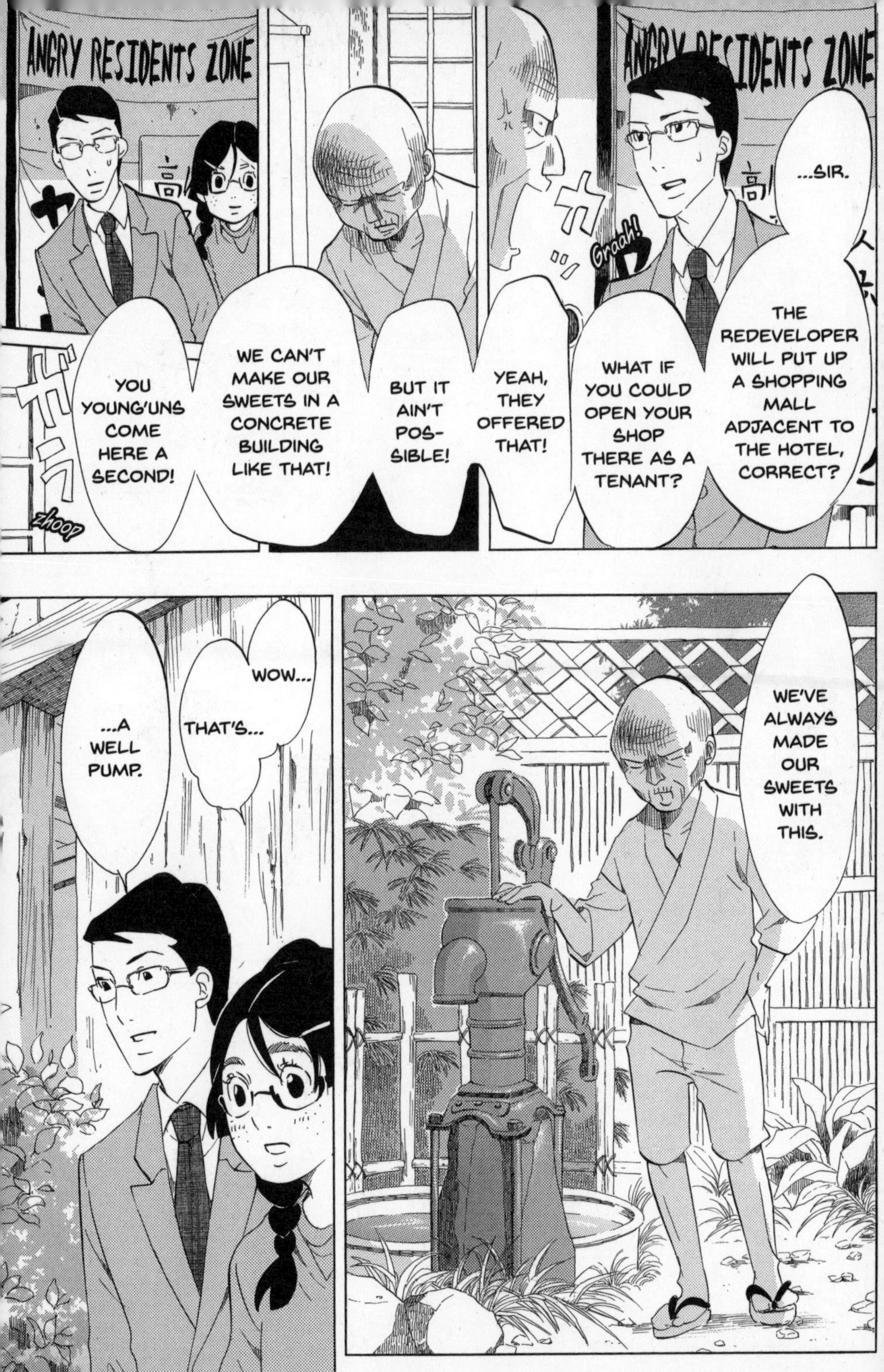
ANGRY RESIDENTS ZONE
...SIR.
THE REDEVELOPER WILL PUT UP A SHOPPING MALL ADJACENT TO THE HOTEL, CORRECT?
WHAT IF YOU COULD OPEN YOUR SHOP THERE AS A TENANT?
Graah!
YEAH, THEY OFFERED THAT!
BUT IT AIN'T POS-SIBLE!
WE CAN'T MAKE OUR SWEETS IN A CONCRETE BUILDING LIKE THAT!
ANGRY RESIDENTS ZONE
zhoop
YOU YOUNG'UNS COME HERE A SECOND!
WE'VE ALWAYS MADE OUR SWEETS WITH THIS.
WOW...
THAT'S...
...A WELL PUMP.

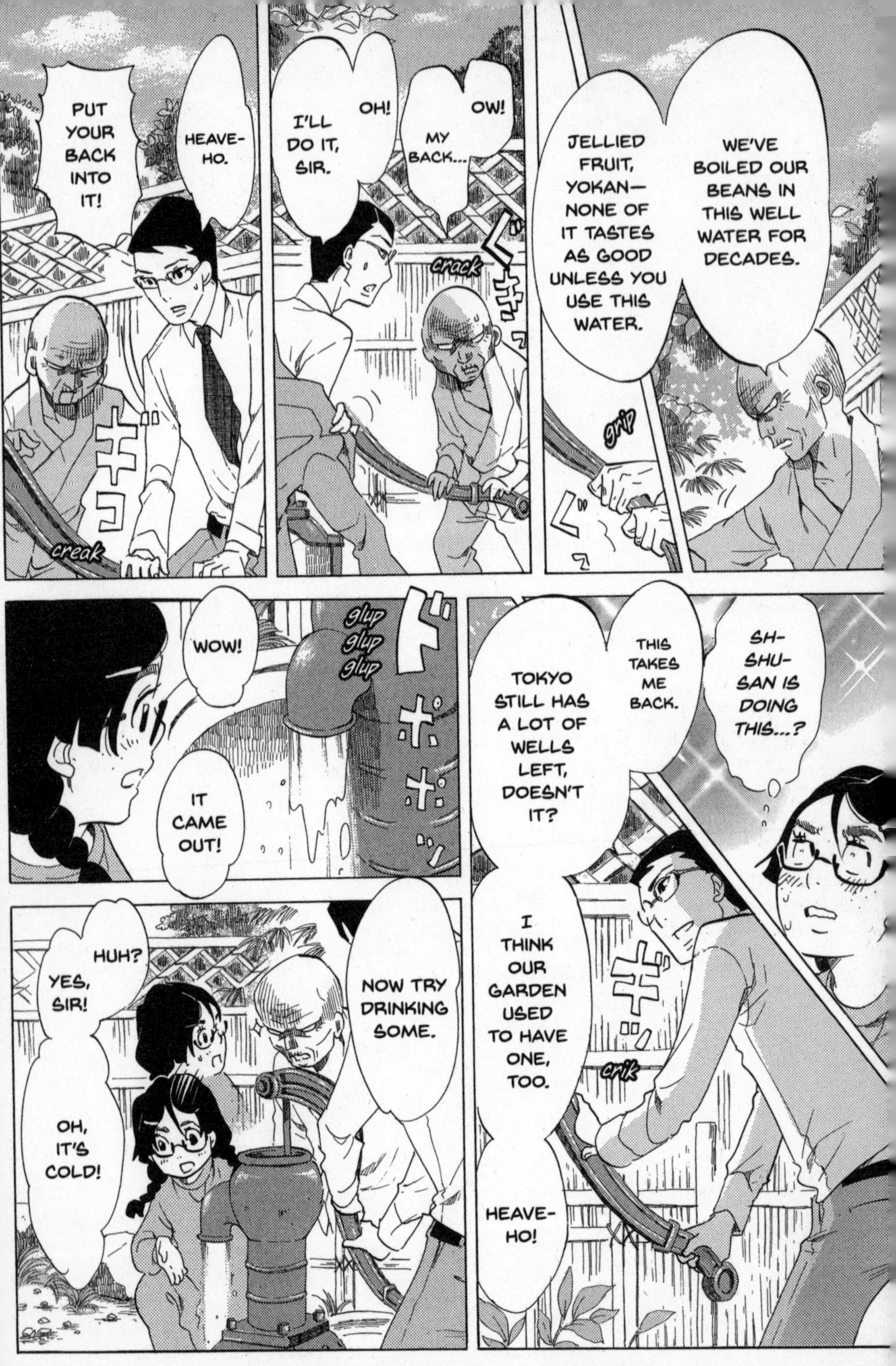
WE'VE BOILED OUR BEANS IN THIS WELL WATER FOR DECADES.
JELLIED FRUIT, YOKAN—NONE OF IT TASTES AS GOOD UNLESS YOU USE THIS WATER.
grip
OW! MY BACK...
OH! I'LL DO IT, SIR.
crack
HEAVE-HO.
PUT YOUR BACK INTO IT!
creak
SH-SHU-SAN IS DOING THIS...?
THIS TAKES ME BACK.
TOKYO STILL HAS A LOT OF WELLS LEFT, DOESN'T IT?
I THINK OUR GARDEN USED TO HAVE ONE, TOO.
crik
HEAVE-HO!
glup glup glup
WOW!
IT CAME OUT!
NOW TRY DRINKING SOME.
HUH? YES, SIR!
OH, IT'S COLD!

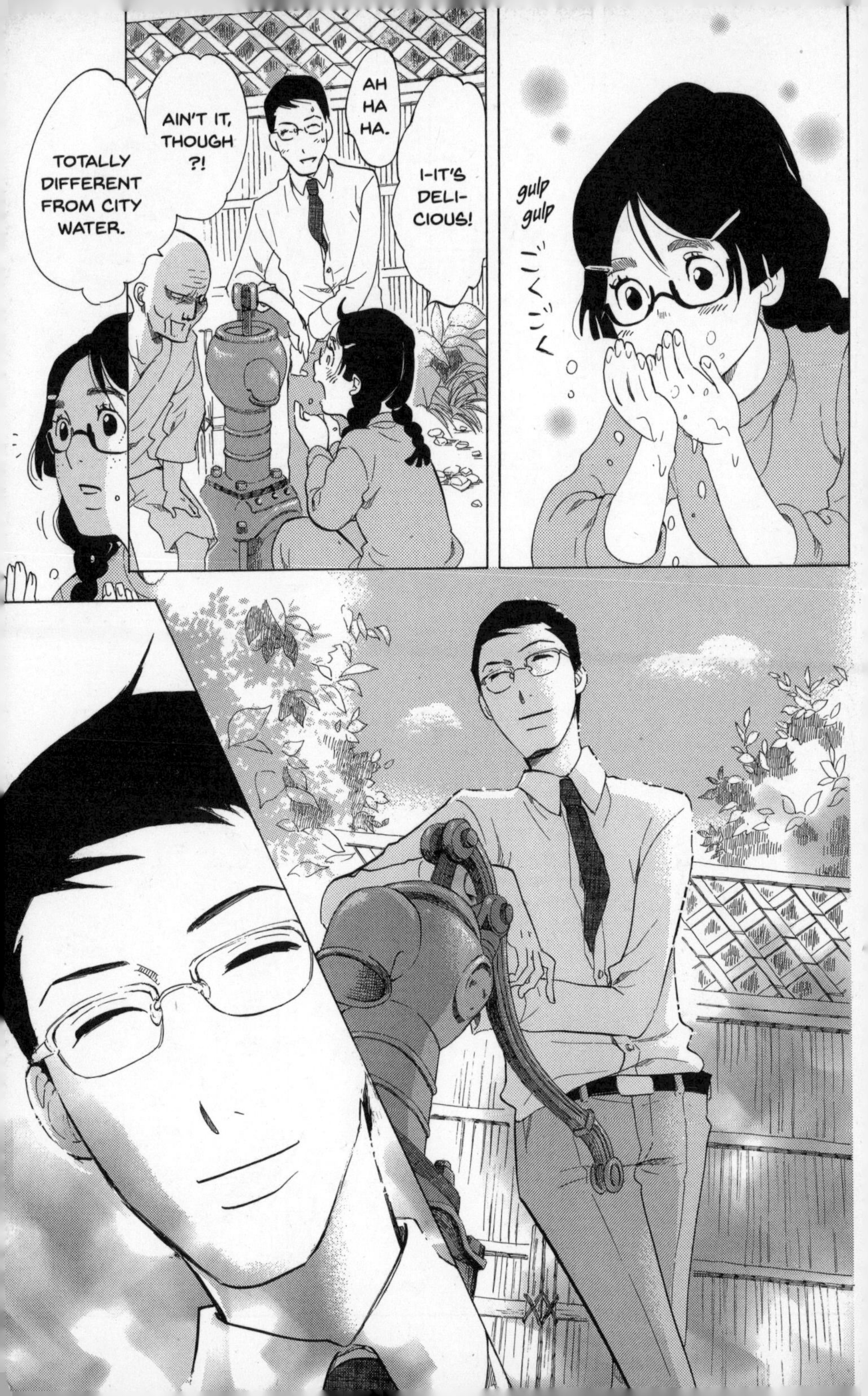
gulp gulp
I-IT'S DELICIOUS!
AH HA HA.
AIN'T IT, THOUGH?!
TOTALLY DIFFERENT FROM CITY WATER.

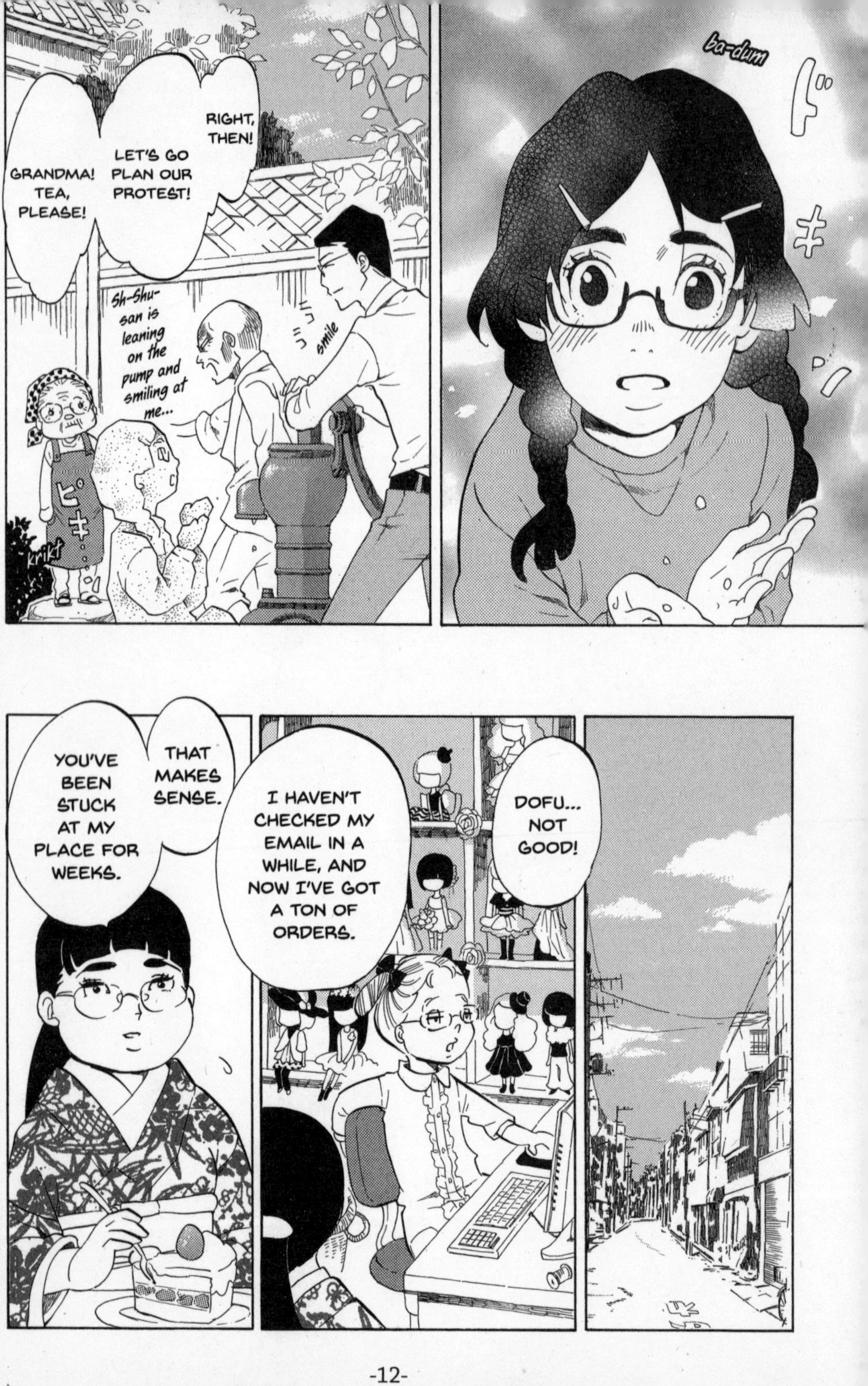
ba-dum
RIGHT, THEN!
LET'S GO PLAN OUR PROTEST!
GRANDMA! TEA, PLEASE!
smile
Sh-Shu-san is leaning on the pump and smiling at me...
krikt
DOFU... NOT GOOD!
I HAVEN'T CHECKED MY EMAIL IN A WHILE, AND NOW I'VE GOT A TON OF ORDERS.
THAT MAKES SENSE.
YOU'VE BEEN STUCK AT MY PLACE FOR WEEKS.

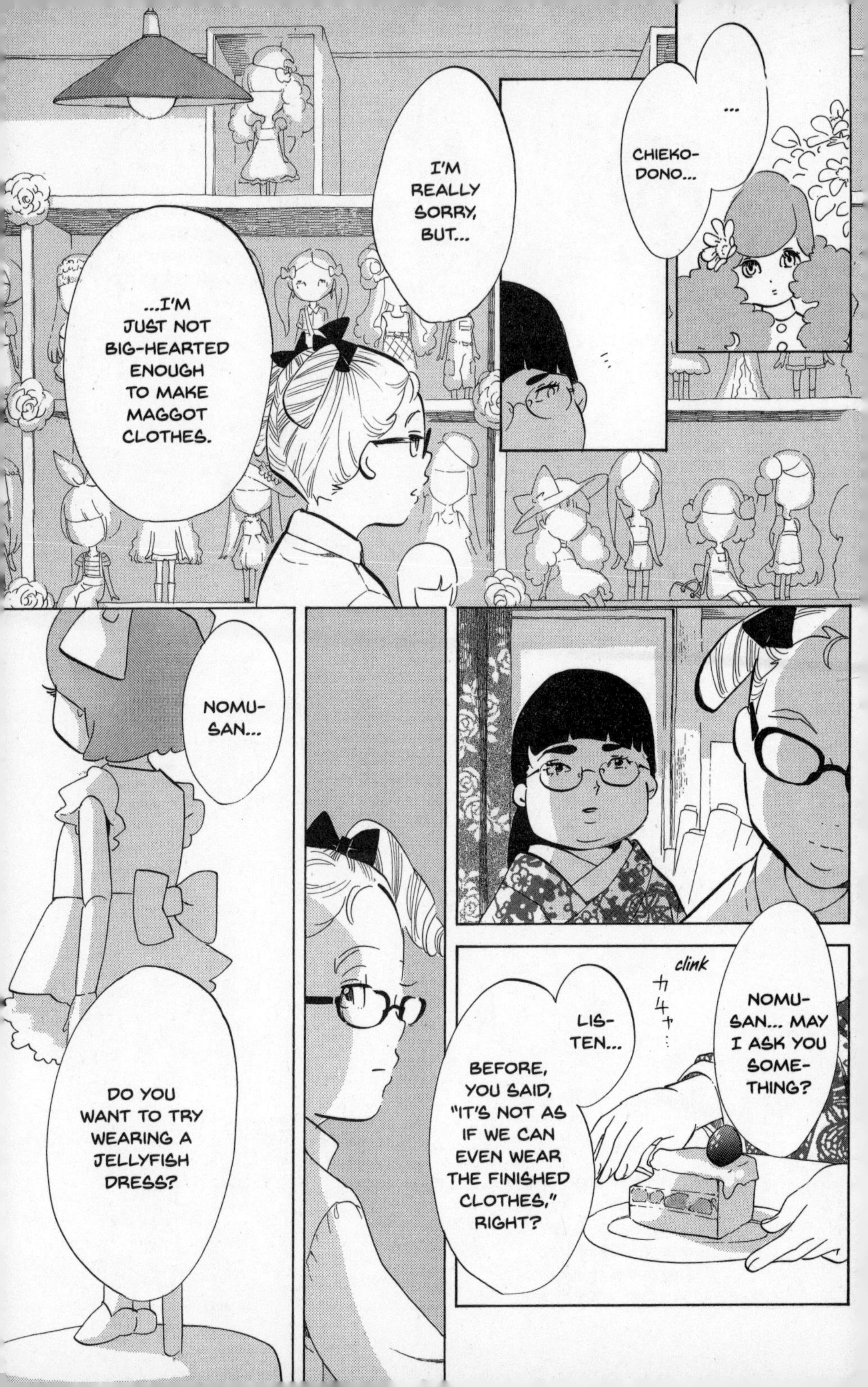
... CHIEKO-DONO...
I'M REALLY SORRY, BUT...
...I'M JUST NOT BIG-HEARTED ENOUGH TO MAKE MAGGOT CLOTHES.
NOMU-SAN... MAY I ASK YOU SOMETHING?
clink
カチャ
LIS-TEN...
BEFORE, YOU SAID, "IT'S NOT AS IF WE CAN EVEN WEAR THE FINISHED CLOTHES," RIGHT?
NOMU-SAN...
DO YOU WANT TO TRY WEARING A JELLYFISH DRESS?

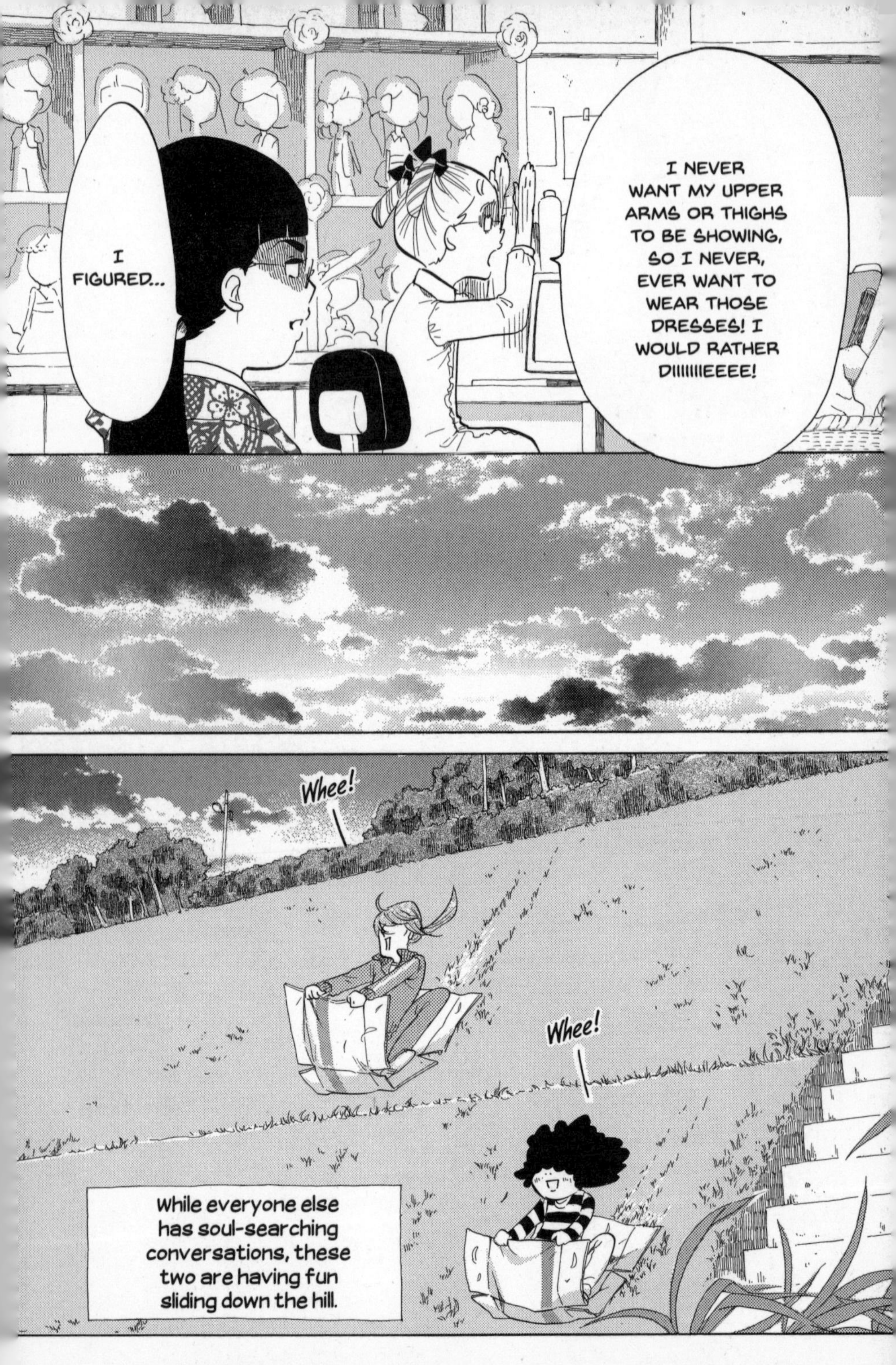
I NEVER WANT MY UPPER ARMS OR THIGHS TO BE SHOWING, SO I NEVER, EVER WANT TO WEAR THOSE DRESSES! I WOULD RATHER DIIIIIIEEEE!
I FIGURED...
Whee!
Whee!
While everyone else has soul-searching conversations, these two are having fun sliding down the hill.

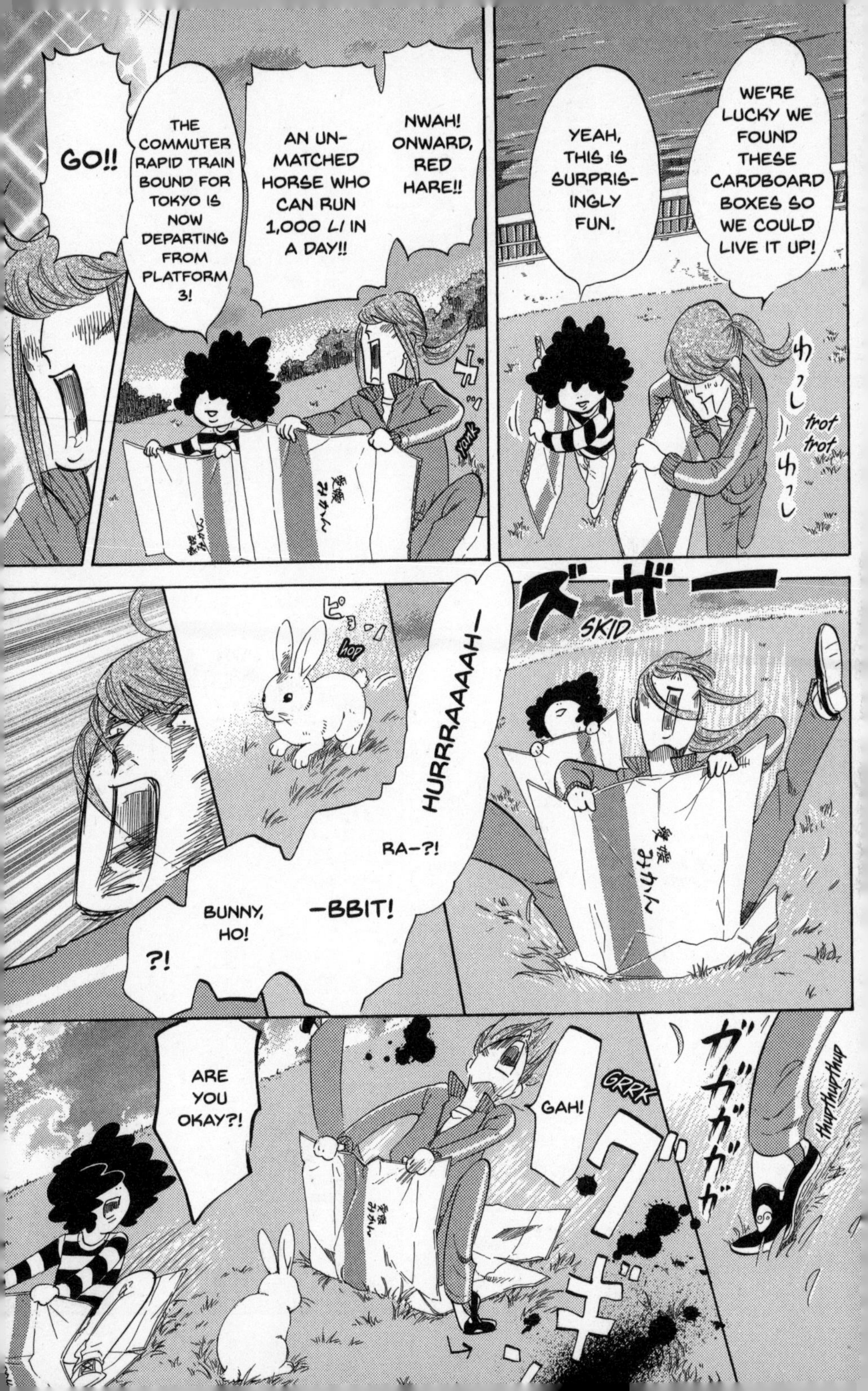
WE'RE LUCKY WE FOUND THESE CARDBOARD BOXES SO WE COULD LIVE IT UP!
YEAH, THIS IS SURPRIS- INGLY FUN.
trot trot
NWAH! ONWARD, RED HARE!!
AN UN- MATCHED HORSE WHO CAN RUN 1,000 LI IN A DAY!!
yank
THE COMMUTER RAPID TRAIN BOUND FOR TOKYO IS NOW DEPARTING FROM PLATFORM 3!
GO!!
SKID
HURRRAAAAH—
hop
RA–?!
–BBIT!
BUNNY, HO!
?!
thupthupthup
GRRK
GAH!
ARE YOU OKAY?!

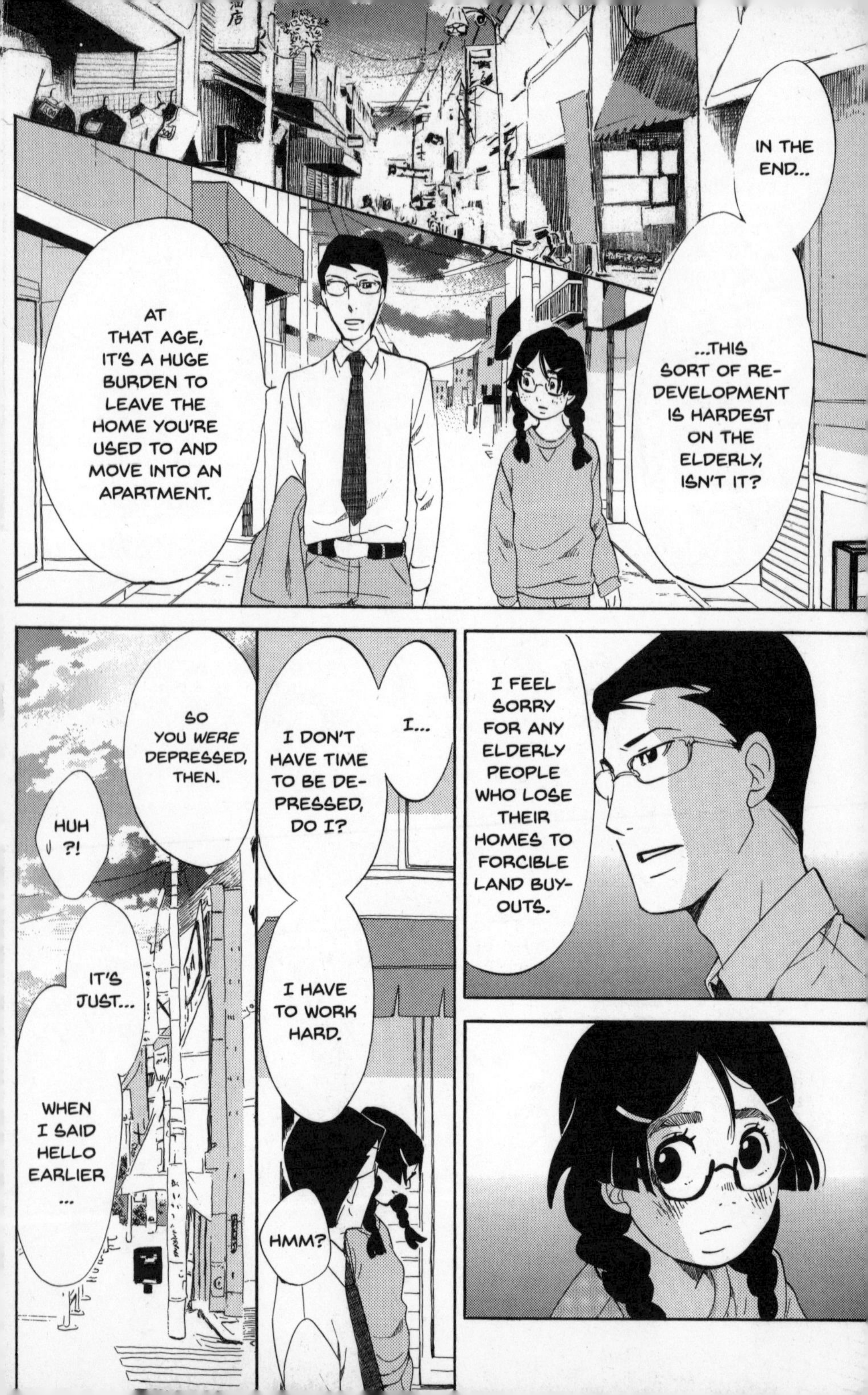
IN THE END...
...THIS SORT OF RE-DEVELOPMENT IS HARDEST ON THE ELDERLY, ISN'T IT?
AT THAT AGE, IT'S A HUGE BURDEN TO LEAVE THE HOME YOU'RE USED TO AND MOVE INTO AN APARTMENT.
I FEEL SORRY FOR ANY ELDERLY PEOPLE WHO LOSE THEIR HOMES TO FORCIBLE LAND BUY-OUTS.
I...
I DON'T HAVE TIME TO BE DE-PRESSED, DO I?
I HAVE TO WORK HARD.
HMM?
SO YOU *WERE* DEPRESSED, THEN.
HUH ?!
IT'S JUST...
WHEN I SAID HELLO EARLIER ...

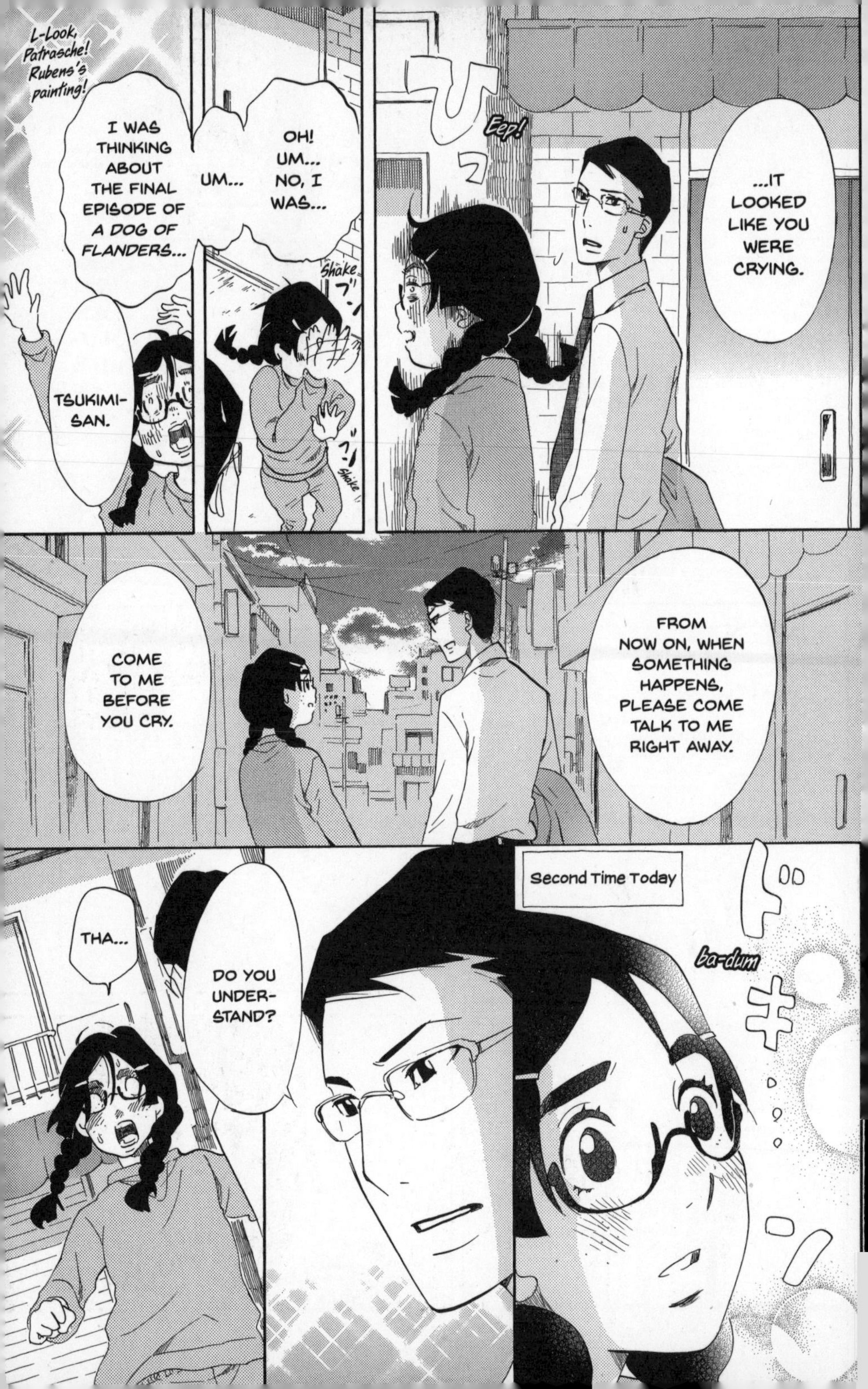
...IT LOOKED LIKE YOU WERE CRYING.
Eep!
OH! UM... NO, I WAS...
UM...
Shake
Shake
I WAS THINKING ABOUT THE FINAL EPISODE OF A DOG OF FLANDERS...
L-Look, Patrasche! Rubens's painting!
TSUKIMI-SAN.
FROM NOW ON, WHEN SOMETHING HAPPENS, PLEASE COME TALK TO ME RIGHT AWAY.
COME TO ME BEFORE YOU CRY.
Second Time Today
ba-dum
DO YOU UNDER-STAND?
THA...

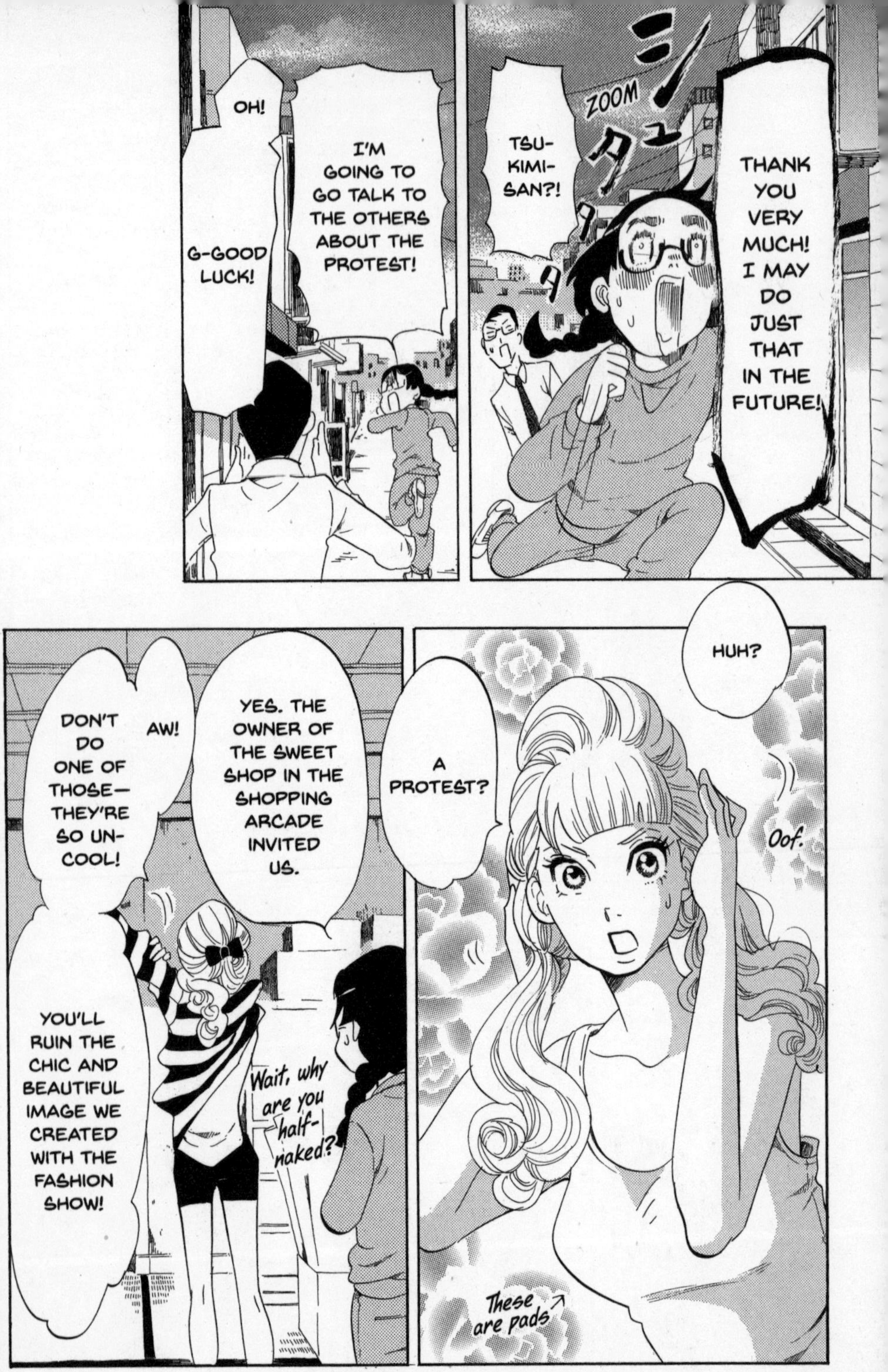
ZOOM
THANK YOU VERY MUCH! I MAY DO JUST THAT IN THE FUTURE!
TSU-KIMI-SAN?!
OH!
I'M GOING TO GO TALK TO THE OTHERS ABOUT THE PROTEST!
G-GOOD LUCK!
HUH?
Oof.
A PROTEST?
These are pads
YES. THE OWNER OF THE SWEET SHOP IN THE SHOPPING ARCADE INVITED US.
AW!
DON'T DO ONE OF THOSE—THEY'RE SO UN-COOL!
YOU'LL RUIN THE CHIC AND BEAUTIFUL IMAGE WE CREATED WITH THE FASHION SHOW!
Wait, why are you half-naked?

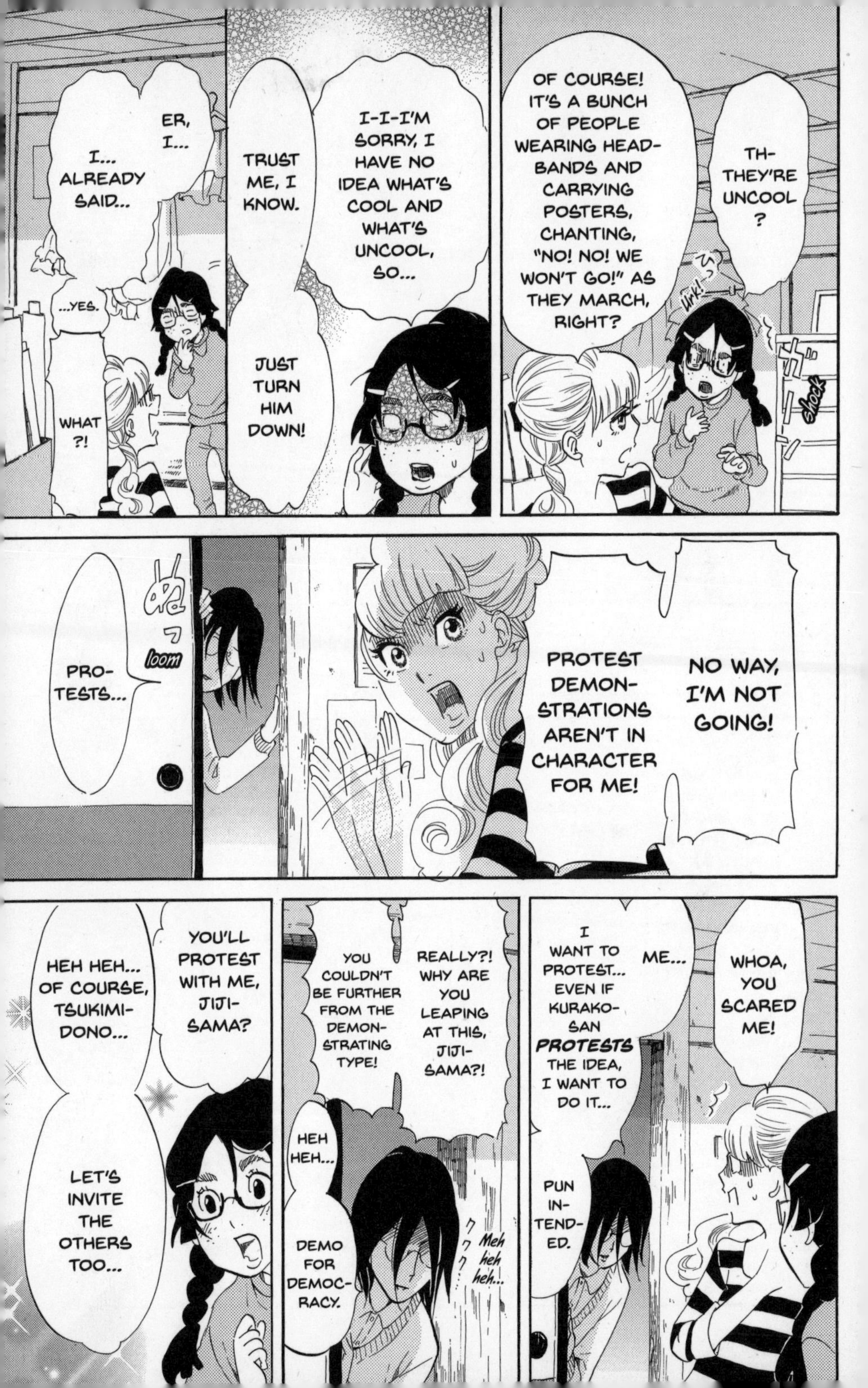
TH- THEY'RE UNCOOL ?
OF COURSE! IT'S A BUNCH OF PEOPLE WEARING HEAD-BANDS AND CARRYING POSTERS, CHANTING, "NO! NO! WE WON'T GO!" AS THEY MARCH, RIGHT?
Urk!
shock
I-I-I'M SORRY, I HAVE NO IDEA WHAT'S COOL AND WHAT'S UNCOOL, SO...
TRUST ME, I KNOW.
JUST TURN HIM DOWN!
ER, I...
I... ALREADY SAID...
...YES.
WHAT ?!
NO WAY, I'M NOT GOING!
PROTEST DEMON-STRATIONS AREN'T IN CHARACTER FOR ME!
loom
PRO-TESTS...
WHOA, YOU SCARED ME!
ME...
I WANT TO PROTEST... EVEN IF KURAKO-SAN PROTESTS THE IDEA, I WANT TO DO IT...
PUN IN-TEND-ED.
REALLY?! WHY ARE YOU LEAPING AT THIS, JIJI-SAMA?!
YOU COULDN'T BE FURTHER FROM THE DEMON-STRATING TYPE!
HEH HEH...
Meh heh heh...
DEMO FOR DEMOC-RACY.
YOU'LL PROTEST WITH ME, JIJI-SAMA?
HEH HEH... OF COURSE, TSUKIMI-DONO...
LET'S INVITE THE OTHERS TOO...

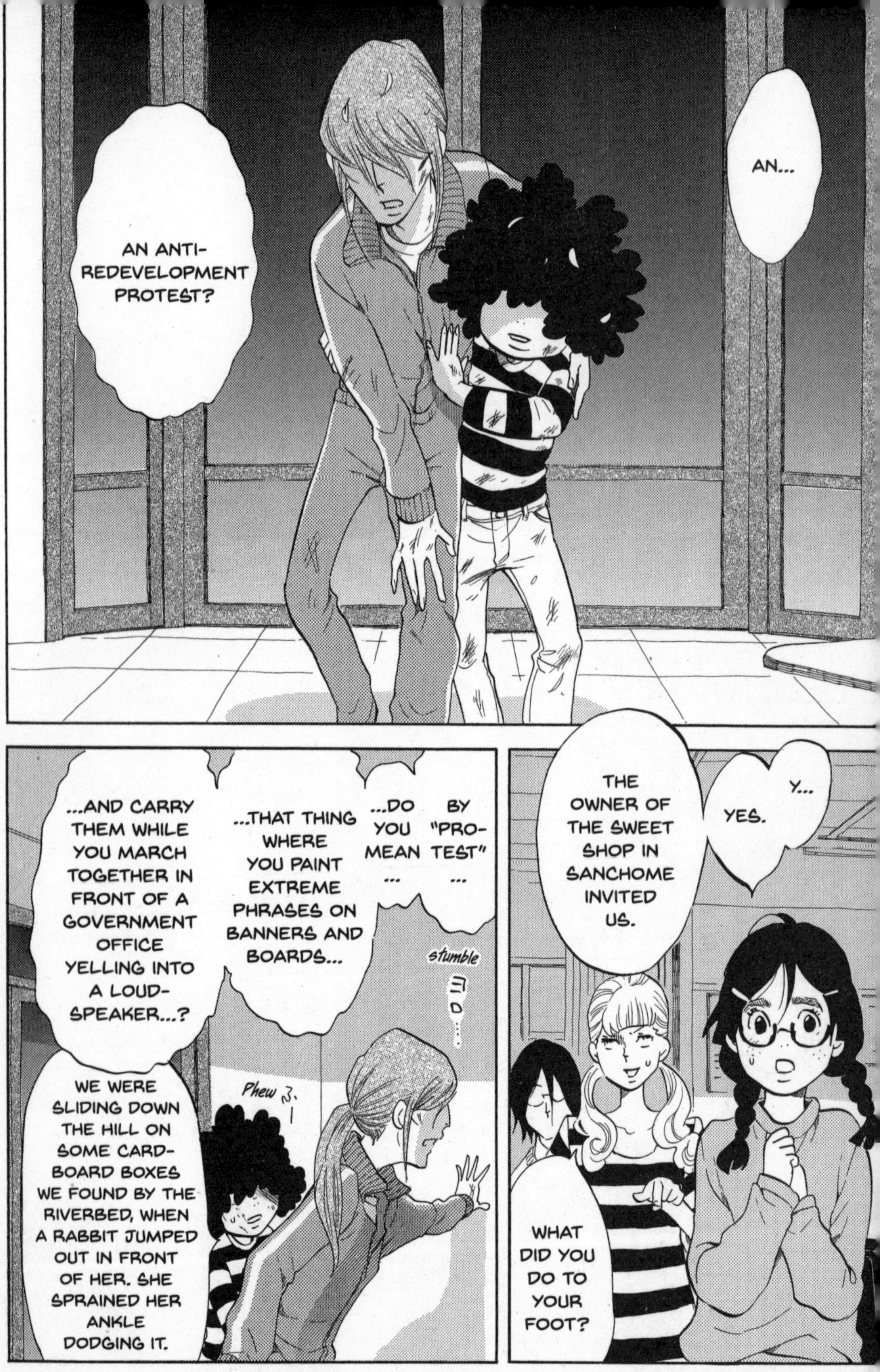
AN...
AN ANTI-REDEVELOPMENT PROTEST?
Y... YES.
THE OWNER OF THE SWEET SHOP IN SANCHOME INVITED US.
WHAT DID YOU DO TO YOUR FOOT?
...DO YOU MEAN BY "PROTEST"...
...THAT THING WHERE YOU PAINT EXTREME PHRASES ON BANNERS AND BOARDS...
...AND CARRY THEM WHILE YOU MARCH TOGETHER IN FRONT OF A GOVERNMENT OFFICE YELLING INTO A LOUD-SPEAKER...?
stumble
Phew
WE WERE SLIDING DOWN THE HILL ON SOME CARD-BOARD BOXES WE FOUND BY THE RIVERBED, WHEN A RABBIT JUMPED OUT IN FRONT OF HER. SHE SPRAINED HER ANKLE DODGING IT.

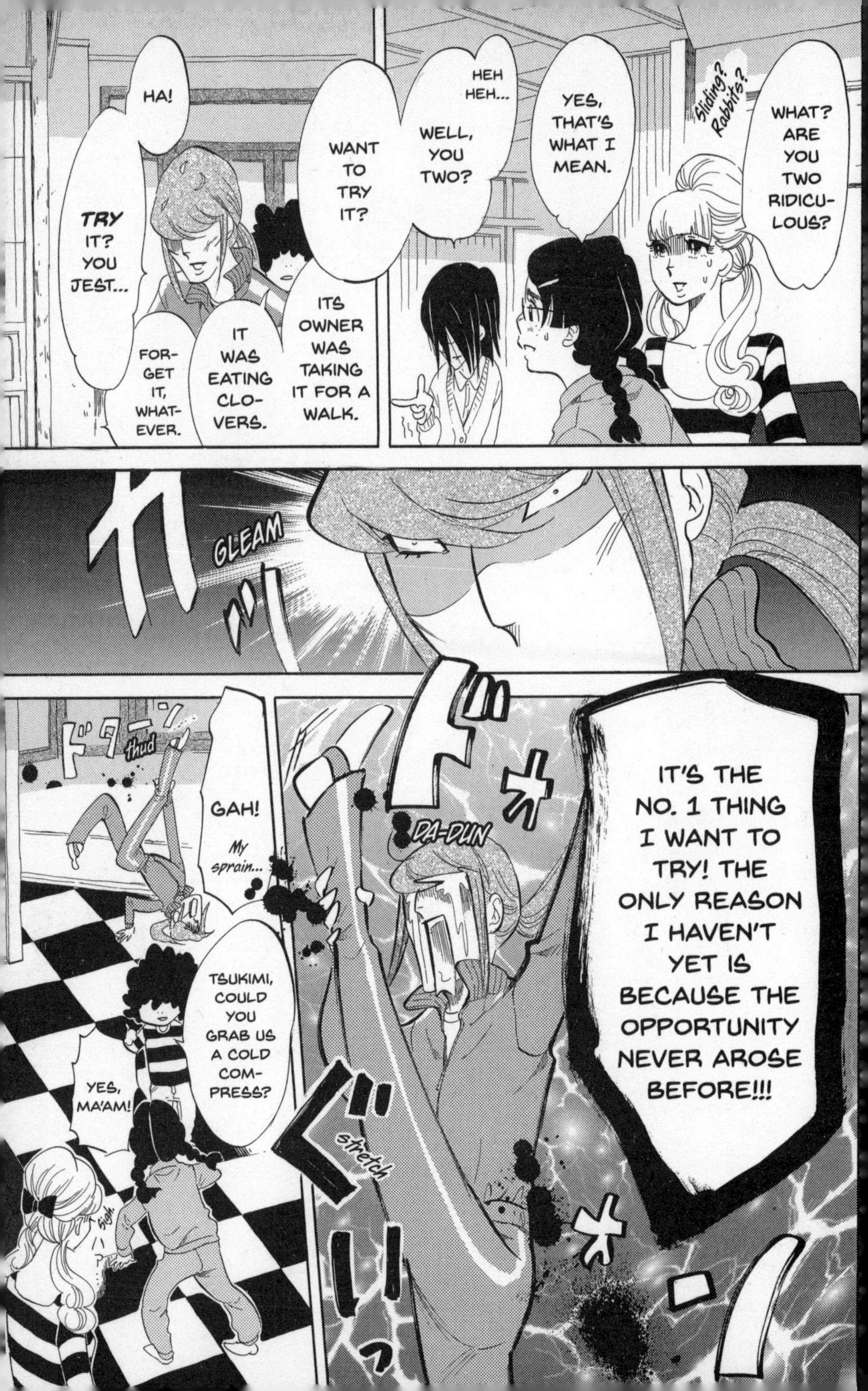
Sliding? Rabbits?
WHAT? ARE YOU TWO RIDICU-LOUS?
YES, THAT'S WHAT I MEAN.
HEH HEH...
WELL, YOU TWO?
WANT TO TRY IT?
HA!
ITS OWNER WAS TAKING IT FOR A WALK.
TRY IT? YOU JEST...
IT WAS EATING CLO-VERS.
FOR-GET IT, WHAT-EVER.
GLEAM
IT'S THE NO. 1 THING I WANT TO TRY! THE ONLY REASON I HAVEN'T YET IS BECAUSE THE OPPORTUNITY NEVER AROSE BEFORE!!!
DA-DUN
stretch
thud
GAH!
My sprain...
TSUKIMI, COULD YOU GRAB US A COLD COM-PRESS?
YES, MA'AM!
Sigh.

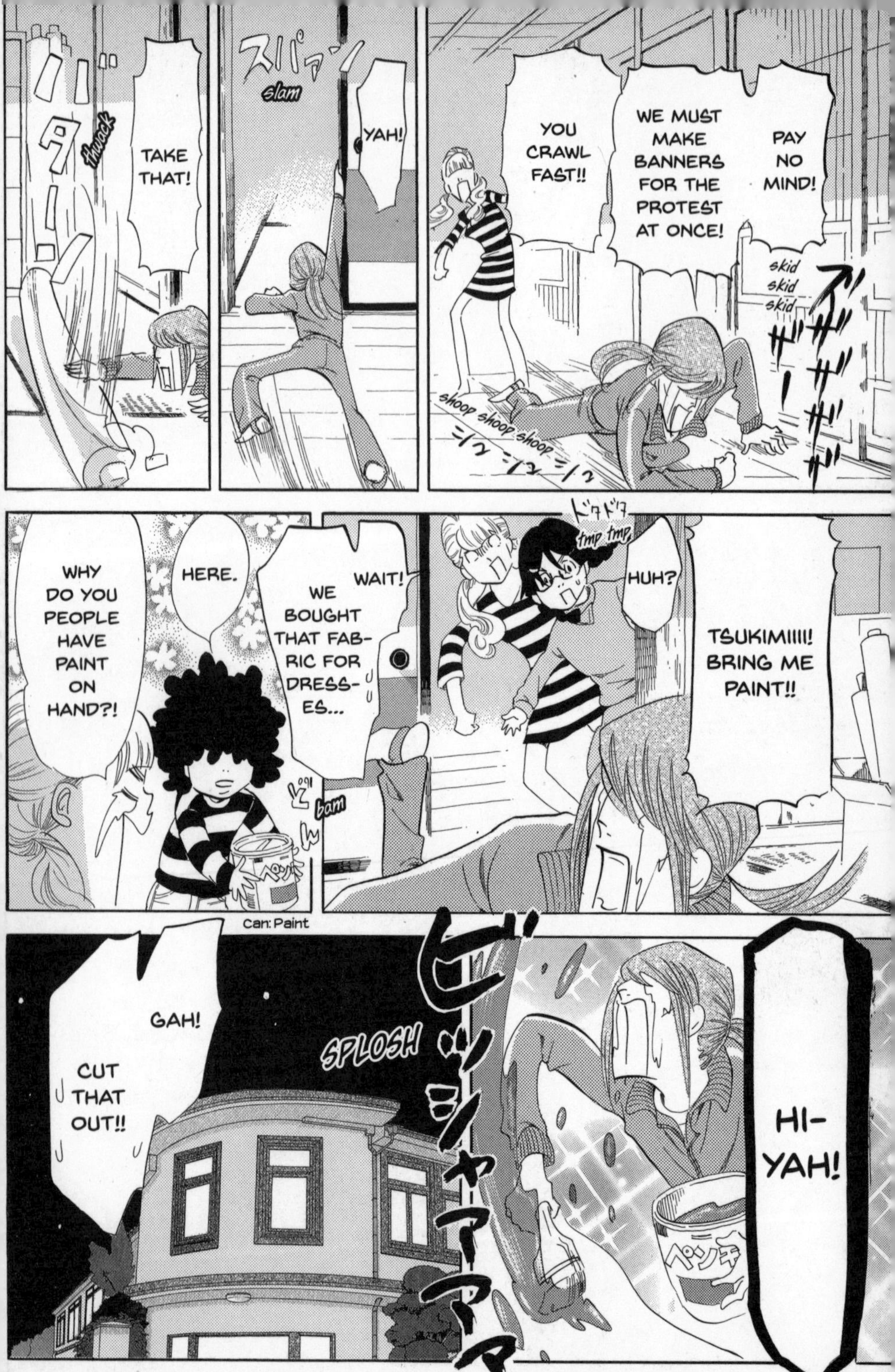
PAY NO MIND!
WE MUST MAKE BANNERS FOR THE PROTEST AT ONCE!
YOU CRAWL FAST!!
skid skid skid
shoop shoop shoop
slam
YAH!
TAKE THAT!
thwack
TSUKIMIIIII! BRING ME PAINT!!
HUH?
tmp tmp
WAIT!
WE BOUGHT THAT FAB-RIC FOR DRESS-ES...
HERE.
WHY DO YOU PEOPLE HAVE PAINT ON HAND?!
bam
Can: Paint
HI-YAH!
SPLOSH
GAH!
CUT THAT OUT!!

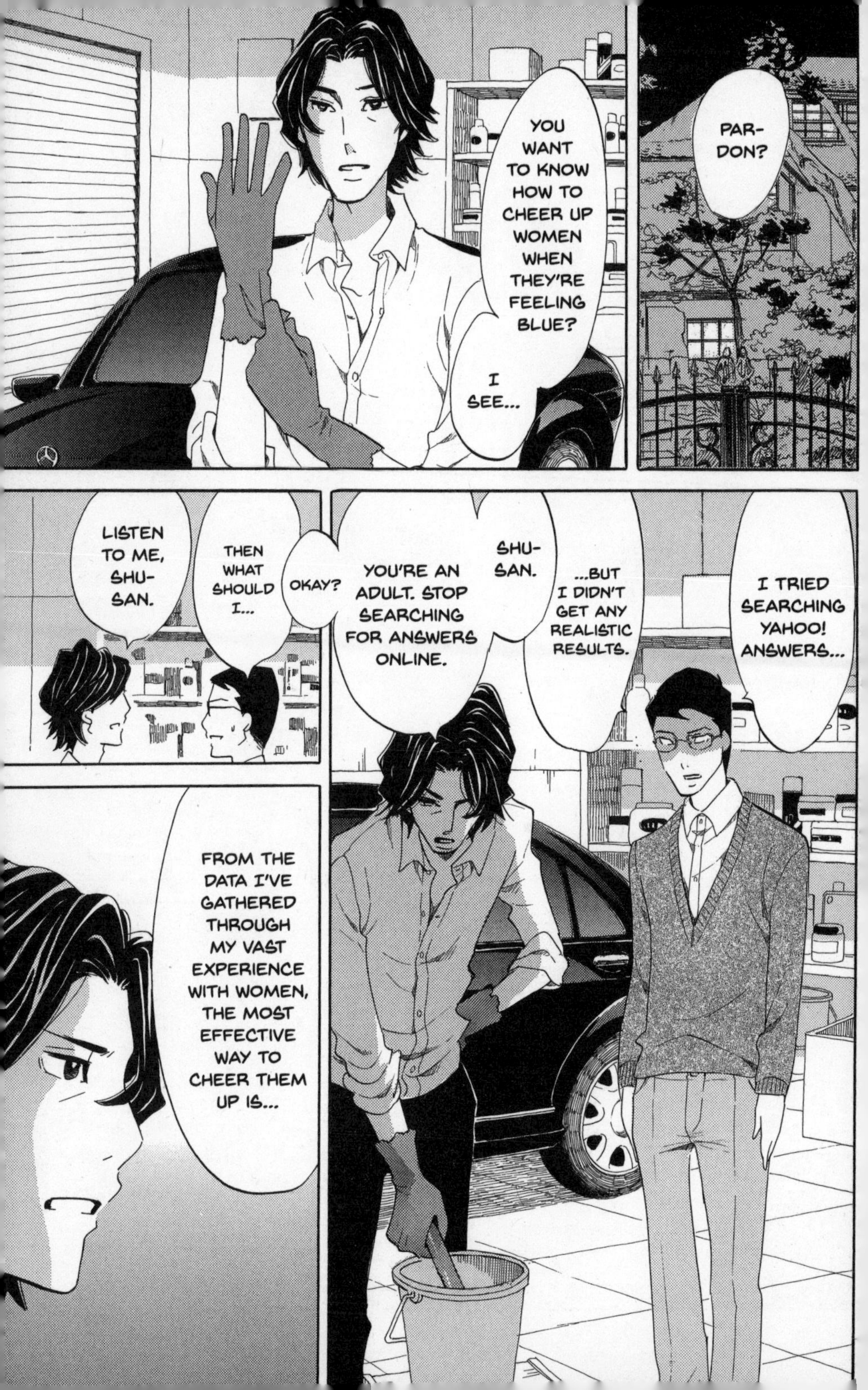
PAR-DON?
YOU WANT TO KNOW HOW TO CHEER UP WOMEN WHEN THEY'RE FEELING BLUE?
I SEE...
I TRIED SEARCHING YAHOO! ANSWERS...
...BUT I DIDN'T GET ANY REALISTIC RESULTS.
SHU-SAN.
YOU'RE AN ADULT. STOP SEARCHING FOR ANSWERS ONLINE.
OKAY?
THEN WHAT SHOULD I...
LISTEN TO ME, SHU-SAN.
FROM THE DATA I'VE GATHERED THROUGH MY VAST EXPERIENCE WITH WOMEN, THE MOST EFFECTIVE WAY TO CHEER THEM UP IS...

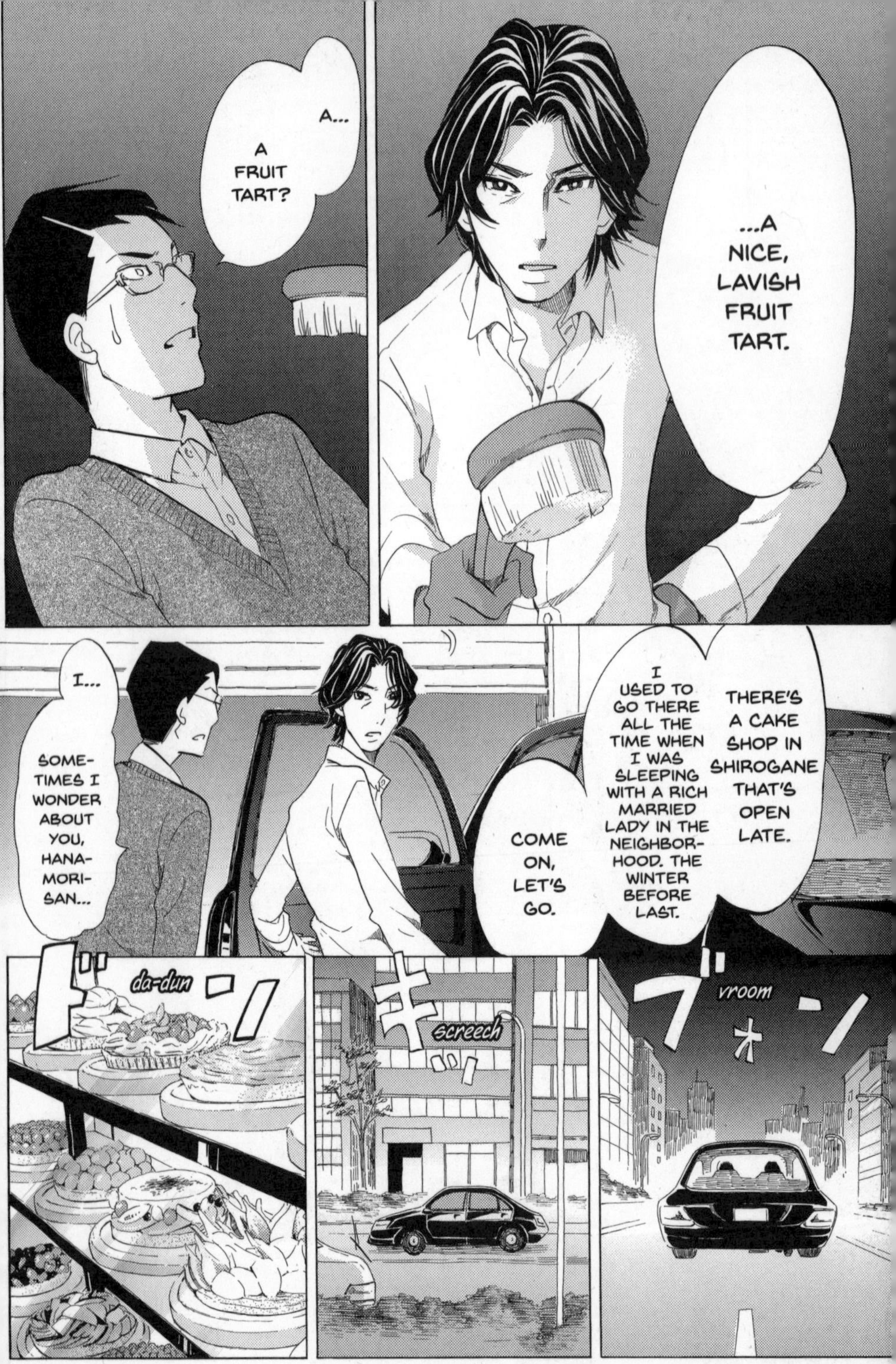
...A NICE, LAVISH FRUIT TART.
A... A FRUIT TART?
THERE'S A CAKE SHOP IN SHIROGANE THAT'S OPEN LATE.
I USED TO GO THERE ALL THE TIME WHEN I WAS SLEEPING WITH A RICH MARRIED LADY IN THE NEIGHBOR-HOOD. THE WINTER BEFORE LAST.
COME ON, LET'S GO.
I...
SOME-TIMES I WONDER ABOUT YOU, HANA-MORI-SAN...
vroom
screech
da-dun

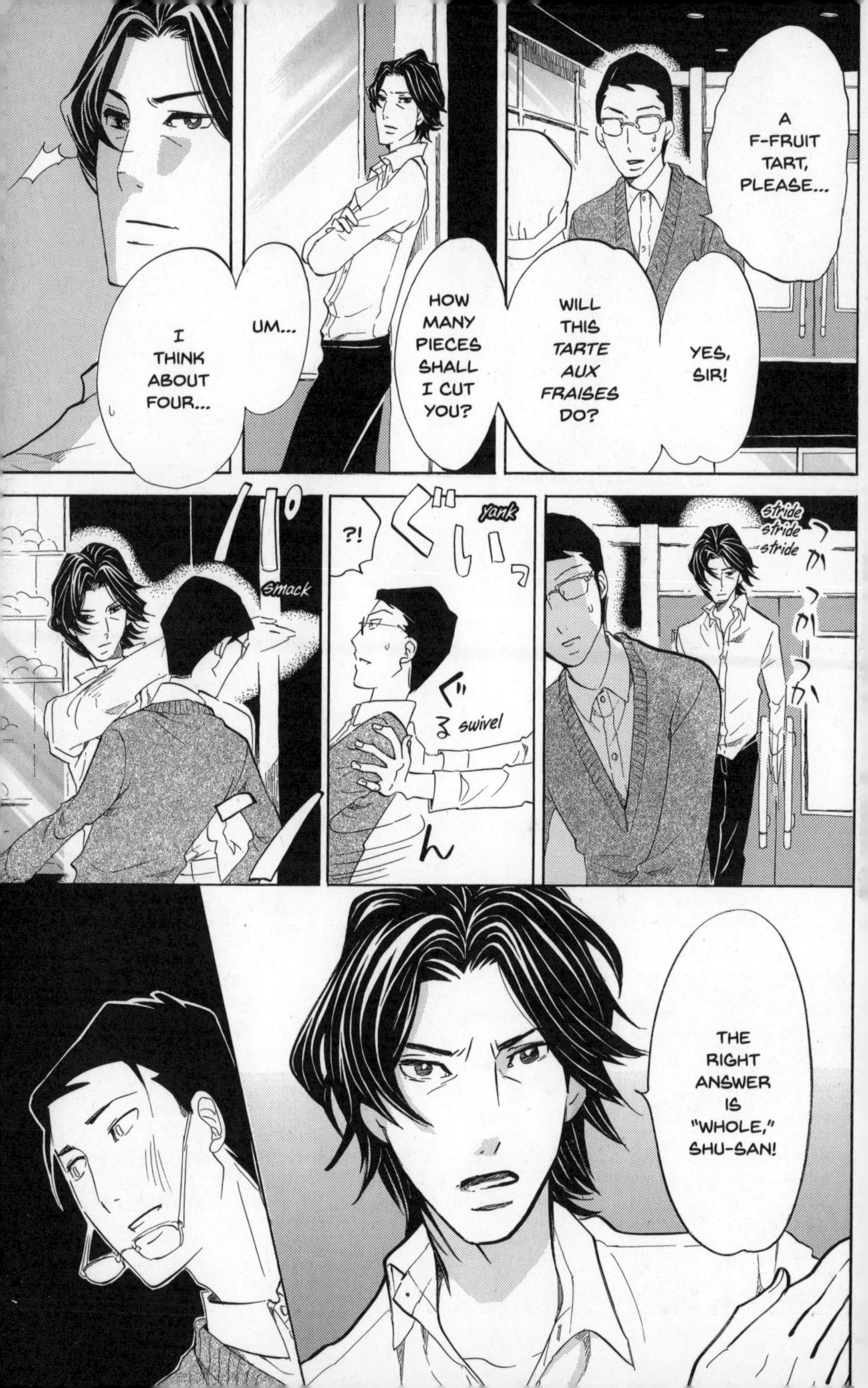
A F-FRUIT TART, PLEASE...
YES, SIR!
WILL THIS TARTE AUX FRAISES DO?
HOW MANY PIECES SHALL I CUT YOU?
UM...
I THINK ABOUT FOUR...
stride stride stride
yank
?!
swivel
smack
THE RIGHT ANSWER IS "WHOLE," SHU-SAN!

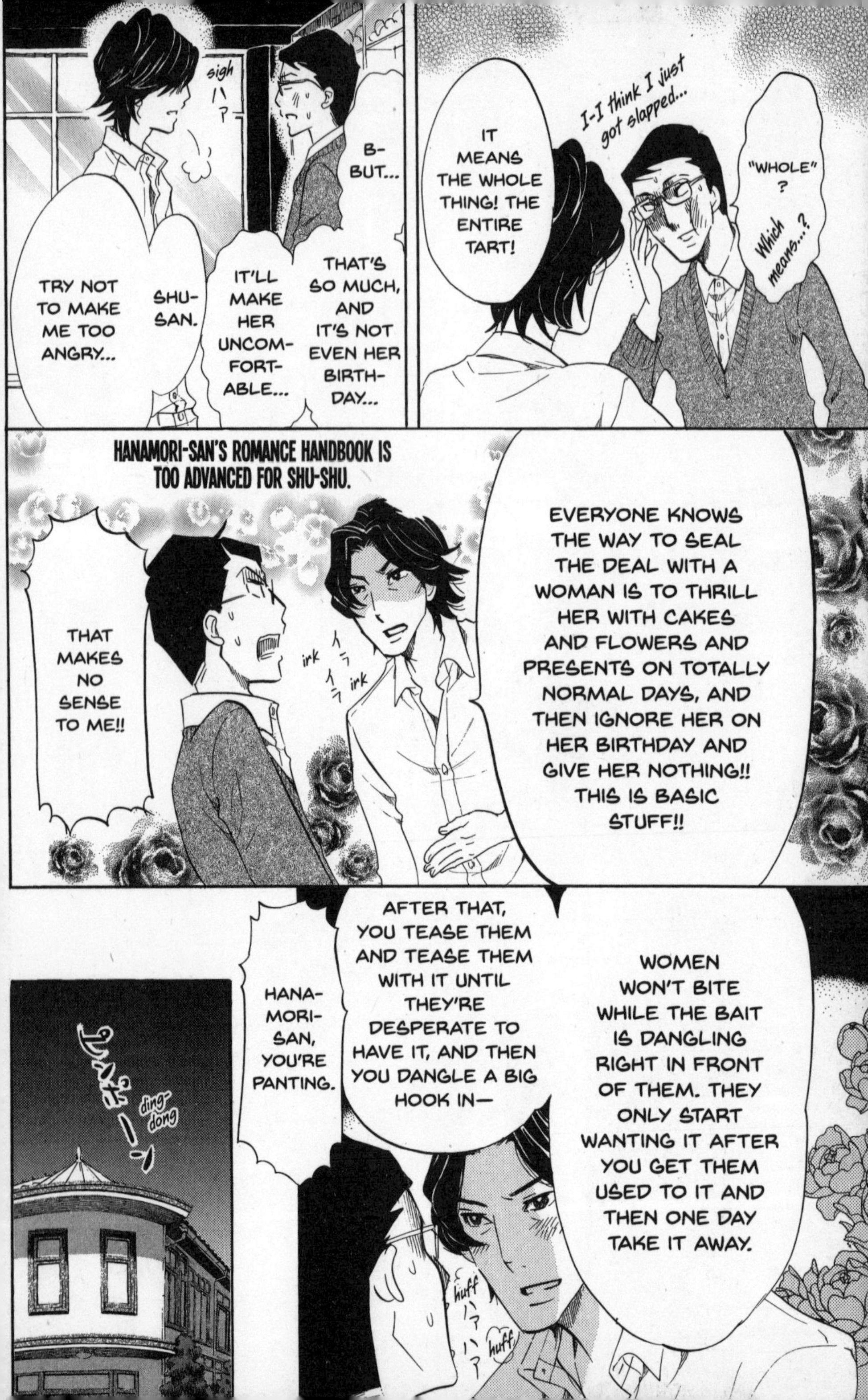
"WHOLE" ?
Which means...?
I-I think I just got slapped...
IT MEANS THE WHOLE THING! THE ENTIRE TART!
sigh
B-BUT...
THAT'S SO MUCH, AND IT'S NOT EVEN HER BIRTHDAY...
IT'LL MAKE HER UNCOMFORTABLE...
SHU-SAN.
TRY NOT TO MAKE ME TOO ANGRY...
EVERYONE KNOWS THE WAY TO SEAL THE DEAL WITH A WOMAN IS TO THRILL HER WITH CAKES AND FLOWERS AND PRESENTS ON TOTALLY NORMAL DAYS, AND THEN IGNORE HER ON HER BIRTHDAY AND GIVE HER NOTHING!! THIS IS BASIC STUFF!!
HANAMORI-SAN'S ROMANCE HANDBOOK IS TOO ADVANCED FOR SHU-SHU.
irk irk
THAT MAKES NO SENSE TO ME!!
WOMEN WON'T BITE WHILE THE BAIT IS DANGLING RIGHT IN FRONT OF THEM. THEY ONLY START WANTING IT AFTER YOU GET THEM USED TO IT AND THEN ONE DAY TAKE IT AWAY.
AFTER THAT, YOU TEASE THEM AND TEASE THEM WITH IT UNTIL THEY'RE DESPERATE TO HAVE IT, AND THEN YOU DANGLE A BIG HOOK IN—
HANAMORI-SAN, YOU'RE PANTING.
huff huff
ding-dong

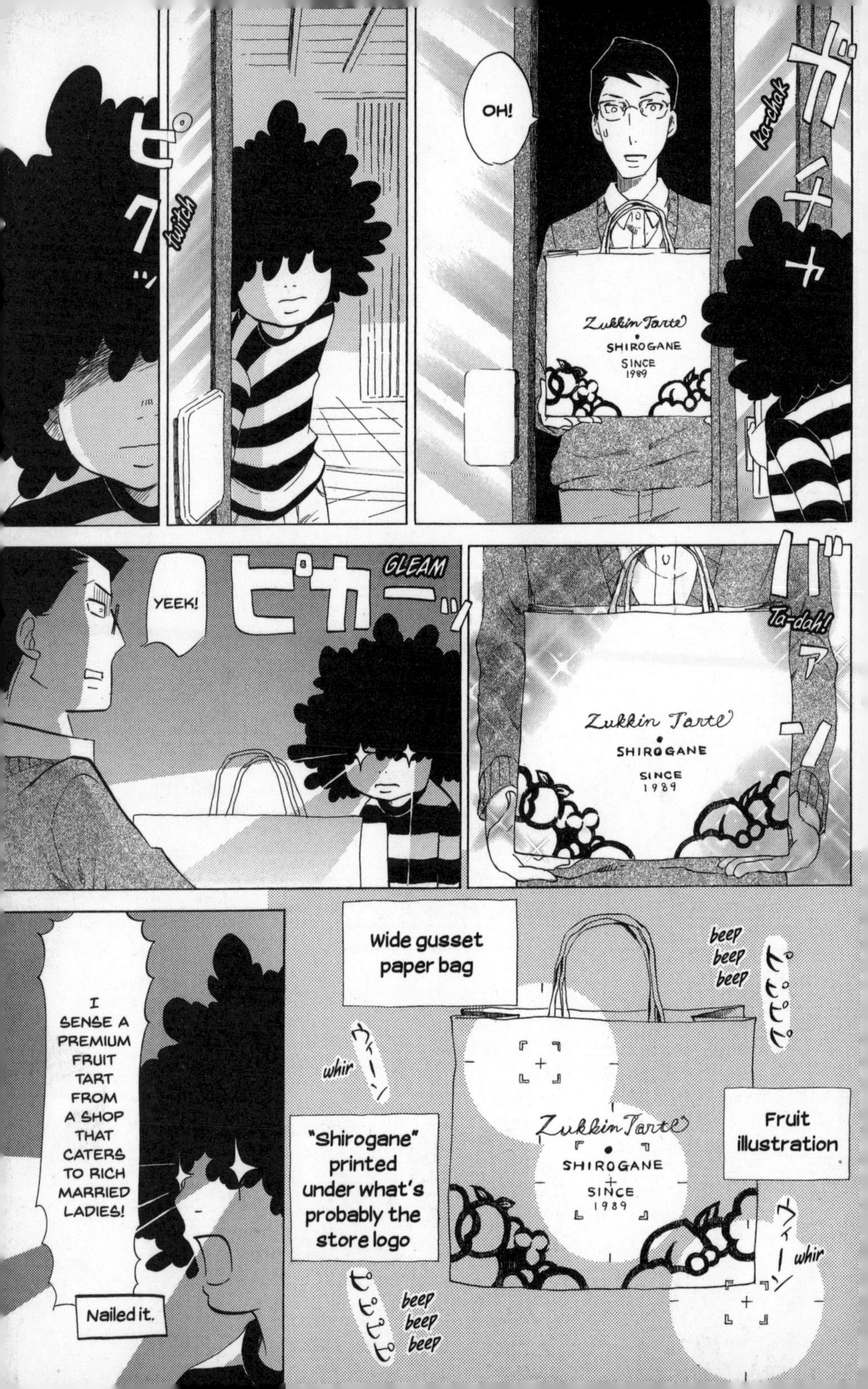
ガチャ
ka-chak
OH!
Zukkin Tarte
SHIROGANE
SINCE 1989
ピクッ
twitch
バァーン
Ta-dah!
Zukkin Tarte
SHIROGANE
SINCE 1989
YEEK!
ピカーン
GLEAM
Wide gusset paper bag
ピピピ
beep beep beep
Fruit illustration
Zukkin Tarte
SHIROGANE
SINCE 1989
ウィーン
whir
"Shirogane" printed under what's probably the store logo
ウィーン
whir
ピピピ
beep beep beep
I SENSE A PREMIUM FRUIT TART FROM A SHOP THAT CATERS TO RICH MARRIED LADIES!
Nailed it.

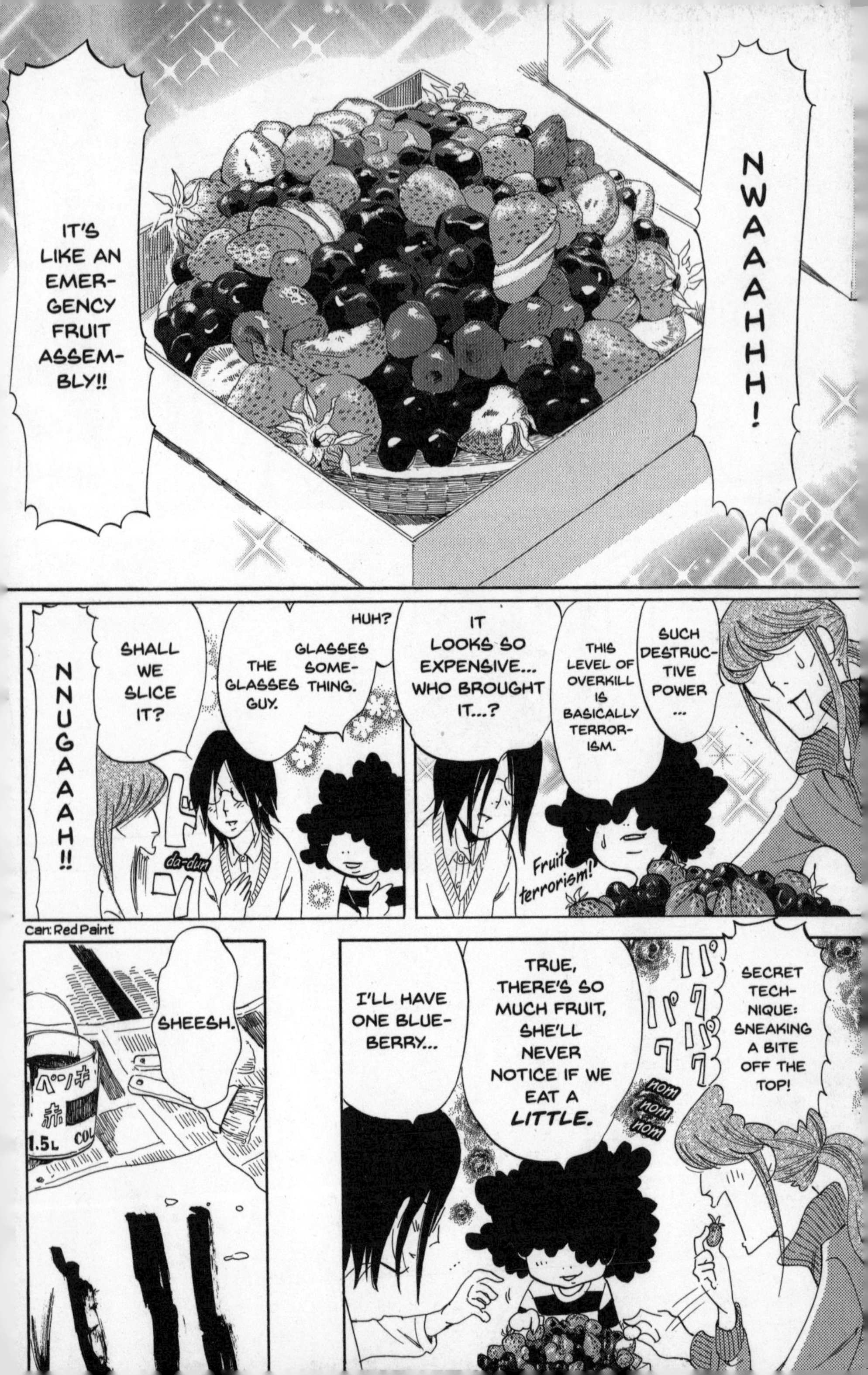
NWAAAAHHH!
IT'S LIKE AN EMERGENCY FRUIT ASSEMBLY!!
SUCH DESTRUCTIVE POWER...
THIS LEVEL OF OVERKILL IS BASICALLY TERRORISM.
IT LOOKS SO EXPENSIVE... WHO BROUGHT IT...?
Fruit terrorism!
HUH?
GLASSES SOMETHING.
THE GLASSES GUY.
SHALL WE SLICE IT?
NNUGAAAAH!!
da-dun
Can: Red Paint
SECRET TECHNIQUE: SNEAKING A BITE OFF THE TOP!
nom nom nom
TRUE, THERE'S SO MUCH FRUIT, SHE'LL NEVER NOTICE IF WE EAT A *LITTLE.*
I'LL HAVE ONE BLUEBERRY...
SHEESH.

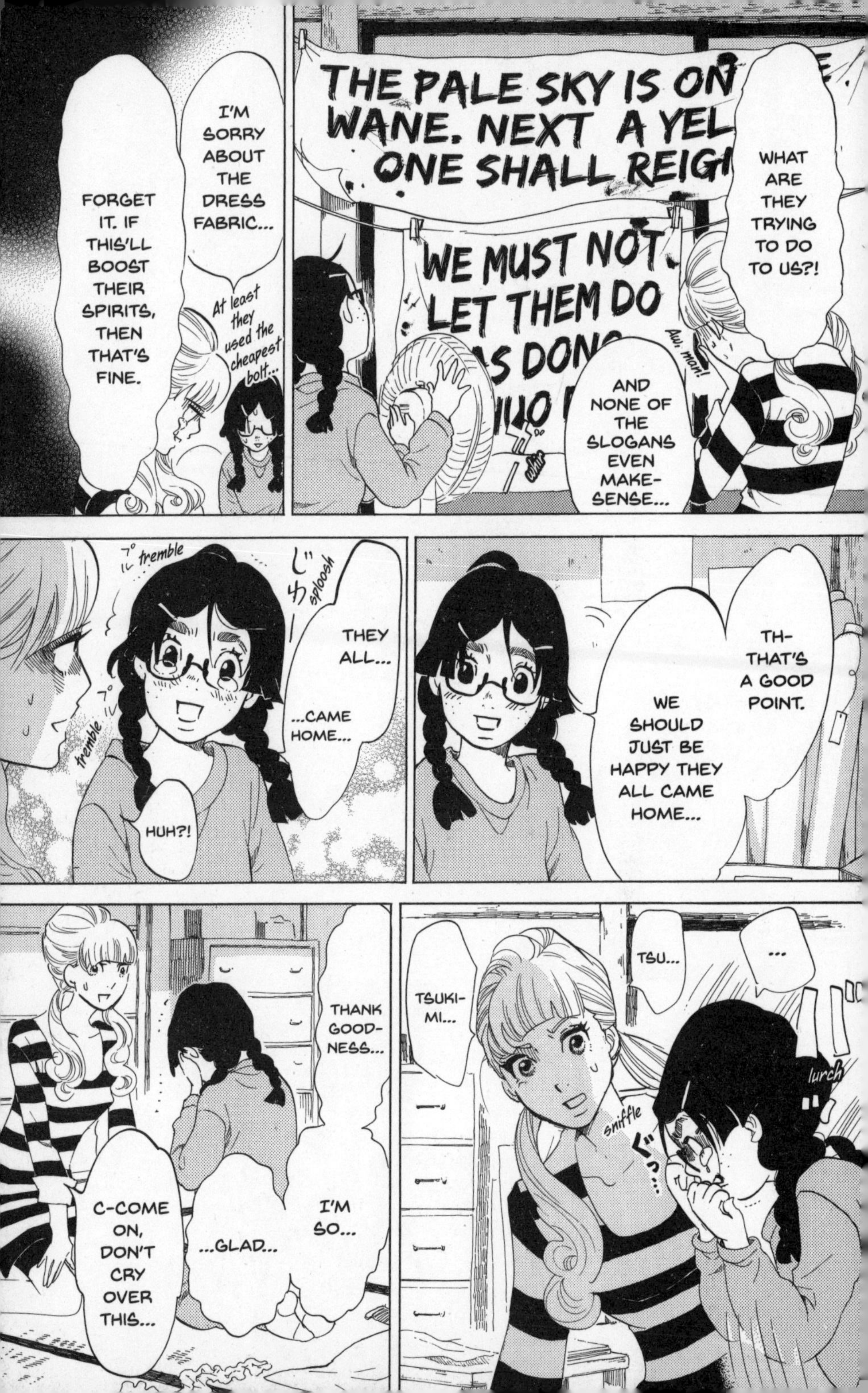
THE PALE SKY IS ON
WANE. NEXT A YEL
ONE SHALL REIG
WE MUST NOT LET THEM DO
WHAT ARE THEY TRYING TO DO TO US?!
Aw, man!
AND NONE OF THE SLOGANS EVEN MAKE-SENSE...
whir
I'M SORRY ABOUT THE DRESS FABRIC...
At least they used the cheapest bolt...
FORGET IT. IF THIS'LL BOOST THEIR SPIRITS, THEN THAT'S FINE.
TH- THAT'S A GOOD POINT.
WE SHOULD JUST BE HAPPY THEY ALL CAME HOME...
sploosh
THEY ALL...
...CAME HOME...
tremble
tremble
HUH?!
...
TSU...
TSUKI-MI...
lurch
sniffle
THANK GOOD-NESS...
I'M SO...
...GLAD...
C-COME ON, DON'T CRY OVER THIS...

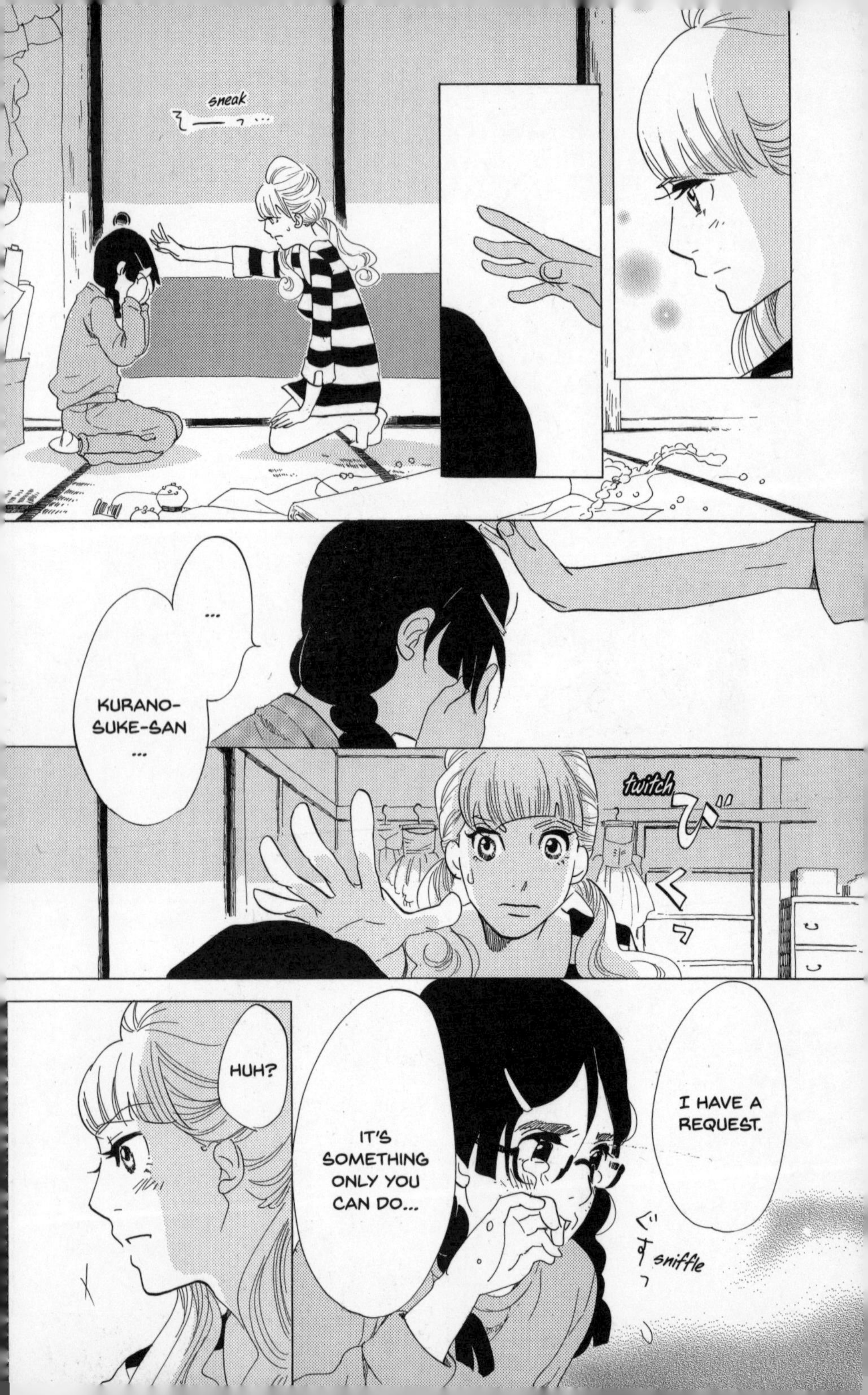
sneak
...
KURANO-SUKE-SAN ...
twitch
I HAVE A REQUEST.
IT'S SOMETHING ONLY YOU CAN DO...
sniffle
HUH?

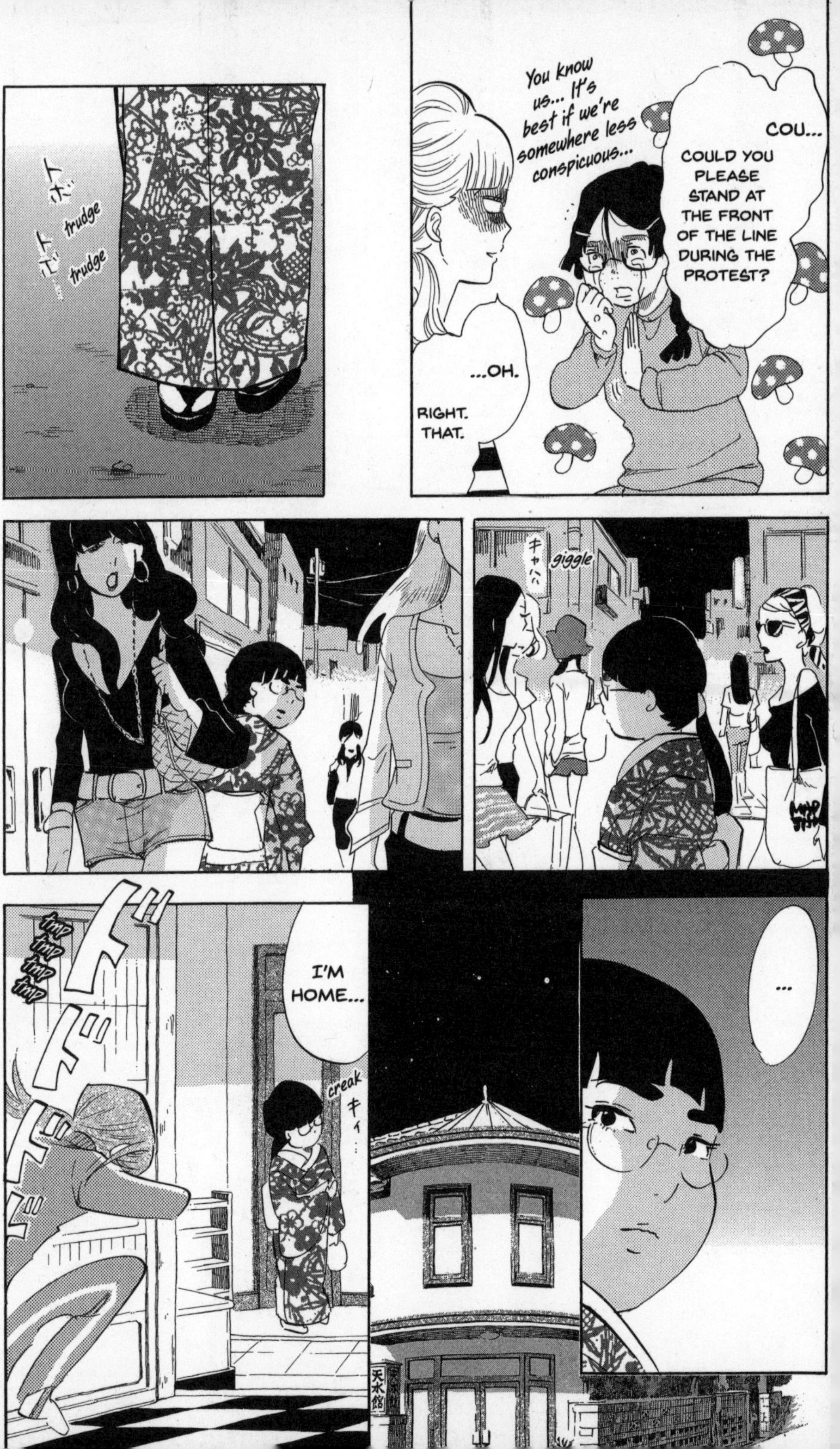
COU...
COULD YOU PLEASE STAND AT THE FRONT OF THE LINE DURING THE PROTEST?
You know us... It's best if we're somewhere less conspicuous...
...OH.
RIGHT. THAT.
トボトボ...
trudge trudge
キャハ
giggle
...
天水館
I'M HOME...
キィ...
creak
ドドドド
tmp tmp tmp tmp

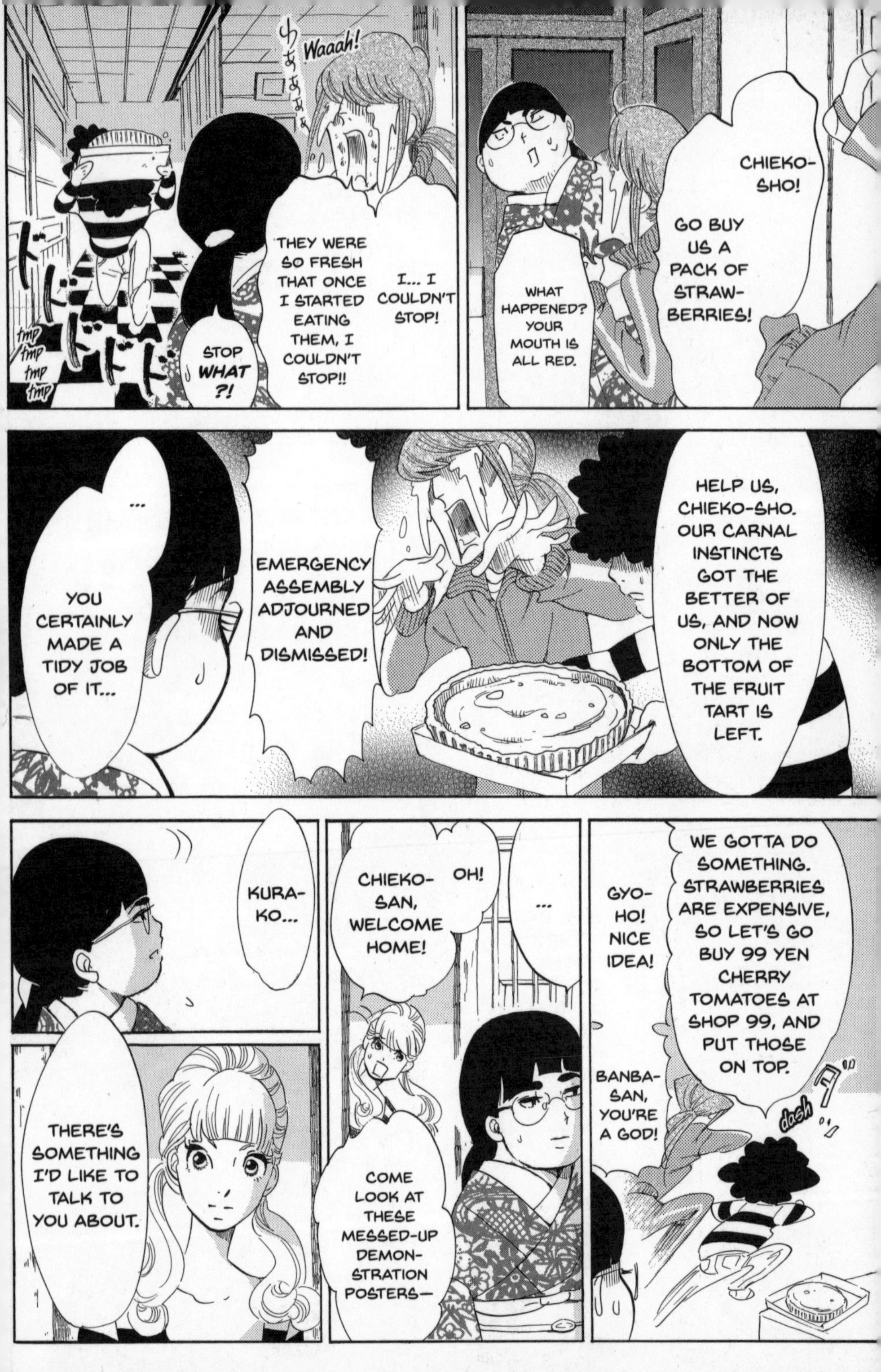
CHIEKO-SHO!
GO BUY US A PACK OF STRAW-BERRIES!
WHAT HAPPENED? YOUR MOUTH IS ALL RED.
Waaah!
I... I COULDN'T STOP!
THEY WERE SO FRESH THAT ONCE I STARTED EATING THEM, I COULDN'T STOP!!
STOP WHAT?!
tmp tmp tmp tmp
HELP US, CHIEKO-SHO. OUR CARNAL INSTINCTS GOT THE BETTER OF US, AND NOW ONLY THE BOTTOM OF THE FRUIT TART IS LEFT.
EMERGENCY ASSEMBLY ADJOURNED AND DISMISSED!
...
YOU CERTAINLY MADE A TIDY JOB OF IT...
WE GOTTA DO SOMETHING. STRAWBERRIES ARE EXPENSIVE, SO LET'S GO BUY 99 YEN CHERRY TOMATOES AT SHOP 99, AND PUT THOSE ON TOP.
GYO-HO! NICE IDEA!
BANBA-SAN, YOU'RE A GOD!
dash
...
OH!
CHIEKO-SAN, WELCOME HOME!
COME LOOK AT THESE MESSED-UP DEMON-STRATION POSTERS—
KURA-KO...
THERE'S SOMETHING I'D LIKE TO TALK TO YOU ABOUT.

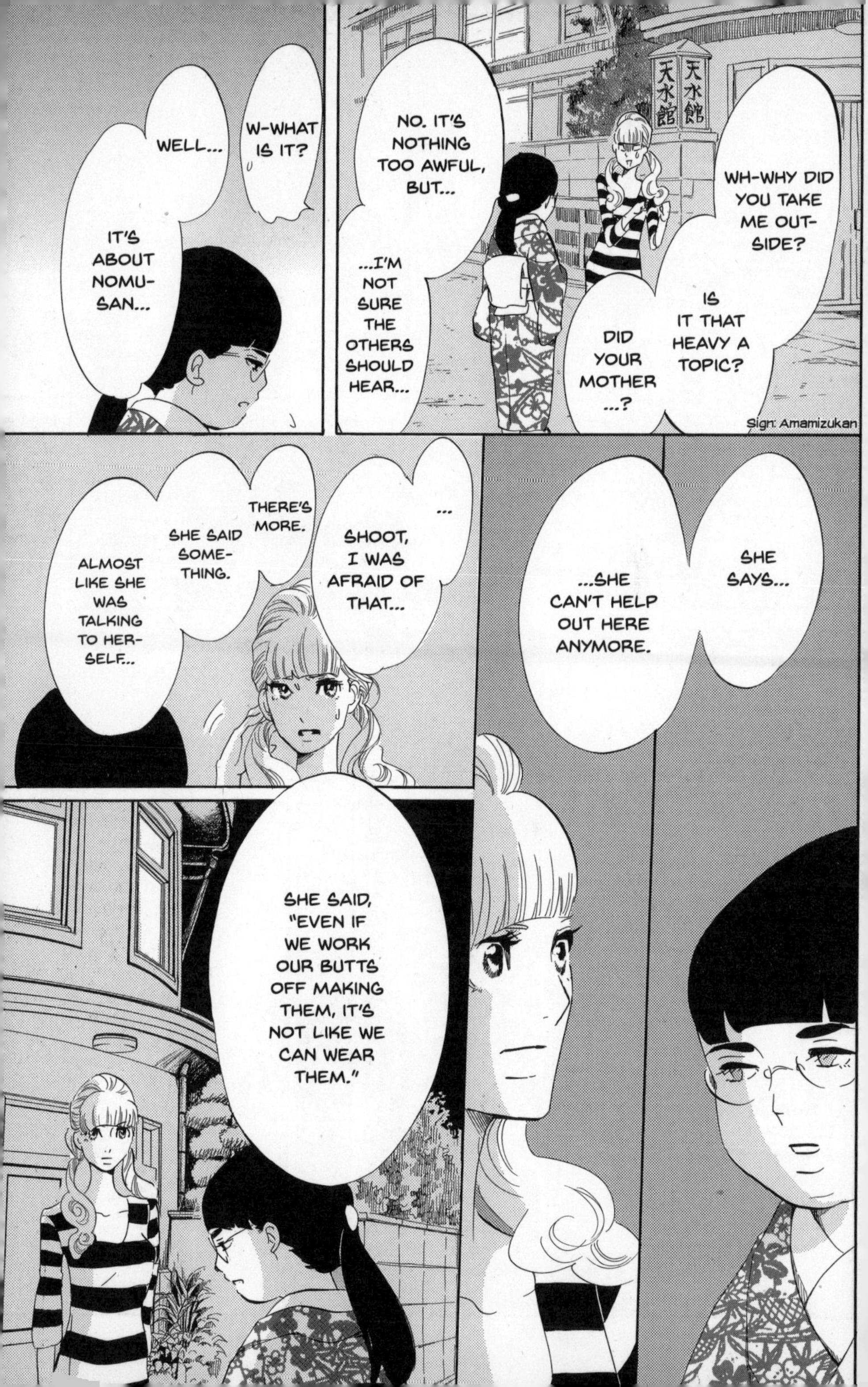
天水館
天水館
WH-WHY DID YOU TAKE ME OUT-SIDE?
IS IT THAT HEAVY A TOPIC?
DID YOUR MOTHER ...?
NO. IT'S NOTHING TOO AWFUL, BUT...
...I'M NOT SURE THE OTHERS SHOULD HEAR...
Sign: Amamizukan
W-WHAT IS IT?
WELL...
IT'S ABOUT NOMU-SAN...
SHE SAYS...
...SHE CAN'T HELP OUT HERE ANYMORE.
...
SHOOT, I WAS AFRAID OF THAT...
THERE'S MORE.
SHE SAID SOME-THING.
ALMOST LIKE SHE WAS TALKING TO HER-SELF...
SHE SAID, "EVEN IF WE WORK OUR BUTTS OFF MAKING THEM, IT'S NOT LIKE WE CAN WEAR THEM."

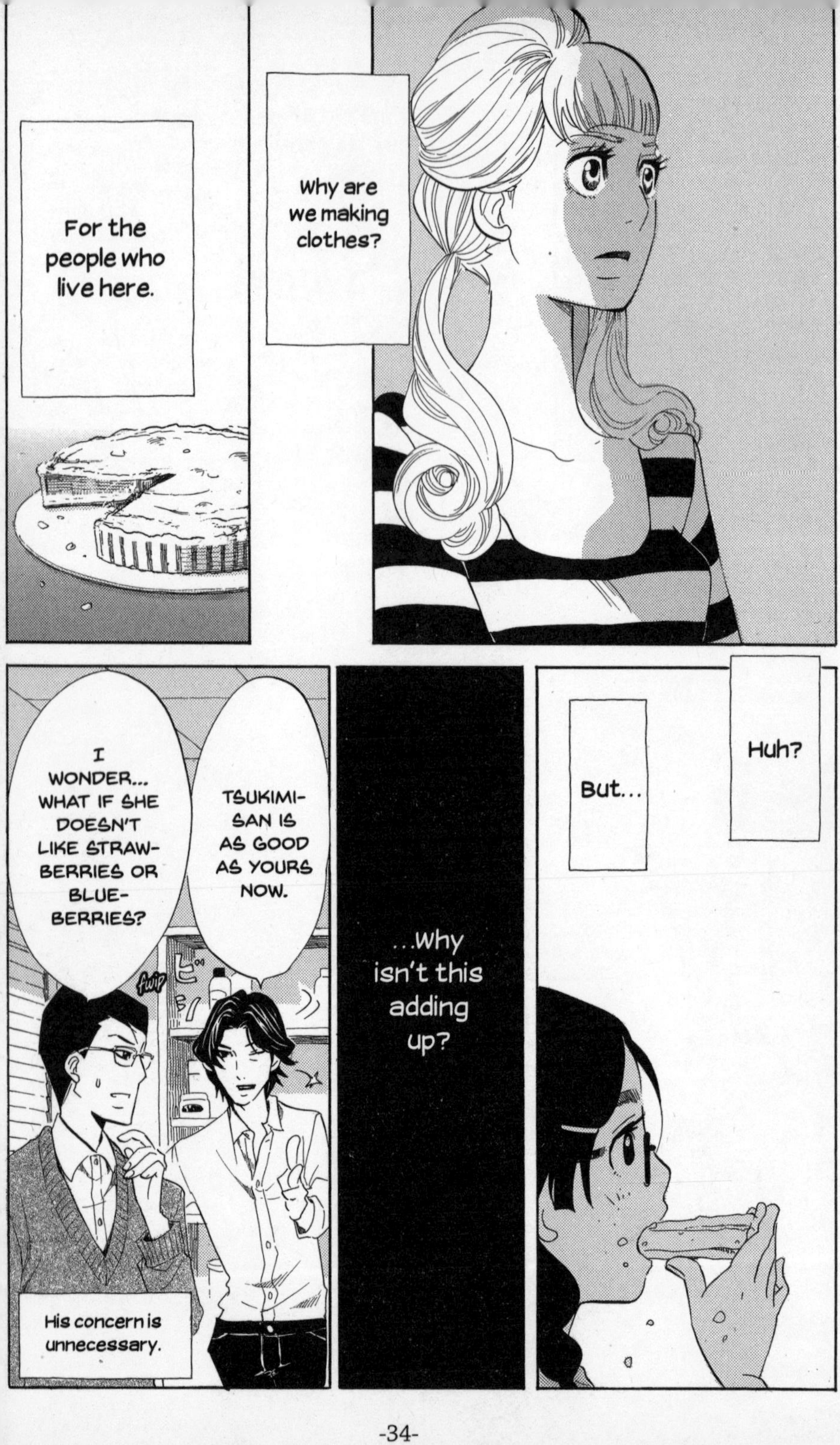
Why are we making clothes?
For the people who live here.
Huh?
But...
...Why isn't this adding up?
TSUKIMI-SAN IS AS GOOD AS YOURS NOW.
I WONDER... WHAT IF SHE DOESN'T LIKE STRAW-BERRIES OR BLUE-BERRIES?
His concern is unnecessary.

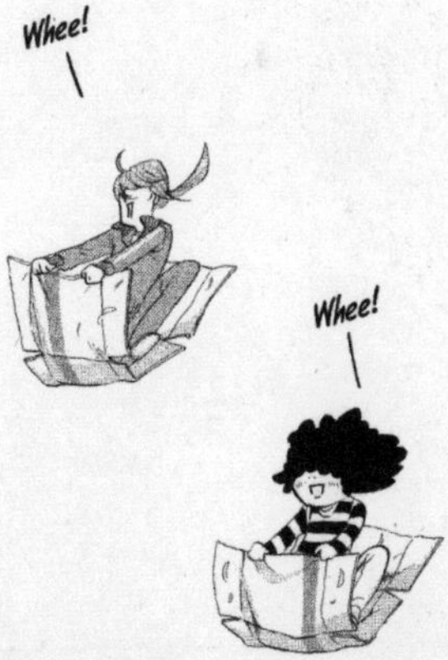
Whee!
Whee!

Episode 46
Girls Just Wanna Have Fun

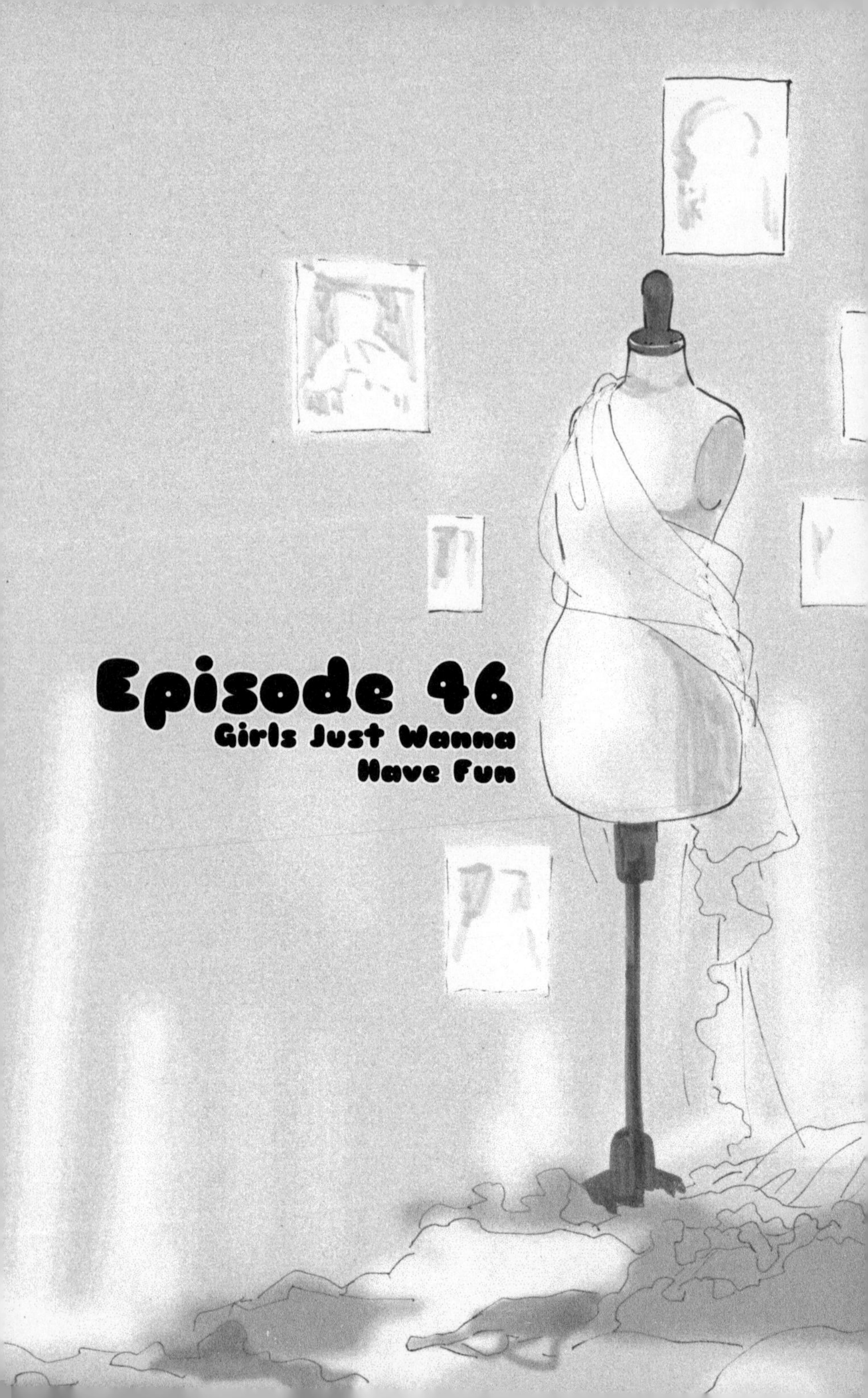

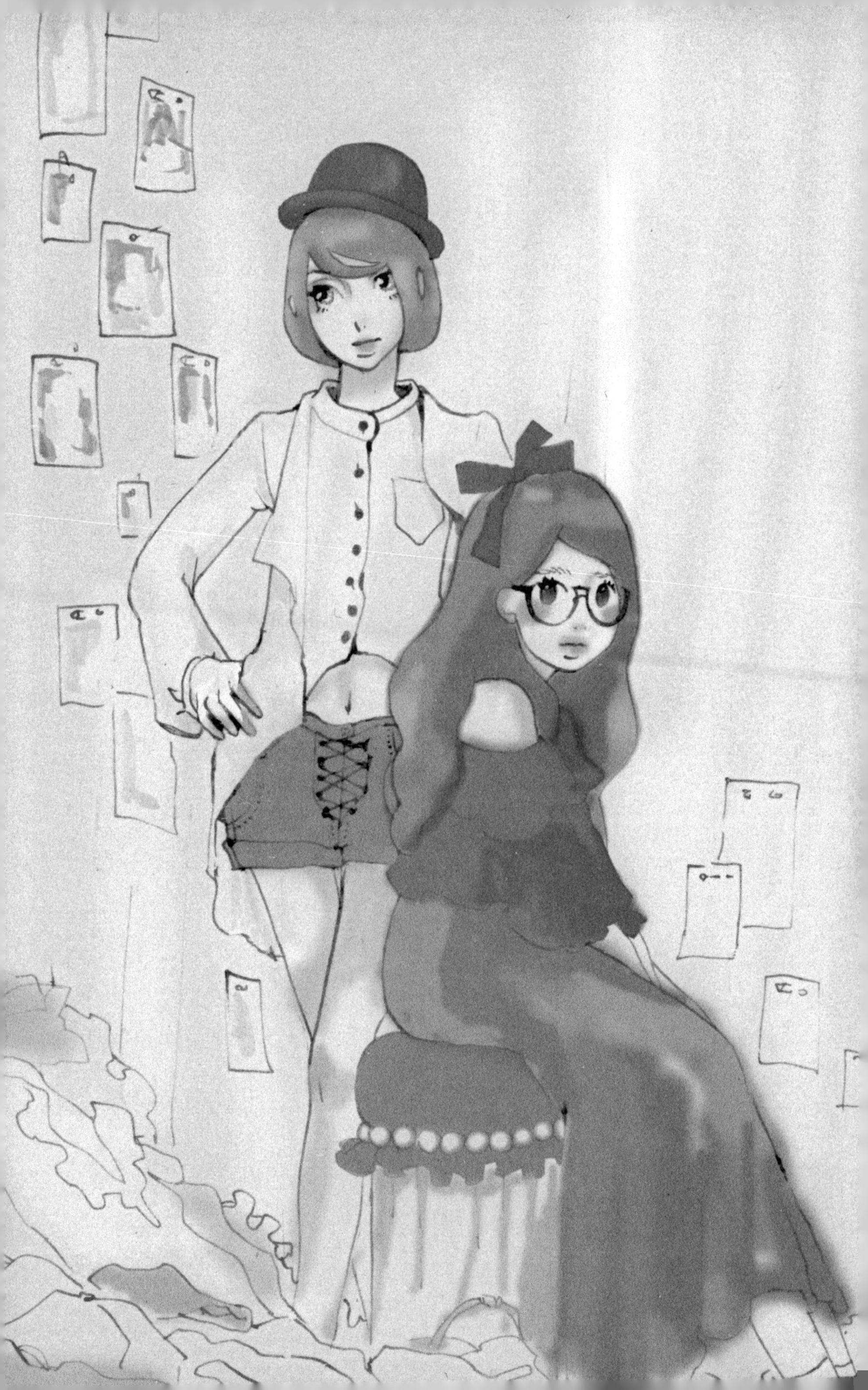

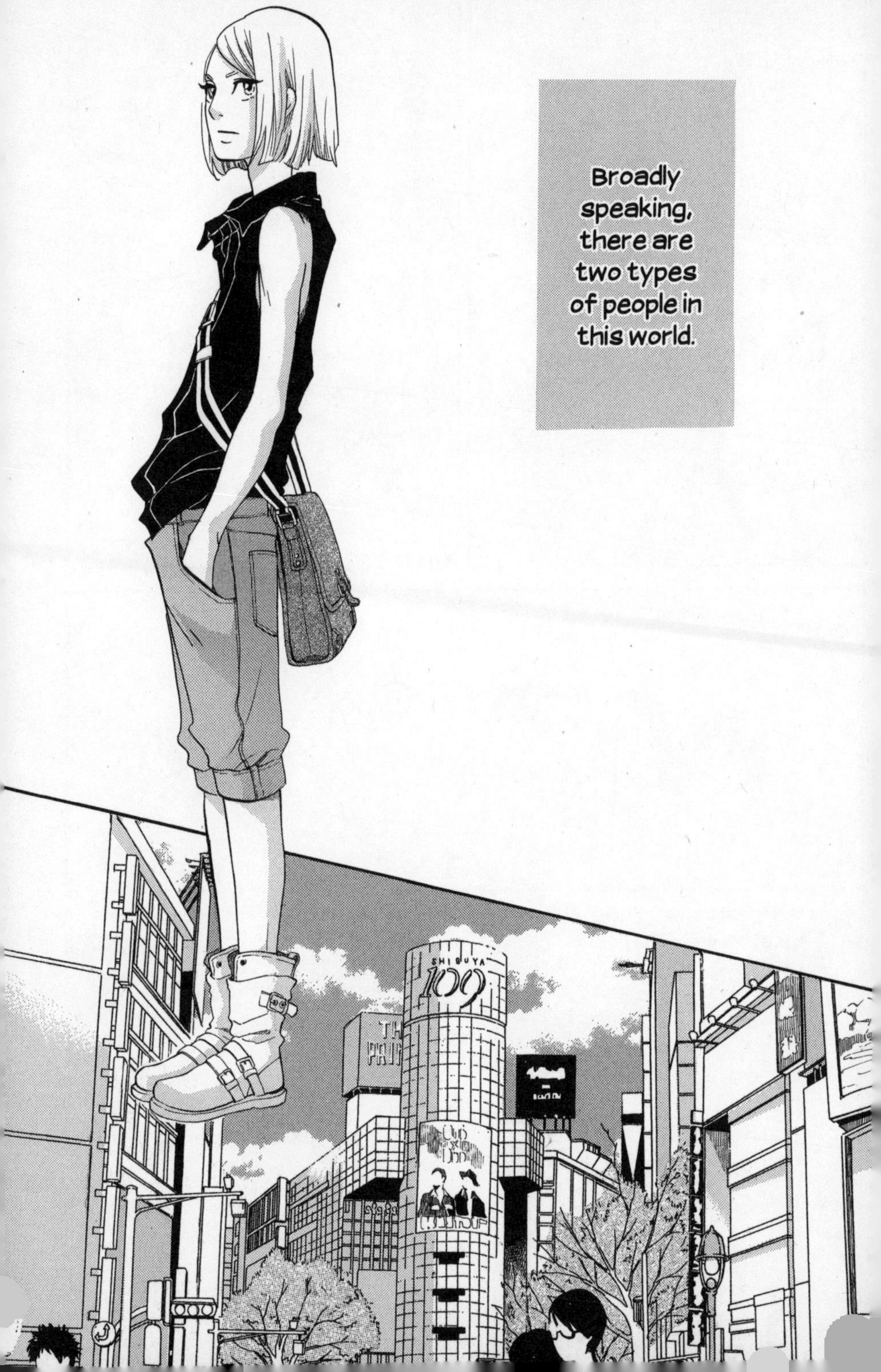
Broadly speaking, there are two types of people in this world.
SHIBUYA 109

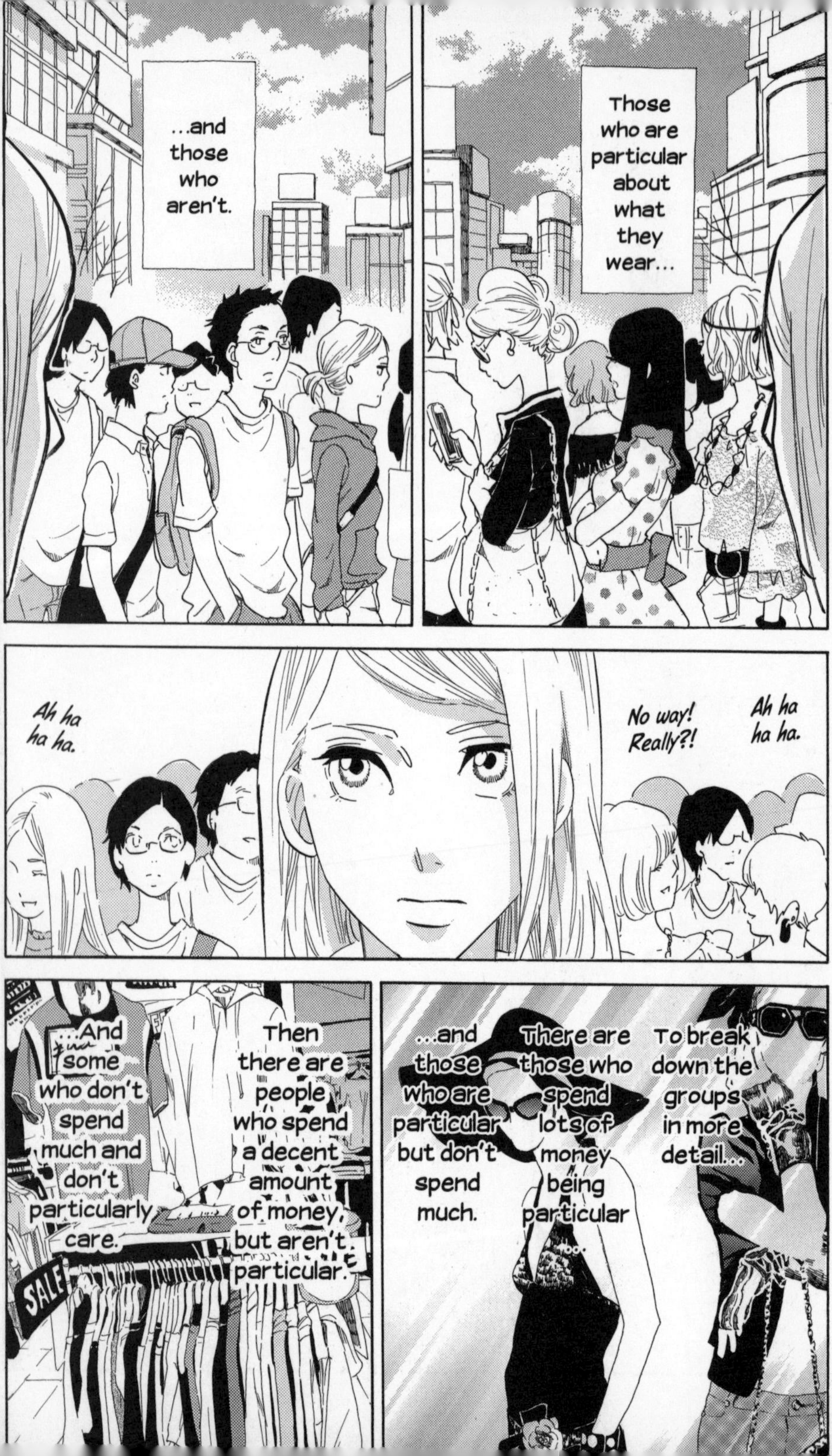
Those who are particular about what they wear...
...and those who aren't.
Ah ha ha ha.
No way! Really?!
Ah ha ha ha.
To break down the groups in more detail...
There are those who spend lots of money being particular...
...and those who are particular but don't spend much.
Then there are people who spend a decent amount of money, but aren't particular.
...And some who don't spend much and don't particularly care.
SALE

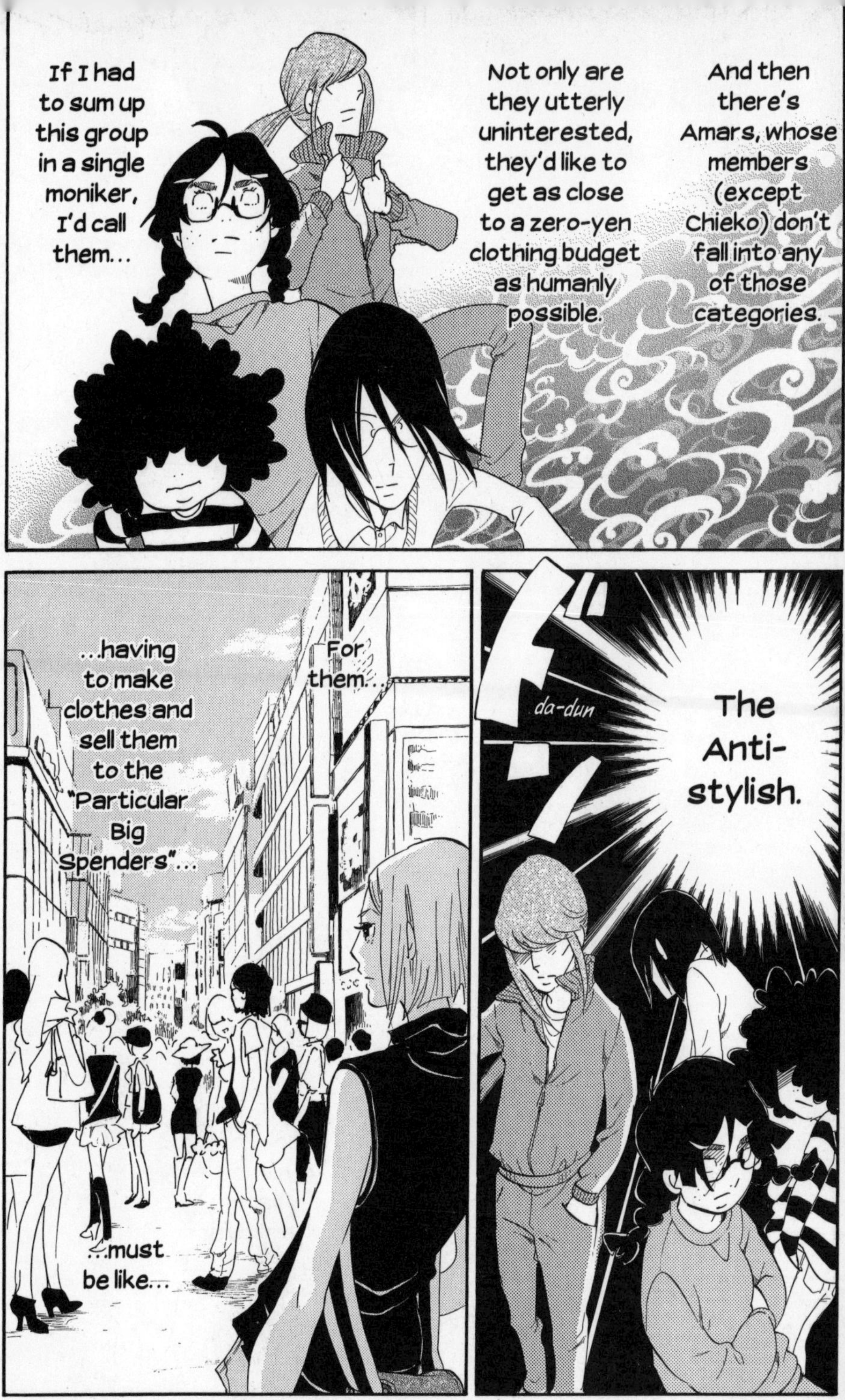
And then there's Amars, whose members (except Chieko) don't fall into any of those categories.
Not only are they utterly uninterested, they'd like to get as close to a zero-yen clothing budget as humanly possible.
If I had to sum up this group in a single moniker, I'd call them...
da-dun
The Anti-stylish.
For them...
...having to make clothes and sell them to the "Particular Big Spenders"...
...must be like...

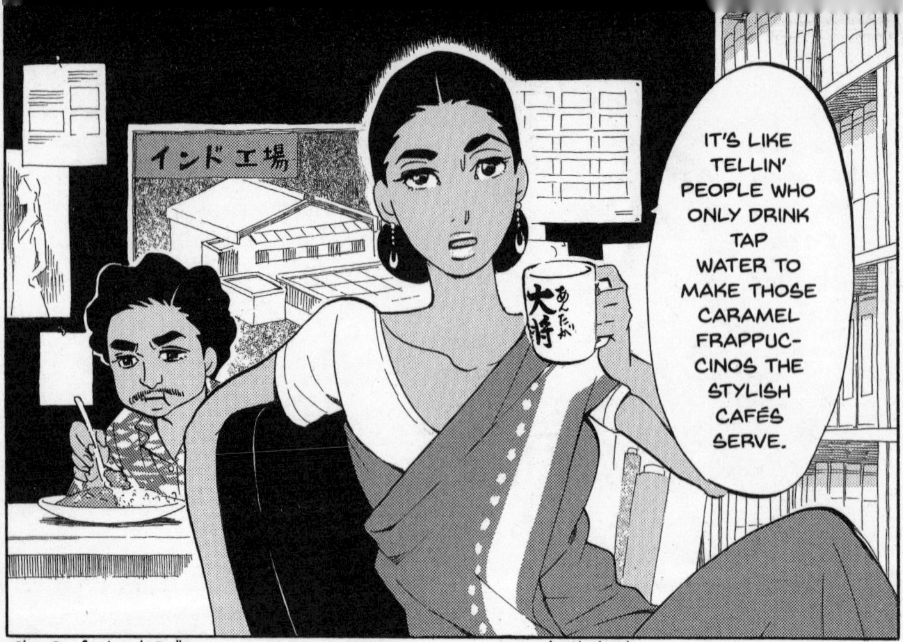
インド工場
あんたが大将
IT'S LIKE TELLIN' PEOPLE WHO ONLY DRINK TAP WATER TO MAKE THOSE CARAMEL FRAPPUC-CINOS THE STYLISH CAFÉS SERVE.

Sign: Our factory in India.

Mug: You're the bomb.

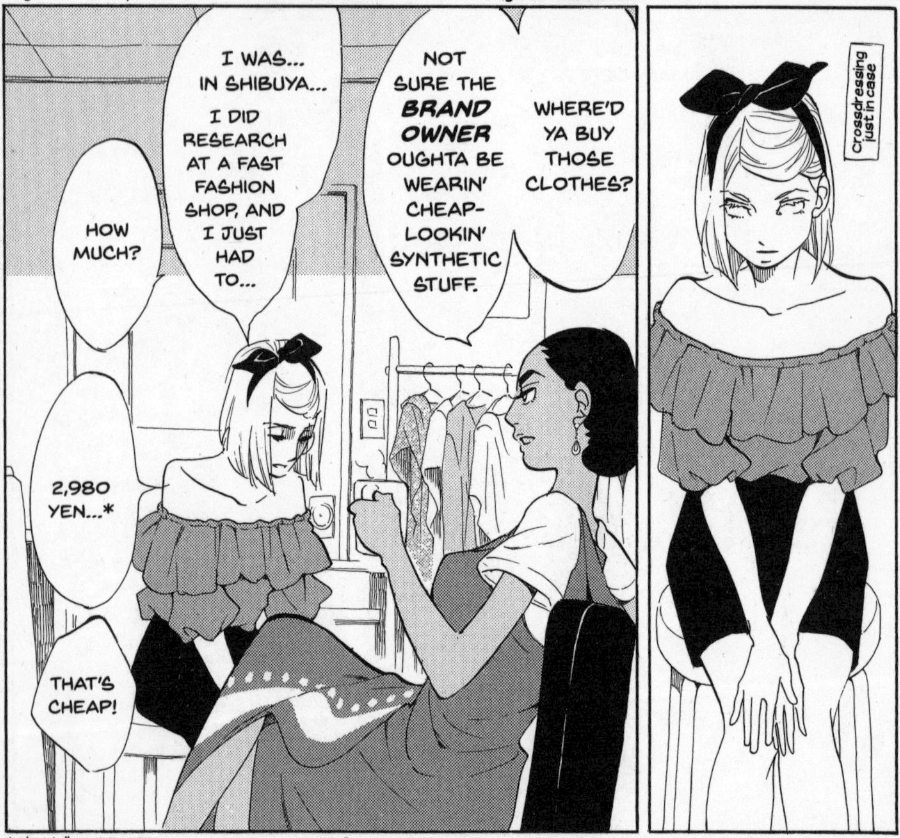
Crossdressing just in case
WHERE'D YA BUY THOSE CLOTHES?
NOT SURE THE **BRAND OWNER** OUGHTA BE WEARIN' CHEAP-LOOKIN' SYNTHETIC STUFF.
I WAS... IN SHIBUYA...
I DID RESEARCH AT A FAST FASHION SHOP, AND I JUST HAD TO...
HOW MUCH?
2,980 YEN...*
THAT'S CHEAP!

*About $29.80 USD.

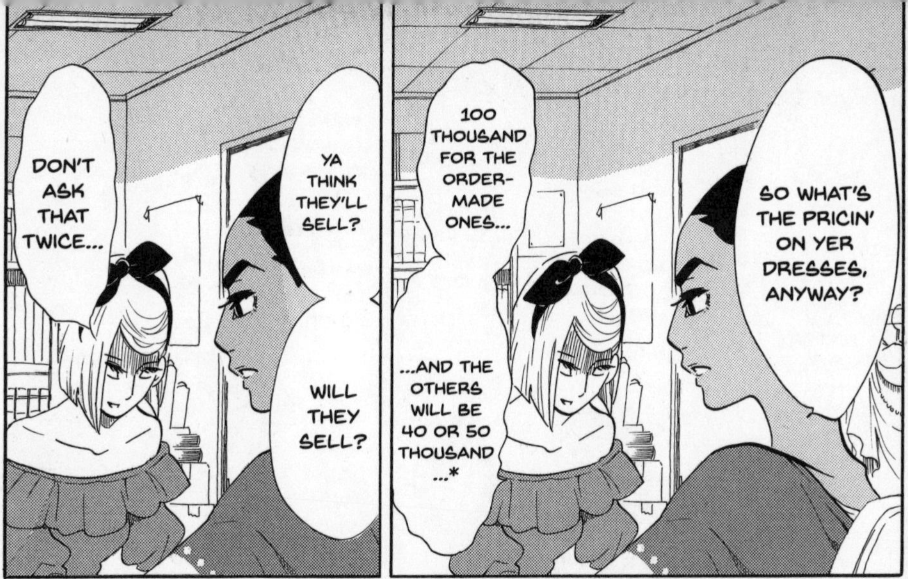
SO WHAT'S THE PRICIN' ON YER DRESSES, ANYWAY?
100 THOUSAND FOR THE ORDER-MADE ONES...
...AND THE OTHERS WILL BE 40 OR 50 THOUSAND ...*
YA THINK THEY'LL SELL?
WILL THEY SELL?
DON'T ASK THAT TWICE...

*About $1,000 USD, $400-500 USD.

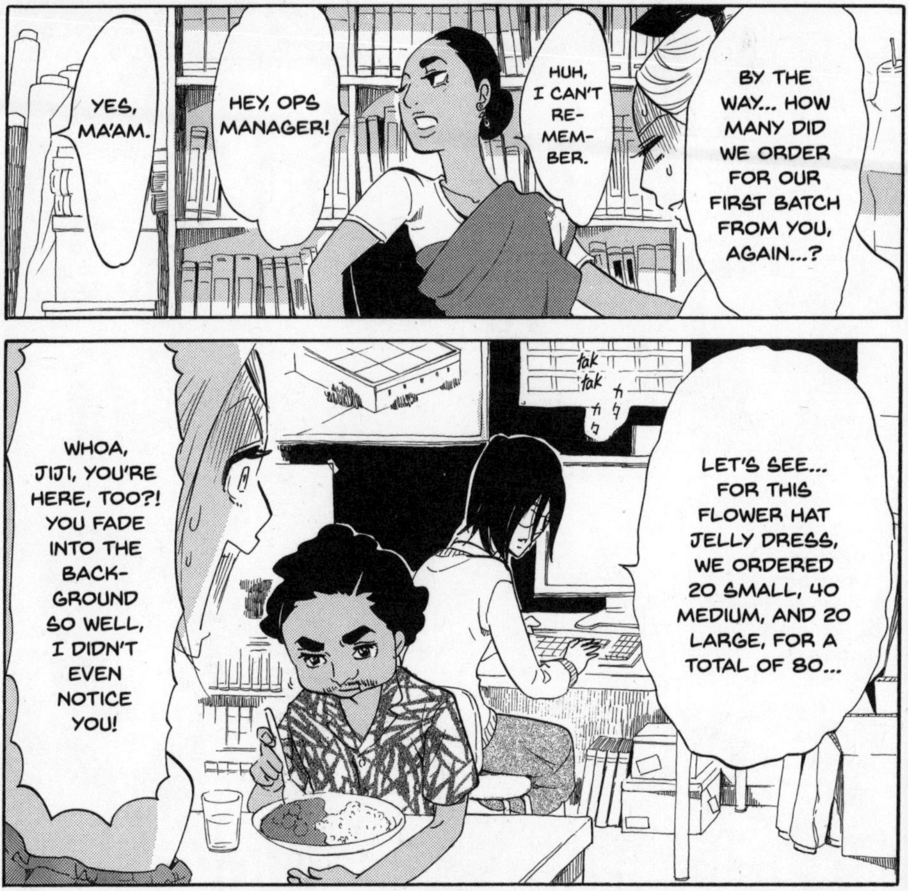
BY THE WAY... HOW MANY DID WE ORDER FOR OUR FIRST BATCH FROM YOU, AGAIN...?
HUH, I CAN'T REMEMBER.
HEY, OPS MANAGER!
YES, MA'AM.
LET'S SEE... FOR THIS FLOWER HAT JELLY DRESS, WE ORDERED 20 SMALL, 40 MEDIUM, AND 20 LARGE, FOR A TOTAL OF 80...
tak tak
カタカタ
WHOA, JIJI, YOU'RE HERE, TOO?! YOU FADE INTO THE BACKGROUND SO WELL, I DIDN'T EVEN NOTICE YOU!

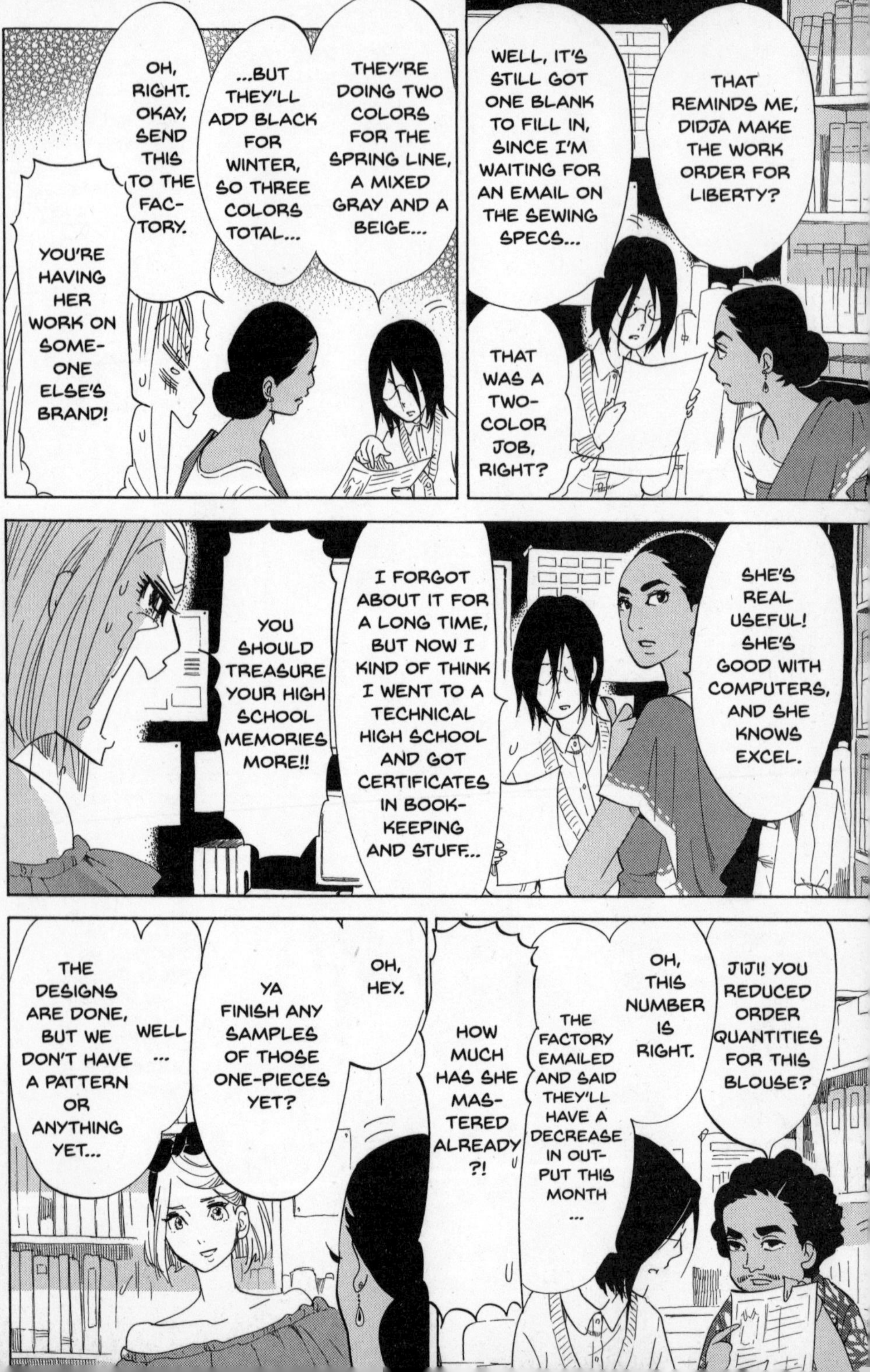
THAT REMINDS ME, DIDJA MAKE THE WORK ORDER FOR LIBERTY?
WELL, IT'S STILL GOT ONE BLANK TO FILL IN, SINCE I'M WAITING FOR AN EMAIL ON THE SEWING SPECS...
THAT WAS A TWO-COLOR JOB, RIGHT?
THEY'RE DOING TWO COLORS FOR THE SPRING LINE, A MIXED GRAY AND A BEIGE...
...BUT THEY'LL ADD BLACK FOR WINTER, SO THREE COLORS TOTAL...
OH, RIGHT. OKAY, SEND THIS TO THE FACTORY.
YOU'RE HAVING HER WORK ON SOMEONE ELSE'S BRAND!
SHE'S REAL USEFUL! SHE'S GOOD WITH COMPUTERS, AND SHE KNOWS EXCEL.
I FORGOT ABOUT IT FOR A LONG TIME, BUT NOW I KIND OF THINK I WENT TO A TECHNICAL HIGH SCHOOL AND GOT CERTIFICATES IN BOOK-KEEPING AND STUFF...
YOU SHOULD TREASURE YOUR HIGH SCHOOL MEMORIES MORE!!
JIJI! YOU REDUCED ORDER QUANTITIES FOR THIS BLOUSE?
OH, THIS NUMBER IS RIGHT.
THE FACTORY EMAILED AND SAID THEY'LL HAVE A DECREASE IN OUT-PUT THIS MONTH ...
HOW MUCH HAS SHE MAS-TERED ALREADY ?!
OH, HEY.
YA FINISH ANY SAMPLES OF THOSE ONE-PIECES YET?
WELL ...
THE DESIGNS ARE DONE, BUT WE DON'T HAVE A PATTERN OR ANYTHING YET...

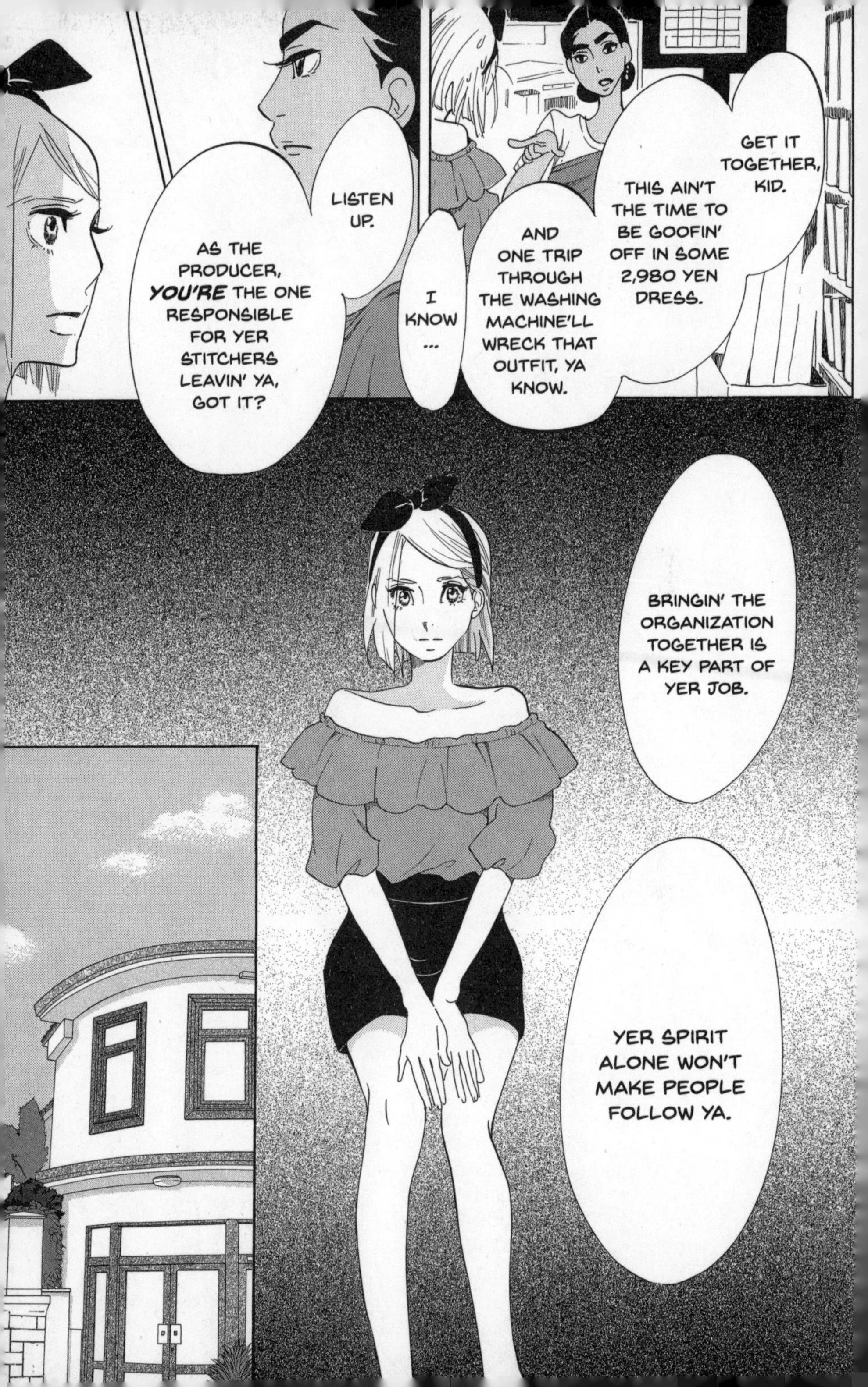
GET IT TOGETHER, KID.
THIS AIN'T THE TIME TO BE GOOFIN' OFF IN SOME 2,980 YEN DRESS.
AND ONE TRIP THROUGH THE WASHING MACHINE'LL WRECK THAT OUTFIT, YA KNOW.
I KNOW ...
LISTEN UP.
AS THE PRODUCER, *YOU'RE* THE ONE RESPONSIBLE FOR YER STITCHERS LEAVIN' YA, GOT IT?
BRINGIN' THE ORGANIZATION TOGETHER IS A KEY PART OF YER JOB.
YER SPIRIT ALONE WON'T MAKE PEOPLE FOLLOW YA.

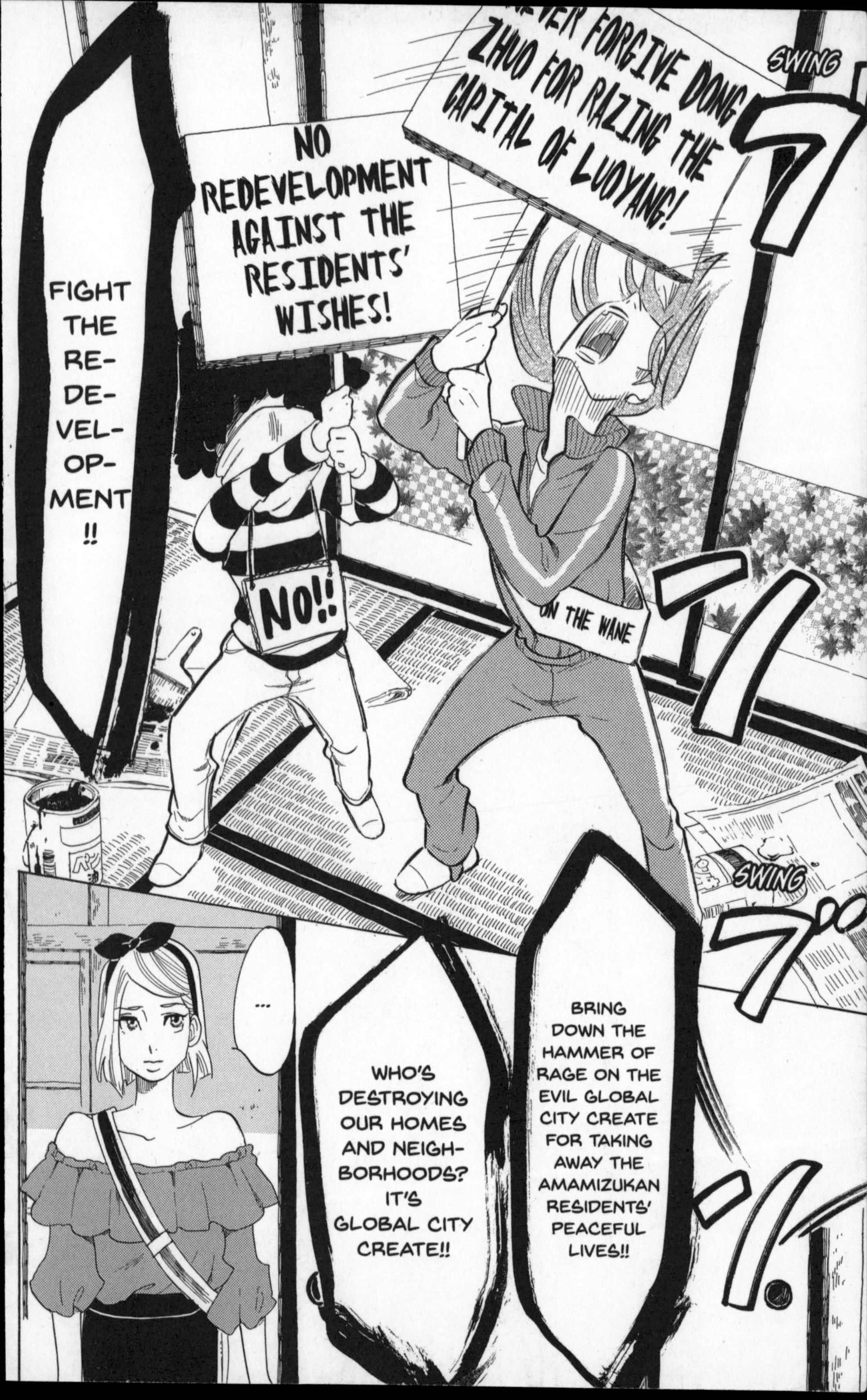
FORGIVE DONG ZHUO FOR RAZING THE CAPITAL OF LUOYANG!
SWING
NO REDEVELOPMENT AGAINST THE RESIDENTS' WISHES!
FIGHT THE RE-DE-VEL-OP-MENT !!
NO!!
ON THE WANE
SWING
BRING DOWN THE HAMMER OF RAGE ON THE EVIL GLOBAL CITY CREATE FOR TAKING AWAY THE AMAMIZUKAN RESIDENTS' PEACEFUL LIVES!!
WHO'S DESTROYING OUR HOMES AND NEIGH-BORHOODS? IT'S GLOBAL CITY CREATE!!
...

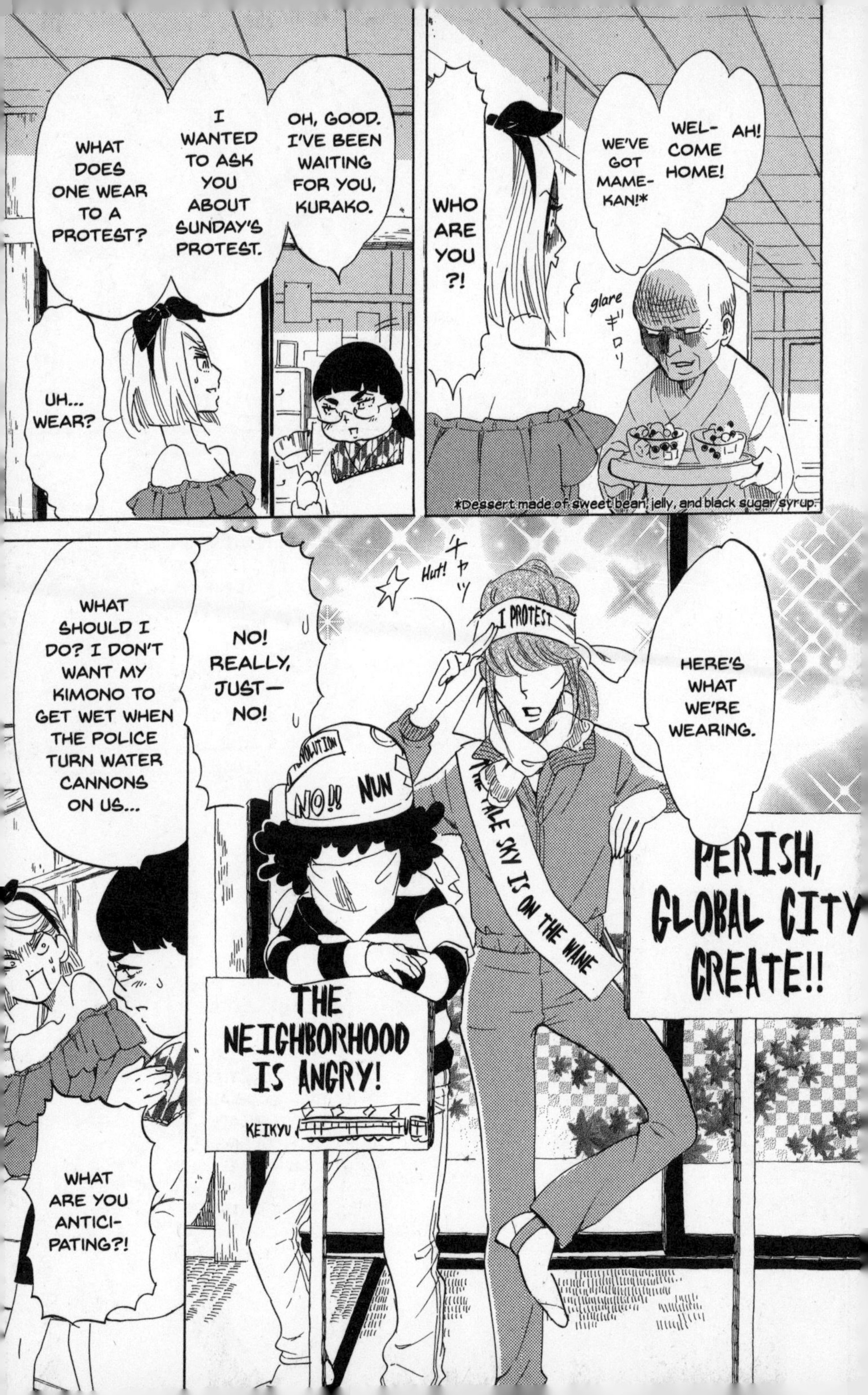
AH!
WEL-COME HOME!
WE'VE GOT MAME-KAN!*
glare
ギロリ
WHO ARE YOU ?!
OH, GOOD. I'VE BEEN WAITING FOR YOU, KURAKO.
I WANTED TO ASK YOU ABOUT SUNDAY'S PROTEST.
WHAT DOES ONE WEAR TO A PROTEST?
UH... WEAR?
HERE'S WHAT WE'RE WEARING.
I PROTEST
Hut!
キャッ
PERISH, GLOBAL CITY CREATE!!
NO!! NUN
THE NEIGHBORHOOD IS ANGRY!
KEIKYU
NO! REALLY, JUST— NO!
WHAT SHOULD I DO? I DON'T WANT MY KIMONO TO GET WET WHEN THE POLICE TURN WATER CANNONS ON US...
WHAT ARE YOU ANTICI-PATING?!
*Dessert made of sweet bean, jelly, and black sugar syrup.

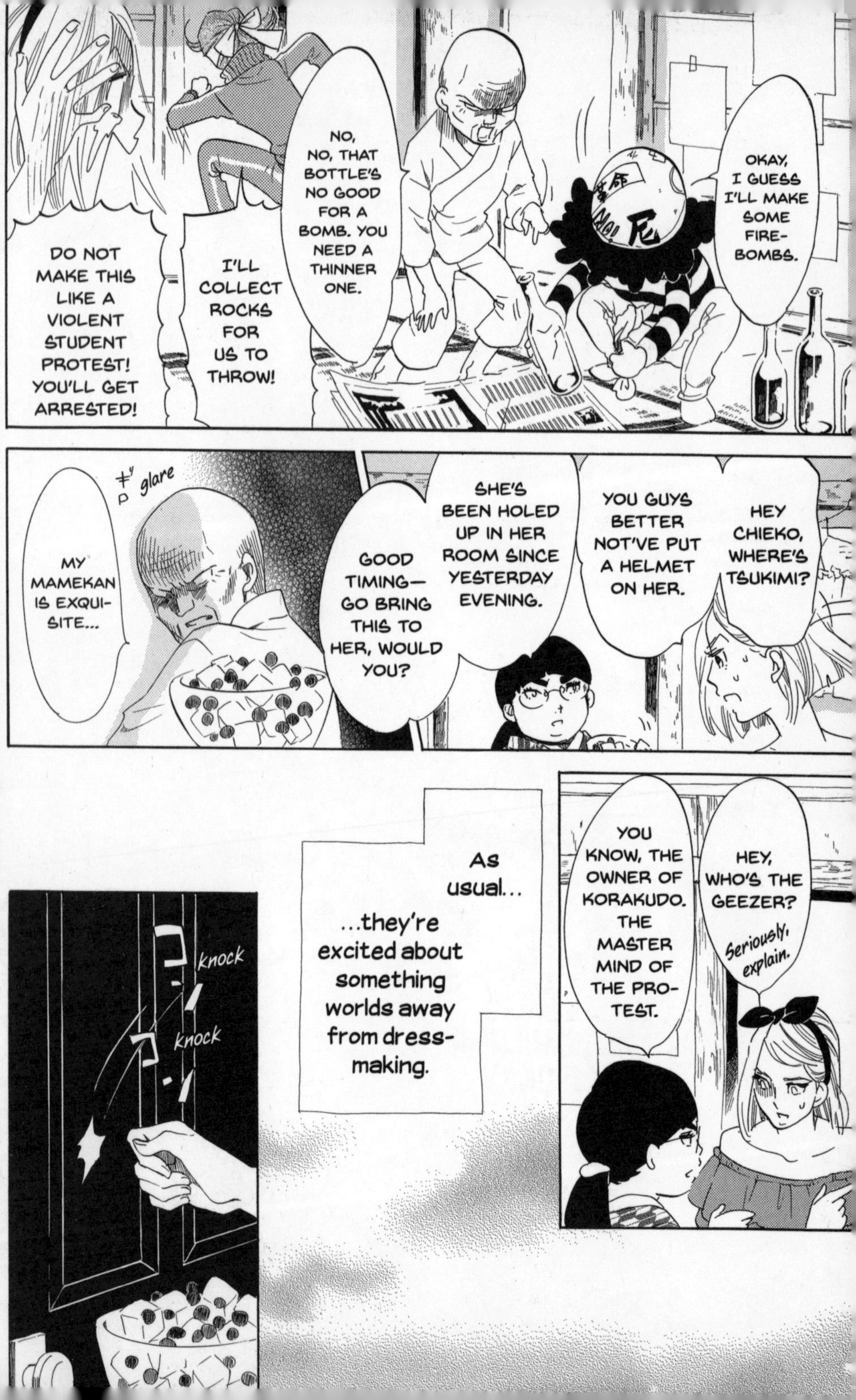
OKAY, I GUESS I'LL MAKE SOME FIRE-BOMBS.
NO, NO, THAT BOTTLE'S NO GOOD FOR A BOMB. YOU NEED A THINNER ONE.
I'LL COLLECT ROCKS FOR US TO THROW!
DO NOT MAKE THIS LIKE A VIOLENT STUDENT PROTEST! YOU'LL GET ARRESTED!
HEY CHIEKO, WHERE'S TSUKIMI?
YOU GUYS BETTER NOT'VE PUT A HELMET ON HER.
SHE'S BEEN HOLED UP IN HER ROOM SINCE YESTERDAY EVENING.
GOOD TIMING—GO BRING THIS TO HER, WOULD YOU?
glare
MY MAMEKAN IS EXQUISITE...
HEY, WHO'S THE GEEZER?
Seriously, explain.
YOU KNOW, THE OWNER OF KORAKUDO. THE MASTER MIND OF THE PRO-TEST.
As usual...
...they're excited about something worlds away from dress-making.
knock
knock

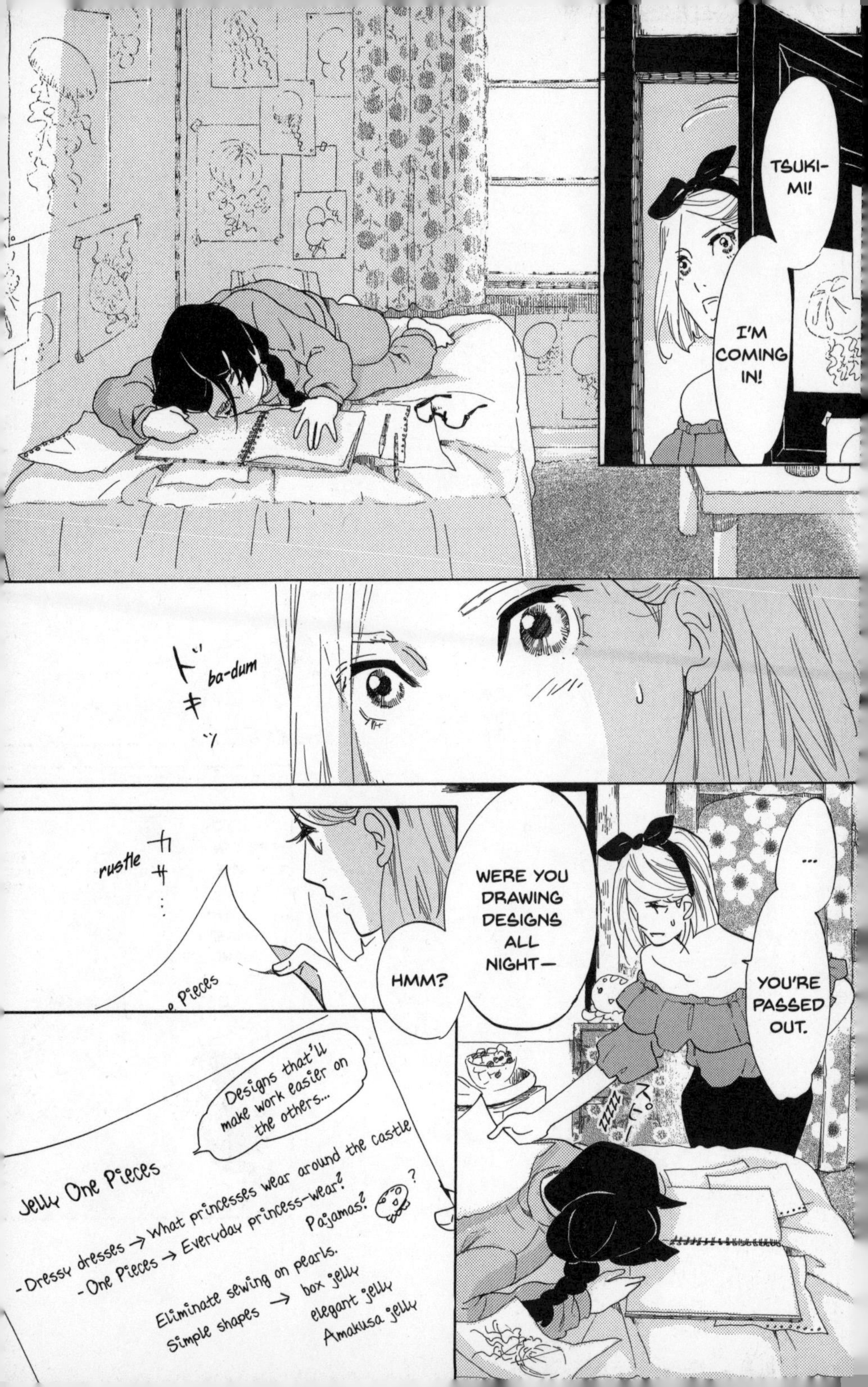
TSUKI-MI!
I'M COMING IN!
ドキッ
ba-dum
...
YOU'RE PASSED OUT.
WERE YOU DRAWING DESIGNS ALL NIGHT—
HMM?
カサ…
rustle
Designs that'll make work easier on the others...
Jelly One Pieces
-Dressy dresses → What princesses wear around the castle
-One Pieces → Everyday princess-wear?
Pajamas?
Eliminate sewing on pearls.
Simple shapes → box jelly
elegant jelly
Amakusa jelly

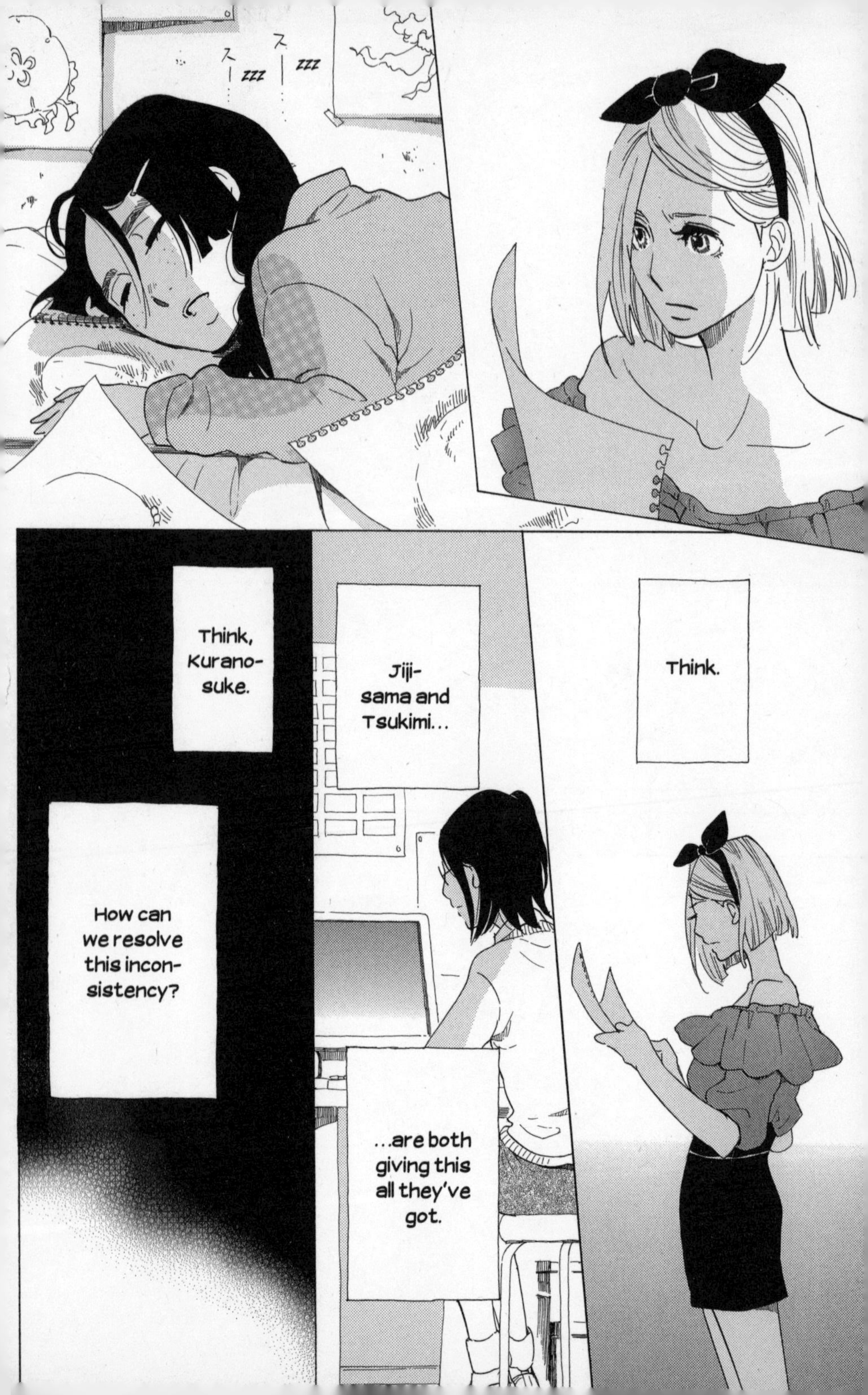
スー
zzz
スー
zzz
Think.
Jiji-sama and Tsukimi...
...are both giving this all they've got.
Think, Kurano-suke.
How can we resolve this inconsistency?

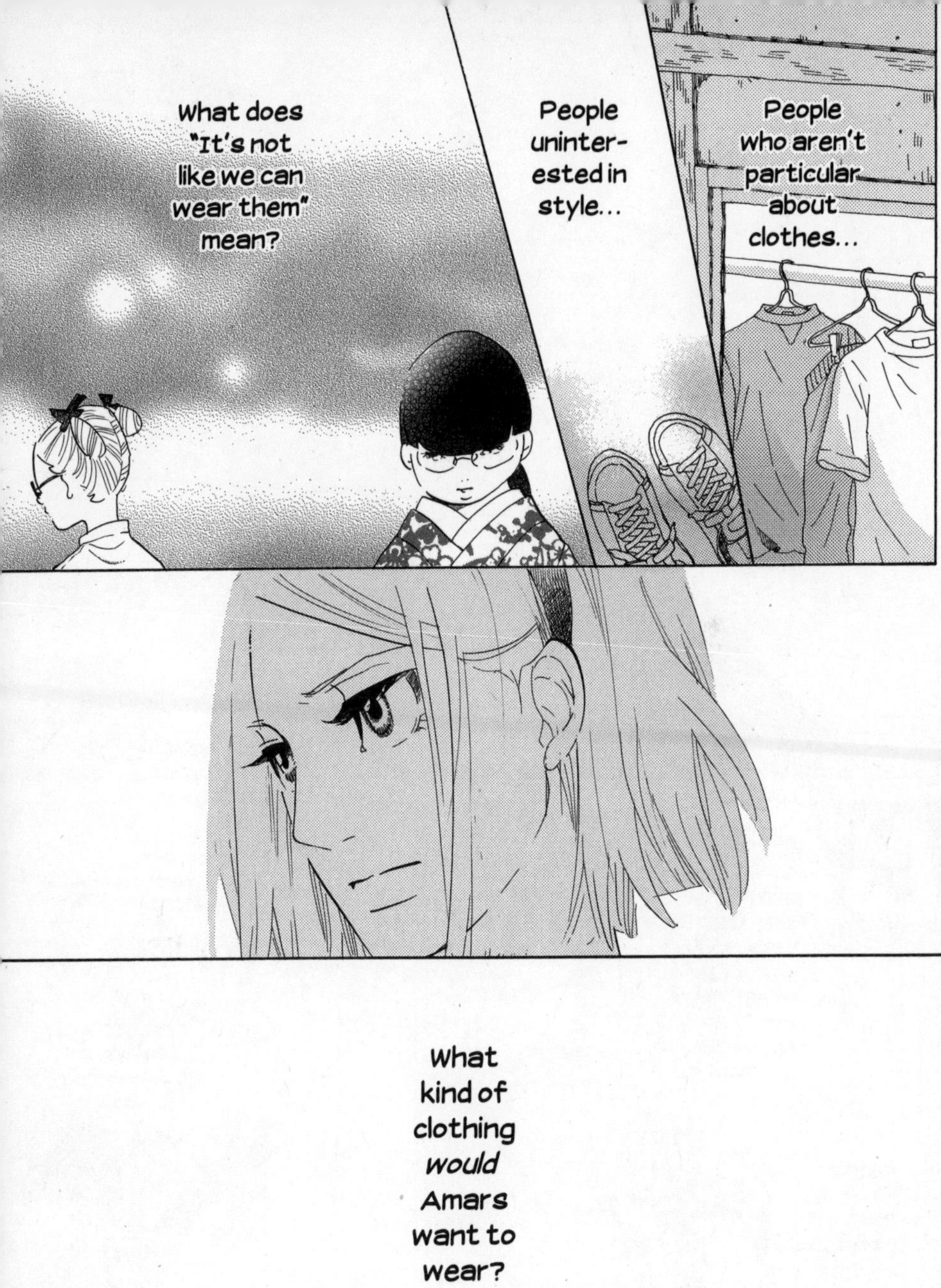
People who aren't particular about clothes...
People uninter-ested in style...
What does "It's not like we can wear them" mean?
What kind of clothing *would* Amars want to wear?

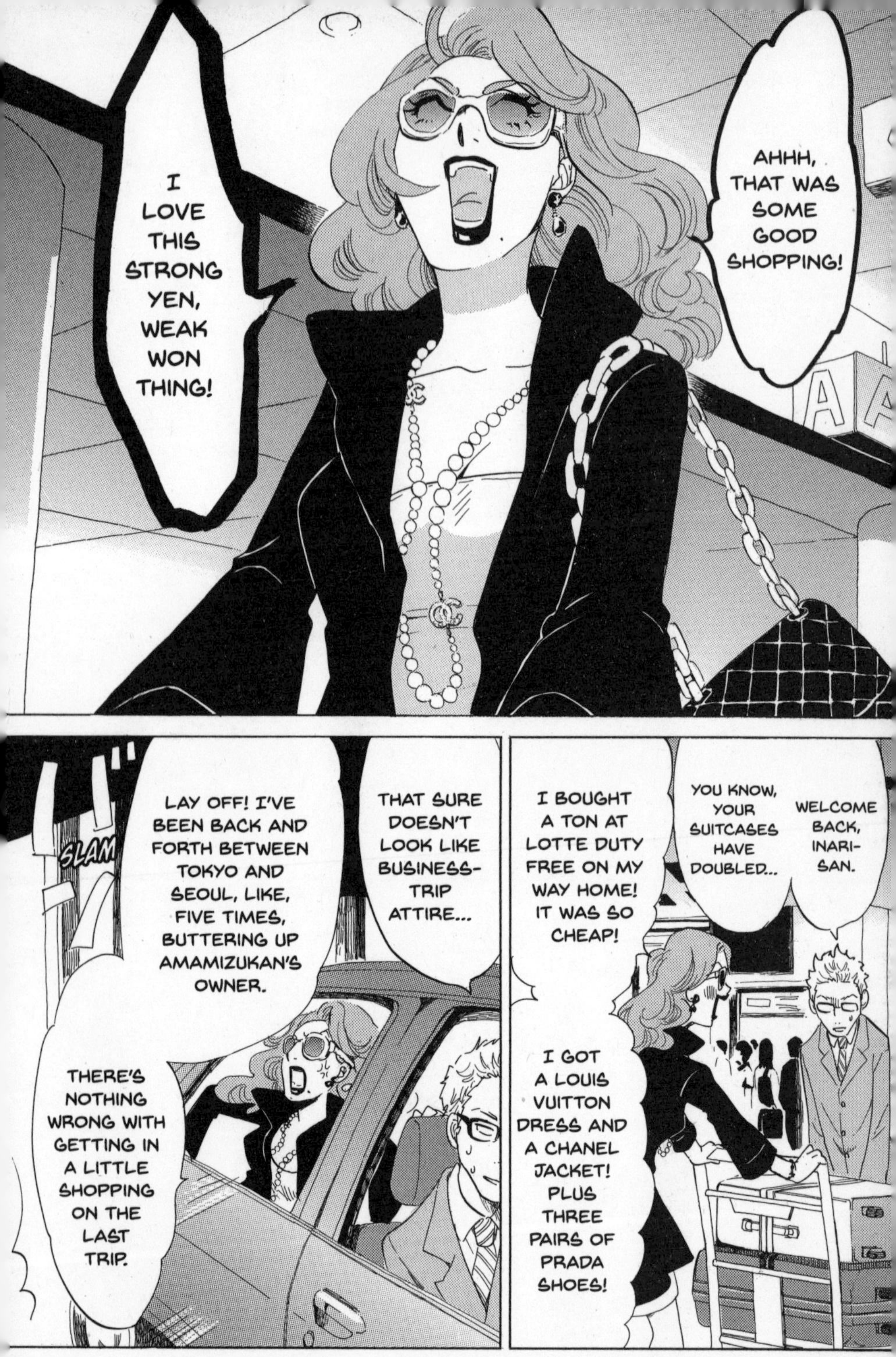
AHHH, THAT WAS SOME GOOD SHOPPING!
I LOVE THIS STRONG YEN, WEAK WON THING!
WELCOME BACK, INARI-SAN.
YOU KNOW, YOUR SUITCASES HAVE DOUBLED...
I BOUGHT A TON AT LOTTE DUTY FREE ON MY WAY HOME! IT WAS SO CHEAP!
I GOT A LOUIS VUITTON DRESS AND A CHANEL JACKET! PLUS THREE PAIRS OF PRADA SHOES!
THAT SURE DOESN'T LOOK LIKE BUSINESS-TRIP ATTIRE...
LAY OFF! I'VE BEEN BACK AND FORTH BETWEEN TOKYO AND SEOUL, LIKE, FIVE TIMES, BUTTERING UP AMAMIZUKAN'S OWNER.
SLAM
THERE'S NOTHING WRONG WITH GETTING IN A LITTLE SHOPPING ON THE LAST TRIP.

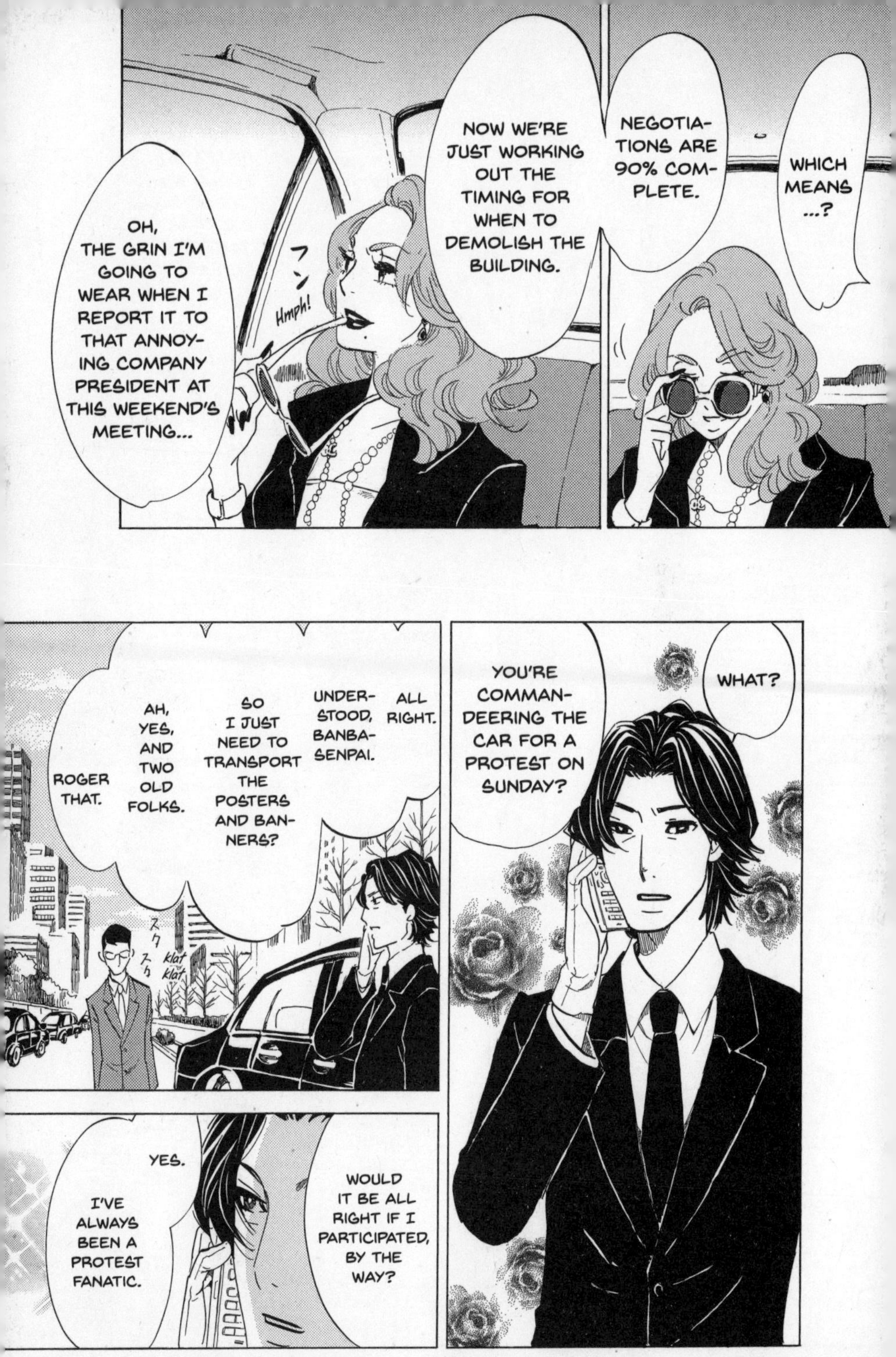
WHICH MEANS ...?
NEGOTIATIONS ARE 90% COMPLETE.
NOW WE'RE JUST WORKING OUT THE TIMING FOR WHEN TO DEMOLISH THE BUILDING.
フン
Hmph!
OH, THE GRIN I'M GOING TO WEAR WHEN I REPORT IT TO THAT ANNOYING COMPANY PRESIDENT AT THIS WEEKEND'S MEETING...
WHAT?
YOU'RE COMMANDEERING THE CAR FOR A PROTEST ON SUNDAY?
ALL RIGHT.
UNDERSTOOD, BANBA-SENPAI.
SO I JUST NEED TO TRANSPORT THE POSTERS AND BANNERS?
AH, YES, AND TWO OLD FOLKS.
ROGER THAT.
スタ
スタ
klat klat
WOULD IT BE ALL RIGHT IF I PARTICIPATED, BY THE WAY?
YES.
I'VE ALWAYS BEEN A PROTEST FANATIC.

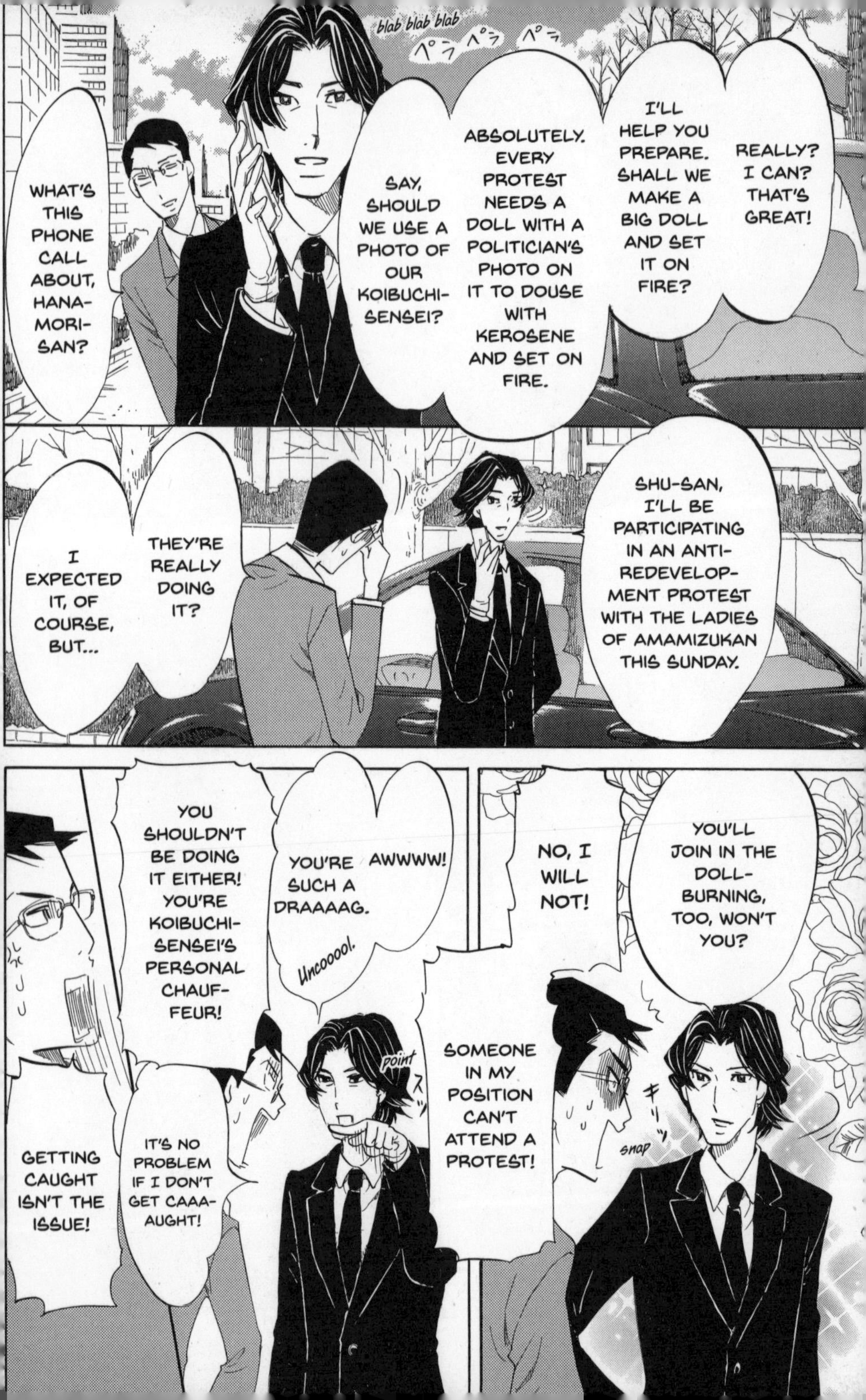
blab blab blab
ペラペラペラ
REALLY? I CAN? THAT'S GREAT!
I'LL HELP YOU PREPARE. SHALL WE MAKE A BIG DOLL AND SET IT ON FIRE?
ABSOLUTELY. EVERY PROTEST NEEDS A DOLL WITH A POLITICIAN'S PHOTO ON IT TO DOUSE WITH KEROSENE AND SET ON FIRE.
SAY, SHOULD WE USE A PHOTO OF OUR KOIBUCHI-SENSEI?
WHAT'S THIS PHONE CALL ABOUT, HANA-MORI-SAN?
SHU-SAN, I'LL BE PARTICIPATING IN AN ANTI-REDEVELOP-MENT PROTEST WITH THE LADIES OF AMAMIZUKAN THIS SUNDAY.
THEY'RE REALLY DOING IT?
I EXPECTED IT, OF COURSE, BUT...
YOU'LL JOIN IN THE DOLL-BURNING, TOO, WON'T YOU?
NO, I WILL NOT!
snap
SOMEONE IN MY POSITION CAN'T ATTEND A PROTEST!
AWWWW!
YOU'RE SUCH A DRAAAAG.
Uncooool.
YOU SHOULDN'T BE DOING IT EITHER! YOU'RE KOIBUCHI-SENSEI'S PERSONAL CHAUF-FEUR!
point
IT'S NO PROBLEM IF I DON'T GET CAAA-AUGHT!
GETTING CAUGHT ISN'T THE ISSUE!

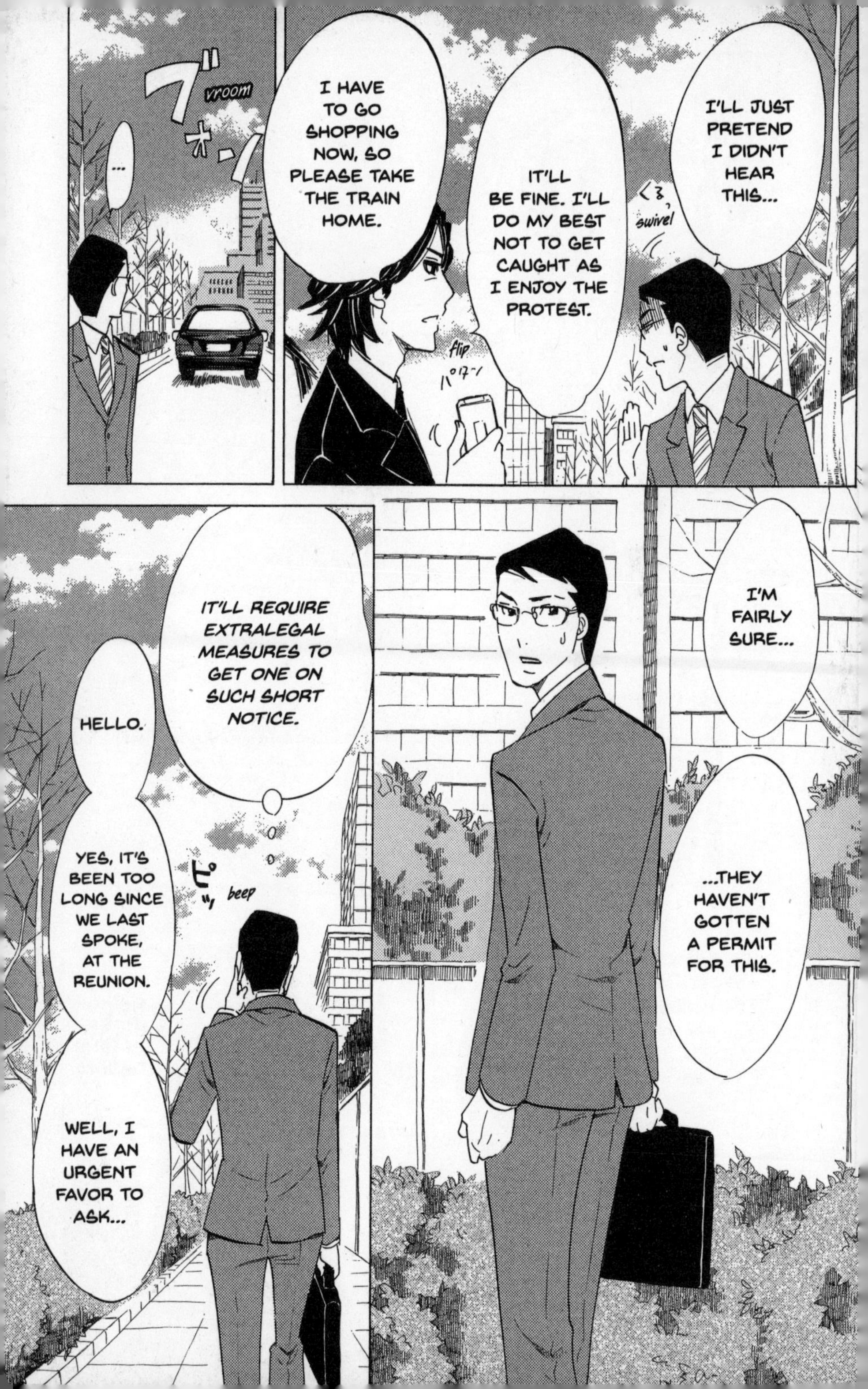
I'LL JUST PRETEND I DIDN'T HEAR THIS...
swivel
IT'LL BE FINE. I'LL DO MY BEST NOT TO GET CAUGHT AS I ENJOY THE PROTEST.
I HAVE TO GO SHOPPING NOW, SO PLEASE TAKE THE TRAIN HOME.
flip
vroom
...
I'M FAIRLY SURE...
...THEY HAVEN'T GOTTEN A PERMIT FOR THIS.
IT'LL REQUIRE EXTRALEGAL MEASURES TO GET ONE ON SUCH SHORT NOTICE.
HELLO.
ピッ
beep
YES, IT'S BEEN TOO LONG SINCE WE LAST SPOKE, AT THE REUNION.
WELL, I HAVE AN URGENT FAVOR TO ASK...

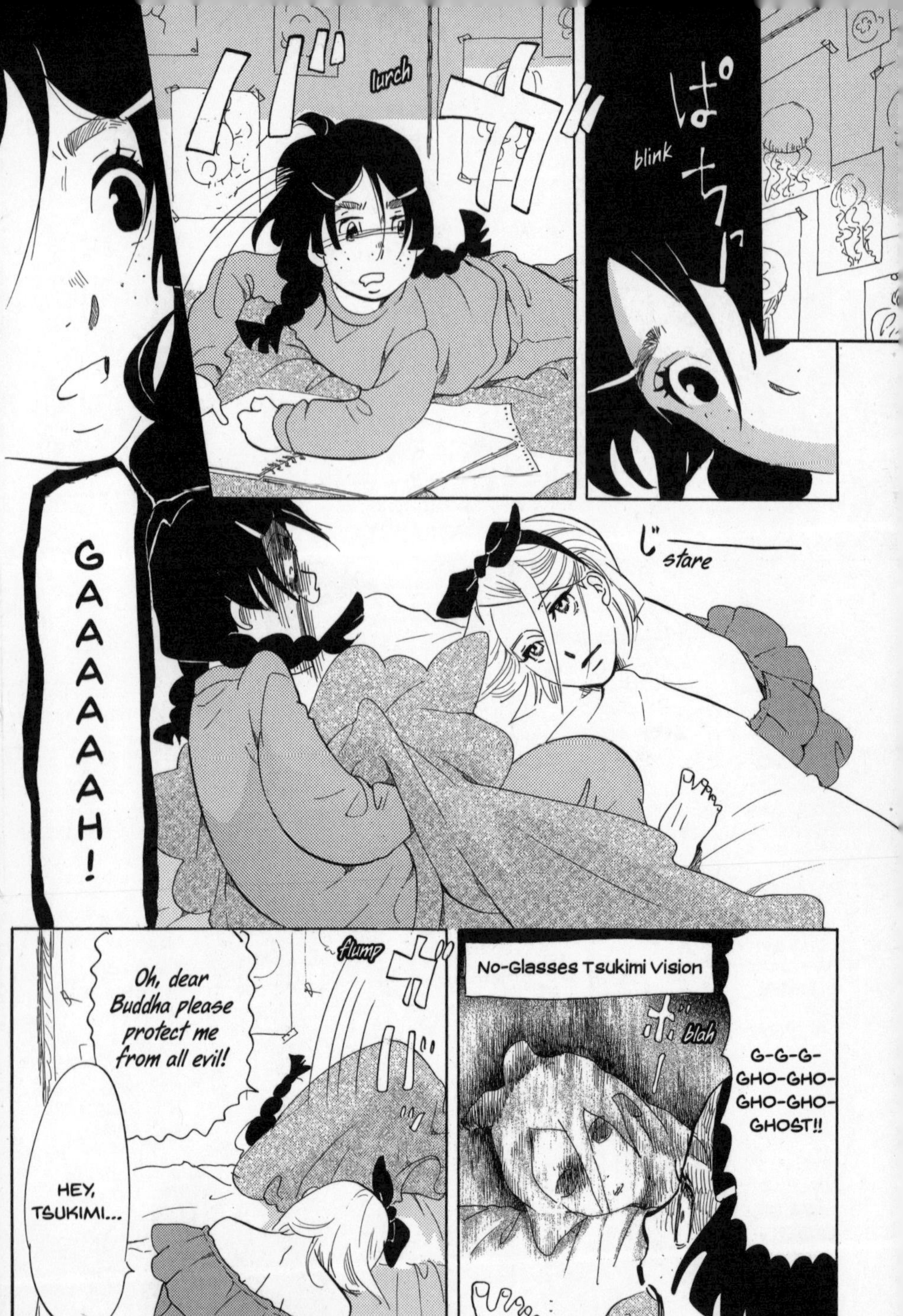

blink
lurch
GAAAAAAAAH!
stare
No-Glasses Tsukimi Vision
blah
G-G-G-GHO-GHO-GHO-GHO-GHOST!!
flump
Oh, dear Buddha please protect me from all evil!
HEY, TSUKIMI...

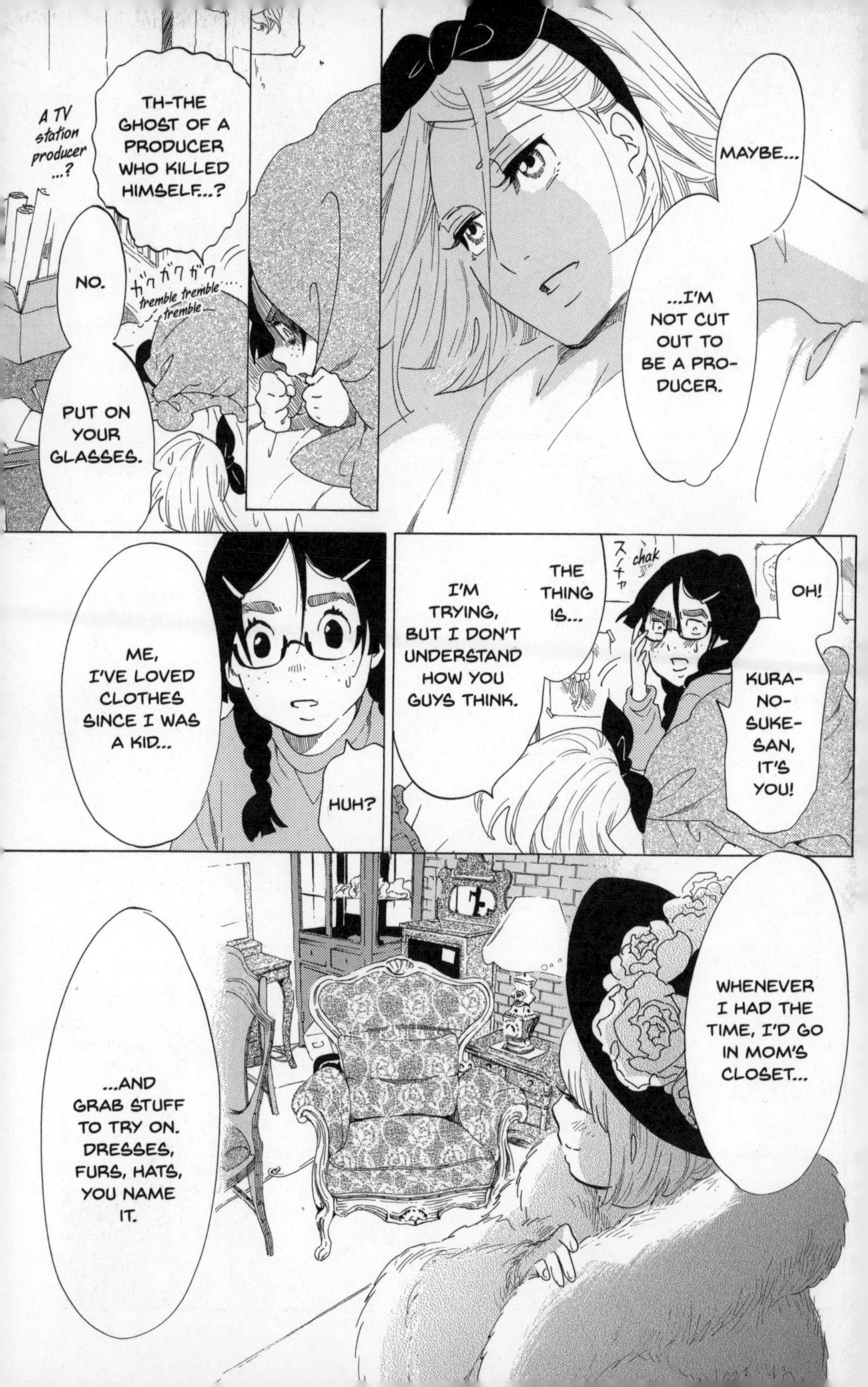
MAYBE...
...I'M NOT CUT OUT TO BE A PRO-DUCER.
TH-THE GHOST OF A PRODUCER WHO KILLED HIMSELF...?
A TV station producer ...?
ガクガクガク tremble tremble tremble
NO.
PUT ON YOUR GLASSES.
OH!
KURA-NO-SUKE-SAN, IT'S YOU!
スチャ chak
THE THING IS...
I'M TRYING, BUT I DON'T UNDERSTAND HOW YOU GUYS THINK.
HUH?
ME, I'VE LOVED CLOTHES SINCE I WAS A KID...
WHENEVER I HAD THE TIME, I'D GO IN MOM'S CLOSET...
...AND GRAB STUFF TO TRY ON. DRESSES, FURS, HATS, YOU NAME IT.

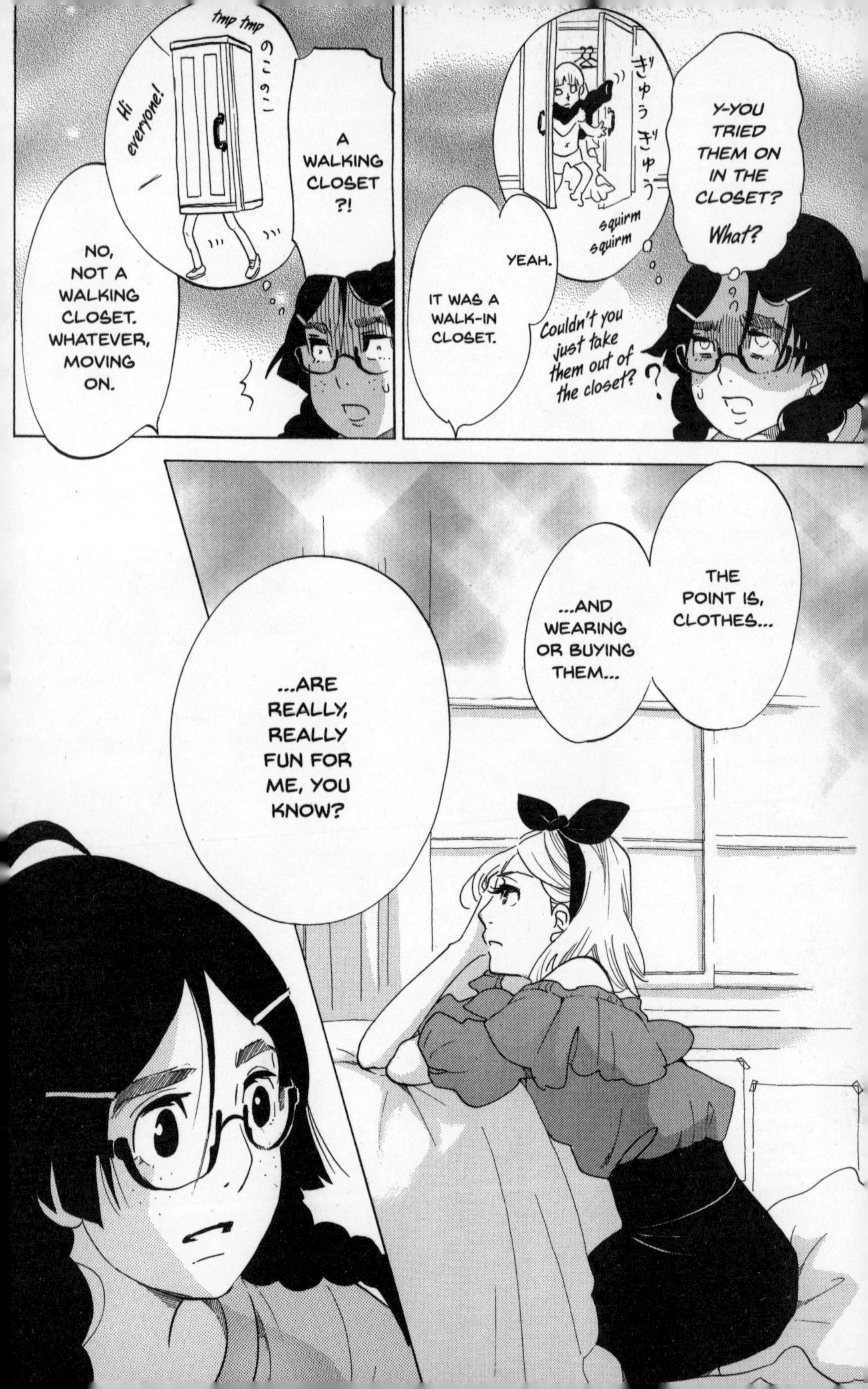
Y-YOU TRIED THEM ON IN THE CLOSET?
What?
ぎゅう ぎゅう
squirm squirm
YEAH.
IT WAS A WALK-IN CLOSET.
Couldn't you just take them out of the closet?
A WALKING CLOSET ?!
tmp tmp
のこのこ
Hi everyone!
NO, NOT A WALKING CLOSET. WHATEVER, MOVING ON.
THE POINT IS, CLOTHES...
...AND WEARING OR BUYING THEM...
...ARE REALLY, REALLY FUN FOR ME, YOU KNOW?

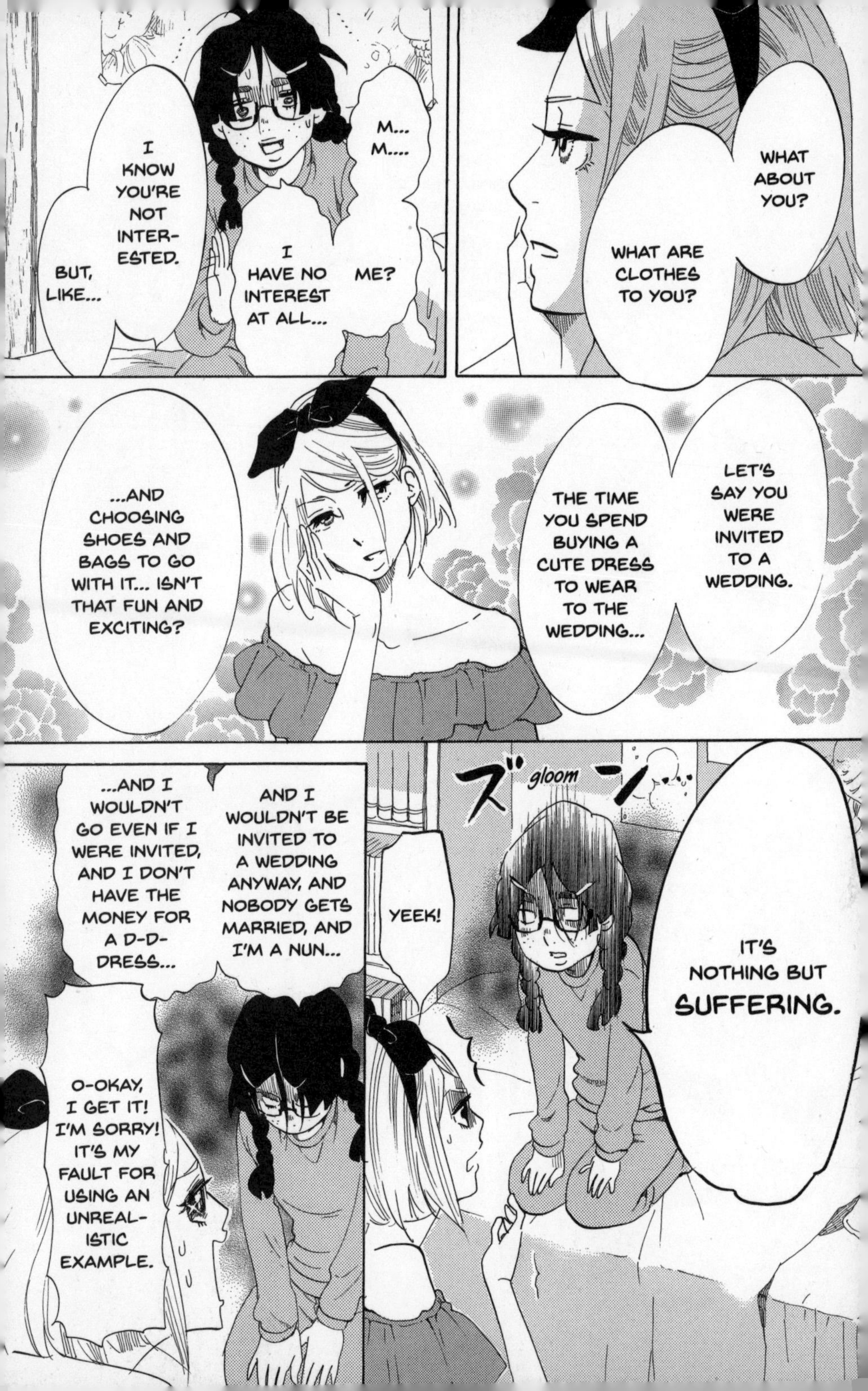
WHAT ABOUT YOU?
WHAT ARE CLOTHES TO YOU?
M... M.... ME?
I HAVE NO INTEREST AT ALL...
I KNOW YOU'RE NOT INTER-ESTED.
BUT, LIKE...
LET'S SAY YOU WERE INVITED TO A WEDDING.
THE TIME YOU SPEND BUYING A CUTE DRESS TO WEAR TO THE WEDDING...
...AND CHOOSING SHOES AND BAGS TO GO WITH IT... ISN'T THAT FUN AND EXCITING?
IT'S NOTHING BUT SUFFERING.
gloom
YEEK!
AND I WOULDN'T BE INVITED TO A WEDDING ANYWAY, AND NOBODY GETS MARRIED, AND I'M A NUN...
...AND I WOULDN'T GO EVEN IF I WERE INVITED, AND I DON'T HAVE THE MONEY FOR A D-D-DRESS...
O-OKAY, I GET IT! I'M SORRY! IT'S MY FAULT FOR USING AN UNREAL-ISTIC EXAMPLE.

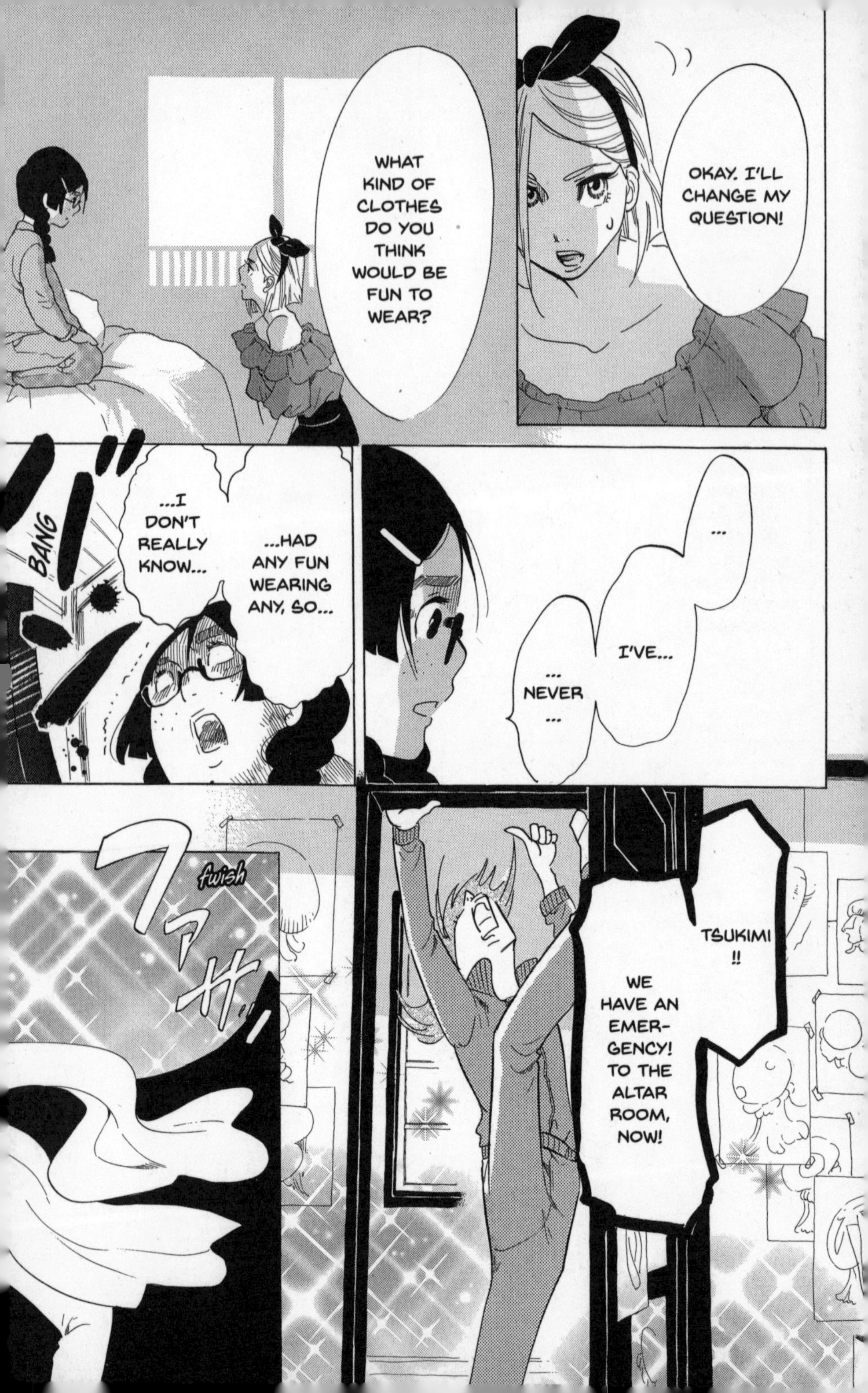
OKAY. I'LL CHANGE MY QUESTION!
WHAT KIND OF CLOTHES DO YOU THINK WOULD BE FUN TO WEAR?
...
I'VE...
...NEVER...
...HAD ANY FUN WEARING ANY, SO...
...I DON'T REALLY KNOW...
BANG
TSUKIMI!!
WE HAVE AN EMERGENCY! TO THE ALTAR ROOM, NOW!
fwish
ファサ

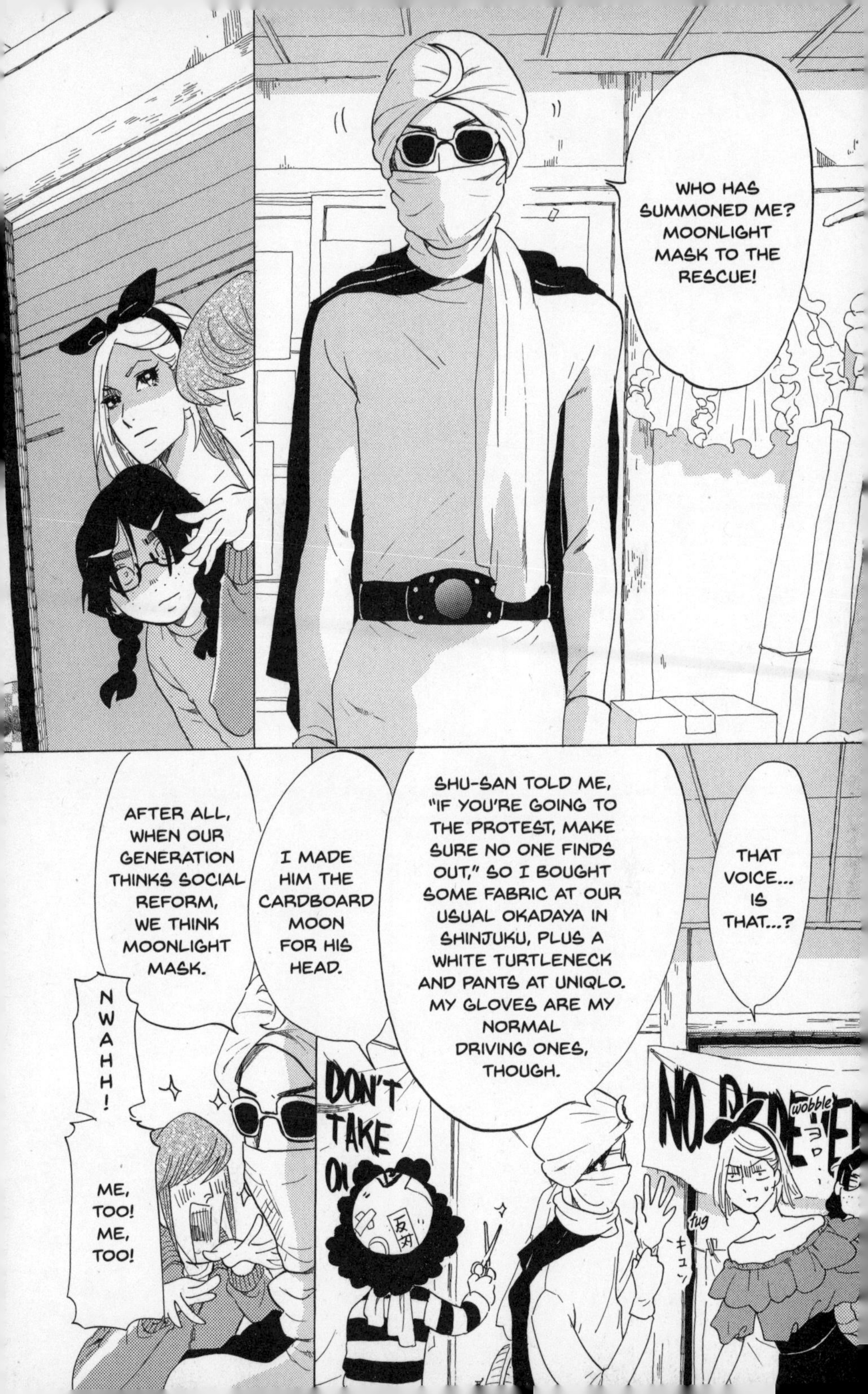
WHO HAS SUMMONED ME? MOONLIGHT MASK TO THE RESCUE!
THAT VOICE... IS THAT...?
SHU-SAN TOLD ME, "IF YOU'RE GOING TO THE PROTEST, MAKE SURE NO ONE FINDS OUT," SO I BOUGHT SOME FABRIC AT OUR USUAL OKADAYA IN SHINJUKU, PLUS A WHITE TURTLENECK AND PANTS AT UNIQLO. MY GLOVES ARE MY NORMAL DRIVING ONES, THOUGH.
I MADE HIM THE CARDBOARD MOON FOR HIS HEAD.
AFTER ALL, WHEN OUR GENERATION THINKS SOCIAL REFORM, WE THINK MOONLIGHT MASK.
wobble
tug
DON'T TAKE ON
反対
NWAHH!
ME, TOO! ME, TOO!

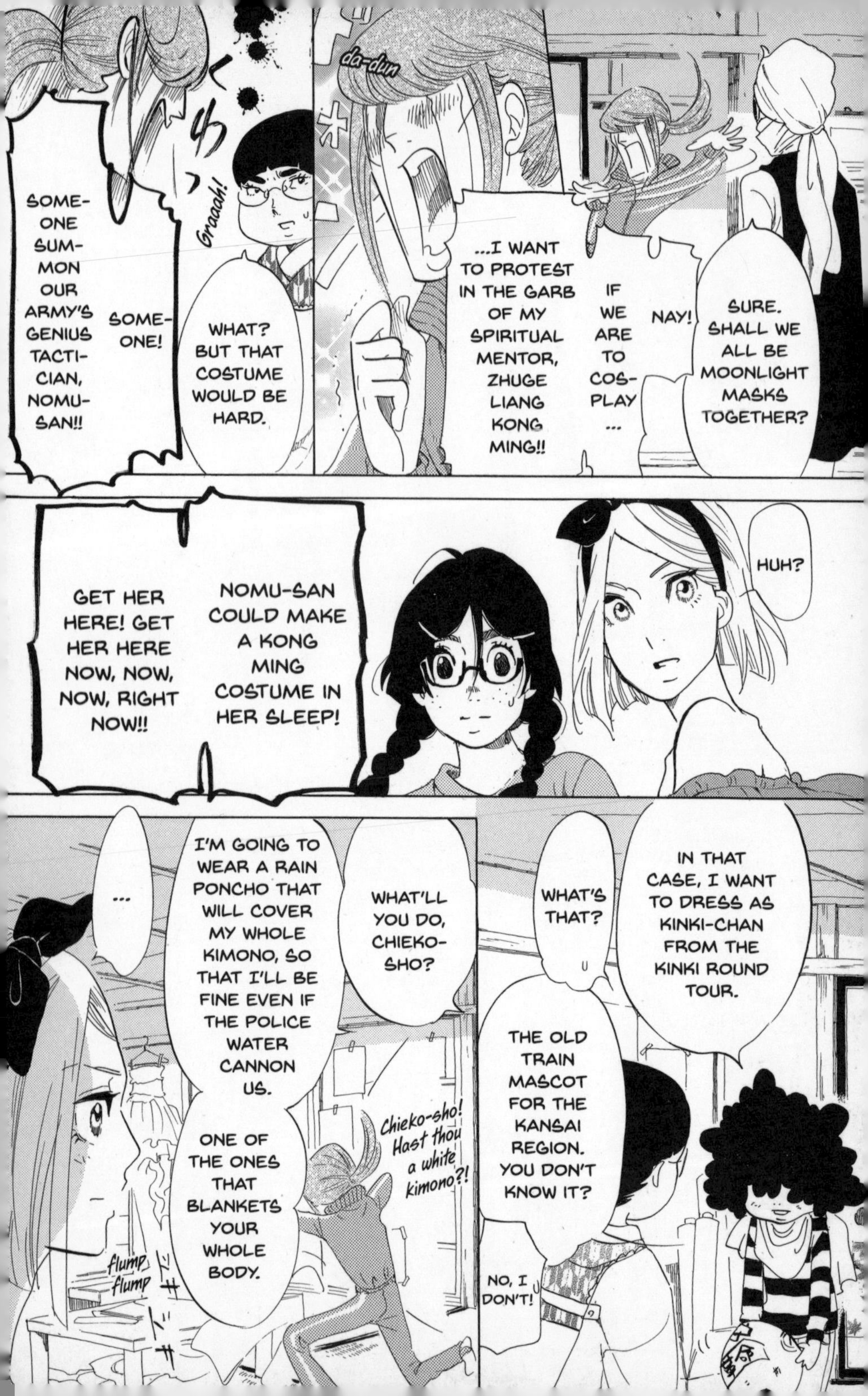
SURE. SHALL WE ALL BE MOONLIGHT MASKS TOGETHER?
NAY!
da-dun
IF WE ARE TO COSPLAY...
...I WANT TO PROTEST IN THE GARB OF MY SPIRITUAL MENTOR, ZHUGE LIANG KONG MING!!
WHAT? BUT THAT COSTUME WOULD BE HARD.
Graaah!
SOMEONE!
SOMEONE SUMMON OUR ARMY'S GENIUS TACTICIAN, NOMU-SAN!!
HUH?
NOMU-SAN COULD MAKE A KONG MING COSTUME IN HER SLEEP!
GET HER HERE! GET HER HERE NOW, NOW, NOW, RIGHT NOW!!
IN THAT CASE, I WANT TO DRESS AS KINKI-CHAN FROM THE KINKI ROUND TOUR.
WHAT'S THAT?
THE OLD TRAIN MASCOT FOR THE KANSAI REGION. YOU DON'T KNOW IT?
NO, I DON'T!
WHAT'LL YOU DO, CHIEKO-SHO?
I'M GOING TO WEAR A RAIN PONCHO THAT WILL COVER MY WHOLE KIMONO, SO THAT I'LL BE FINE EVEN IF THE POLICE WATER CANNON US.
...
Chieko-sho! Hast thou a white kimono?!
ONE OF THE ONES THAT BLANKETS YOUR WHOLE BODY.
flump flump

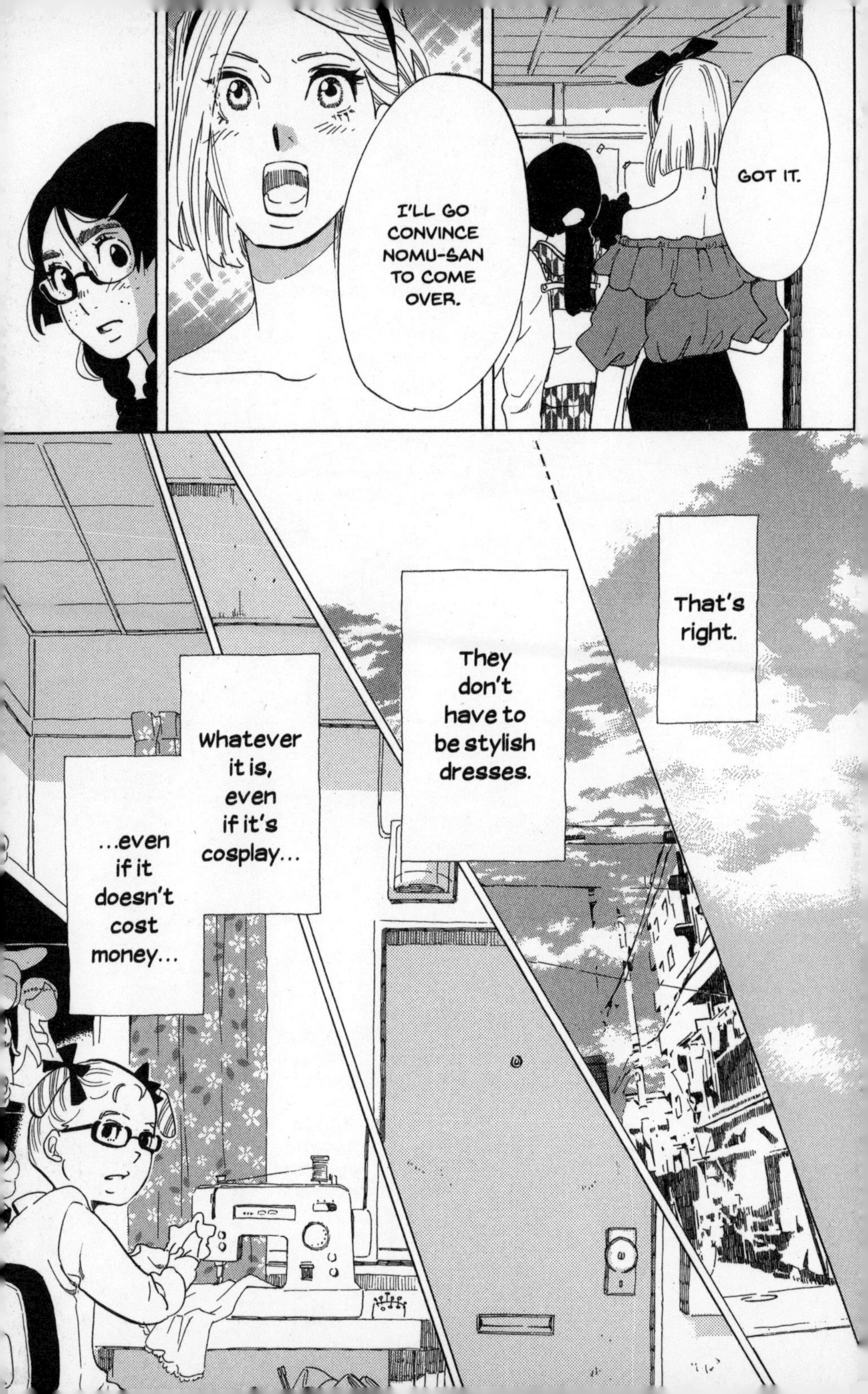
GOT IT.
I'LL GO CONVINCE NOMU-SAN TO COME OVER.
That's right.
They don't have to be stylish dresses.
Whatever it is, even if it's cosplay...
...even if it doesn't cost money...

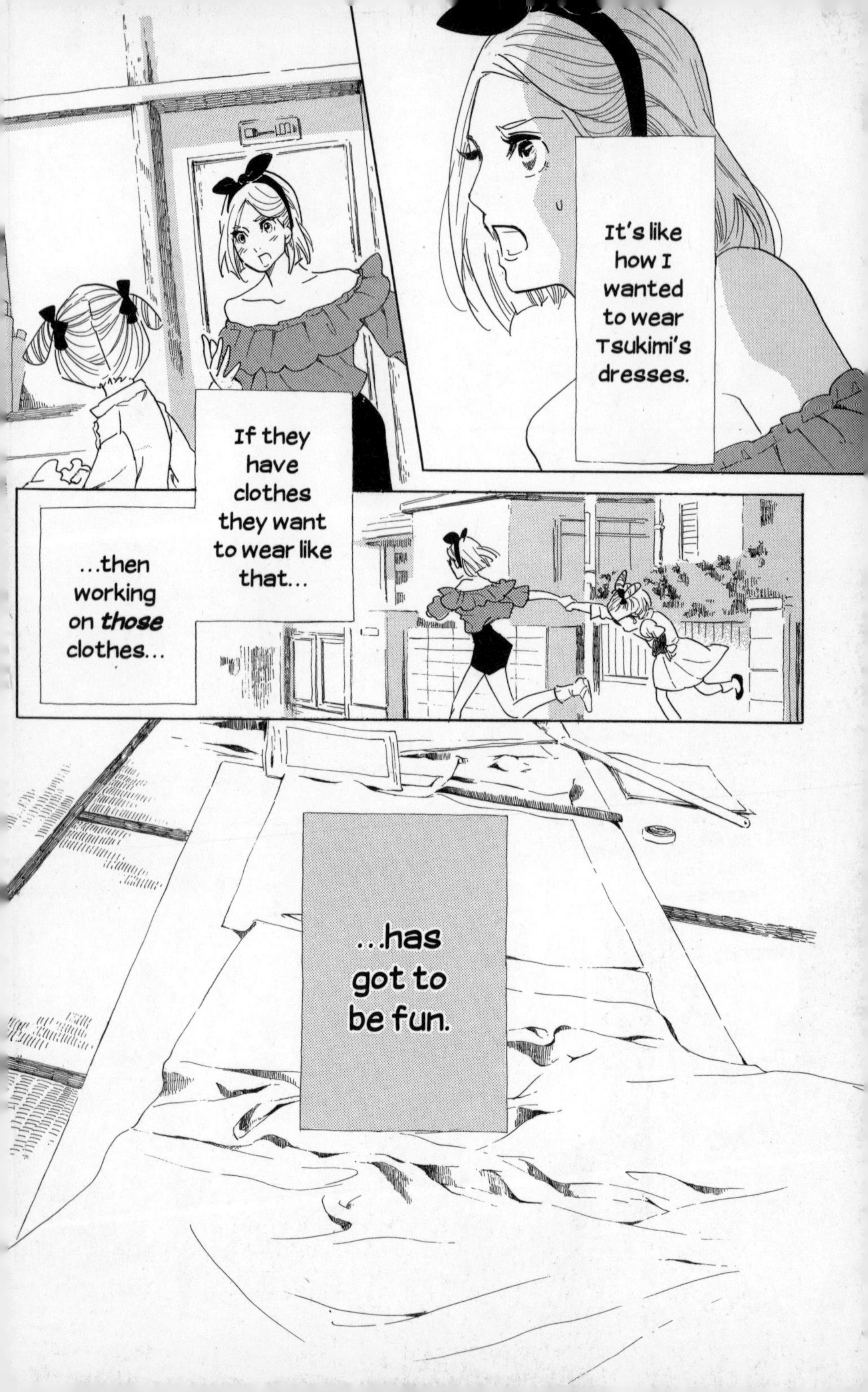
It's like how I wanted to wear Tsukimi's dresses.
If they have clothes they want to wear like that...
...then working on *those* clothes...
...has got to be fun.

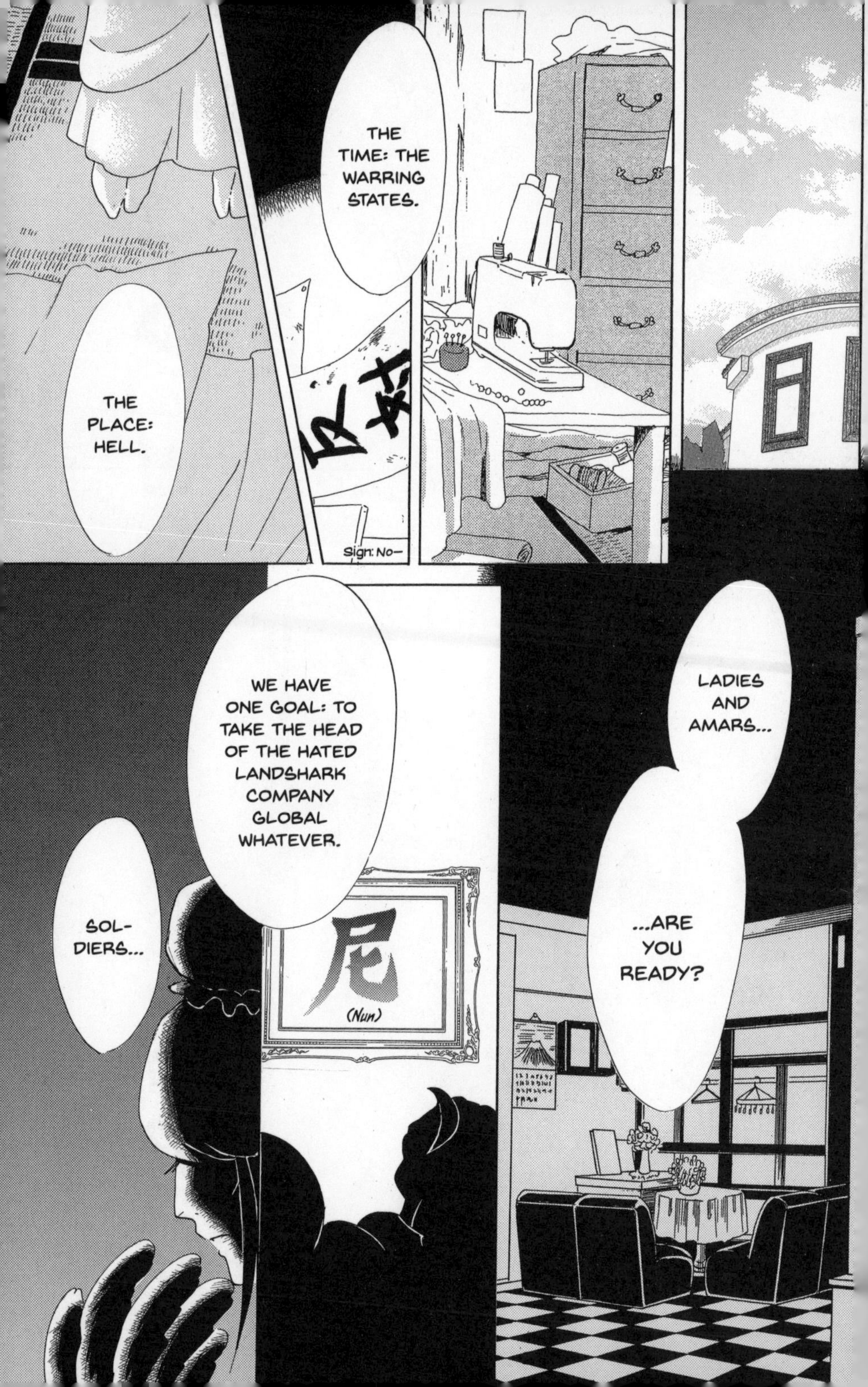
THE TIME: THE WARRING STATES.
THE PLACE: HELL.
Sign: No—
LADIES AND AMARS...
...ARE YOU READY?
WE HAVE ONE GOAL: TO TAKE THE HEAD OF THE HATED LANDSHARK COMPANY GLOBAL WHATEVER.
(Nun)
SOL-DIERS...

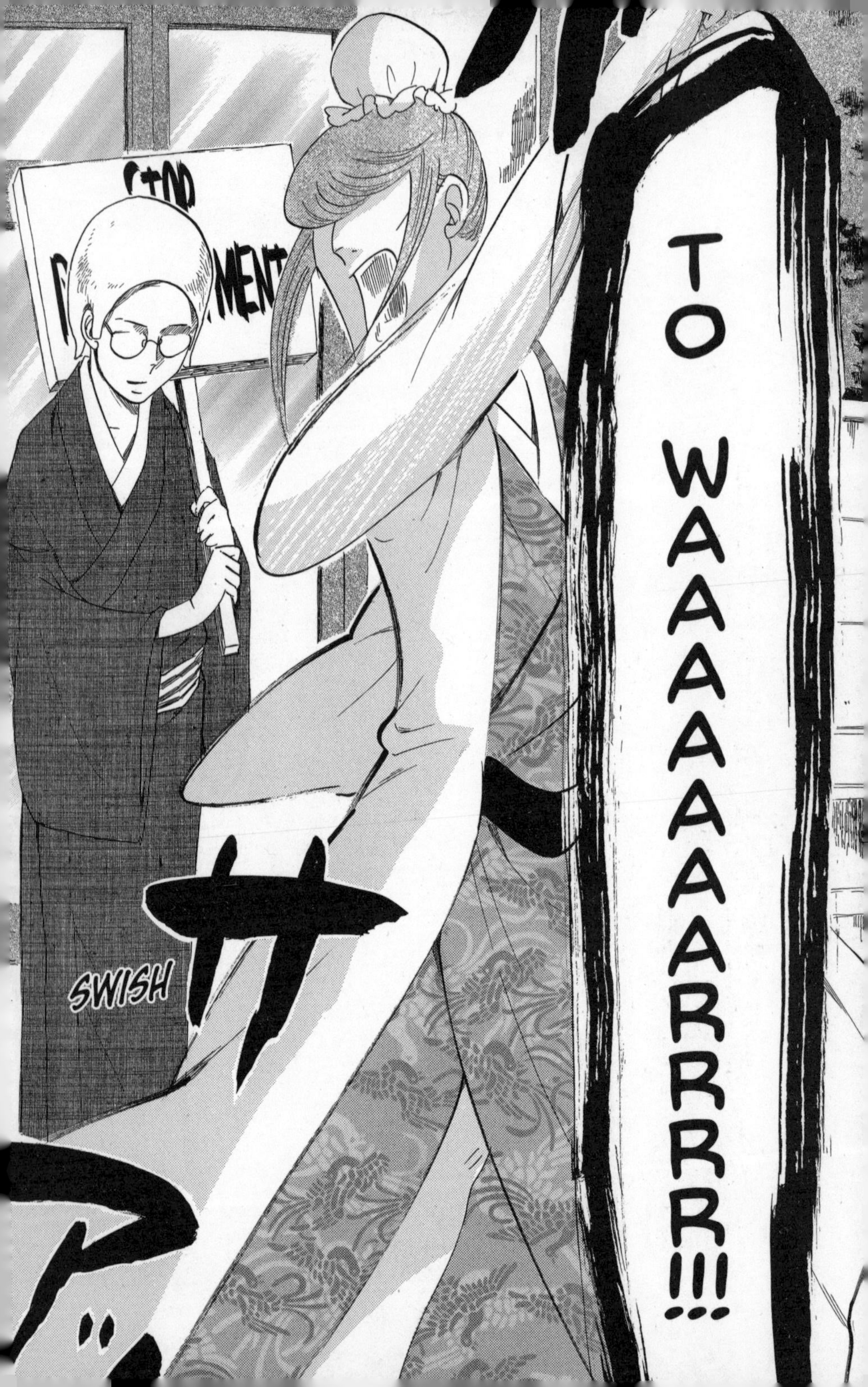
TO WAAAAAARRRR!!!
SWISH

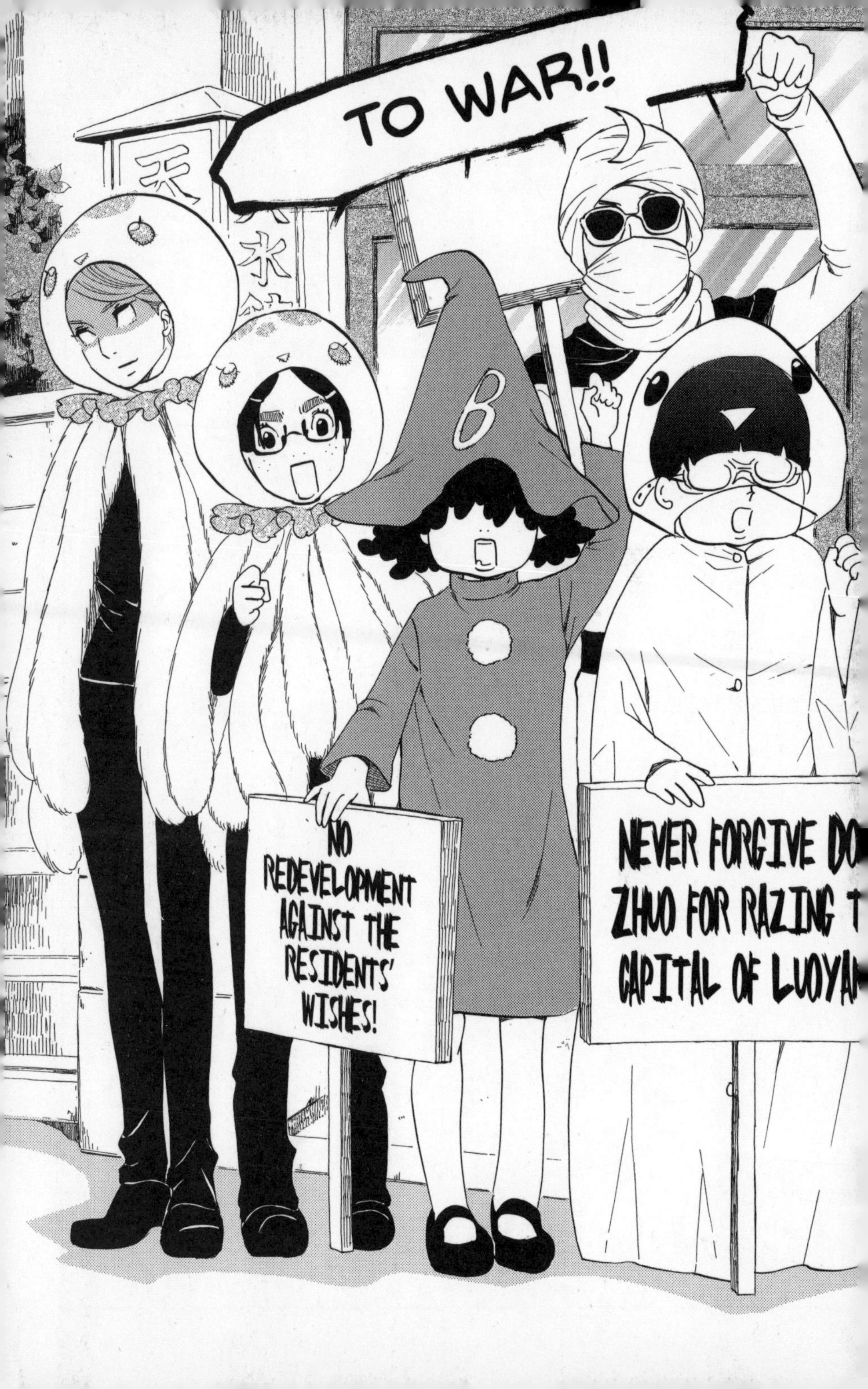
TO WAR!!
NO REDEVELOPMENT AGAINST THE RESIDENTS' WISHES!
NEVER FORGIVE DO
ZHUO FOR RAZING T
CAPITAL OF LUOYAN

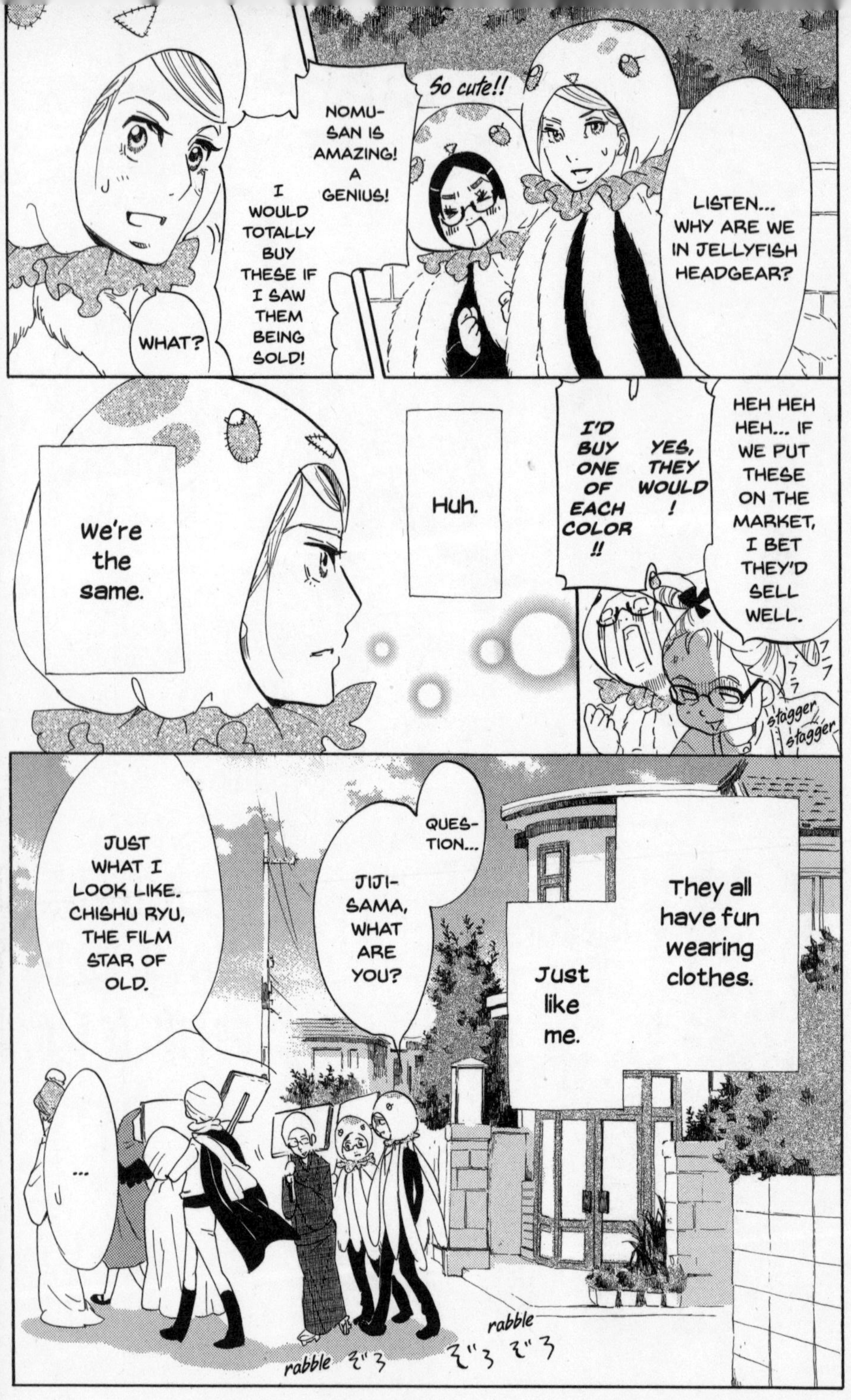
LISTEN... WHY ARE WE IN JELLYFISH HEADGEAR?
So cute!!
NOMU-SAN IS AMAZING! A GENIUS!
I WOULD TOTALLY BUY THESE IF I SAW THEM BEING SOLD!
WHAT?
HEH HEH HEH... IF WE PUT THESE ON THE MARKET, I BET THEY'D SELL WELL.
YES, THEY WOULD!
I'D BUY ONE OF EACH COLOR!!
stagger
stagger
Huh.
We're the same.
They all have fun wearing clothes.
Just like me.
QUESTION...
JIJI-SAMA, WHAT ARE YOU?
JUST WHAT I LOOK LIKE. CHISHU RYU, THE FILM STAR OF OLD.
...
rabble
rabble

Episode 47
Monsieur Hire

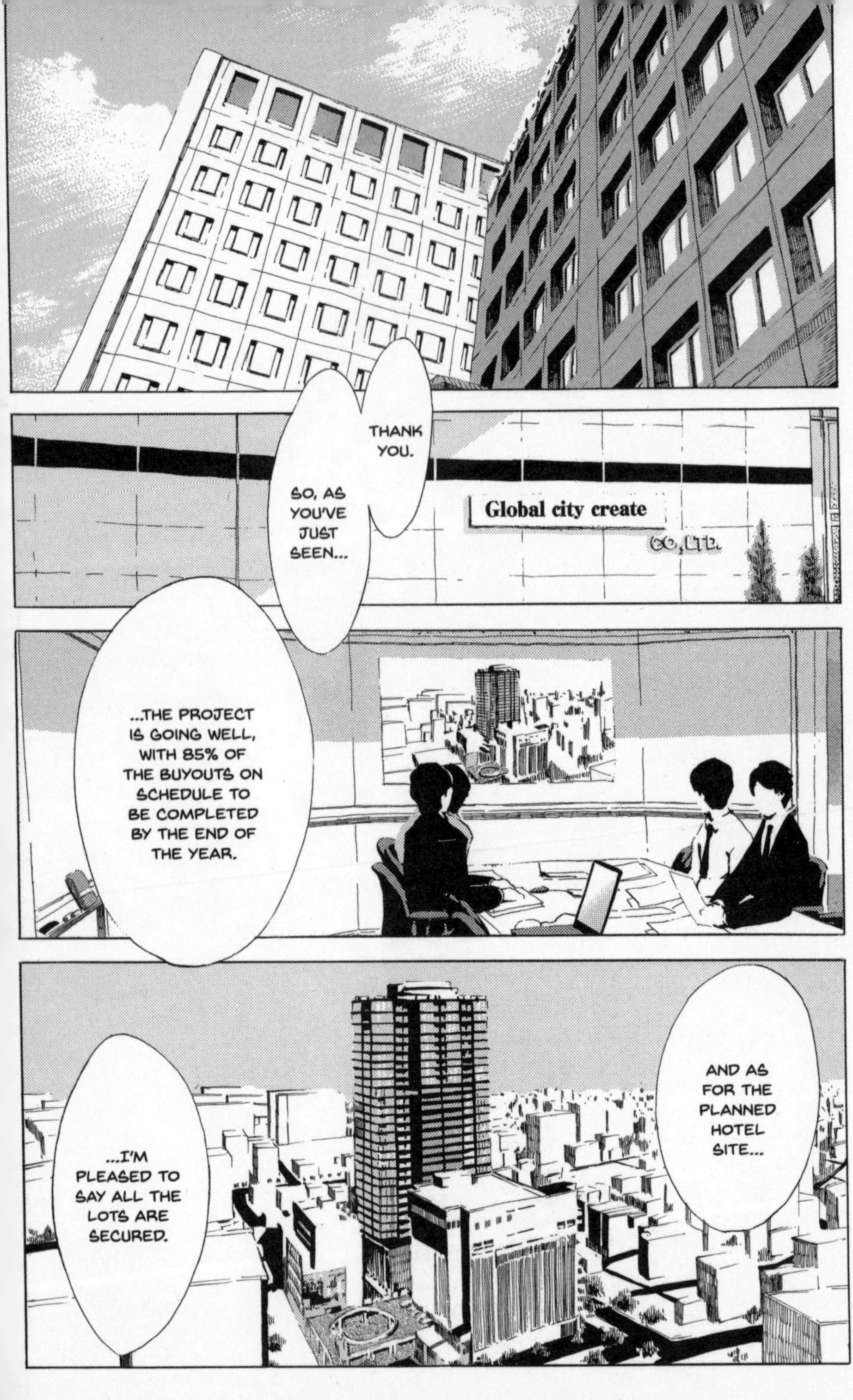
THANK YOU.
SO, AS YOU'VE JUST SEEN...
Global city create
CO.,LTD.
...THE PROJECT IS GOING WELL, WITH 85% OF THE BUYOUTS ON SCHEDULE TO BE COMPLETED BY THE END OF THE YEAR.
AND AS FOR THE PLANNED HOTEL SITE...
...I'M PLEASED TO SAY ALL THE LOTS ARE SECURED.

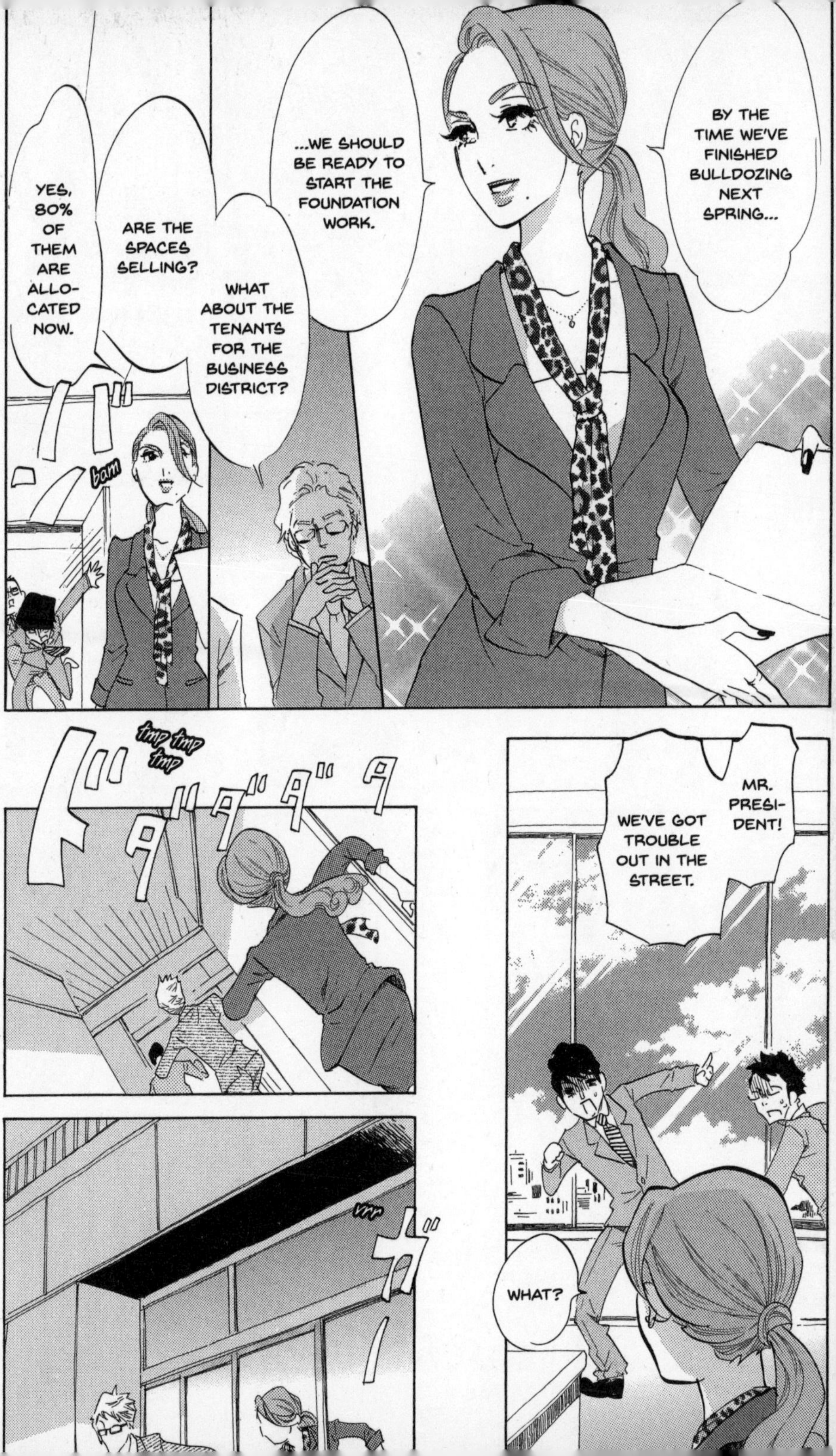
BY THE TIME WE'VE FINISHED BULLDOZING NEXT SPRING...
...WE SHOULD BE READY TO START THE FOUNDATION WORK.
WHAT ABOUT THE TENANTS FOR THE BUSINESS DISTRICT?
ARE THE SPACES SELLING?
YES, 80% OF THEM ARE ALLO-CATED NOW.
bam
MR. PRESI-DENT!
WE'VE GOT TROUBLE OUT IN THE STREET.
WHAT?
tmp tmp tmp
ドダダダダ
vrr
ガ

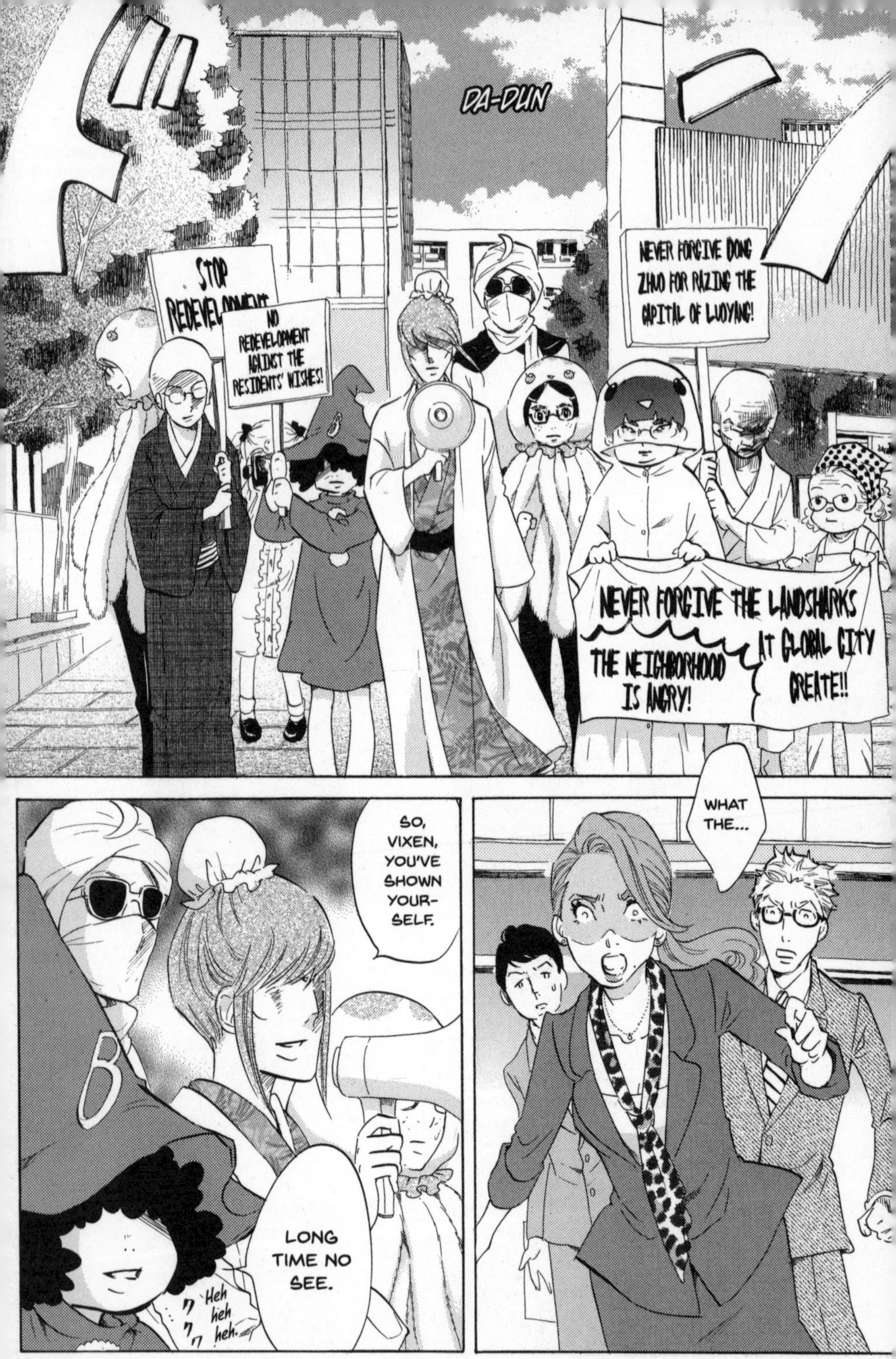
NEVER FORGIVE DONG ZHUO FOR RAZING THE CAPITAL OF LUOYANG!
DA-DUN
STOP REDEVELOPMEN
NO REDEVELOPMENT AGAINST THE RESIDENTS' WISHES!
NEVER FORGIVE THE LANDSHARKS AT GLOBAL CITY CREATE!!
THE NEIGHBORHOOD IS ANGRY!
WHAT THE...
SO, VIXEN, YOU'VE SHOWN YOURSELF.
LONG TIME NO SEE.
ククク
Heh heh heh.

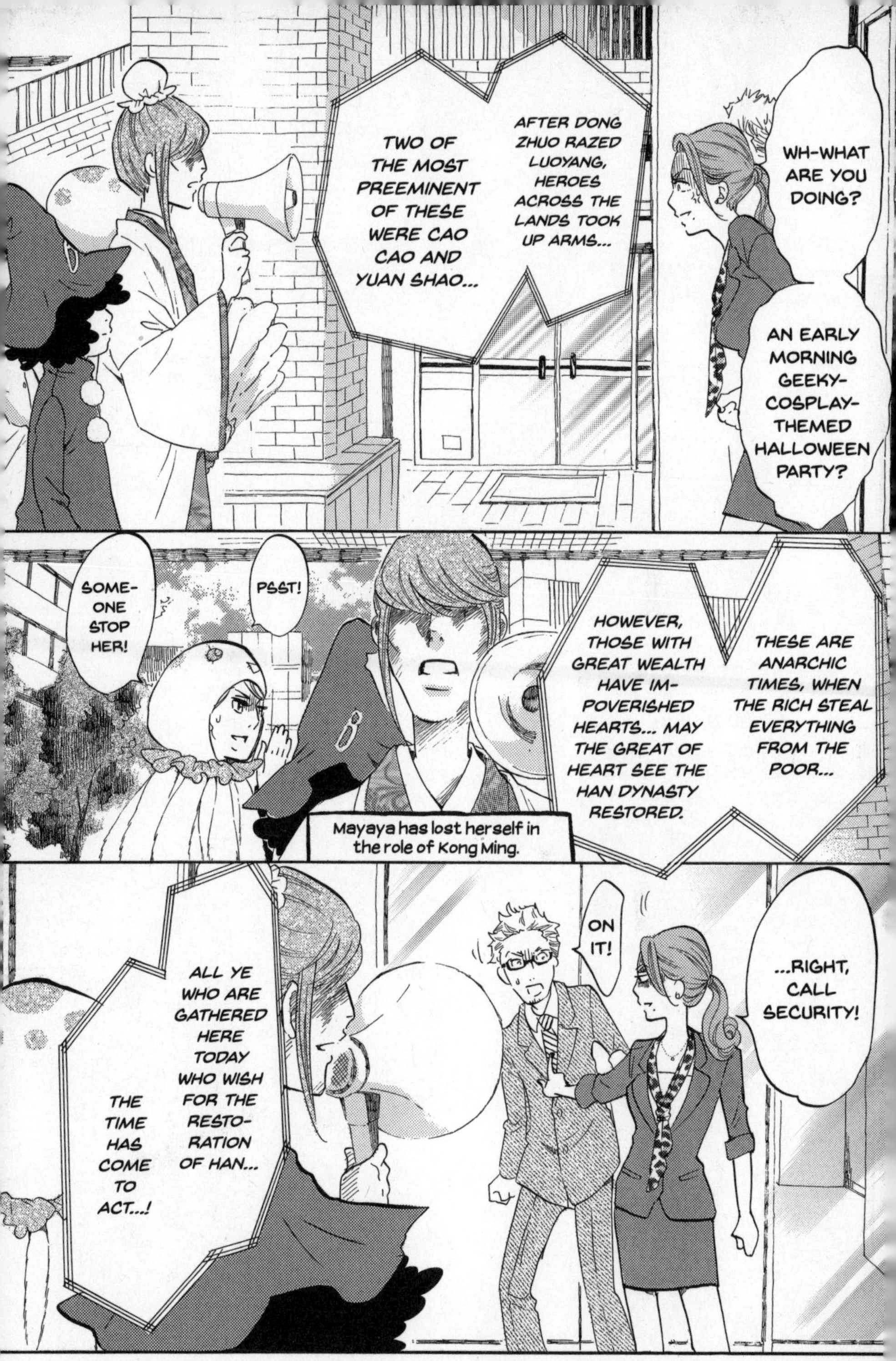
WH-WHAT ARE YOU DOING?
AN EARLY MORNING GEEKY-COSPLAY-THEMED HALLOWEEN PARTY?
AFTER DONG ZHUO RAZED LUOYANG, HEROES ACROSS THE LANDS TOOK UP ARMS... TWO OF THE MOST PREEMINENT OF THESE WERE CAO CAO AND YUAN SHAO...
THESE ARE ANARCHIC TIMES, WHEN THE RICH STEAL EVERYTHING FROM THE POOR... HOWEVER, THOSE WITH GREAT WEALTH HAVE IMPOVERISHED HEARTS... MAY THE GREAT OF HEART SEE THE HAN DYNASTY RESTORED.
Mayaya has lost herself in the role of Kong Ming.
PSST!
SOME-ONE STOP HER!
...RIGHT, CALL SECURITY!
ON IT!
ALL YE WHO ARE GATHERED HERE TODAY WHO WISH FOR THE RESTO-RATION OF HAN... THE TIME HAS COME TO ACT...!

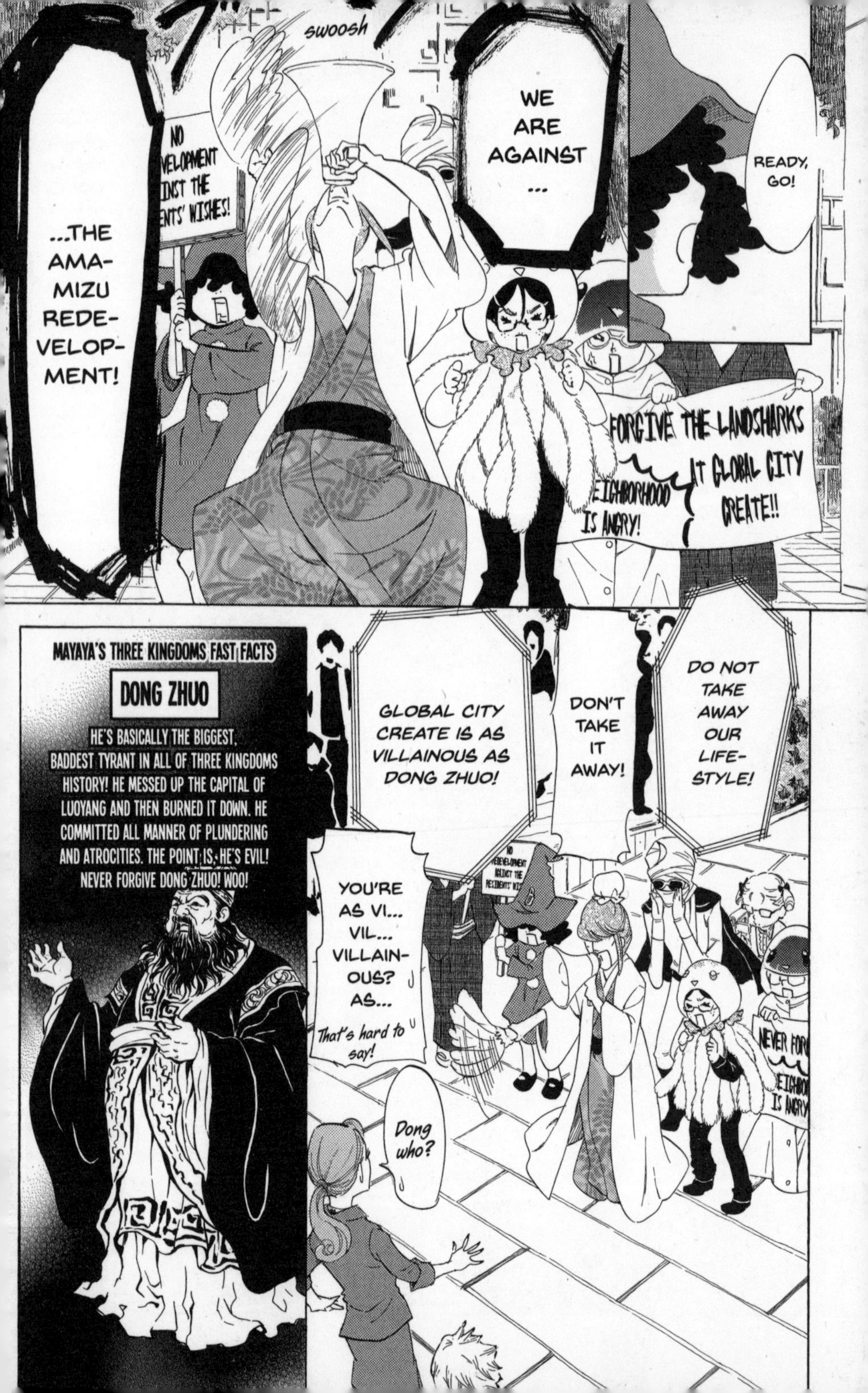
swoosh
READY, GO!
WE ARE AGAINST ...
...THE AMAMIZU REDEVELOPMENT!
FORGIVE THE LANDSHARKS
IT GLOBAL CITY CREATE!!
IS ANGRY!
DO NOT TAKE AWAY OUR LIFESTYLE!
DON'T TAKE IT AWAY!
GLOBAL CITY CREATE IS AS VILLAINOUS AS DONG ZHUO!
YOU'RE AS VI... VIL... VILLAINOUS? AS...
That's hard to say!
Dong who?
MAYAYA'S THREE KINGDOMS FAST FACTS
DONG ZHUO
HE'S BASICALLY THE BIGGEST, BADDEST TYRANT IN ALL OF THREE KINGDOMS HISTORY! HE MESSED UP THE CAPITAL OF LUOYANG AND THEN BURNED IT DOWN. HE COMMITTED ALL MANNER OF PLUNDERING AND ATROCITIES. THE POINT IS, HE'S EVIL! NEVER FORGIVE DONG ZHUO! WOO!

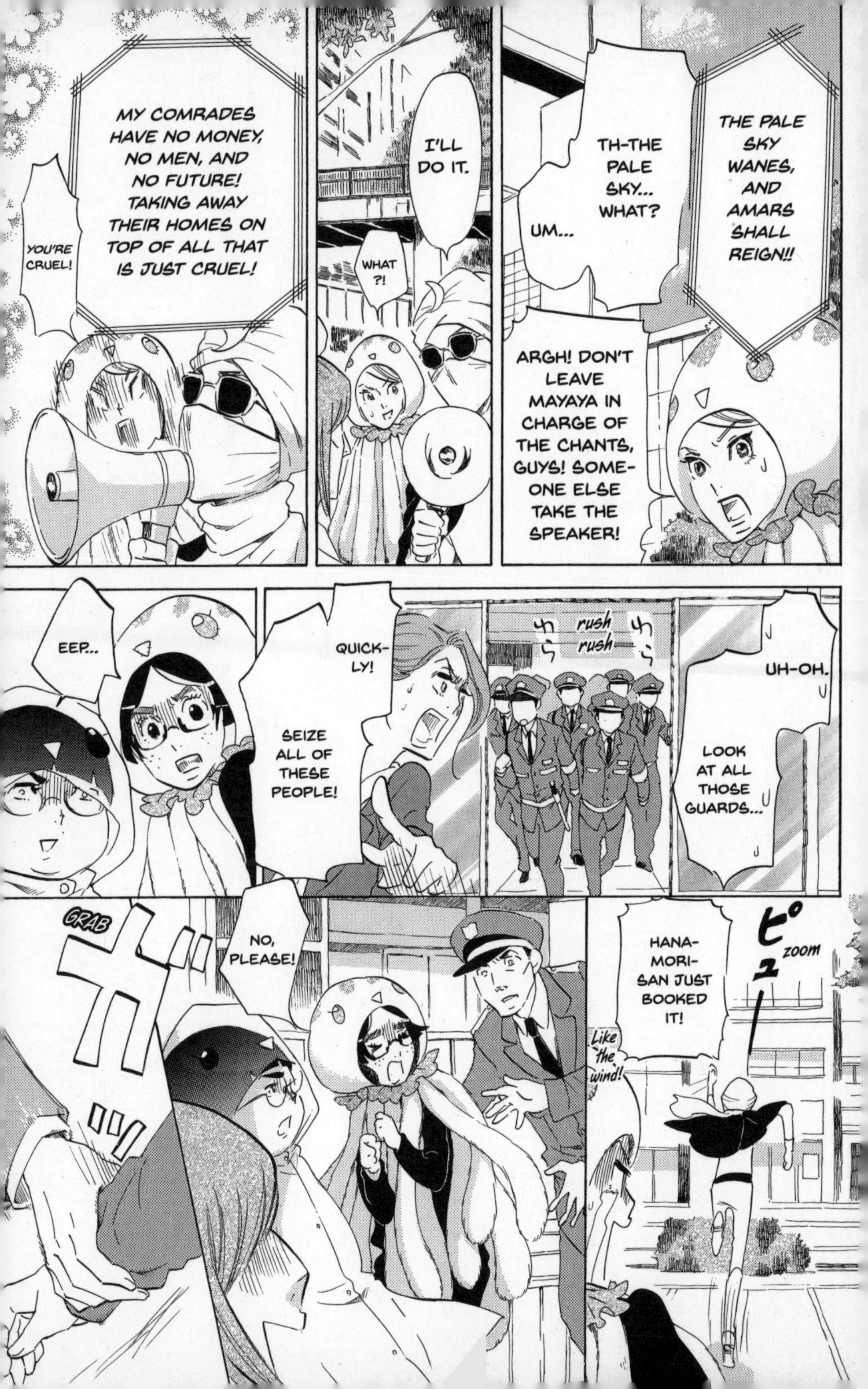
THE PALE SKY WANES, AND AMARS SHALL REIGN!!
TH-THE PALE SKY... WHAT?
UM...
ARGH! DON'T LEAVE MAYAYA IN CHARGE OF THE CHANTS, GUYS! SOMEONE ELSE TAKE THE SPEAKER!
I'LL DO IT.
WHAT?!
MY COMRADES HAVE NO MONEY, NO MEN, AND NO FUTURE! TAKING AWAY THEIR HOMES ON TOP OF ALL THAT IS JUST CRUEL!
YOU'RE CRUEL!
UH-OH.
LOOK AT ALL THOSE GUARDS...
rush rush
QUICKLY!
SEIZE ALL OF THESE PEOPLE!
EEP...
HANAMORI-SAN JUST BOOKED IT!
zoom
Like the wind!
NO, PLEASE!
GRAB

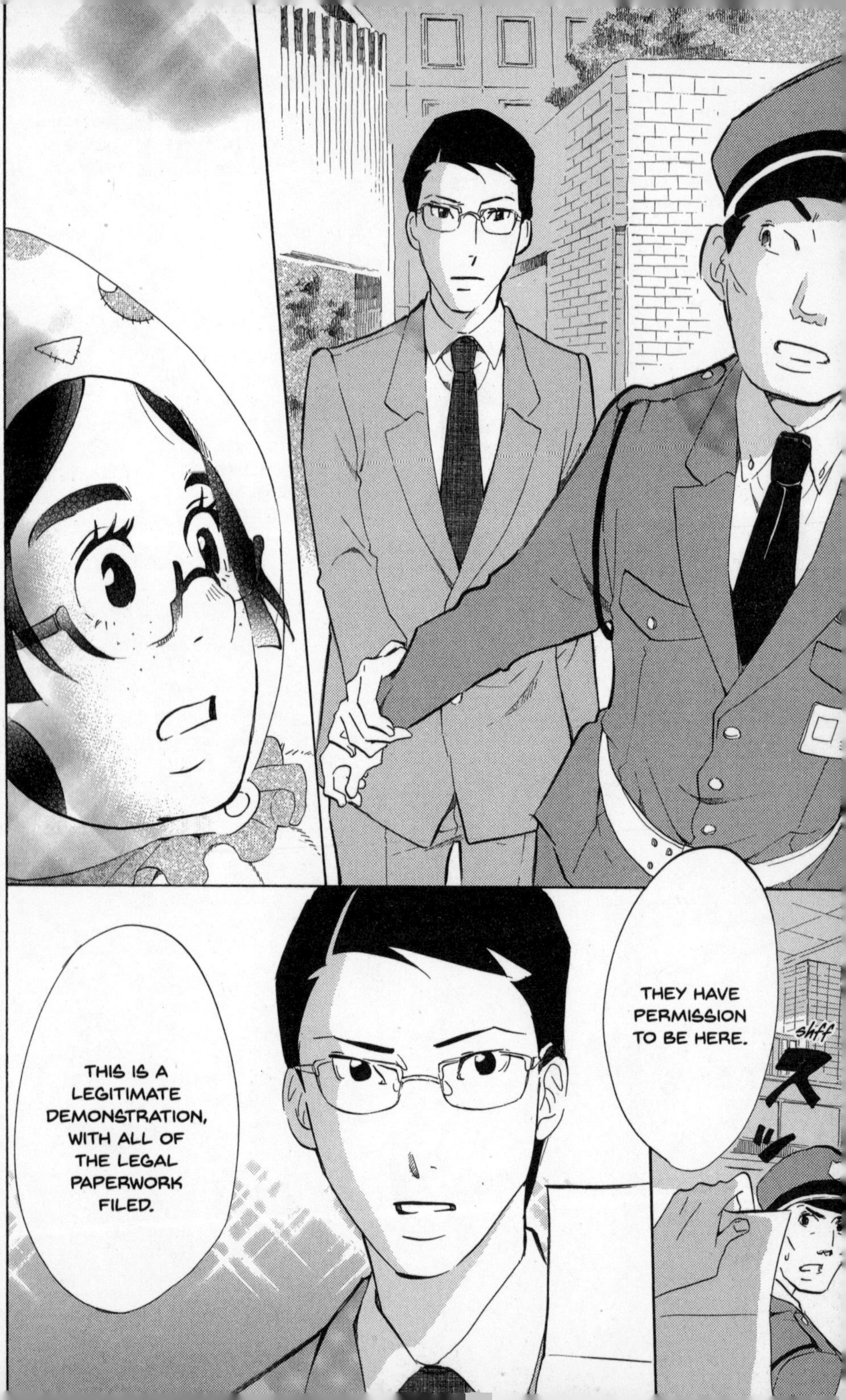
THEY HAVE PERMISSION TO BE HERE.
shff
THIS IS A LEGITIMATE DEMONSTRATION, WITH ALL OF THE LEGAL PAPERWORK FILED.

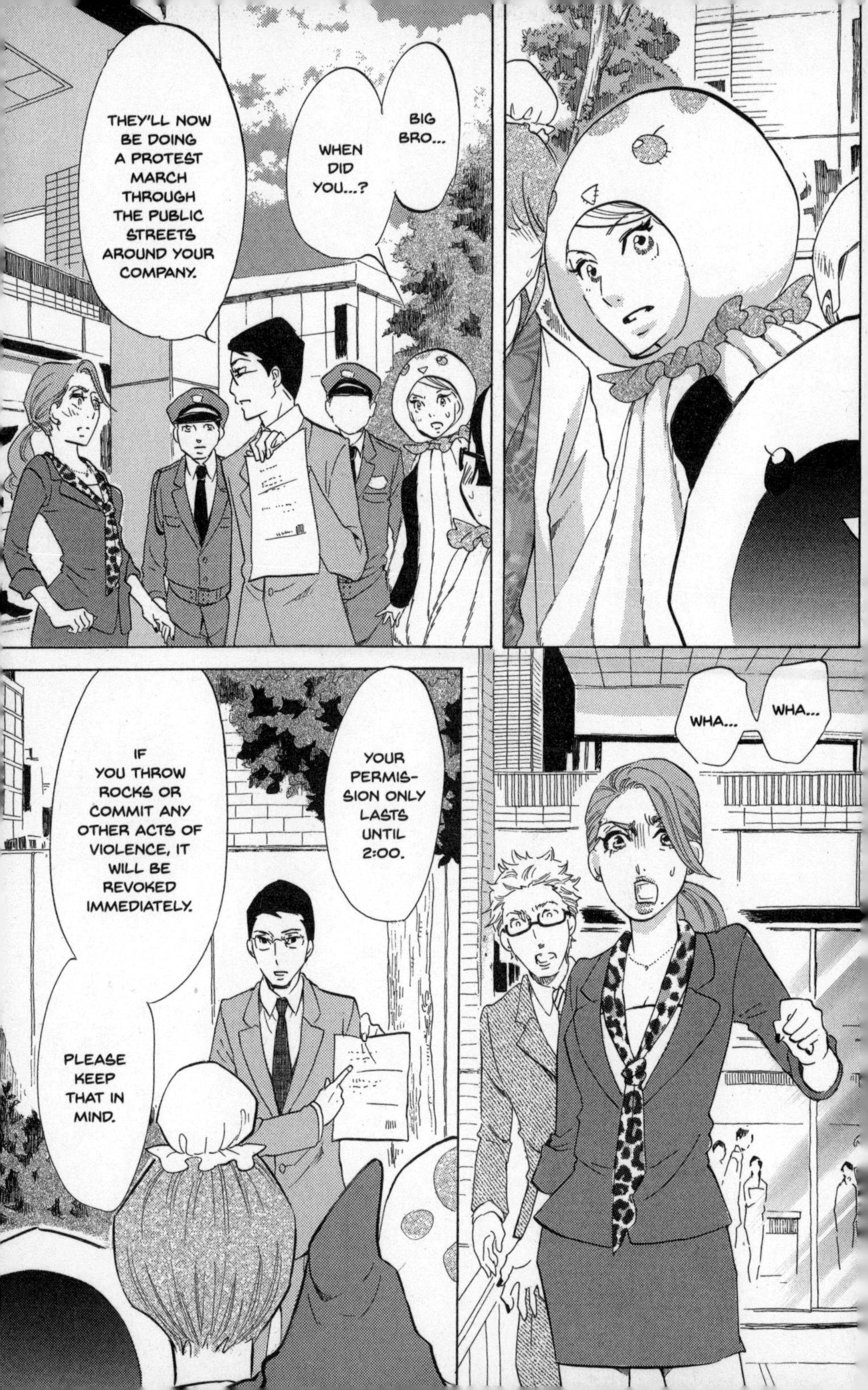
BIG BRO...
WHEN DID YOU...?
THEY'LL NOW BE DOING A PROTEST MARCH THROUGH THE PUBLIC STREETS AROUND YOUR COMPANY.
WHA...
WHA...
YOUR PERMISSION ONLY LASTS UNTIL 2:00.
IF YOU THROW ROCKS OR COMMIT ANY OTHER ACTS OF VIOLENCE, IT WILL BE REVOKED IMMEDIATELY.
PLEASE KEEP THAT IN MIND.

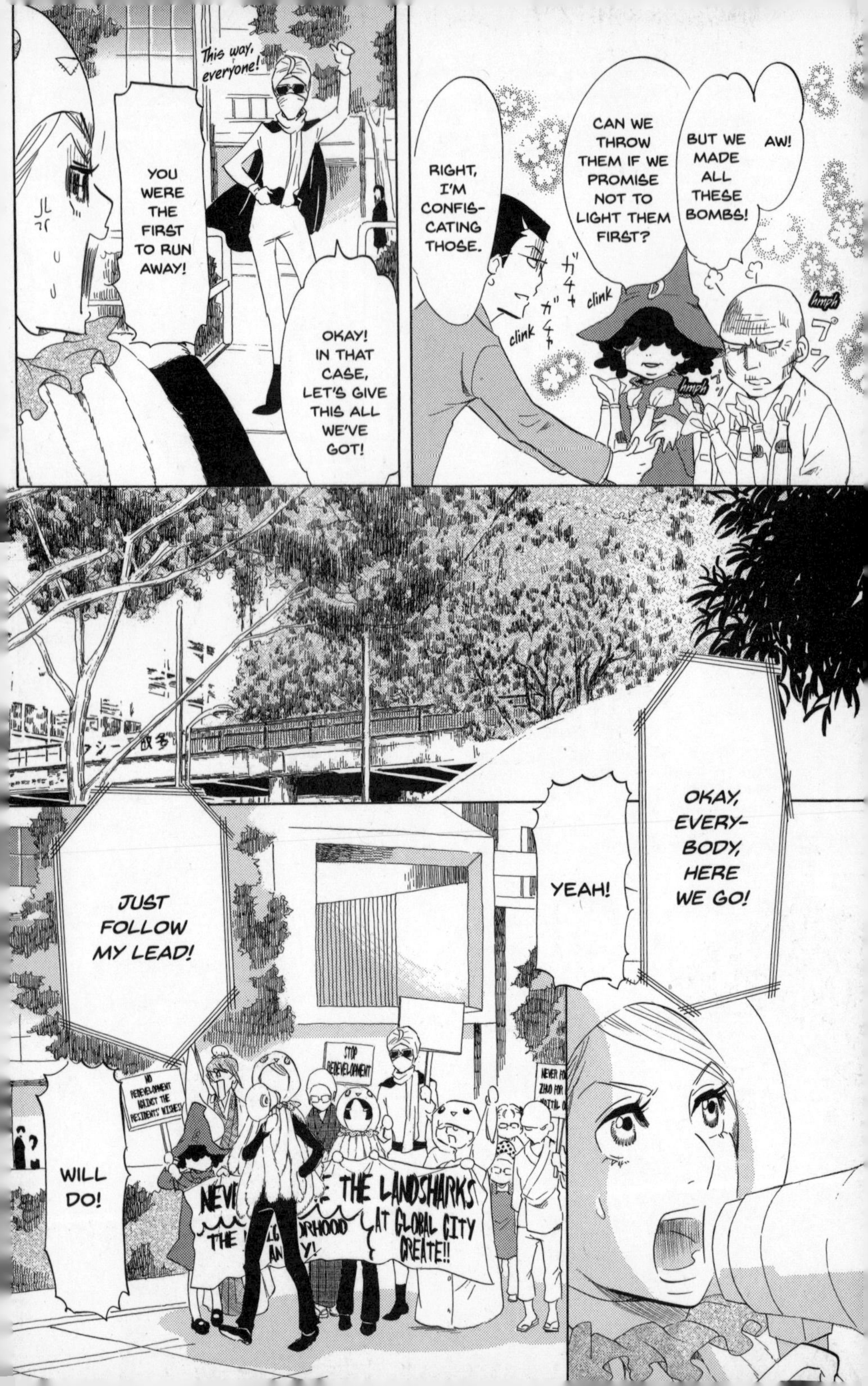
AW!
BUT WE MADE ALL THESE BOMBS!
CAN WE THROW THEM IF WE PROMISE NOT TO LIGHT THEM FIRST?
hmph
hmph
clink
clink
RIGHT, I'M CONFIS-CATING THOSE.
This way, everyone!
YOU WERE THE FIRST TO RUN AWAY!
OKAY! IN THAT CASE, LET'S GIVE THIS ALL WE'VE GOT!
OKAY, EVERY-BODY, HERE WE GO!
YEAH!
JUST FOLLOW MY LEAD!
STOP REDEVELOPMENT
NO REDEVELOPMENT AGAINST THE RESIDENTS' WISHES
THE LANDSHARKS
AT GLOBAL CITY CREATE!!
WILL DO!

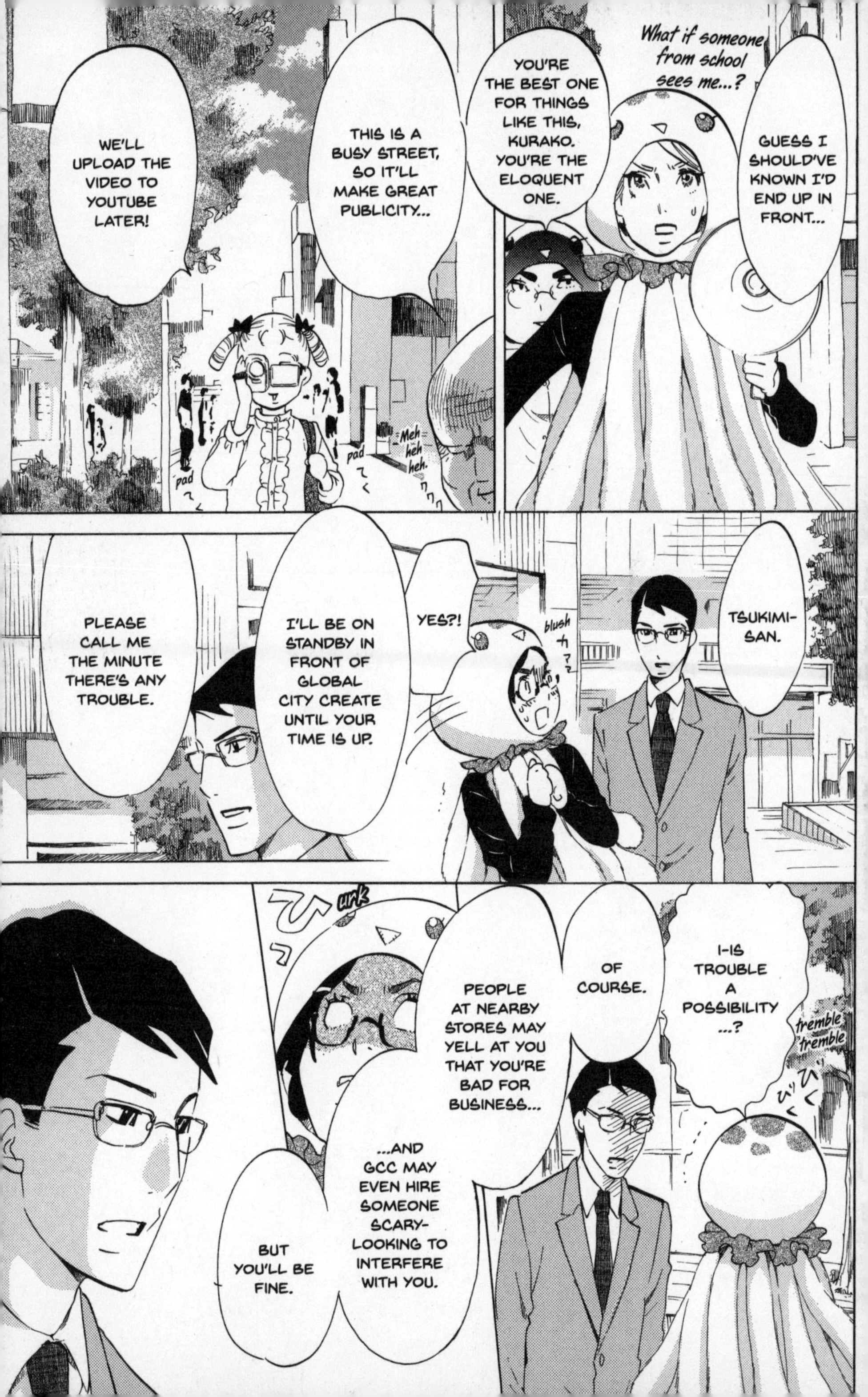
What if someone from school sees me...?
GUESS I SHOULD'VE KNOWN I'D END UP IN FRONT...
YOU'RE THE BEST ONE FOR THINGS LIKE THIS, KURAKO. YOU'RE THE ELOQUENT ONE.
THIS IS A BUSY STREET, SO IT'LL MAKE GREAT PUBLICITY...
Meh heh heh.
pad
pad
WE'LL UPLOAD THE VIDEO TO YOUTUBE LATER!
TSUKIMI-SAN.
blush
YES?!
I'LL BE ON STANDBY IN FRONT OF GLOBAL CITY CREATE UNTIL YOUR TIME IS UP.
PLEASE CALL ME THE MINUTE THERE'S ANY TROUBLE.
I-IS TROUBLE A POSSIBILITY ...?
tremble tremble
OF COURSE.
PEOPLE AT NEARBY STORES MAY YELL AT YOU THAT YOU'RE BAD FOR BUSINESS...
urk
...AND GCC MAY EVEN HIRE SOMEONE SCARY-LOOKING TO INTERFERE WITH YOU.
BUT YOU'LL BE FINE.

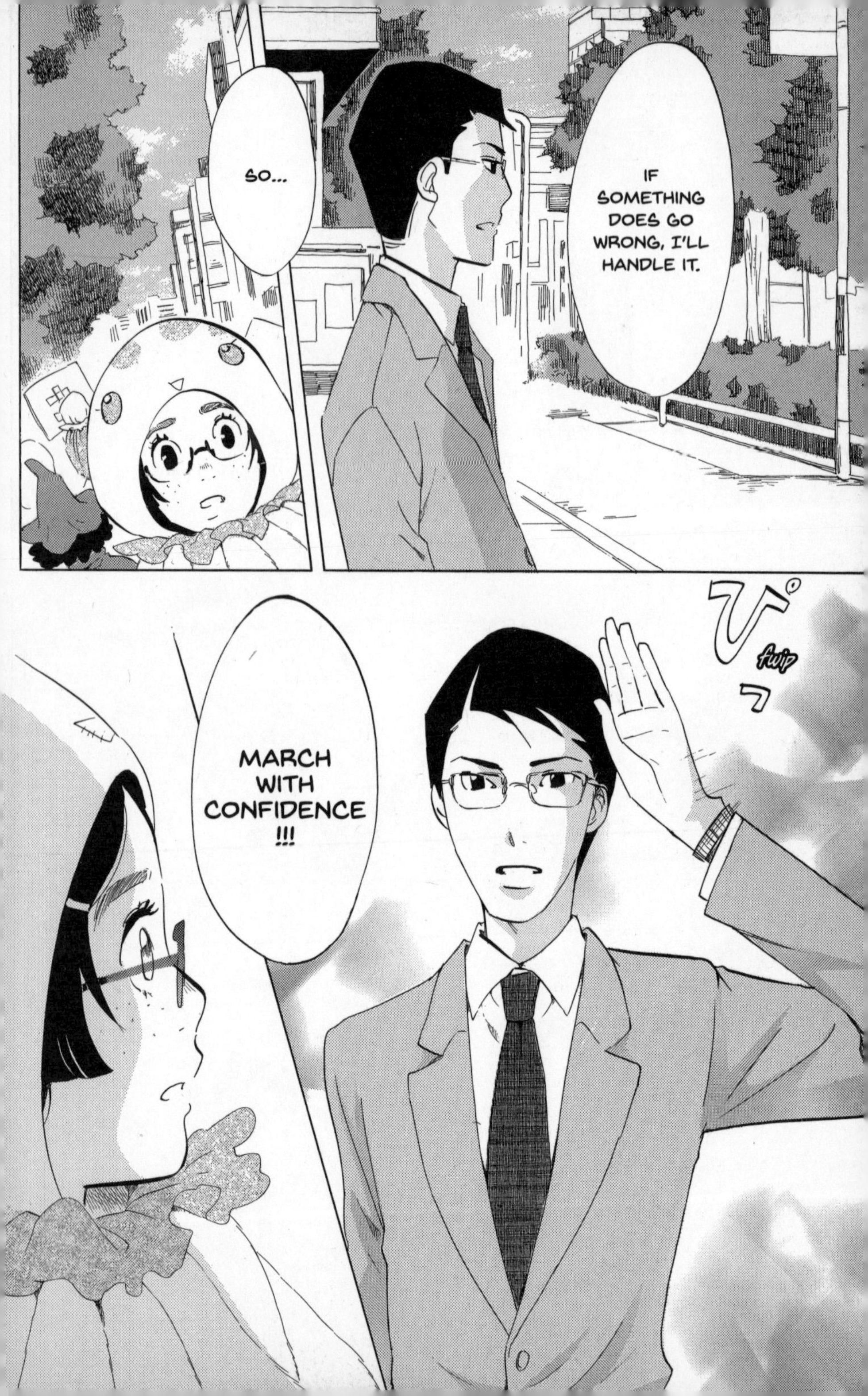
IF SOMETHING DOES GO WRONG, I'LL HANDLE IT.
SO...
ぴっ
fwip
MARCH WITH CONFIDENCE !!!

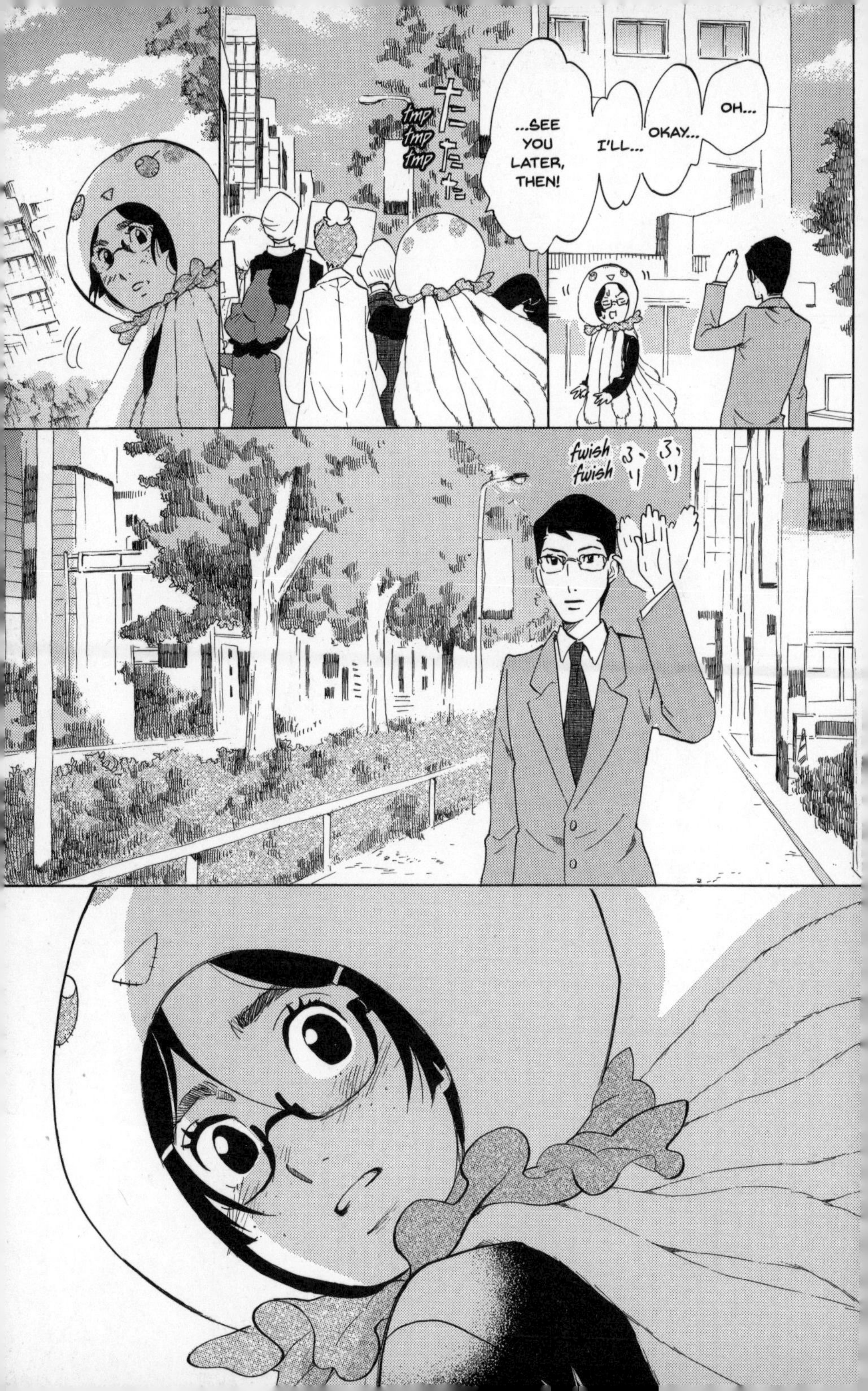
OH...
OKAY...
I'LL...
...SEE YOU LATER, THEN!
tmp tmp tmp
fwish fwish
ふり ふり

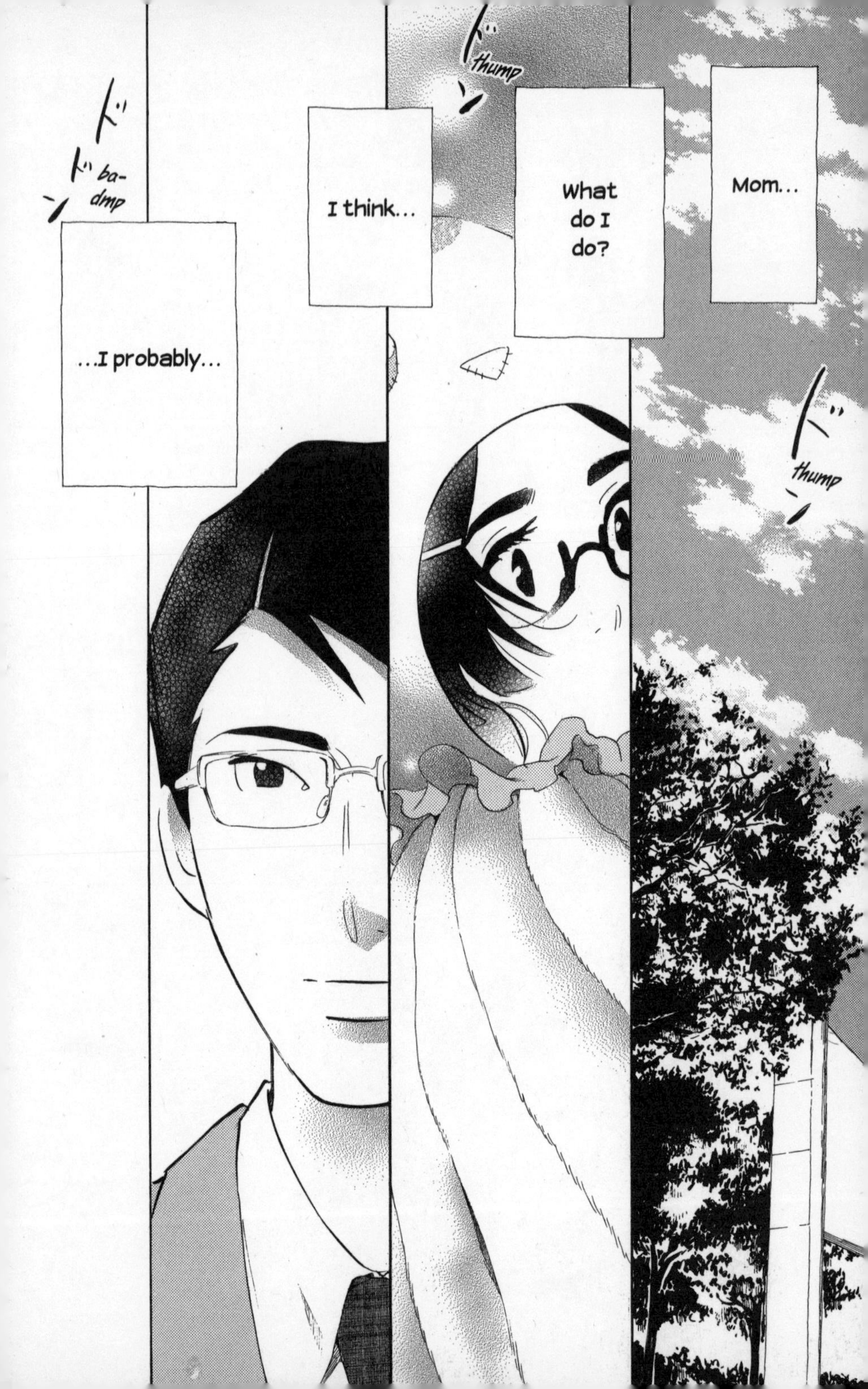
Mom...
ド
thump
What do I do?
ド
thump
I think...
...I probably...
ドド
ba-dmp

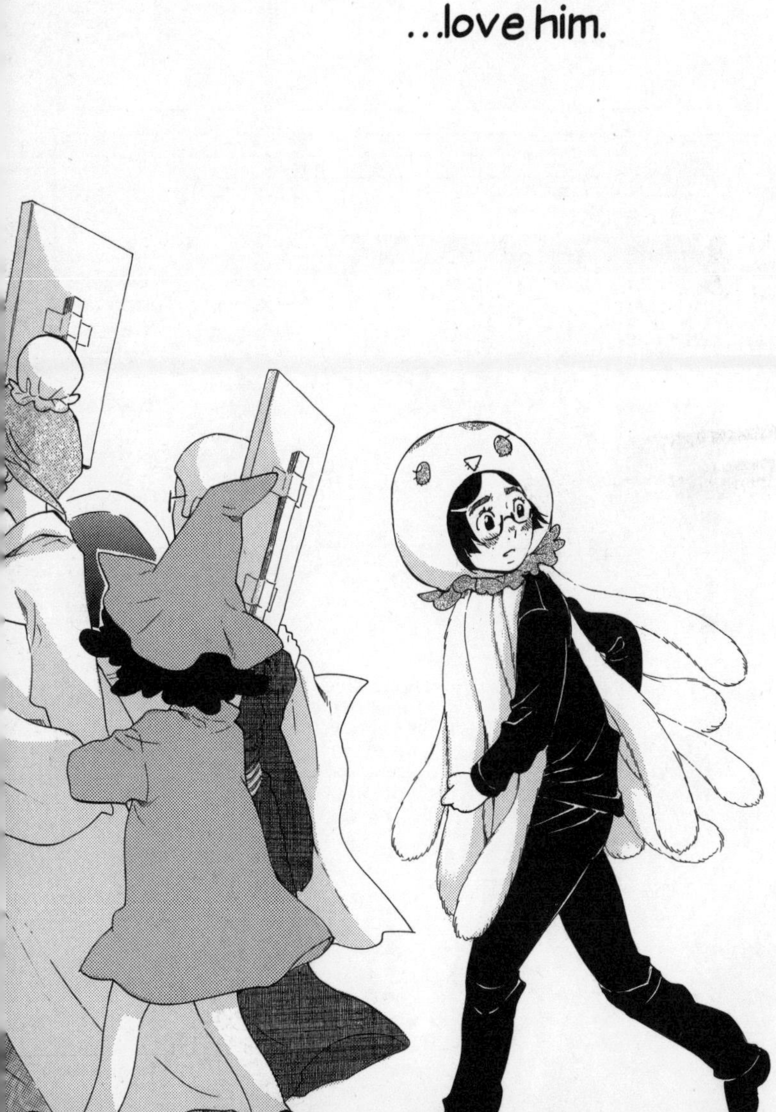
...love him.

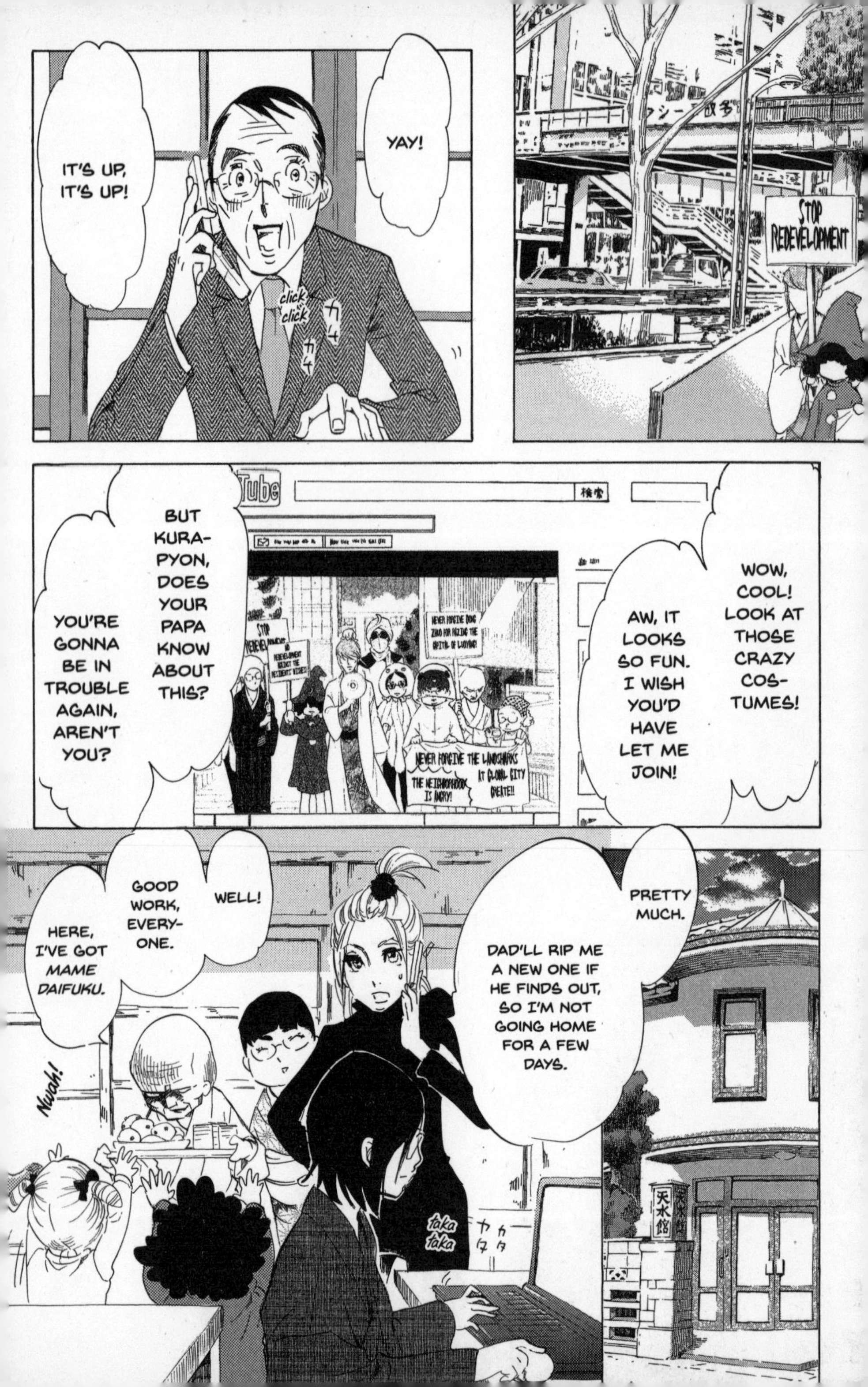
STOP REDEVELOPMENT
YAY!
IT'S UP, IT'S UP!
click click
WOW, COOL! LOOK AT THOSE CRAZY COSTUMES!
AW, IT LOOKS SO FUN. I WISH YOU'D HAVE LET ME JOIN!
BUT KURA-PYON, DOES YOUR PAPA KNOW ABOUT THIS?
YOU'RE GONNA BE IN TROUBLE AGAIN, AREN'T YOU?
NEVER FORGIVE THE LANDSHARKS
AT GLOBAL CITY CREATE!!
THE NEIGHBORHOOD IS ANGRY!
PRETTY MUCH.
DAD'LL RIP ME A NEW ONE IF HE FINDS OUT, SO I'M NOT GOING HOME FOR A FEW DAYS.
WELL!
GOOD WORK, EVERYONE.
HERE, I'VE GOT MAME DAIFUKU.
Nwah!
taka taka

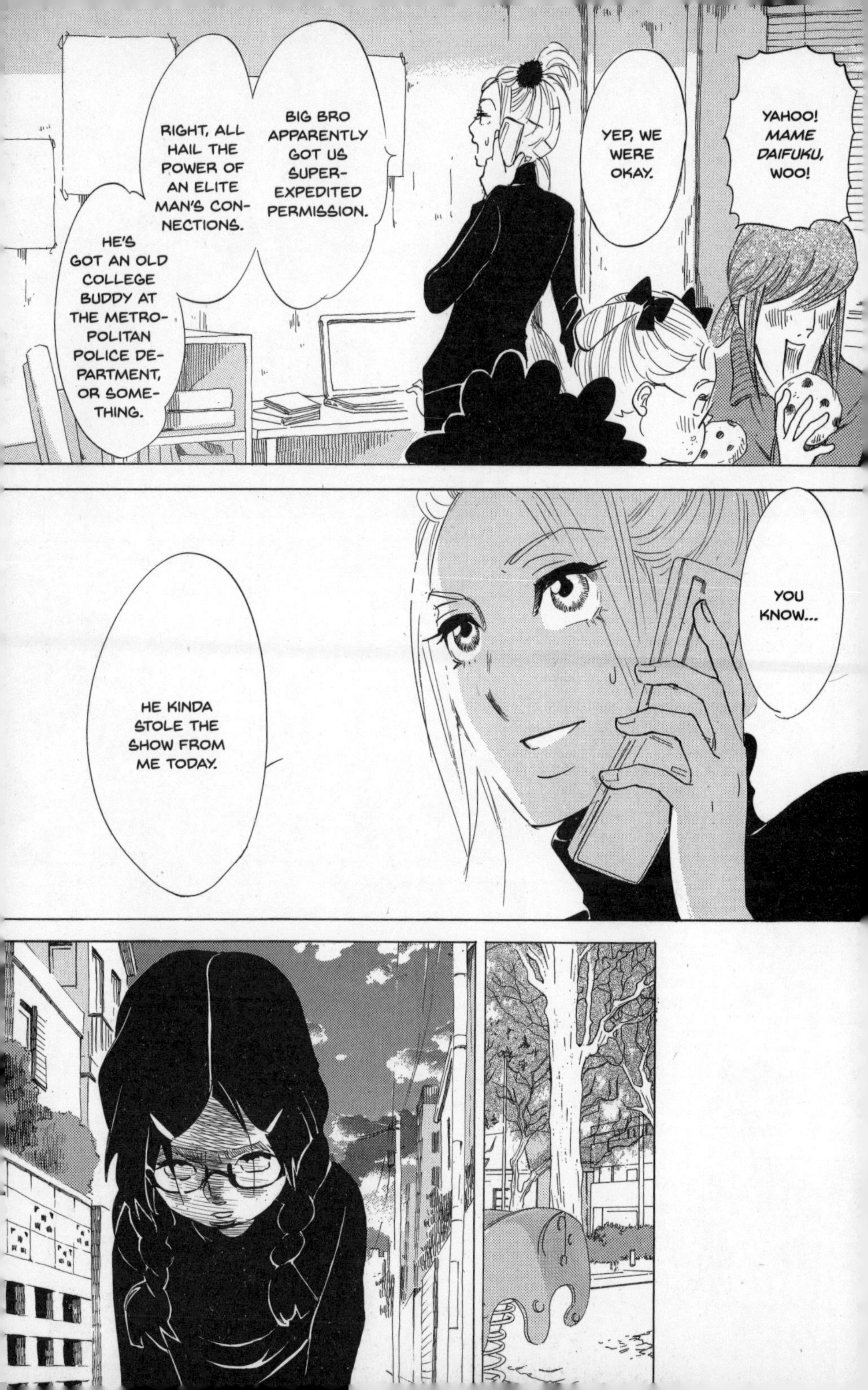
YAHOO! MAME DAIFUKU, WOO!
YEP, WE WERE OKAY.
BIG BRO APPARENTLY GOT US SUPER-EXPEDITED PERMISSION.
RIGHT, ALL HAIL THE POWER OF AN ELITE MAN'S CONNECTIONS.
HE'S GOT AN OLD COLLEGE BUDDY AT THE METROPOLITAN POLICE DEPARTMENT, OR SOMETHING.
YOU KNOW...
HE KINDA STOLE THE SHOW FROM ME TODAY.

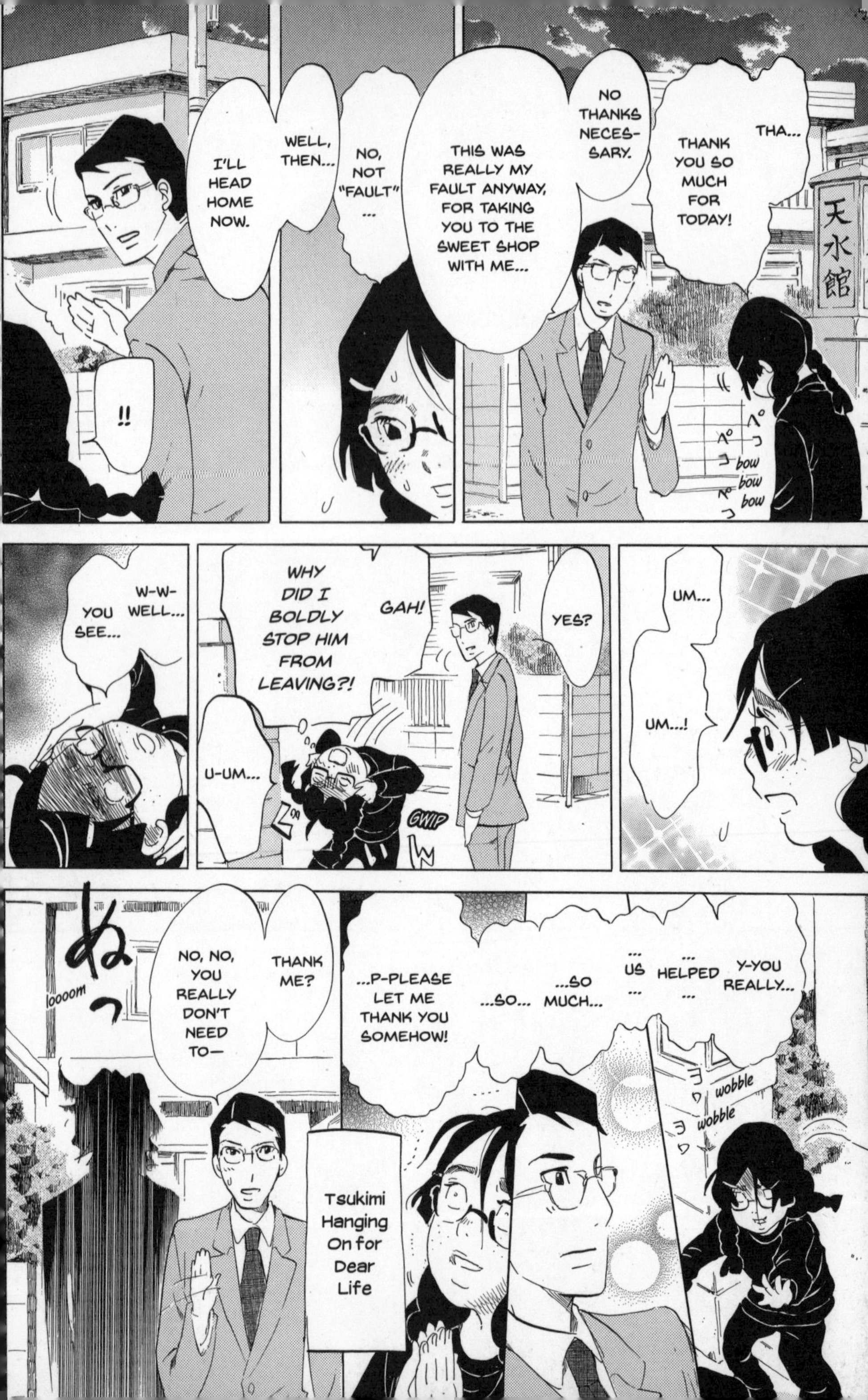
THA...
THANK YOU SO MUCH FOR TODAY!
天水館
ペコ bow ペコ bow ペコ bow
NO THANKS NECES-SARY.
THIS WAS REALLY MY FAULT ANYWAY, FOR TAKING YOU TO THE SWEET SHOP WITH ME...
NO, NOT "FAULT"...
WELL, THEN...
I'LL HEAD HOME NOW.
!!
UM...
UM...!
YES?
GAH!
WHY DID I BOLDLY STOP HIM FROM LEAVING?!
U-UM...
GWIP
W-W-WELL...
YOU SEE...
Y-YOU REALLY...
...HELPED...
...US...
...SO MUCH...
...SO...
...P-PLEASE LET ME THANK YOU SOMEHOW!
ヨロ wobble ヨロ wobble
THANK ME?
NO, NO, YOU REALLY DON'T NEED TO—
Tsukimi Hanging On for Dear Life
ぬっ looooom

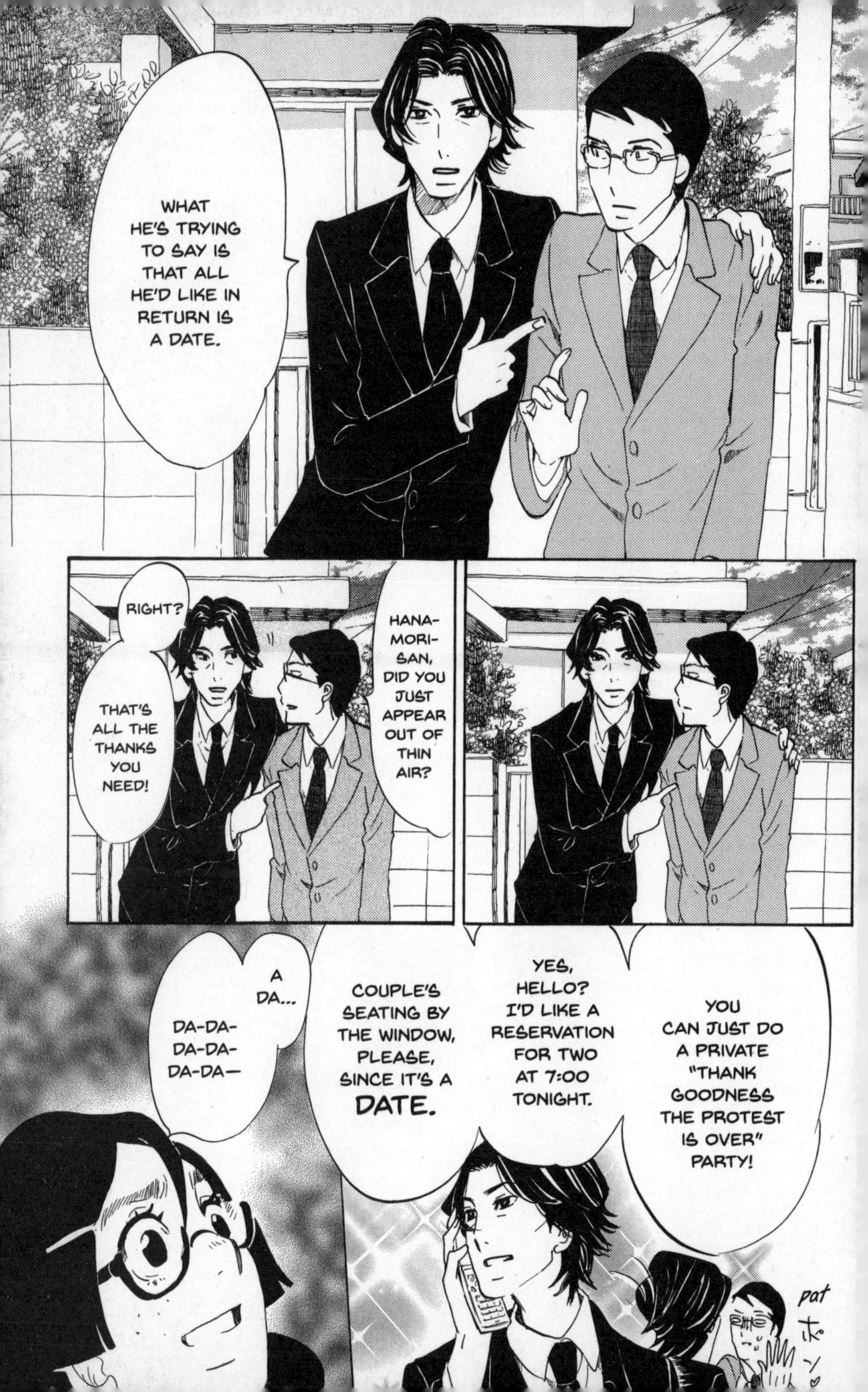
WHAT HE'S TRYING TO SAY IS THAT ALL HE'D LIKE IN RETURN IS A DATE.
HANA-MORI-SAN, DID YOU JUST APPEAR OUT OF THIN AIR?
RIGHT?
THAT'S ALL THE THANKS YOU NEED!
YOU CAN JUST DO A PRIVATE "THANK GOODNESS THE PROTEST IS OVER" PARTY!
YES, HELLO? I'D LIKE A RESERVATION FOR TWO AT 7:00 TONIGHT.
COUPLE'S SEATING BY THE WINDOW, PLEASE, SINCE IT'S A DATE.
A DA...
DA-DA-DA-DA-DA-DA—
pat

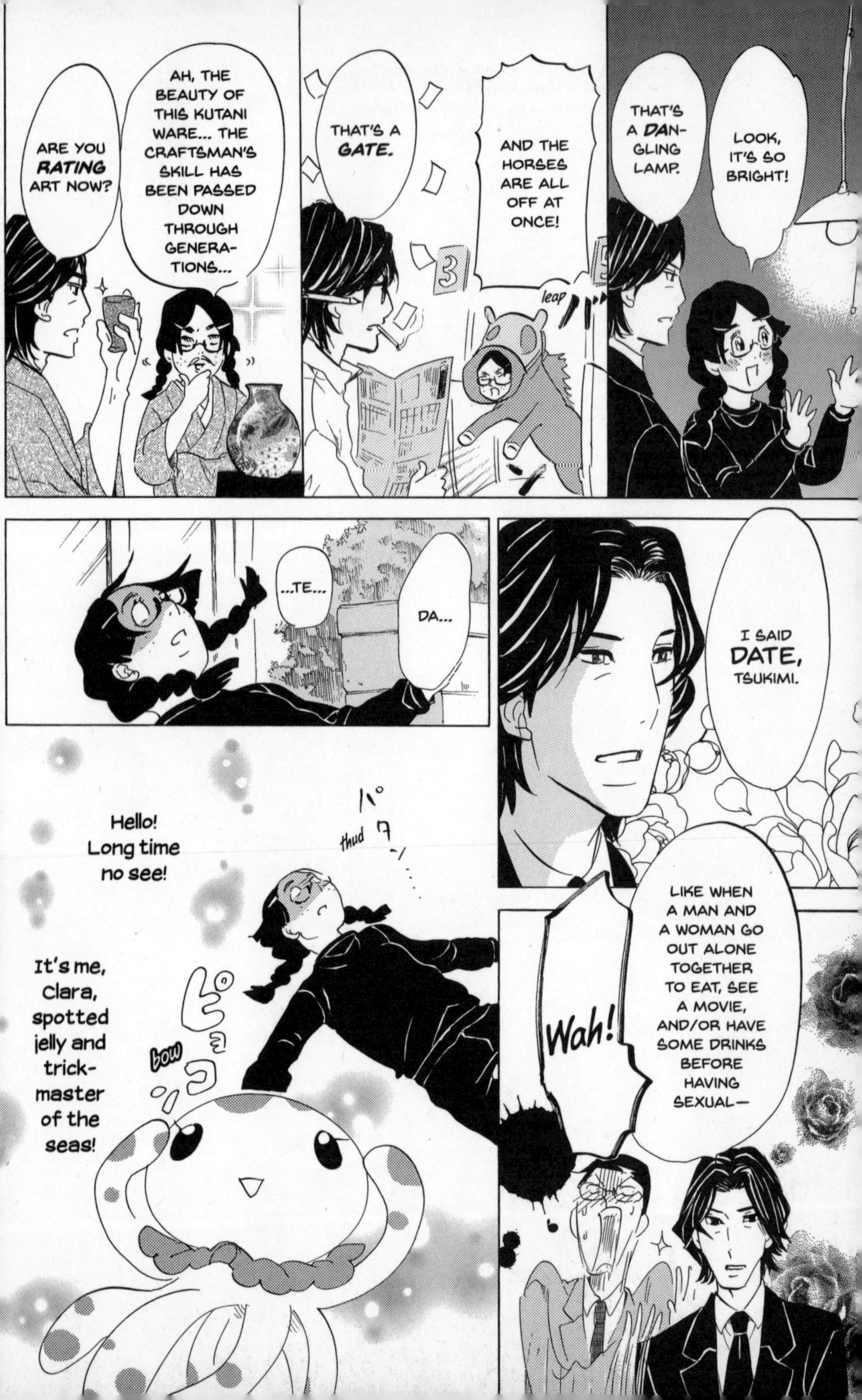
LOOK, IT'S SO BRIGHT!
THAT'S A DAN-GLING LAMP.
AND THE HORSES ARE ALL OFF AT ONCE!
leap
THAT'S A GATE.
AH, THE BEAUTY OF THIS KUTANI WARE... THE CRAFTSMAN'S SKILL HAS BEEN PASSED DOWN THROUGH GENERA-TIONS...
ARE YOU RATING ART NOW?
I SAID DATE, TSUKIMI.
DA...
...TE...
LIKE WHEN A MAN AND A WOMAN GO OUT ALONE TOGETHER TO EAT, SEE A MOVIE, AND/OR HAVE SOME DRINKS BEFORE HAVING SEXUAL—
Wah!
パ
thud
ピョコ
bow
Hello! Long time no see!
It's me, Clara, spotted jelly and trick-master of the seas!

TOP 10 EVENTS AN AMARS WILL PROBABLY NEVER EXPERIENCE

○	1.	**DATE**
○	2.	**MIXER**
○	3.	**BEAUTY SALON**

Here it goes... Bam!

Okay, let's jump wight to our usual list!

bing

crumble *crumble*

crumble

Instead of petrification, it's erosion.

Tsukimi-tan was so shocked that she didn't just turn to stone; she dissolved into sand.

It goes without saying that number 1 is "date"!!

SAY WHAT?

...ON A DATE WITH TSUKIMI THANKS TO THE PROTEST?

BIG BRO IS GOING...

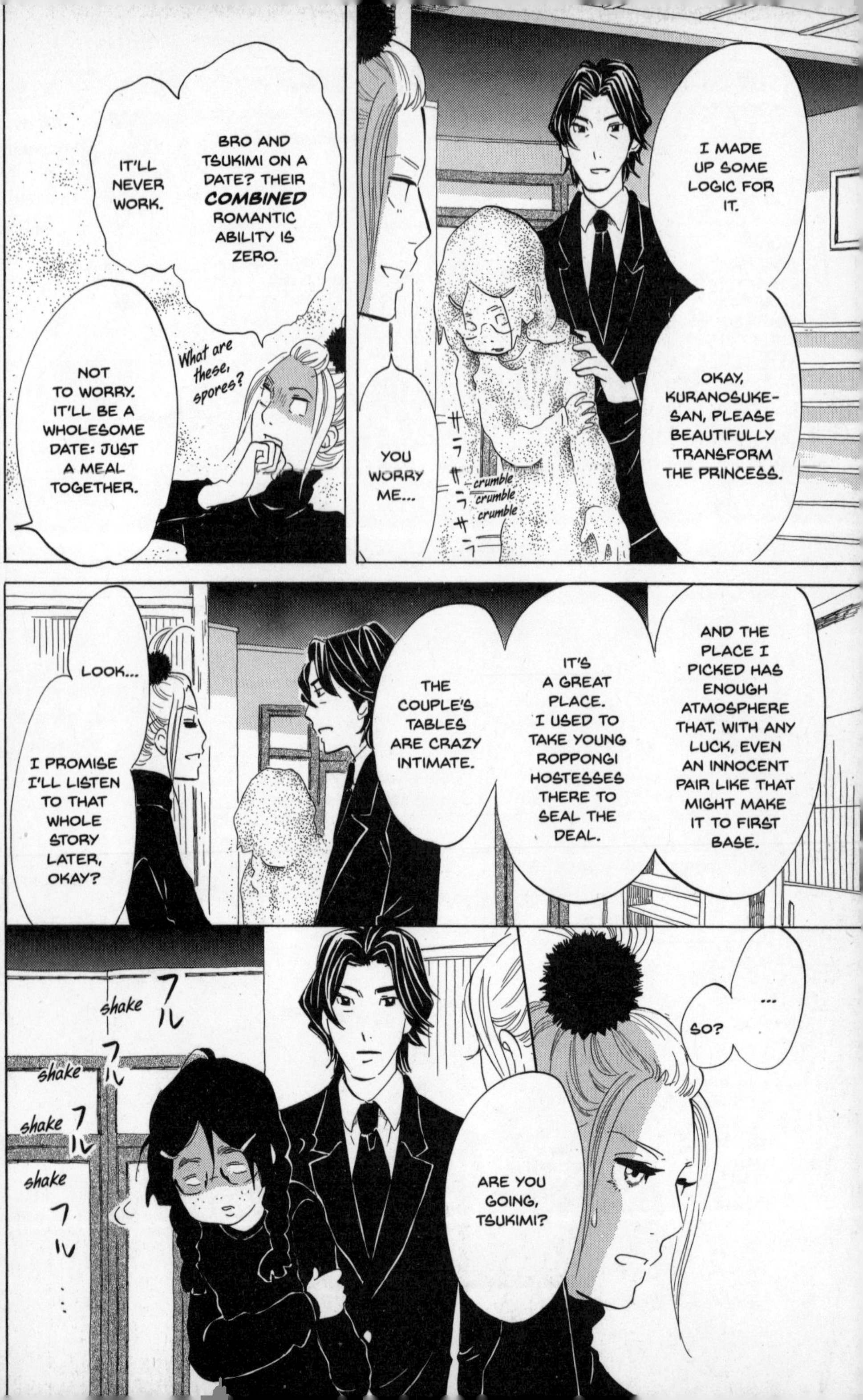
I MADE UP SOME LOGIC FOR IT.
OKAY, KURANOSUKE-SAN, PLEASE BEAUTIFULLY TRANSFORM THE PRINCESS.
YOU WORRY ME...
crumble crumble crumble
BRO AND TSUKIMI ON A DATE? THEIR **COMBINED** ROMANTIC ABILITY IS ZERO.
IT'LL NEVER WORK.
What are these, spores?
NOT TO WORRY. IT'LL BE A WHOLESOME DATE: JUST A MEAL TOGETHER.
AND THE PLACE I PICKED HAS ENOUGH ATMOSPHERE THAT, WITH ANY LUCK, EVEN AN INNOCENT PAIR LIKE THAT MIGHT MAKE IT TO FIRST BASE.
IT'S A GREAT PLACE. I USED TO TAKE YOUNG ROPPONGI HOSTESSES THERE TO SEAL THE DEAL.
THE COUPLE'S TABLES ARE CRAZY INTIMATE.
LOOK...
I PROMISE I'LL LISTEN TO THAT WHOLE STORY LATER, OKAY?
... SO?
ARE YOU GOING, TSUKIMI?
shake
shake
shake
shake

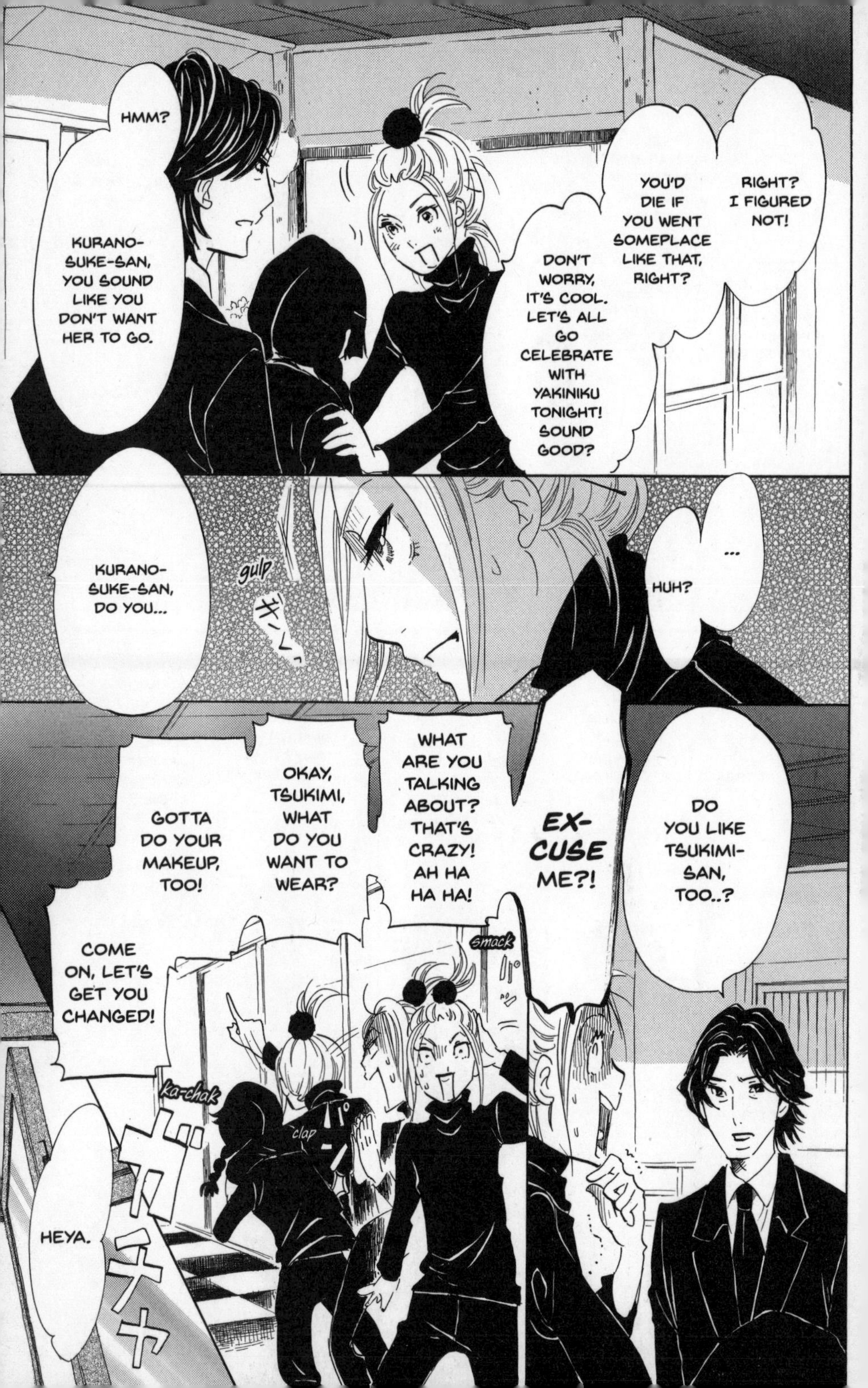
RIGHT? I FIGURED NOT!
YOU'D DIE IF YOU WENT SOMEPLACE LIKE THAT, RIGHT?
DON'T WORRY, IT'S COOL. LET'S ALL GO CELEBRATE WITH YAKINIKU TONIGHT! SOUND GOOD?
HMM?
KURANO-SUKE-SAN, YOU SOUND LIKE YOU DON'T WANT HER TO GO.
...
HUH?
gulp
ギクッ
KURANO-SUKE-SAN, DO YOU...
DO YOU LIKE TSUKIMI-SAN, TOO..?
EX-CUSE ME?!
smack
WHAT ARE YOU TALKING ABOUT? THAT'S CRAZY! AH HA HA HA!
OKAY, TSUKIMI, WHAT DO YOU WANT TO WEAR?
GOTTA DO YOUR MAKEUP, TOO!
COME ON, LET'S GET YOU CHANGED!
clap
ka-chak
ガチャ
HEYA.

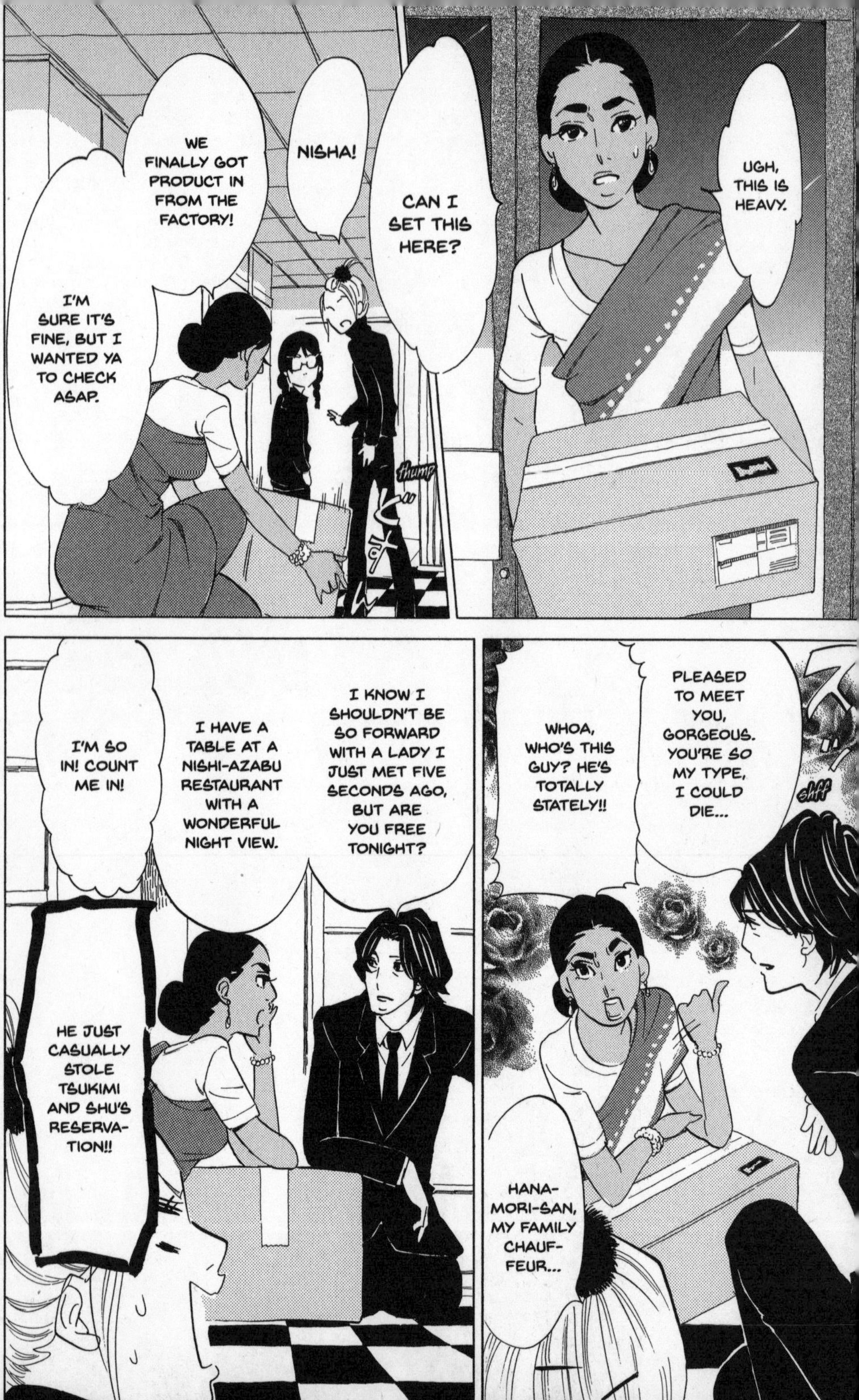
UGH, THIS IS HEAVY.
CAN I SET THIS HERE?
NISHA!
WE FINALLY GOT PRODUCT IN FROM THE FACTORY!
I'M SURE IT'S FINE, BUT I WANTED YA TO CHECK ASAP.
thump
PLEASED TO MEET YOU, GORGEOUS. YOU'RE SO MY TYPE, I COULD DIE...
WHOA, WHO'S THIS GUY? HE'S TOTALLY STATELY!!
shff
HANA-MORI-SAN, MY FAMILY CHAUF-FEUR...
I KNOW I SHOULDN'T BE SO FORWARD WITH A LADY I JUST MET FIVE SECONDS AGO, BUT ARE YOU FREE TONIGHT?
I HAVE A TABLE AT A NISHI-AZABU RESTAURANT WITH A WONDERFUL NIGHT VIEW.
I'M SO IN! COUNT ME IN!
HE JUST CASUALLY STOLE TSUKIMI AND SHU'S RESERVA-TION!!

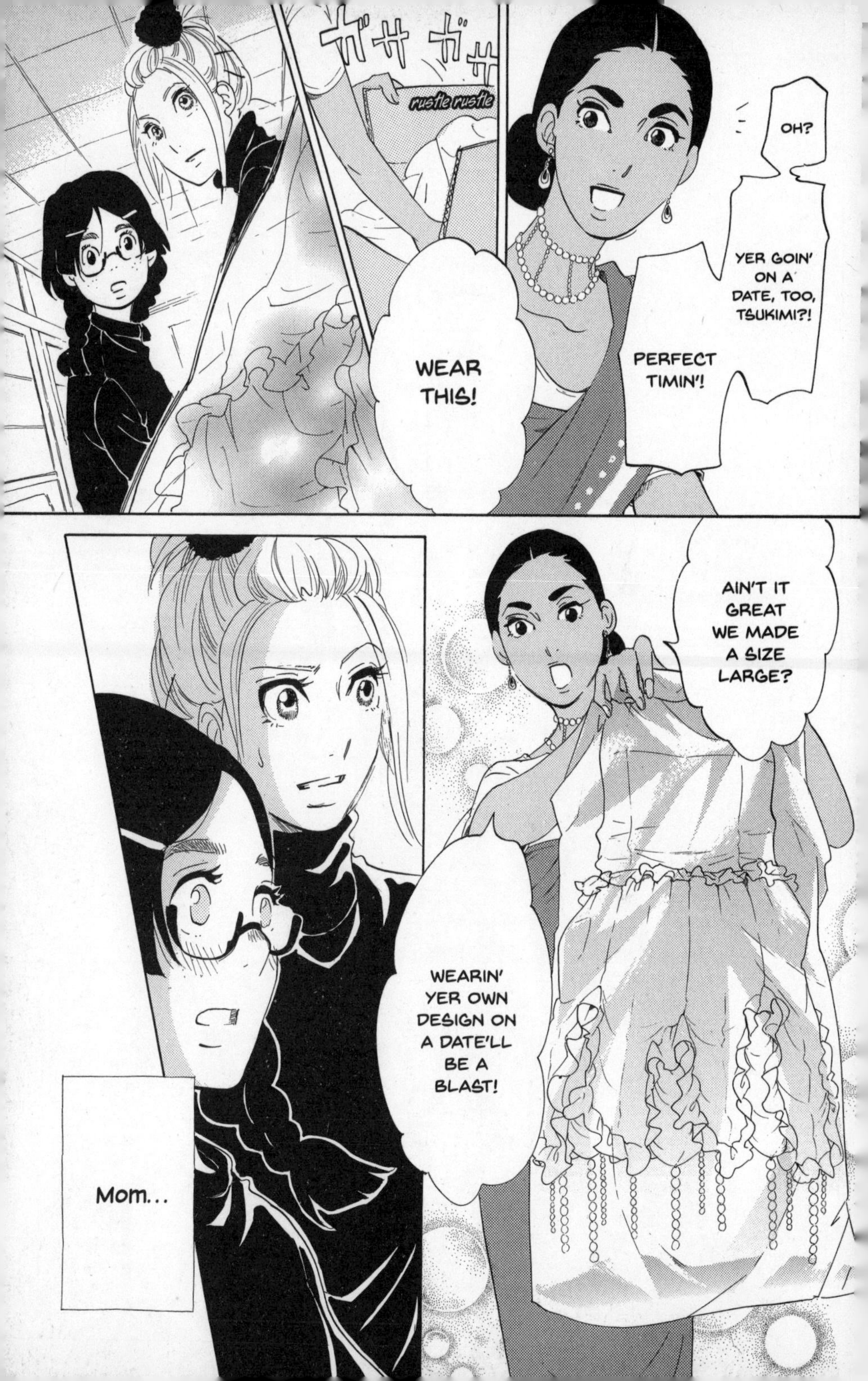
OH?
YER GOIN' ON A DATE, TOO, TSUKIMI?!
PERFECT TIMIN'!
ガサガサ
rustle rustle
WEAR THIS!
AIN'T IT GREAT WE MADE A SIZE LARGE?
WEARIN' YER OWN DESIGN ON A DATE'LL BE A BLAST!
Mom...

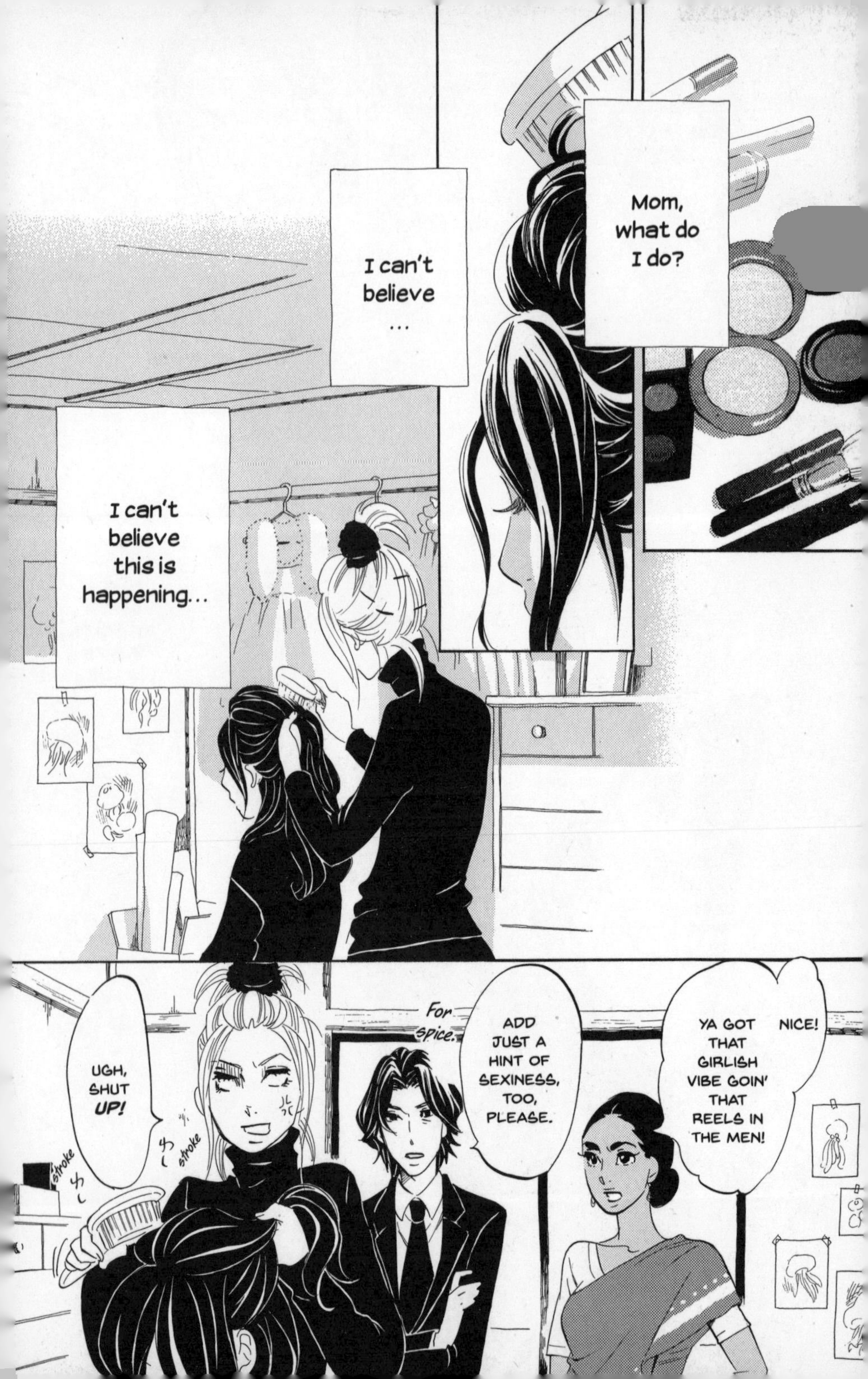
Mom, what do I do?
I can't believe …
I can't believe this is happening…
NICE!
YA GOT THAT GIRLISH VIBE GOIN' THAT REELS IN THE MEN!
ADD JUST A HINT OF SEXINESS, TOO, PLEASE.
For spice.
UGH, SHUT UP!
stroke
stroke

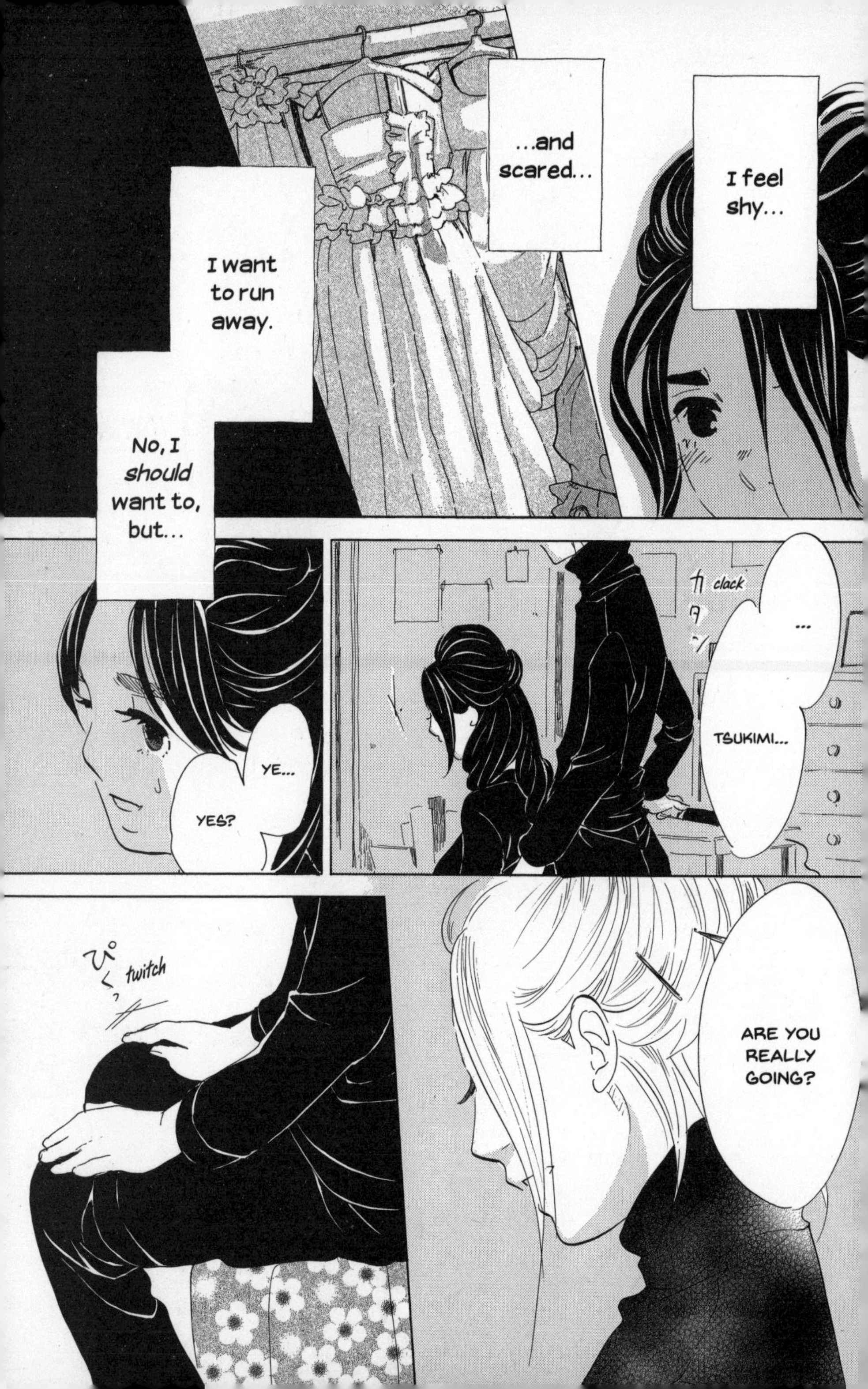
I feel shy...
...and scared...
I want to run away.
No, I *should* want to, but...
カタン clack
...
TSUKIMI...
YE... YES?
ARE YOU REALLY GOING?
ぴくっ twitch

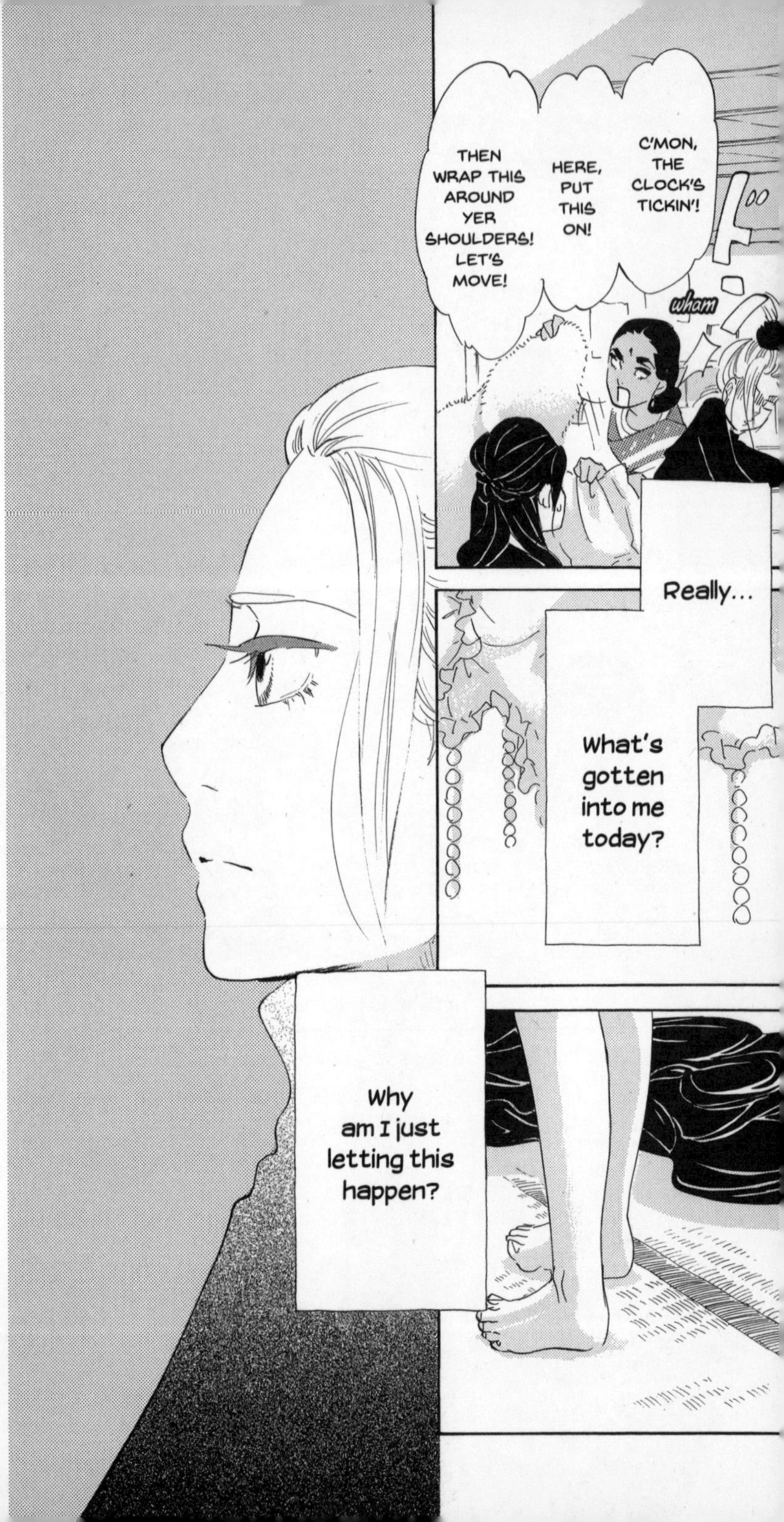
C'MON, THE CLOCK'S TICKIN'!
HERE, PUT THIS ON!
THEN WRAP THIS AROUND YER SHOULDERS! LET'S MOVE!
wham
Really...
What's gotten into me today?
Why am I just letting this happen?

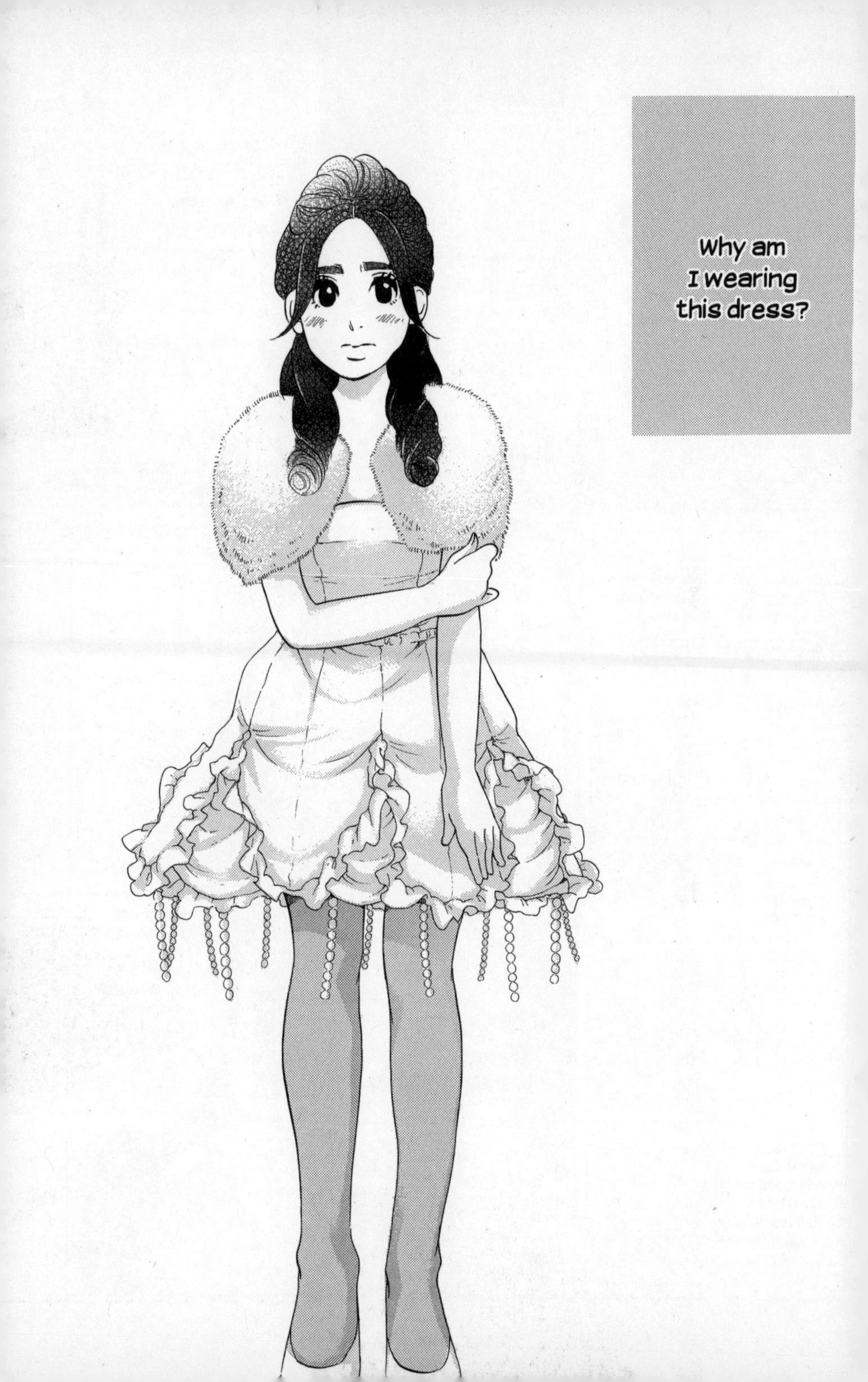
Why am I wearing this dress?

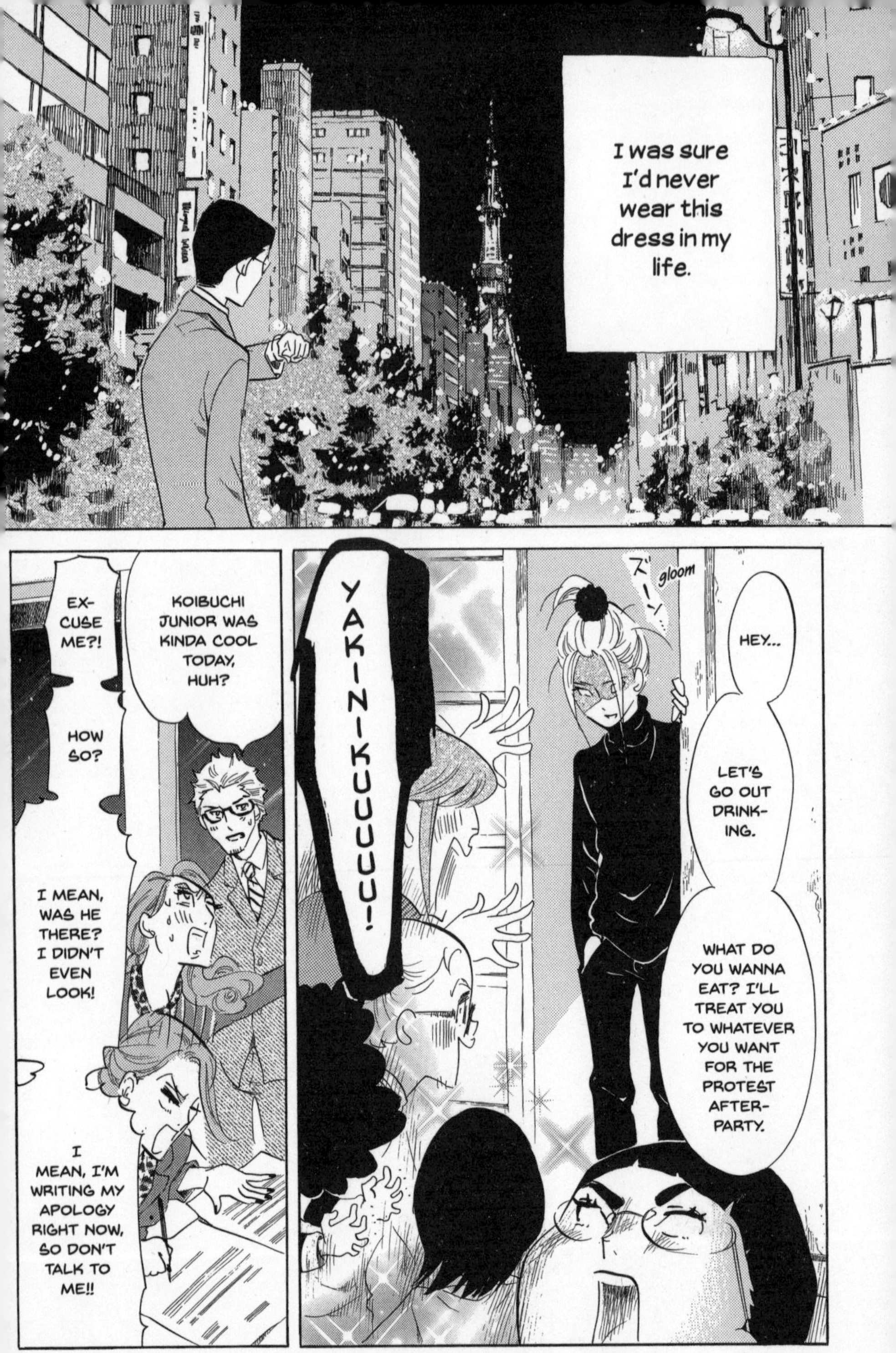
I was sure I'd never wear this dress in my life.
gloom
HEY...
LET'S GO OUT DRINKING.
WHAT DO YOU WANNA EAT? I'LL TREAT YOU TO WHATEVER YOU WANT FOR THE PROTEST AFTER-PARTY.
YAKINIKUUUUU!
KOIBUCHI JUNIOR WAS KINDA COOL TODAY, HUH?
EX-CUSE ME?!
HOW SO?
I MEAN, WAS HE THERE? I DIDN'T EVEN LOOK!
I MEAN, I'M WRITING MY APOLOGY RIGHT NOW, SO DON'T TALK TO ME!!

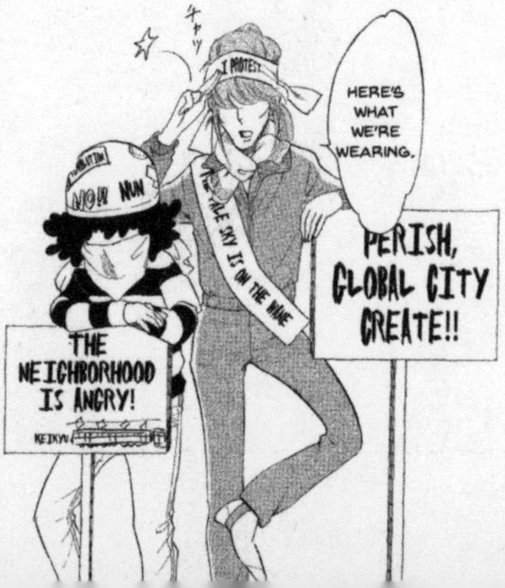
HERE'S WHAT WE'RE WEARING.
I PROTEST
PERISH, GLOBAL CITY CREATE!!
THE NEIGHBORHOOD IS ANGRY!
KEIKYU

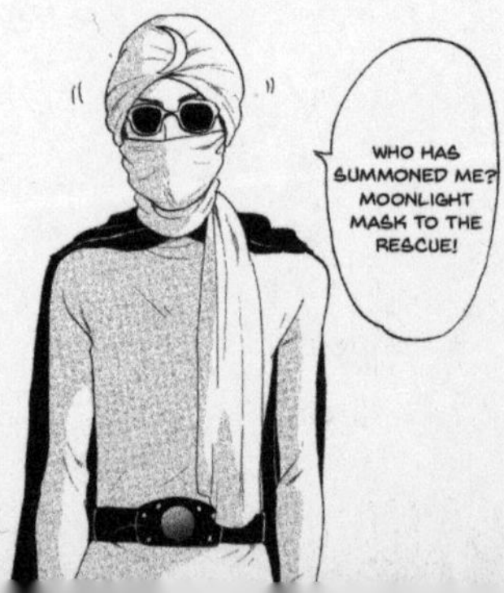
WHO HAS SUMMONED ME? MOONLIGHT MASK TO THE RESCUE!

Episode 48

My Date with Shu-Shu

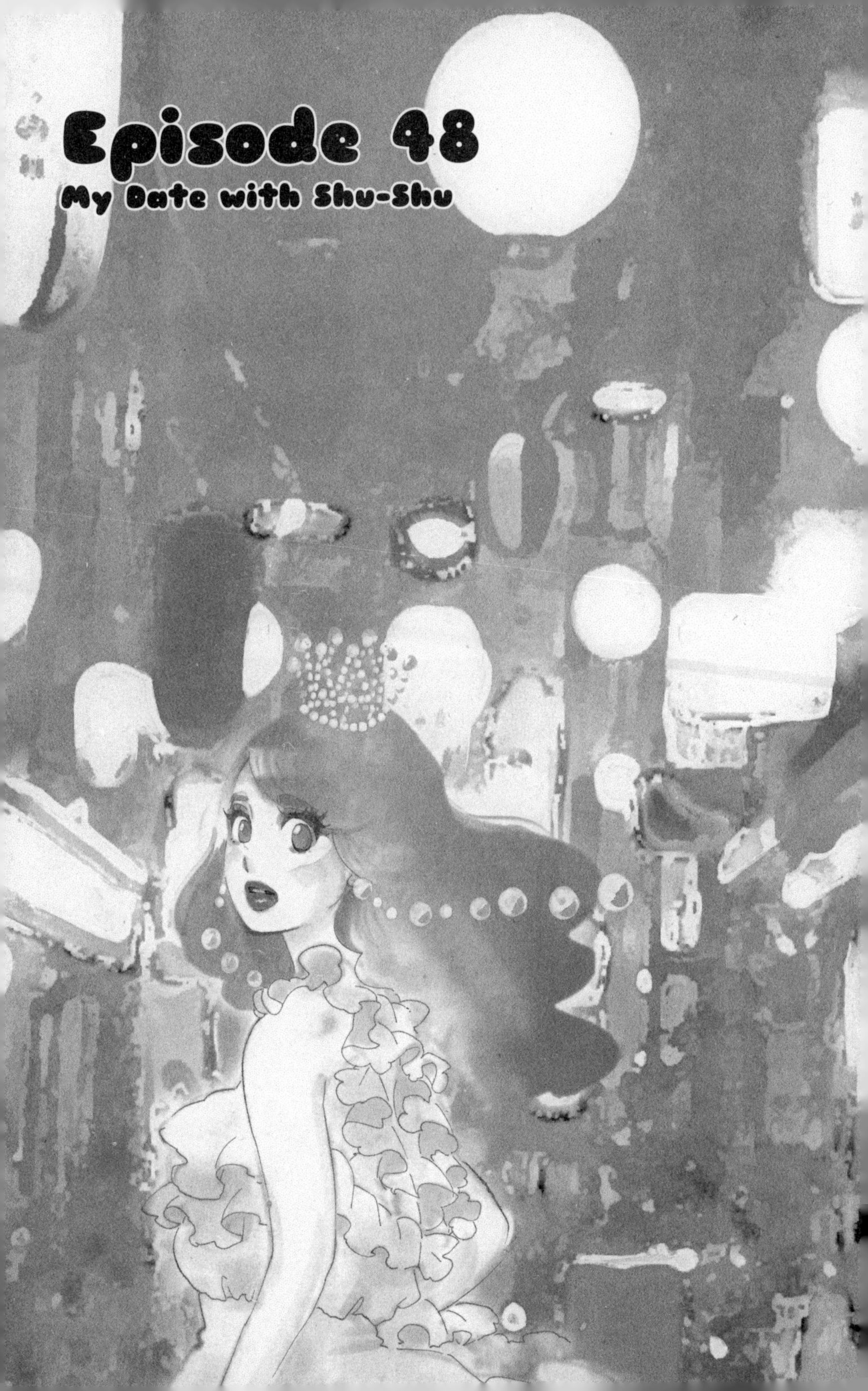

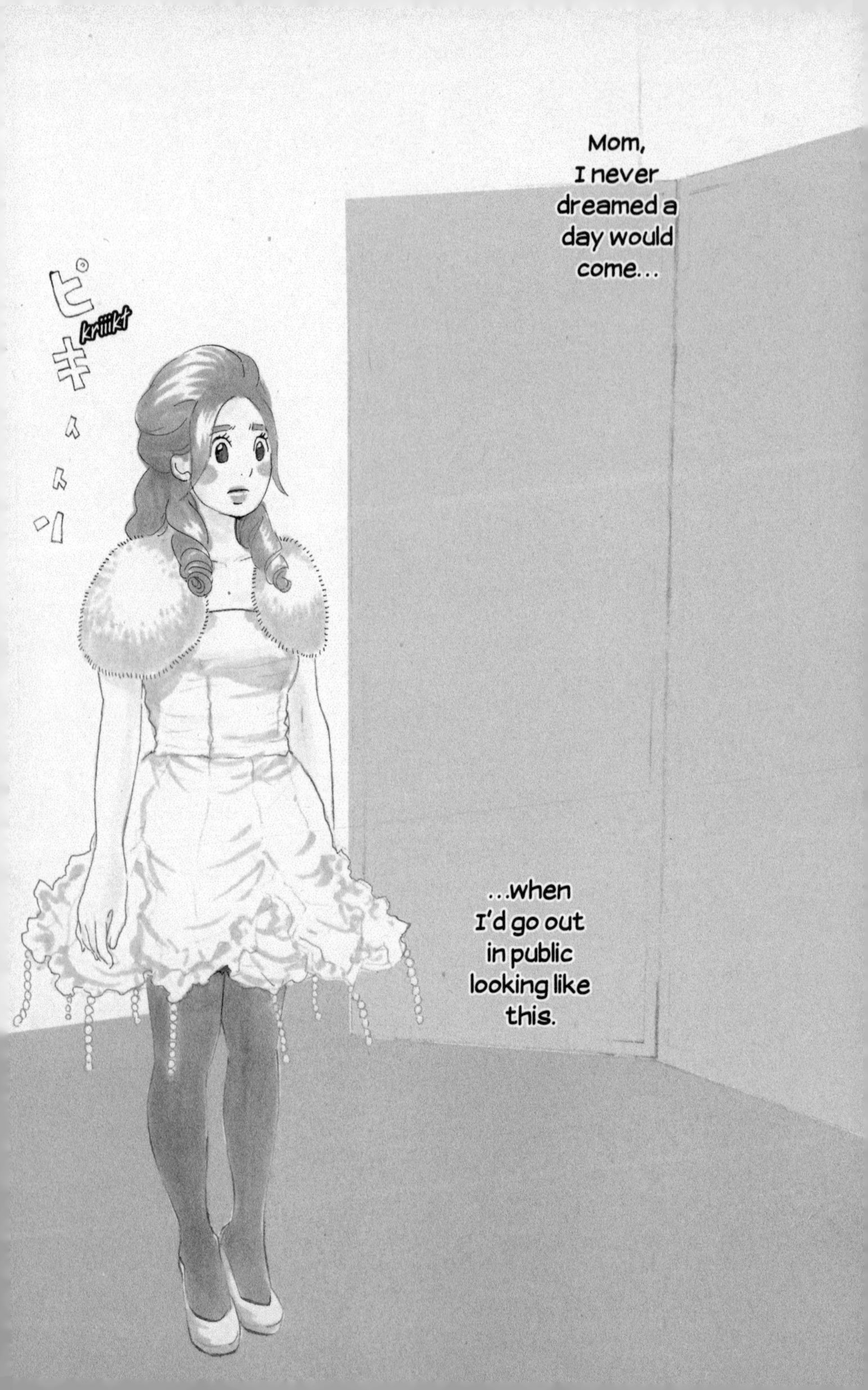
Mom,
I never dreamed a day would come...
ピキィィン
kriiikt
...when I'd go out in public looking like this.

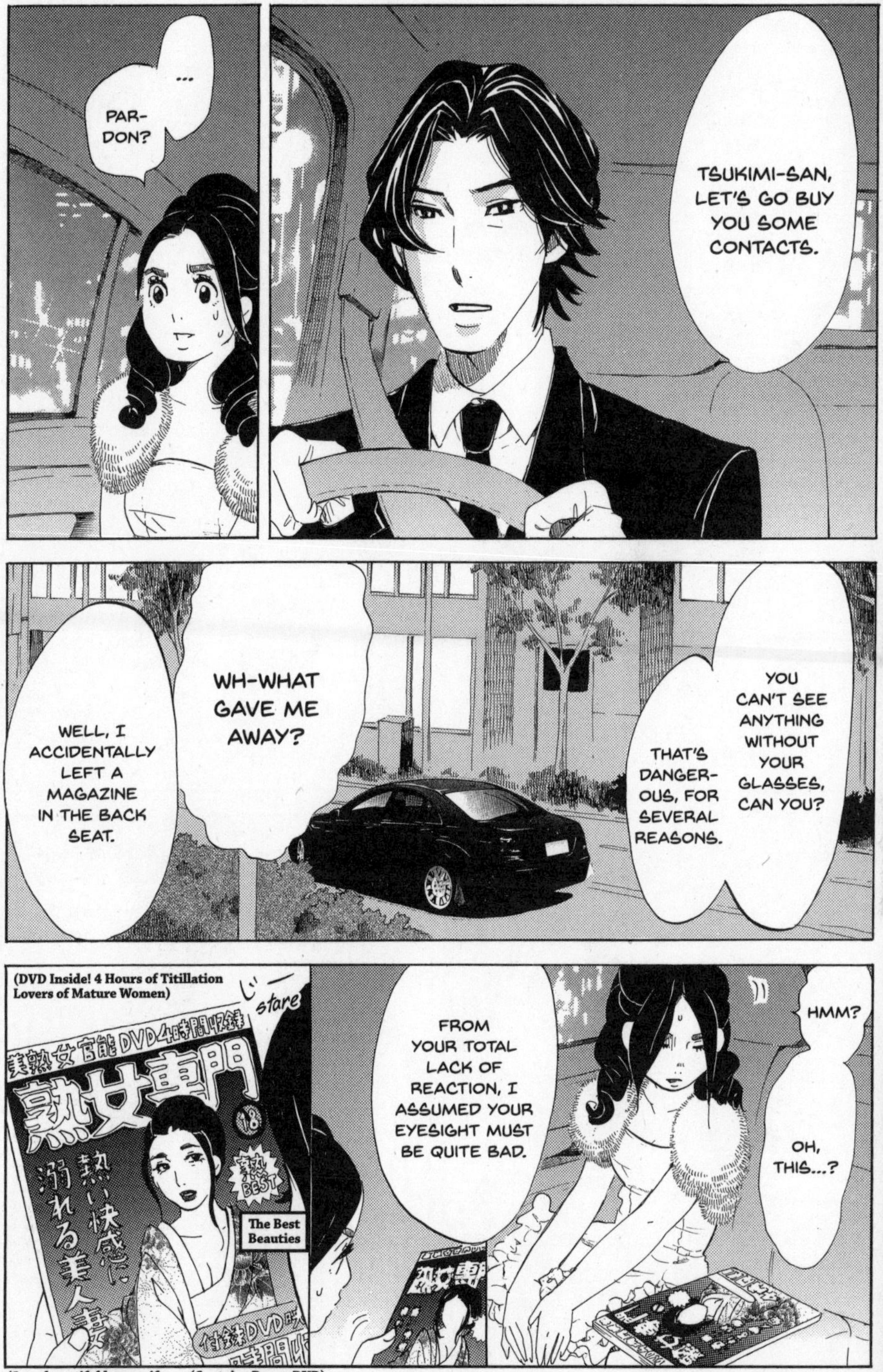
TSUKIMI-SAN, LET'S GO BUY YOU SOME CONTACTS.
...
PAR-DON?
YOU CAN'T SEE ANYTHING WITHOUT YOUR GLASSES, CAN YOU?
THAT'S DANGER-OUS, FOR SEVERAL REASONS.
WH-WHAT GAVE ME AWAY?
WELL, I ACCIDENTALLY LEFT A MAGAZINE IN THE BACK SEAT.
HMM?
OH, THIS...?
FROM YOUR TOTAL LACK OF REACTION, I ASSUMED YOUR EYESIGHT MUST BE QUITE BAD.
(DVD Inside! 4 Hours of Titillation Lovers of Mature Women)
じー
stare
熟女専門
The Best Beauties
(See a beautiful housewife abandon herself to passion!)
(Contains Bonus DVD)

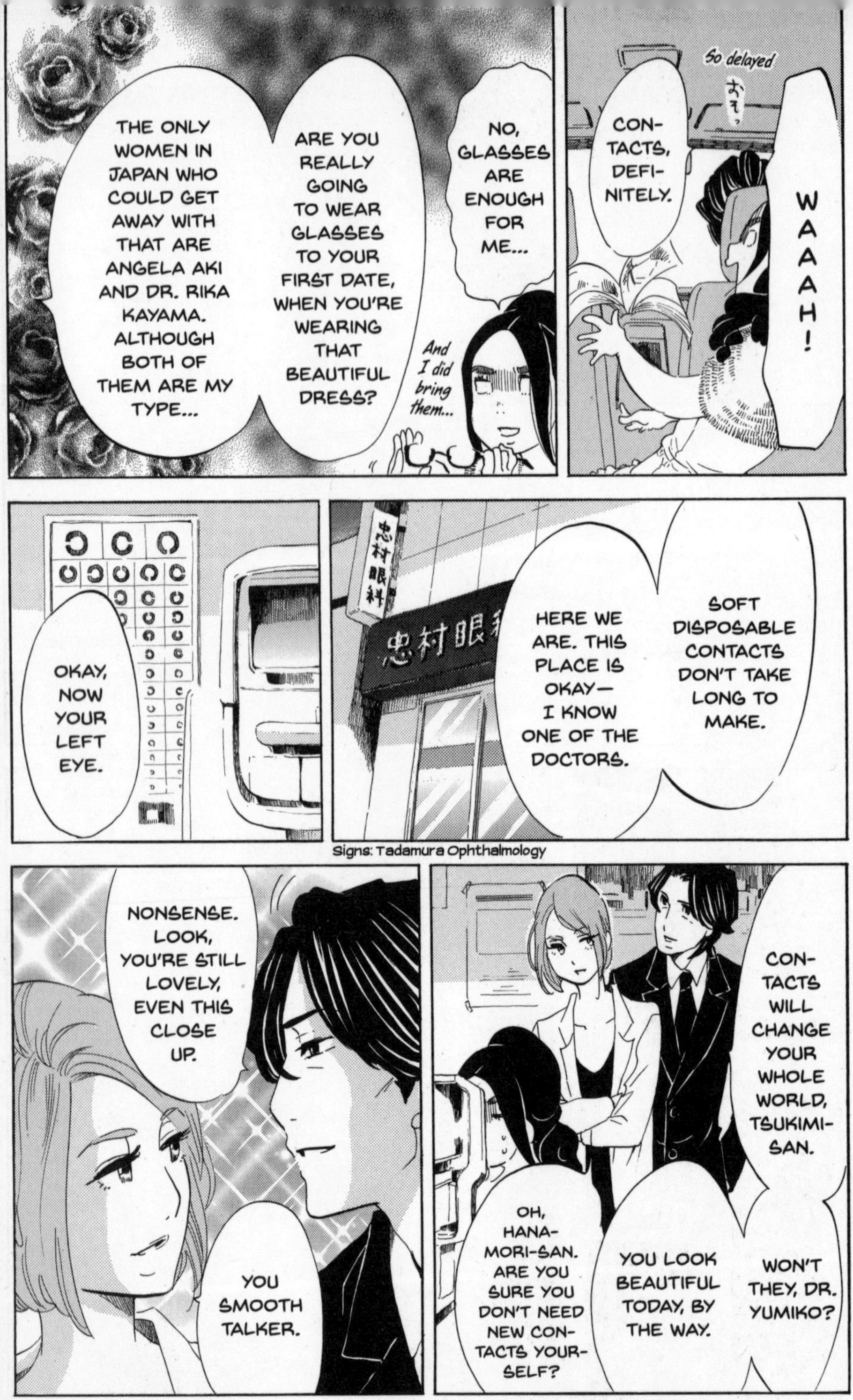
So delayed
おそっ
WAAAH!
CONTACTS, DEFINITELY.
NO, GLASSES ARE ENOUGH FOR ME...
And I did bring them...
ARE YOU REALLY GOING TO WEAR GLASSES TO YOUR FIRST DATE, WHEN YOU'RE WEARING THAT BEAUTIFUL DRESS?
THE ONLY WOMEN IN JAPAN WHO COULD GET AWAY WITH THAT ARE ANGELA AKI AND DR. RIKA KAYAMA. ALTHOUGH BOTH OF THEM ARE MY TYPE...
忠村眼科
忠村眼
SOFT DISPOSABLE CONTACTS DON'T TAKE LONG TO MAKE.
HERE WE ARE. THIS PLACE IS OKAY— I KNOW ONE OF THE DOCTORS.
OKAY, NOW YOUR LEFT EYE.
Signs: Tadamura Ophthalmology
CONTACTS WILL CHANGE YOUR WHOLE WORLD, TSUKIMI-SAN.
WON'T THEY, DR. YUMIKO?
YOU LOOK BEAUTIFUL TODAY, BY THE WAY.
OH, HANAMORI-SAN. ARE YOU SURE YOU DON'T NEED NEW CONTACTS YOURSELF?
NONSENSE. LOOK, YOU'RE STILL LOVELY, EVEN THIS CLOSE UP.
YOU SMOOTH TALKER.

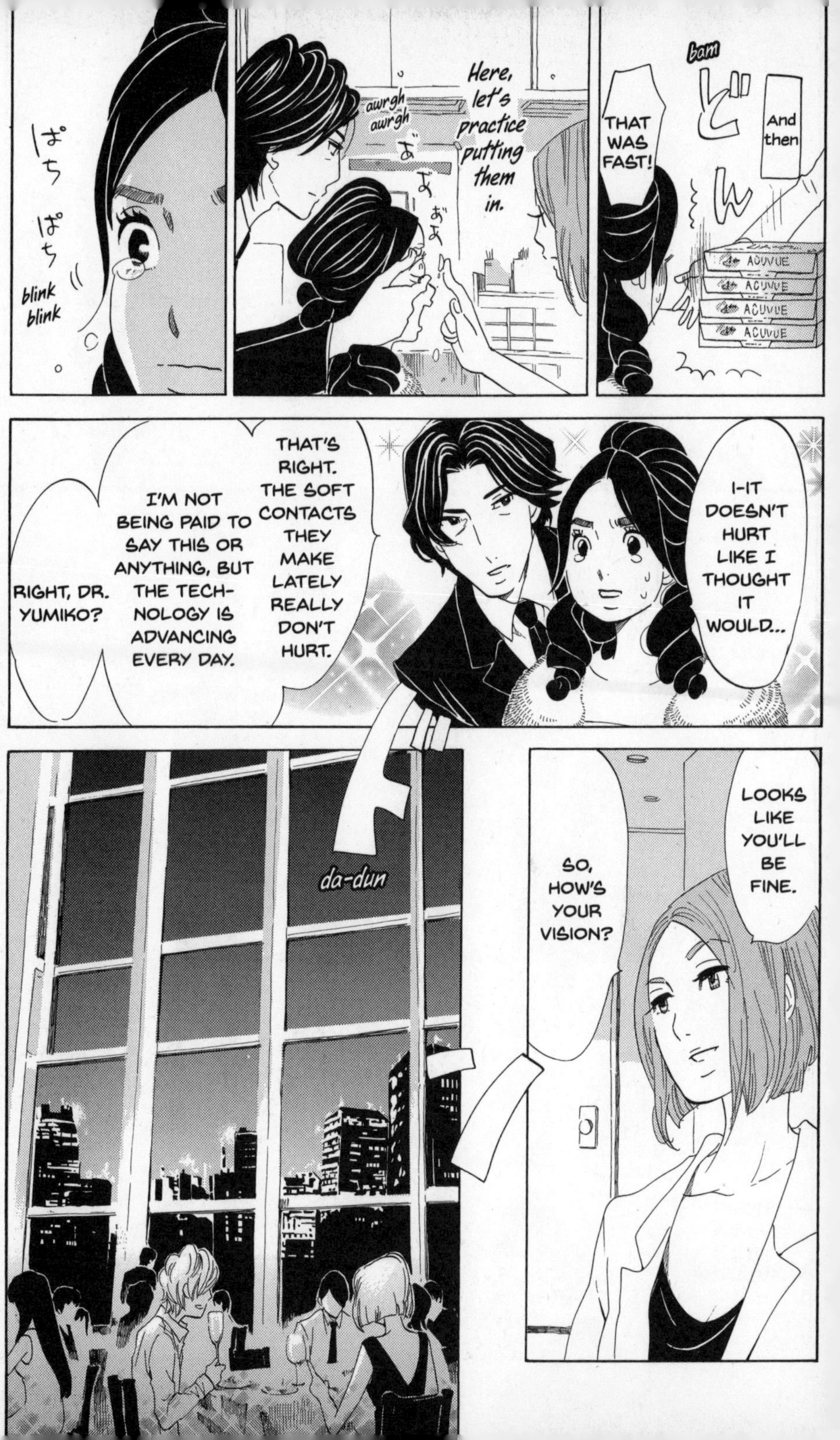
And then
bam
どん
THAT WAS FAST!
ACUVUE
ACUVUE
ACUVUE
ACUVUE
Here, let's practice putting them in.
awrgh awrgh
ぉぉぉぉ
ぱち ぱち
blink blink
I-IT DOESN'T HURT LIKE I THOUGHT IT WOULD...
THAT'S RIGHT. THE SOFT CONTACTS THEY MAKE LATELY REALLY DON'T HURT.
I'M NOT BEING PAID TO SAY THIS OR ANYTHING, BUT THE TECH-NOLOGY IS ADVANCING EVERY DAY.
RIGHT, DR. YUMIKO?
LOOKS LIKE YOU'LL BE FINE.
SO, HOW'S YOUR VISION?
da-dun

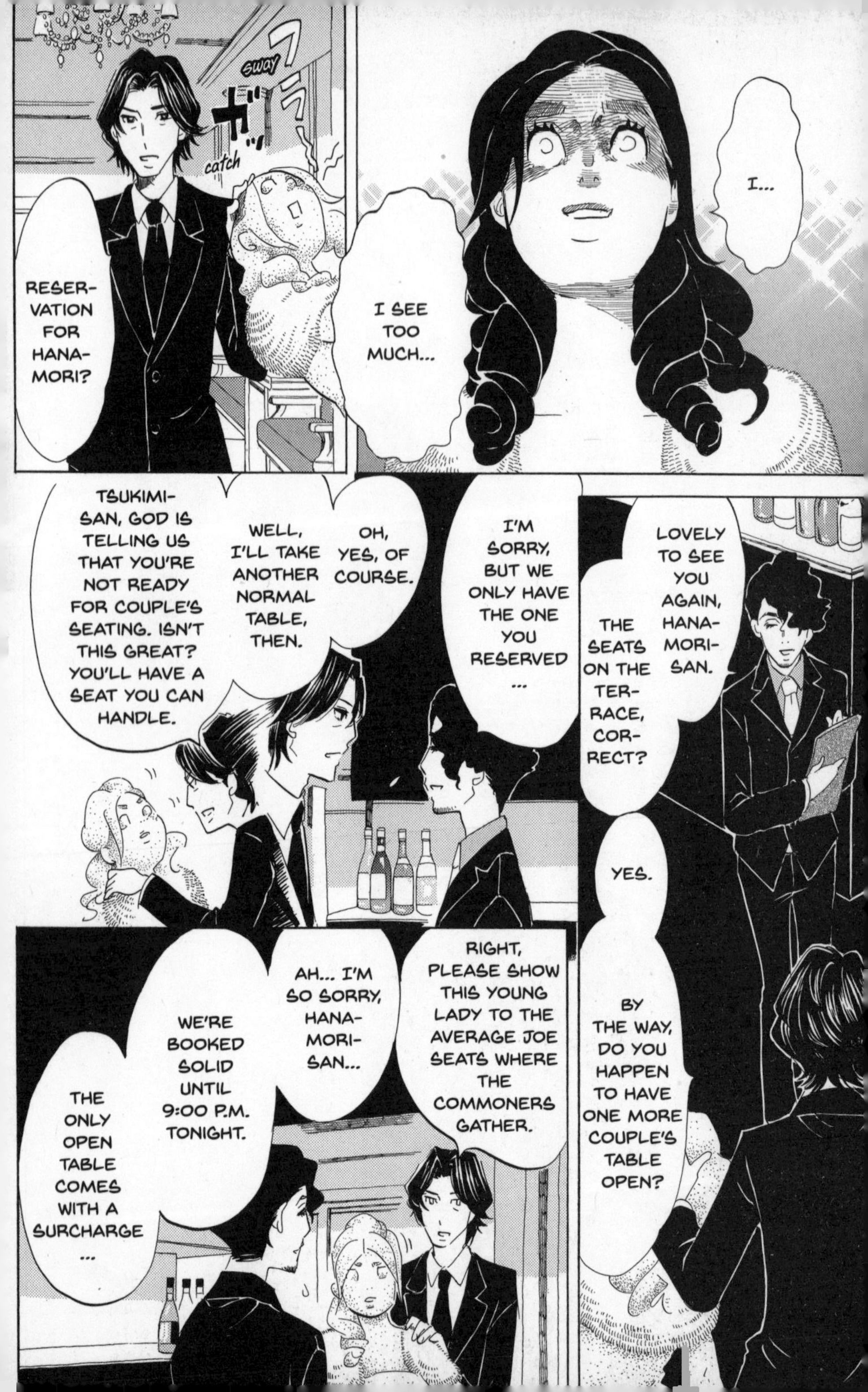
I...
I SEE TOO MUCH...
sway
catch
RESERVATION FOR HANAMORI?
LOVELY TO SEE YOU AGAIN, HANAMORI-SAN.
THE SEATS ON THE TERRACE, CORRECT?
YES.
BY THE WAY, DO YOU HAPPEN TO HAVE ONE MORE COUPLE'S TABLE OPEN?
I'M SORRY, BUT WE ONLY HAVE THE ONE YOU RESERVED ...
OH, YES, OF COURSE.
WELL, I'LL TAKE ANOTHER NORMAL TABLE, THEN.
TSUKIMI-SAN, GOD IS TELLING US THAT YOU'RE NOT READY FOR COUPLE'S SEATING. ISN'T THIS GREAT? YOU'LL HAVE A SEAT YOU CAN HANDLE.
RIGHT, PLEASE SHOW THIS YOUNG LADY TO THE AVERAGE JOE SEATS WHERE THE COMMONERS GATHER.
AH... I'M SO SORRY, HANAMORI-SAN...
WE'RE BOOKED SOLID UNTIL 9:00 P.M. TONIGHT.
THE ONLY OPEN TABLE COMES WITH A SURCHARGE ...

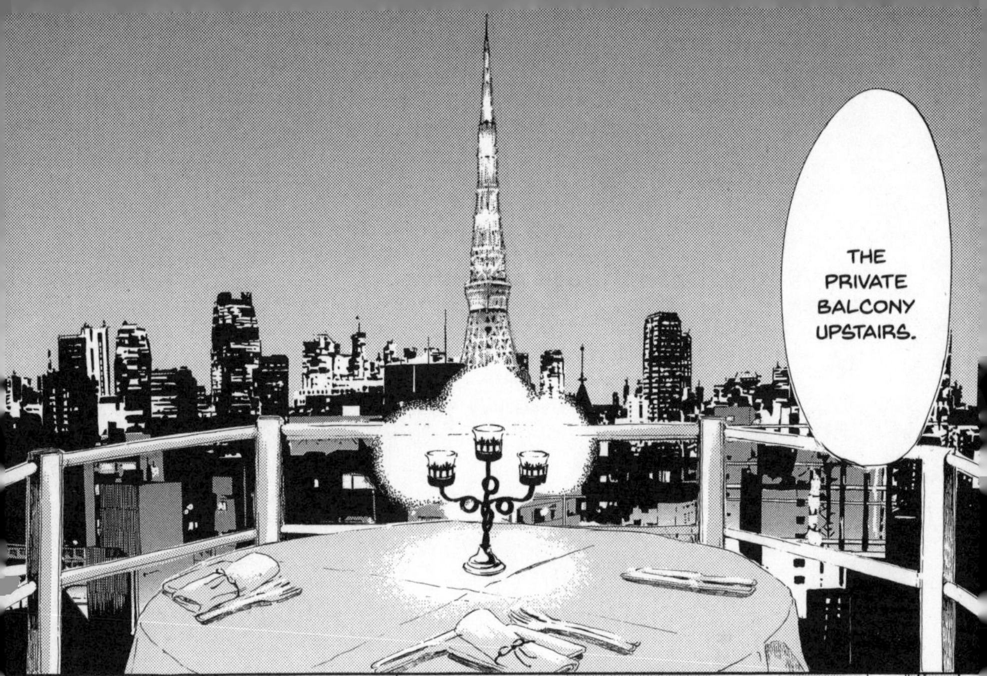
THE PRIVATE BALCONY UPSTAIRS.

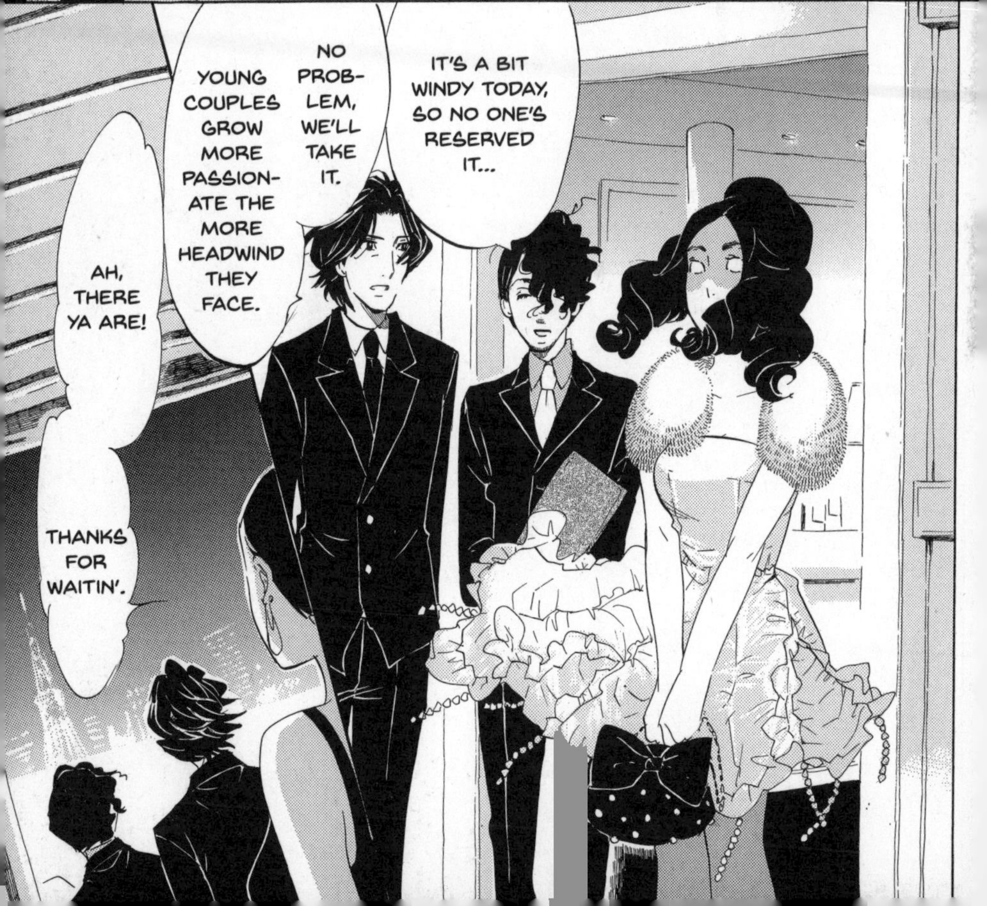
IT'S A BIT WINDY TODAY, SO NO ONE'S RESERVED IT...
NO PROB-LEM, WE'LL TAKE IT.
YOUNG COUPLES GROW MORE PASSION-ATE THE MORE HEADWIND THEY FACE.
AH, THERE YA ARE!
THANKS FOR WAITIN'.

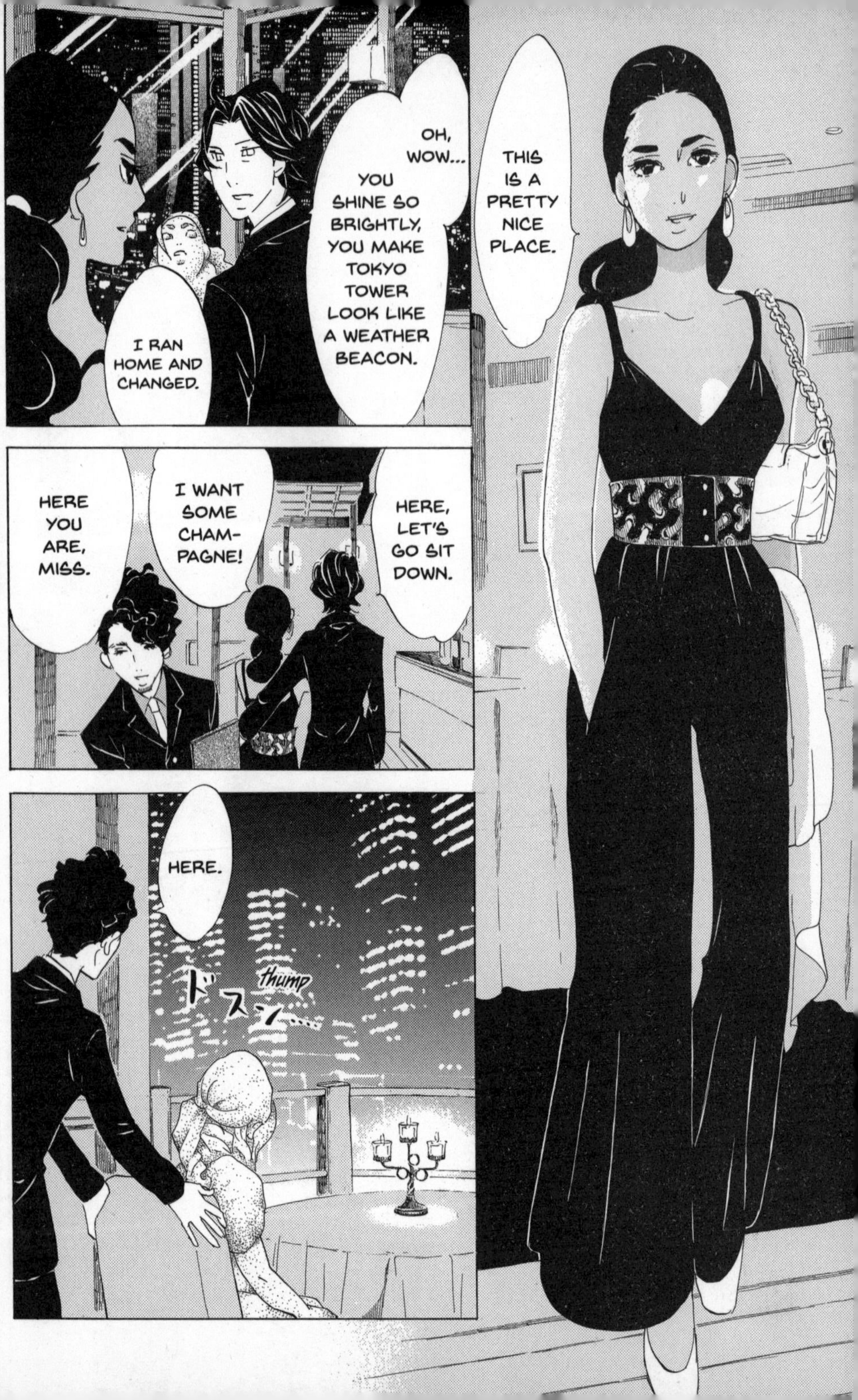
THIS IS A PRETTY NICE PLACE.
OH, WOW...
YOU SHINE SO BRIGHTLY, YOU MAKE TOKYO TOWER LOOK LIKE A WEATHER BEACON.
I RAN HOME AND CHANGED.
HERE, LET'S GO SIT DOWN.
I WANT SOME CHAM-PAGNE!
HERE YOU ARE, MISS.
HERE.
ドスン…
thump

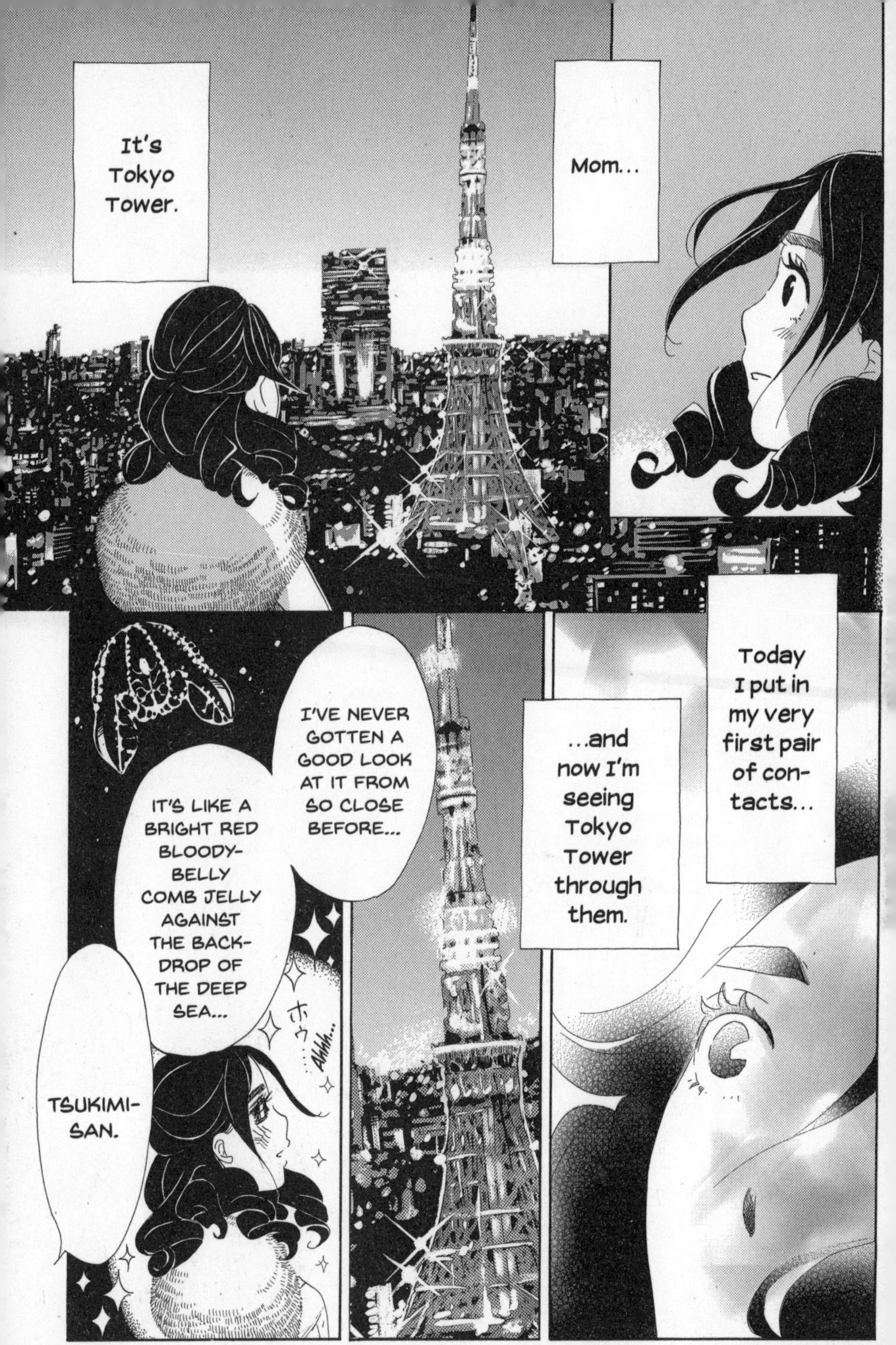
Mom...
It's Tokyo Tower.
Today I put in my very first pair of contacts...
...and now I'm seeing Tokyo Tower through them.
I'VE NEVER GOTTEN A GOOD LOOK AT IT FROM SO CLOSE BEFORE...
IT'S LIKE A BRIGHT RED BLOODY-BELLY COMB JELLY AGAINST THE BACKDROP OF THE DEEP SEA...
ホウ…
Ahhh...
TSUKIMI-SAN.

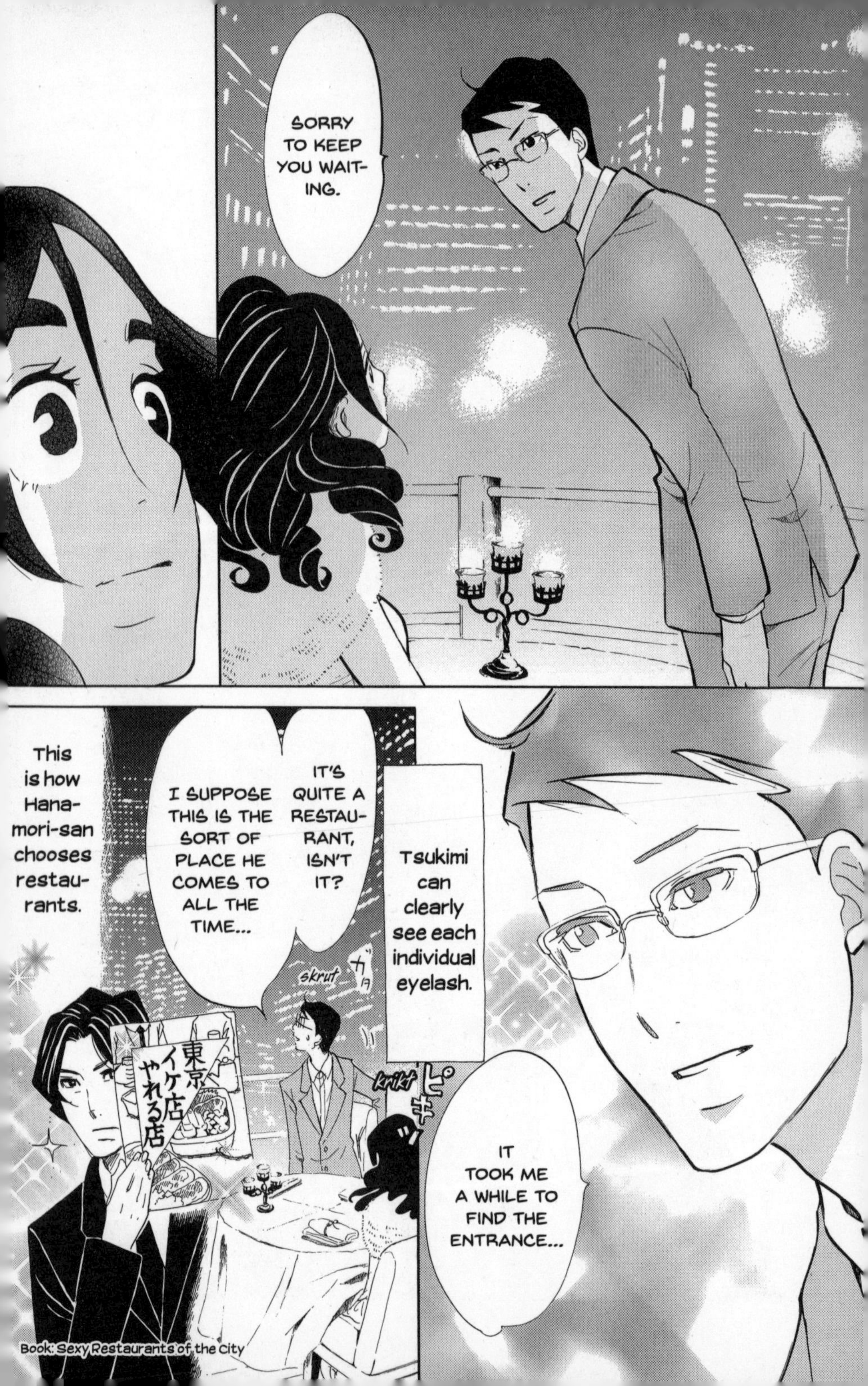
SORRY TO KEEP YOU WAIT-ING.
Tsukimi can clearly see each individual eyelash.
IT TOOK ME A WHILE TO FIND THE ENTRANCE...
IT'S QUITE A RESTAU-RANT, ISN'T IT?
I SUPPOSE THIS IS THE SORT OF PLACE HE COMES TO ALL THE TIME...
This is how Hana-mori-san chooses restau-rants.
skrut
krikt
東京イケ店やれる店
Book: Sexy Restaurants of the City

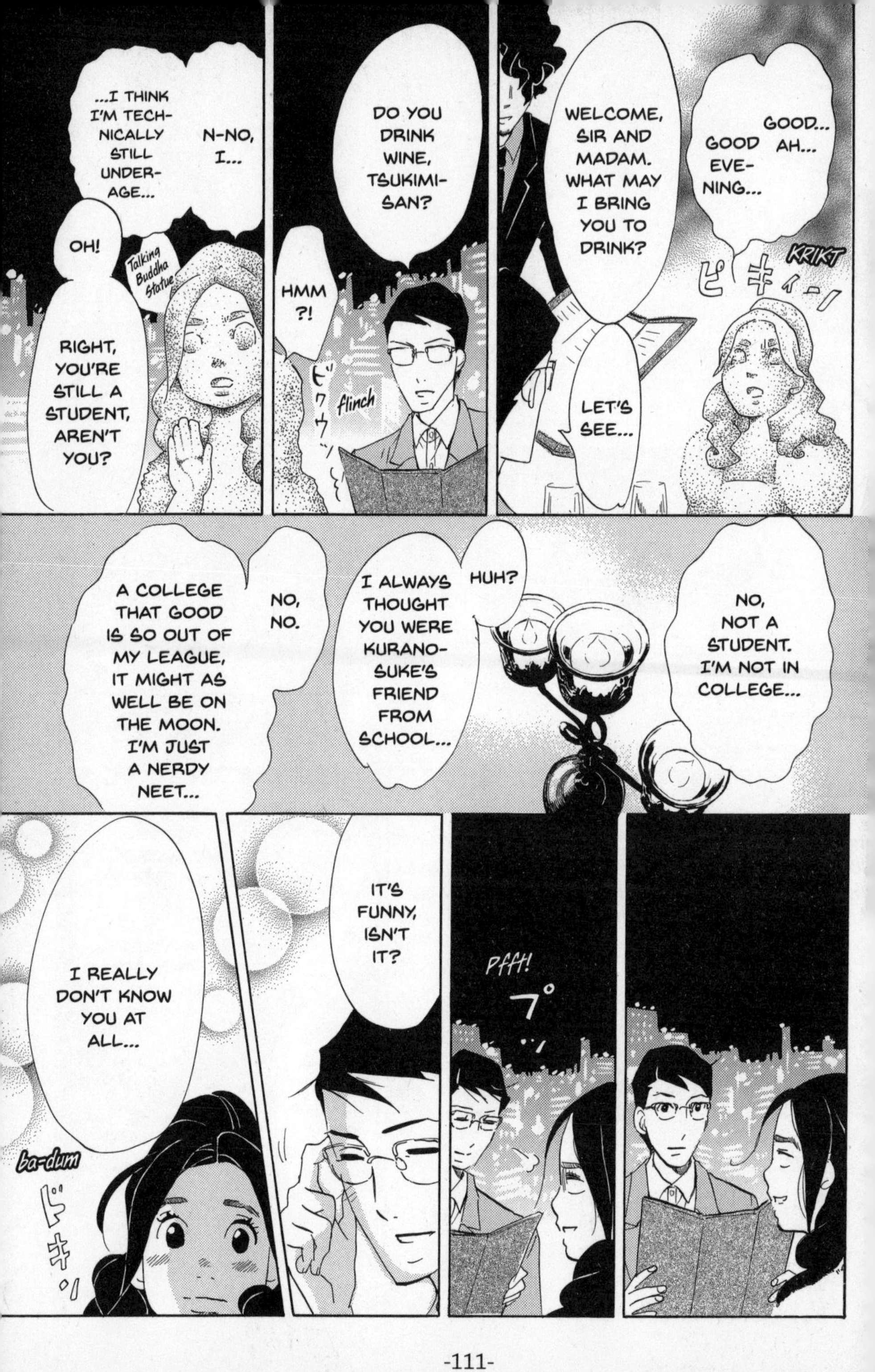
GOOD... AH...
GOOD EVE-NING...
KRIKT
ピキィーン
WELCOME, SIR AND MADAM. WHAT MAY I BRING YOU TO DRINK?
LET'S SEE...
DO YOU DRINK WINE, TSUKIMI-SAN?
HMM ?!
ビクゥッ
flinch
N-NO, I...
...I THINK I'M TECH-NICALLY STILL UNDER-AGE...
OH!
Talking Buddha Statue
RIGHT, YOU'RE STILL A STUDENT, AREN'T YOU?
NO, NOT A STUDENT. I'M NOT IN COLLEGE...
HUH?
I ALWAYS THOUGHT YOU WERE KURANO-SUKE'S FRIEND FROM SCHOOL...
NO, NO.
A COLLEGE THAT GOOD IS SO OUT OF MY LEAGUE, IT MIGHT AS WELL BE ON THE MOON. I'M JUST A NERDY NEET...
Pfft!
プッ
IT'S FUNNY, ISN'T IT?
I REALLY DON'T KNOW YOU AT ALL...
ba-dum
ドキッ

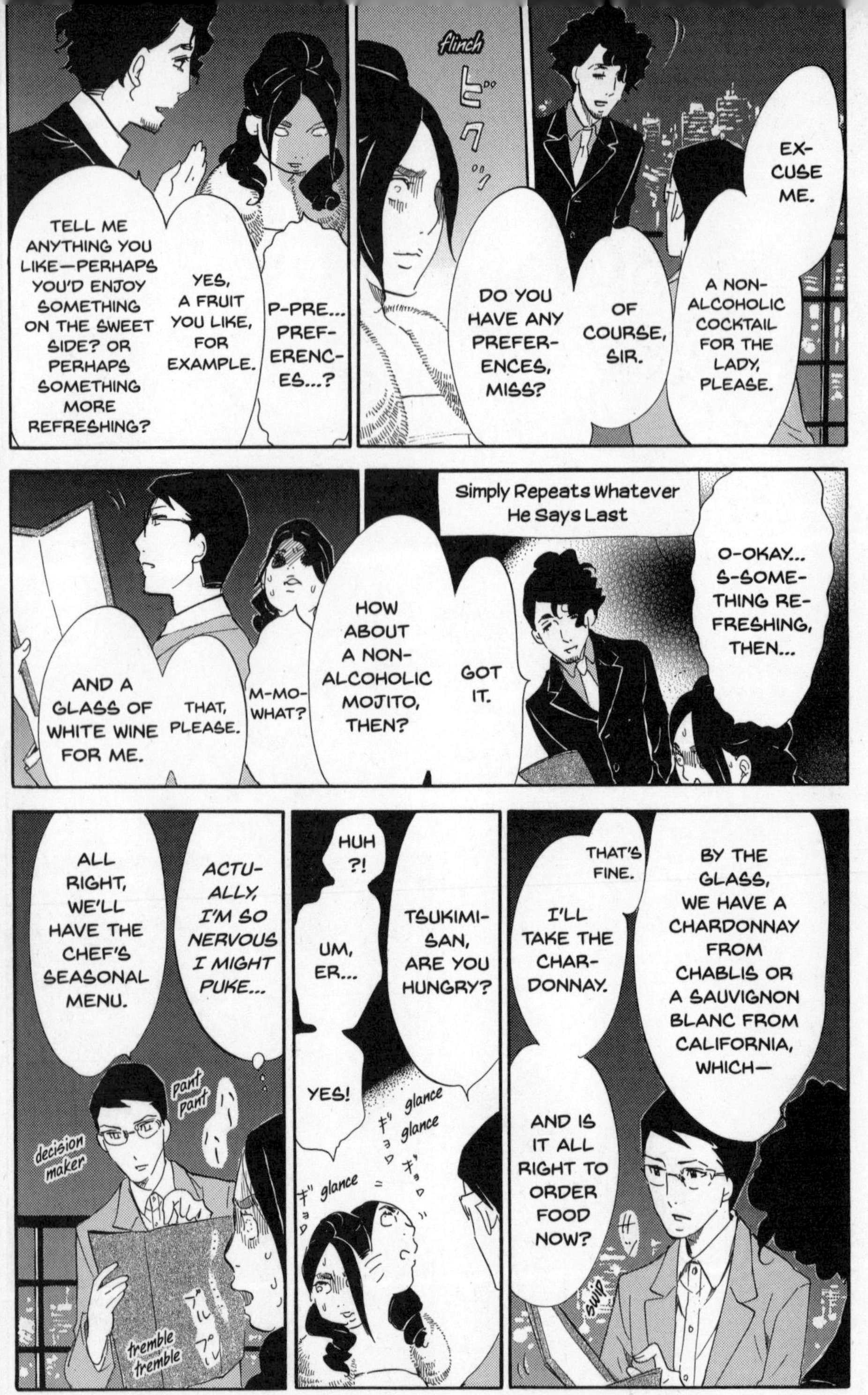
EX-CUSE ME.
A NON-ALCOHOLIC COCKTAIL FOR THE LADY, PLEASE.
OF COURSE, SIR.
DO YOU HAVE ANY PREFER-ENCES, MISS?
flinch
P-PRE... PREF-ERENC-ES...?
YES, A FRUIT YOU LIKE, FOR EXAMPLE.
TELL ME ANYTHING YOU LIKE—PERHAPS YOU'D ENJOY SOMETHING ON THE SWEET SIDE? OR PERHAPS SOMETHING MORE REFRESHING?
Simply Repeats Whatever He Says Last
O-OKAY... S-SOME-THING RE-FRESHING, THEN...
GOT IT.
HOW ABOUT A NON-ALCOHOLIC MOJITO, THEN?
M-MO-WHAT?
THAT, PLEASE.
AND A GLASS OF WHITE WINE FOR ME.
BY THE GLASS, WE HAVE A CHARDONNAY FROM CHABLIS OR A SAUVIGNON BLANC FROM CALIFORNIA, WHICH—
THAT'S FINE.
I'LL TAKE THE CHAR-DONNAY.
AND IS IT ALL RIGHT TO ORDER FOOD NOW?
swip
TSUKIMI-SAN, ARE YOU HUNGRY?
HUH ?!
UM, ER...
YES!
glance
glance
glance
ACTU-ALLY, I'M SO NERVOUS I MIGHT PUKE...
ALL RIGHT, WE'LL HAVE THE CHEF'S SEASONAL MENU.
pant pant
decision maker
tremble tremble

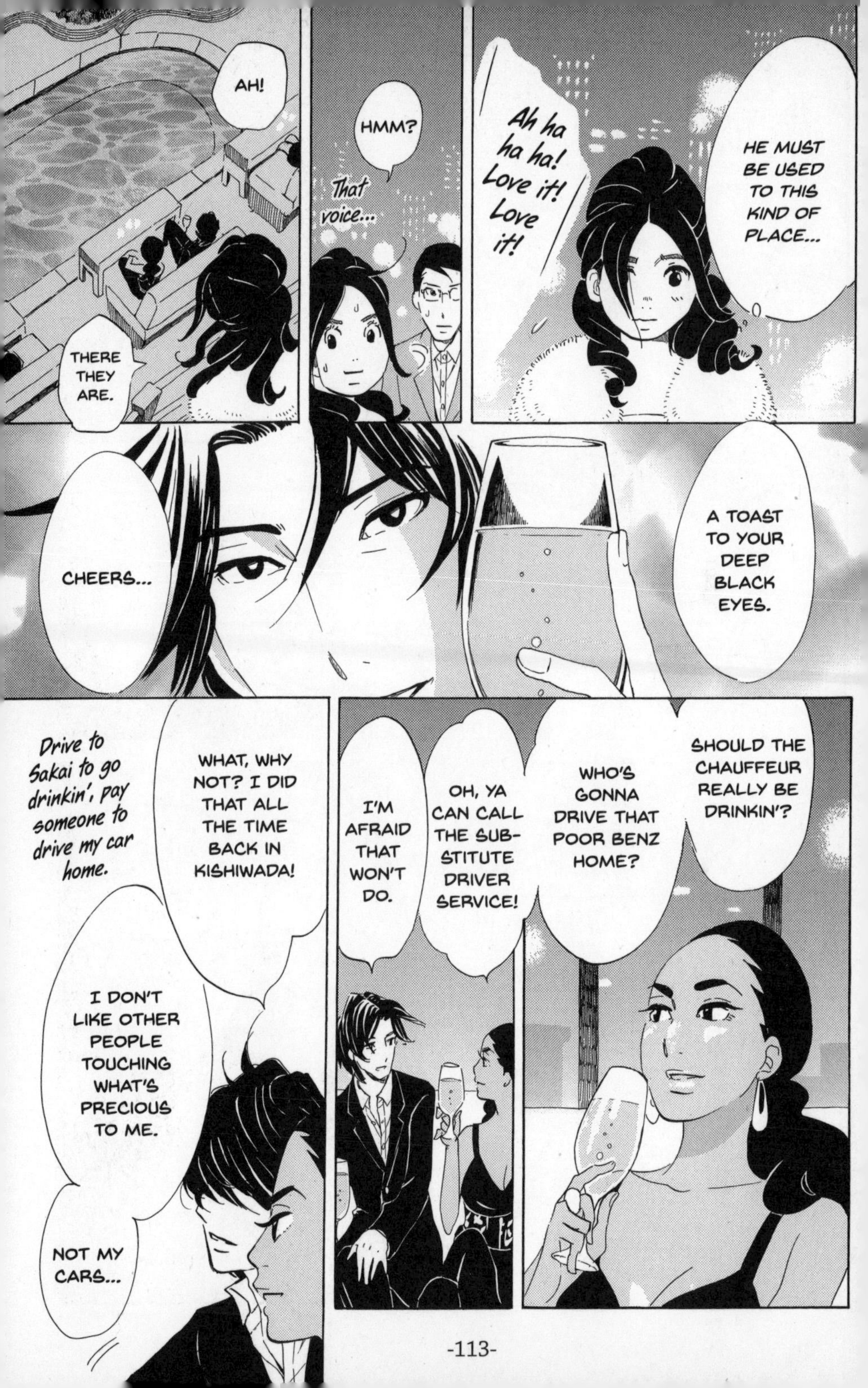
HE MUST BE USED TO THIS KIND OF PLACE...
Ah ha ha ha! Love it! Love it!
HMM?
That voice...
AH!
THERE THEY ARE.
A TOAST TO YOUR DEEP BLACK EYES.
CHEERS...
SHOULD THE CHAUFFEUR REALLY BE DRINKIN'?
WHO'S GONNA DRIVE THAT POOR BENZ HOME?
OH, YA CAN CALL THE SUB-STITUTE DRIVER SERVICE!
I'M AFRAID THAT WON'T DO.
WHAT, WHY NOT? I DID THAT ALL THE TIME BACK IN KISHIWADA!
Drive to Sakai to go drinkin', pay someone to drive my car home.
I DON'T LIKE OTHER PEOPLE TOUCHING WHAT'S PRECIOUS TO ME.
NOT MY CARS...

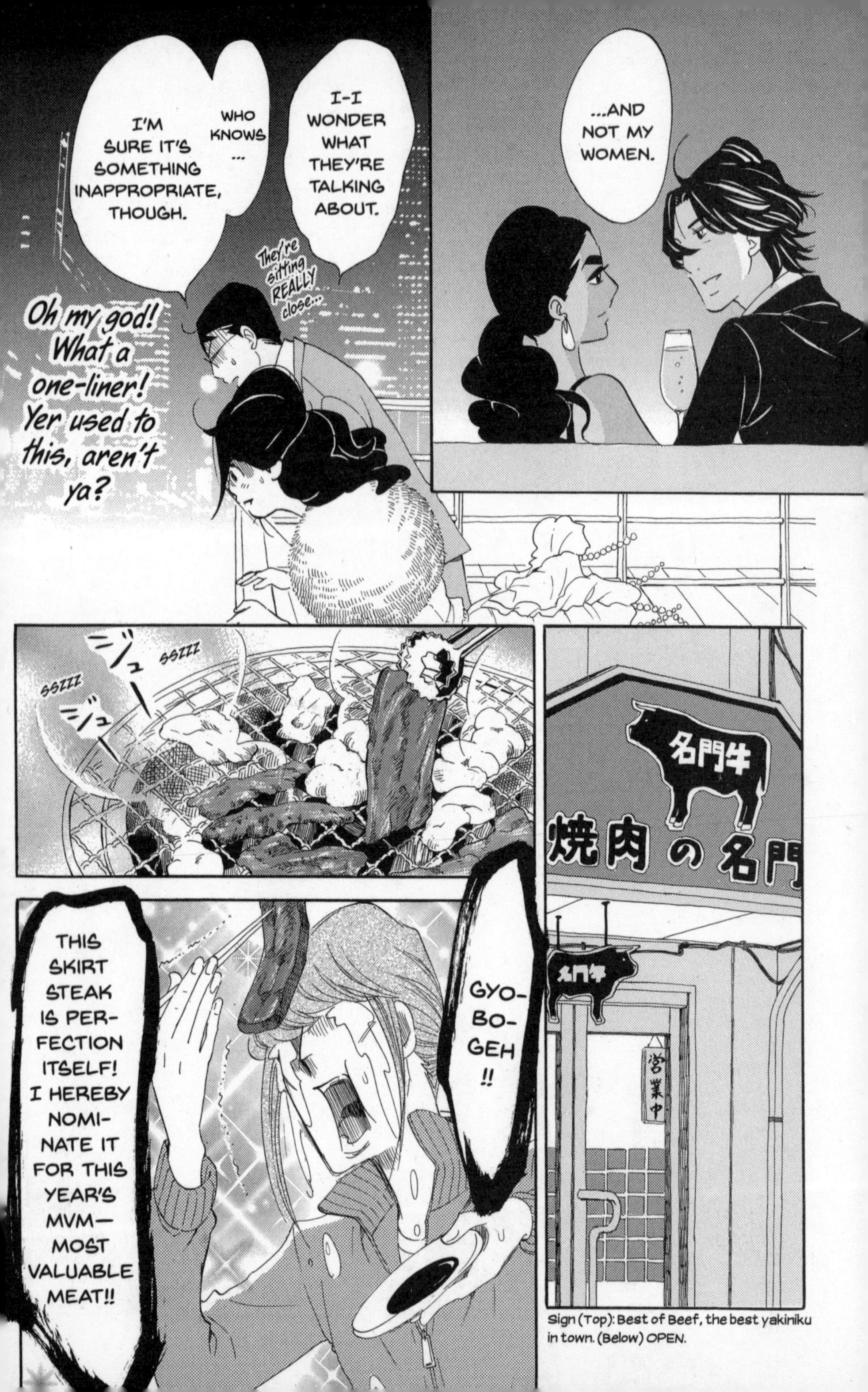
...AND NOT MY WOMEN.
I-I WONDER WHAT THEY'RE TALKING ABOUT.
WHO KNOWS ...
I'M SURE IT'S SOMETHING INAPPROPRIATE, THOUGH.
They're sitting REALLY close...
Oh my god! What a one-liner! Yer used to this, aren't ya?
名門牛
焼肉の名門
名門牛
営業中
ジュ
SSZZZ
SSZZZ
ジュ
GYO-BO-GEH!!
THIS SKIRT STEAK IS PER-FECTION ITSELF! I HEREBY NOMI-NATE IT FOR THIS YEAR'S MVM—MOST VALUABLE MEAT!!

Sign (Top): Best of Beef, the best yakiniku in town. (Below) OPEN.

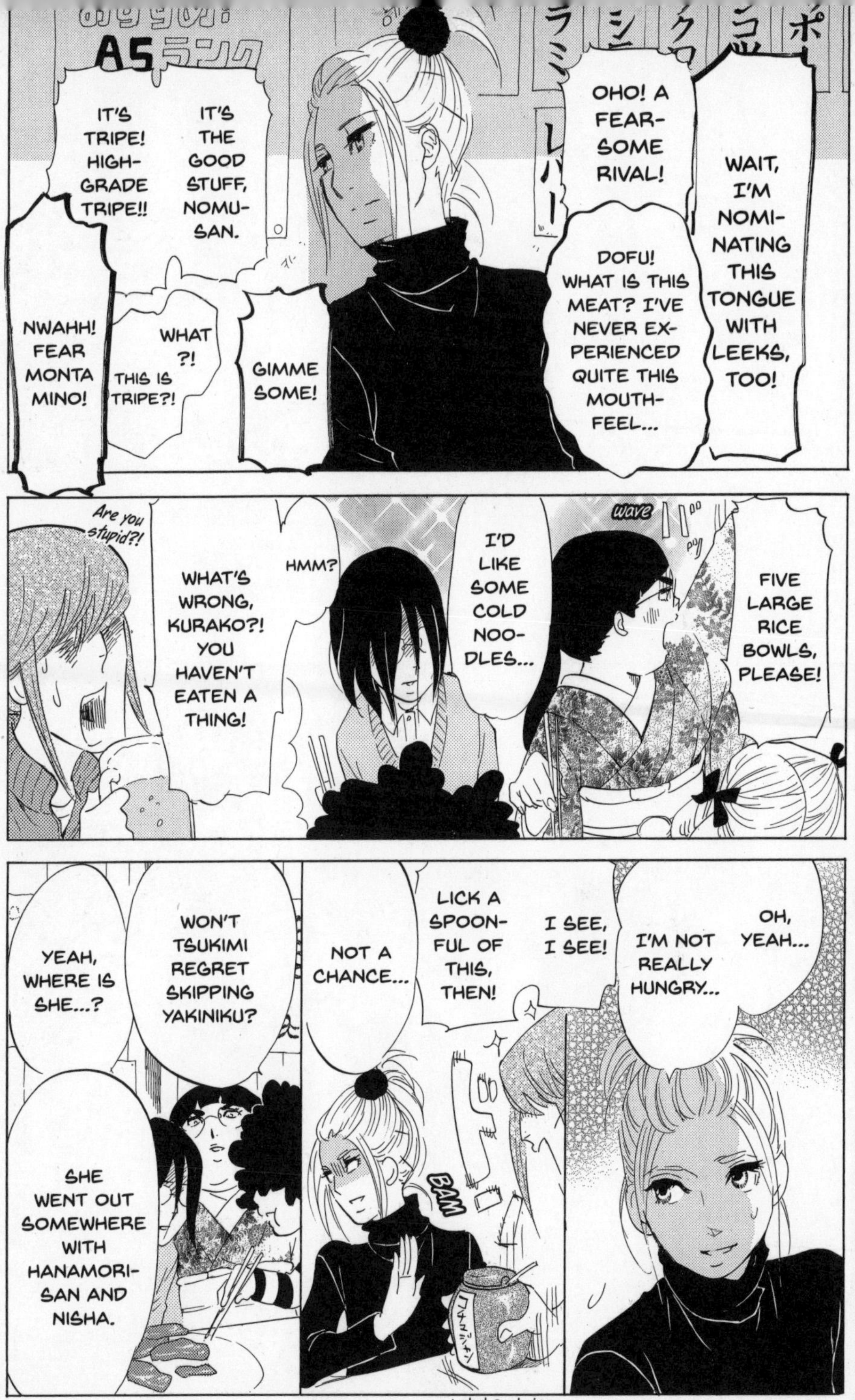
WAIT, I'M NOMINATING THIS TONGUE WITH LEEKS, TOO!
OHO! A FEARSOME RIVAL!
DOFU! WHAT IS THIS MEAT? I'VE NEVER EXPERIENCED QUITE THIS MOUTHFEEL...
IT'S THE GOOD STUFF, NOMU-SAN.
IT'S TRIPE! HIGH-GRADE TRIPE!!
GIMME SOME!
WHAT?!
THIS IS TRIPE?!
NWAHH! FEAR MONTA MINO!
wave
FIVE LARGE RICE BOWLS, PLEASE!
I'D LIKE SOME COLD NOODLES...
HMM?
WHAT'S WRONG, KURAKO?! YOU HAVEN'T EATEN A THING!
Are you stupid?!
OH, YEAH...
I'M NOT REALLY HUNGRY...
I SEE, I SEE!
LICK A SPOONFUL OF THIS, THEN!
NOT A CHANCE...
BAM
WON'T TSUKIMI REGRET SKIPPING YAKINIKU?
YEAH, WHERE IS SHE...?
SHE WENT OUT SOMEWHERE WITH HANAMORI-SAN AND NISHA.

Label: Gochujang

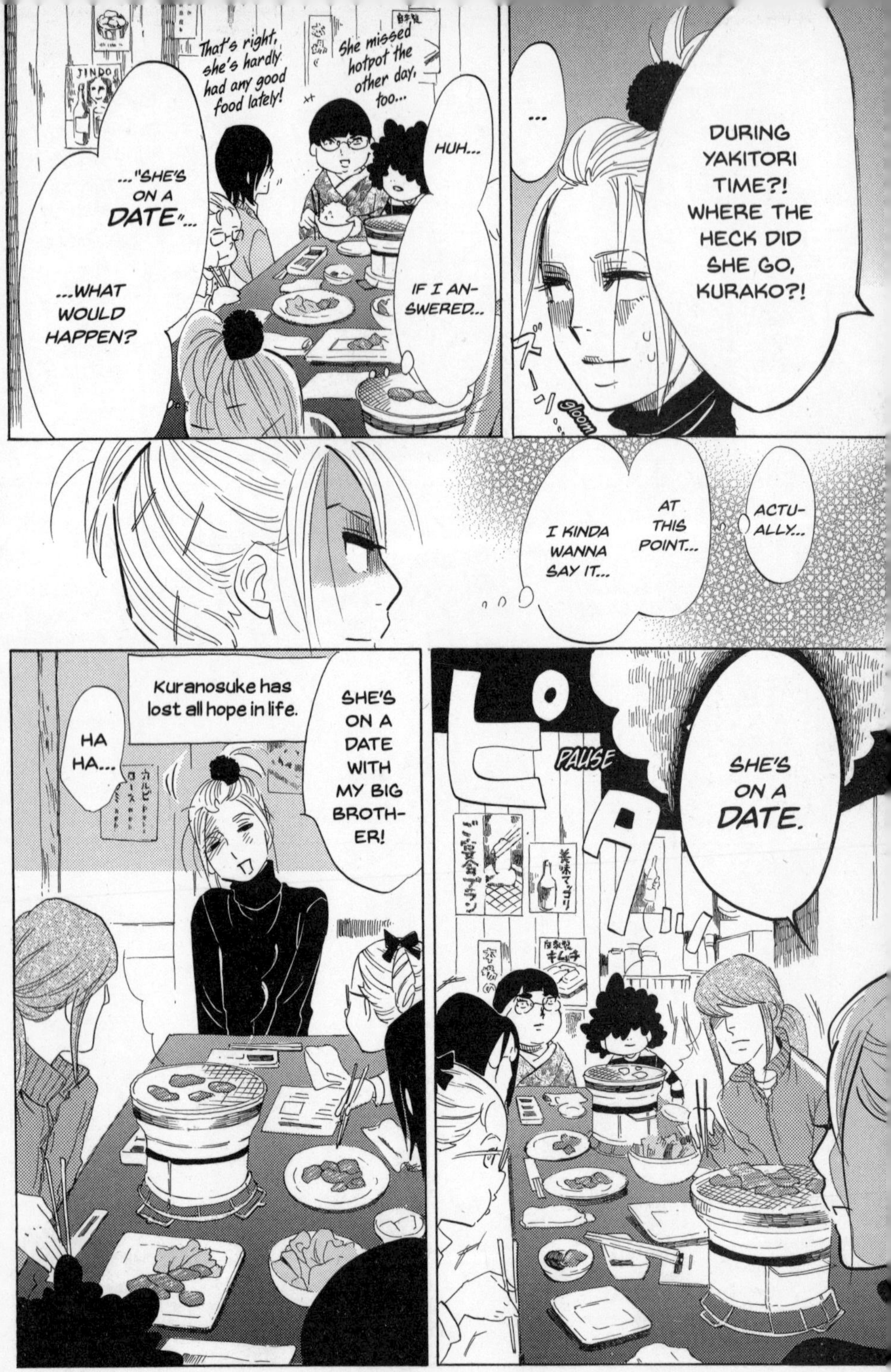
...
DURING YAKITORI TIME?! WHERE THE HECK DID SHE GO, KURAKO?!
gloom
That's right, she's hardly had any good food lately!
She missed hotpot the other day, too...
HUH...
IF I AN-SWERED...
..."SHE'S ON A DATE"...
...WHAT WOULD HAPPEN?
ACTU-ALLY...
AT THIS POINT...
I KINDA WANNA SAY IT...
PAUSE
SHE'S ON A DATE.
SHE'S ON A DATE WITH MY BIG BROTH-ER!
Kuranosuke has lost all hope in life.
HA HA...

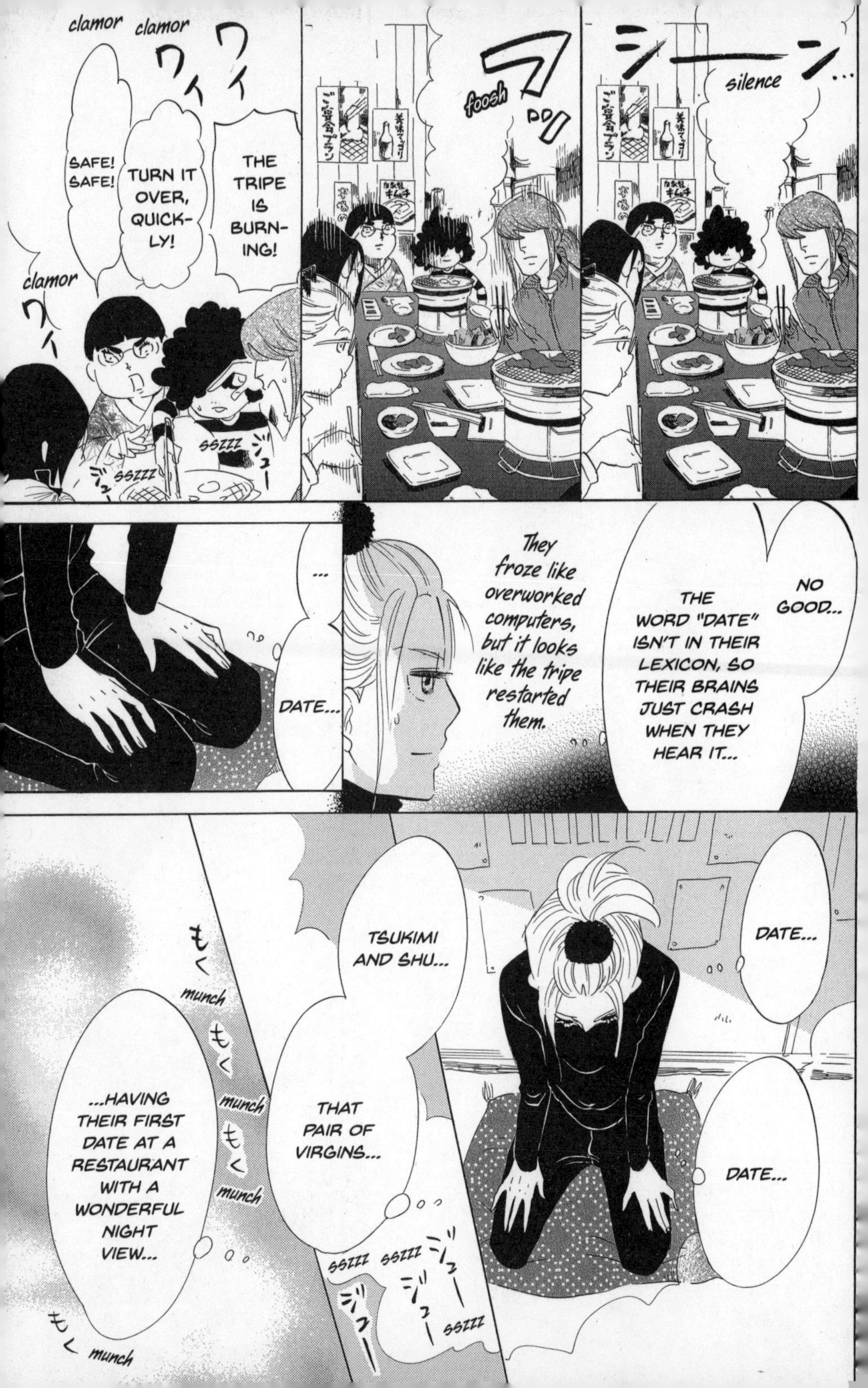
シーン…
silence
ワッ
foosh
ワイワイ
clamor clamor
THE TRIPE IS BURNING!
TURN IT OVER, QUICKLY!
SAFE! SAFE!
ワイ
clamor
ジュー
SSZZZ
SSZZZ
NO GOOD...
THE WORD "DATE" ISN'T IN THEIR LEXICON, SO THEIR BRAINS JUST CRASH WHEN THEY HEAR IT...
They froze like overworked computers, but it looks like the tripe restarted them.
...
DATE...
DATE...
DATE...
TSUKIMI AND SHU...
THAT PAIR OF VIRGINS...
...HAVING THEIR FIRST DATE AT A RESTAURANT WITH A WONDERFUL NIGHT VIEW...
もく munch
もく munch
もく munch
もく munch
SSZZZ SSZZZ SSZZZ
ジュー ジュー ジュー

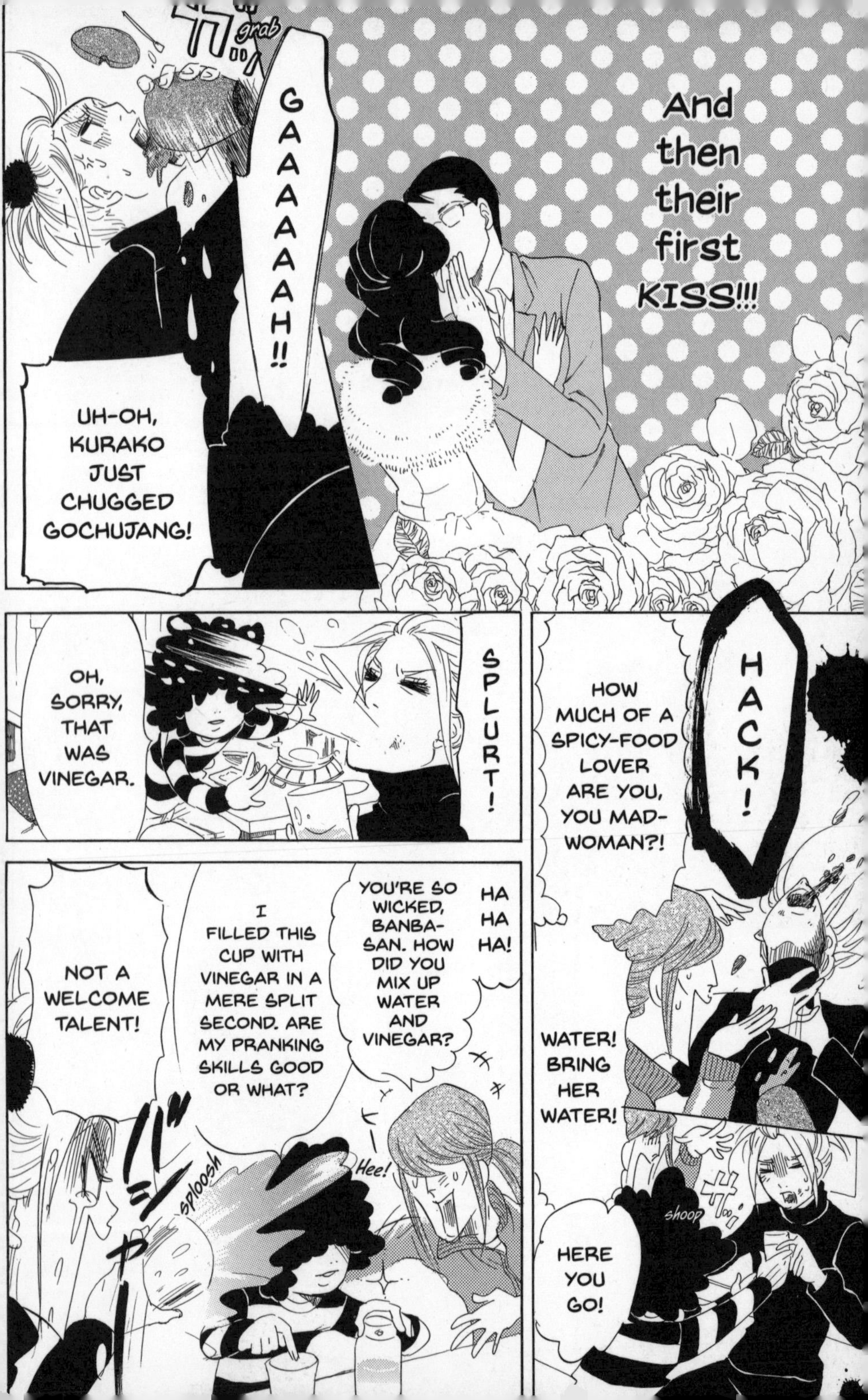
grab
And then their first KISS!!!
GAAAAAAAH!!
UH-OH, KURAKO JUST CHUGGED GOCHUJANG!
HACK!
HOW MUCH OF A SPICY-FOOD LOVER ARE YOU, YOU MAD-WOMAN?!
WATER! BRING HER WATER!
shoop
HERE YOU GO!
SPLURT!
OH, SORRY, THAT WAS VINEGAR.
HA HA HA!
YOU'RE SO WICKED, BANBA-SAN. HOW DID YOU MIX UP WATER AND VINEGAR?
I FILLED THIS CUP WITH VINEGAR IN A MERE SPLIT SECOND. ARE MY PRANKING SKILLS GOOD OR WHAT?
Hee!
NOT A WELCOME TALENT!
sploosh

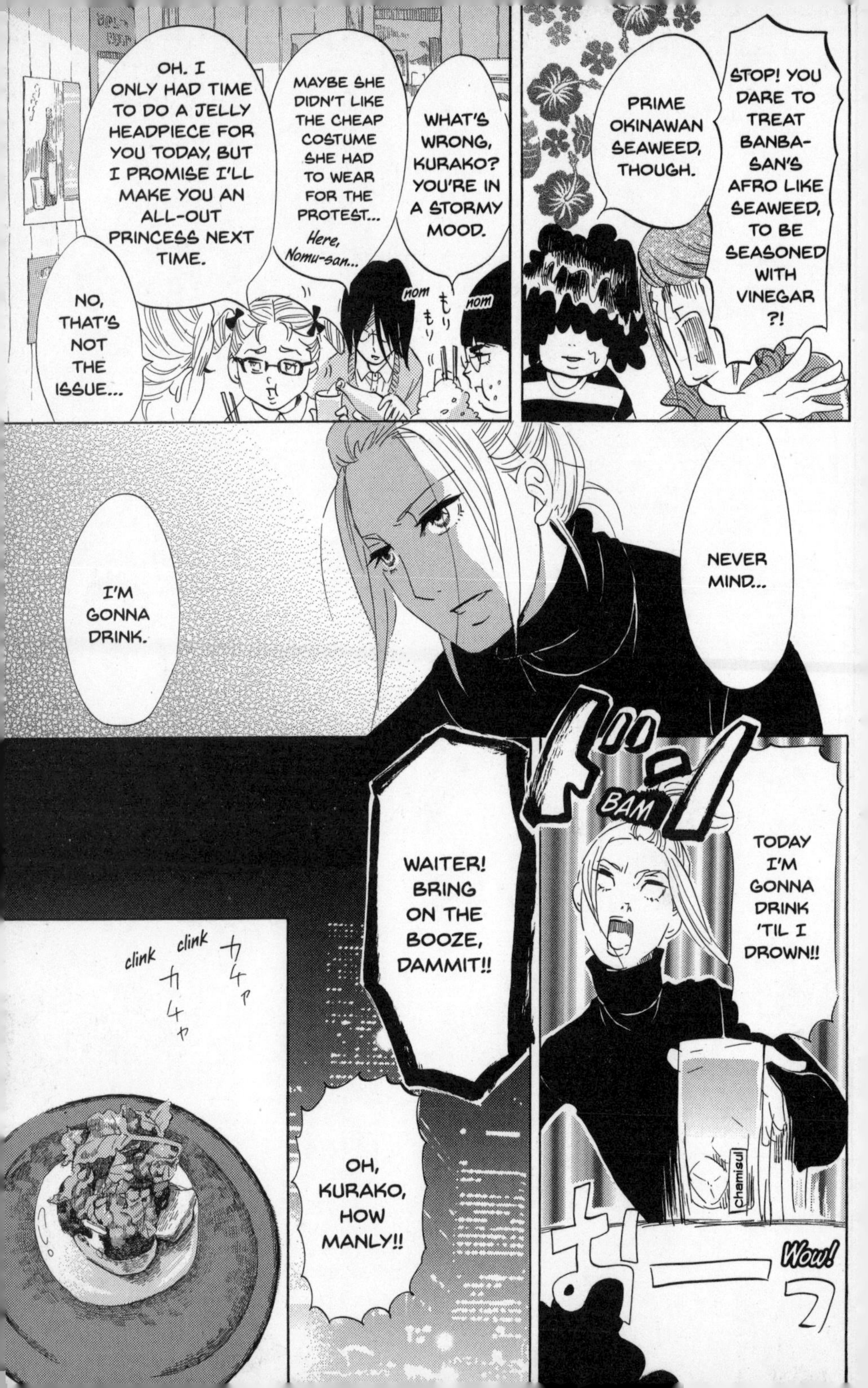
STOP! YOU DARE TO TREAT BANBA-SAN'S AFRO LIKE SEAWEED, TO BE SEASONED WITH VINEGAR ?!
PRIME OKINAWAN SEAWEED, THOUGH.
WHAT'S WRONG, KURAKO? YOU'RE IN A STORMY MOOD.
nom
nom
MAYBE SHE DIDN'T LIKE THE CHEAP COSTUME SHE HAD TO WEAR FOR THE PROTEST...
Here, Nomu-san...
OH. I ONLY HAD TIME TO DO A JELLY HEADPIECE FOR YOU TODAY, BUT I PROMISE I'LL MAKE YOU AN ALL-OUT PRINCESS NEXT TIME.
NO, THAT'S NOT THE ISSUE...
NEVER MIND...
I'M GONNA DRINK.
BAM
TODAY I'M GONNA DRINK 'TIL I DROWN!!
WAITER! BRING ON THE BOOZE, DAMMIT!!
Chamisul
Wow!
clink
clink
OH, KURAKO, HOW MANLY!!

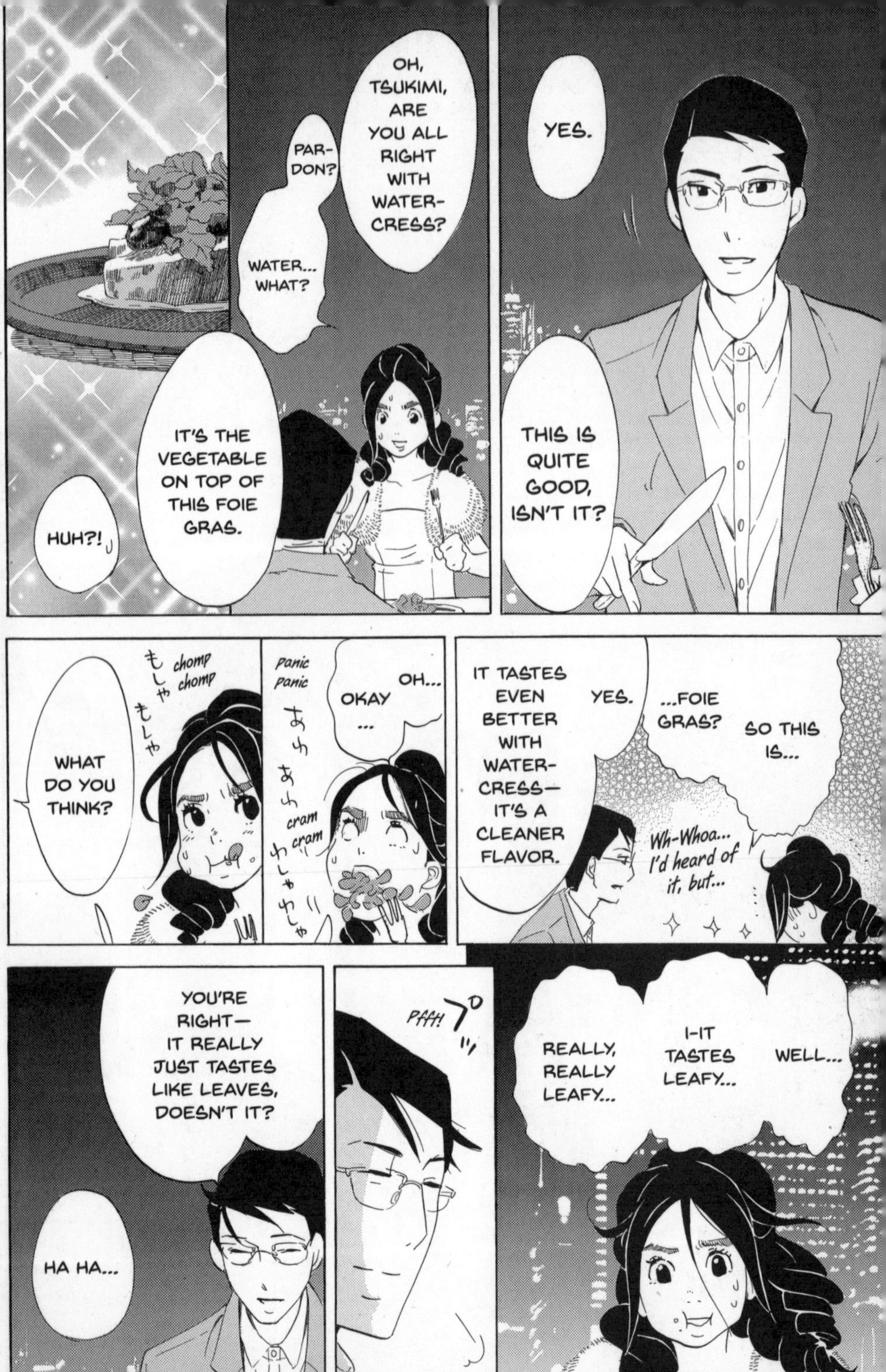
YES.
THIS IS QUITE GOOD, ISN'T IT?
OH, TSUKIMI, ARE YOU ALL RIGHT WITH WATER-CRESS?
PAR-DON?
WATER... WHAT?
IT'S THE VEGETABLE ON TOP OF THIS FOIE GRAS.
HUH?!
SO THIS IS...
...FOIE GRAS?
Wh-Whoa... I'd heard of it, but...
YES.
IT TASTES EVEN BETTER WITH WATER-CRESS— IT'S A CLEANER FLAVOR.
OH...
OKAY...
panic panic
あわあわ
cram cram
わしゃわしゃ
もしゃもしゃ
chomp chomp
WHAT DO YOU THINK?
WELL...
I-IT TASTES LEAFY...
REALLY, REALLY LEAFY...
Pfft!
YOU'RE RIGHT— IT REALLY JUST TASTES LIKE LEAVES, DOESN'T IT?
HA HA...

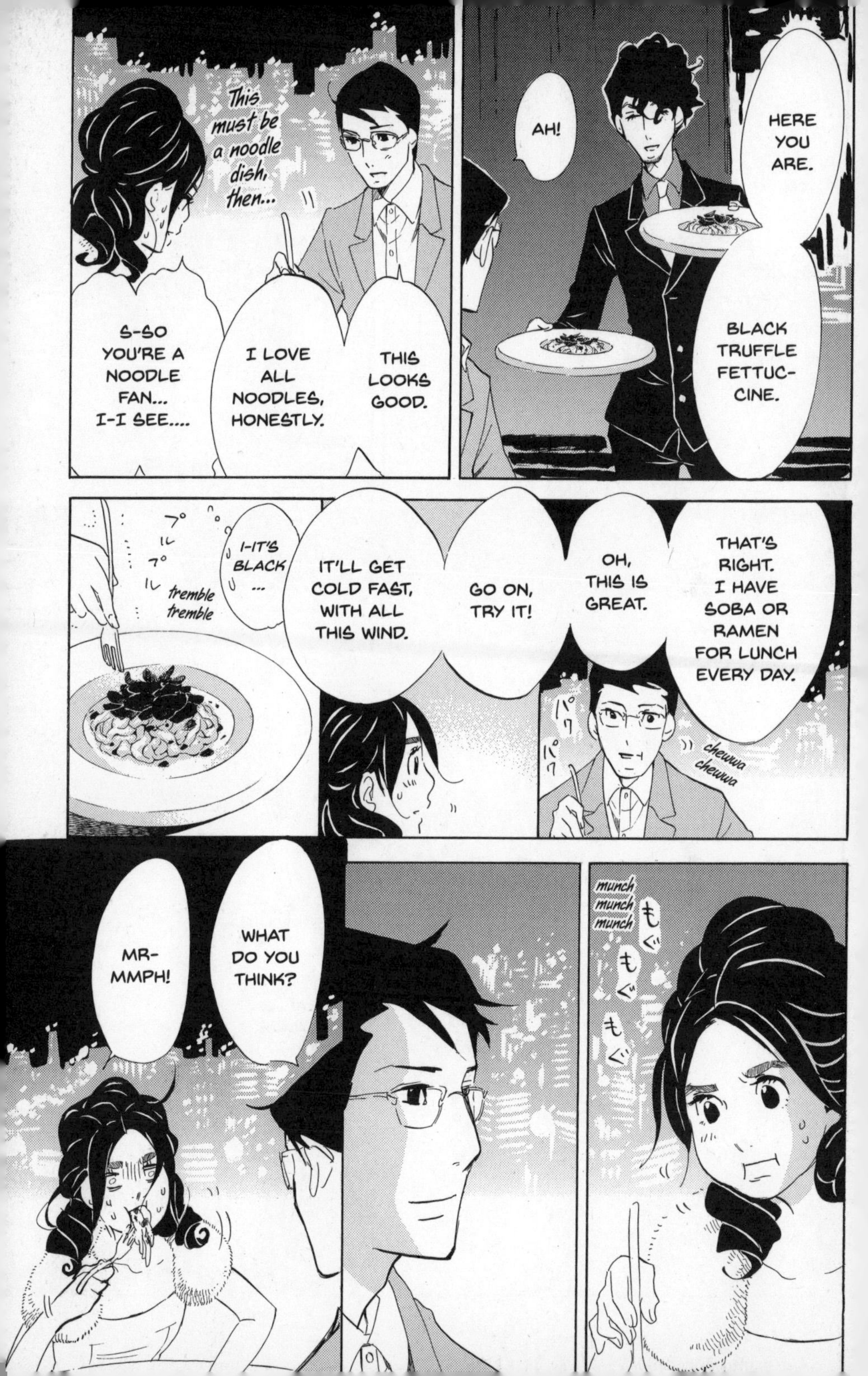
HERE YOU ARE.
BLACK TRUFFLE FETTUC-CINE.
AH!
This must be a noodle dish, then...
THIS LOOKS GOOD.
I LOVE ALL NOODLES, HONESTLY.
S-SO YOU'RE A NOODLE FAN... I-I SEE....
THAT'S RIGHT. I HAVE SOBA OR RAMEN FOR LUNCH EVERY DAY.
OH, THIS IS GREAT.
パク パク
chewwa chewwa
GO ON, TRY IT!
IT'LL GET COLD FAST, WITH ALL THIS WIND.
I-IT'S BLACK ...
プルプル
tremble tremble
もぐ もぐ もぐ
munch munch munch
WHAT DO YOU THINK?
MR-MMPH!

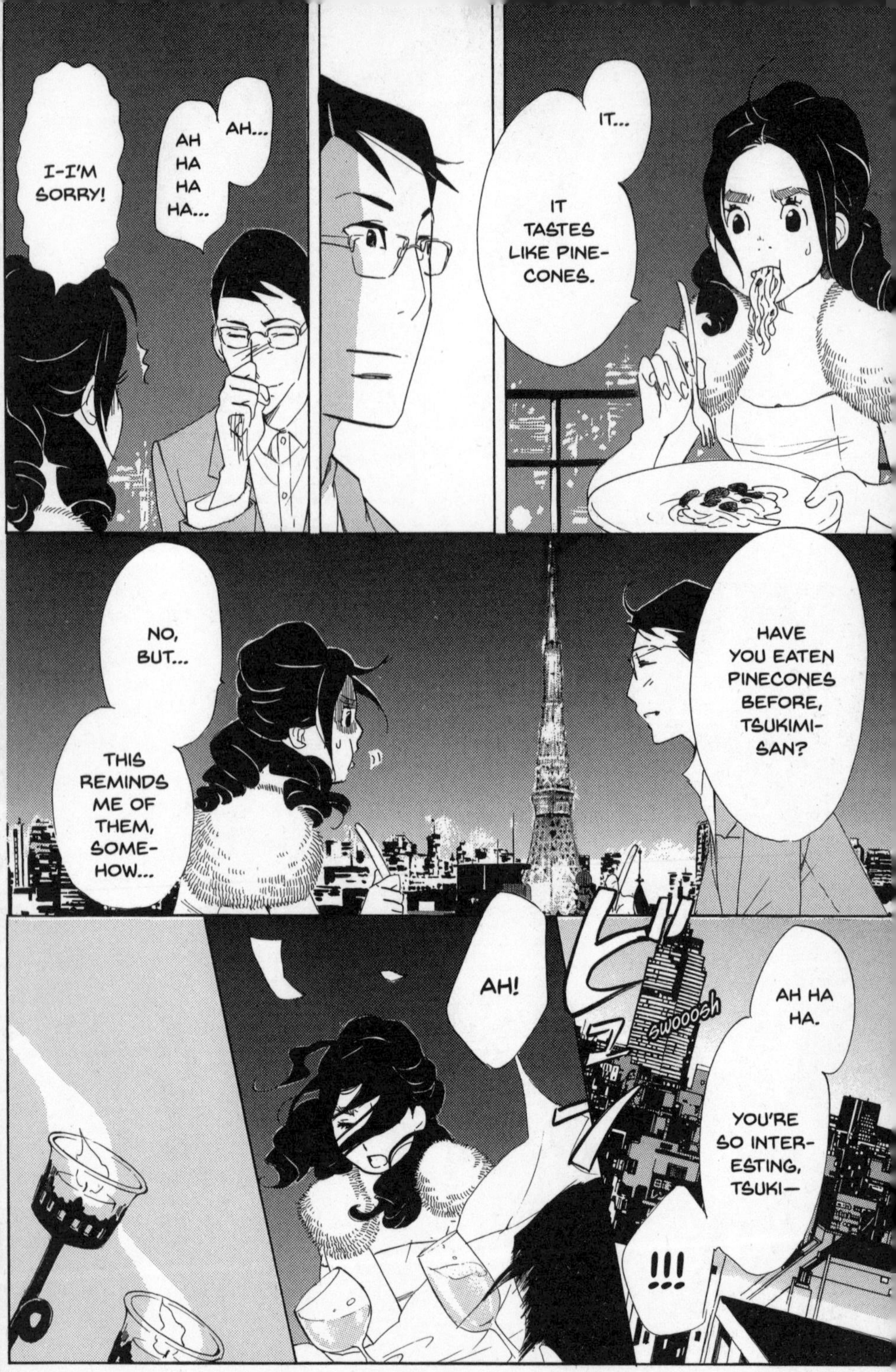
IT...
IT TASTES LIKE PINE-CONES.
AH... AH HA HA HA...
I-I'M SORRY!
HAVE YOU EATEN PINECONES BEFORE, TSUKIMI-SAN?
NO, BUT...
THIS REMINDS ME OF THEM, SOMEHOW...
AH HA HA.
YOU'RE SO INTER-ESTING, TSUKI—
swooosh
AH!
!!!

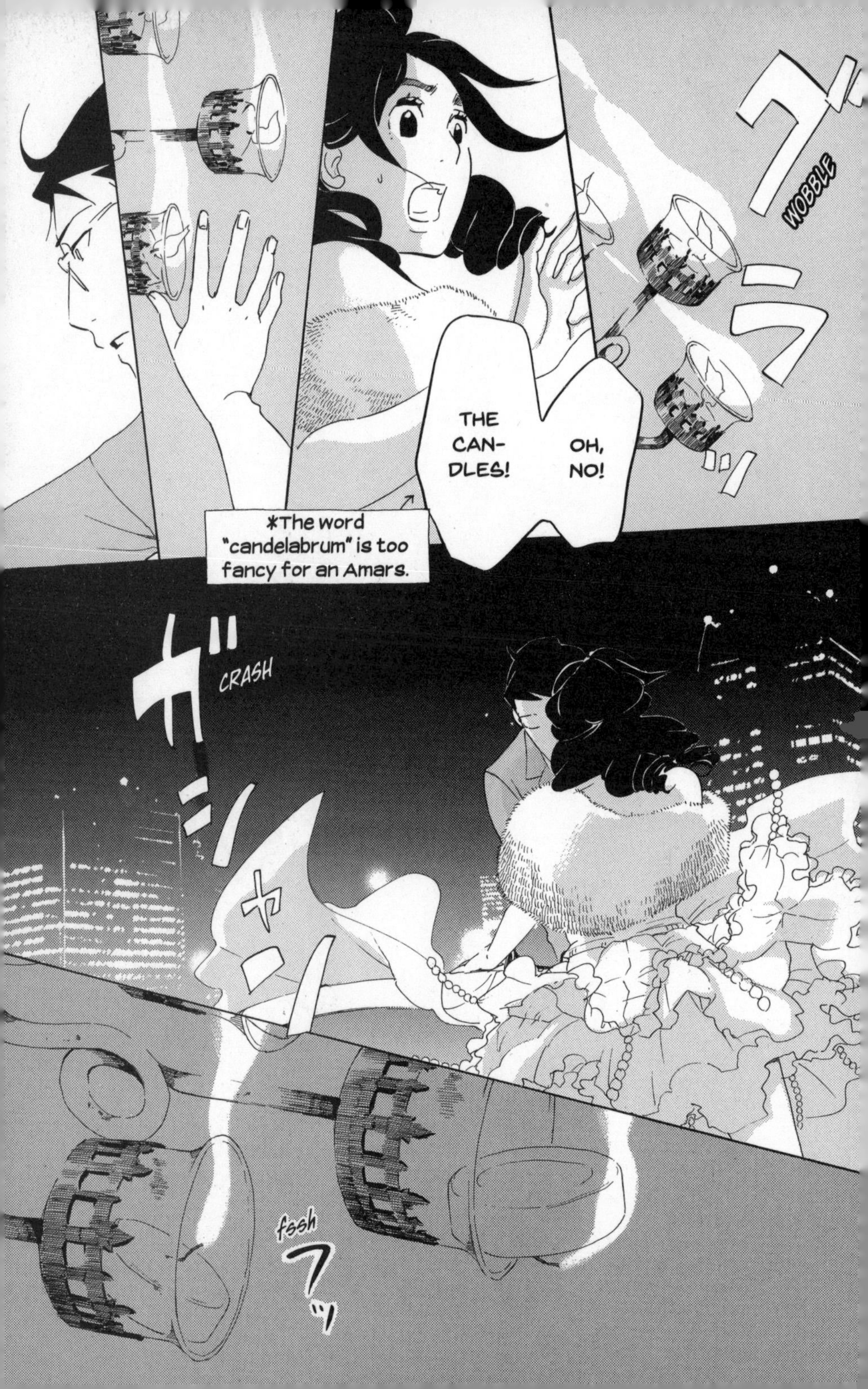
WOBBLE
THE CAN-DLES! OH, NO!
*The word "candelabrum" is too fancy for an Amars.
CRASH
fssh

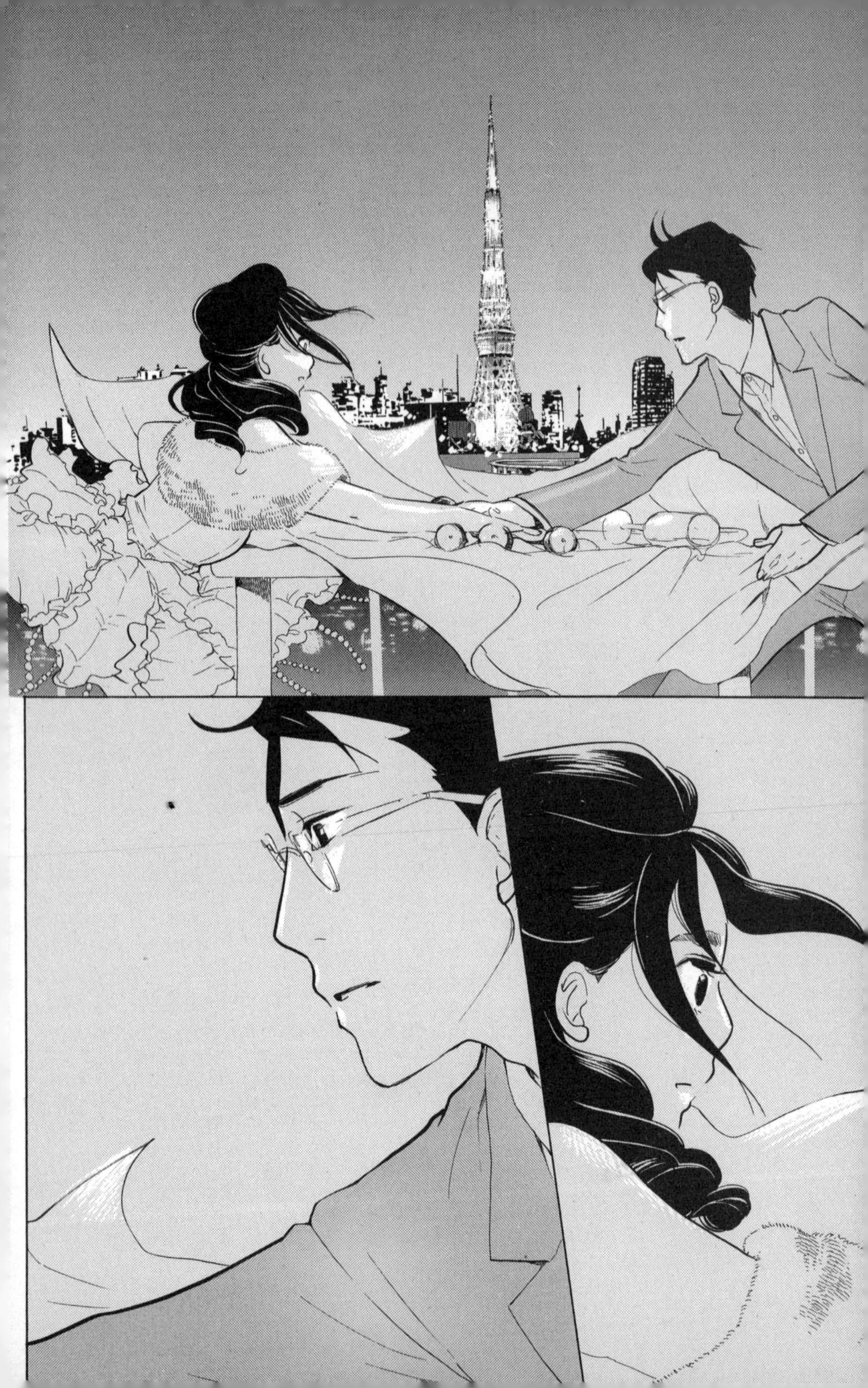

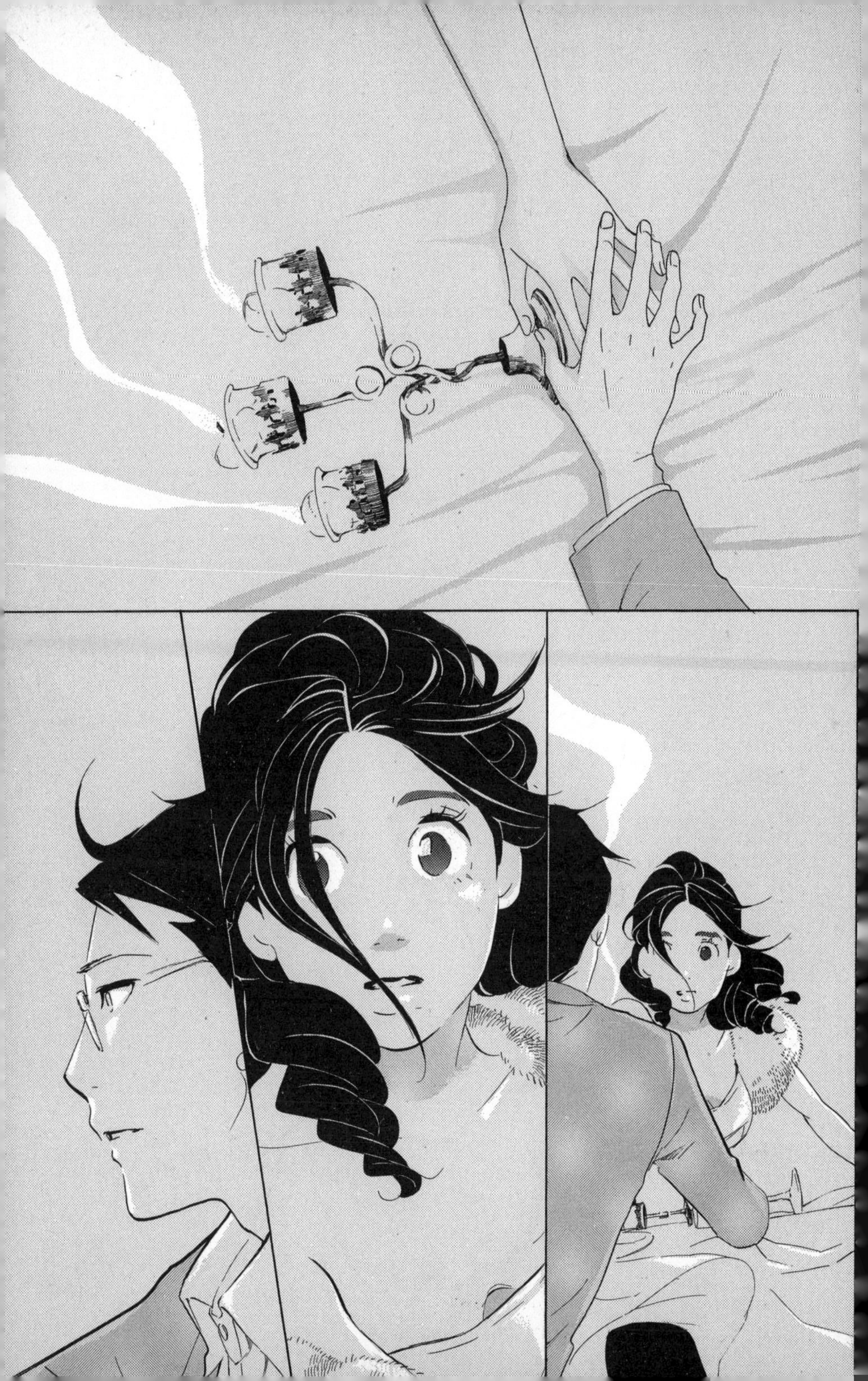

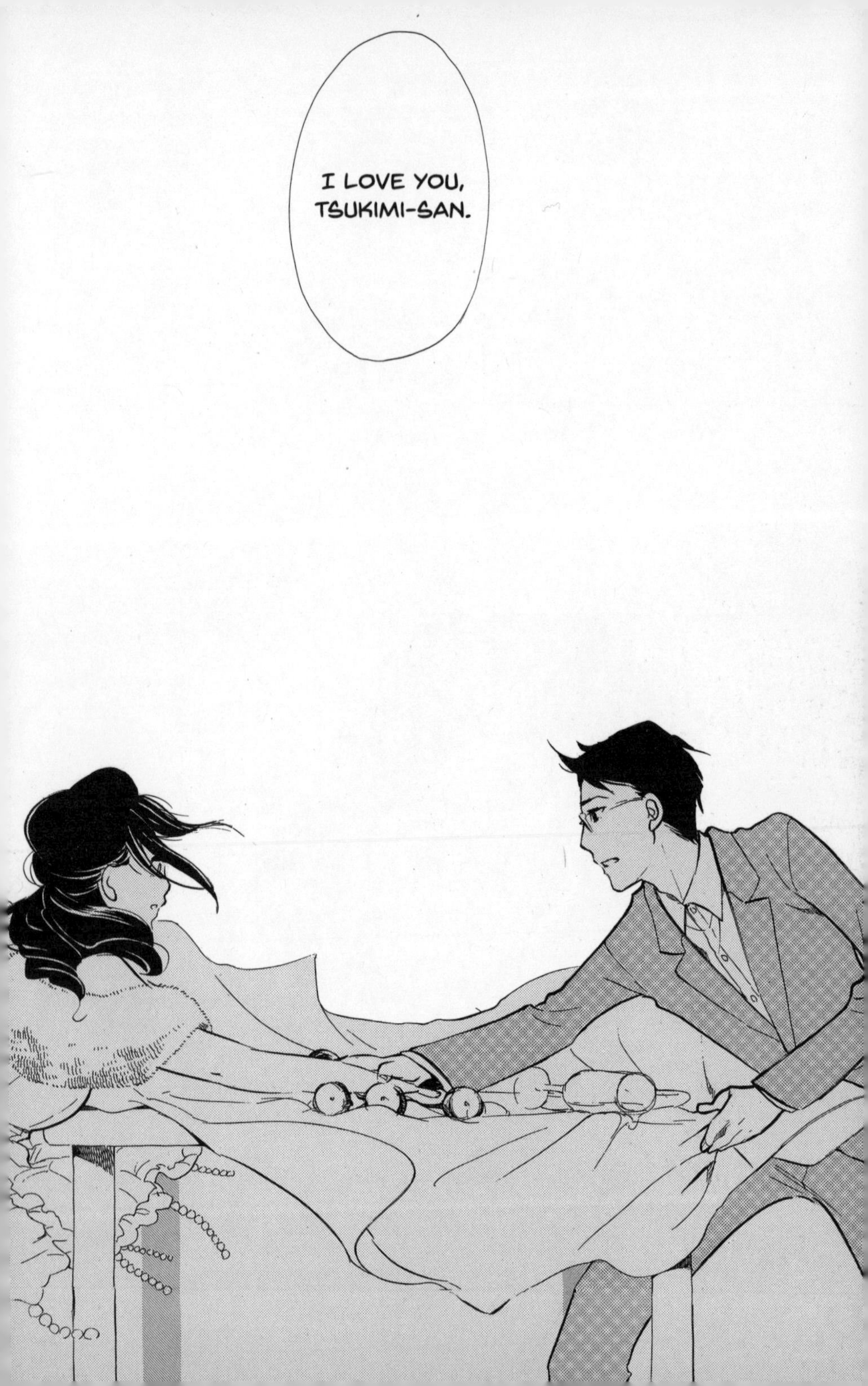
I LOVE YOU, TSUKIMI-SAN.

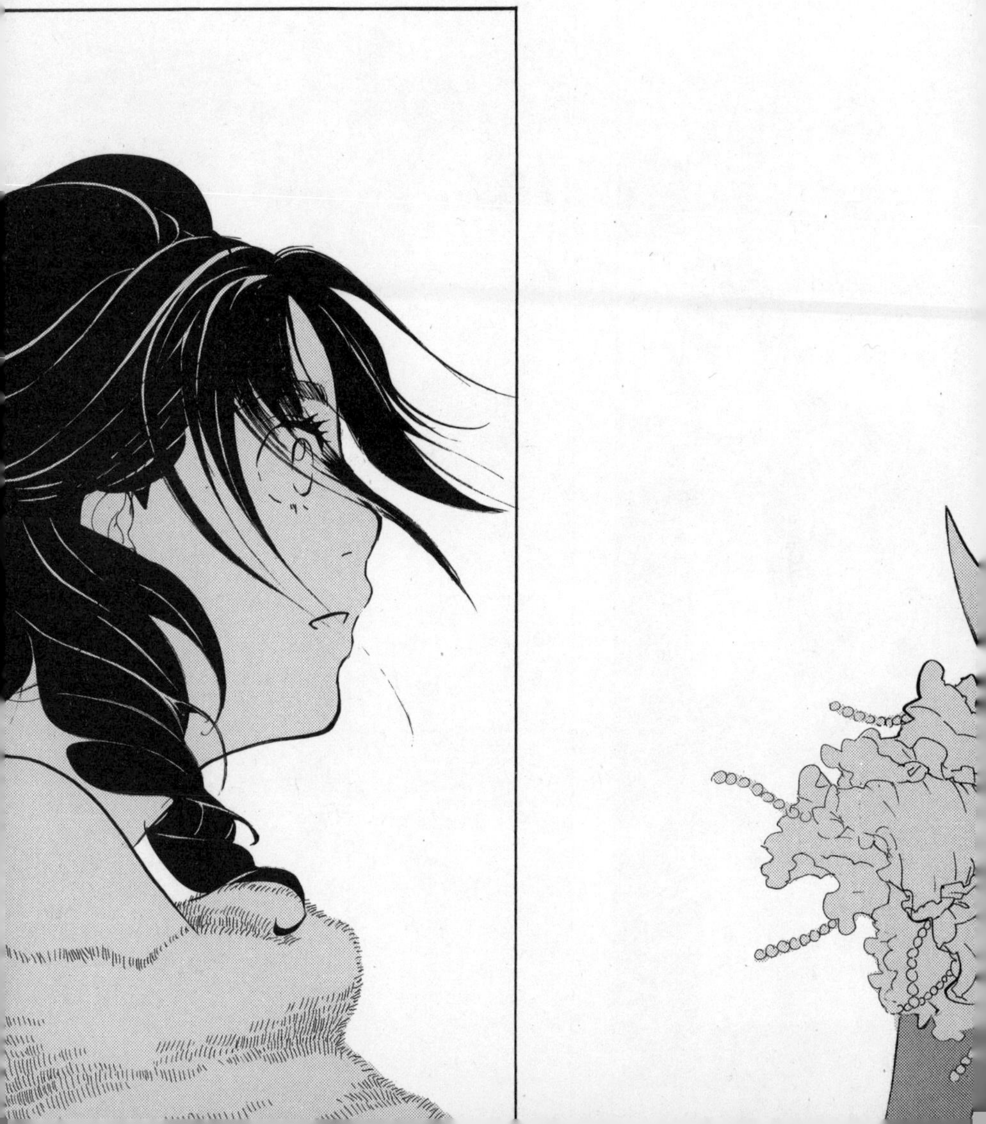

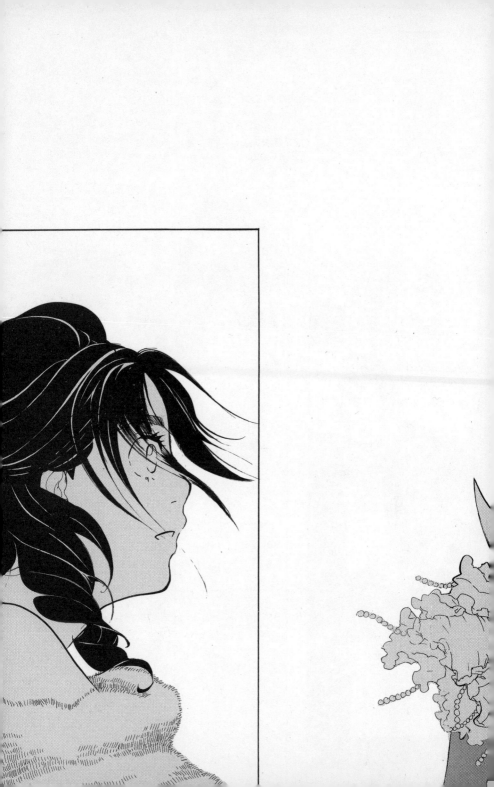

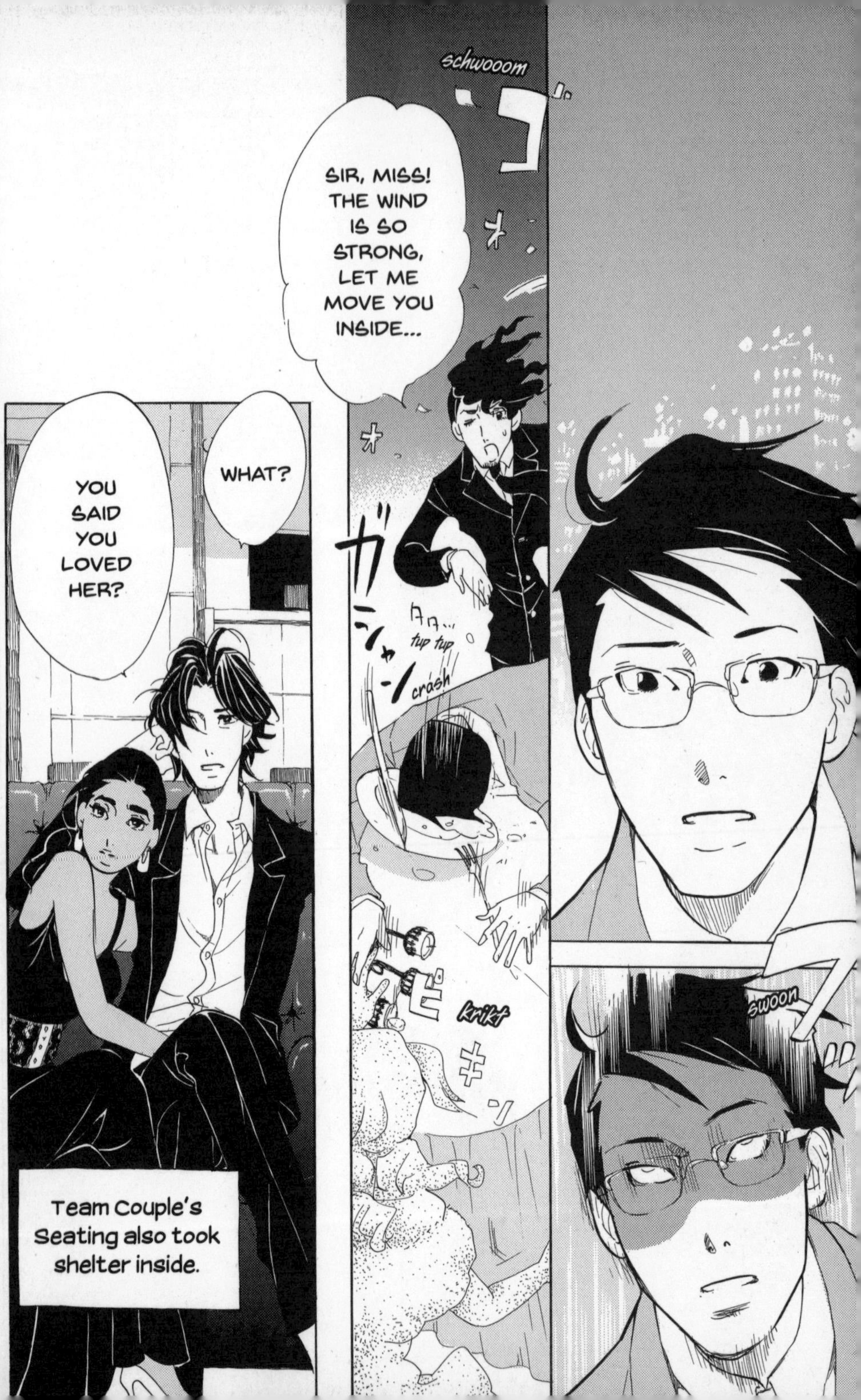
swoon
schwooom
SIR, MISS! THE WIND IS SO STRONG, LET ME MOVE YOU INSIDE...
tup tup
crash
krikt
WHAT?
YOU SAID YOU LOVED HER?
Team Couple's Seating also took shelter inside.

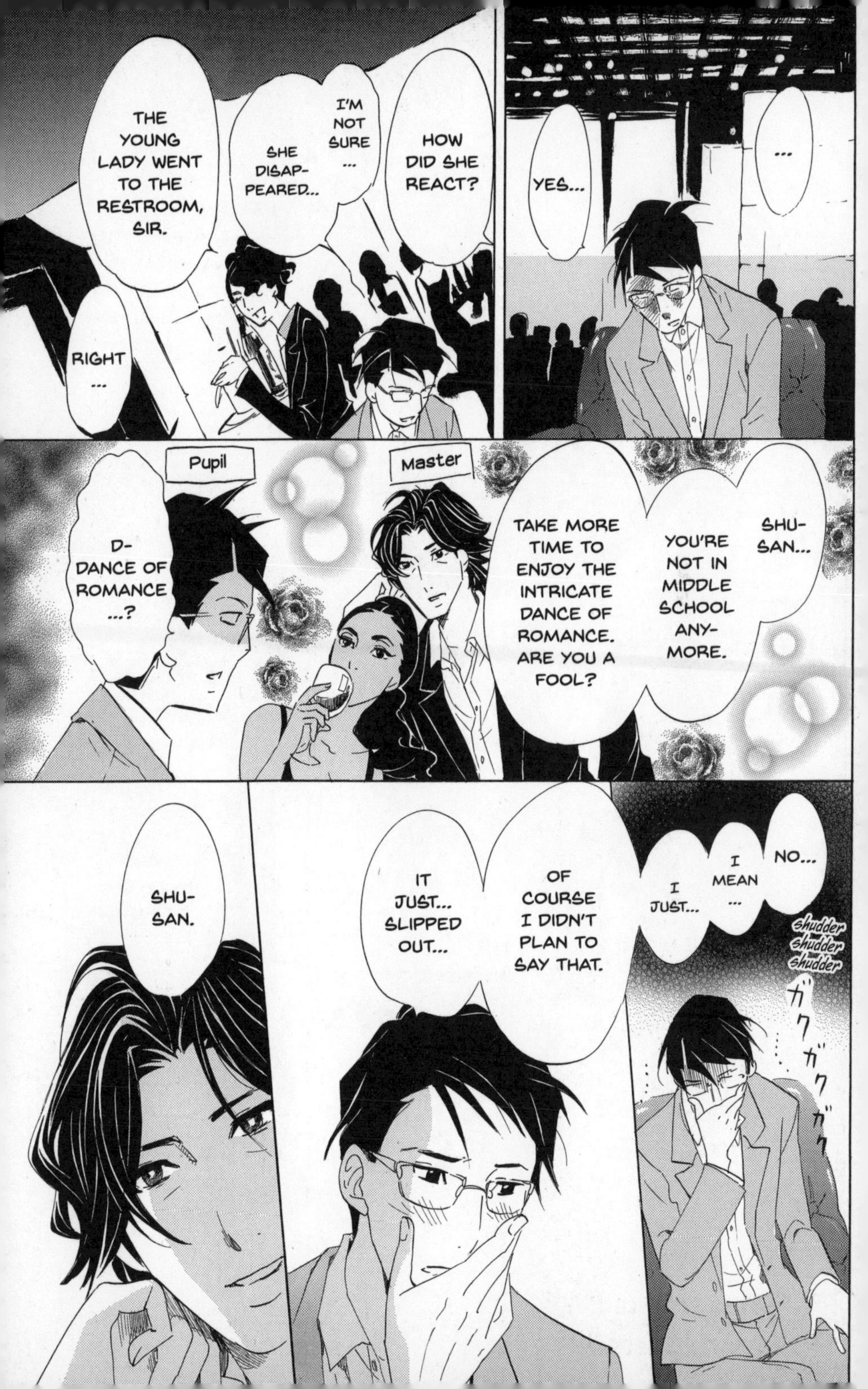
...
YES...
HOW DID SHE REACT?
I'M NOT SURE ...
SHE DISAP-PEARED...
THE YOUNG LADY WENT TO THE RESTROOM, SIR.
RIGHT ...
SHU-SAN...
YOU'RE NOT IN MIDDLE SCHOOL ANY-MORE.
TAKE MORE TIME TO ENJOY THE INTRICATE DANCE OF ROMANCE. ARE YOU A FOOL?
Master
Pupil
D-DANCE OF ROMANCE ...?
NO...
I MEAN ...
I JUST...
shudder shudder shudder
ガクガクガク
OF COURSE I DIDN'T PLAN TO SAY THAT.
IT JUST... SLIPPED OUT...
SHU-SAN.

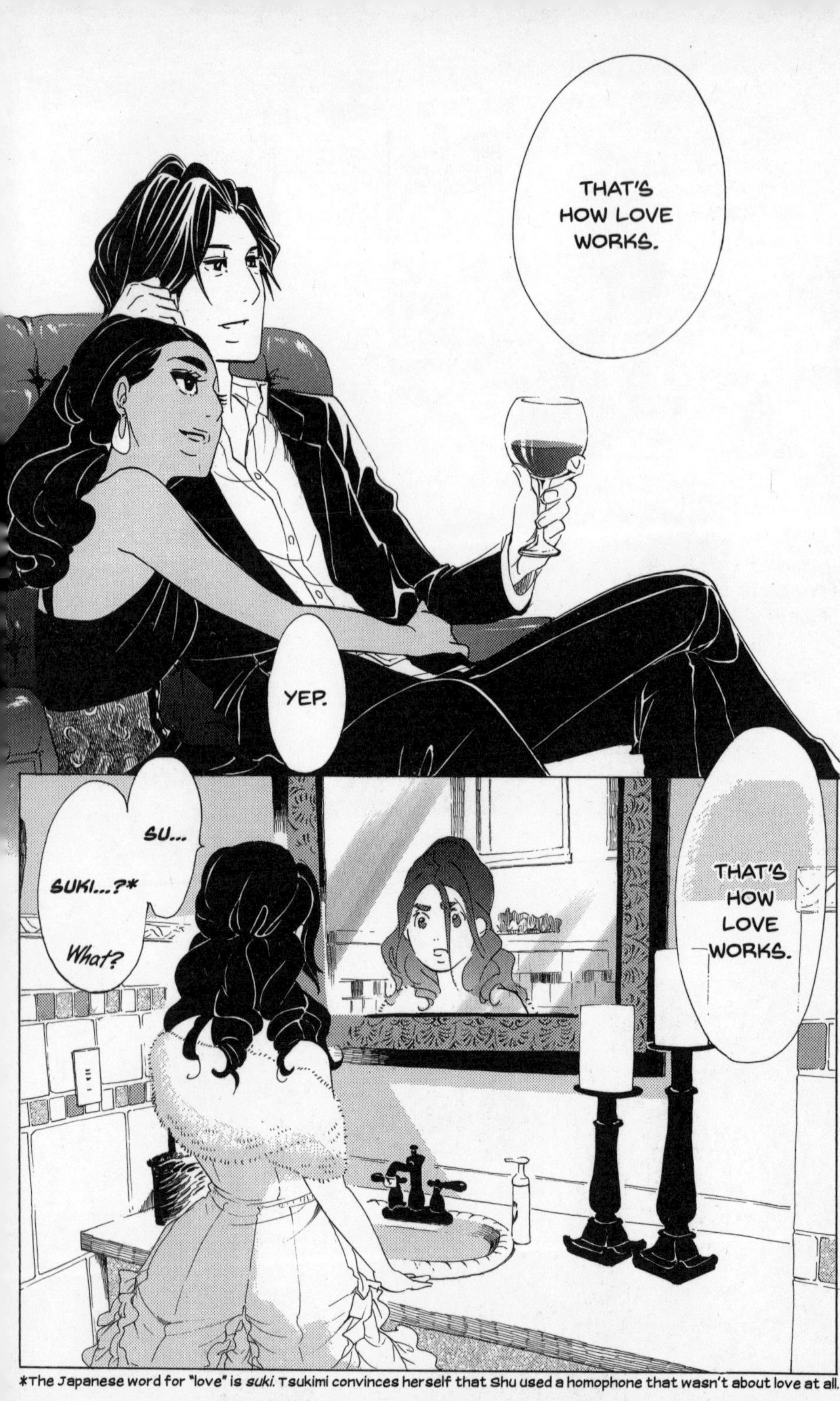
THAT'S HOW LOVE WORKS.
YEP.
THAT'S HOW LOVE WORKS.
SU...
SUKI...?*
What?

*The Japanese word for "love" is *suki*. Tsukimi convinces herself that Shu used a homophone that wasn't about love at all.

Episode 49

About a Pureboy

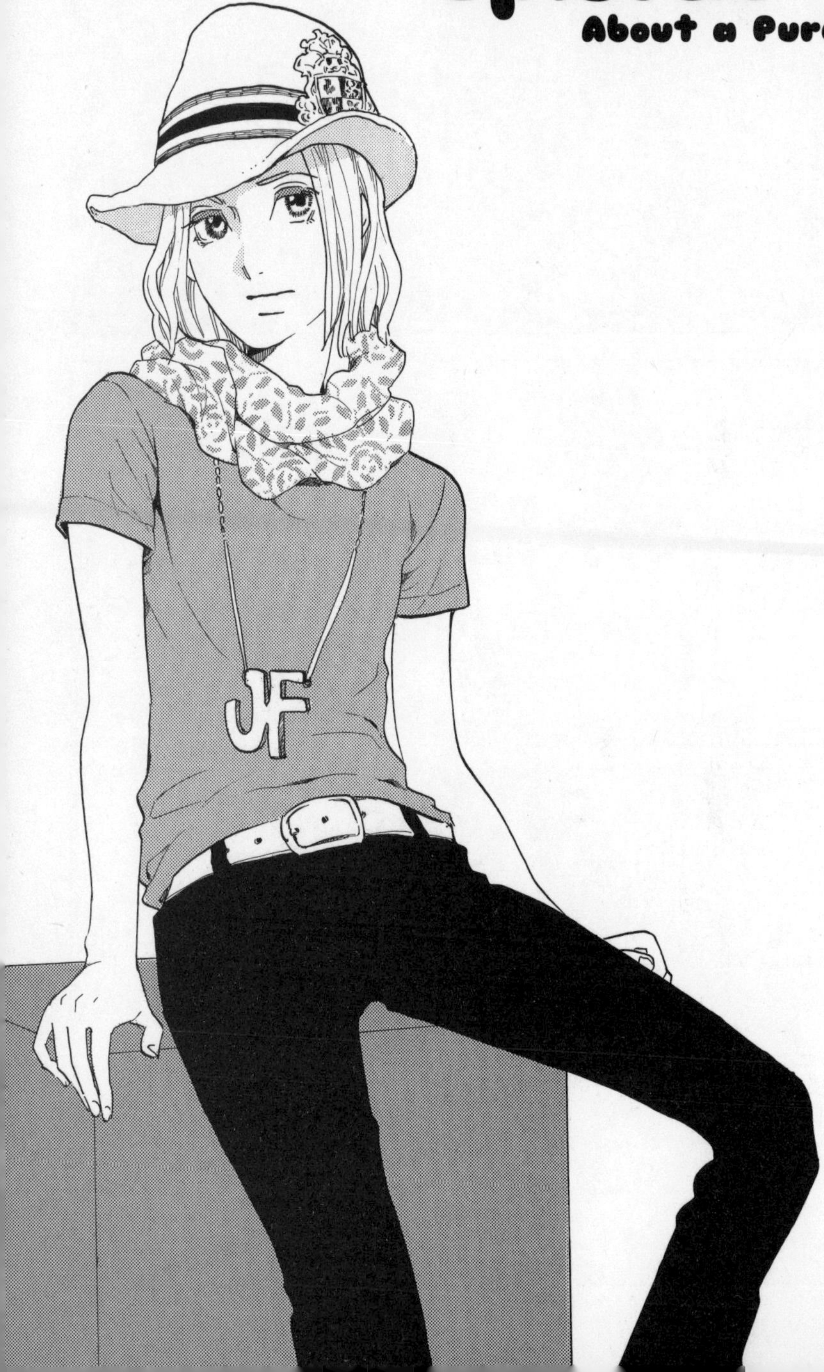

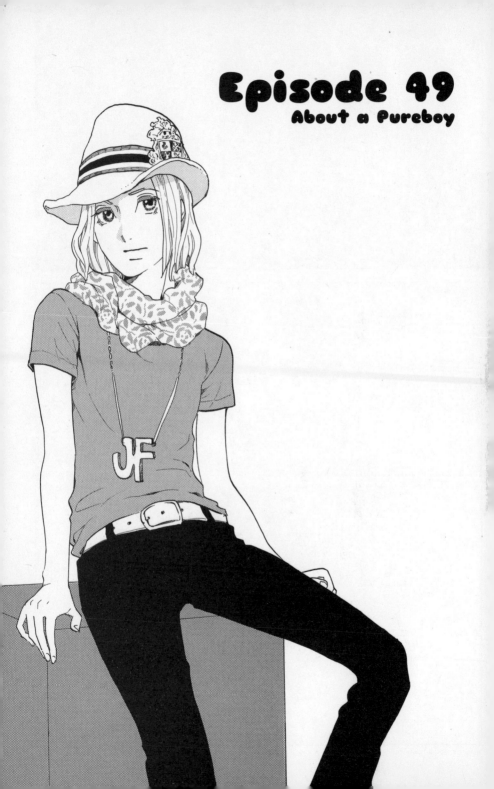

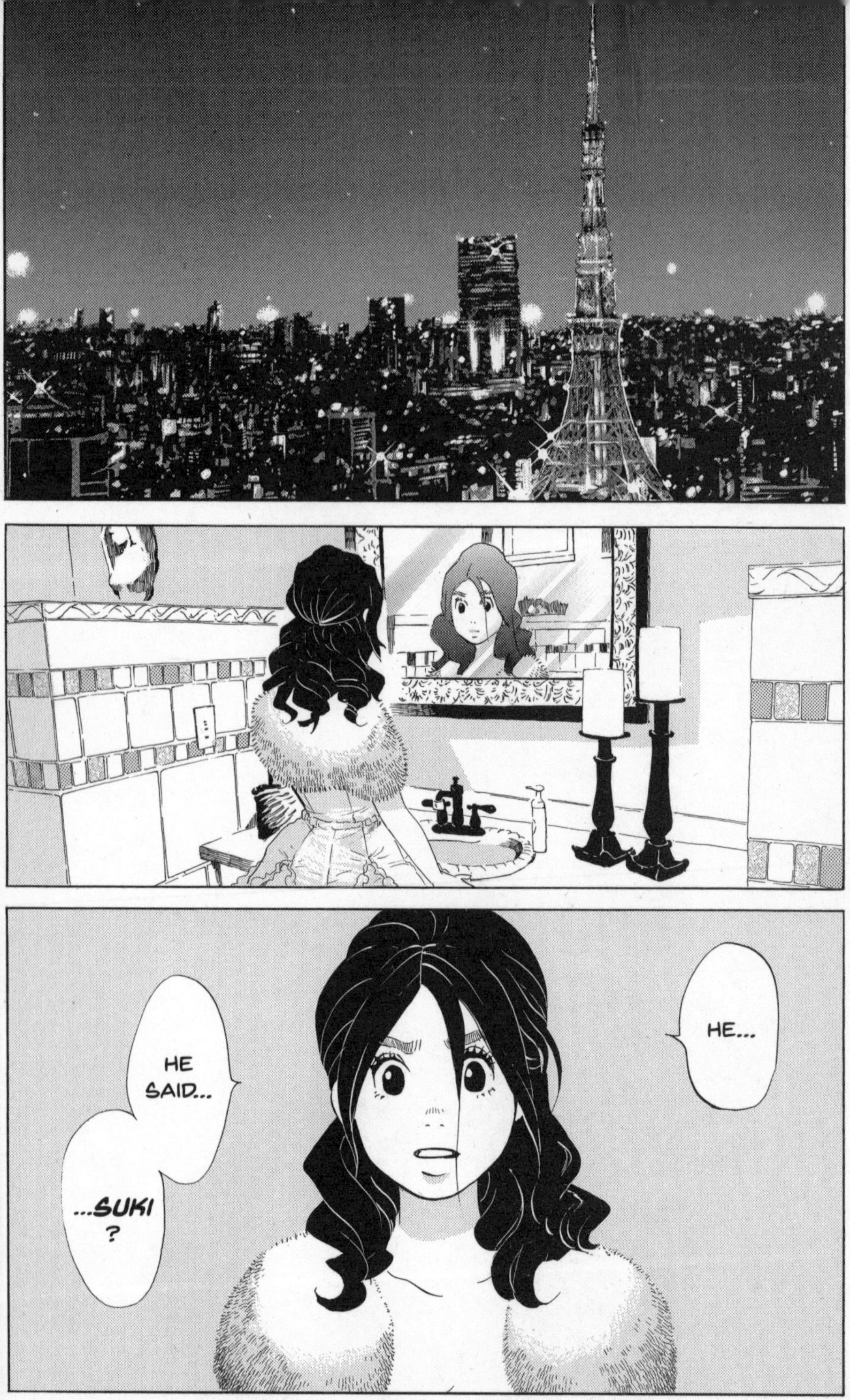
HE...
HE SAID...
...SUKI ?

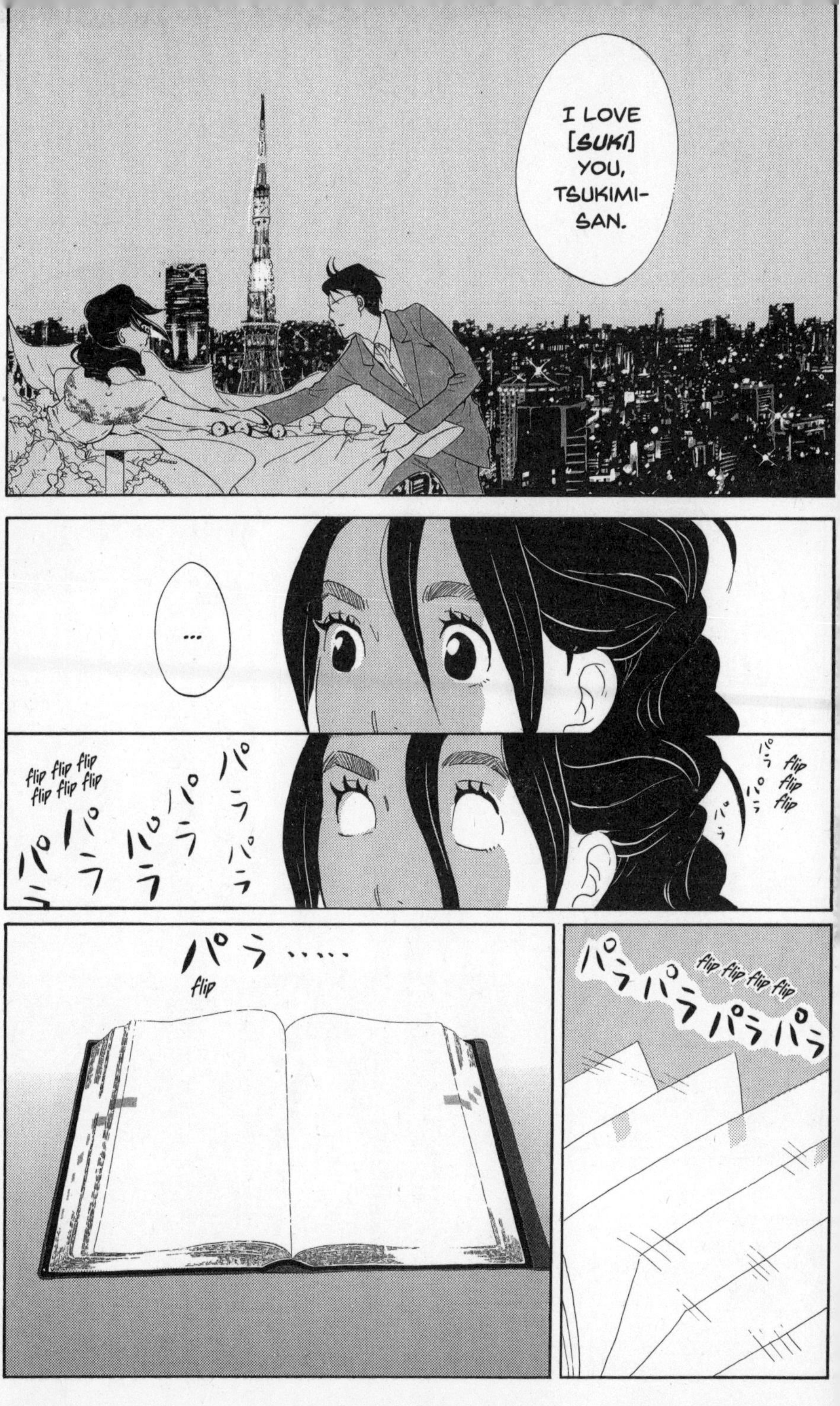
I LOVE [SUKI] YOU, TSUKIMI-SAN.
...
パラ
flip flip flip
パラパラ
パラパラ
パラパラ
flip flip flip
flip flip flip
パラパラパラパラ
flip flip flip flip
パラ.....
flip

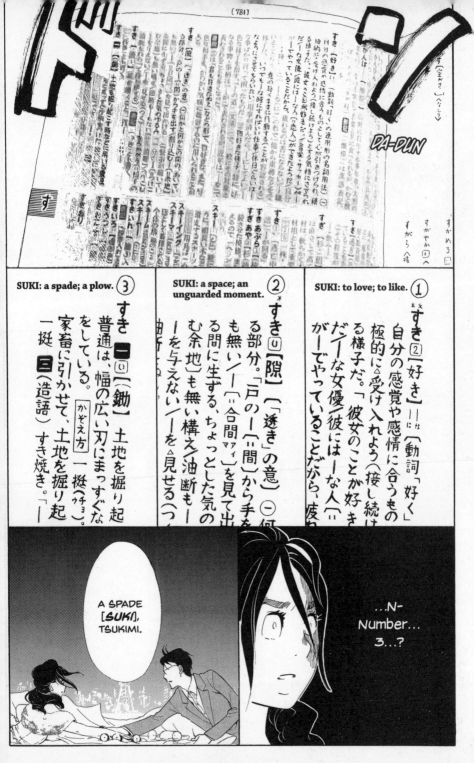

DA-DUN

(781)

SUKI: a spade; a plow. ③

すき 一〇〔〔鋤〕 土地を掘り起
普通は 幅の広い刃にまっすぐな
をしている。
家畜に引かせて、土地を掘り起
かぞえ方 一挺（イッチョ
一挺 三（造語）すき焼き。「―

SUKI: a space; an unguarded moment. ②

すき〇〔隙〕 〔「透き」の意〕 〇何
る部分。「戸の―〔=間〕
も無い／―〔=合間アイ〕を見て出
る間に生ずる、ちょっとした気の
む余地）も無い 構え／油断も―
―を与えない／―を△見せる（つ

SUKI: to love; to like. ①

すき〇〔好き〕 ―に〔動詞「好く」
自分の感覚や感情に合うもの
極的に△受け入れよう（接し続け
る様子だ。「彼女のことが好き
だ／―な女優／彼には―な人〔=
がーでやっていることだから、疲

A SPADE
[SUKI],
TSUKIMI.

...N-
Number...
3...?

-134-

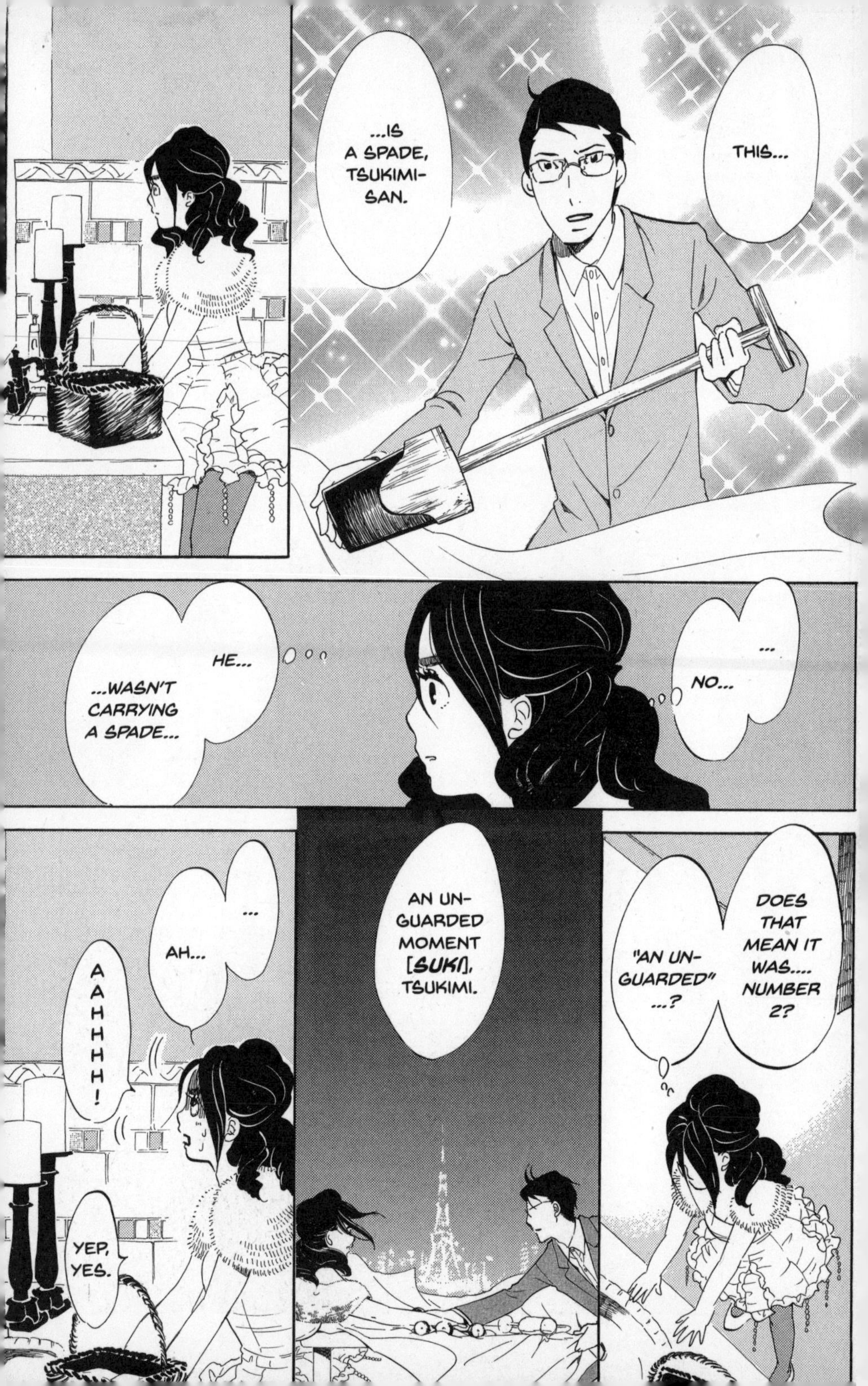
THIS...
...IS A SPADE, TSUKIMI-SAN.
... NO...
HE... ...WASN'T CARRYING A SPADE...
DOES THAT MEAN IT WAS.... NUMBER 2?
"AN UN-GUARDED" ...?
AN UN-GUARDED MOMENT [SUKI], TSUKIMI.
... AH...
AAHHHHH!
YEP, YES.

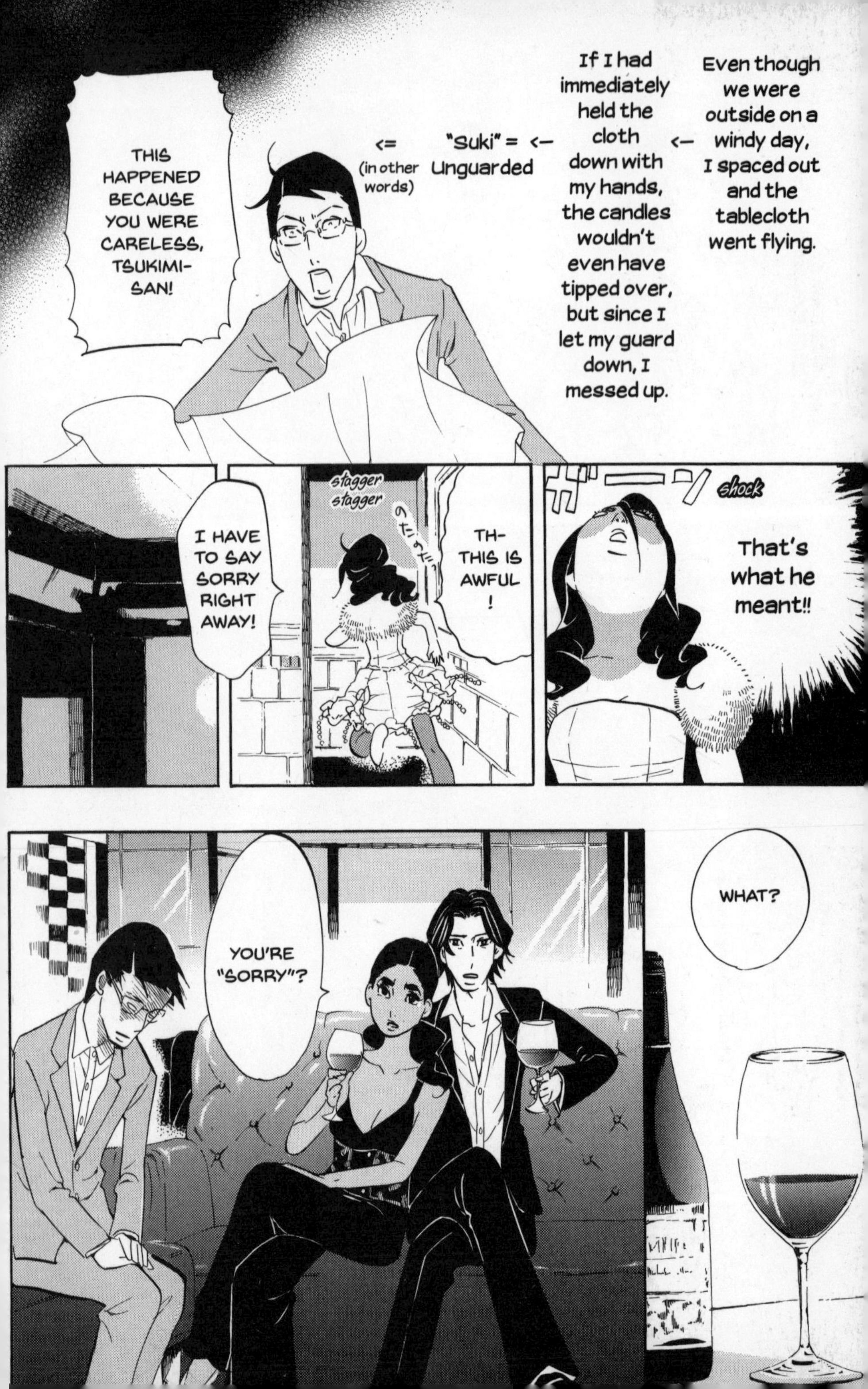
Even though we were outside on a windy day, I spaced out and the tablecloth went flying.
<-
If I had immediately held the cloth down with my hands, the candles wouldn't even have tipped over, but since I let my guard down, I messed up.
<-
"Suki" = Unguarded
<= (in other words)
THIS HAPPENED BECAUSE YOU WERE CARELESS, TSUKIMI-SAN!
shock
That's what he meant!!
stagger stagger
TH-THIS IS AWFUL!
I HAVE TO SAY SORRY RIGHT AWAY!
WHAT?
YOU'RE "SORRY"?

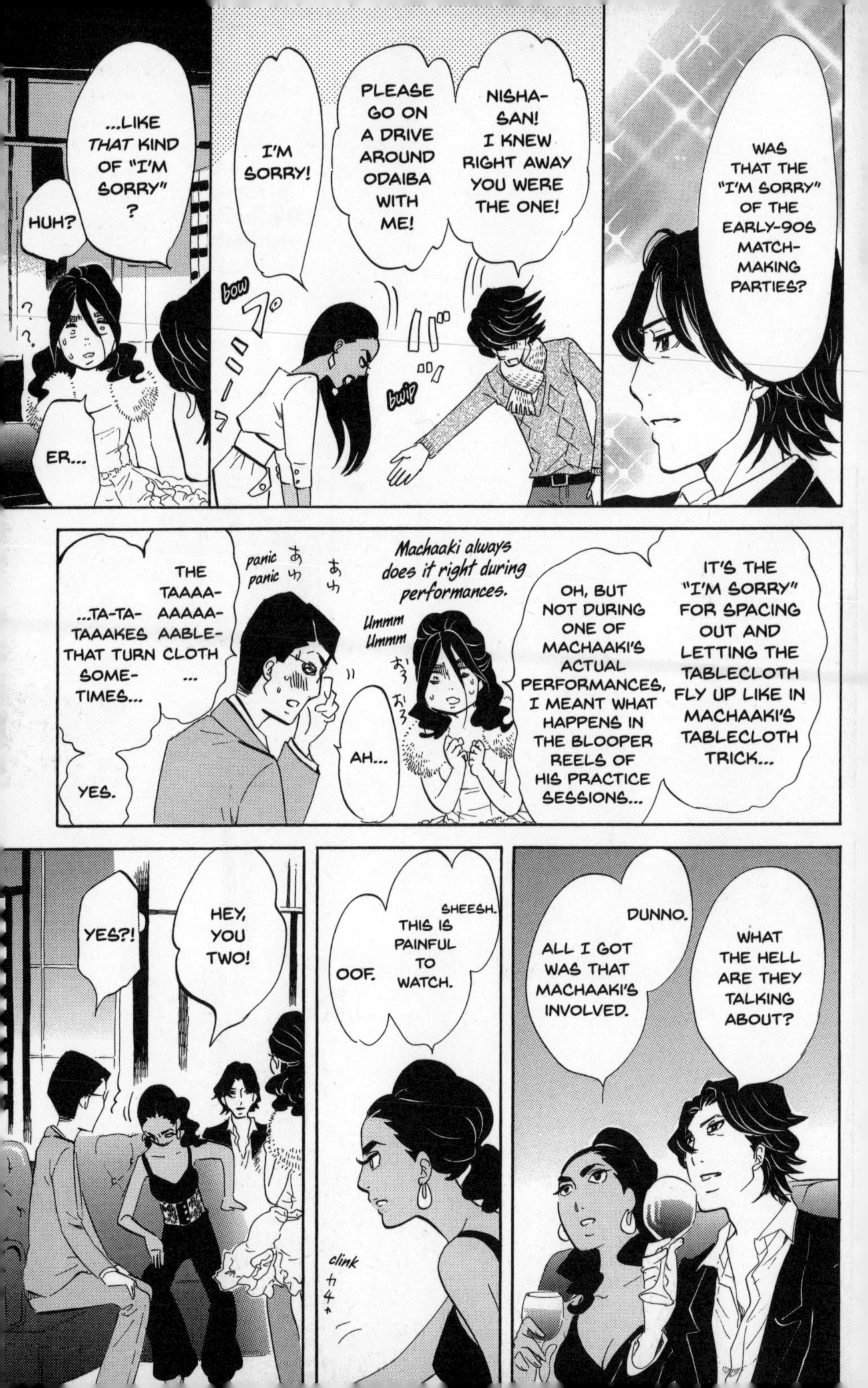
WAS THAT THE "I'M SORRY" OF THE EARLY-90S MATCH-MAKING PARTIES?
NISHA-SAN! I KNEW RIGHT AWAY YOU WERE THE ONE!
PLEASE GO ON A DRIVE AROUND ODAIBA WITH ME!
I'M SORRY!
bow
bwip
...LIKE THAT KIND OF "I'M SORRY"?
HUH?
ER...
IT'S THE "I'M SORRY" FOR SPACING OUT AND LETTING THE TABLECLOTH FLY UP LIKE IN MACHAAKI'S TABLECLOTH TRICK...
OH, BUT NOT DURING ONE OF MACHAAKI'S ACTUAL PERFORMANCES, I MEANT WHAT HAPPENS IN THE BLOOPER REELS OF HIS PRACTICE SESSIONS...
Machaaki always does it right during performances.
Ummm Ummm
AH...
panic panic
THE TAAAA-AAAAA-AABLE-CLOTH...
...TA-TA-TAAAKES THAT TURN SOME-TIMES...
YES.
WHAT THE HELL ARE THEY TALKING ABOUT?
DUNNO.
ALL I GOT WAS THAT MACHAAKI'S INVOLVED.
SHEESH.
THIS IS PAINFUL TO WATCH.
OOF.
clink
HEY, YOU TWO!
YES?!

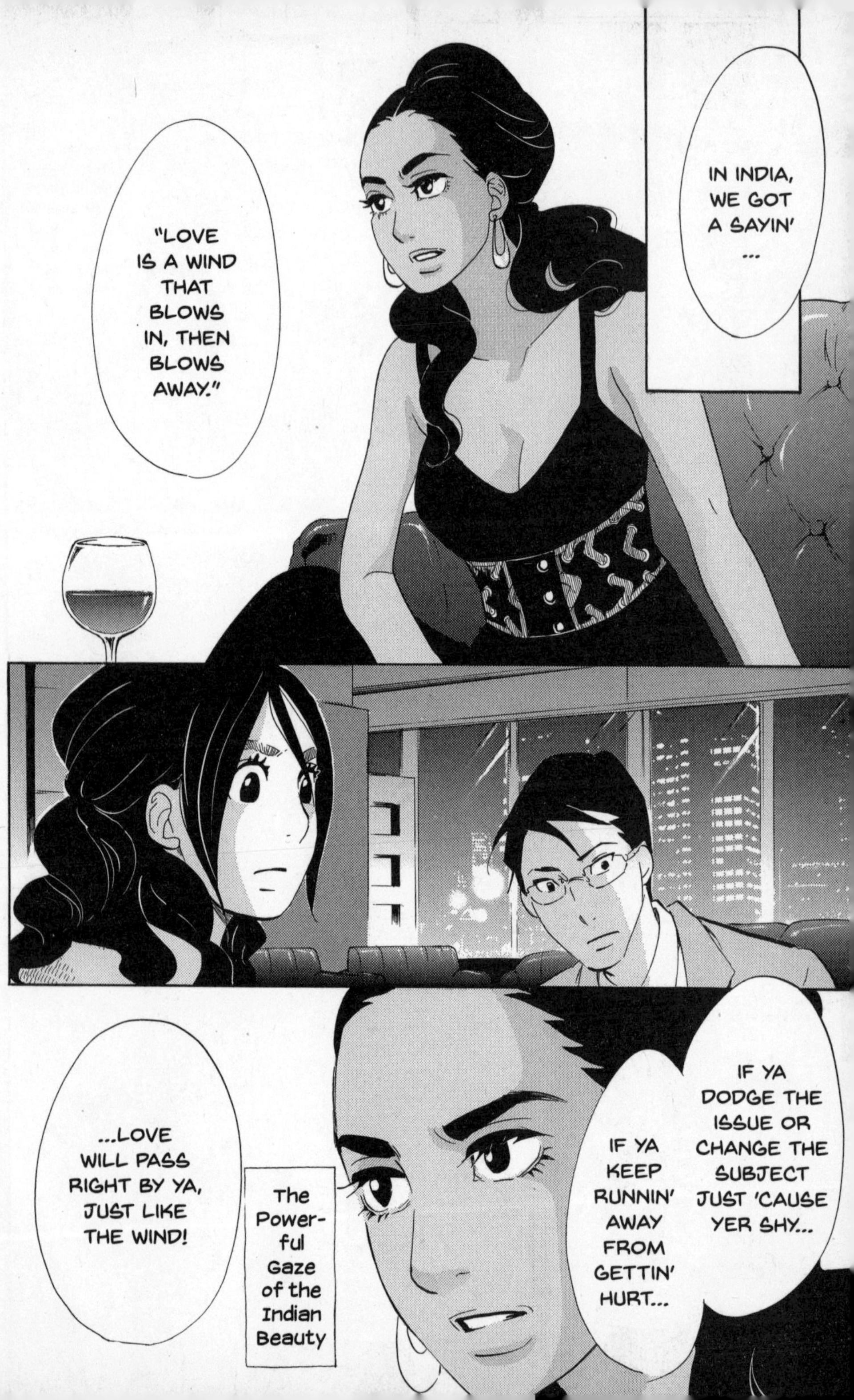
IN INDIA, WE GOT A SAYIN' ...
"LOVE IS A WIND THAT BLOWS IN, THEN BLOWS AWAY."
IF YA DODGE THE ISSUE OR CHANGE THE SUBJECT JUST 'CAUSE YER SHY...
IF YA KEEP RUNNIN' AWAY FROM GETTIN' HURT...
The Power-ful Gaze of the Indian Beauty
...LOVE WILL PASS RIGHT BY YA, JUST LIKE THE WIND!

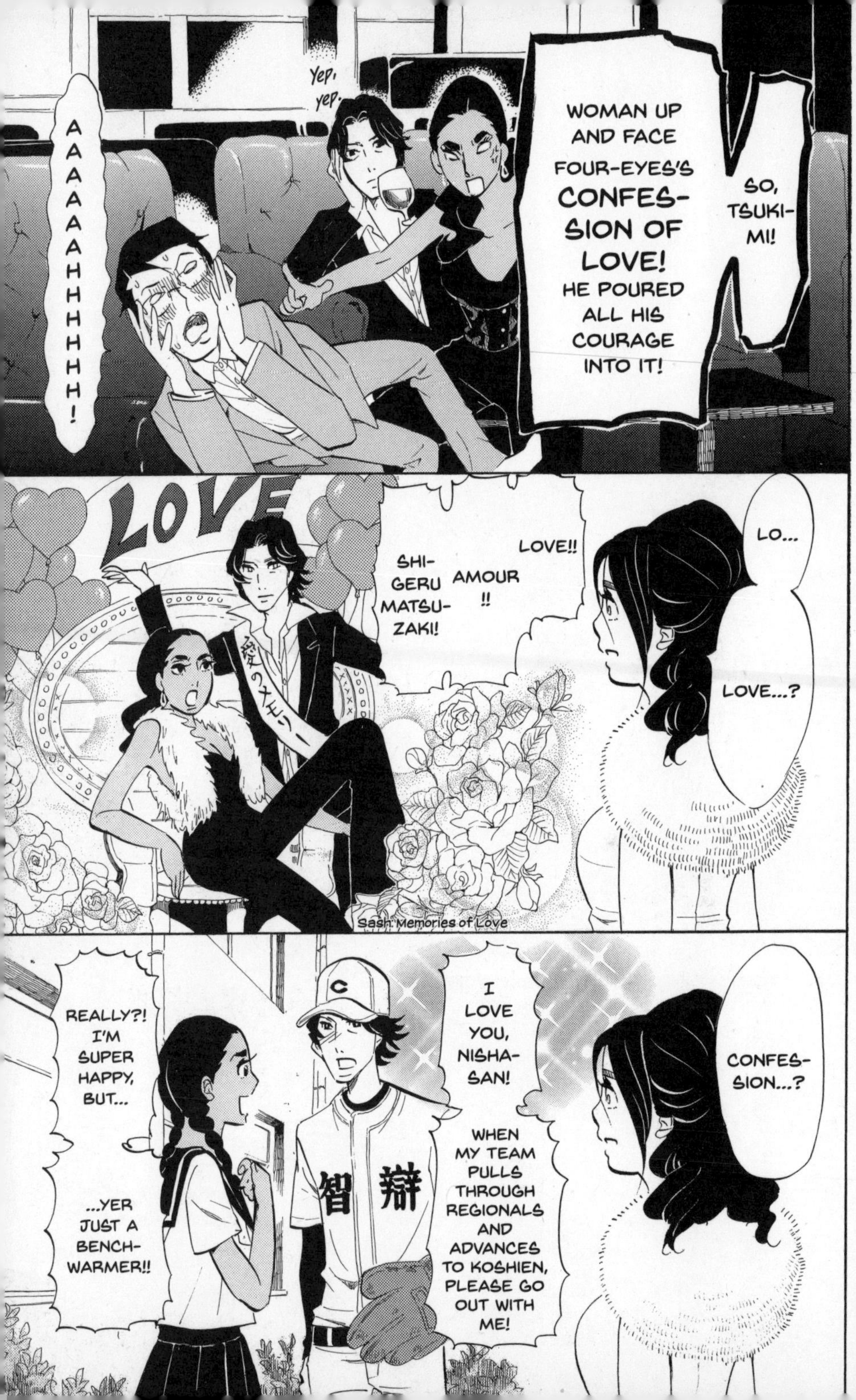
SO, TSUKIMI!
WOMAN UP AND FACE FOUR-EYES'S CONFESSION OF LOVE! HE POURED ALL HIS COURAGE INTO IT!
Yep, yep.
AAAAAAHHHHHHHH!
LO...
LOVE...?
LOVE!!
AMOUR!!
SHIGERU MATSUZAKI!
LOVE
Sash: Memories of Love
CONFESSION...?
I LOVE YOU, NISHA-SAN!
WHEN MY TEAM PULLS THROUGH REGIONALS AND ADVANCES TO KOSHIEN, PLEASE GO OUT WITH ME!
REALLY?! I'M SUPER HAPPY, BUT...
...YER JUST A BENCH-WARMER!!

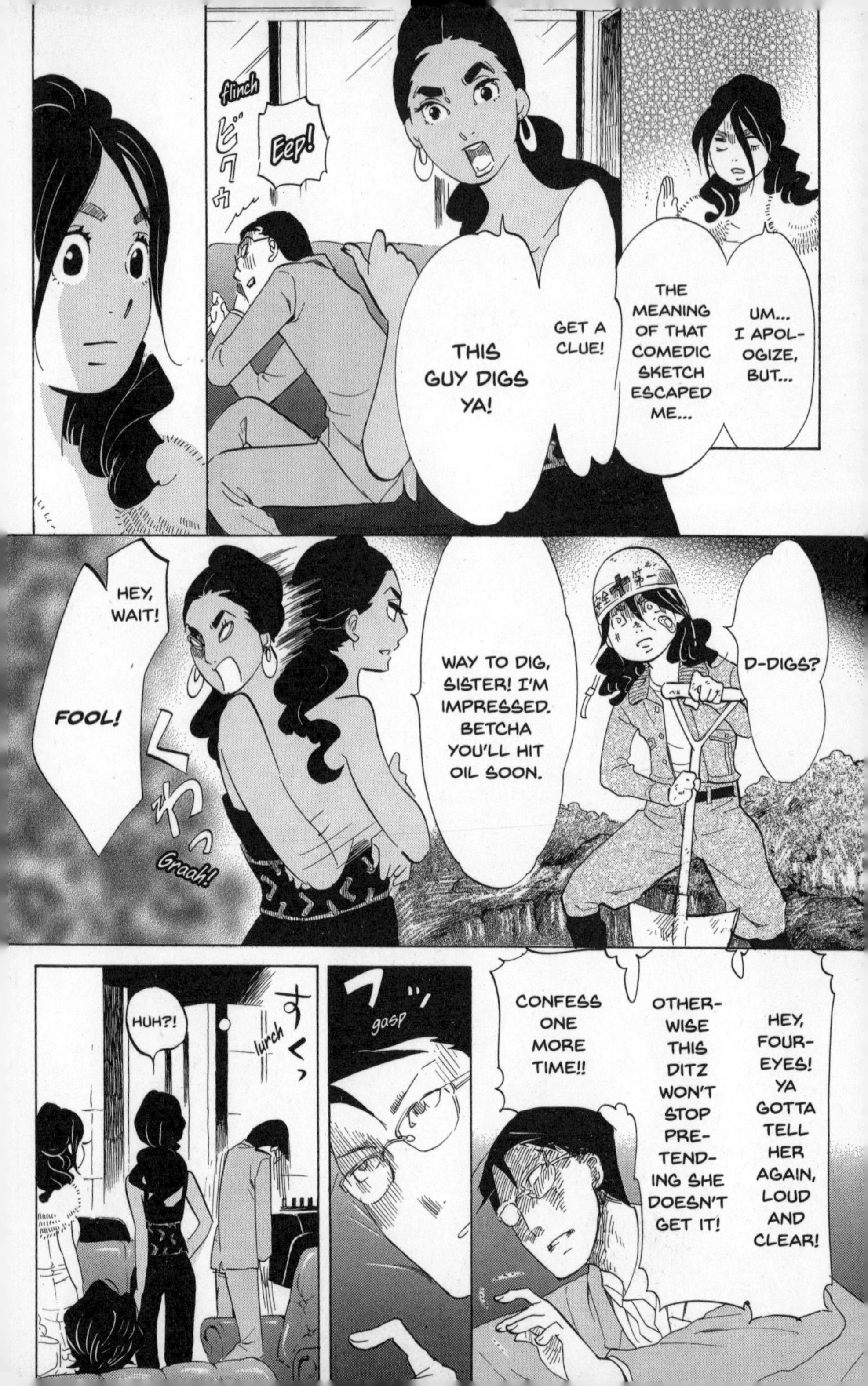
UM... I APOLOGIZE, BUT...
THE MEANING OF THAT COMEDIC SKETCH ESCAPED ME...
GET A CLUE!
THIS GUY DIGS YA!
Eep!
flinch
D-DIGS?
WAY TO DIG, SISTER! I'M IMPRESSED. BETCHA YOU'LL HIT OIL SOON.
HEY, WAIT!
FOOL!
Graah!
HEY, FOUR-EYES! YA GOTTA TELL HER AGAIN, LOUD AND CLEAR!
OTHER-WISE THIS DITZ WON'T STOP PRE-TEND-ING SHE DOESN'T GET IT!
CONFESS ONE MORE TIME!!
gasp
lurch
HUH?!

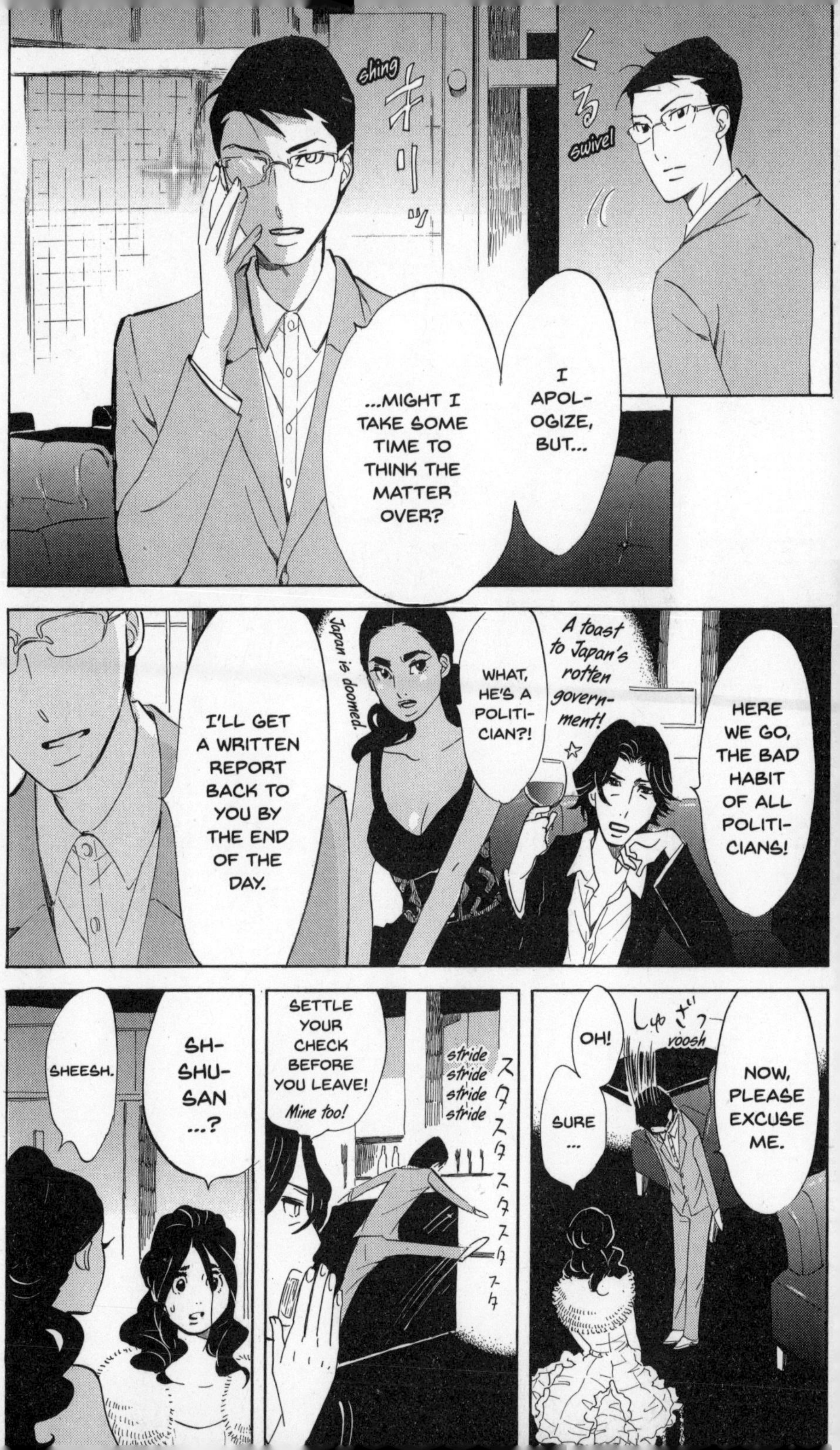
くる
swivel
I APOLOGIZE, BUT...
キリッ
shing
...MIGHT I TAKE SOME TIME TO THINK THE MATTER OVER?
HERE WE GO, THE BAD HABIT OF ALL POLITICIANS!
A toast to Japan's rotten government! ☆
WHAT, HE'S A POLITICIAN?!
Japan is doomed.
I'LL GET A WRITTEN REPORT BACK TO YOU BY THE END OF THE DAY.
しゅざっ
voosh
NOW, PLEASE EXCUSE ME.
OH!
SURE...
スタスタスタスタ
stride stride stride stride
SETTLE YOUR CHECK BEFORE YOU LEAVE!
Mine too!
SH-SHU-SAN...?
SHEESH.

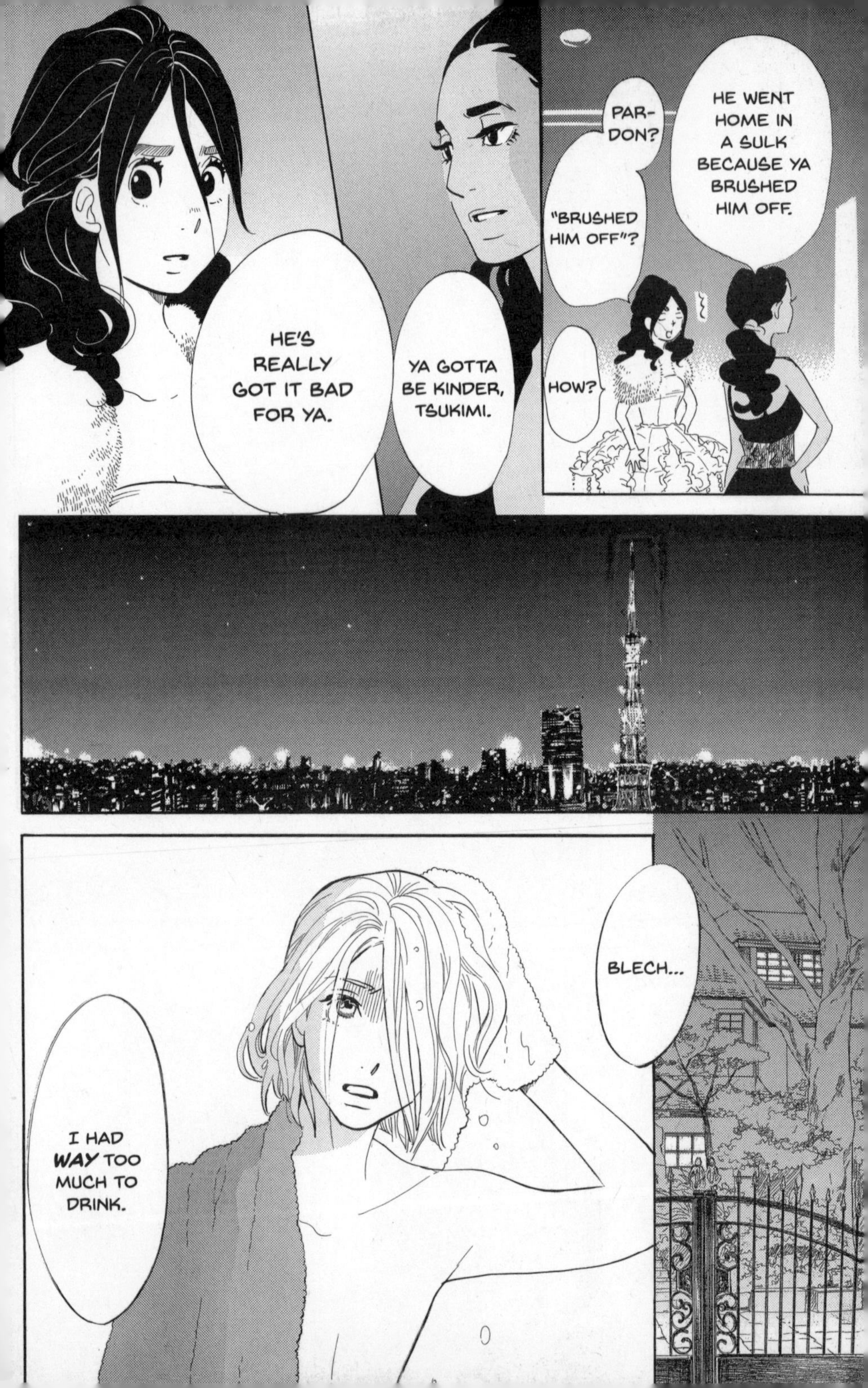
HE WENT HOME IN A SULK BECAUSE YA BRUSHED HIM OFF.
PARDON?
"BRUSHED HIM OFF"?
HOW?
YA GOTTA BE KINDER, TSUKIMI.
HE'S REALLY GOT IT BAD FOR YA.
BLECH...
I HAD **WAY** TOO MUCH TO DRINK.

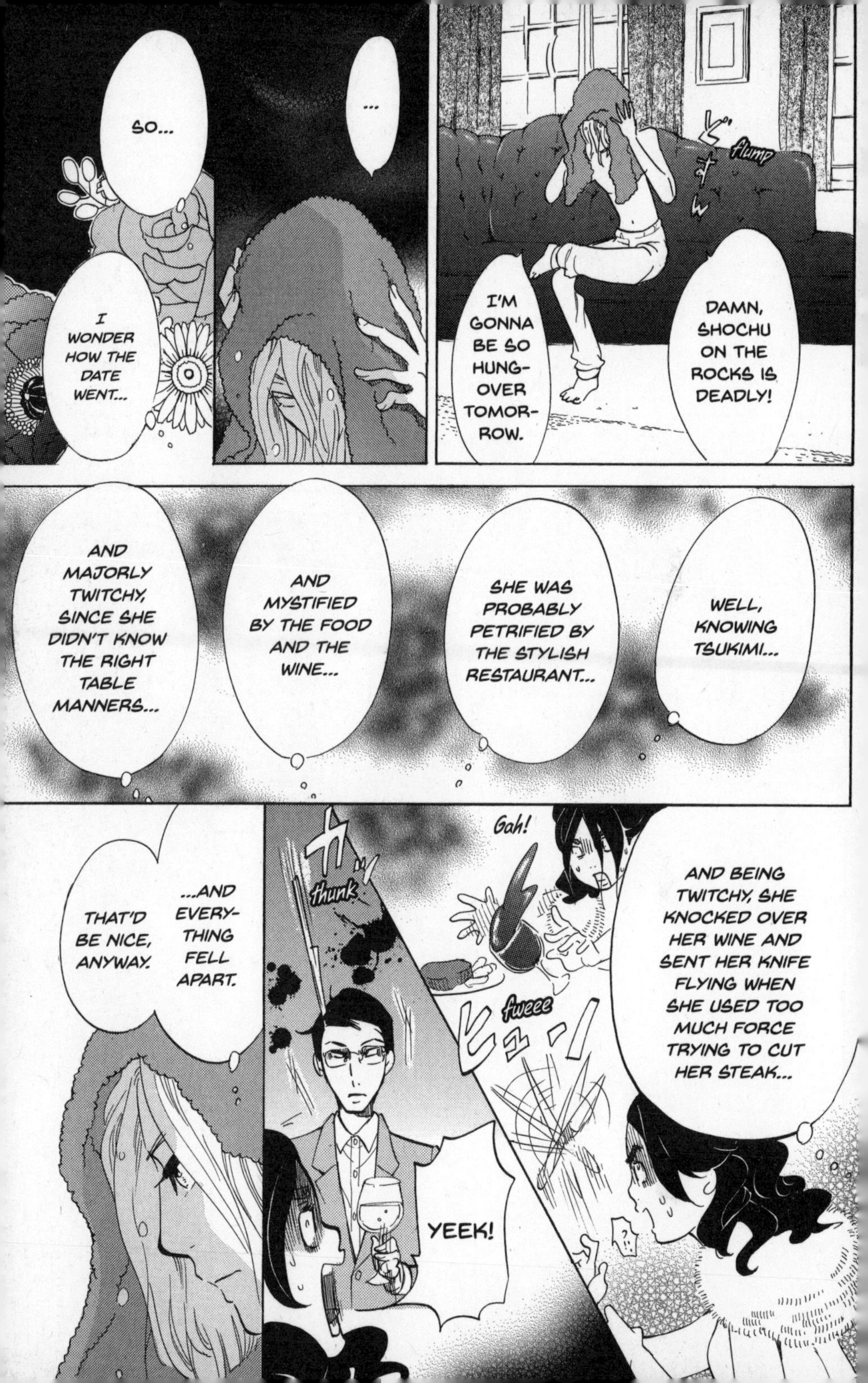

Flump
DAMN, SHOCHU ON THE ROCKS IS DEADLY!
I'M GONNA BE SO HUNG-OVER TOMORROW.
...
SO...
I WONDER HOW THE DATE WENT...
WELL, KNOWING TSUKIMI...
SHE WAS PROBABLY PETRIFIED BY THE STYLISH RESTAURANT...
AND MYSTIFIED BY THE FOOD AND THE WINE...
AND MAJORLY TWITCHY, SINCE SHE DIDN'T KNOW THE RIGHT TABLE MANNERS...
AND BEING TWITCHY, SHE KNOCKED OVER HER WINE AND SENT HER KNIFE FLYING WHEN SHE USED TOO MUCH FORCE TRYING TO CUT HER STEAK...
Gah!
fweee
thunk
?!
YEEK!
...AND EVERYTHING FELL APART.
THAT'D BE NICE, ANYWAY.

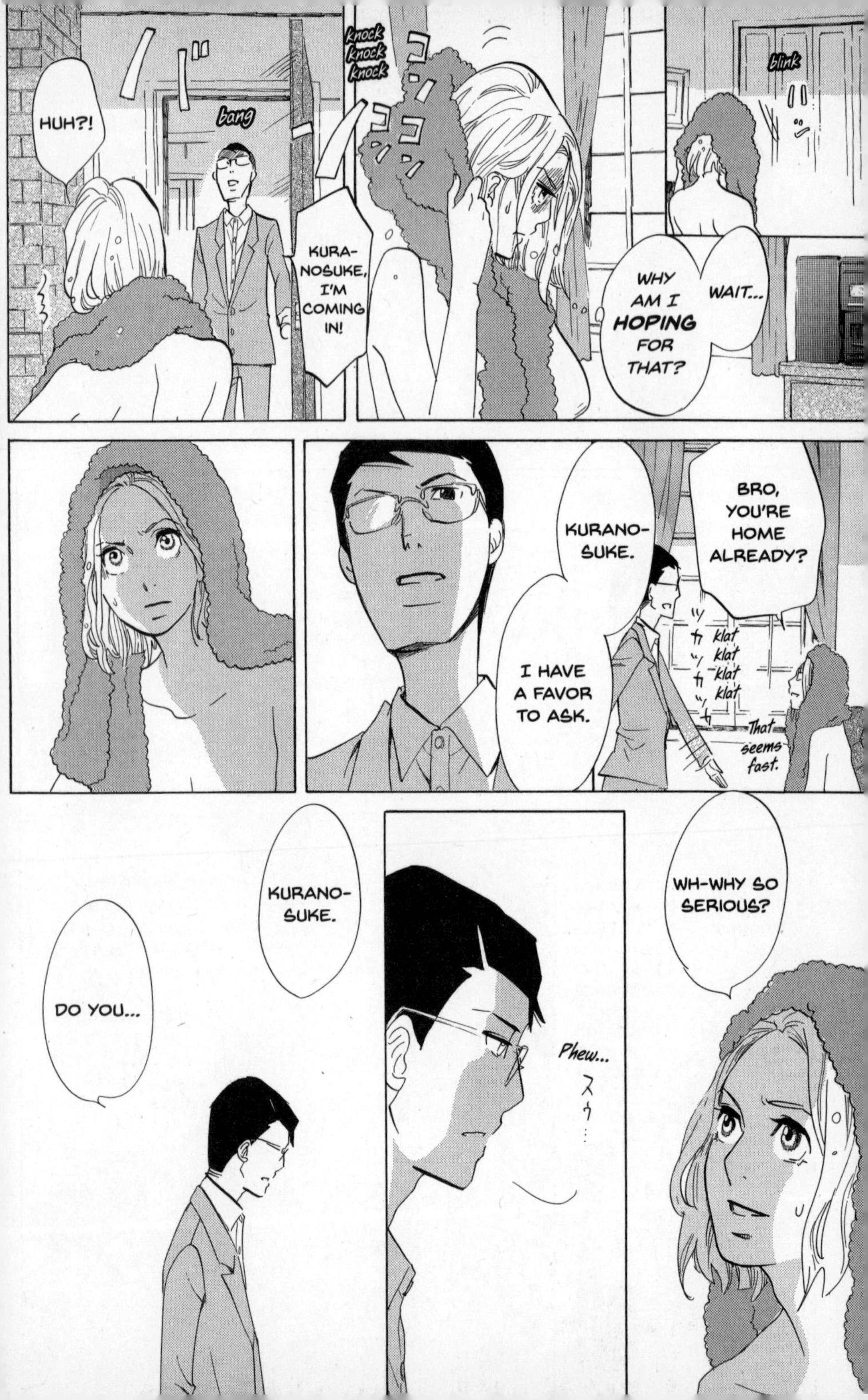
blink
WAIT...
WHY AM I HOPING FOR THAT?
knock knock knock
KURA-NOSUKE, I'M COMING IN!
bang
HUH?!
BRO, YOU'RE HOME ALREADY?
klat klat klat klat
That seems fast.
KURANO-SUKE.
I HAVE A FAVOR TO ASK.
WH-WHY SO SERIOUS?
Phew...
KURANO-SUKE.
DO YOU...

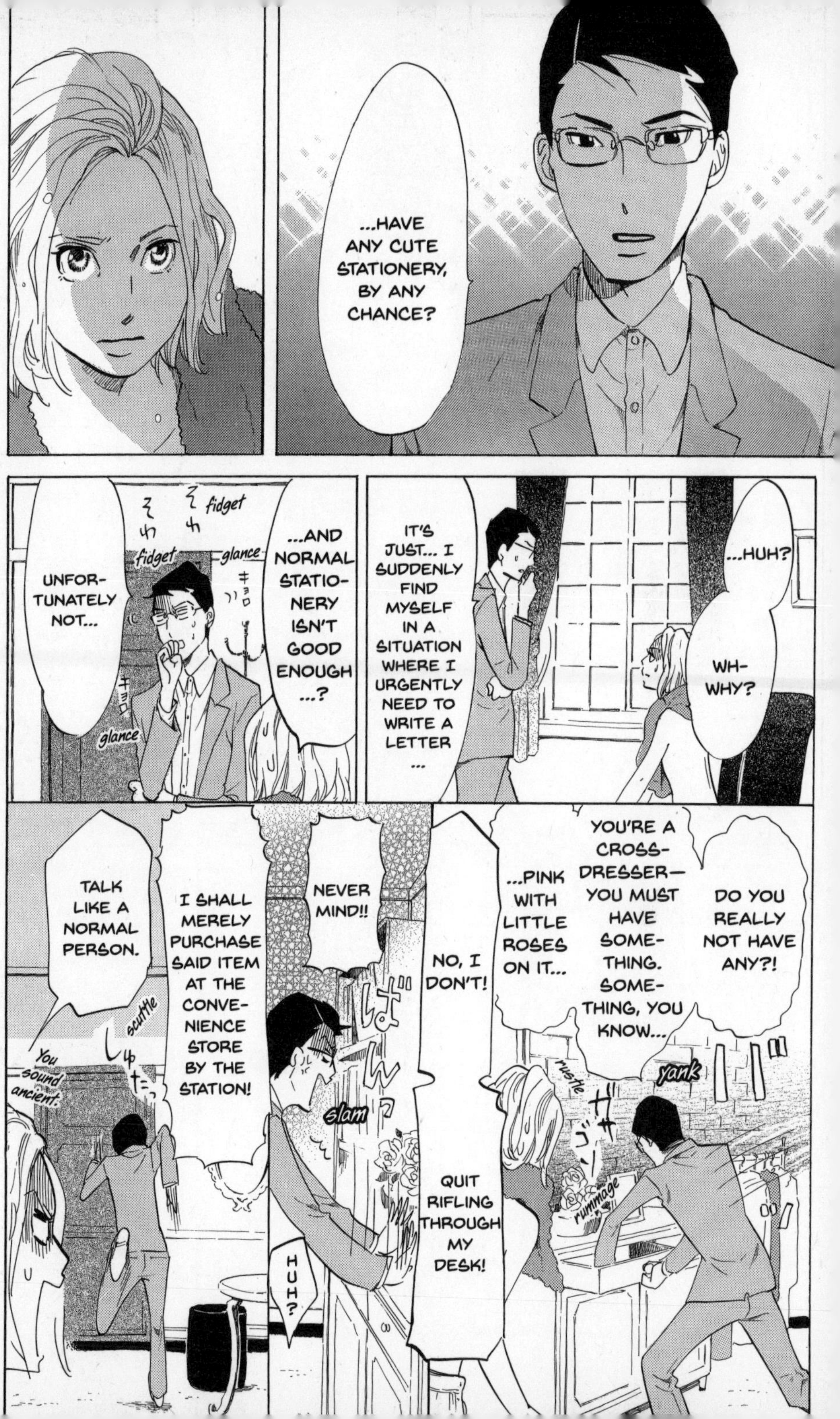
...HAVE ANY CUTE STATIONERY, BY ANY CHANCE?
...HUH?
WH-WHY?
IT'S JUST... I SUDDENLY FIND MYSELF IN A SITUATION WHERE I URGENTLY NEED TO WRITE A LETTER...
...AND NORMAL STATIONERY ISN'T GOOD ENOUGH...?
fidget
fidget
glance
UNFORTUNATELY NOT...
glance
DO YOU REALLY NOT HAVE ANY?!
YOU'RE A CROSS-DRESSER—YOU MUST HAVE SOMETHING. SOMETHING, YOU KNOW...
...PINK WITH LITTLE ROSES ON IT...
yank
rustle
rummage
NO, I DON'T!
QUIT RIFLING THROUGH MY DESK!
NEVER MIND!!
slam
HUH?
I SHALL MERELY PURCHASE SAID ITEM AT THE CONVENIENCE STORE BY THE STATION!
TALK LIKE A NORMAL PERSON.
scuttle
You sound ancient.

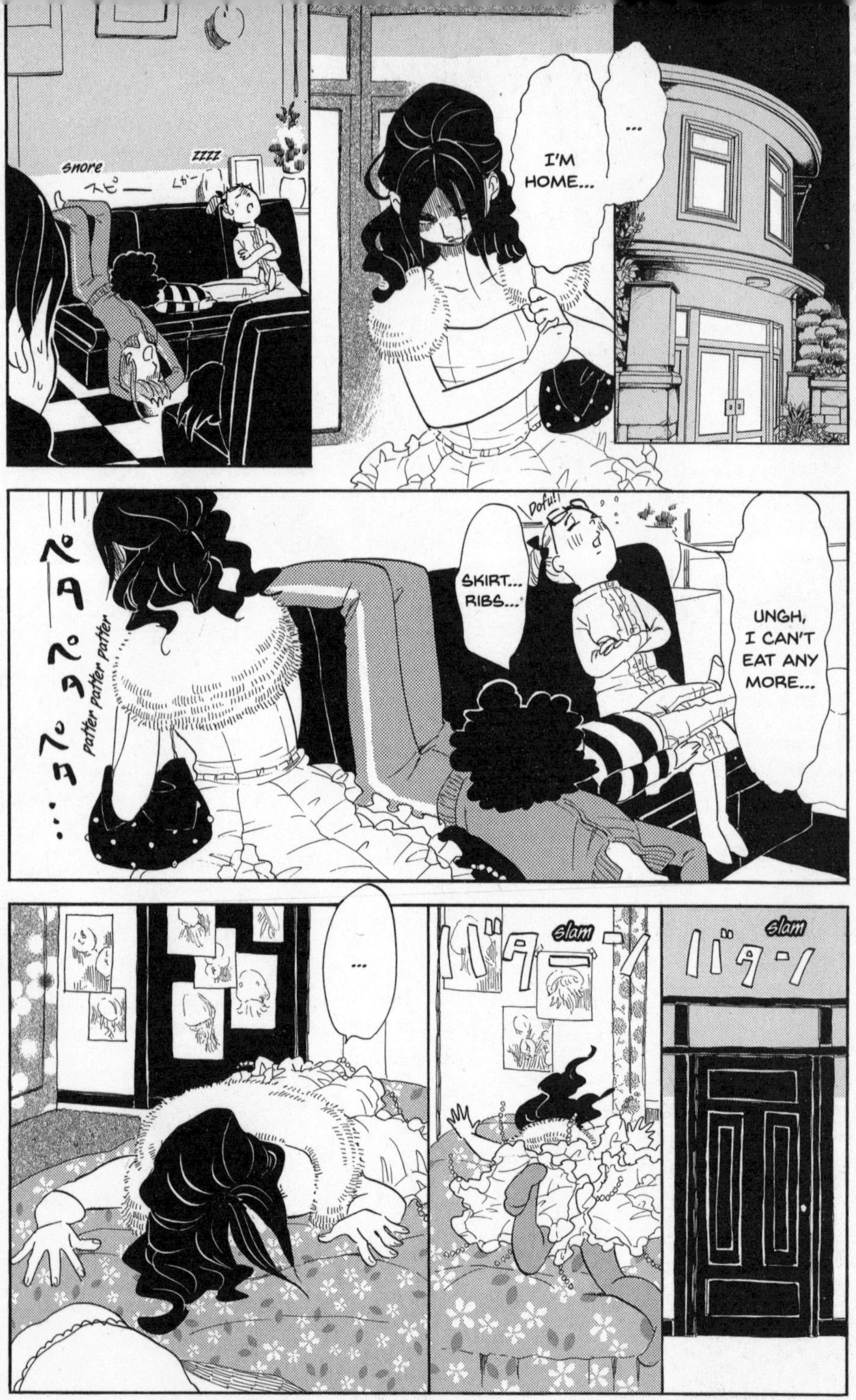
...
I'M HOME...
ZZZZ
ムガー
snore
スピー
UNGH, I CAN'T EAT ANY MORE...
Dofu!
SKIRT... RIBS...
ペタペタ...
patter patter patter
slam
バターン
slam
バターン
...

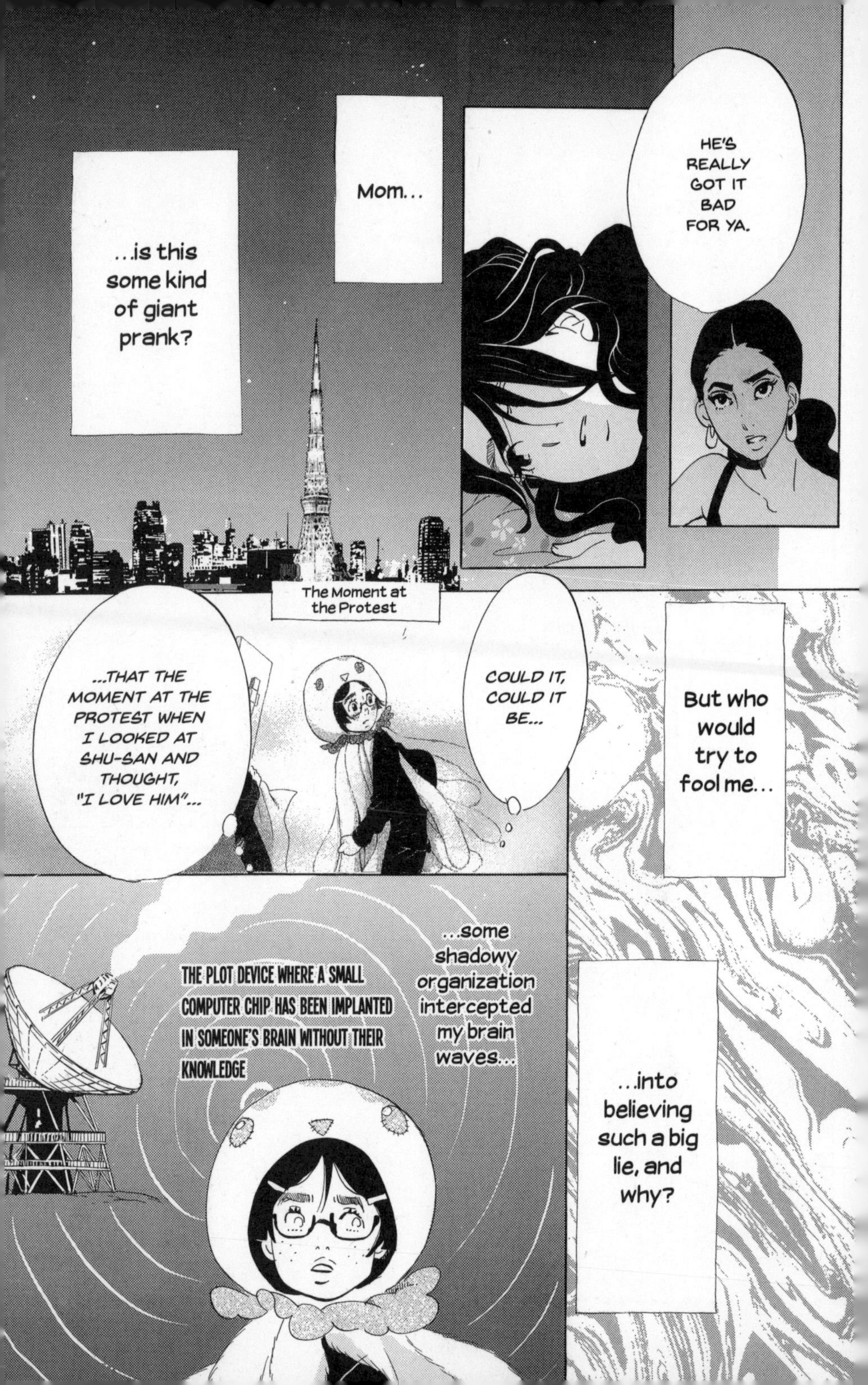
HE'S REALLY GOT IT BAD FOR YA.
Mom...
...is this some kind of giant prank?
But who would try to fool me...
...into believing such a big lie, and why?
The Moment at the Protest
COULD IT, COULD IT BE...
...THAT THE MOMENT AT THE PROTEST WHEN I LOOKED AT SHU-SAN AND THOUGHT, "I LOVE HIM"...
...some shadowy organization intercepted my brain waves...
THE PLOT DEVICE WHERE A SMALL COMPUTER CHIP HAS BEEN IMPLANTED IN SOMEONE'S BRAIN WITHOUT THEIR KNOWLEDGE

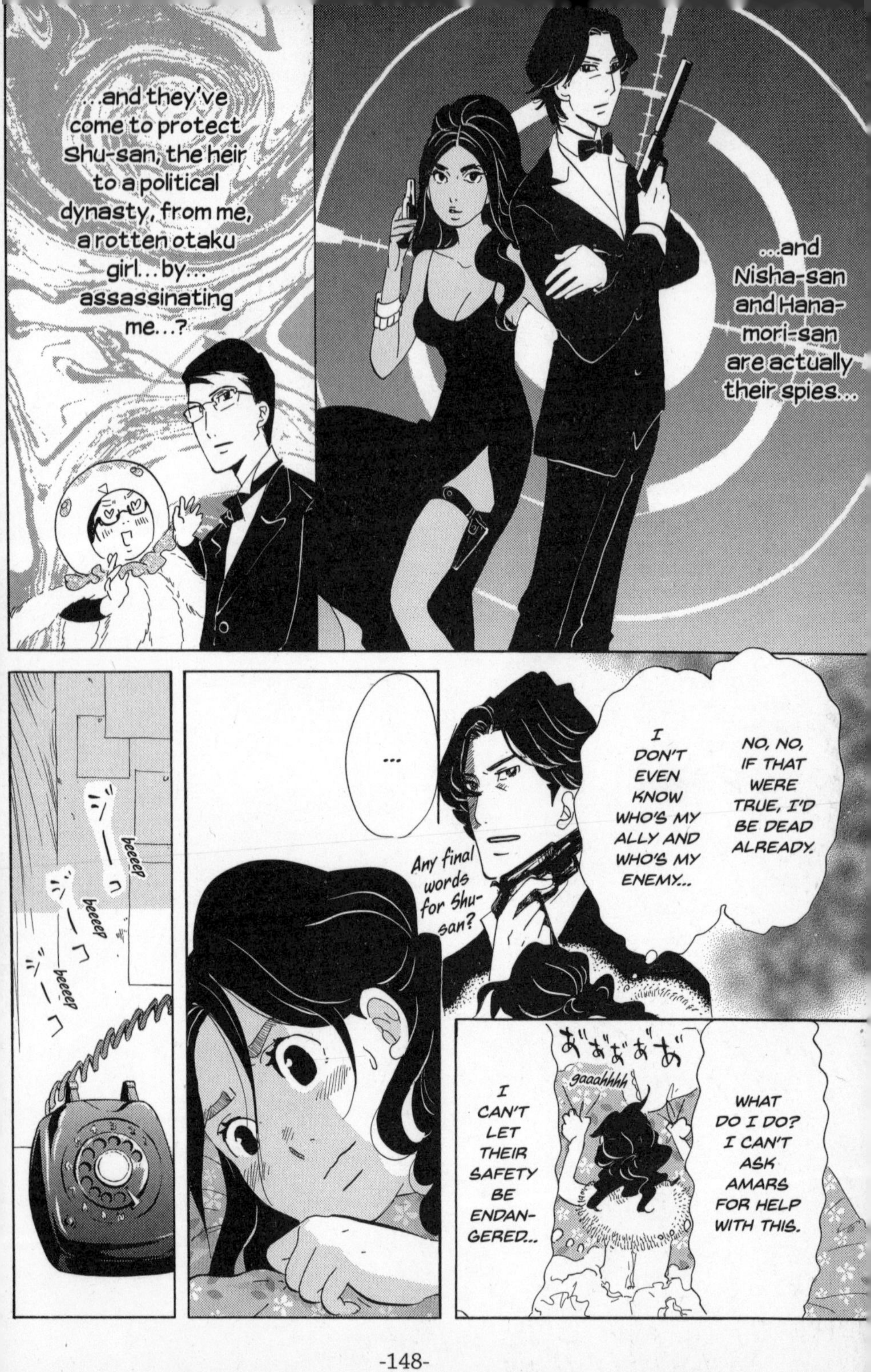

...and Nisha-san and Hana-mori-san are actually their spies...
...and they've come to protect Shu-san, the heir to a political dynasty, from me, a rotten otaku girl... by... assassinating me...?
Any final words for Shu-san?
NO, NO, IF THAT WERE TRUE, I'D BE DEAD ALREADY.
I DON'T EVEN KNOW WHO'S MY ALLY AND WHO'S MY ENEMY...
gaaahhhh
WHAT DO I DO? I CAN'T ASK AMARS FOR HELP WITH THIS.
I CAN'T LET THEIR SAFETY BE ENDAN-GERED...
...
beeeep
beeeep
beeeep

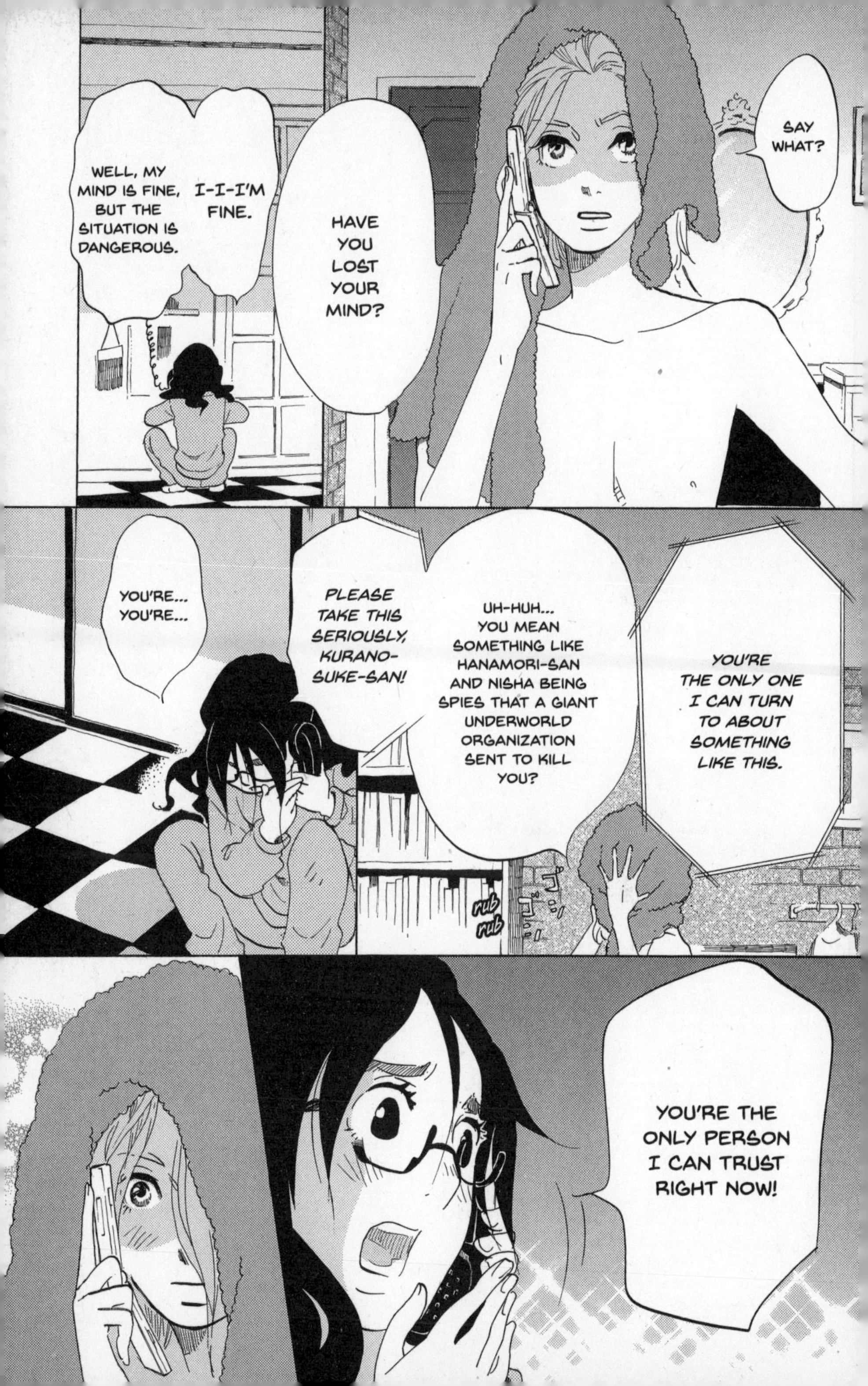
SAY WHAT?
HAVE YOU LOST YOUR MIND?
I-I-I'M FINE.
WELL, MY MIND IS FINE, BUT THE SITUATION IS DANGEROUS.
YOU'RE THE ONLY ONE I CAN TURN TO ABOUT SOMETHING LIKE THIS.
UH-HUH... YOU MEAN SOMETHING LIKE HANAMORI-SAN AND NISHA BEING SPIES THAT A GIANT UNDERWORLD ORGANIZATION SENT TO KILL YOU?
rub rub
PLEASE TAKE THIS SERIOUSLY, KURANO-SUKE-SAN!
YOU'RE... YOU'RE...
YOU'RE THE ONLY PERSON I CAN TRUST RIGHT NOW!

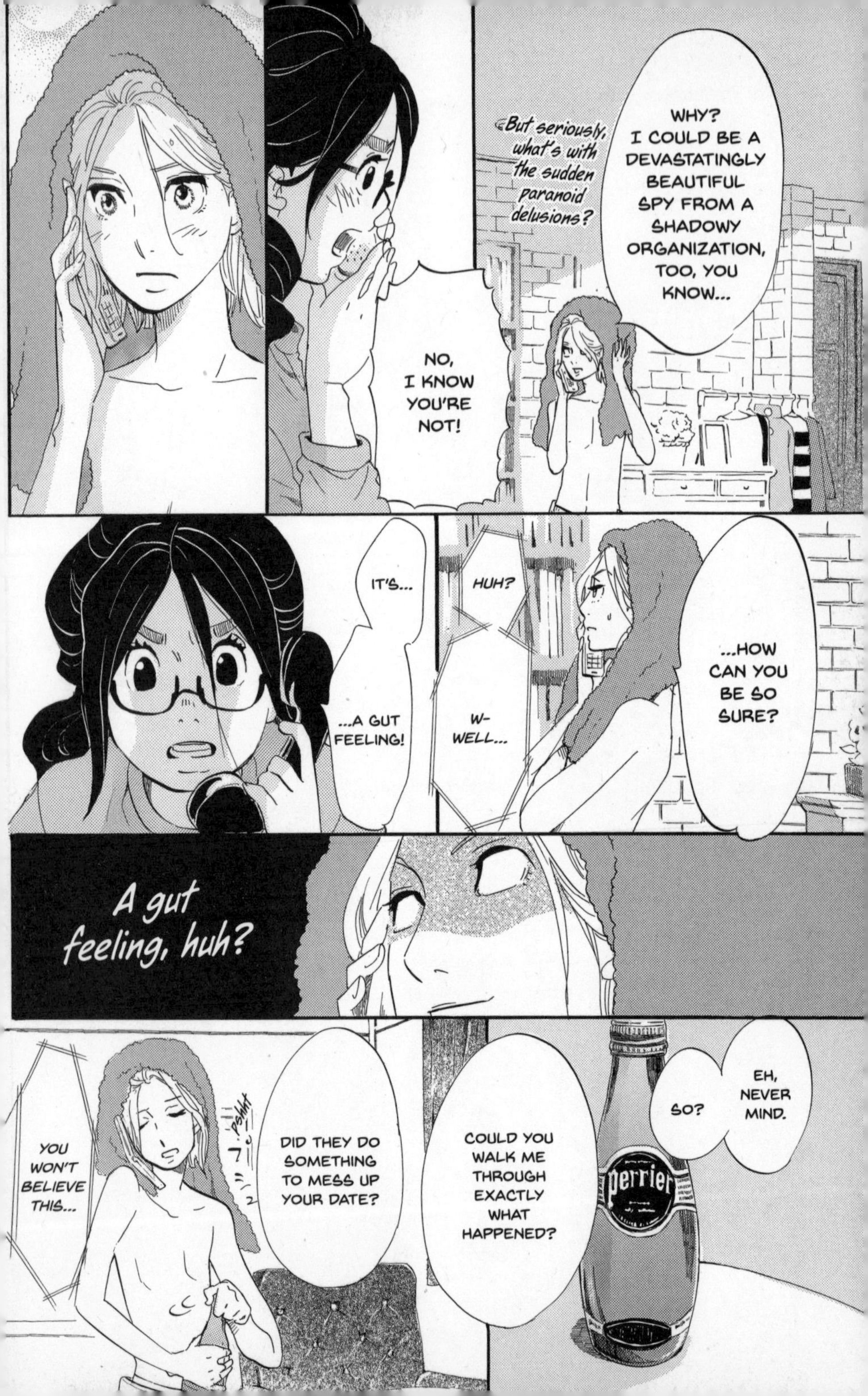

But seriously, what's with the sudden paranoid delusions?
WHY? I COULD BE A DEVASTATINGLY BEAUTIFUL SPY FROM A SHADOWY ORGANIZATION, TOO, YOU KNOW...
NO, I KNOW YOU'RE NOT!
...HOW CAN YOU BE SO SURE?
HUH?
W-WELL...
IT'S...
...A GUT FEELING!
A gut feeling, huh?
EH, NEVER MIND.
SO?
COULD YOU WALK ME THROUGH EXACTLY WHAT HAPPENED?
DID THEY DO SOMETHING TO MESS UP YOUR DATE?
pshht
YOU WON'T BELIEVE THIS...

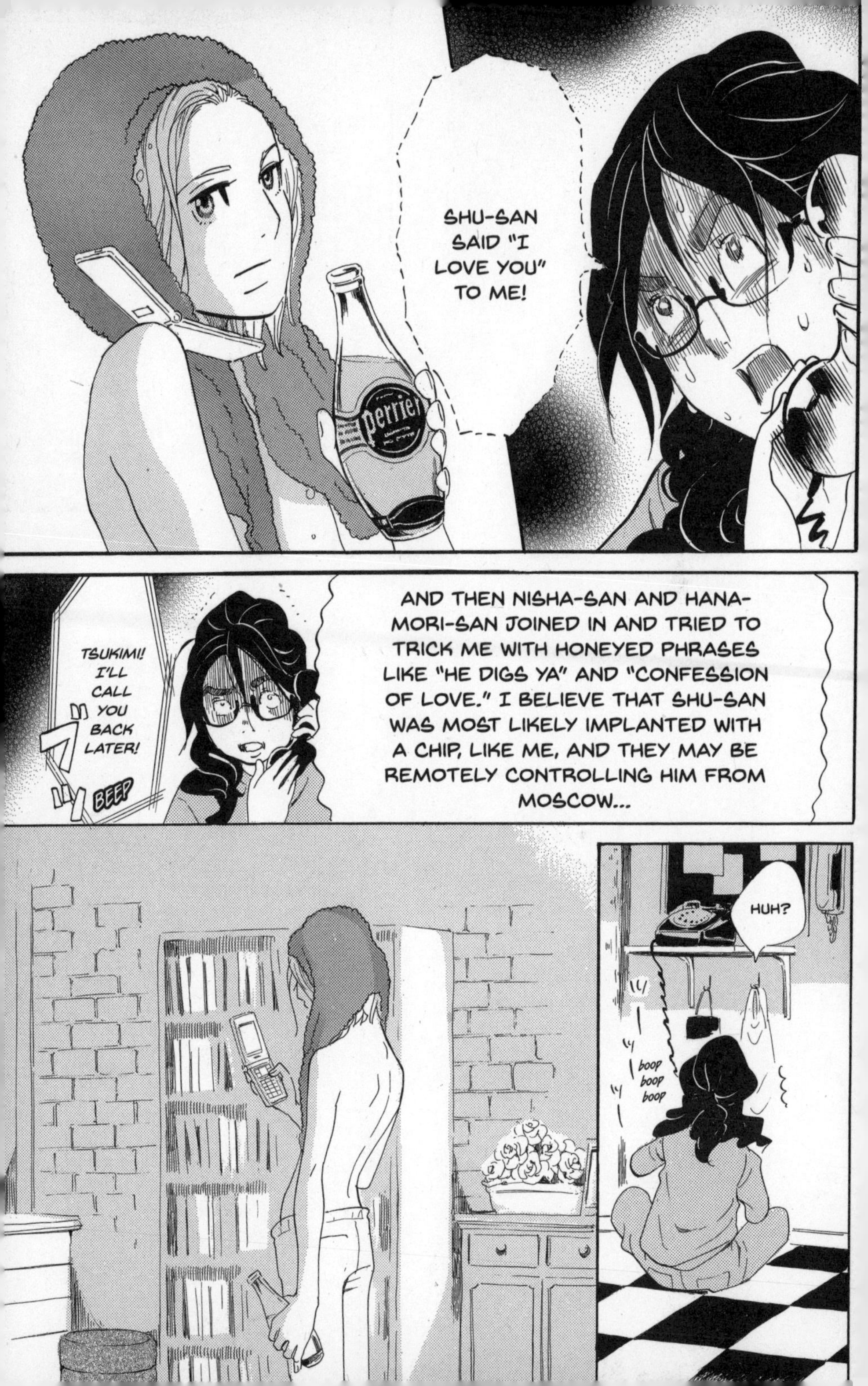
SHU-SAN SAID "I LOVE YOU" TO ME!
AND THEN NISHA-SAN AND HANA-MORI-SAN JOINED IN AND TRIED TO TRICK ME WITH HONEYED PHRASES LIKE "HE DIGS YA" AND "CONFESSION OF LOVE." I BELIEVE THAT SHU-SAN WAS MOST LIKELY IMPLANTED WITH A CHIP, LIKE ME, AND THEY MAY BE REMOTELY CONTROLLING HIM FROM MOSCOW...
TSUKIMI! I'LL CALL YOU BACK LATER!
BEEP
HUH?
boop boop boop

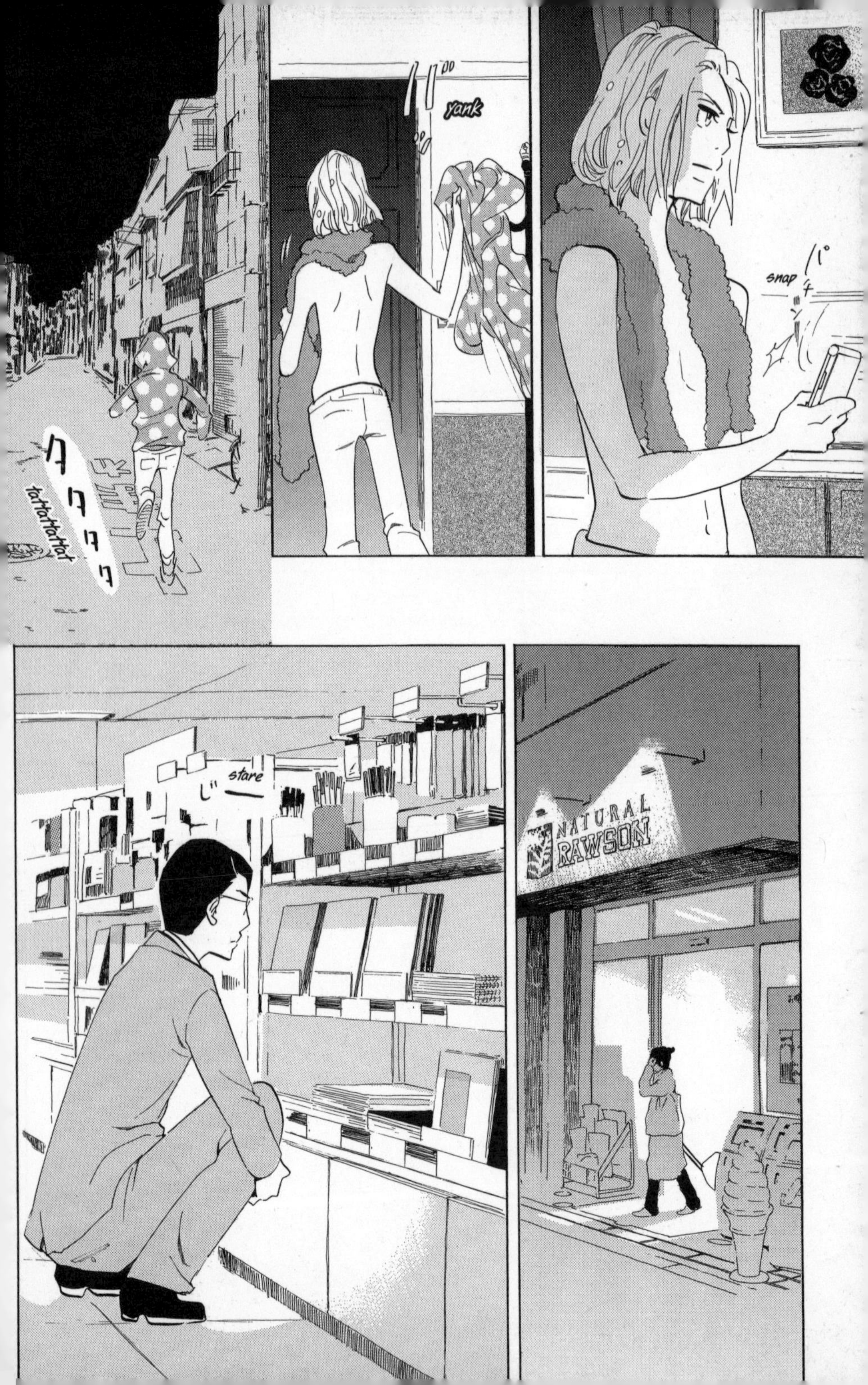
パチン
snap
yank
タタタタ
tattattattat
NATURAL
RAWSON
じー
stare

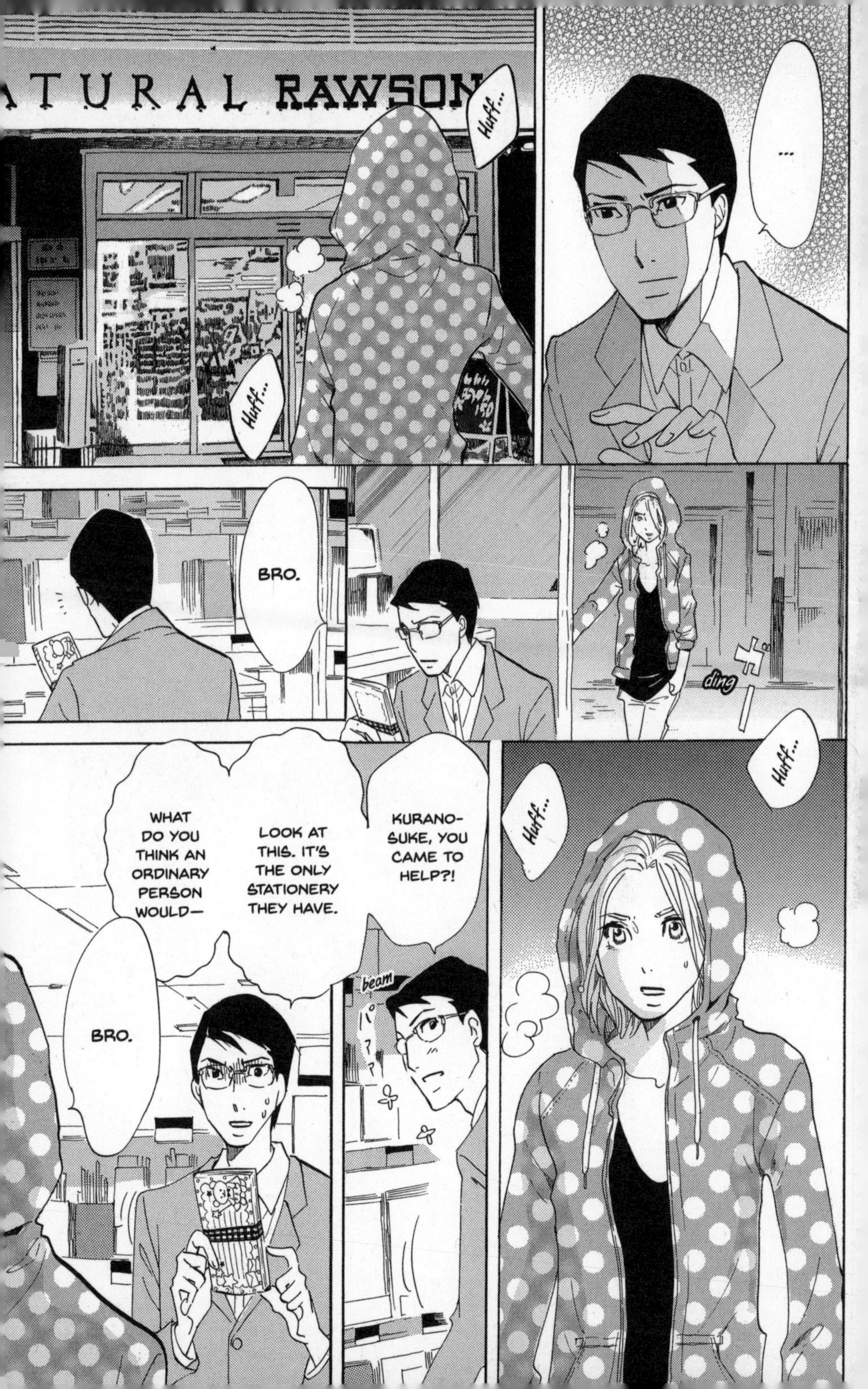
...
ATURAL RAWSON
Huff...
Huff...
ding
BRO.
Huff...
Huff...
KURANO-SUKE, YOU CAME TO HELP?!
beam
LOOK AT THIS. IT'S THE ONLY STATIONERY THEY HAVE.
WHAT DO YOU THINK AN ORDINARY PERSON WOULD—
BRO.

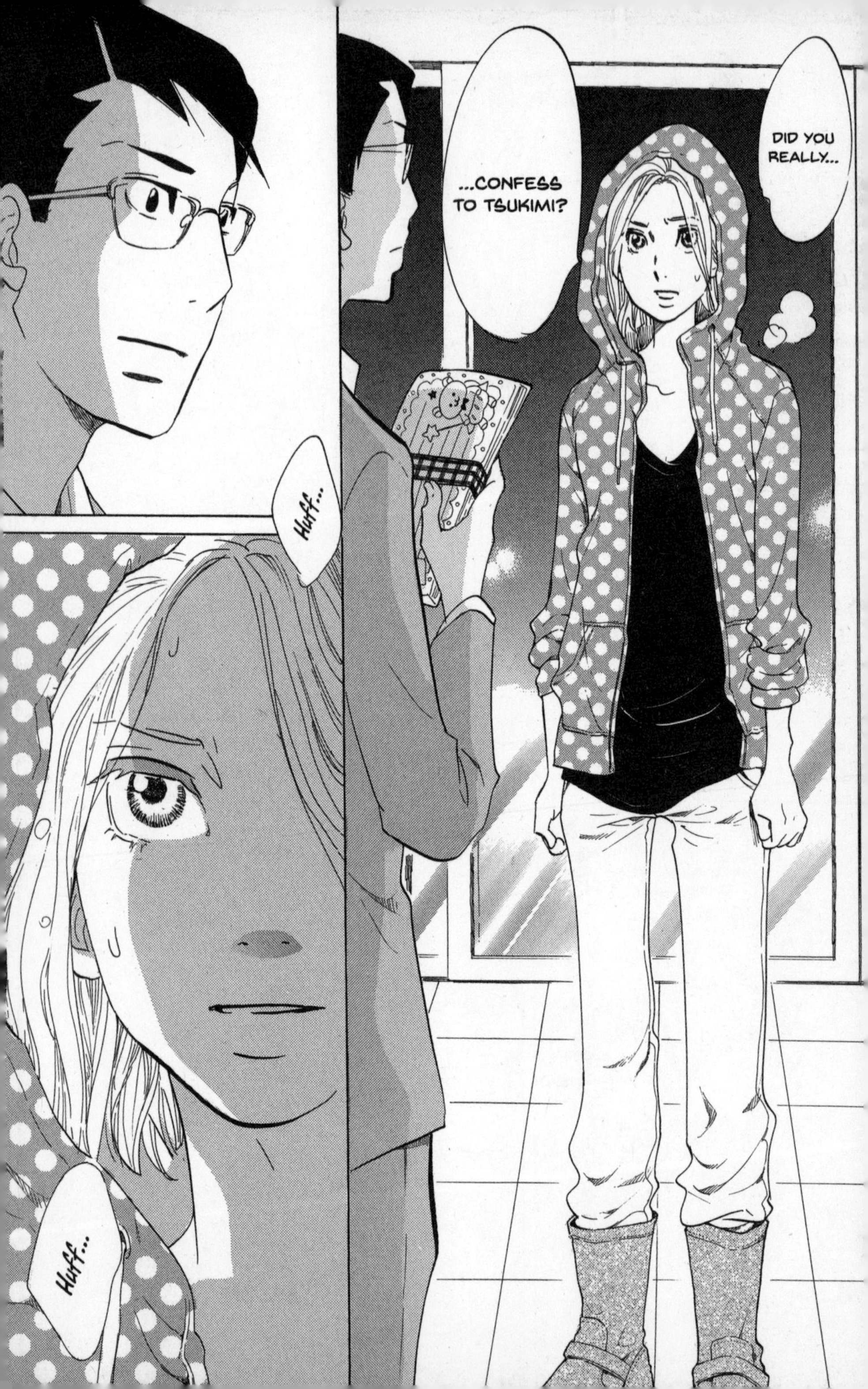
DID YOU REALLY...
...CONFESS TO TSUKIMI?
Huff...
Huff...

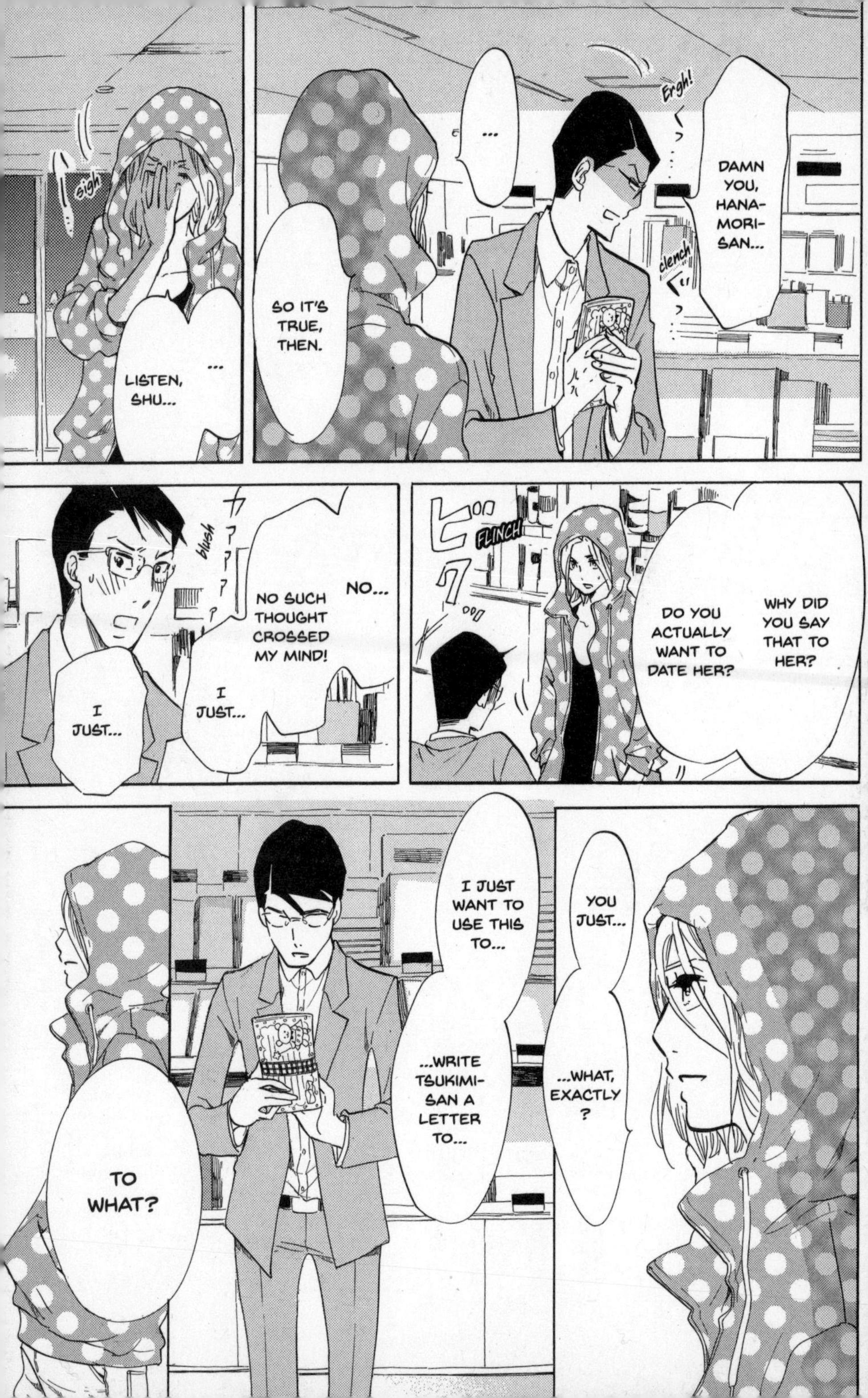
Ergh!
DAMN YOU, HANAMORI-SAN...
clench
...
SO IT'S TRUE, THEN.
sigh
LISTEN, SHU... ...
WHY DID YOU SAY THAT TO HER?
DO YOU ACTUALLY WANT TO DATE HER?
FLINCH
blush
NO...
NO SUCH THOUGHT CROSSED MY MIND!
I JUST...
I JUST...
YOU JUST...
...WHAT, EXACTLY?
I JUST WANT TO USE THIS TO...
...WRITE TSUKIMI-SAN A LETTER TO...
TO WHAT?

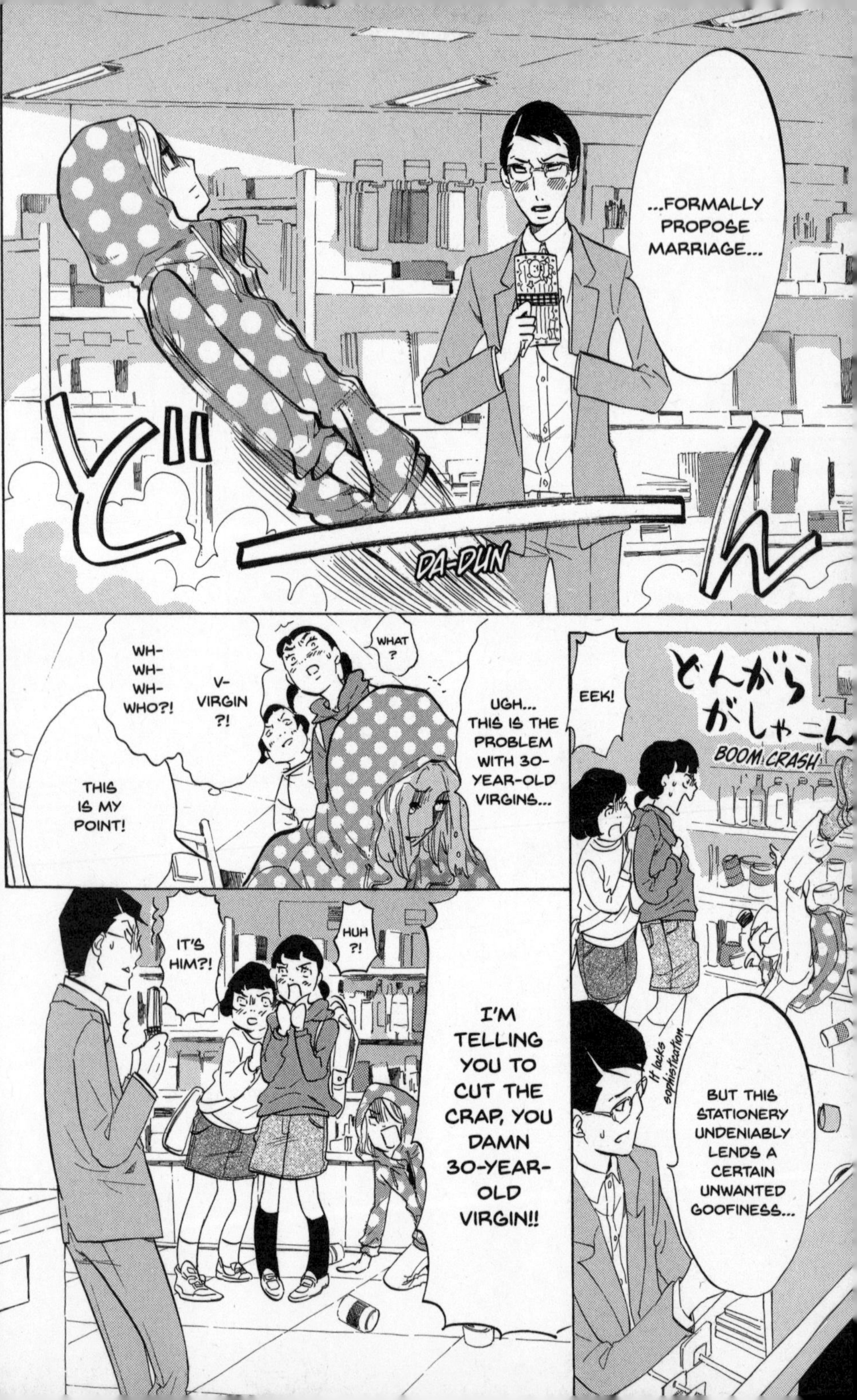

...FORMALLY PROPOSE MARRIAGE...
どーん
DA-DUN
どんがらがしゃーん
BOOM CRASH
EEK!
WHAT?
UGH... THIS IS THE PROBLEM WITH 30-YEAR-OLD VIRGINS...
WH-WH-WH-WHO?!
V-VIRGIN?!
THIS IS MY POINT!
BUT THIS STATIONERY UNDENIABLY LENDS A CERTAIN UNWANTED GOOFINESS...
It lacks sophistication.
HUH?!
IT'S HIM?!
I'M TELLING YOU TO CUT THE CRAP, YOU DAMN 30-YEAR-OLD VIRGIN!!

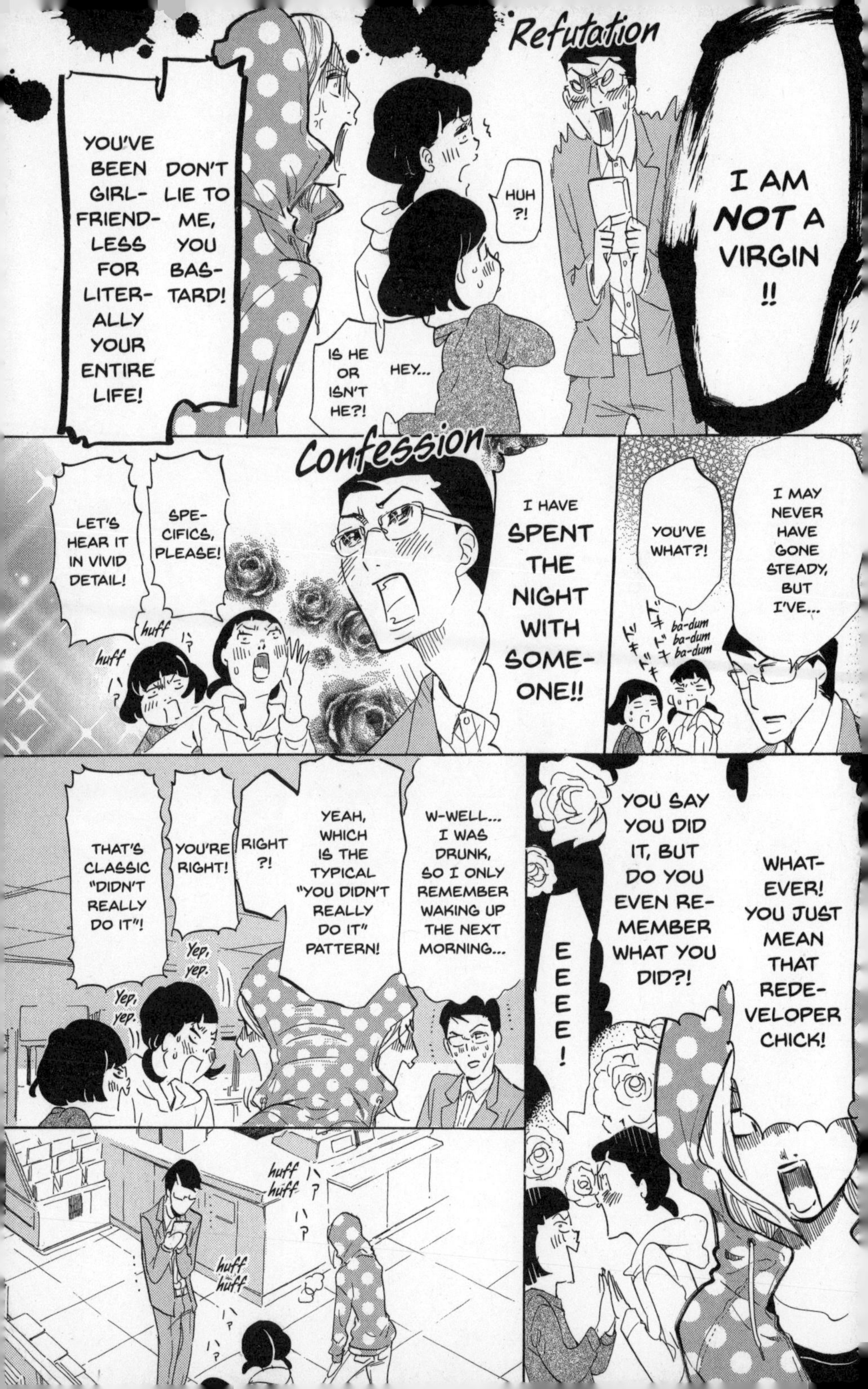
Refutation
I AM NOT A VIRGIN!!
HUH?!
HEY...
IS HE OR ISN'T HE?!
DON'T LIE TO ME, YOU BASTARD!
YOU'VE BEEN GIRLFRIEND-LESS FOR LITERALLY YOUR ENTIRE LIFE!
I MAY NEVER HAVE GONE STEADY, BUT I'VE...
YOU'VE WHAT?!
ba-dum ba-dum ba-dum
Confession
I HAVE SPENT THE NIGHT WITH SOMEONE!!
SPECIFICS, PLEASE!
LET'S HEAR IT IN VIVID DETAIL!
huff
huff
WHATEVER! YOU JUST MEAN THAT REDEVELOPER CHICK!
YOU SAY YOU DID IT, BUT DO YOU EVEN REMEMBER WHAT YOU DID?!
EEEEE!
W-WELL... I WAS DRUNK, SO I ONLY REMEMBER WAKING UP THE NEXT MORNING...
YEAH, WHICH IS THE TYPICAL "YOU DIDN'T REALLY DO IT" PATTERN!
RIGHT?!
YOU'RE RIGHT!
THAT'S CLASSIC "DIDN'T REALLY DO IT"!
Yep, yep.
Yep, yep.
huff huff
huff huff

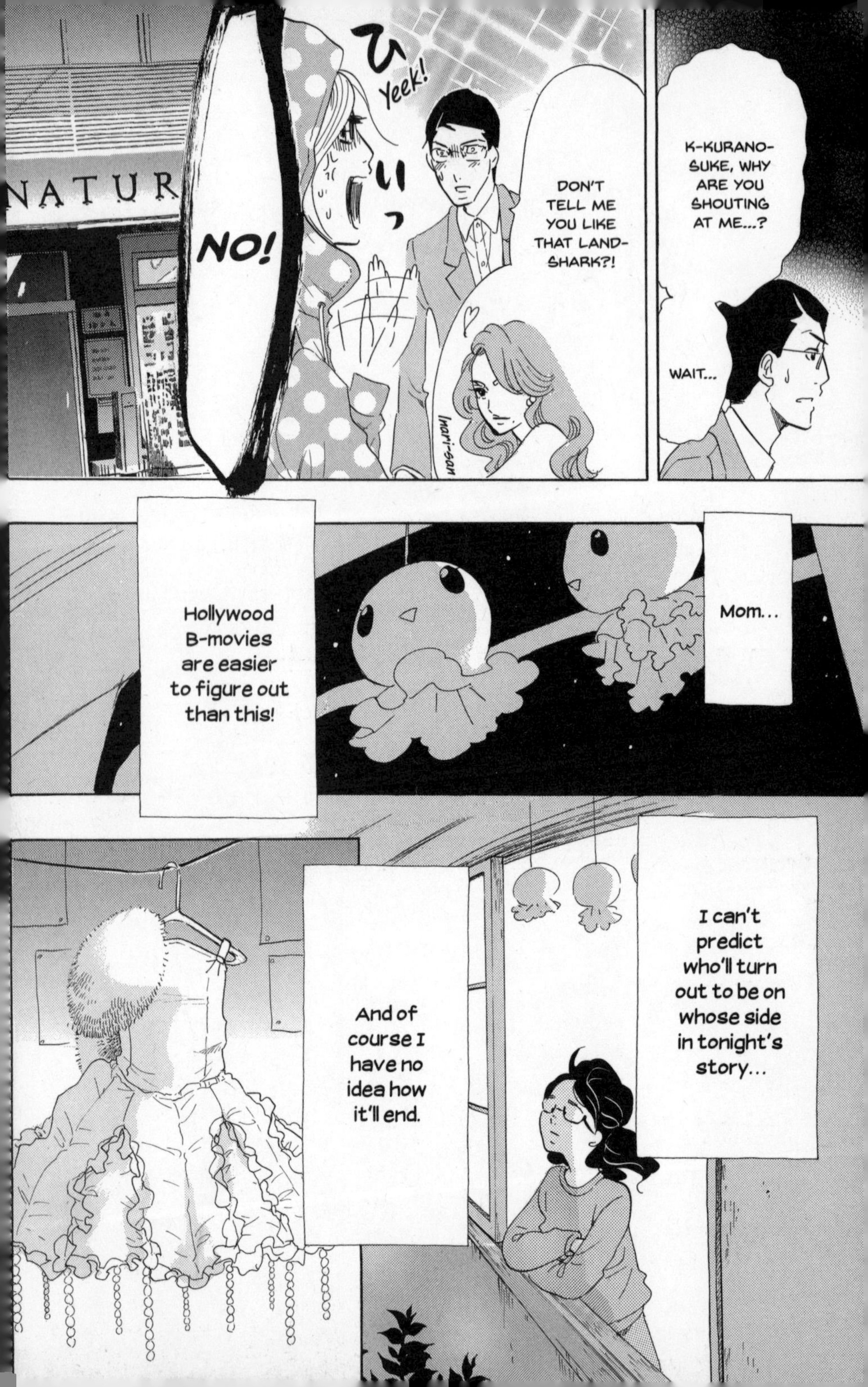
K-KURANO-SUKE, WHY ARE YOU SHOUTING AT ME...?
WAIT...
DON'T TELL ME YOU LIKE THAT LAND-SHARK?!
ひ
Yeek!
いっ
Inari-san
NATUR
NO!
Mom...
Hollywood B-movies are easier to figure out than this!
I can't predict who'll turn out to be on whose side in tonight's story...
And of course I have no idea how it'll end.

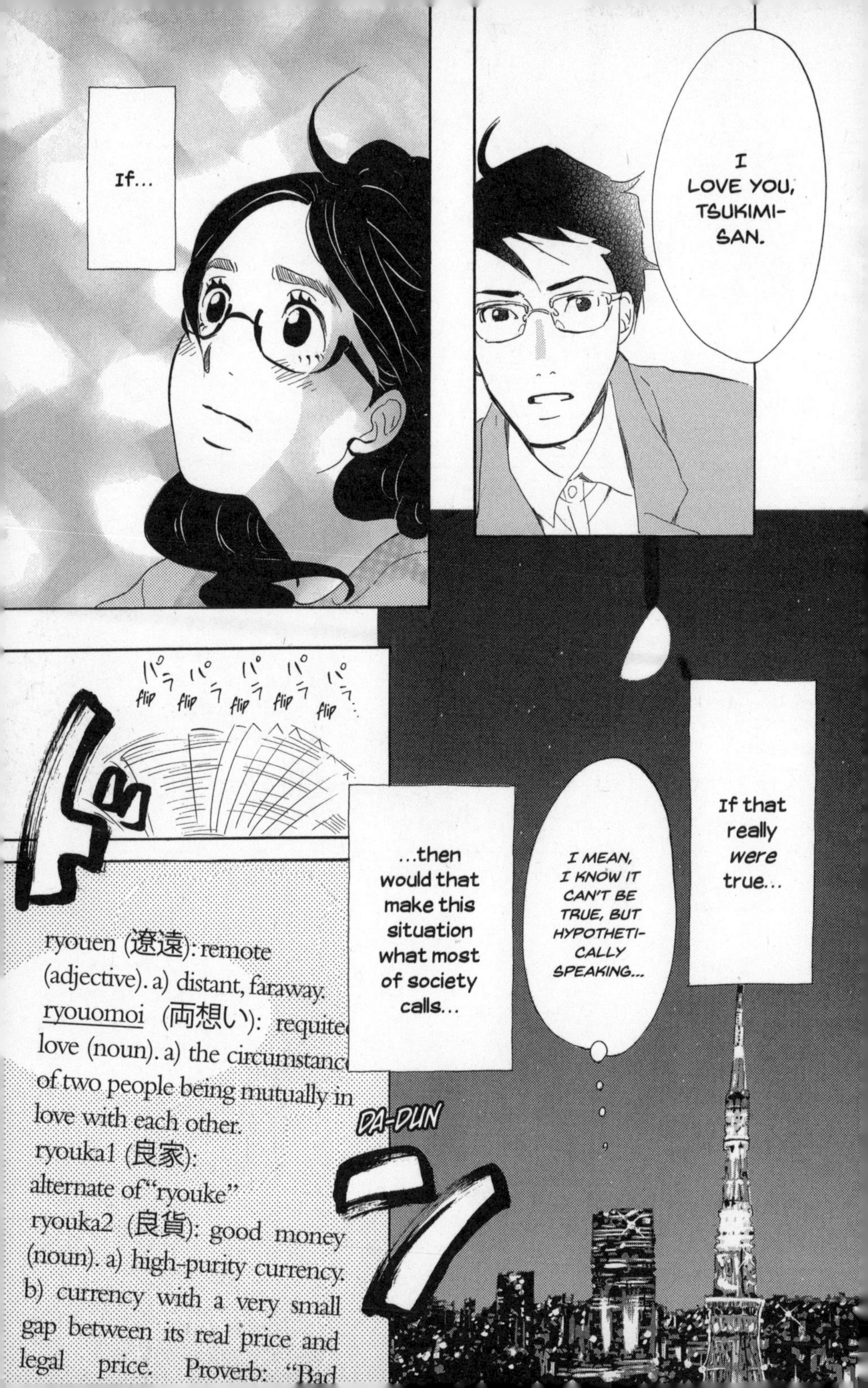

I LOVE YOU, TSUKIMI-SAN.
If...
If that really were true...
I MEAN, I KNOW IT CAN'T BE TRUE, BUT HYPOTHETICALLY SPEAKING...
...then would that make this situation what most of society calls...
パラ flip パラ flip パラ flip パラ flip パラ... flip
ryouen (遼遠): remote (adjective). a) distant, faraway.
ryouomoi (両想い): requited love (noun). a) the circumstance of two people being mutually in love with each other.
ryouka1 (良家): alternate of "ryouke"
ryouka2 (良貨): good money (noun). a) high-purity currency. b) currency with a very small gap between its real price and legal price. Proverb: "Bad
DA-DUN

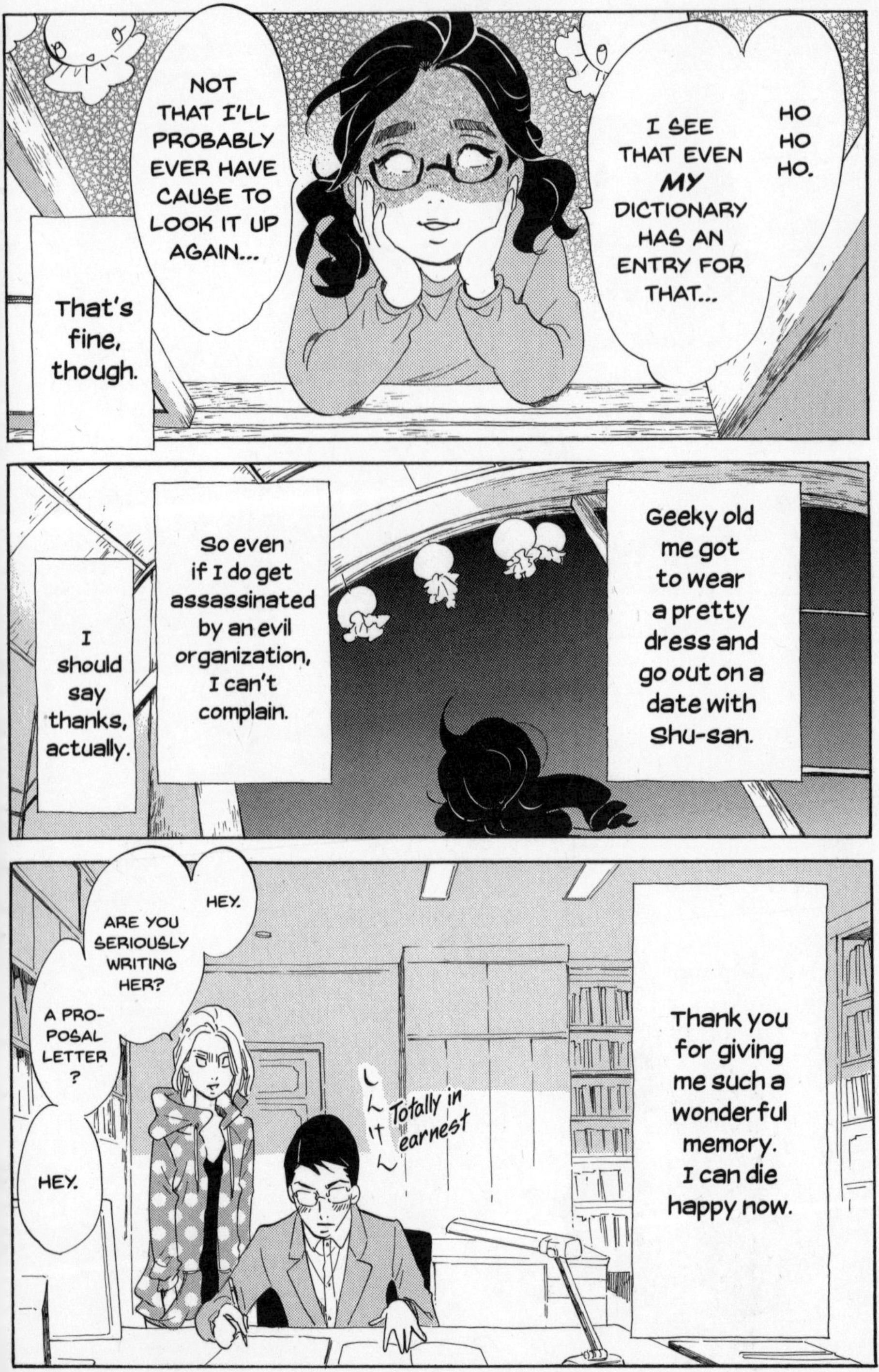
HO HO HO.
I SEE THAT EVEN MY DICTIONARY HAS AN ENTRY FOR THAT...
NOT THAT I'LL PROBABLY EVER HAVE CAUSE TO LOOK IT UP AGAIN...
That's fine, though.
Geeky old me got to wear a pretty dress and go out on a date with Shu-san.
So even if I do get assassinated by an evil organization, I can't complain.
I should say thanks, actually.
Thank you for giving me such a wonderful memory. I can die happy now.
しんけん
Totally in earnest
HEY.
ARE YOU SERIOUSLY WRITING HER? A PRO-POSAL LETTER?
HEY.

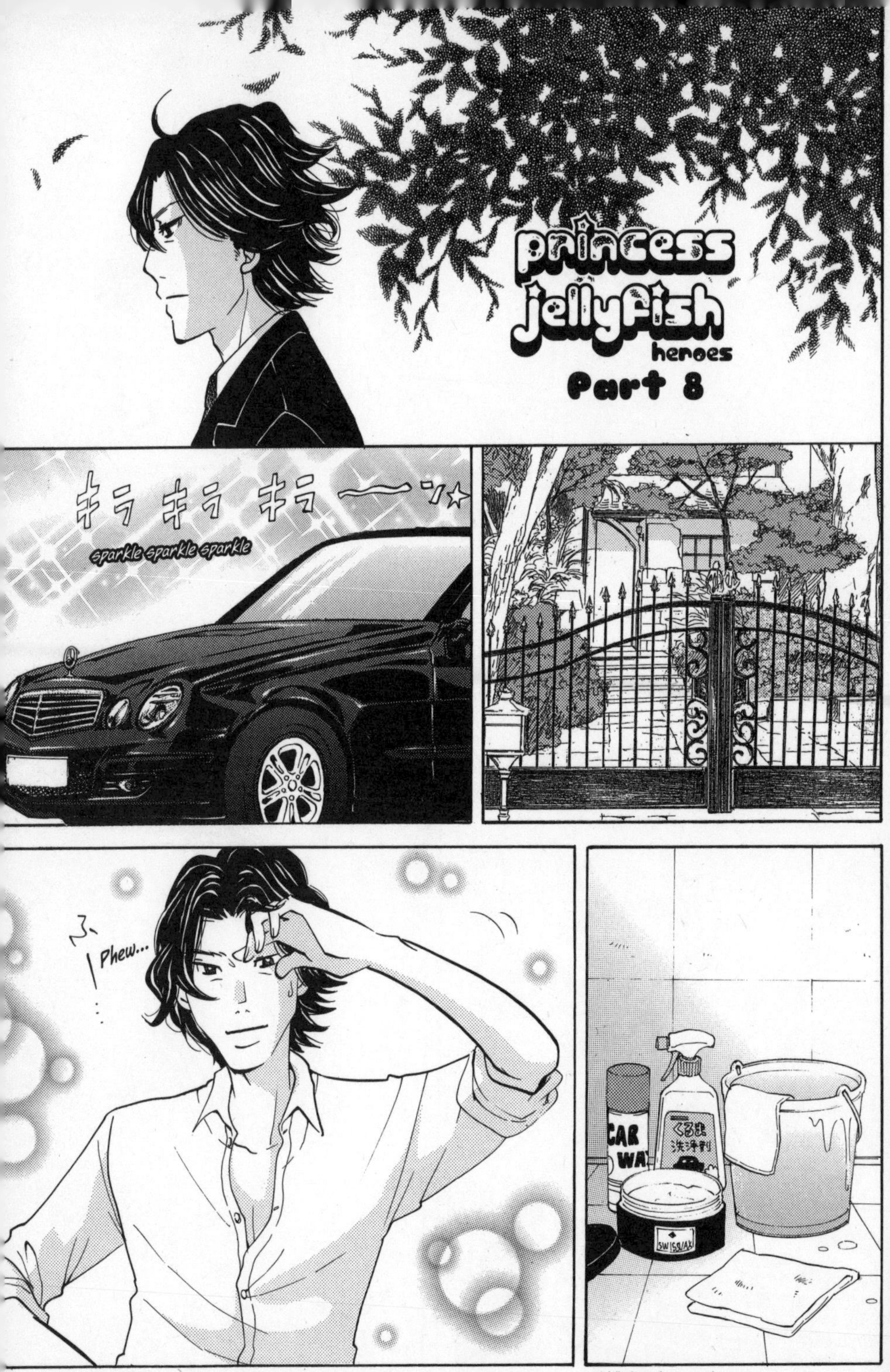
princess jellyfish heroes
Part 8
キラキラキラ〜〜ン☆
sparkle sparkle sparkle
ふ…
Phew...

Middle bottle: Car Cleaner

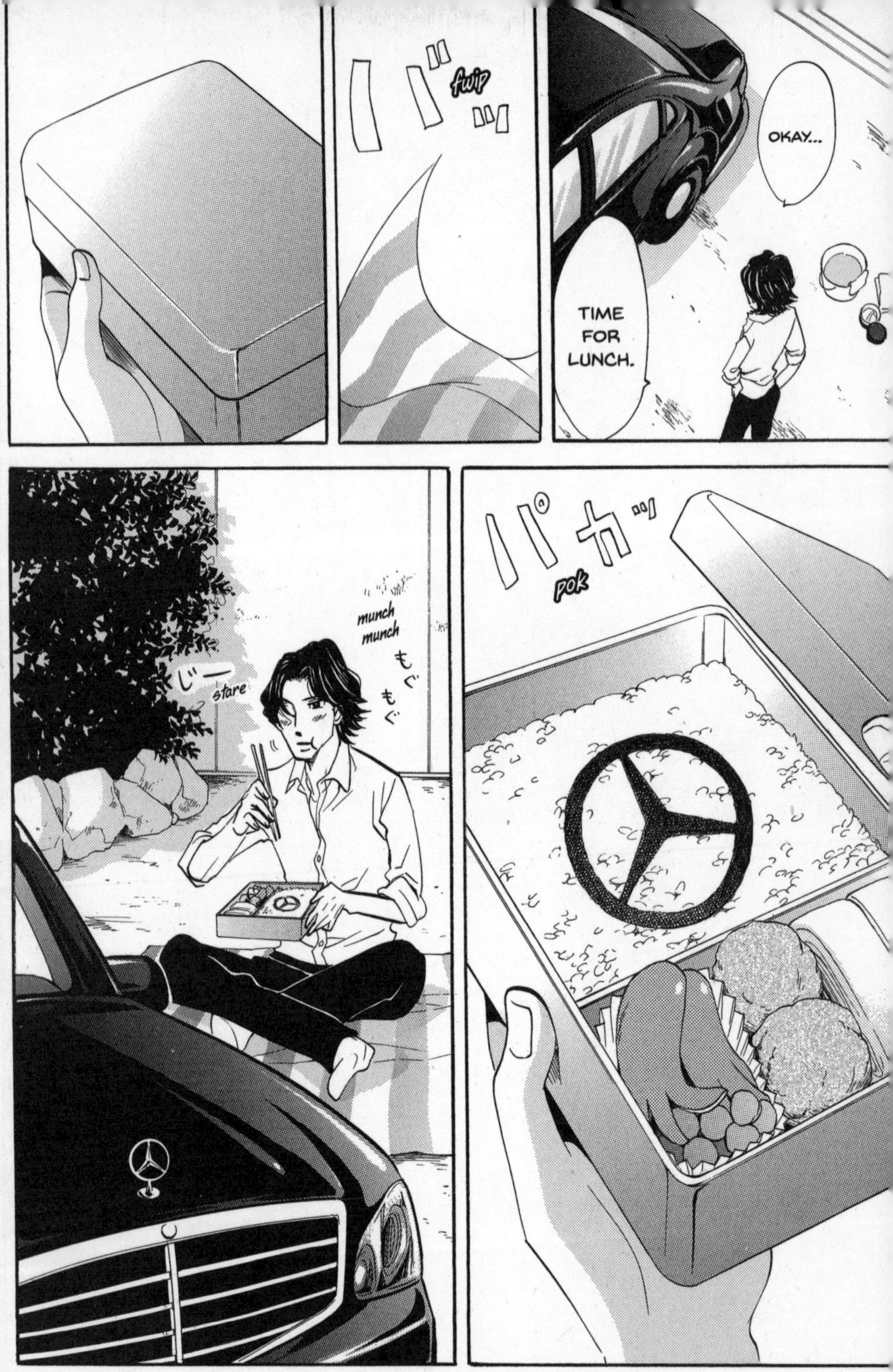
OKAY...
TIME FOR LUNCH.
fwip
パカッ
pok
munch munch
もぐもぐ
じー
stare

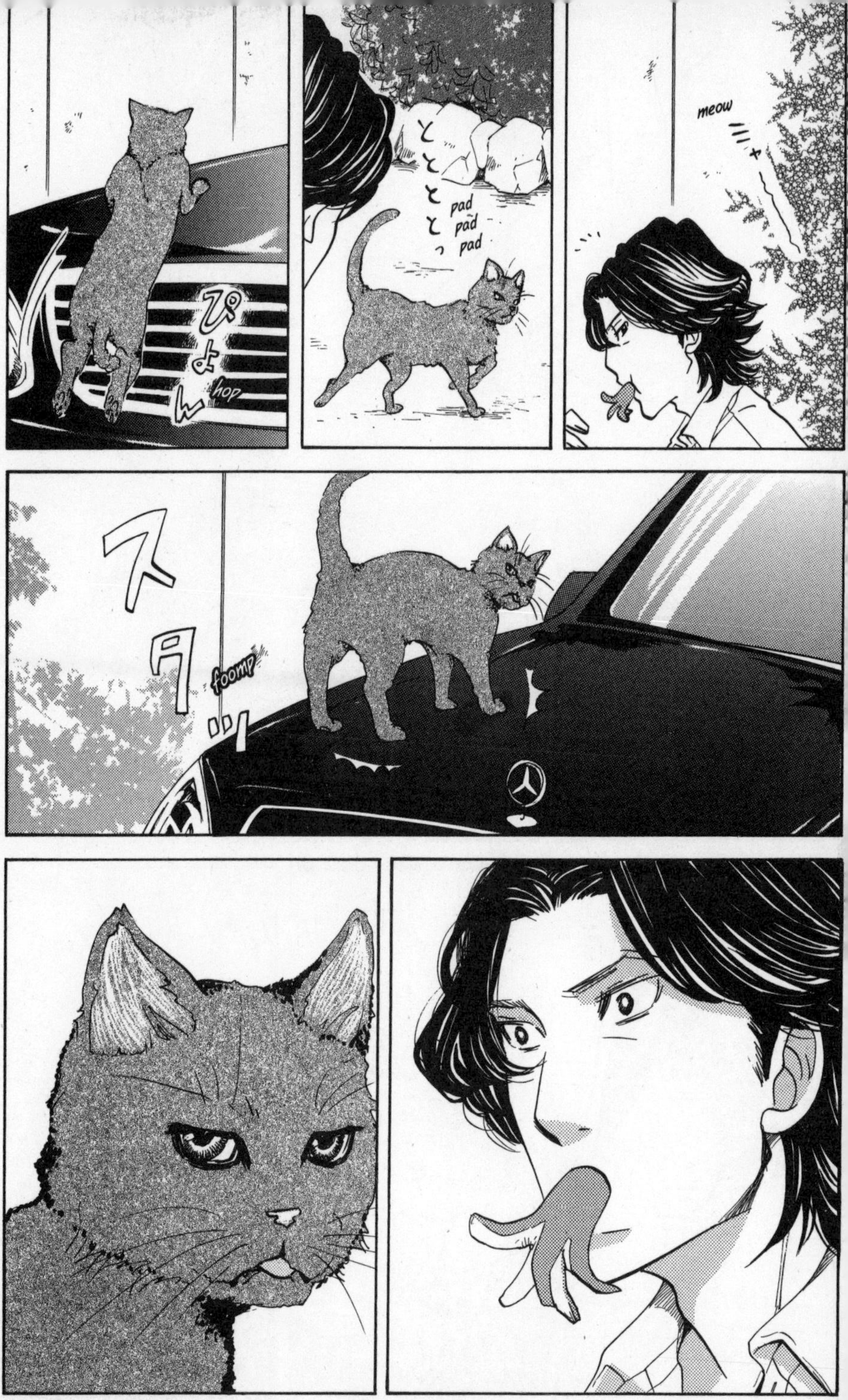
ニャ〜
meow
ととととっ
pad pad pad
ぴょん
hop
スタッ
foomp

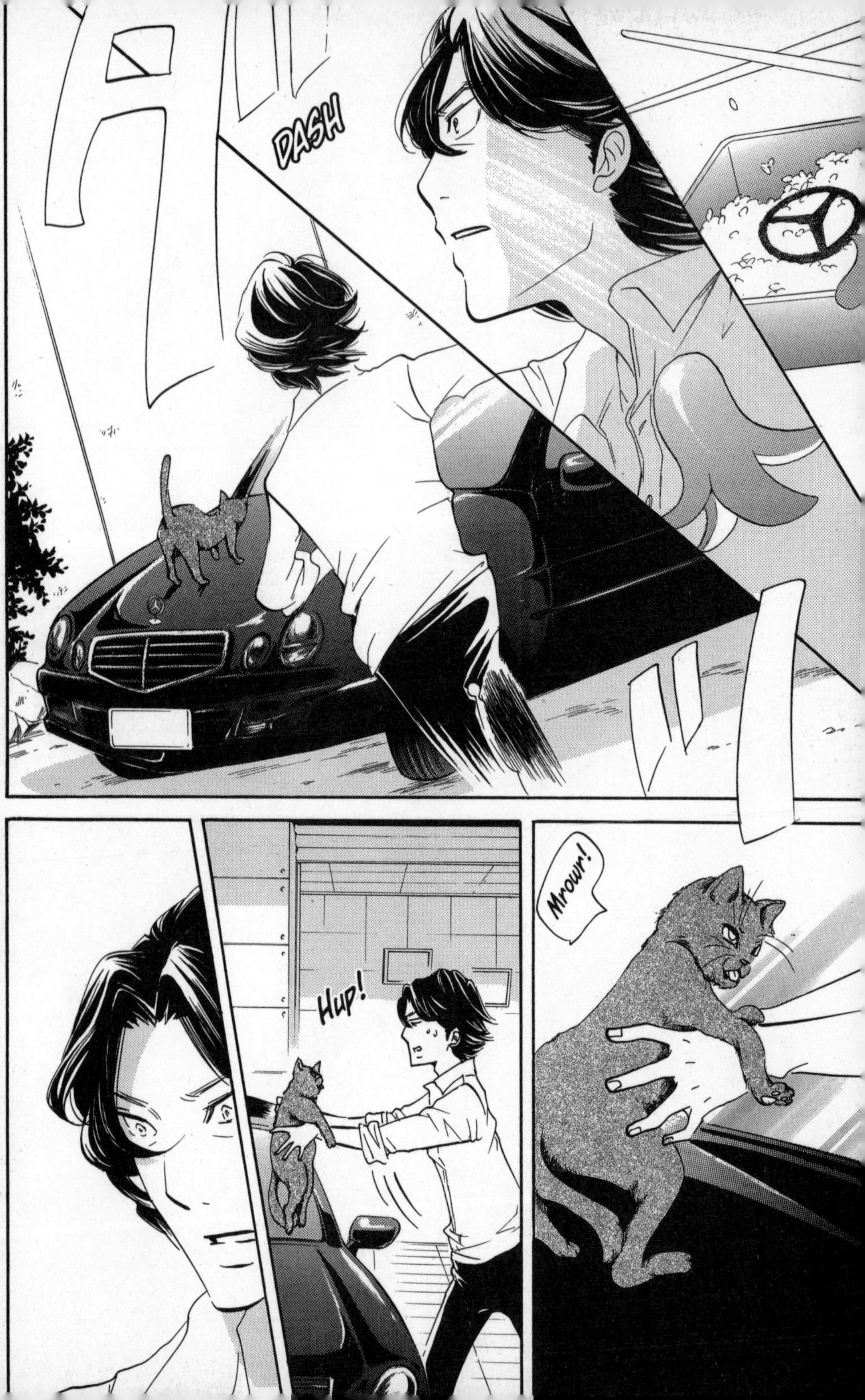
DASH
Mrowr!
Hup!

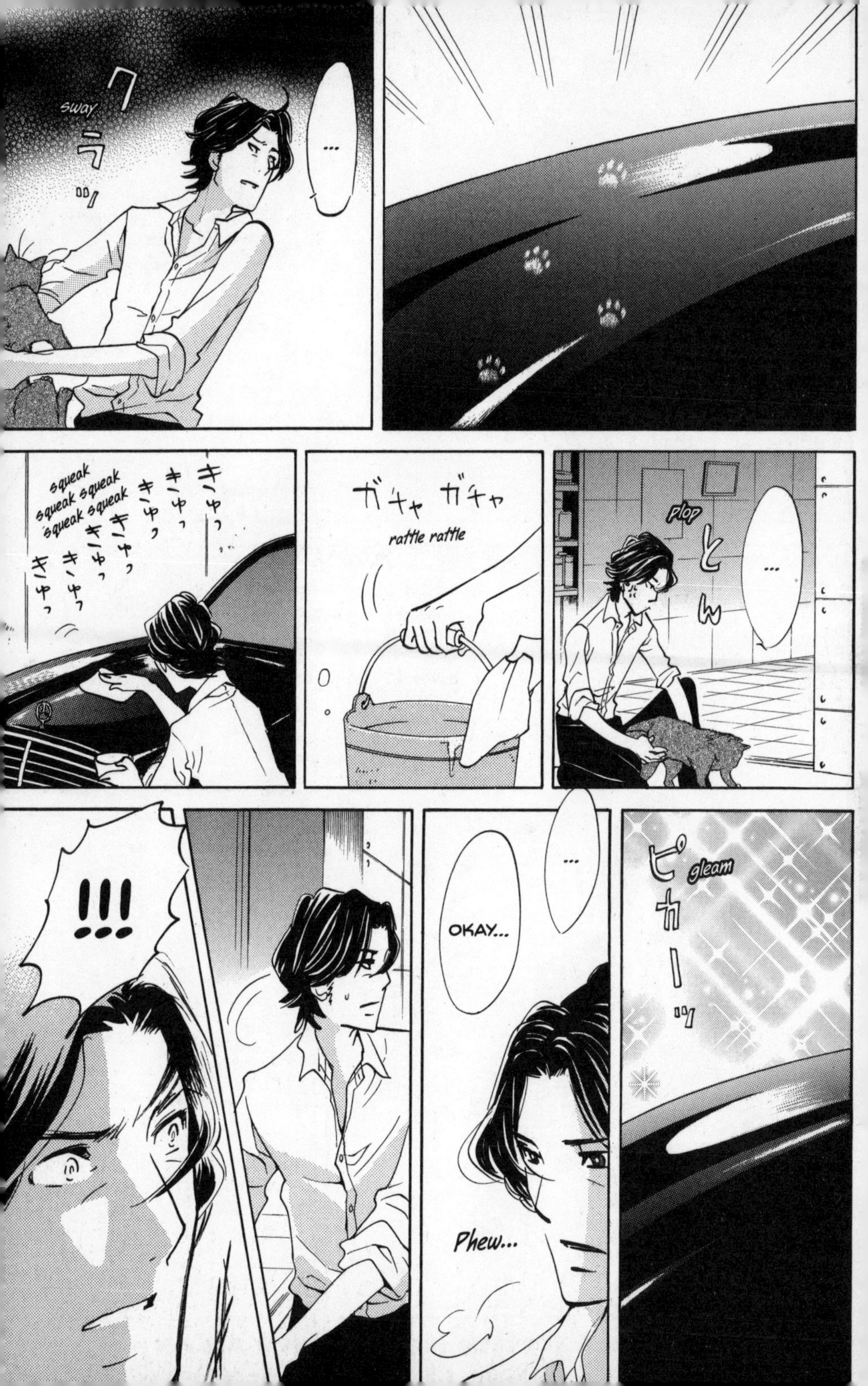
...
sway
クラッ
...
Plop
とん
ガチャ ガチャ
rattle rattle
squeak squeak squeak squeak squeak
キュッ キュッ キュッ キュッ キュッ キュッ キュッ
gleam
ピカーッ
...
OKAY...
Phew...
!!!

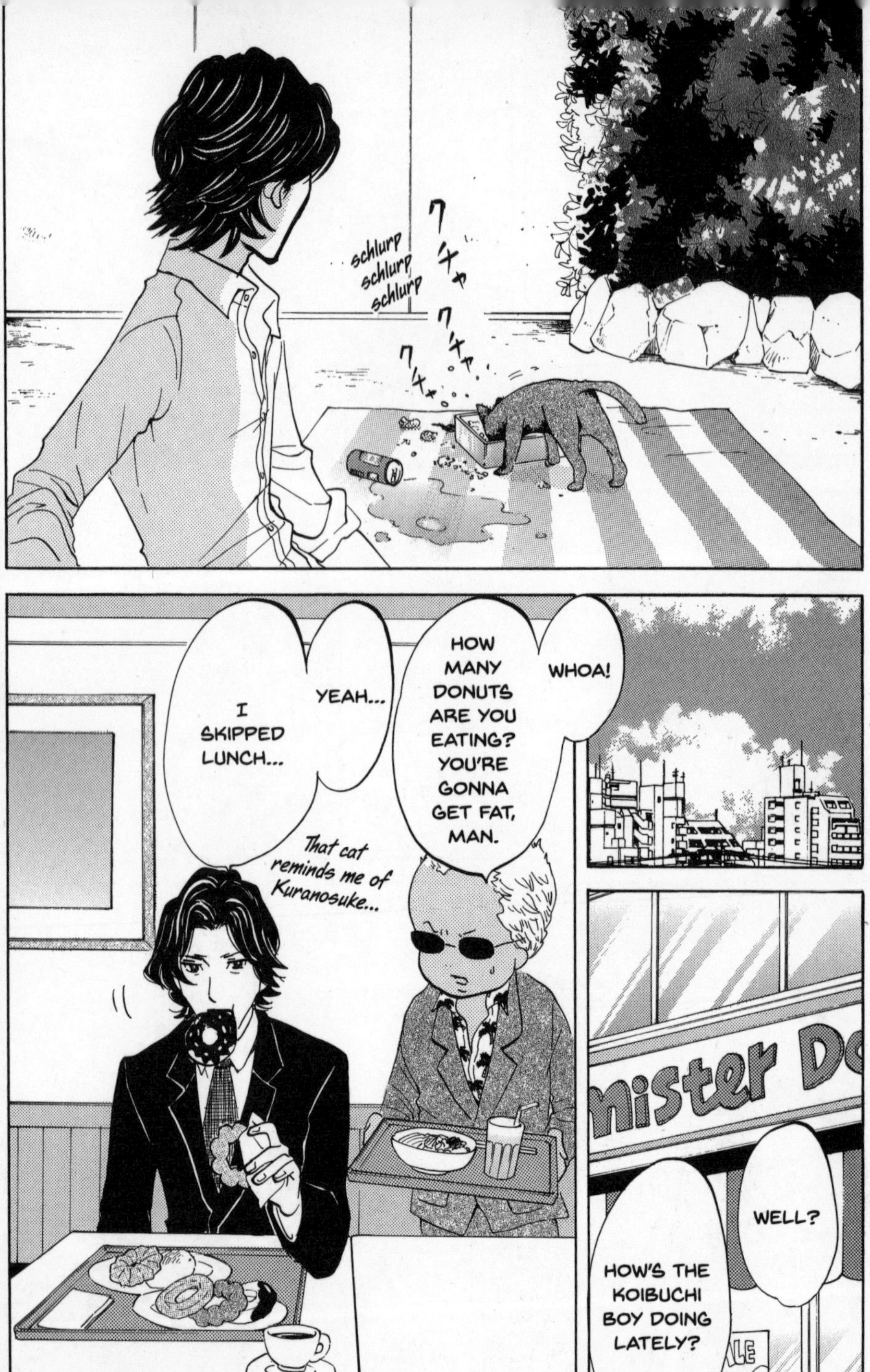
schlurp schlurp schlurp
mister Do
WELL?
HOW'S THE KOIBUCHI BOY DOING LATELY?
WHOA!
HOW MANY DONUTS ARE YOU EATING? YOU'RE GONNA GET FAT, MAN.
YEAH...
I SKIPPED LUNCH...
That cat reminds me of Kuranosuke...

Princess Jellyfish Heroes Part 8/End

...A NICE, LAVISH FRUIT TART.

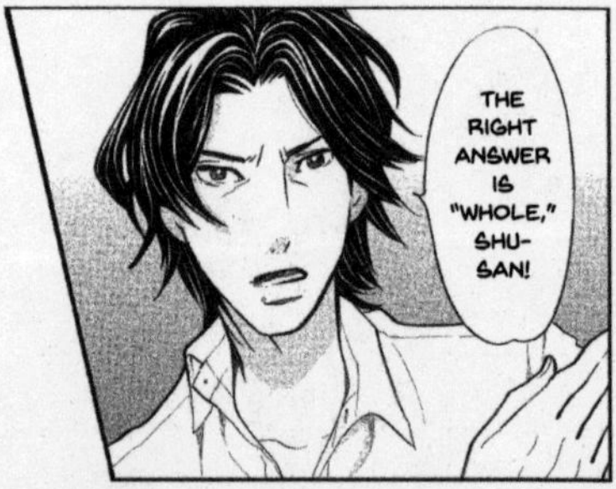
THE RIGHT ANSWER IS "WHOLE," SHU-SAN!

Bonus Manga: There's No Cure for Amars

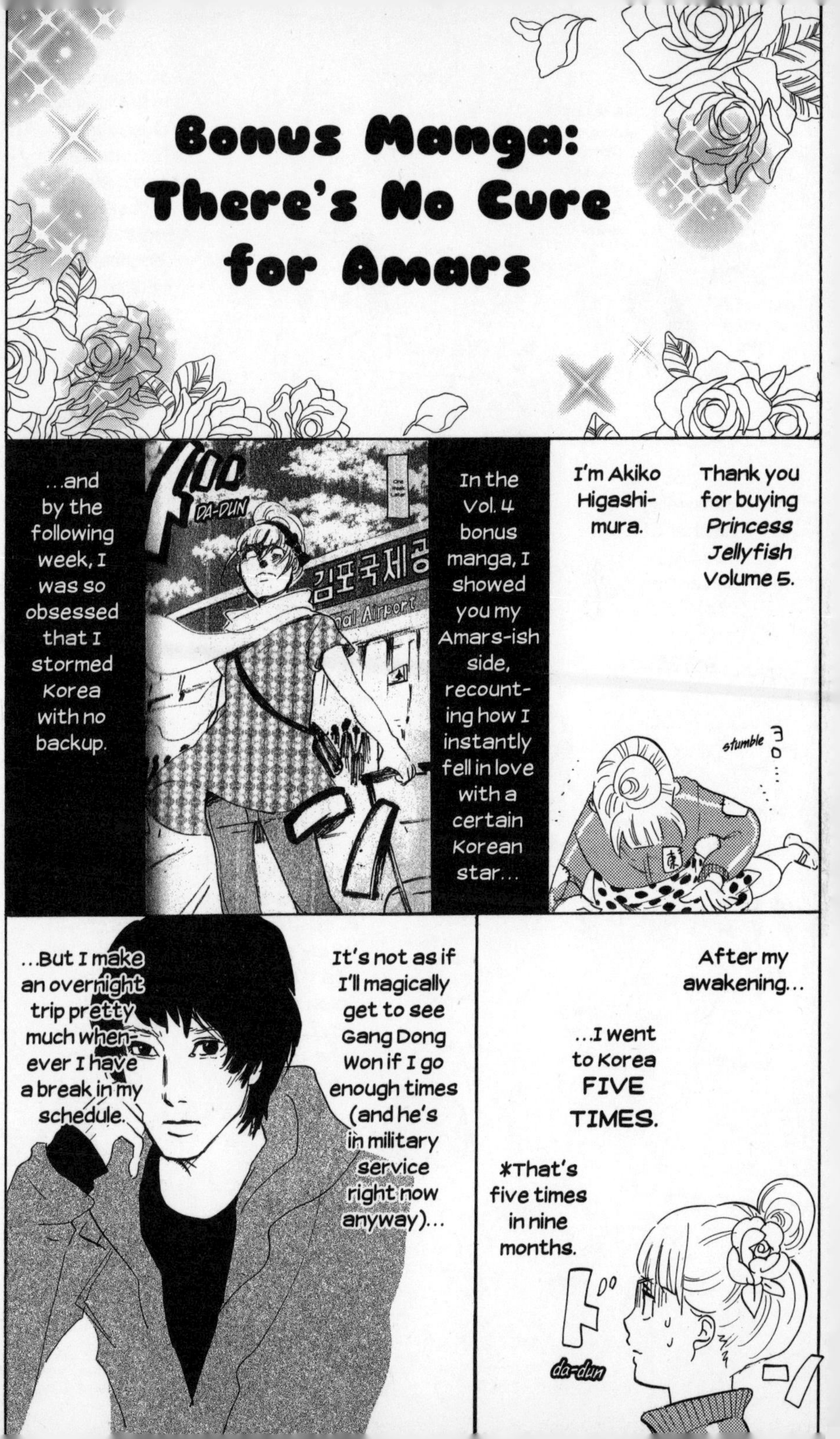
Thank you for buying *Princess Jellyfish* Volume 5.
I'm Akiko Higashi-mura.
stumble
In the Vol. 4 bonus manga, I showed you my Amars-ish side, recount-ing how I instantly fell in love with a certain Korean star...
DA-DUN
김포국제공
...and by the following week, I was so obsessed that I stormed Korea with no backup.
After my awakening...
...I went to Korea FIVE TIMES.
*That's five times in nine months.
da-dun
It's not as if I'll magically get to see Gang Dong Won if I go enough times (and he's in military service right now anyway)...
...But I make an overnight trip pretty much when-ever I have a break in my schedule.

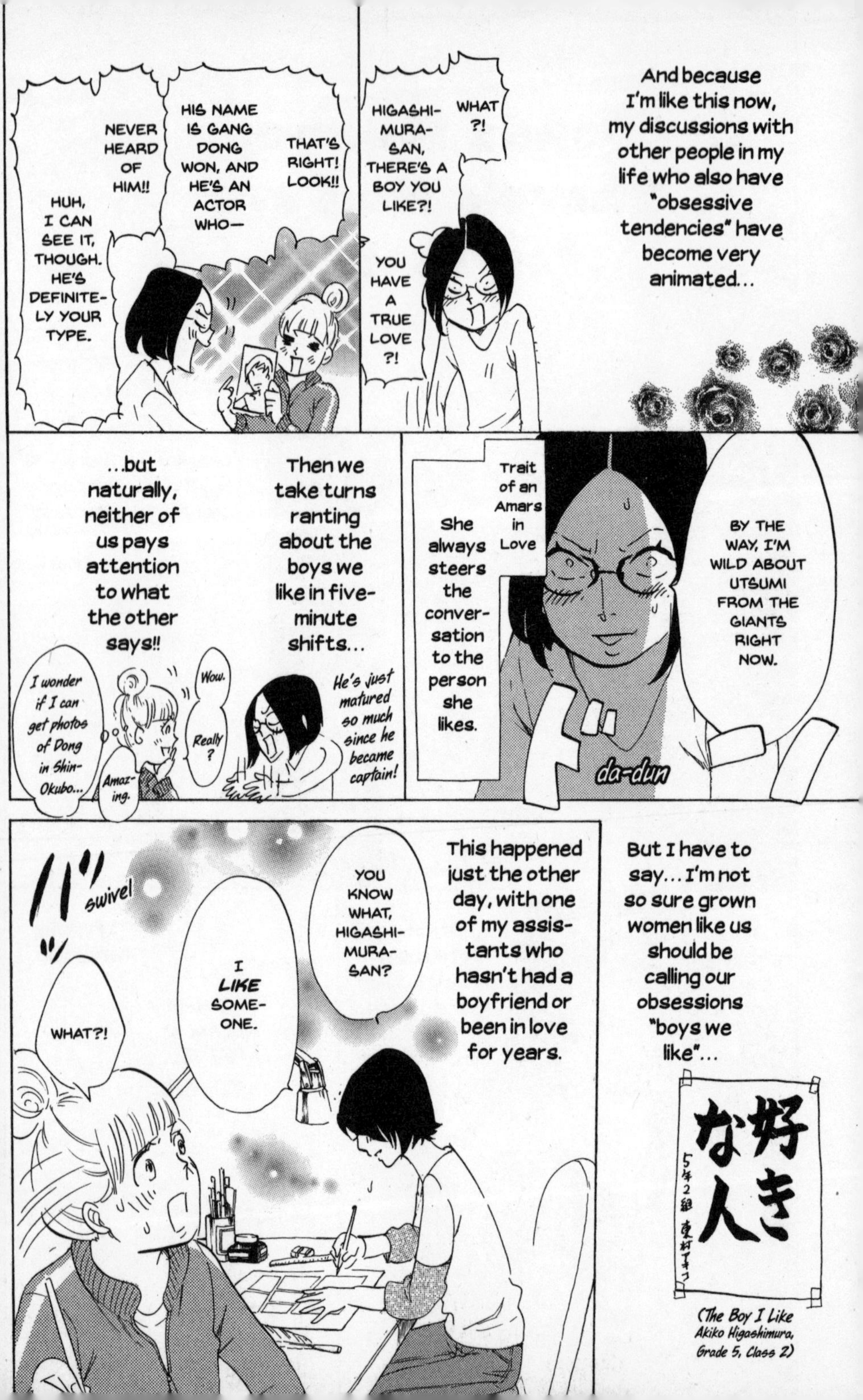
And because I'm like this now, my discussions with other people in my life who also have "obsessive tendencies" have become very animated...
WHAT?!
HIGASHIMURA-SAN, THERE'S A BOY YOU LIKE?!
YOU HAVE A TRUE LOVE?!
THAT'S RIGHT! LOOK!!
HIS NAME IS GANG DONG WON, AND HE'S AN ACTOR WHO—
NEVER HEARD OF HIM!!
HUH, I CAN SEE IT, THOUGH. HE'S DEFINITELY YOUR TYPE.
BY THE WAY, I'M WILD ABOUT UTSUMI FROM THE GIANTS RIGHT NOW.
Trait of an Amars in Love
She always steers the conversation to the person she likes.
da-dun
Then we take turns ranting about the boys we like in five-minute shifts...
...but naturally, neither of us pays attention to what the other says!!
He's just matured so much since he became captain!
Wow.
Really?
Amazing.
I wonder if I can get photos of Dong in Shin-Okubo...
But I have to say... I'm not so sure grown women like us should be calling our obsessions "boys we like"...
好きな人
5年2組 東村アキコ
(The Boy I Like Akiko Higashimura, Grade 5, Class 2)
This happened just the other day, with one of my assistants who hasn't had a boyfriend or been in love for years.
YOU KNOW WHAT, HIGASHIMURA-SAN?
I *LIKE* SOMEONE.
swivel
WHAT?!

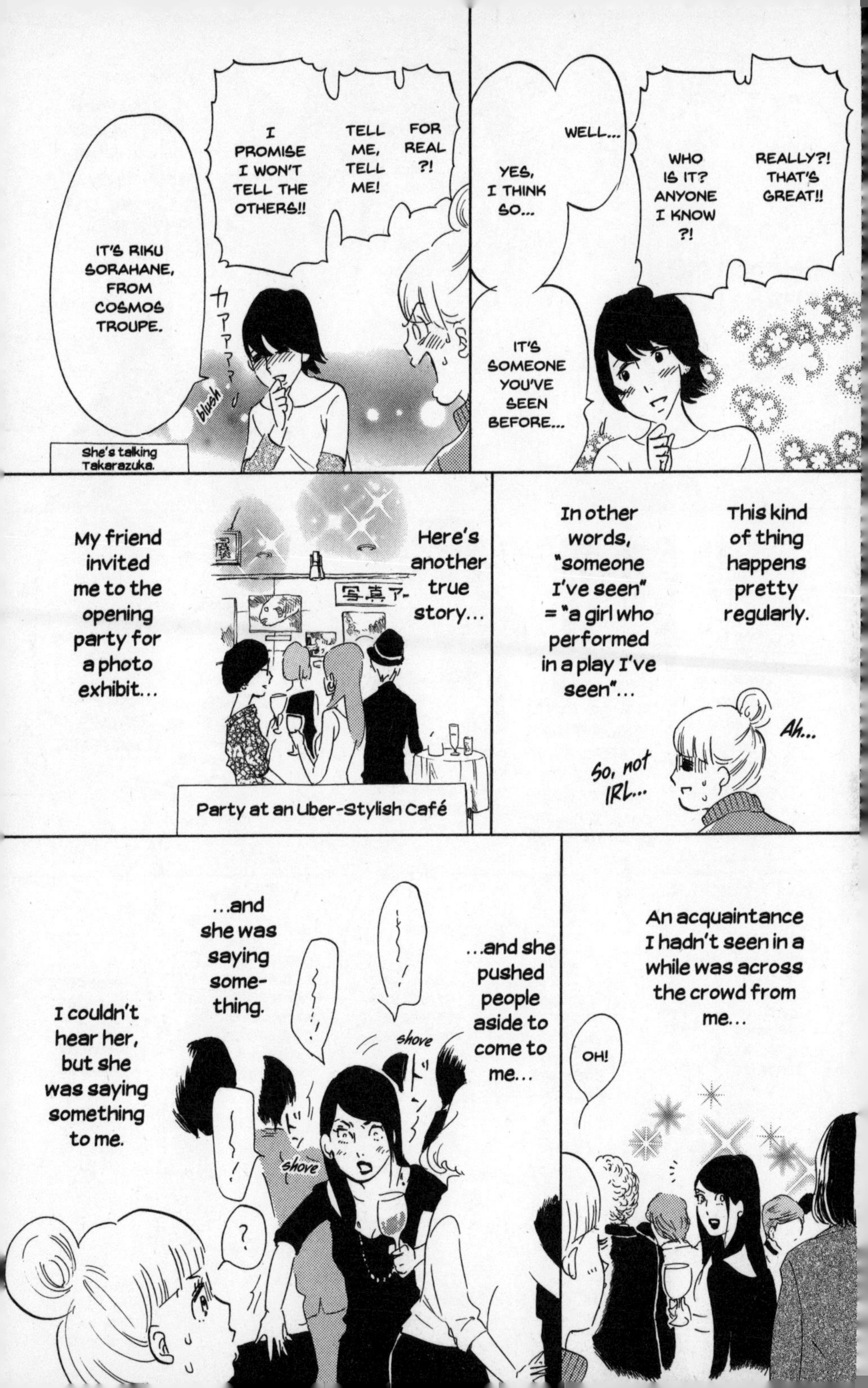
REALLY?! THAT'S GREAT!!
WHO IS IT? ANYONE I KNOW ?!
WELL...
YES, I THINK SO...
IT'S SOMEONE YOU'VE SEEN BEFORE...
FOR REAL ?!
TELL ME, TELL ME!
I PROMISE I WON'T TELL THE OTHERS!!
IT'S RIKU SORAHANE, FROM COSMOS TROUPE.
カアアア
blush
She's talking Takarazuka.
This kind of thing happens pretty regularly.
In other words, "someone I've seen" = "a girl who performed in a play I've seen"...
Ah...
So, not IRL...
Here's another true story...
My friend invited me to the opening party for a photo exhibit...
写真ア
Party at an Uber-Stylish Café
An acquaintance I hadn't seen in a while was across the crowd from me...
OH!
...and she pushed people aside to come to me...
shove
...and she was saying some-thing.
I couldn't hear her, but she was saying something to me.
shove
?

huff huff
I wondered what it could be, and then...
OMG CHANSUNG.
OMG CHANSUNG OMG CHANSUNG.
CHA...?
OMG CHANSUNG CHANSUNG OMG OMG OMG OMG.
huff huff
huff huff
WHO IS CHANSUNG, AGAIN? IS HE IN TVXQ? NO, THAT'S CHANGMIN...
OH, HE'S IN THE BAND 2AM, RIGHT? NO, THAT'S ANOTHER CHANGMIN...
CHANSUNG! CHANSUNG!
THE YOUNGEST MEMBER OF 2PM!
HE'S SO HOT! HE'S SO CUTE! I WANT TO MARRY HIM! I WANT TO MARRY HIM! OMG I CAN'T DEAL WITH IT!!
In that moment, I experienced the full force of the K-pop craze that's swept Japan these past few years.
Moreover, thanks to our hopeless Amars nature...
Later
2PM, EH?
ONE OF MY ASSISTANTS WAS INTO THEM, BUT I'VE NEVER REALLY WATCHED THEM...
I CAN'T EVEN REMEMBER WHICH ONE IS CHANSUNG...
WELL, I'M ALL ABOUT DONG WON RIGHT NOW, SO I WON'T FEEL ANYTHING EVEN IF I DO WATCH THEM...
BUT SHE SAID...
YOU BETTER AT LEAST WATCH CHANSUNG IN THAT PROMO VIDEO AT 1 MINUTE AND 45 SECONDS!!
SO I GUESS I'D BETTER...
click click

I'LL GET SOME COFFEE...

skrut

...

Phew...

*It's now 1:00am, and I've put my son to bed.

strum strum

thrum

YEP. THIS MUST BE IT...

Right, I do know these guys.

'75.8.18

...

...

...

blup blup

sprinkle sprinkle

You see, we Amars are hopelessly vulnerable to the "obsession germ," which infects us with the loves of its other carriers. Someone please find a cure.

I'M SORRY, DONG! I LIKE YOU *AND* CHANSUNG NOW!!

ken-splash

じー
stare
美熟女官能DVD4時間収録
熟女専門
18
熱い快感に
溺れる美人妻
美熟BEST
付録DVD

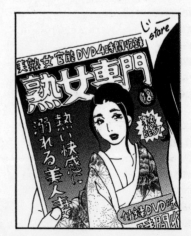

Translation Notes

For the Sake of Others, page 3
In Japanese, the title is *"Taga Tame,"* which has two possible references: The title to the 1979 opening song to *Cyborg 009*, or Taro Hyugaji's 1995 film, also known as *Portrait of the Wind*.

Chii Sanpo, page 15
Chii Sanpo was a popular TV show that featured walks through the smaller neighborhoods of Tokyo. Its star, Takeo Chii (a.k.a. "Chii-Chii"), unfortunately passed away at 70 years old, shortly after this volume of *Princess Jellyfish* was published in Japan. He appeared on the program until shortly before his death. He sometimes ended the program with a watercolor painting.

"The pale sky is on the wane / Next, a yellow one shall reign", page 27
This is a quote from a song in the first chapter of *Romance of the Three Kingdoms (Three Kingdoms.* Luo Guanzhong, translated by Moss Roberts, 1993, pg. 4). It's actually a pretty good slogan to choose for this type of demonstration, since in the novel this song is sung by civilians revolting against the government. The yellow sky mentioned refers to the Yellow Turbans, the civilians who initiated the revolt, commonly called the "Yellow Turban Rebellion." There's little chance of Global City Create detecting what Mayaya means by this reference, of course...

Girls Just Wanna Have Fun, page 34
This chapter's title translates to "What's Wrong with Just Having Fun?" Here, it is localized to "Girls Just Wanna Have Fun."

Do not make this like a violent student protest! You'll get arrested!, page 46
Although Japan saw student protests during the 1940s and '50s as well, the most famous ones today are the protests of the 1960s. These were largely focused on opposition to the renewals of the Japan-U.S. Joint Security Treaty in 1960 and 1970, but other treaties and proposed laws were also subjects of protests both on and off college campuses, along with the Vietnam War, environmental issues, tuition hikes and various local issues affecting particular colleges. The level of violence steadily escalated as the decade went on, with many injuries and even a few fatalities recorded before the protests died down. "Student protest" and "violence" are associated concepts in the minds of many to this day. However, this may yet change: in 2015, student protests against new security legislation expanding the role of the military were peaceful.

Moonlight Mask, page 61
Moonlight Mask is Japan's first live-action *tokusatsu* superhero. He first appeared

in a TV drama in 1958, and has since been seen in film, anime, and manga adaptations. *Tokusatsu* literally translates to "special filming" and is a genre of Japanese live-action that uses special effects. The genre can include titles such as Moonlight Mask, Power Rangers, Godzilla, and more.

Chishu Ryu, page 68
Chishu Ryu was a prolific actor who was in many movies and TV shows, starting in 1928. He was known for his rural Kumamoto accent. Jiji is dressed up as his character, a Buddhist priest, from the popular Tora-san film series *"It's Tough Being A Man"* or *"Otoko wa Tsurai yo"*—a famous role which Chishu Ryu played until his passing in 1993.

Sexy Restaurants of the City, page 108
This is a parody of an actual book called *Tokyo Ii Mise Yareru Mise*. The original 1994 edition was called *Tokyo Beauty & the Beast* in its English subtitle, while the updated edition published in 2012 was subtitled *Sex & the City & the Restaurants*. Both editions are restaurant guides heavily crossed with dating guides, with extensive tips on the where, when, and how of wining and dining a woman on a date and winning her over.

Monta Mino, page 113
Monta Mino is a television personality most associated with emcee, newscaster, and announcer-style roles on live television. His skill and stamina are worth fearing: among other things, he has won the Guinness World Record for most hours of live television by a host in one week (awarded March 31, 2008). As for why he suddenly comes up in a conversation about meat, tripe made from the rumen stomach is called *mino* in Japanese, which is where Mayaya's association comes from.

Suki...?, page 128
The Japanese language is infamous for having a high number of homophones. Since each homophone of *suki* uses a different Japanese *kanji* when written down, readers can feel complete confidence that Shu said "love."

Machaaki's Tablecloth Trick, page 135
"Machaaki" here is a nickname for the singer, actor, and all-around entertainer Masaaki Sakai. In addition to his stint in the band The Spiders and his leading role in the 1978-1980 TV series *Monkey*, he's also well-known in Japan for the many talent shows he's entered. One of his staples is pulling a tablecloth off of a set table without disturbing any of the dishes.

Love!! Amour!! Shigeru Matsuzaki!!, page 137
Shigeru Matsuzaki, a famous Japanese singer with a long and twinkling-eyed career, sings "Memories of Love" as one of his standards. Many may recognize his voice from the *Katamari Damacy* soundtracks.

There's No Cure for Amars, page 169
This title is a riff on the common Japanese proverb "There's no cure for idiocy."

The K-Pop Craze, page 172
Higashimura-sensei isn't exaggerating about Korean pop or "K-pop" being a huge social force in Japan! So many popular Korean bands are jumbled together in Higashimura's mind that she initially thinks of Max Changmin of the boy-band-turned-duo TVXQ and Lee Changmin of the mostly-still-a-boy-band 2AM before she arrives at the right answer: Hwang Chansung of the (you guessed it) boy band 2PM. Now, if you're thinking that two different Korean bands named "2AM" and "2PM" sounds like it can't be a coincidence, you're right—these two groups began as one larger group called "One Day."

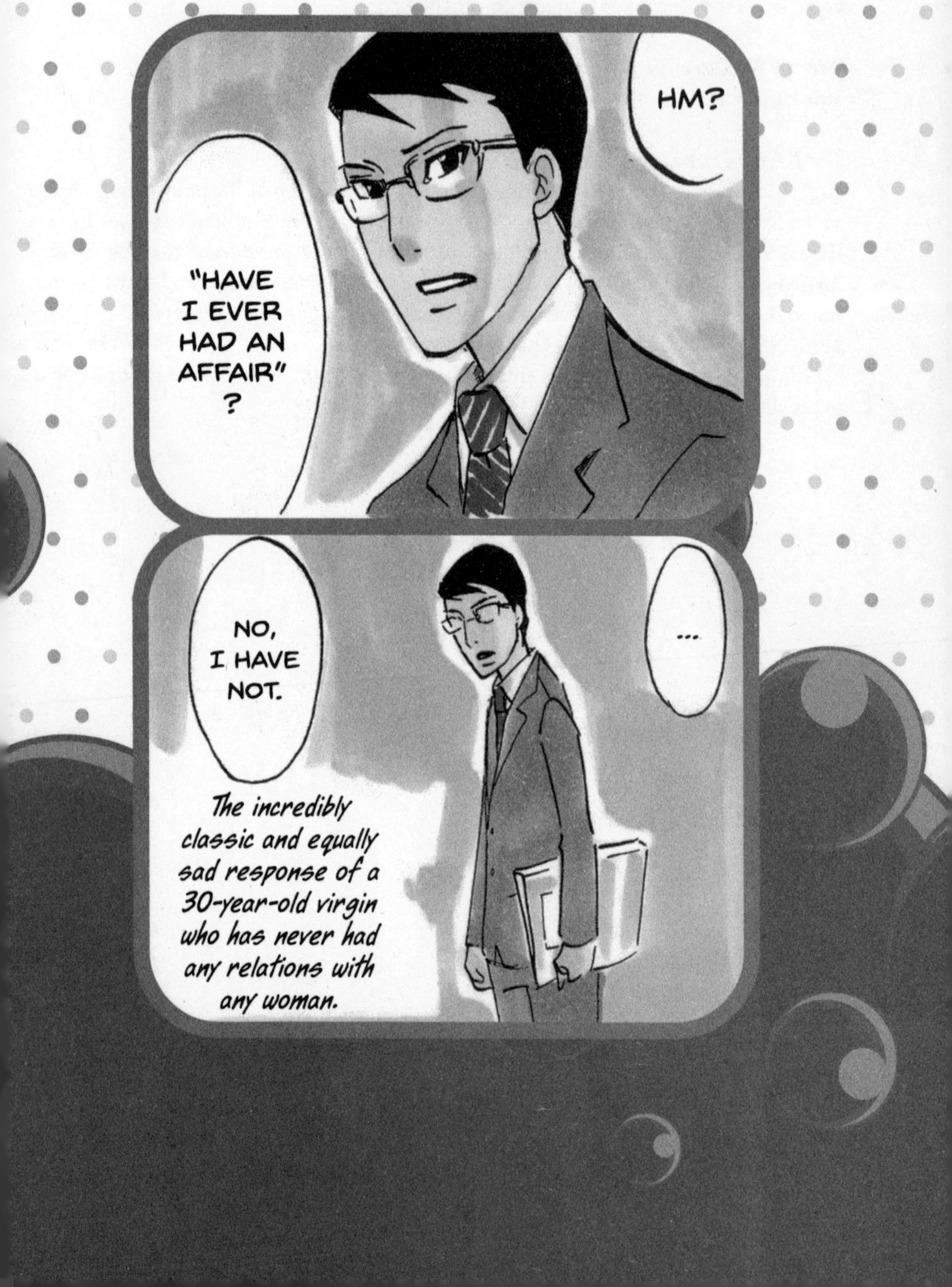
HM?
"HAVE I EVER HAD AN AFFAIR"?
...
NO, I HAVE NOT.
The incredibly classic and equally sad response of a 30-year-old virgin who has never had any relations with any woman.

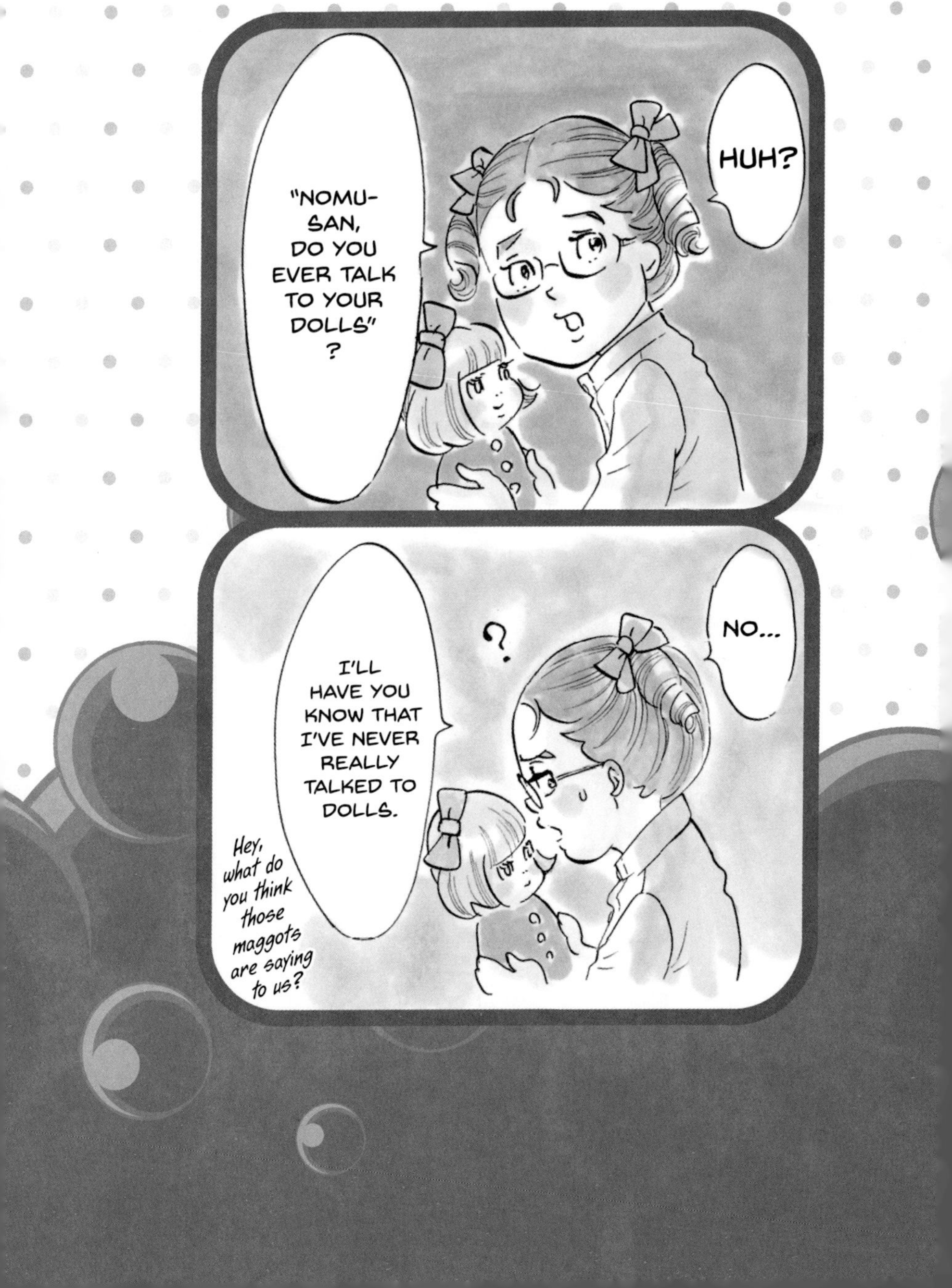
HUH?
"NOMU-SAN, DO YOU EVER TALK TO YOUR DOLLS"?
NO...
I'LL HAVE YOU KNOW THAT I'VE NEVER REALLY TALKED TO DOLLS.
Hey, what do you think those maggots are saying to us?

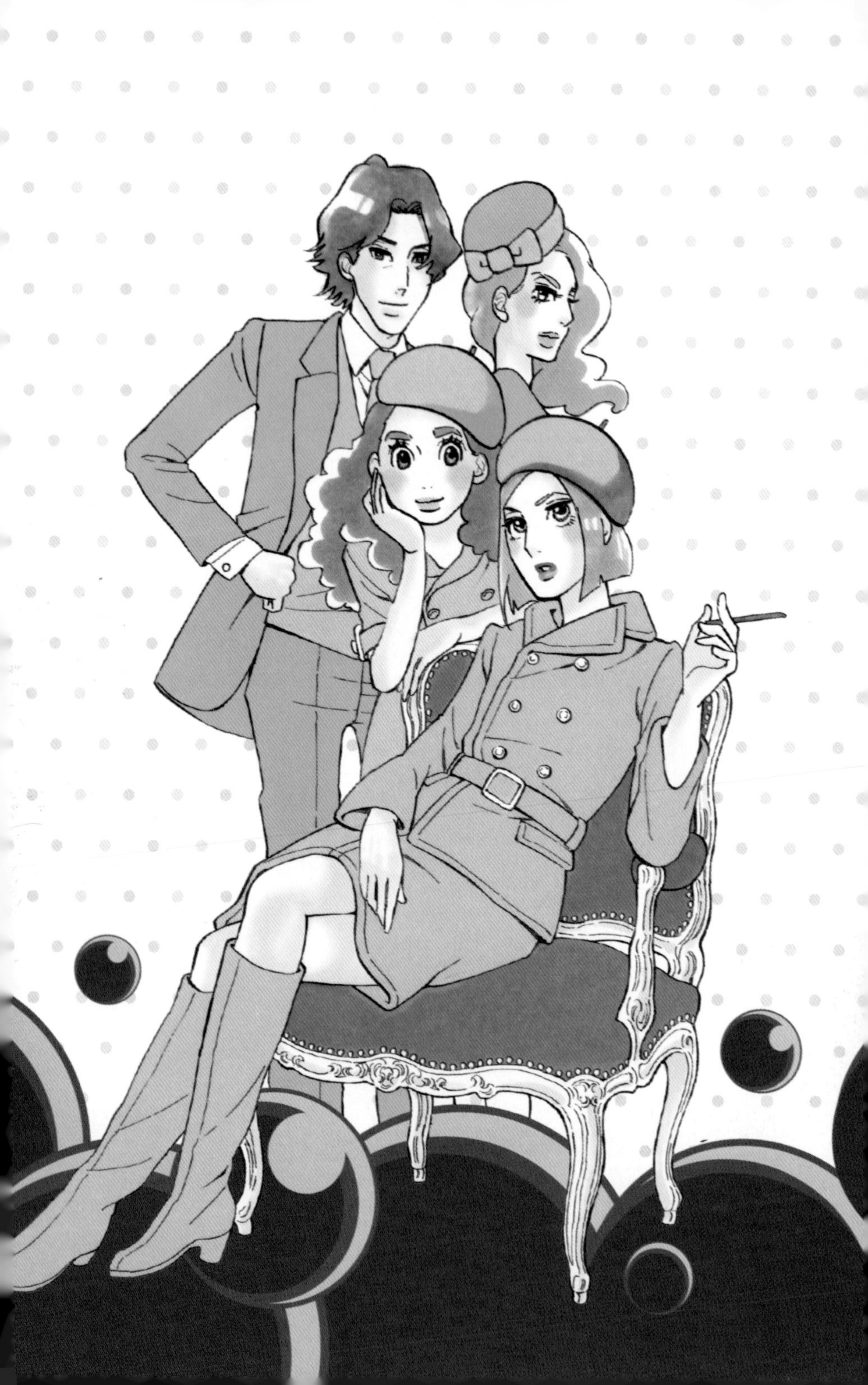

DEAREST READERS!

I HOPE YOU'RE WELL!
I FINALLY DECIDED TO FULFILL
MY DESTINY OF INSTALLING
A HOME AQUARIUM AND
GETTING A PET JELLYFISH!
OR SO I THOUGHT...
THE GUY WHO WORKS AT
THE AQUA CORNER IN THE
HOME IMPROVEMENT STORE
SAID, "YOU HAVE TO START
WITH A FRESHWATER TANK."
I SOMEHOW ENDED UP
BUYING PET *CRAYFISH!*
THEY'RE *SO* BORING!

-AKIKO HIGASHIMURA

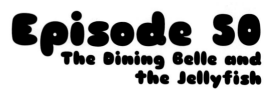

Episode 50
The Dining Belle and the Jellyfish

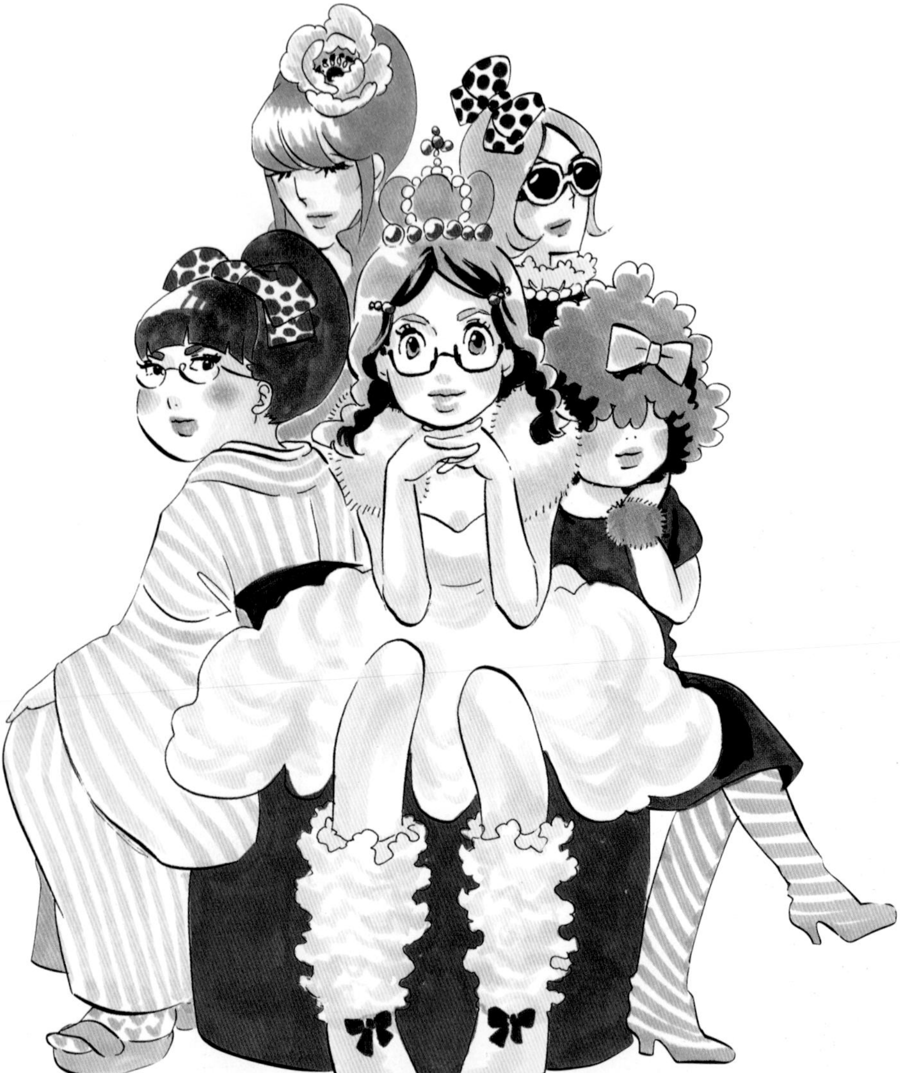

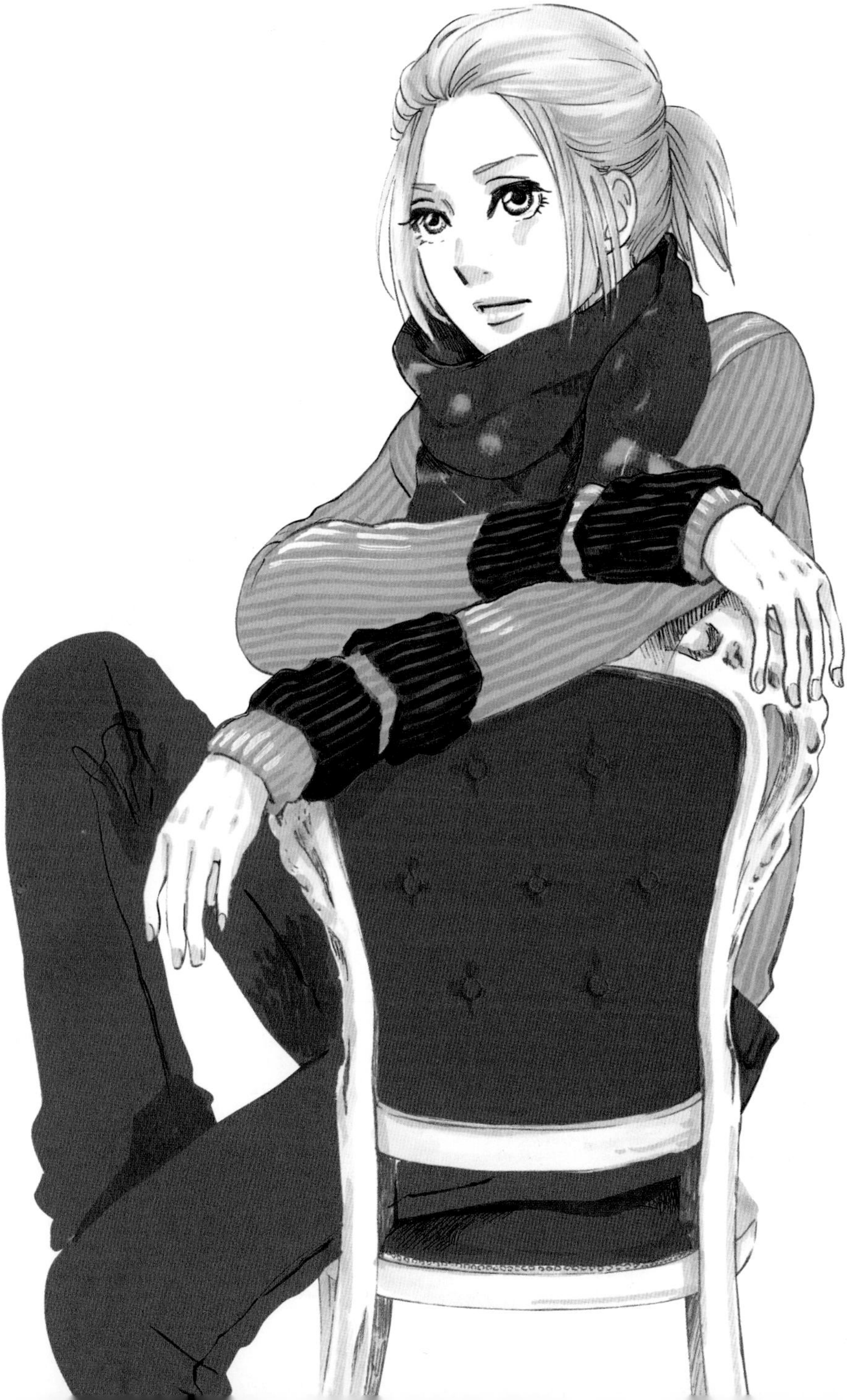

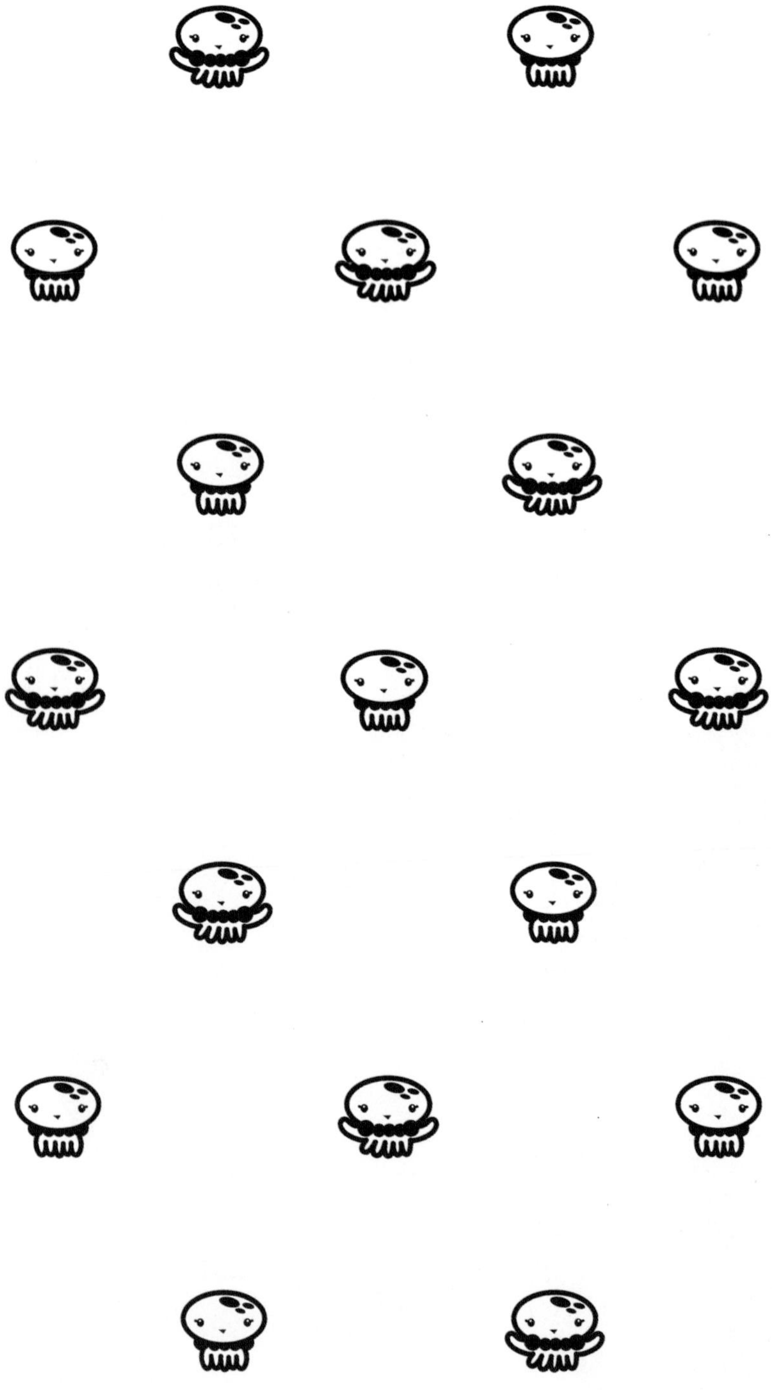

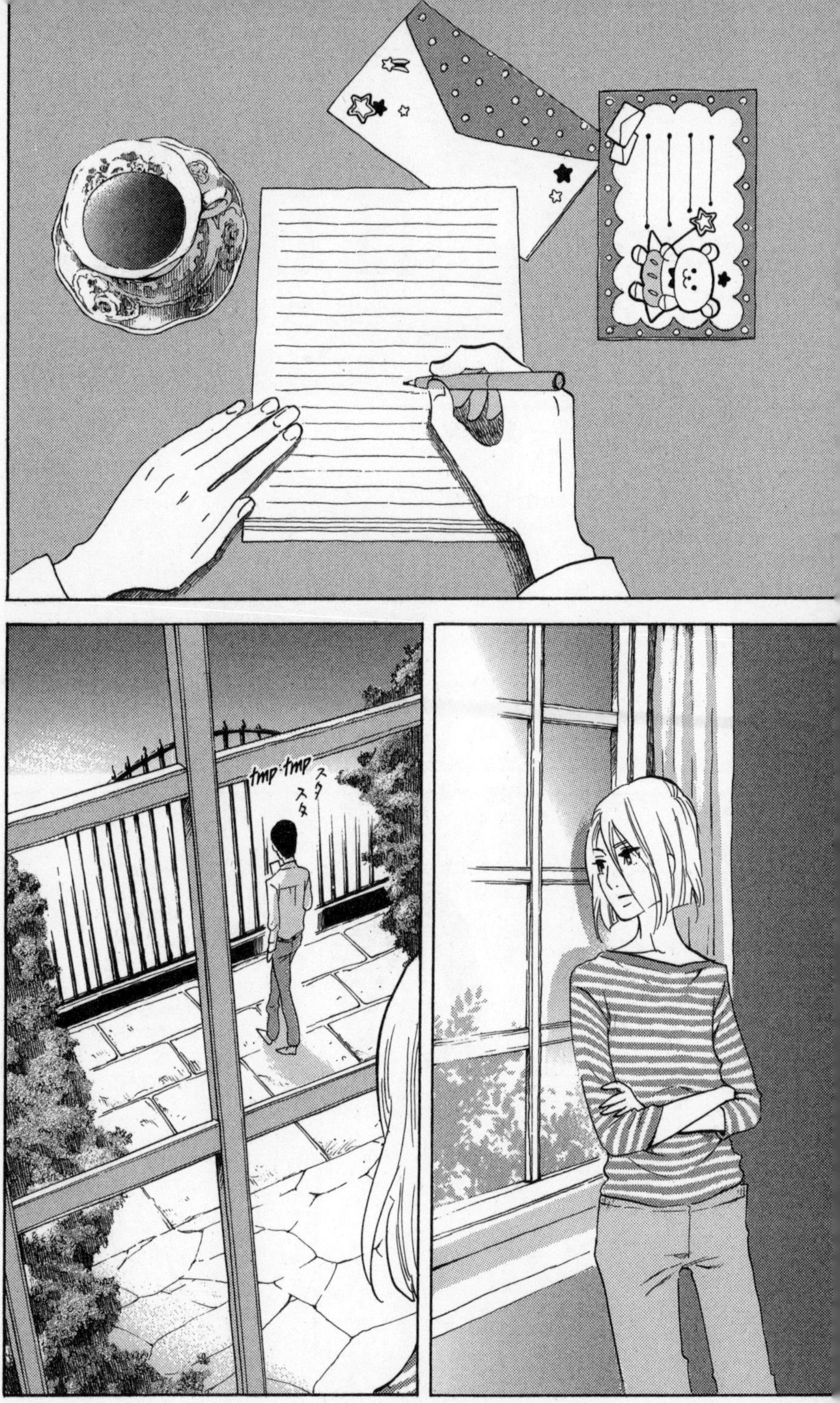
tmp tmp
スタスタ

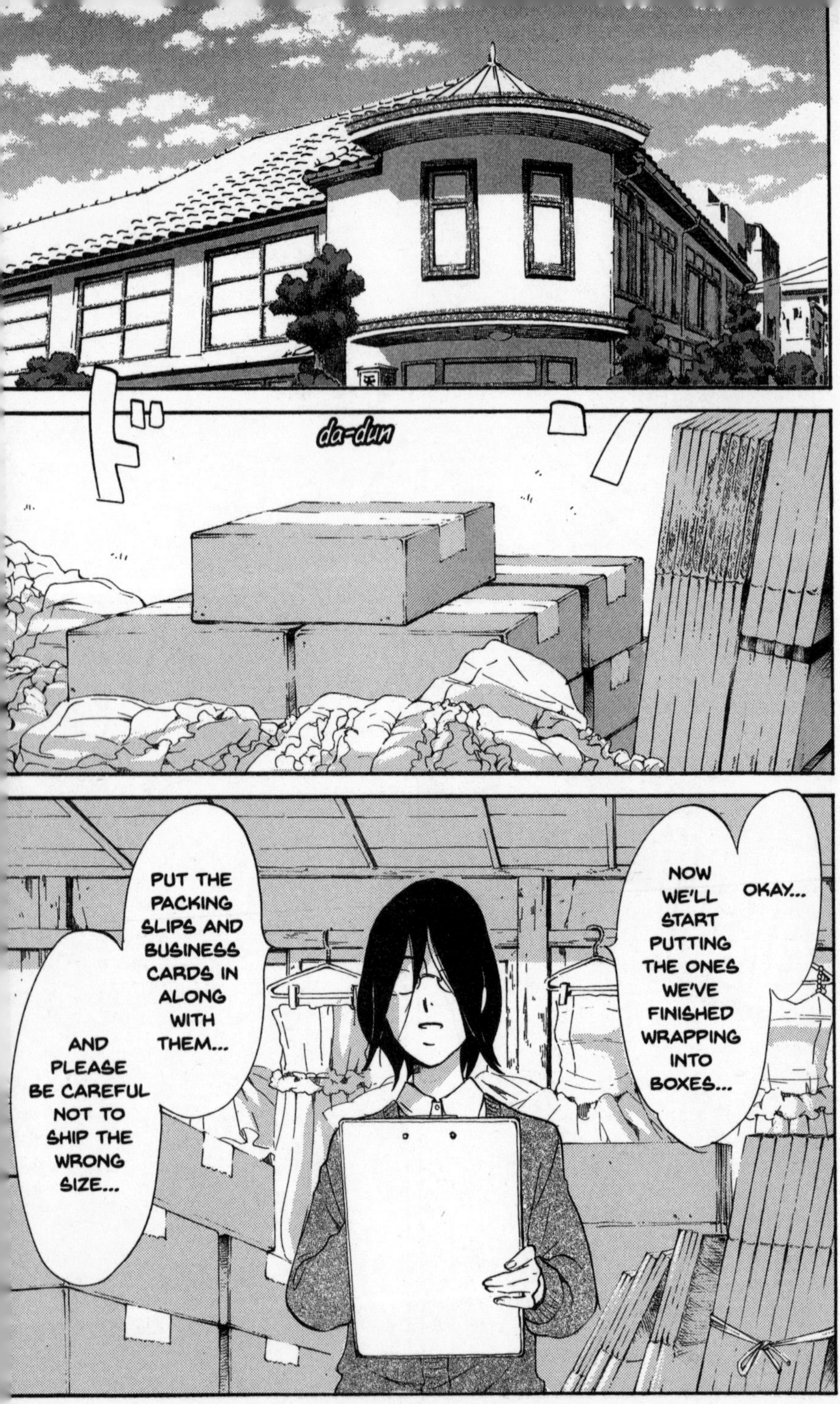
da-dun
OKAY...
NOW WE'LL START PUTTING THE ONES WE'VE FINISHED WRAPPING INTO BOXES...
PUT THE PACKING SLIPS AND BUSINESS CARDS IN ALONG WITH THEM...
AND PLEASE BE CAREFUL NOT TO SHIP THE WRONG SIZE...

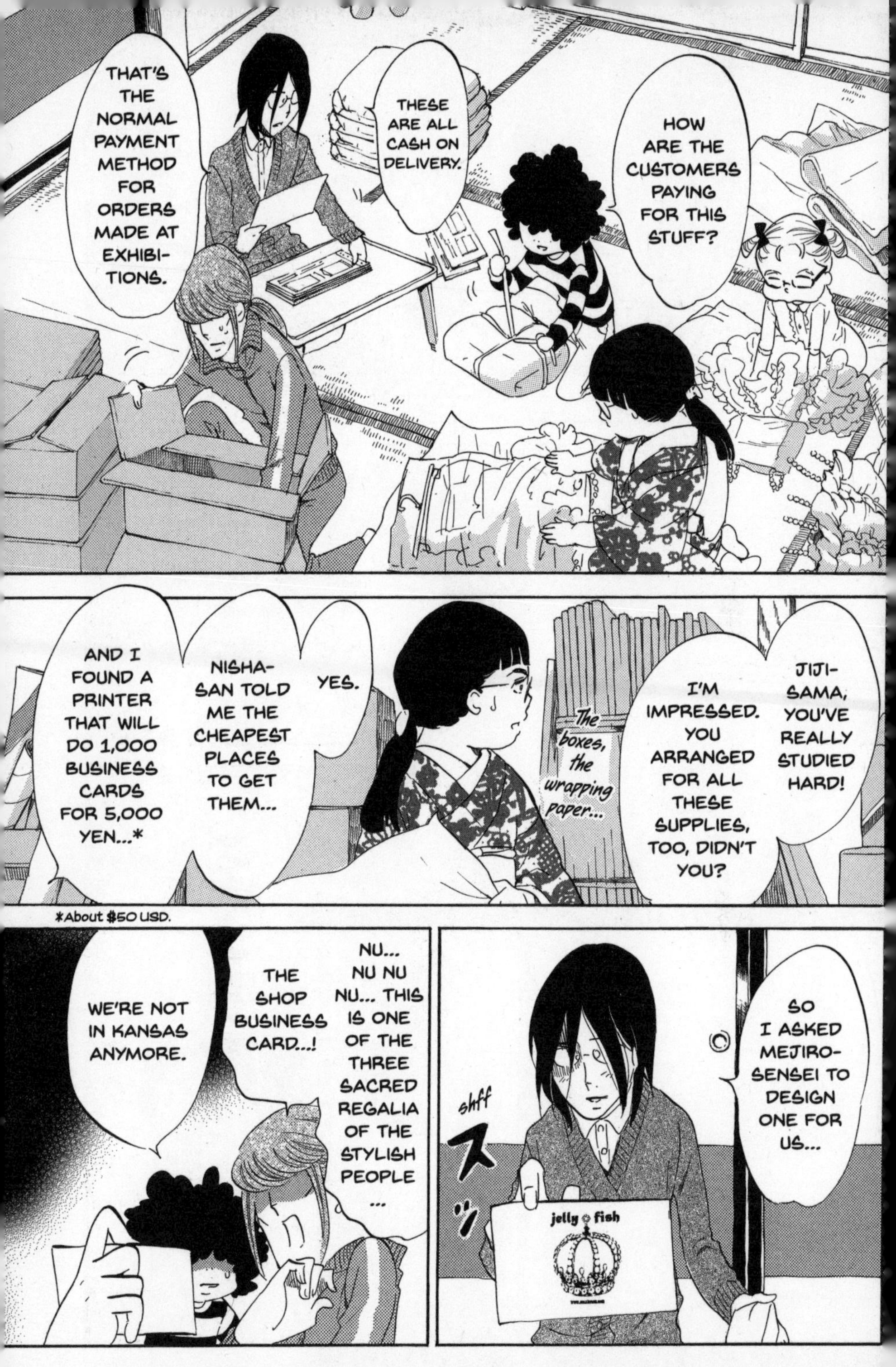
HOW ARE THE CUSTOMERS PAYING FOR THIS STUFF?
THESE ARE ALL CASH ON DELIVERY.
THAT'S THE NORMAL PAYMENT METHOD FOR ORDERS MADE AT EXHIBITIONS.
JIJI-SAMA, YOU'VE REALLY STUDIED HARD!
I'M IMPRESSED. YOU ARRANGED FOR ALL THESE SUPPLIES, TOO, DIDN'T YOU?
The boxes, the wrapping paper...
YES.
NISHA-SAN TOLD ME THE CHEAPEST PLACES TO GET THEM...
AND I FOUND A PRINTER THAT WILL DO 1,000 BUSINESS CARDS FOR 5,000 YEN...*
SO I ASKED MEJIRO-SENSEI TO DESIGN ONE FOR US...
shff
jelly fish
NU... NU NU NU... THIS IS ONE OF THE THREE SACRED REGALIA OF THE STYLISH PEOPLE...
THE SHOP BUSINESS CARD...!
WE'RE NOT IN KANSAS ANYMORE.

*About $50 USD.

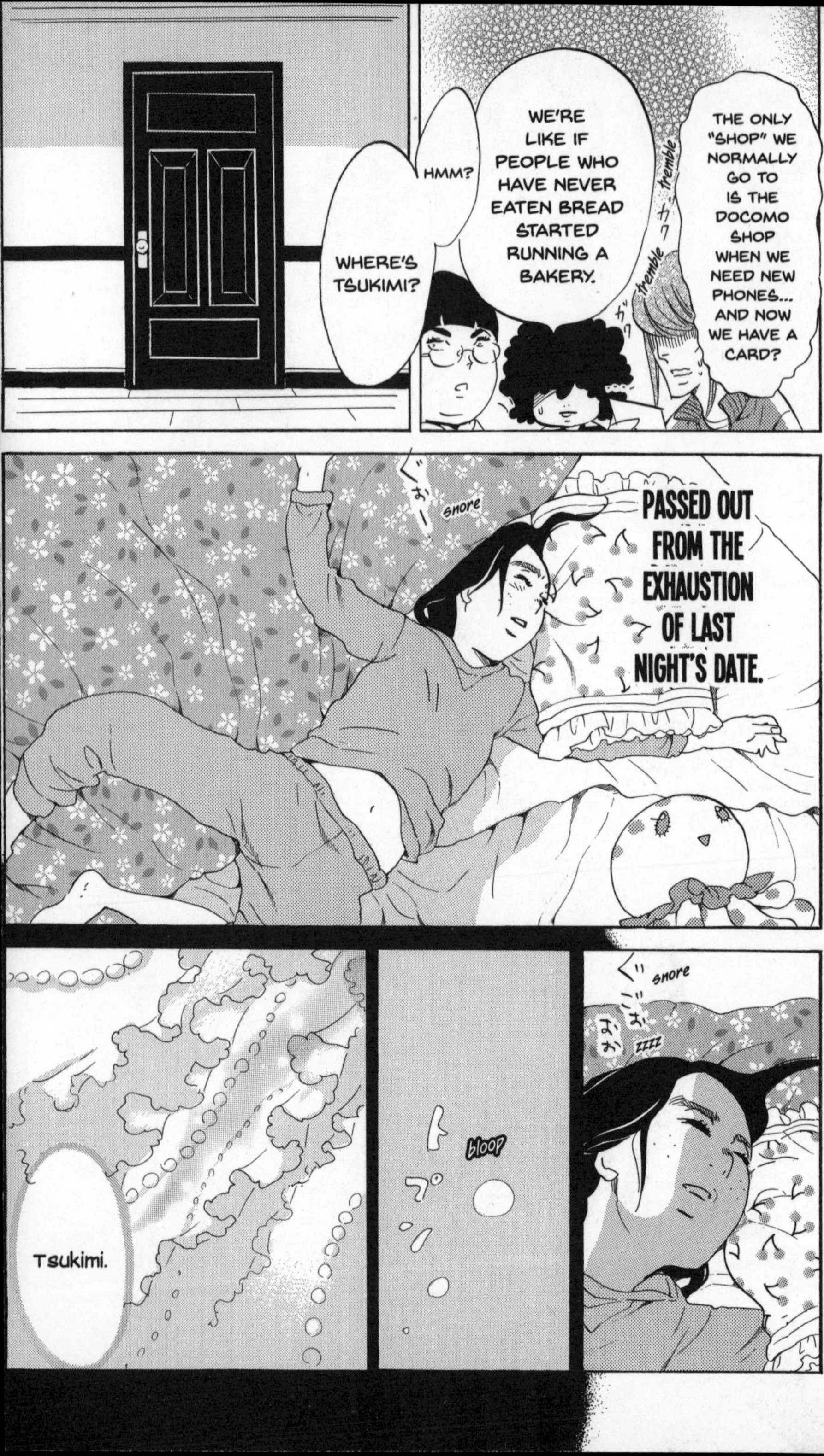
THE ONLY "SHOP" WE NORMALLY GO TO IS THE DOCOMO SHOP WHEN WE NEED NEW PHONES... AND NOW WE HAVE A CARD?
tremble
tremble
WE'RE LIKE IF PEOPLE WHO HAVE NEVER EATEN BREAD STARTED RUNNING A BAKERY.
HMM?
WHERE'S TSUKIMI?
snore
PASSED OUT FROM THE EXHAUSTION OF LAST NIGHT'S DATE.
snore
zzzz
bloop
Tsukimi.

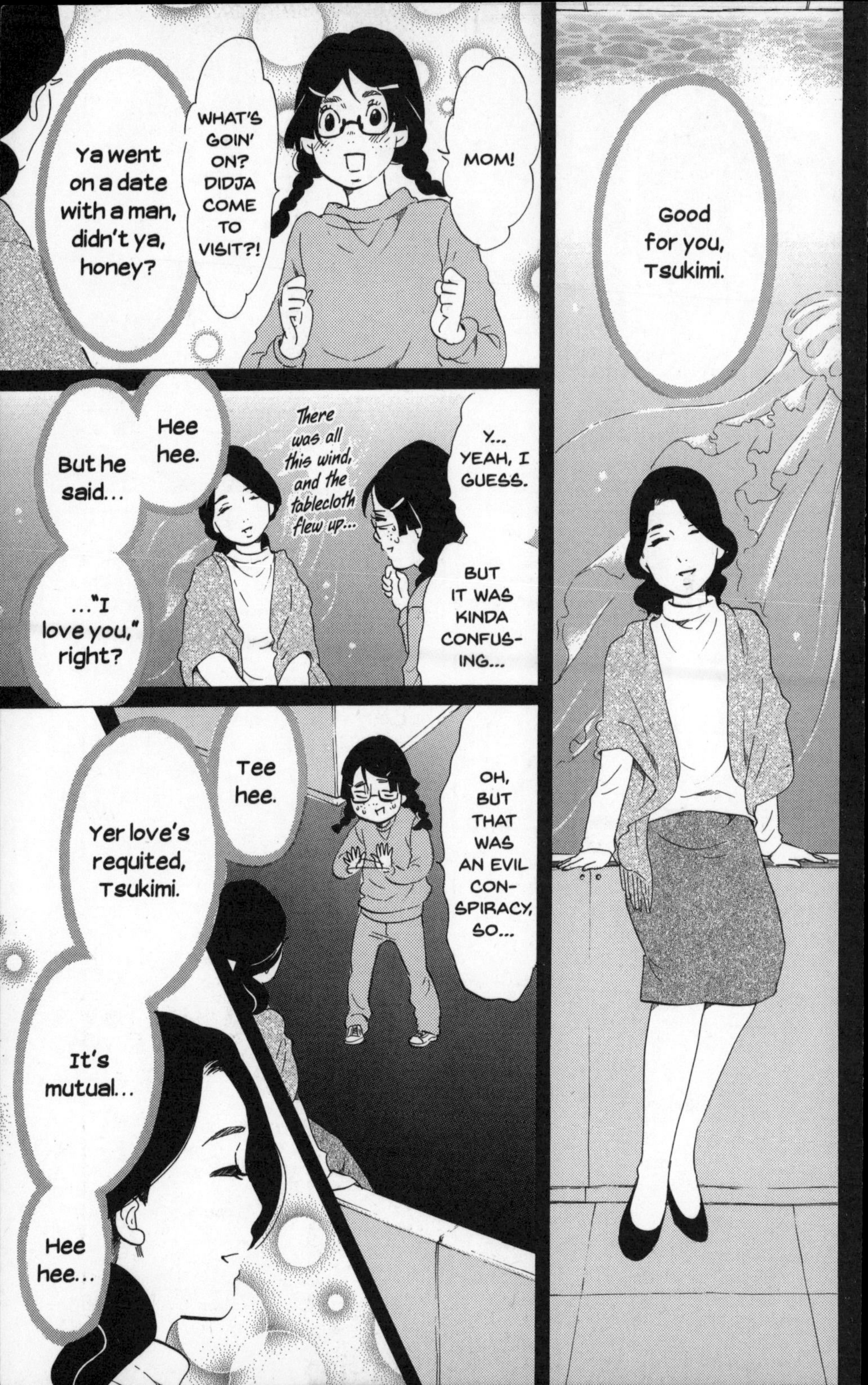
Good for you, Tsukimi.
MOM!
WHAT'S GOIN' ON? DIDJA COME TO VISIT?!
Ya went on a date with a man, didn't ya, honey?
Y... YEAH, I GUESS.
BUT IT WAS KINDA CONFUS-ING...
There was all this wind, and the tablecloth flew up...
Hee hee.
But he said...
..."I love you," right?
OH, BUT THAT WAS AN EVIL CON-SPIRACY, SO...
Tee hee.
Yer love's requited, Tsukimi.
It's mutual...
Hee hee...

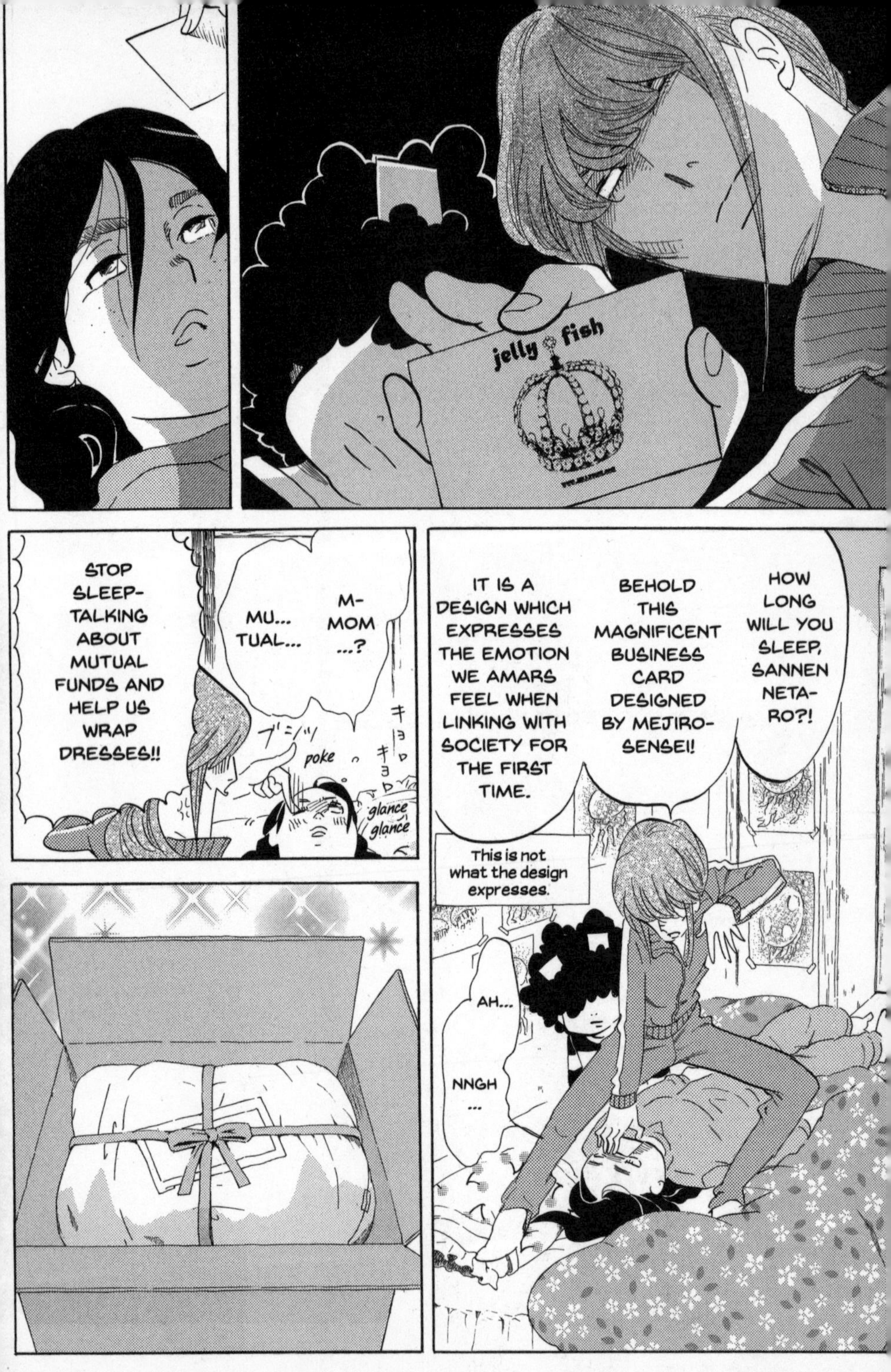
jelly fish
HOW LONG WILL YOU SLEEP, SANNEN NETA-RO?!
BEHOLD THIS MAGNIFICENT BUSINESS CARD DESIGNED BY MEJIRO-SENSEI!
IT IS A DESIGN WHICH EXPRESSES THE EMOTION WE AMARS FEEL WHEN LINKING WITH SOCIETY FOR THE FIRST TIME.
This is not what the design expresses.
AH...
NNGH...
M-MOM...?
MU... TUAL...
glance glance
poke
STOP SLEEP-TALKING ABOUT MUTUAL FUNDS AND HELP US WRAP DRESSES!!

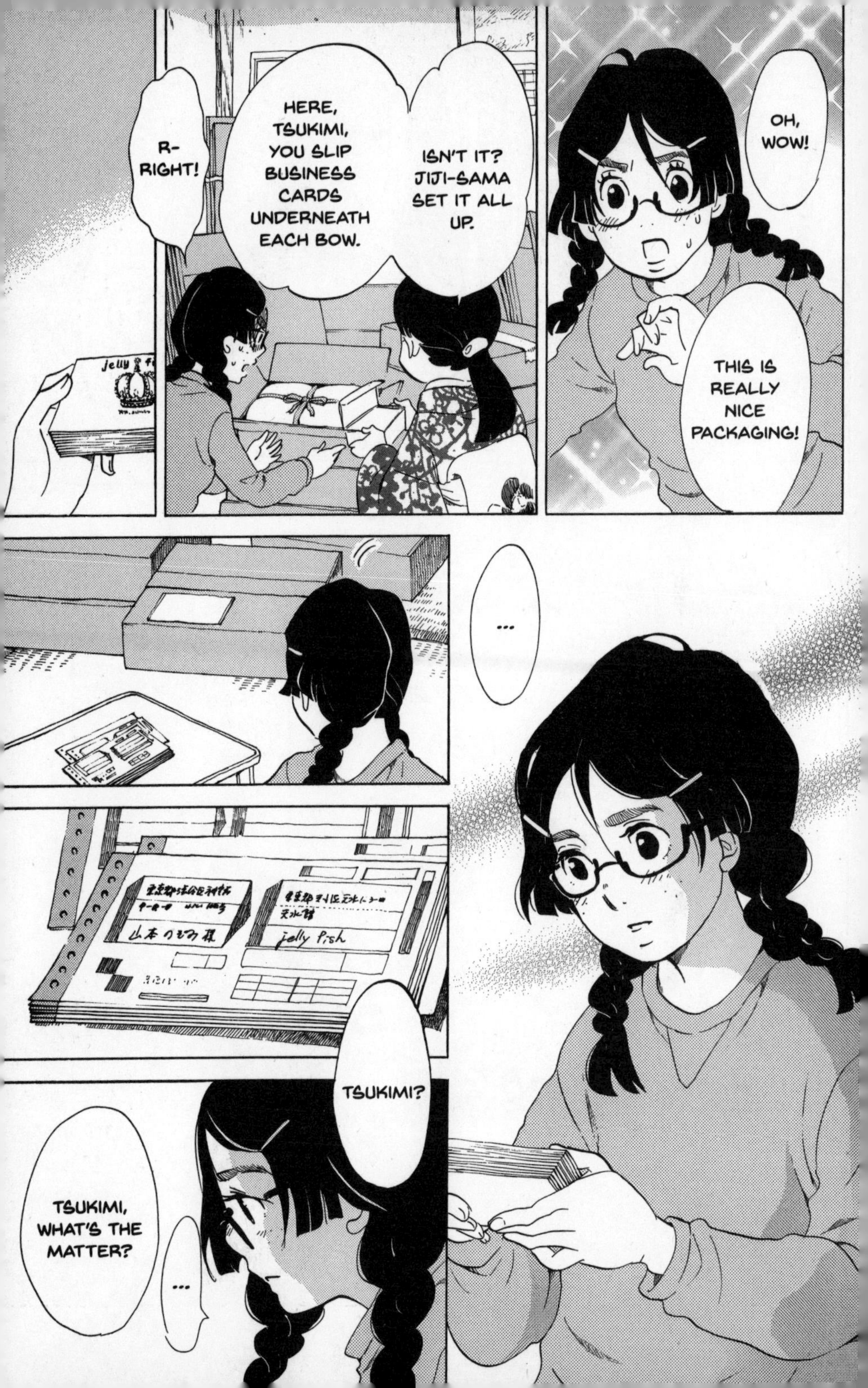
OH, WOW!
THIS IS REALLY NICE PACKAGING!
ISN'T IT? JIJI-SAMA SET IT ALL UP.
HERE, TSUKIMI, YOU SLIP BUSINESS CARDS UNDERNEATH EACH BOW.
R-RIGHT!
...
TSUKIMI?
TSUKIMI, WHAT'S THE MATTER?
...

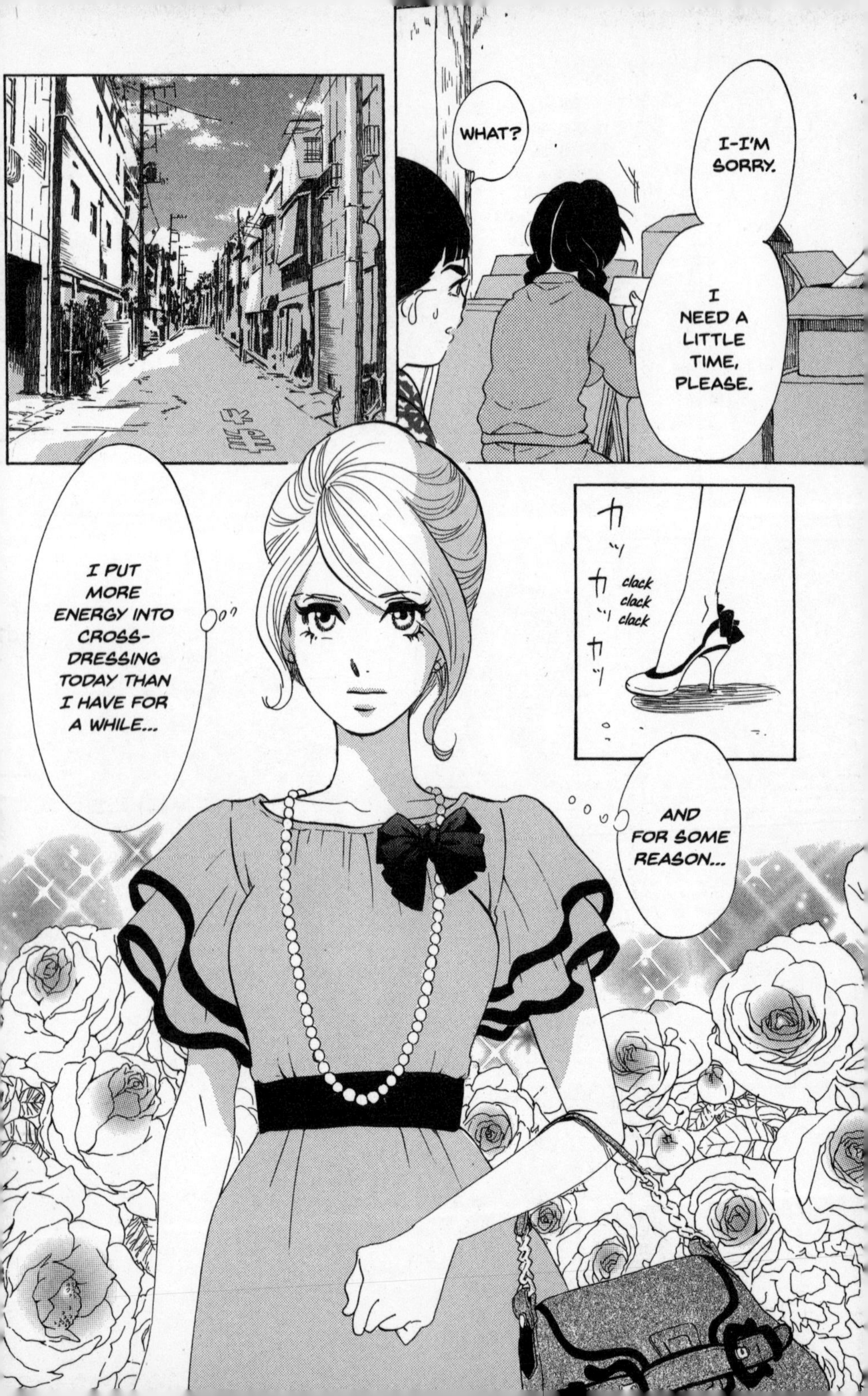
I-I'M SORRY.
I NEED A LITTLE TIME, PLEASE.
WHAT?
カッカッカッ
clack clack clack
I PUT MORE ENERGY INTO CROSS-DRESSING TODAY THAN I HAVE FOR A WHILE...
AND FOR SOME REASON...

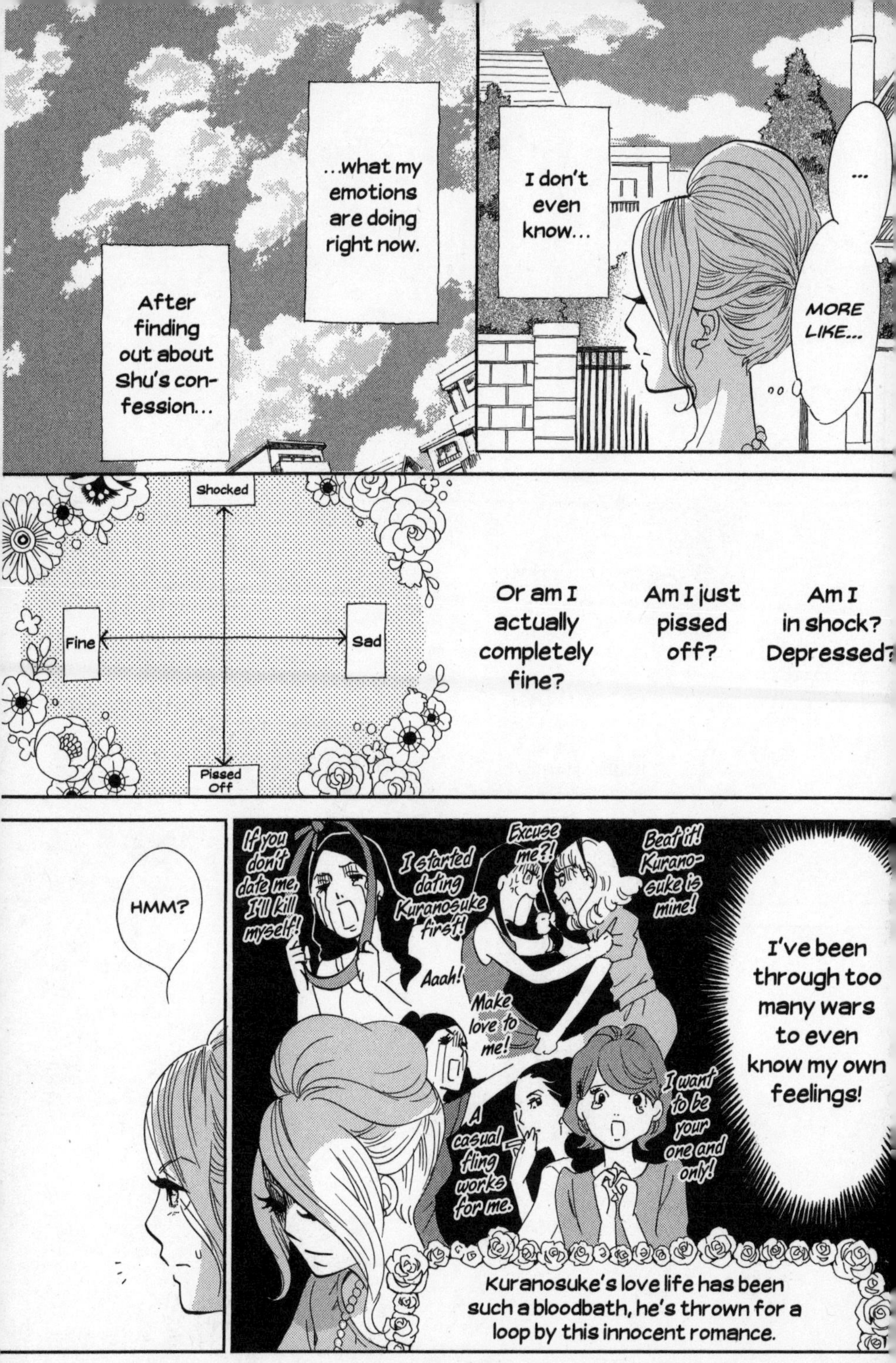
...
MORE LIKE...
I don't even know...
...what my emotions are doing right now.
After finding out about Shu's confession...
Am I in shock? Depressed?
Am I just pissed off?
Or am I actually completely fine?
Shocked
Sad
Fine
Pissed Off
I've been through too many wars to even know my own feelings!
Beat it! Kuranosuke is mine!
Excuse me?!
I started dating Kuranosuke first!
If you don't date me, I'll kill myself!
Aaah!
Make love to me!
I want to be your one and only!
A casual fling works for me.
Kuranosuke's love life has been such a bloodbath, he's thrown for a loop by this innocent romance.
HMM?

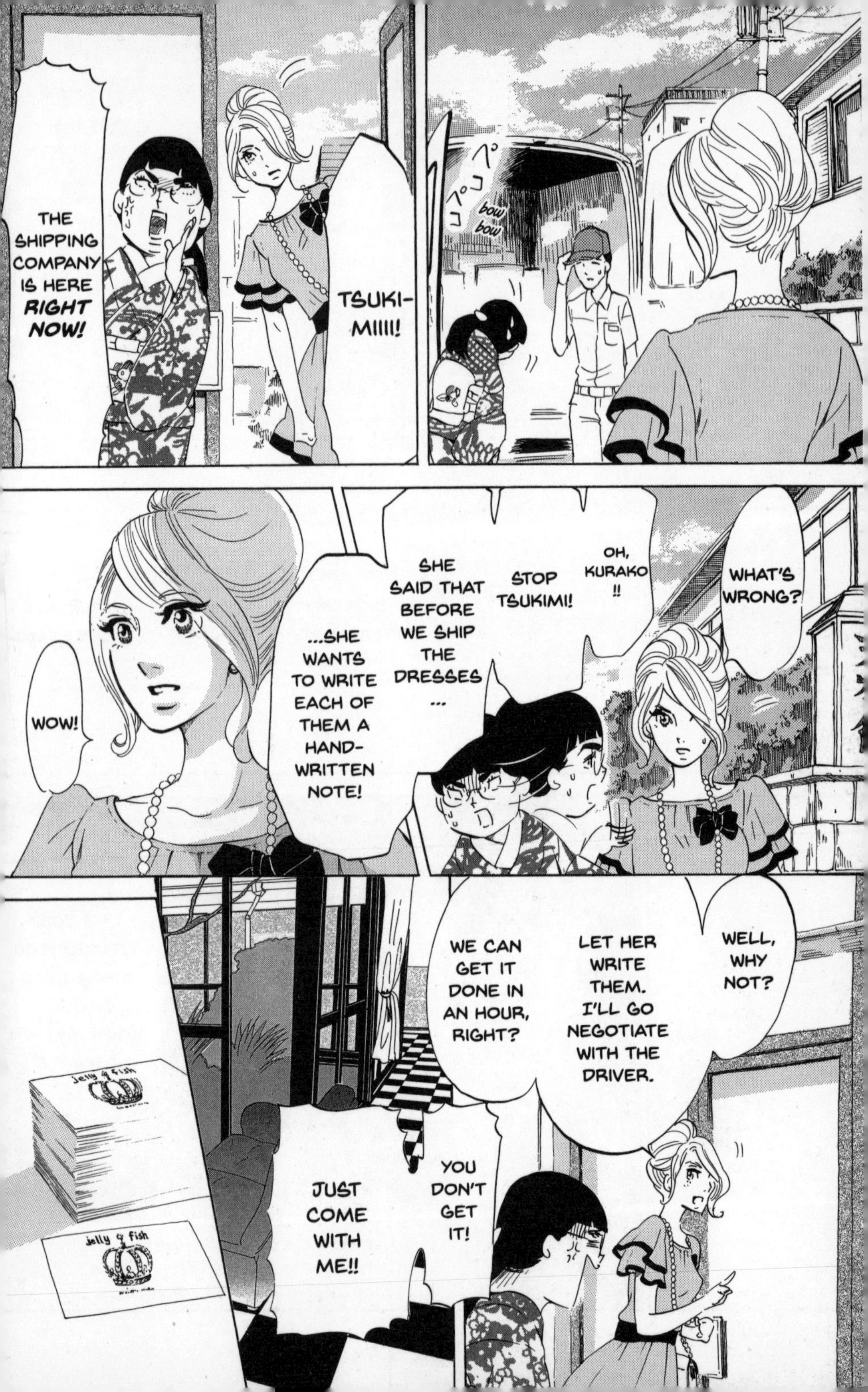
ペコ
ペコ
bow bow
TSUKI-MIIII!
THE SHIPPING COMPANY IS HERE RIGHT NOW!
WHAT'S WRONG?
OH, KURAKO!!
STOP TSUKIMI!
SHE SAID THAT BEFORE WE SHIP THE DRESSES...
...SHE WANTS TO WRITE EACH OF THEM A HAND-WRITTEN NOTE!
WOW!
WELL, WHY NOT?
LET HER WRITE THEM. I'LL GO NEGOTIATE WITH THE DRIVER.
WE CAN GET IT DONE IN AN HOUR, RIGHT?
YOU DON'T GET IT!
JUST COME WITH ME!!

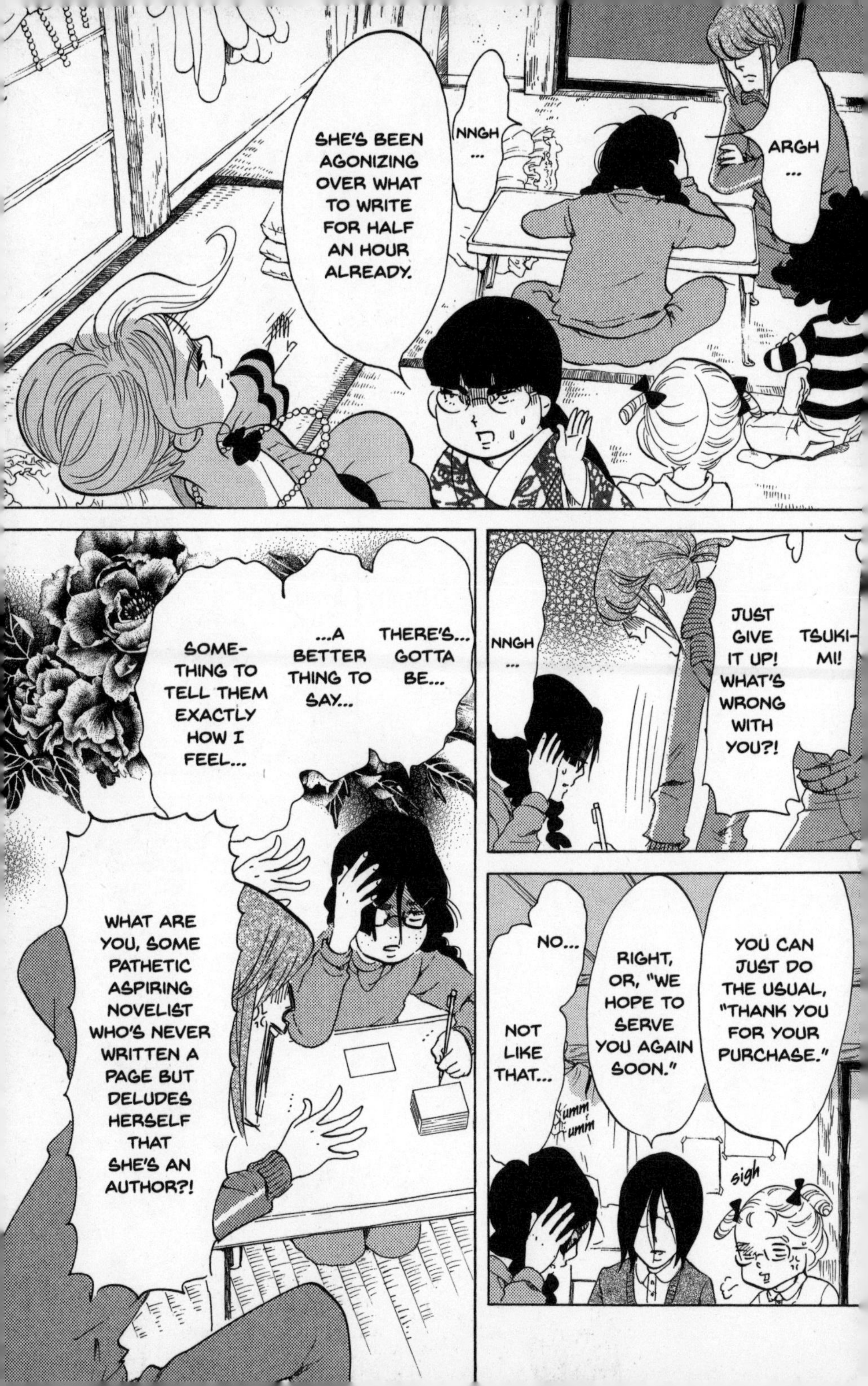
ARGH ...
NNGH ...
SHE'S BEEN AGONIZING OVER WHAT TO WRITE FOR HALF AN HOUR ALREADY.
TSUKI-MI!
JUST GIVE IT UP! WHAT'S WRONG WITH YOU?!
NNGH ...
YOU CAN JUST DO THE USUAL, "THANK YOU FOR YOUR PURCHASE."
RIGHT, OR, "WE HOPE TO SERVE YOU AGAIN SOON."
NO...
NOT LIKE THAT...
umm umm
sigh
THERE'S... GOTTA BE...
...A BETTER THING TO SAY...
SOME-THING TO TELL THEM EXACTLY HOW I FEEL...
WHAT ARE YOU, SOME PATHETIC ASPIRING NOVELIST WHO'S NEVER WRITTEN A PAGE BUT DELUDES HERSELF THAT SHE'S AN AUTHOR?!

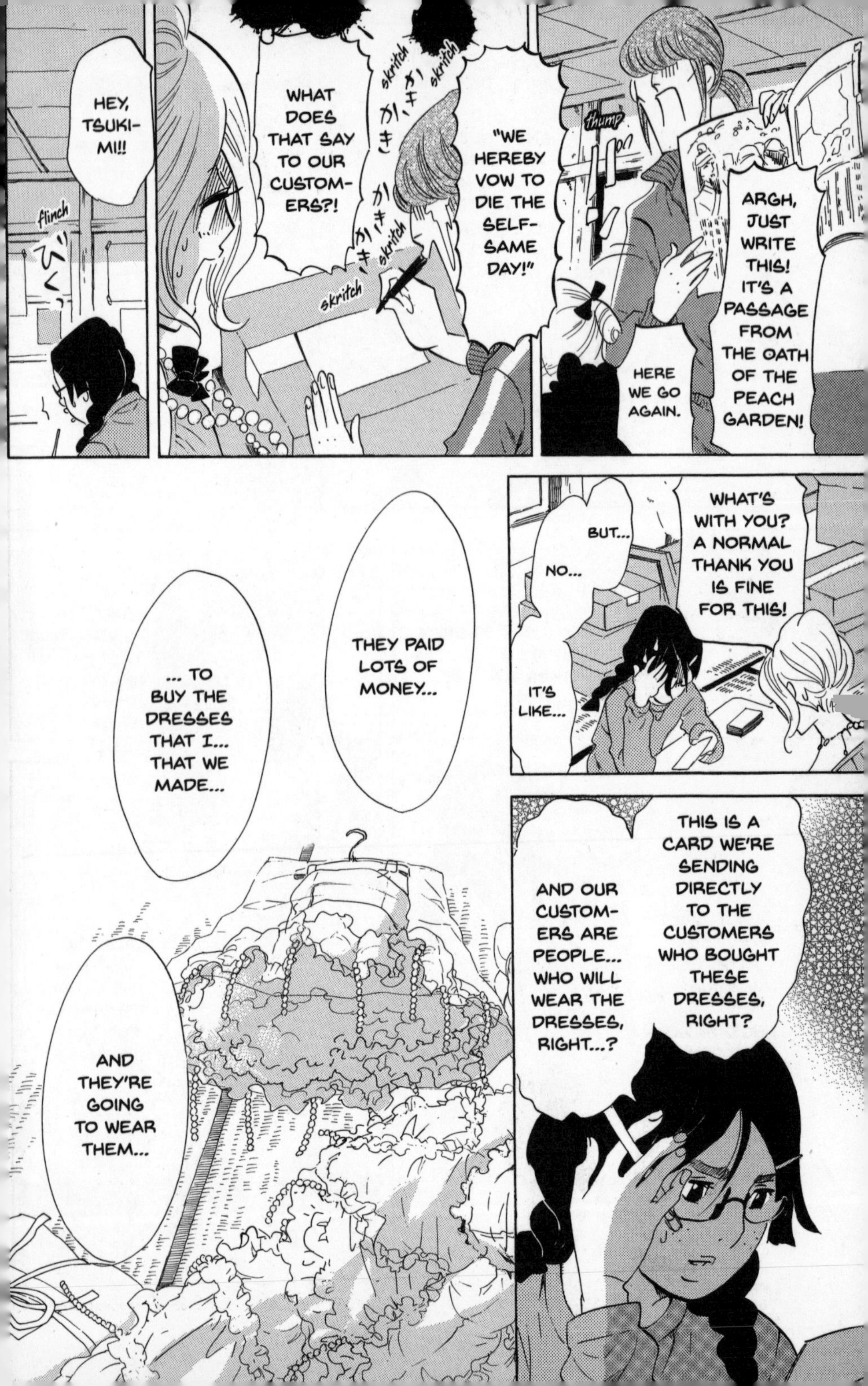
ARGH, JUST WRITE THIS! IT'S A PASSAGE FROM THE OATH OF THE PEACH GARDEN!
thump
HERE WE GO AGAIN.
"WE HEREBY VOW TO DIE THE SELF-SAME DAY!"
skritch
skritch
skritch
skritch
WHAT DOES THAT SAY TO OUR CUSTOMERS?!
HEY, TSUKIMI!!
flinch
WHAT'S WITH YOU? A NORMAL THANK YOU IS FINE FOR THIS!
BUT... NO...
IT'S LIKE...
THIS IS A CARD WE'RE SENDING DIRECTLY TO THE CUSTOMERS WHO BOUGHT THESE DRESSES, RIGHT?
AND OUR CUSTOMERS ARE PEOPLE... WHO WILL WEAR THE DRESSES, RIGHT...?
THEY PAID LOTS OF MONEY...
... TO BUY THE DRESSES THAT I... THAT WE MADE...
AND THEY'RE GOING TO WEAR THEM...

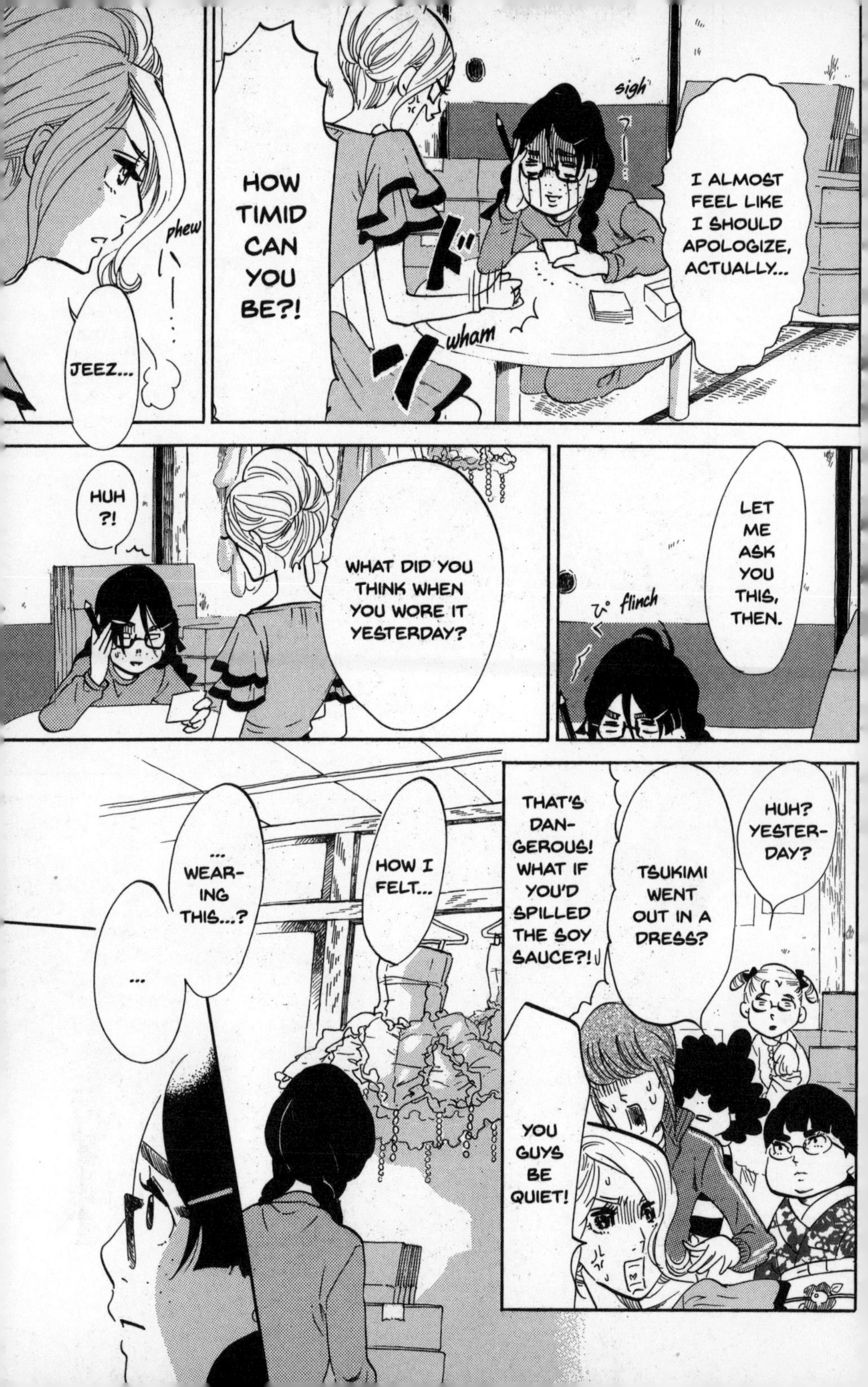
sigh
I ALMOST FEEL LIKE I SHOULD APOLOGIZE, ACTUALLY...
HOW TIMID CAN YOU BE?!
wham
phew
JEEZ...
LET ME ASK YOU THIS, THEN.
flinch
WHAT DID YOU THINK WHEN YOU WORE IT YESTERDAY?
HUH ?!
HUH? YESTER-DAY?
TSUKIMI WENT OUT IN A DRESS?
THAT'S DAN-GEROUS! WHAT IF YOU'D SPILLED THE SOY SAUCE?!
YOU GUYS BE QUIET!
HOW I FELT...
... WEAR-ING THIS...?
...

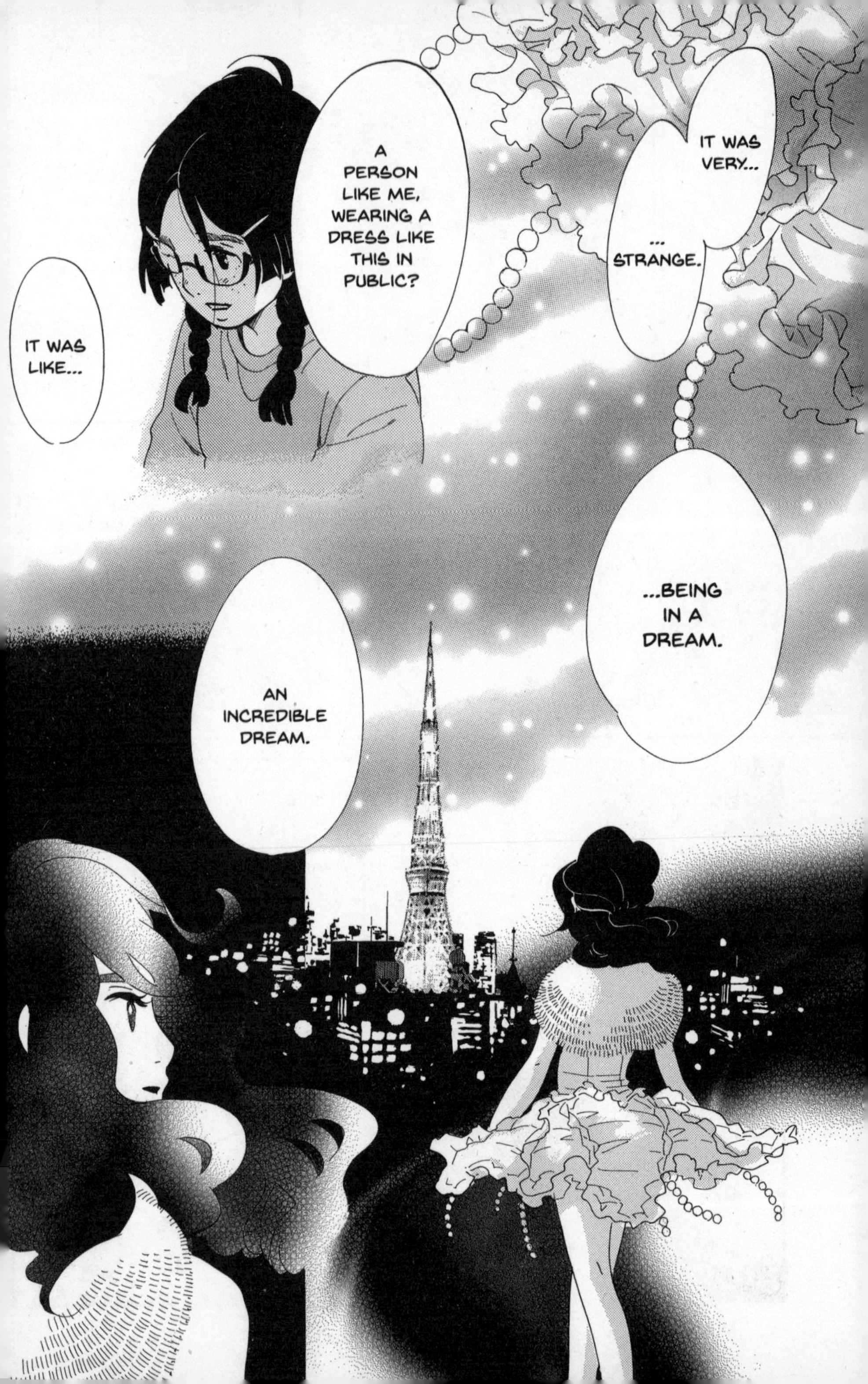
IT WAS VERY...
...STRANGE.
A PERSON LIKE ME, WEARING A DRESS LIKE THIS IN PUBLIC?
IT WAS LIKE...
...BEING IN A DREAM.
AN INCREDIBLE DREAM.

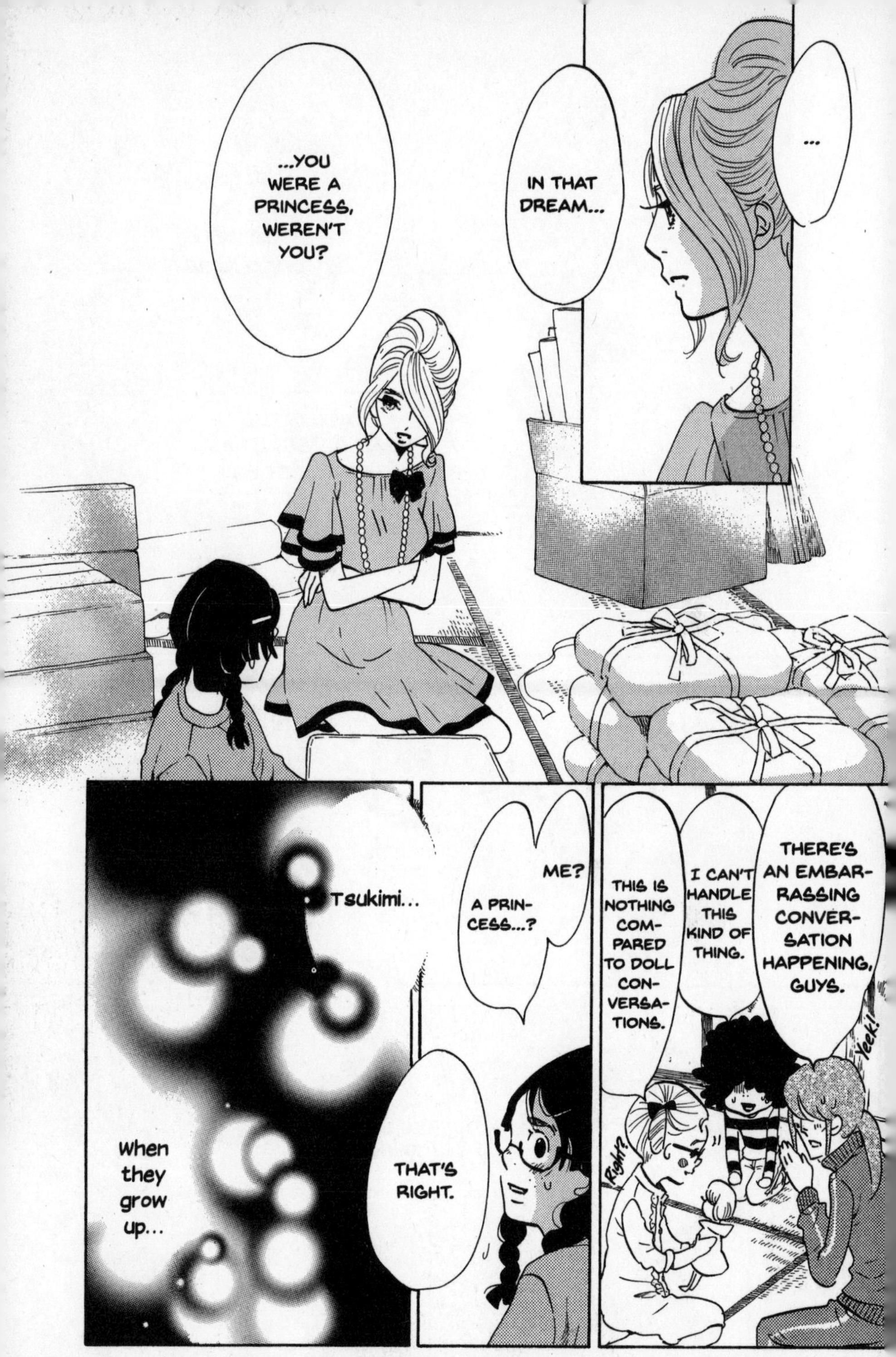
...
IN THAT DREAM...
...YOU WERE A PRINCESS, WEREN'T YOU?
THERE'S AN EMBARRASSING CONVERSATION HAPPENING, GUYS.
I CAN'T HANDLE THIS KIND OF THING.
THIS IS NOTHING COMPARED TO DOLL CONVERSATIONS.
Yeek!
Right!?
ME?
A PRINCESS...?
THAT'S RIGHT.
Tsukimi...
When they grow up...

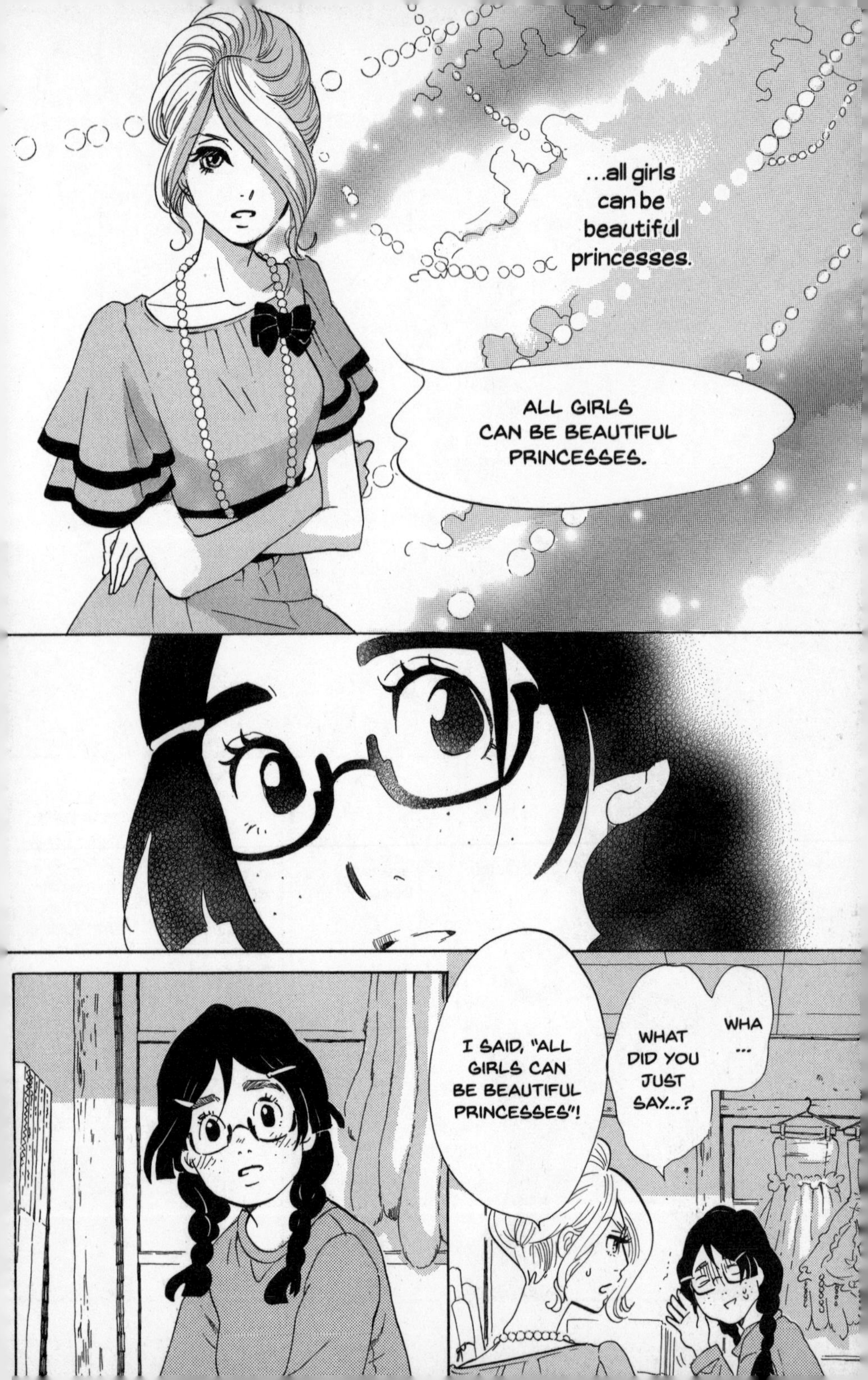
...all girls can be beautiful princesses.
ALL GIRLS CAN BE BEAUTIFUL PRINCESSES.
WHA ...
WHAT DID YOU JUST SAY...?
I SAID, "ALL GIRLS CAN BE BEAUTIFUL PRINCESSES"!

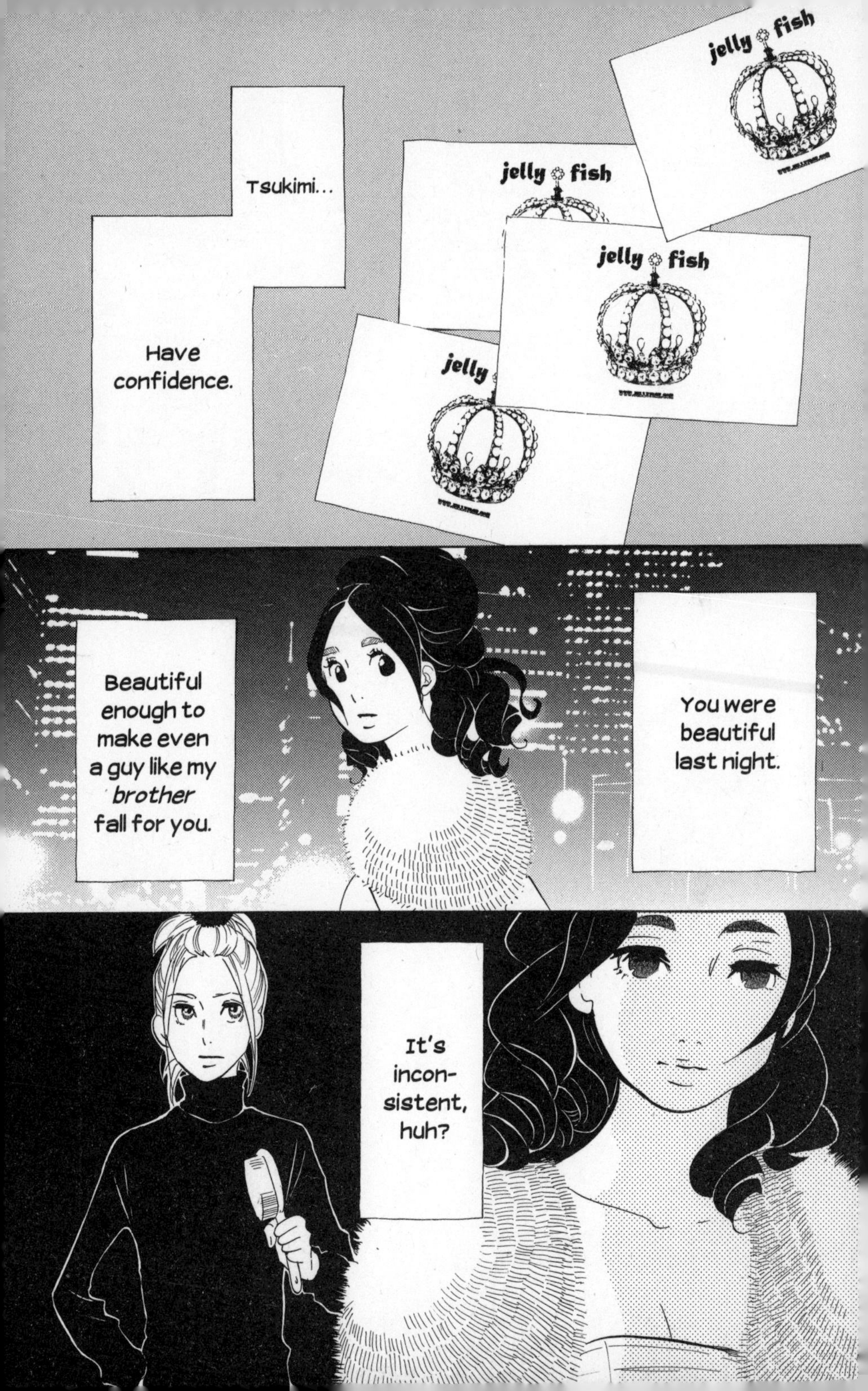
jelly fish
jelly fish
jelly fish
jelly
Tsukimi…
Have confidence.
You were beautiful last night.
Beautiful enough to make even a guy like my *brother* fall for you.
It's incon-sistent, huh?

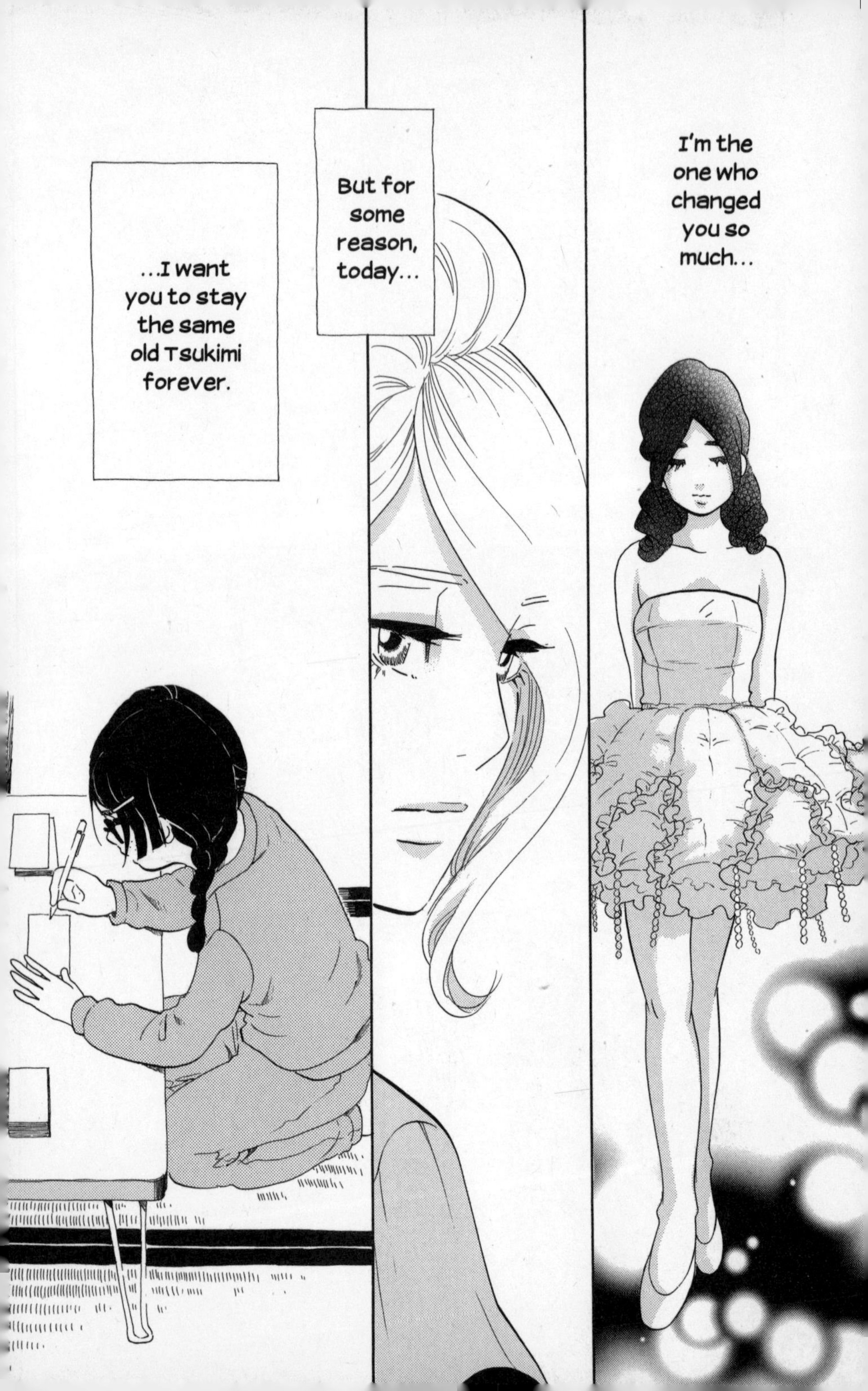
I'm the one who changed you so much...
But for some reason, today...
...I want you to stay the same old Tsukimi forever.

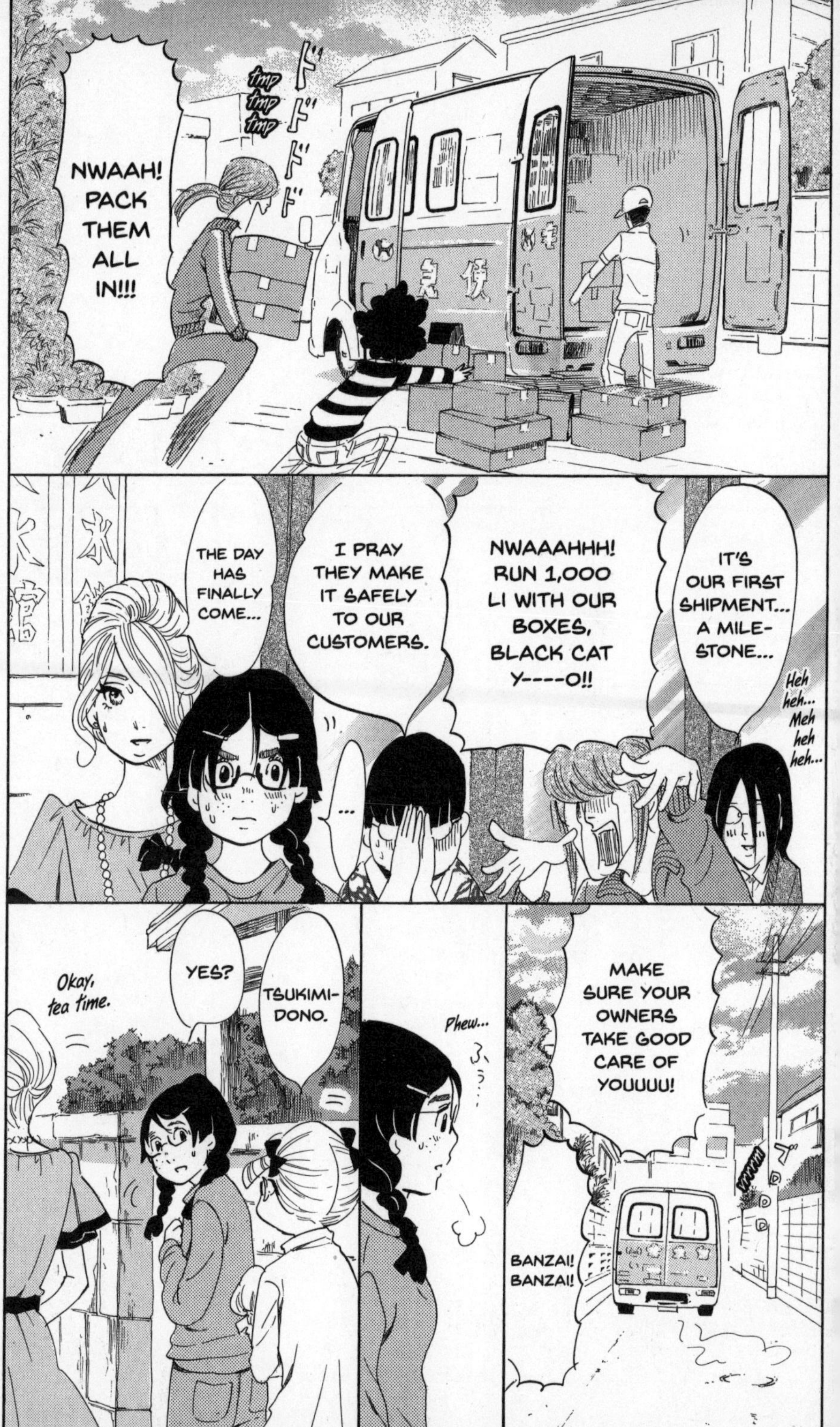

tmp tmp tmp
ドドドド
NWAAH! PACK THEM ALL IN!!!
Heh heh... Meh heh heh...
IT'S OUR FIRST SHIPMENT... A MILE-STONE...
NWAAAHHH! RUN 1,000 LI WITH OUR BOXES, BLACK CAT Y----O!!
I PRAY THEY MAKE IT SAFELY TO OUR CUSTOMERS.
...
THE DAY HAS FINALLY COME...
MAKE SURE YOUR OWNERS TAKE GOOD CARE OF YOUUUU!
BANZAI! BANZAI!
Phew...
ふぅ...
TSUKIMI-DONO.
YES?
Okay, tea time.

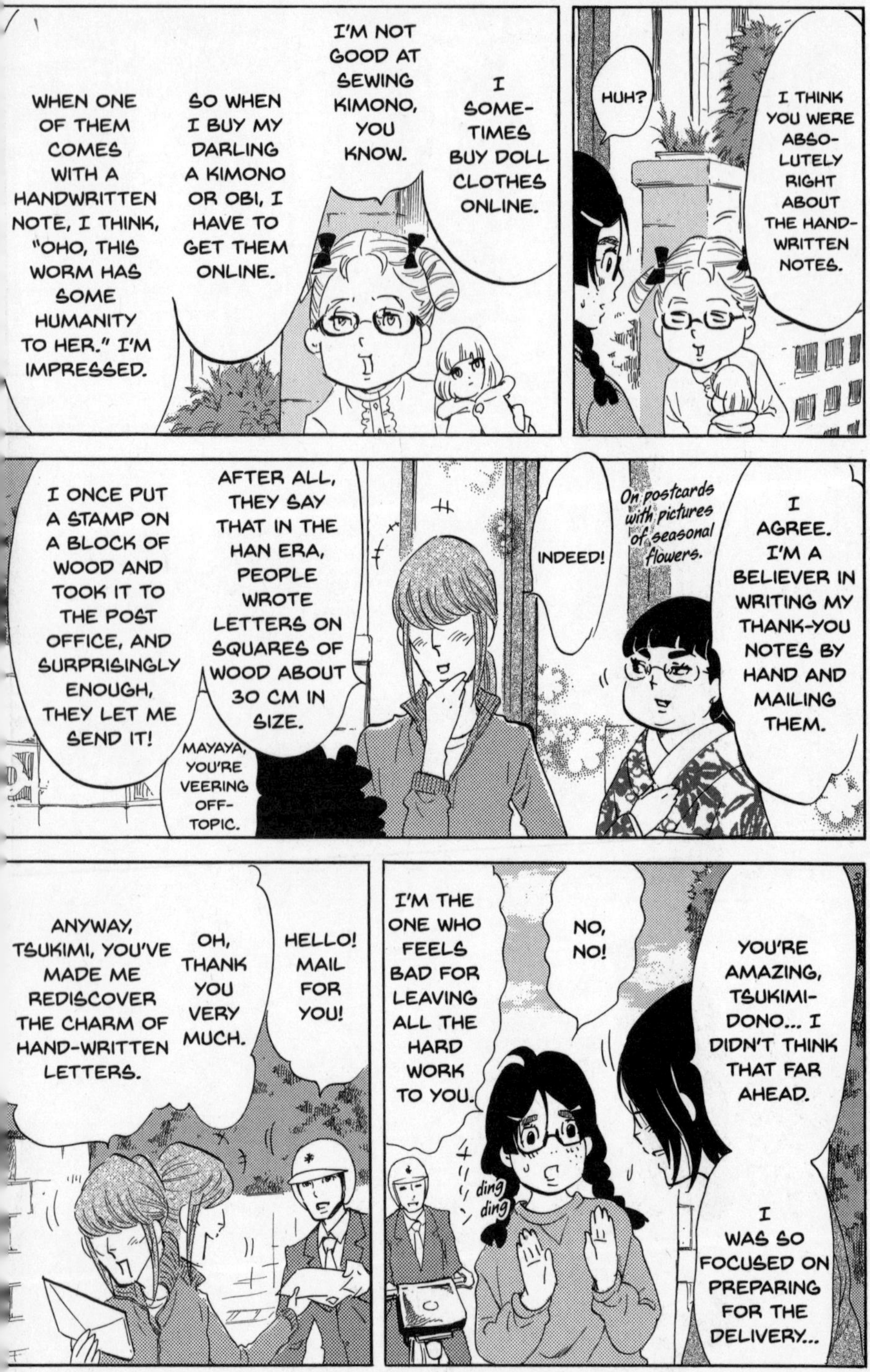
I THINK YOU WERE ABSOLUTELY RIGHT ABOUT THE HAND-WRITTEN NOTES.
HUH?
I SOMETIMES BUY DOLL CLOTHES ONLINE.
I'M NOT GOOD AT SEWING KIMONO, YOU KNOW.
SO WHEN I BUY MY DARLING A KIMONO OR OBI, I HAVE TO GET THEM ONLINE.
WHEN ONE OF THEM COMES WITH A HANDWRITTEN NOTE, I THINK, "OHO, THIS WORM HAS SOME HUMANITY TO HER." I'M IMPRESSED.
I AGREE. I'M A BELIEVER IN WRITING MY THANK-YOU NOTES BY HAND AND MAILING THEM.
On postcards with pictures of seasonal flowers.
INDEED!
AFTER ALL, THEY SAY THAT IN THE HAN ERA, PEOPLE WROTE LETTERS ON SQUARES OF WOOD ABOUT 30 CM IN SIZE.
I ONCE PUT A STAMP ON A BLOCK OF WOOD AND TOOK IT TO THE POST OFFICE, AND SURPRISINGLY ENOUGH, THEY LET ME SEND IT!
MAYAYA, YOU'RE VEERING OFF-TOPIC.
YOU'RE AMAZING, TSUKIMI-DONO... I DIDN'T THINK THAT FAR AHEAD.
I WAS SO FOCUSED ON PREPARING FOR THE DELIVERY...
NO, NO!
I'M THE ONE WHO FEELS BAD FOR LEAVING ALL THE HARD WORK TO YOU.
ding ding
HELLO! MAIL FOR YOU!
OH, THANK YOU VERY MUCH.
ANYWAY, TSUKIMI, YOU'VE MADE ME REDISCOVER THE CHARM OF HAND-WRITTEN LETTERS.

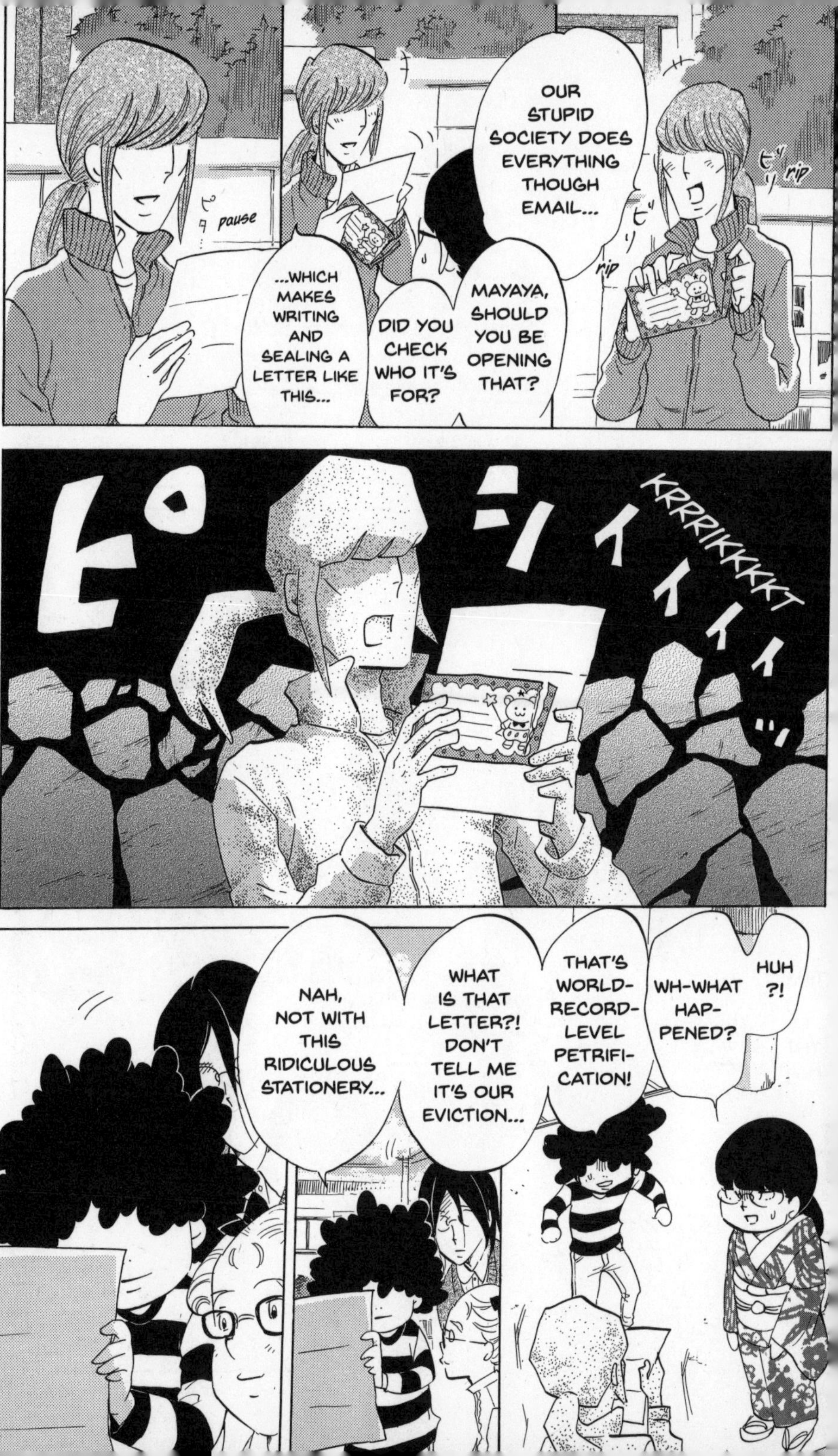
ビリ rip
ビリ rip
OUR STUPID SOCIETY DOES EVERYTHING THOUGH EMAIL...
MAYAYA, SHOULD YOU BE OPENING THAT?
DID YOU CHECK WHO IT'S FOR?
...WHICH MAKES WRITING AND SEALING A LETTER LIKE THIS...
ピタ pause
ピシイイイッ
KRRRIKKKKT
HUH?!
WH-WHAT HAPPENED?
THAT'S WORLD-RECORD-LEVEL PETRIFICATION!
WHAT IS THAT LETTER?! DON'T TELL ME IT'S OUR EVICTION...
NAH, NOT WITH THIS RIDICULOUS STATIONERY...

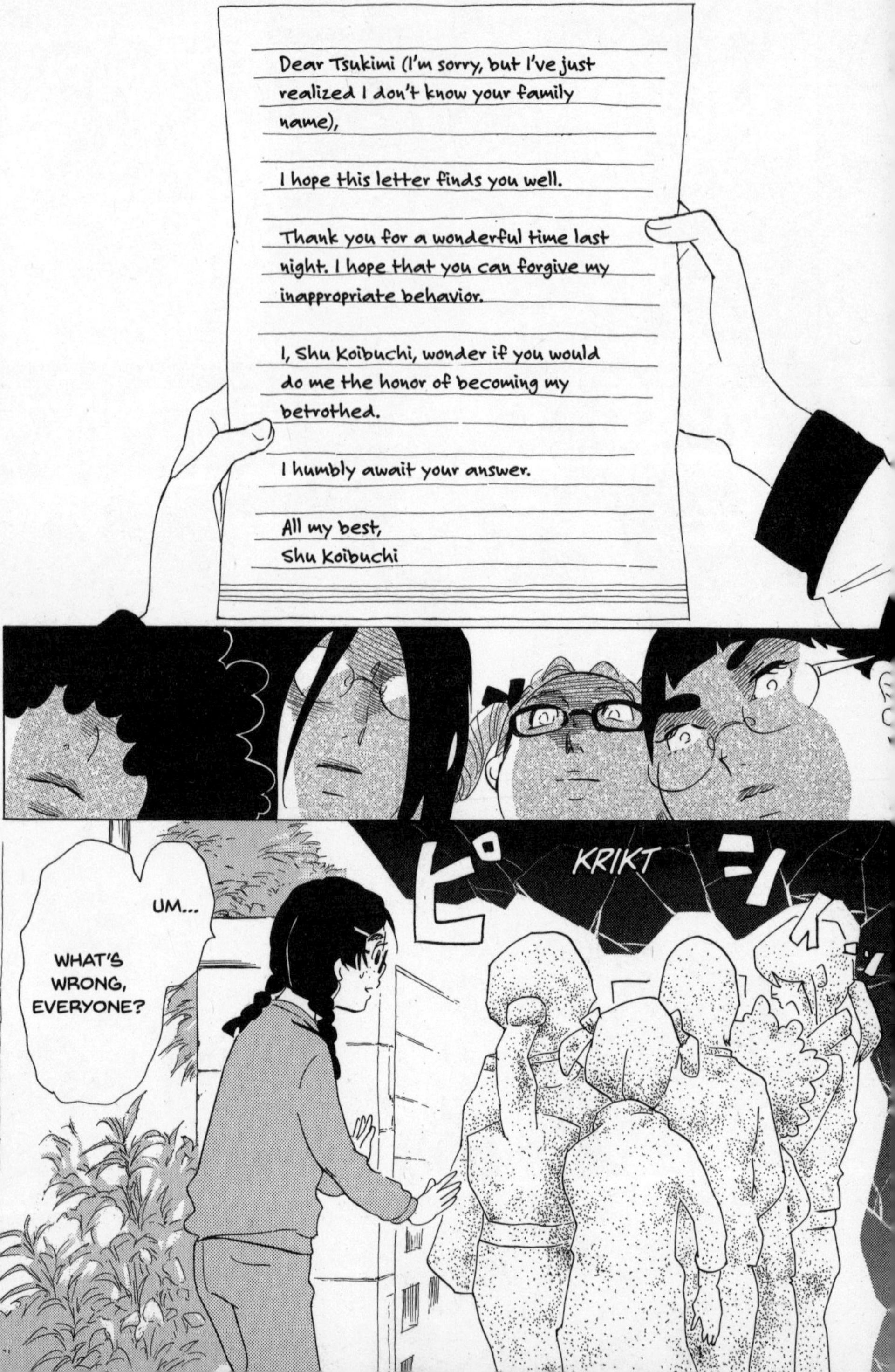
Dear Tsukimi (I'm sorry, but I've just realized I don't know your family name),
I hope this letter finds you well.
Thank you for a wonderful time last night. I hope that you can forgive my inappropriate behavior.
I, Shu Koibuchi, wonder if you would do me the honor of becoming my betrothed.
I humbly await your answer.
All my best,
Shu Koibuchi
KRIKT
UM... WHAT'S WRONG, EVERYONE?

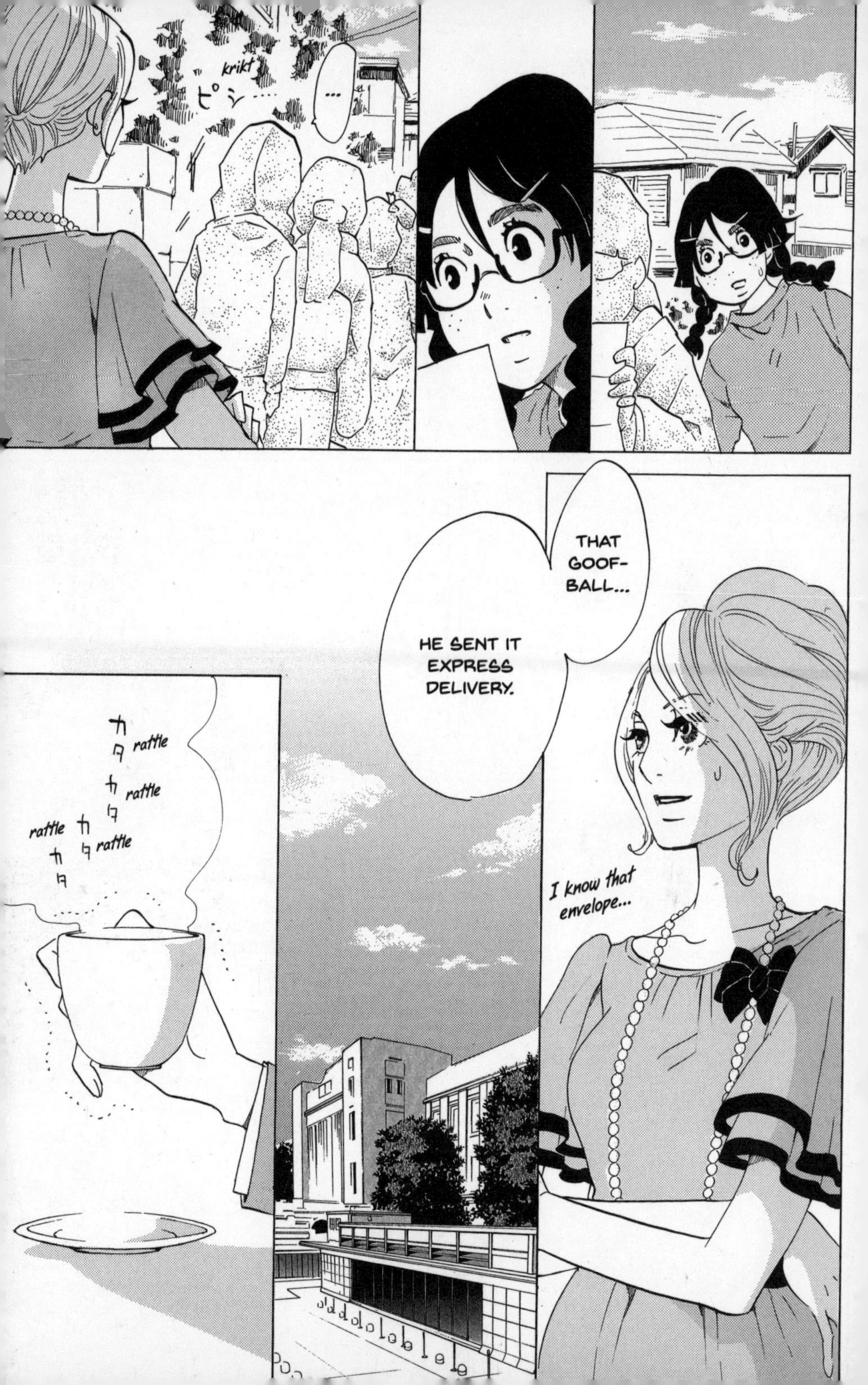
...
ピシ…
krikt
THAT GOOF-BALL...
HE SENT IT EXPRESS DELIVERY.
I know that envelope...
カタ
rattle
カタ
rattle
カタ
rattle
カタ
rattle

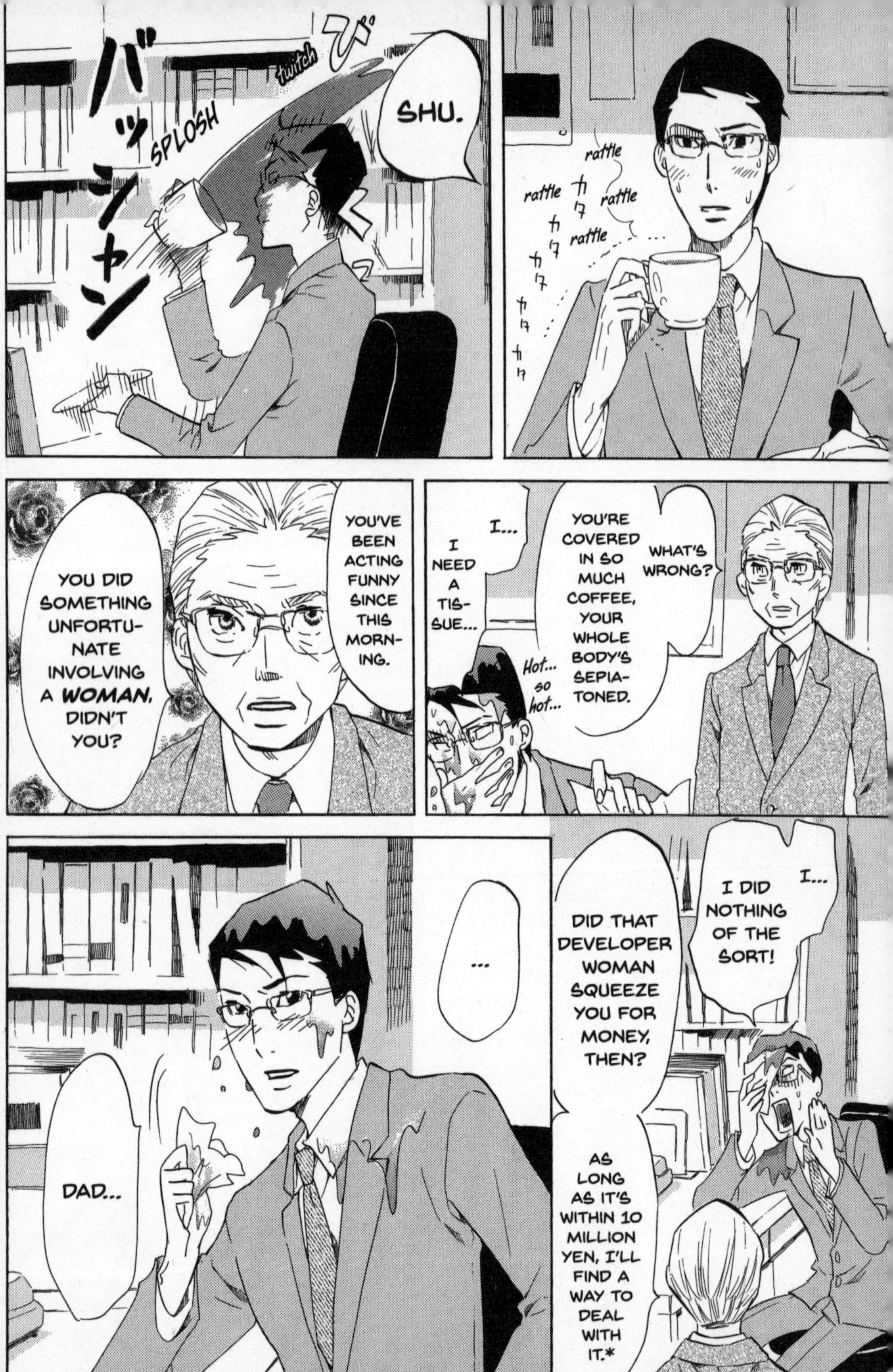

rattle
カタ
rattle
カタ
rattle
カタ
rattle
カタ
カタ
SHU.
ぴ
twitch
バッシャン
SPLOSH
WHAT'S WRONG?
YOU'RE COVERED IN SO MUCH COFFEE, YOUR WHOLE BODY'S SEPIA-TONED.
I...
I NEED A TIS-SUE...
Hot... so hot...
YOU'VE BEEN ACTING FUNNY SINCE THIS MORN-ING.
YOU DID SOMETHING UNFORTU-NATE INVOLVING A **WOMAN**, DIDN'T YOU?
I...
I DID NOTHING OF THE SORT!
DID THAT DEVELOPER WOMAN SQUEEZE YOU FOR MONEY, THEN?
AS LONG AS IT'S WITHIN 10 MILLION YEN, I'LL FIND A WAY TO DEAL WITH IT.*
...
DAD...

*About $100,000 USD.

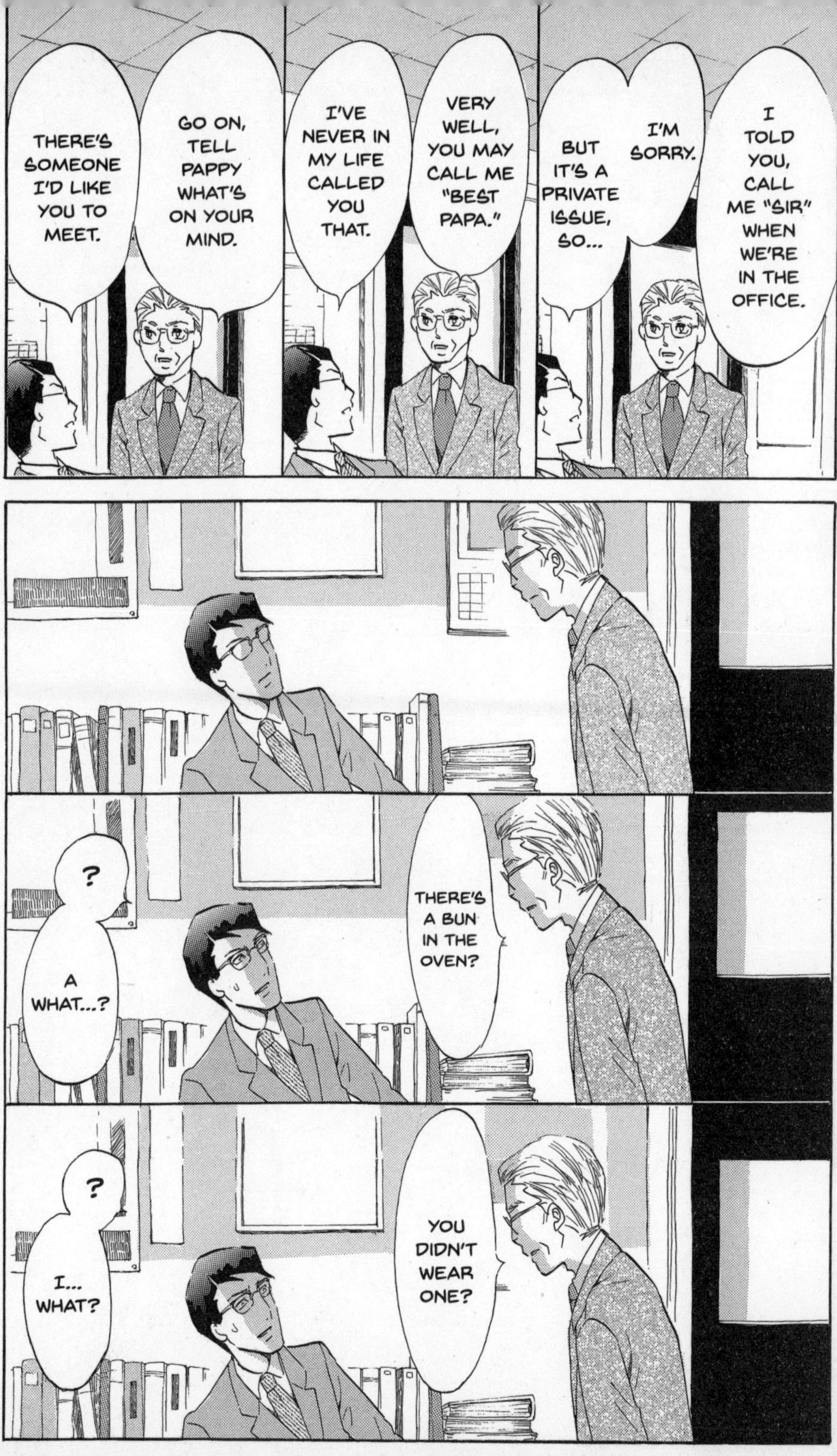
I TOLD YOU, CALL ME "SIR" WHEN WE'RE IN THE OFFICE.
I'M SORRY.
BUT IT'S A PRIVATE ISSUE, SO...
VERY WELL, YOU MAY CALL ME "BEST PAPA."
I'VE NEVER IN MY LIFE CALLED YOU THAT.
GO ON, TELL PAPPY WHAT'S ON YOUR MIND.
THERE'S SOMEONE I'D LIKE YOU TO MEET.
THERE'S A BUN IN THE OVEN?
?
A WHAT...?
YOU DIDN'T WEAR ONE?
?
I... WHAT?

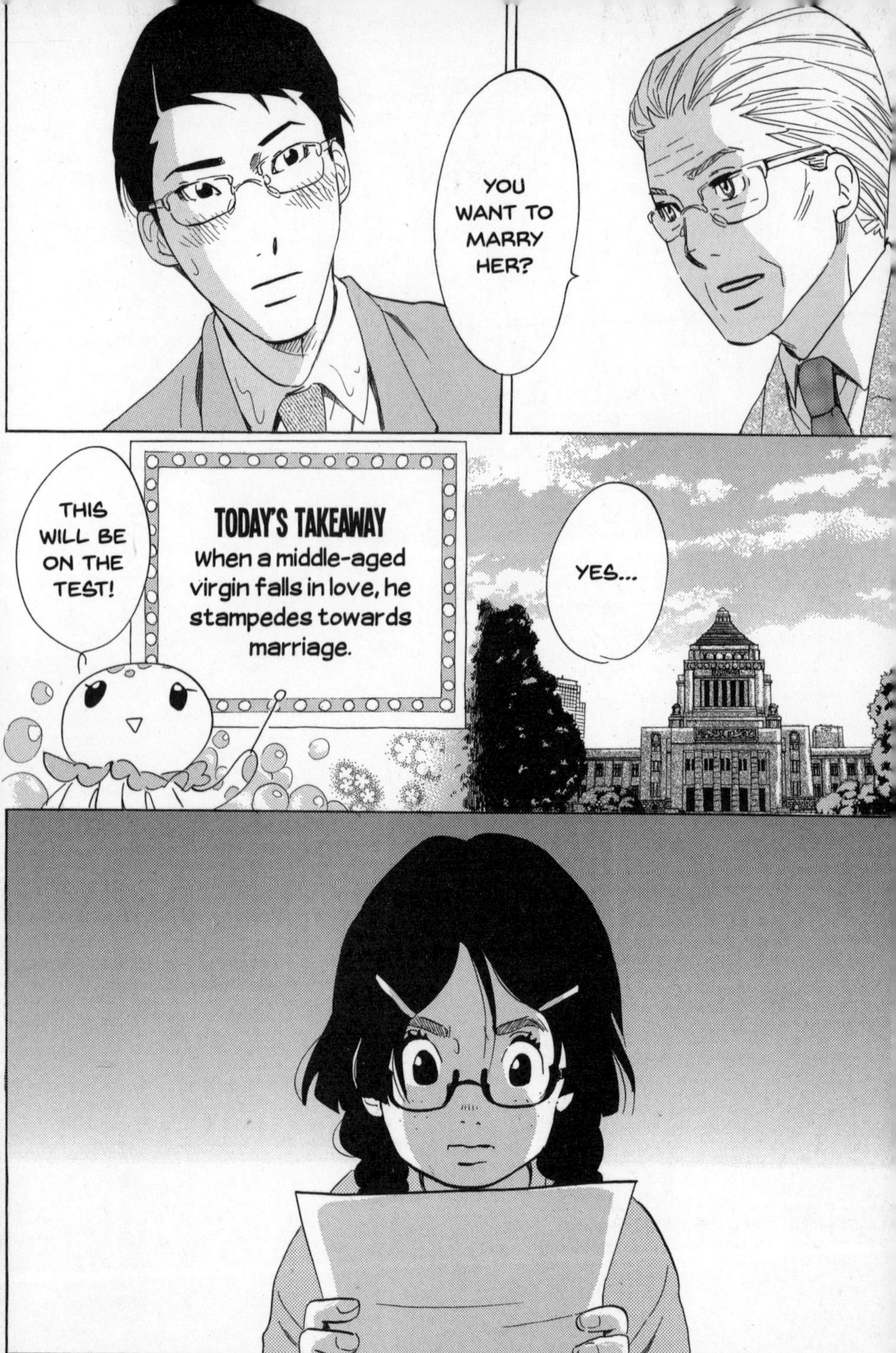
YOU WANT TO MARRY HER?
YES...
TODAY'S TAKEAWAY
When a middle-aged virgin falls in love, he stampedes towards marriage.
THIS WILL BE ON THE TEST!

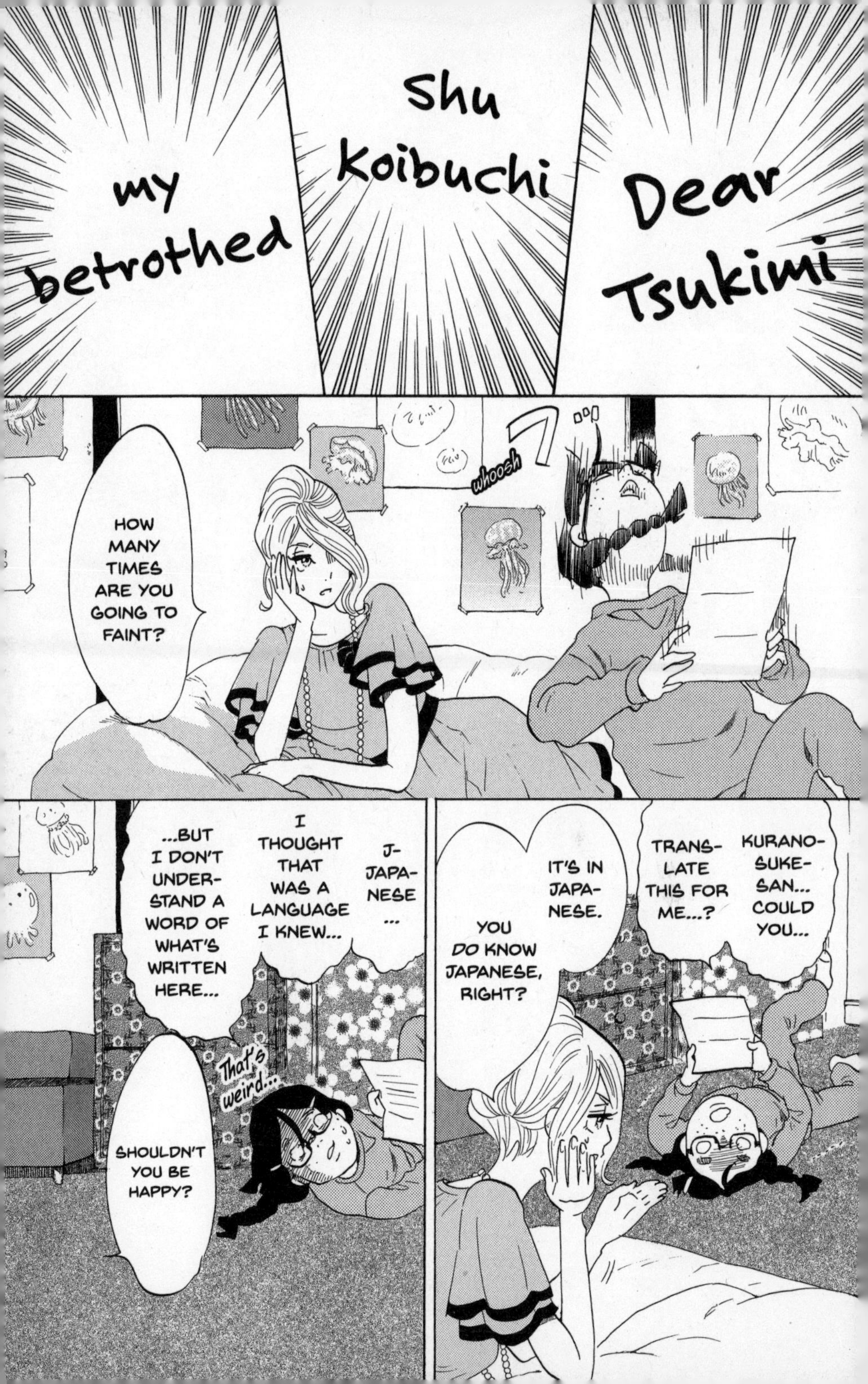
Dear Tsukimi
Shu Koibuchi
my betrothed
whoosh
HOW MANY TIMES ARE YOU GOING TO FAINT?
KURANO-SUKE-SAN... COULD YOU...
TRANS-LATE THIS FOR ME...?
IT'S IN JAPA-NESE.
YOU *DO* KNOW JAPANESE, RIGHT?
J-JAPA-NESE...
I THOUGHT THAT WAS A LANGUAGE I KNEW...
...BUT I DON'T UNDER-STAND A WORD OF WHAT'S WRITTEN HERE...
That's weird...
SHOULDN'T YOU BE HAPPY?

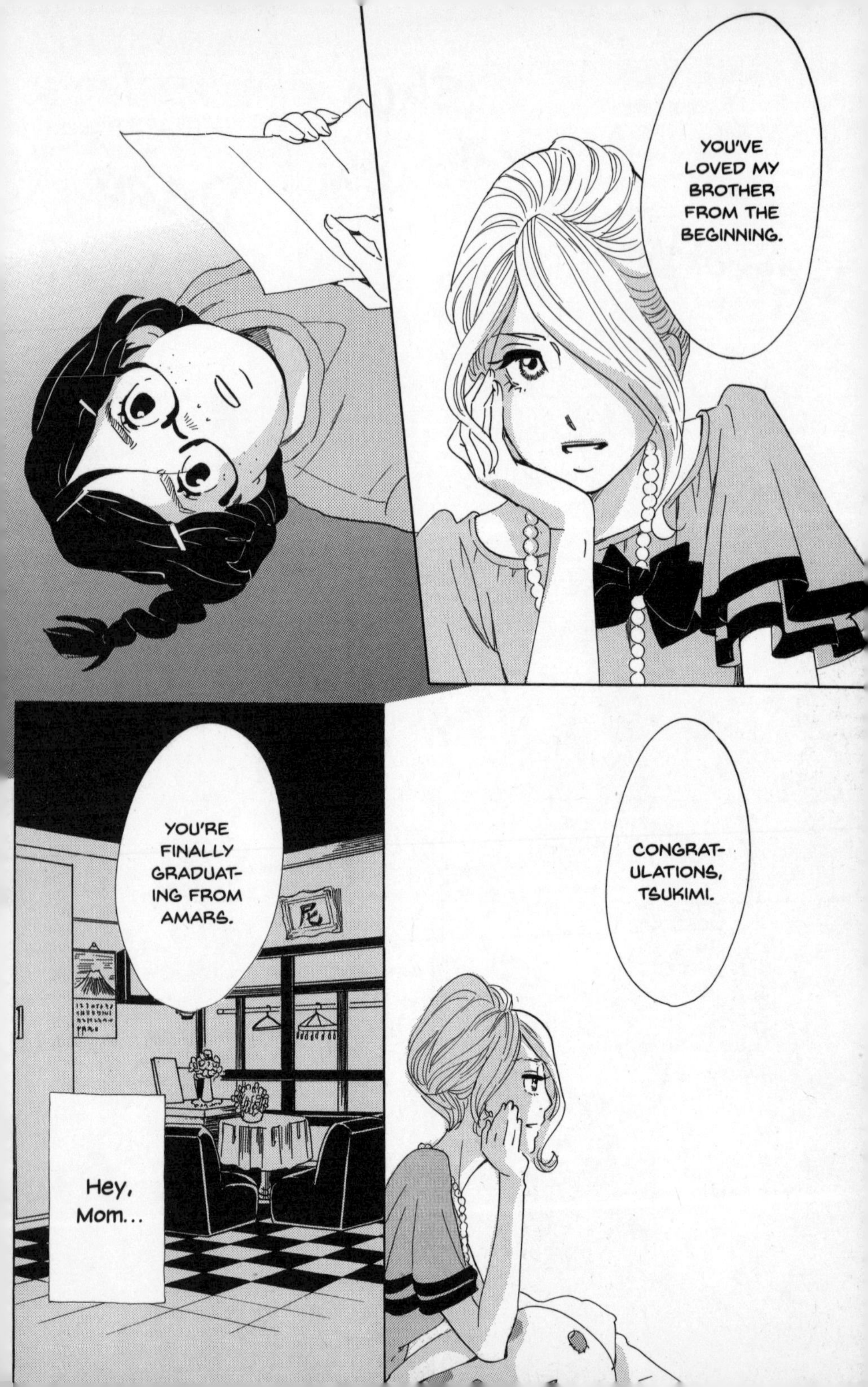
YOU'VE LOVED MY BROTHER FROM THE BEGINNING.
CONGRATULATIONS, TSUKIMI.
YOU'RE FINALLY GRADUATING FROM AMARS.
Hey, Mom...

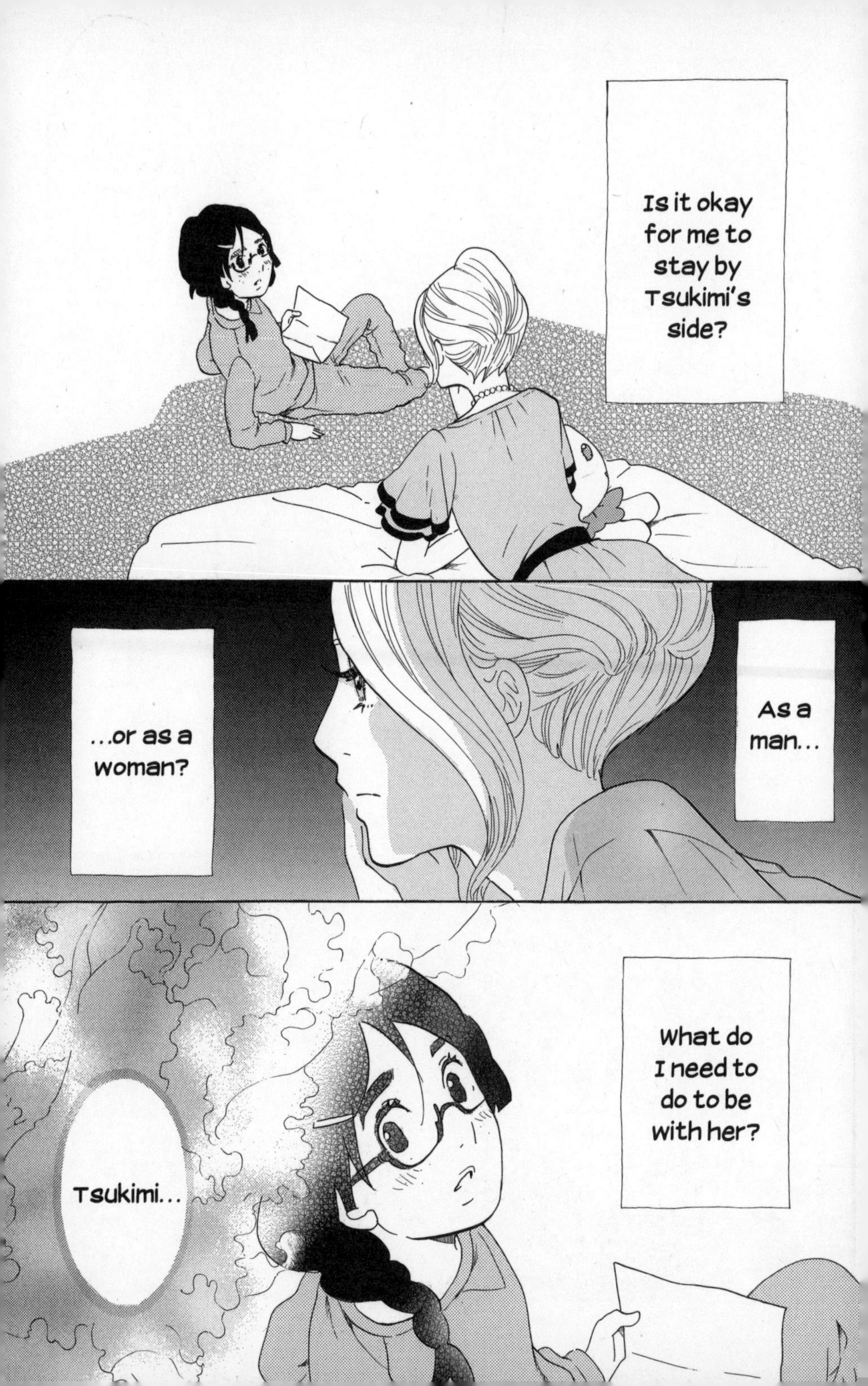
Is it okay for me to stay by Tsukimi's side?
As a man...
...or as a woman?
What do I need to do to be with her?
Tsukimi...

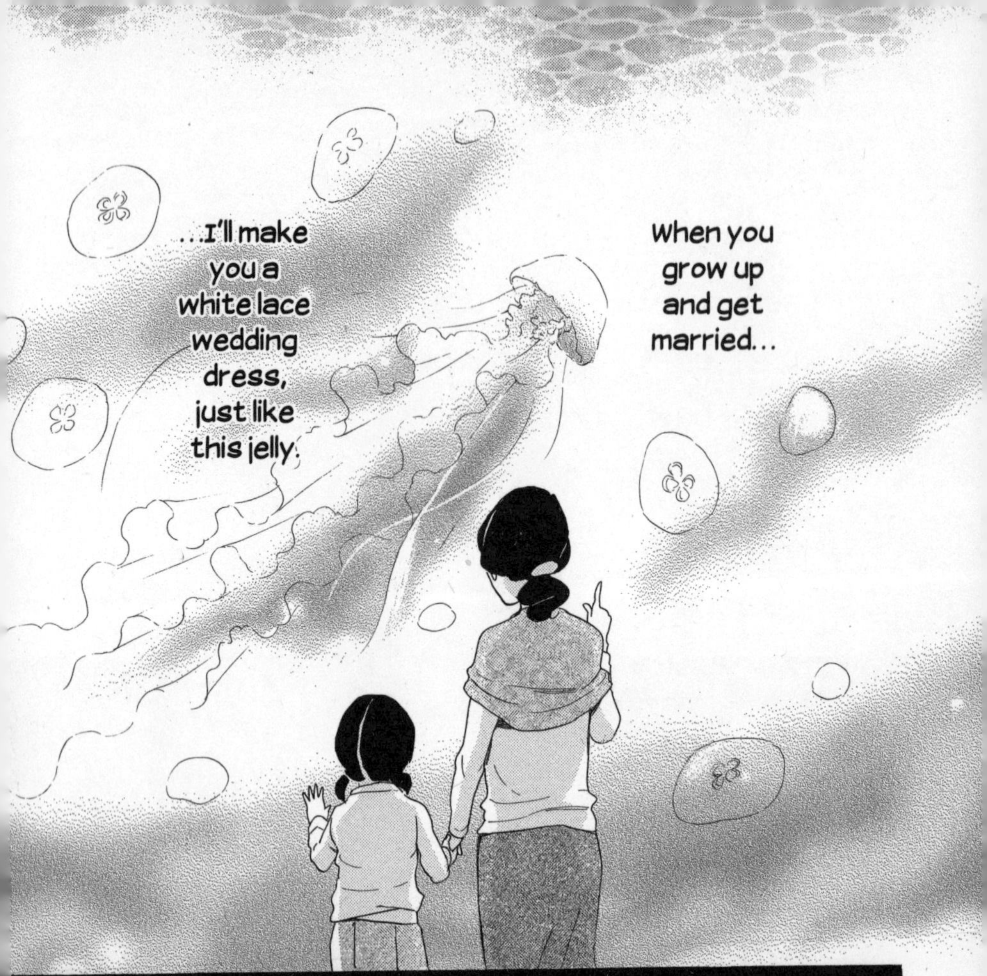
When you grow up and get married...
...I'll make you a white lace wedding dress, just like this jelly.

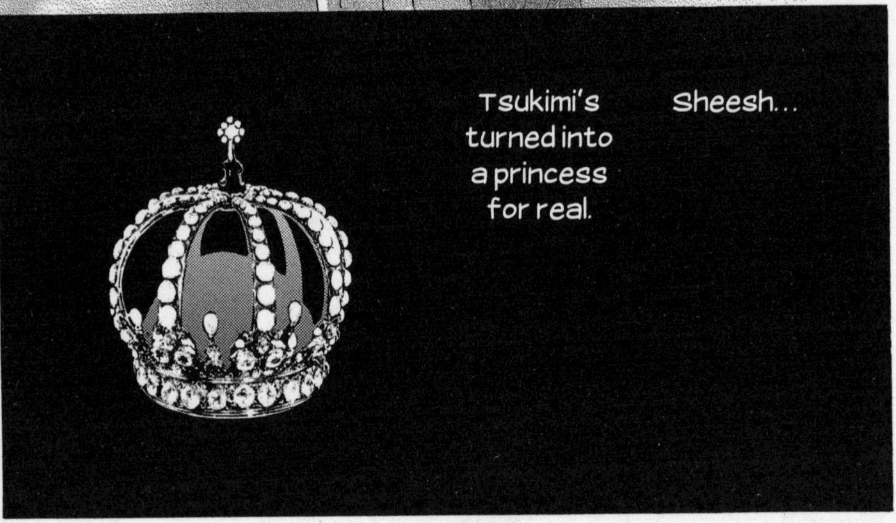
Sheesh...
Tsukimi's turned into a princess for real.

Episode 51
The Sorcerer's Younger Brother

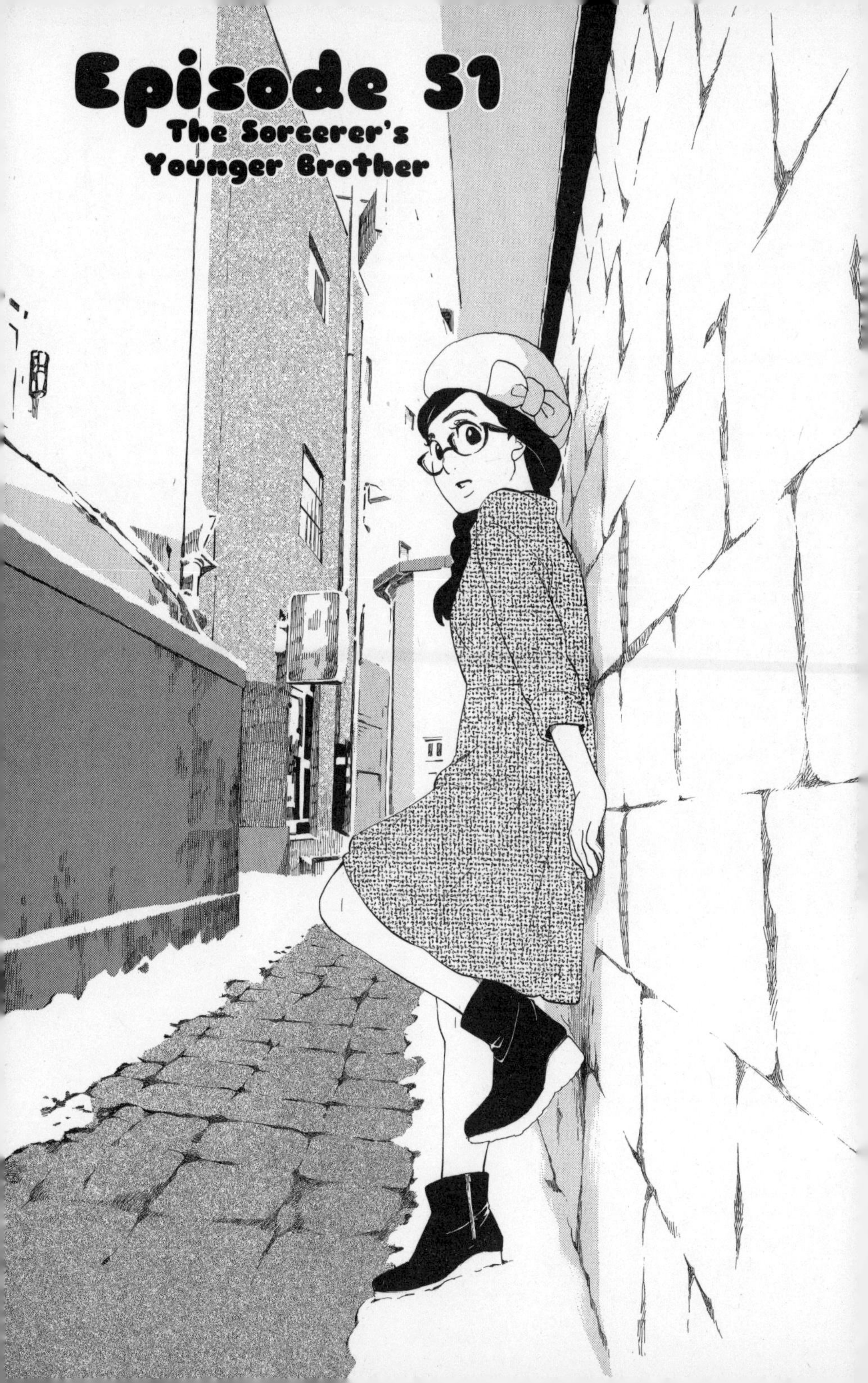

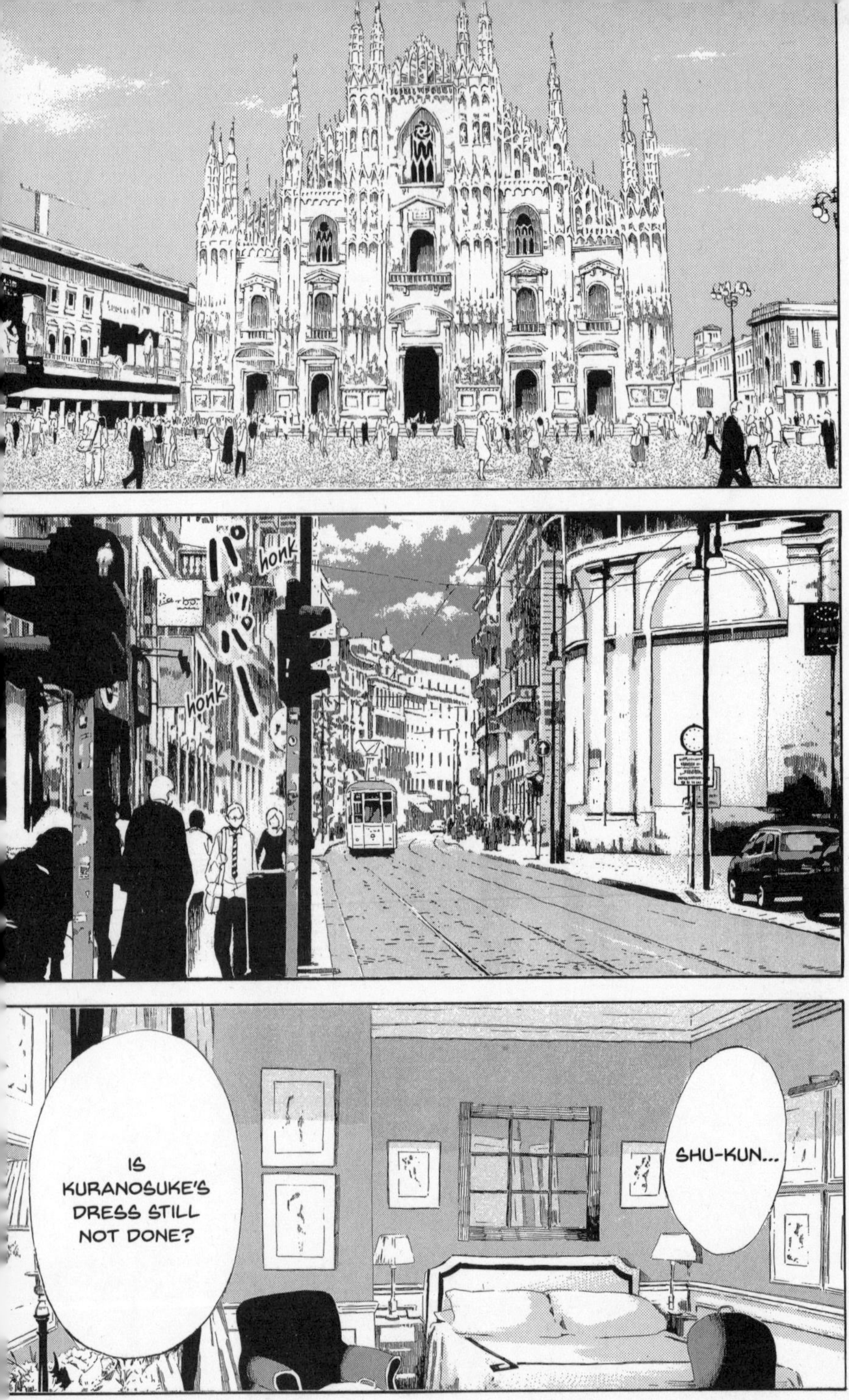
honk
honk
SHU-KUN...
IS KURANOSUKE'S DRESS STILL NOT DONE?

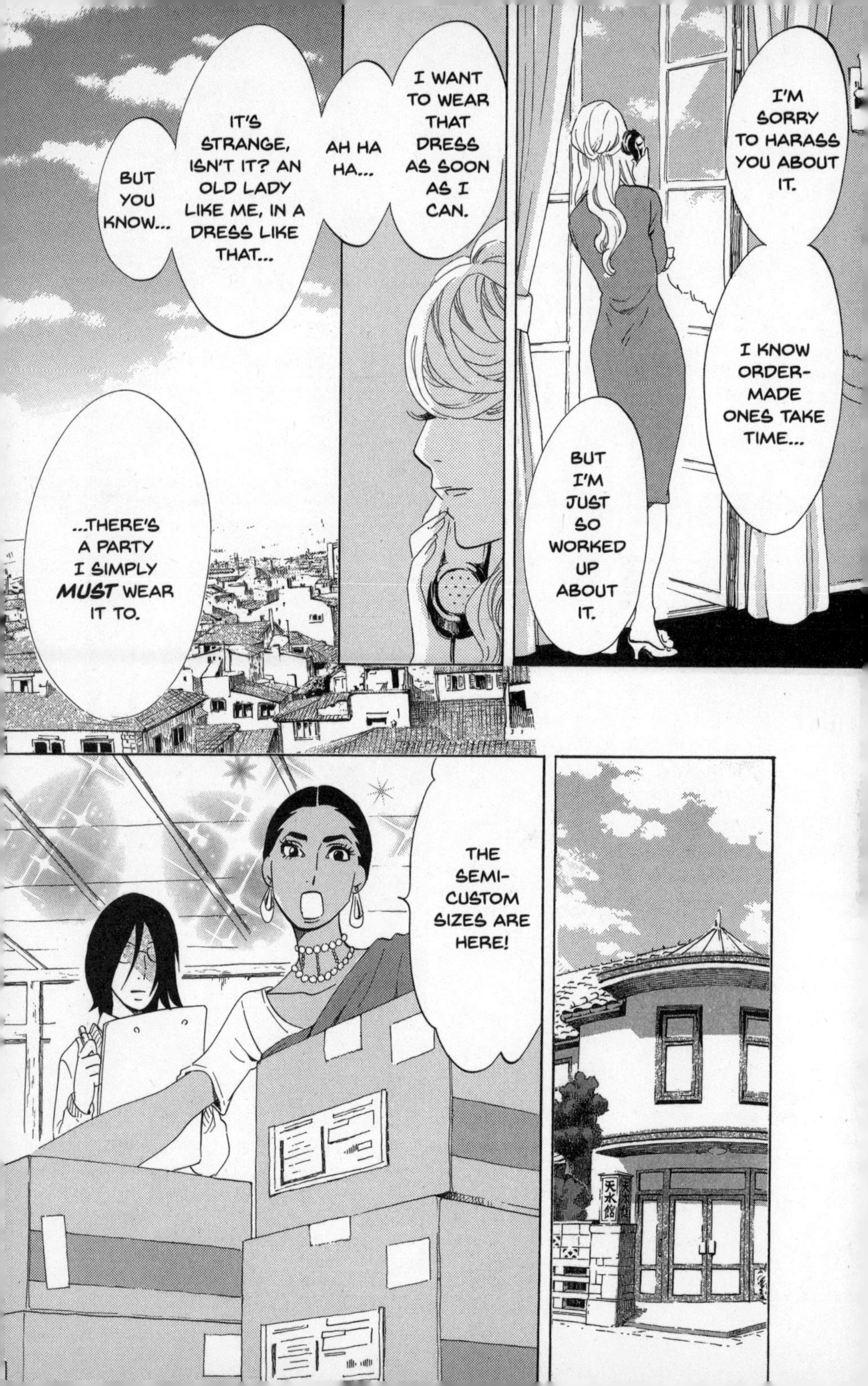

I'M SORRY TO HARASS YOU ABOUT IT.
I KNOW ORDER-MADE ONES TAKE TIME...
BUT I'M JUST SO WORKED UP ABOUT IT.
I WANT TO WEAR THAT DRESS AS SOON AS I CAN.
AH HA HA...
IT'S STRANGE, ISN'T IT? AN OLD LADY LIKE ME, IN A DRESS LIKE THAT...
BUT YOU KNOW...
...THERE'S A PARTY I SIMPLY *MUST* WEAR IT TO.
天水館
THE SEMI-CUSTOM SIZES ARE HERE!

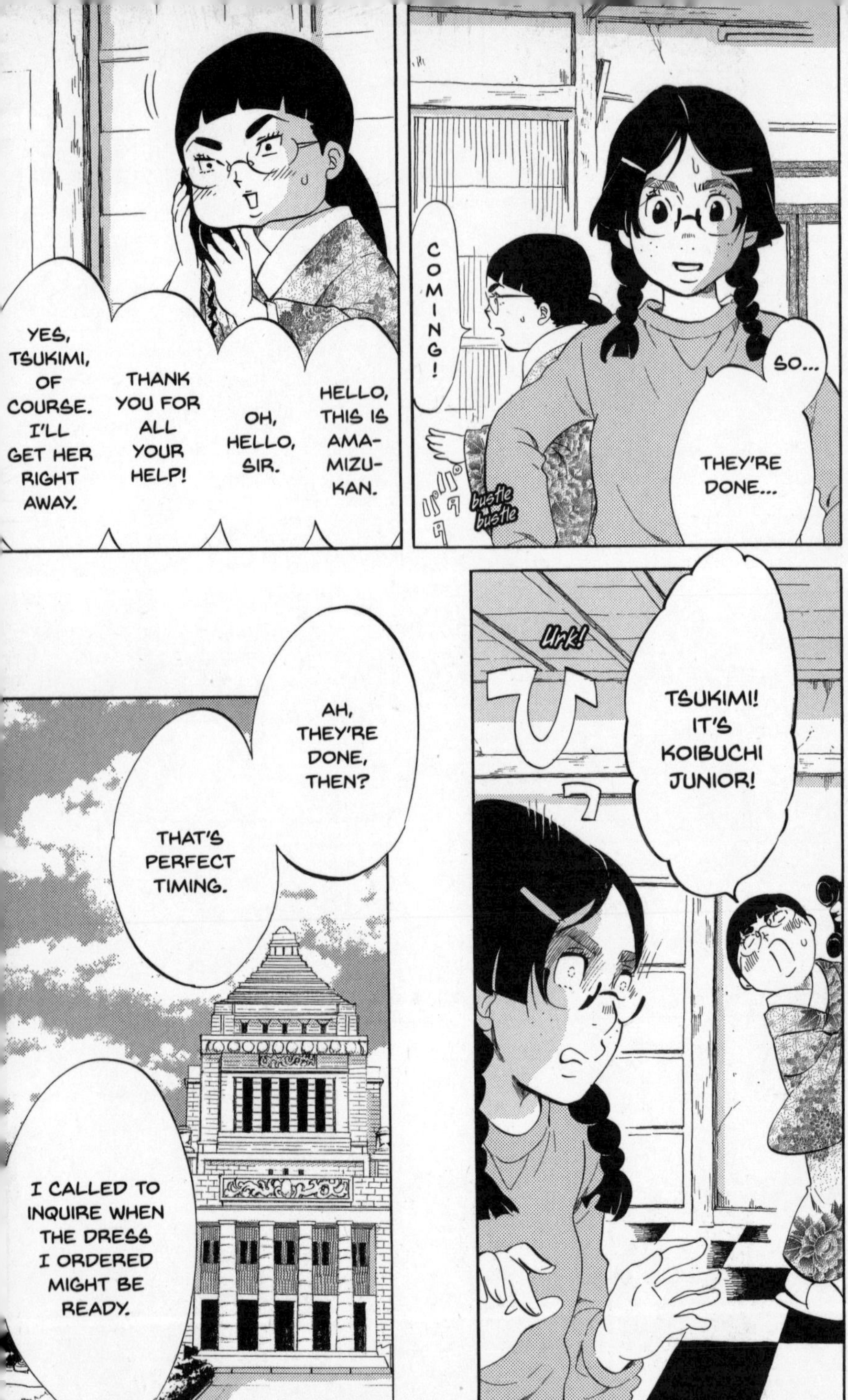
SO...
THEY'RE DONE...
COMING!
bustle bustle
HELLO, THIS IS AMAMIZUKAN.
OH, HELLO, SIR.
THANK YOU FOR ALL YOUR HELP!
YES, TSUKIMI, OF COURSE. I'LL GET HER RIGHT AWAY.
TSUKIMI! IT'S KOIBUCHI JUNIOR!
Urk!
AH, THEY'RE DONE, THEN?
THAT'S PERFECT TIMING.
I CALLED TO INQUIRE WHEN THE DRESS I ORDERED MIGHT BE READY.

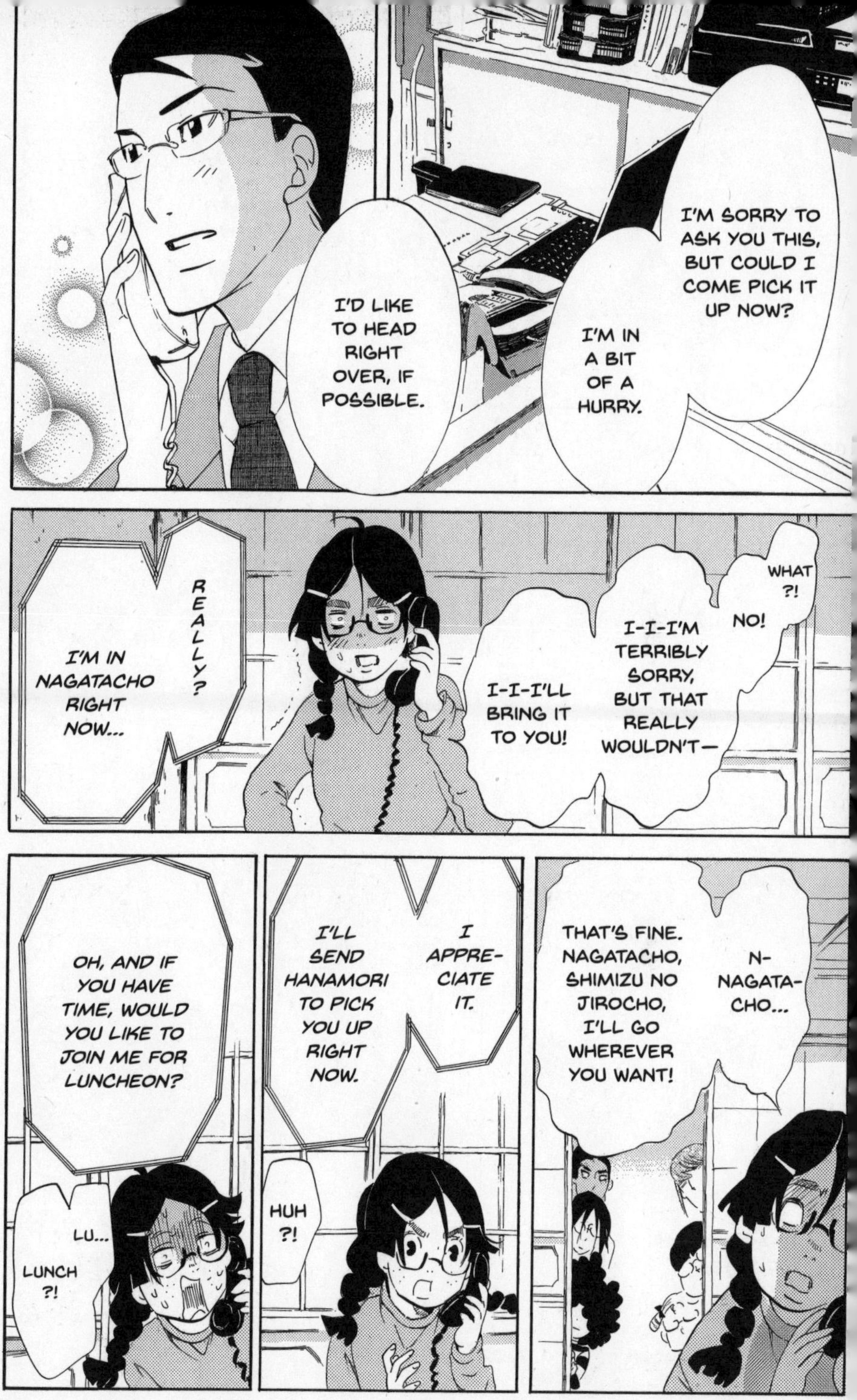
I'M SORRY TO ASK YOU THIS, BUT COULD I COME PICK IT UP NOW?
I'M IN A BIT OF A HURRY.
I'D LIKE TO HEAD RIGHT OVER, IF POSSIBLE.
WHAT?!
NO!
I-I-I'M TERRIBLY SORRY, BUT THAT REALLY WOULDN'T—
I-I-I'LL BRING IT TO YOU!
REALLY?
I'M IN NAGATACHO RIGHT NOW...
N-NAGATACHO...
THAT'S FINE. NAGATACHO, SHIMIZU NO JIROCHO, I'LL GO WHEREVER YOU WANT!
I APPRECIATE IT.
I'LL SEND HANAMORI TO PICK YOU UP RIGHT NOW.
HUH?!
OH, AND IF YOU HAVE TIME, WOULD YOU LIKE TO JOIN ME FOR LUNCHEON?
LU...
LUNCH?!

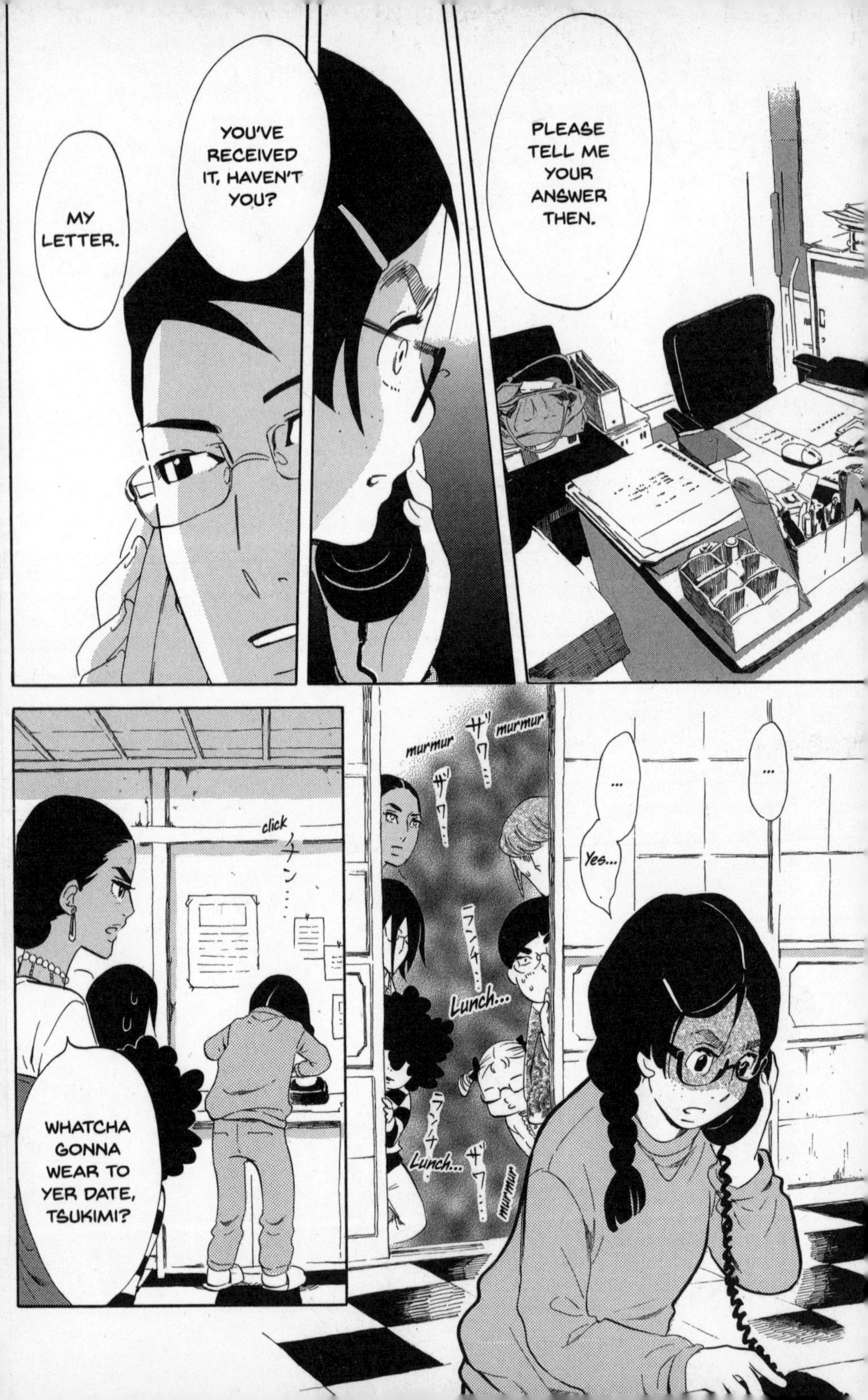
PLEASE TELL ME YOUR ANSWER THEN.
YOU'VE RECEIVED IT, HAVEN'T YOU?
MY LETTER.
...
...
Yes...
murmur
murmur
Lunch...
Lunch...
murmur
click
WHATCHA GONNA WEAR TO YER DATE, TSUKIMI?

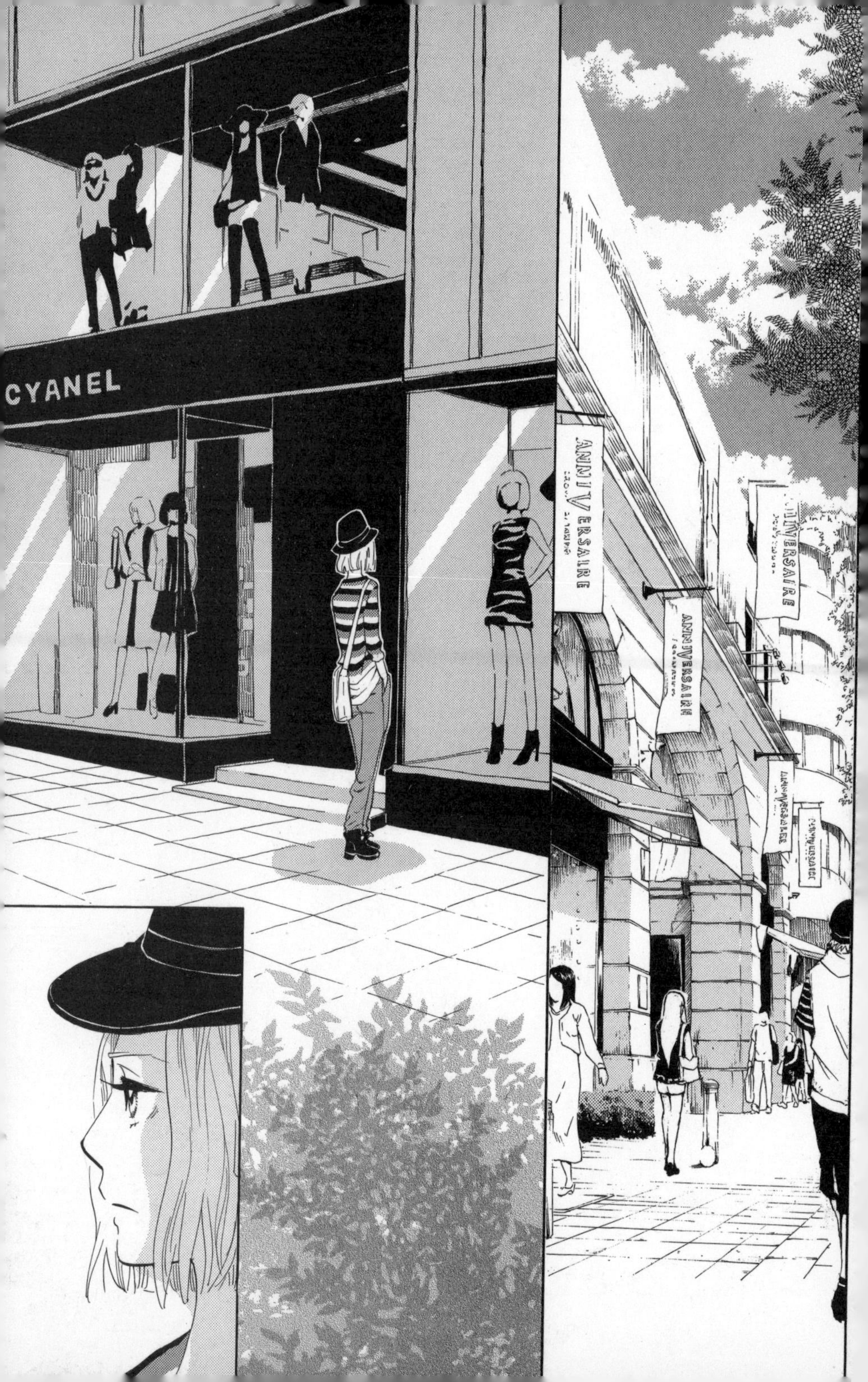
ANNIVERSAIRE
ANNIVERSAIRE
CYANEL

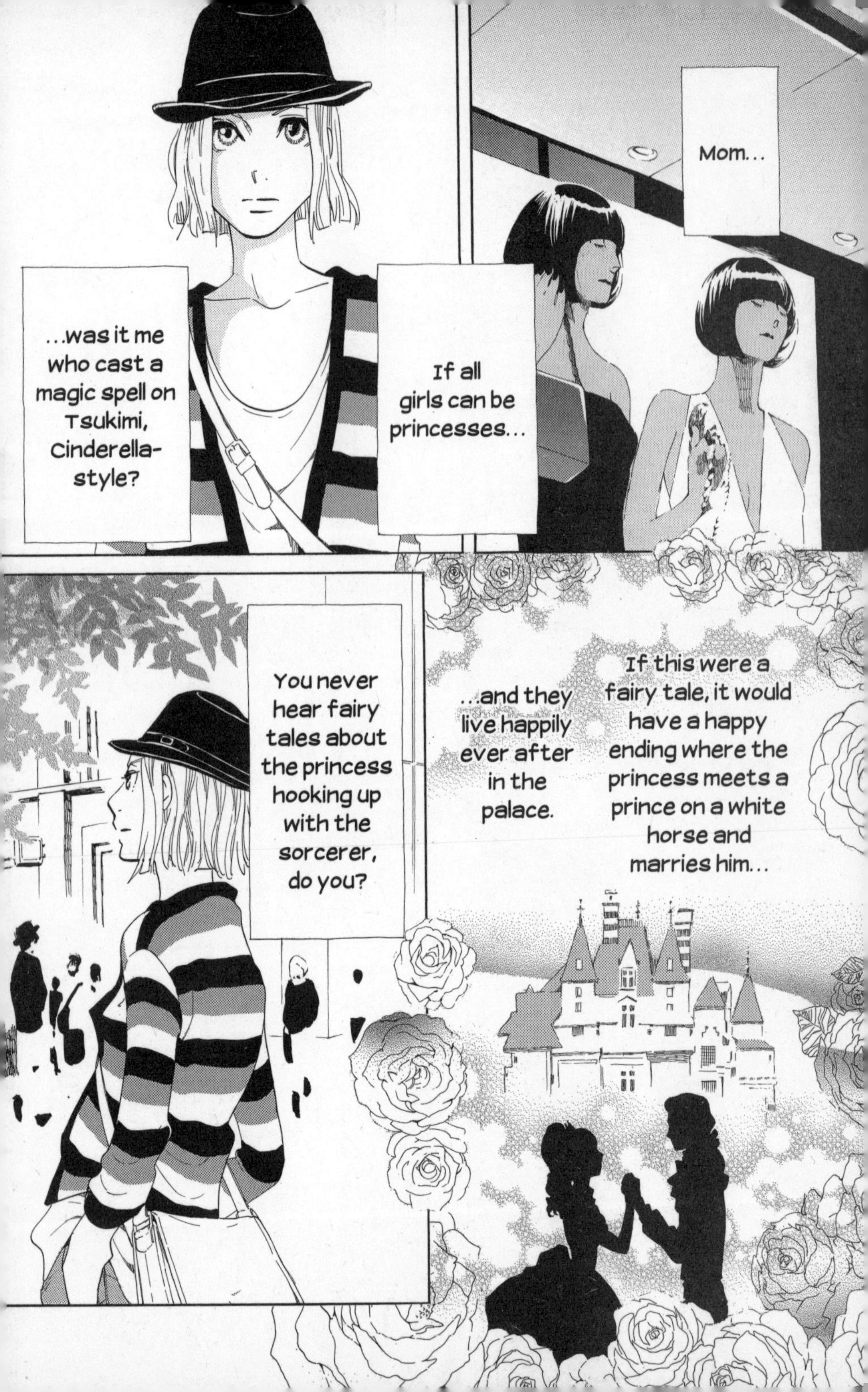
Mom...
If all girls can be princesses...
...was it me who cast a magic spell on Tsukimi, Cinderella-style?
If this were a fairy tale, it would have a happy ending where the princess meets a prince on a white horse and marries him...
...and they live happily ever after in the palace.
You never hear fairy tales about the princess hooking up with the sorcerer, do you?

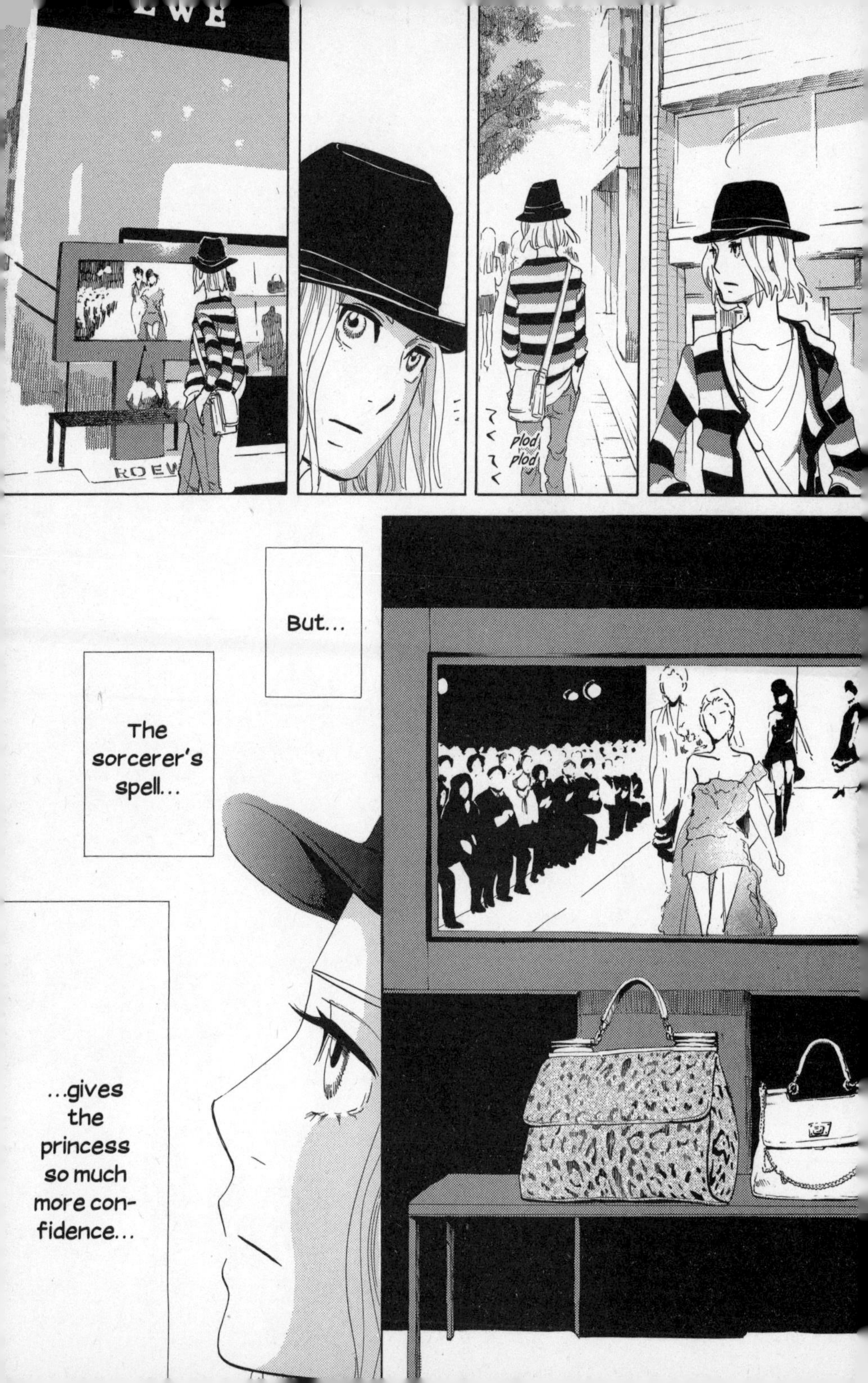

plod
plod
EWE
ROEW
But...
The sorcerer's spell...
...gives the princess so much more confidence...

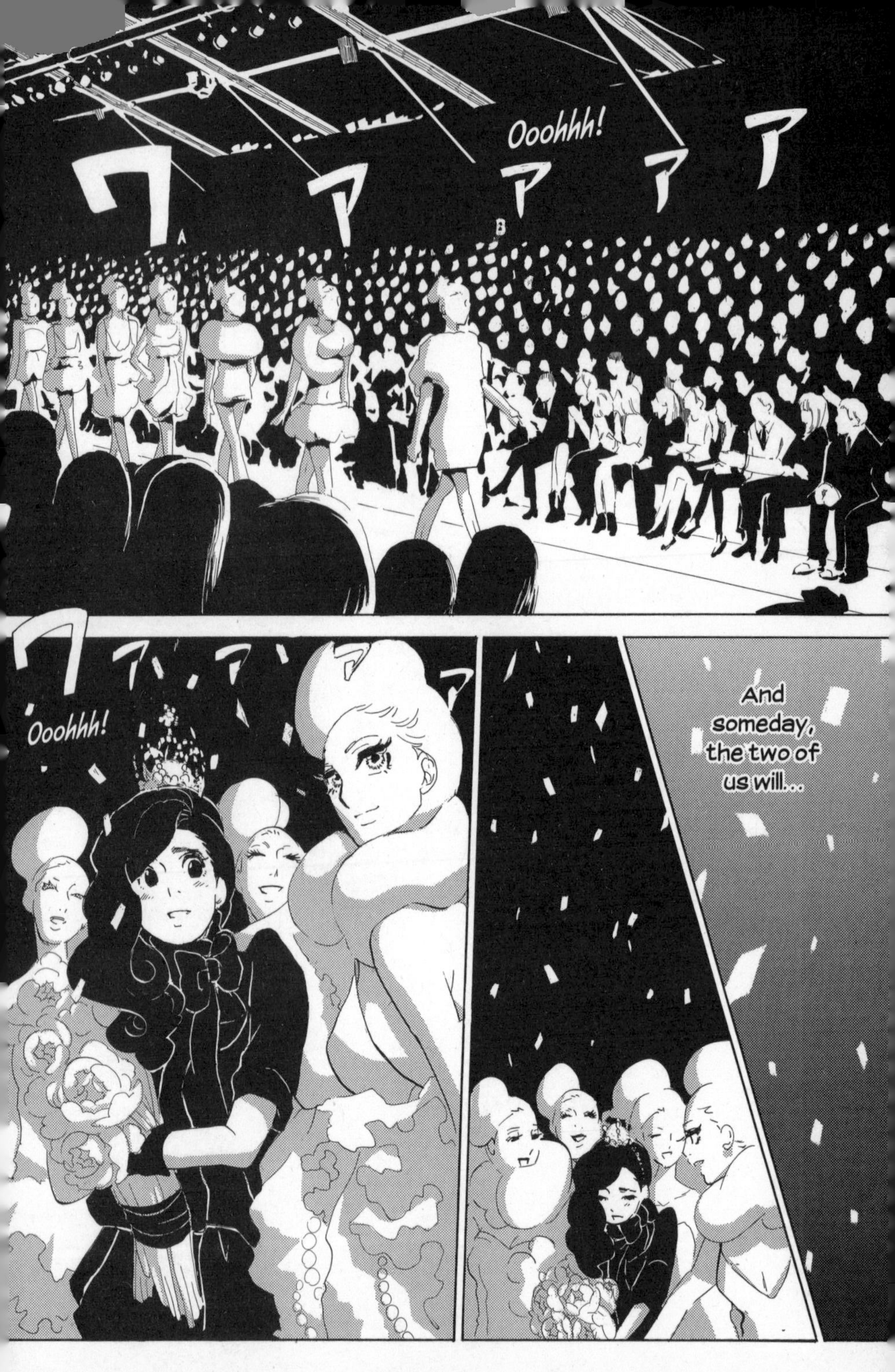
Ooohhh!
ワアアアア
And someday, the two of us will...
Ooohhh!
ワァァァァ

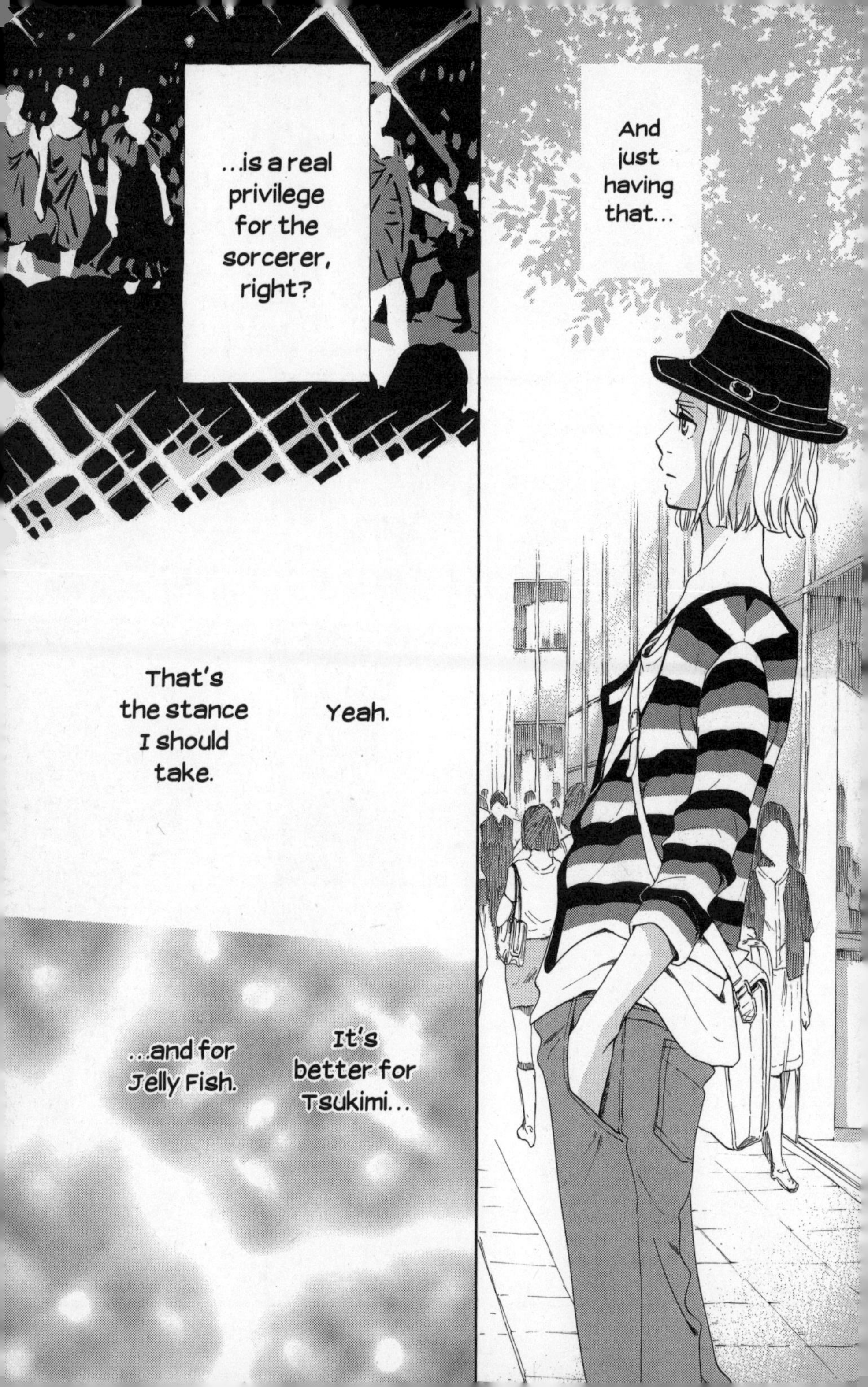
And just having that…
…is a real privilege for the sorcerer, right?
Yeah.
That's the stance I should take.
It's better for Tsukimi…
…and for Jelly Fish.

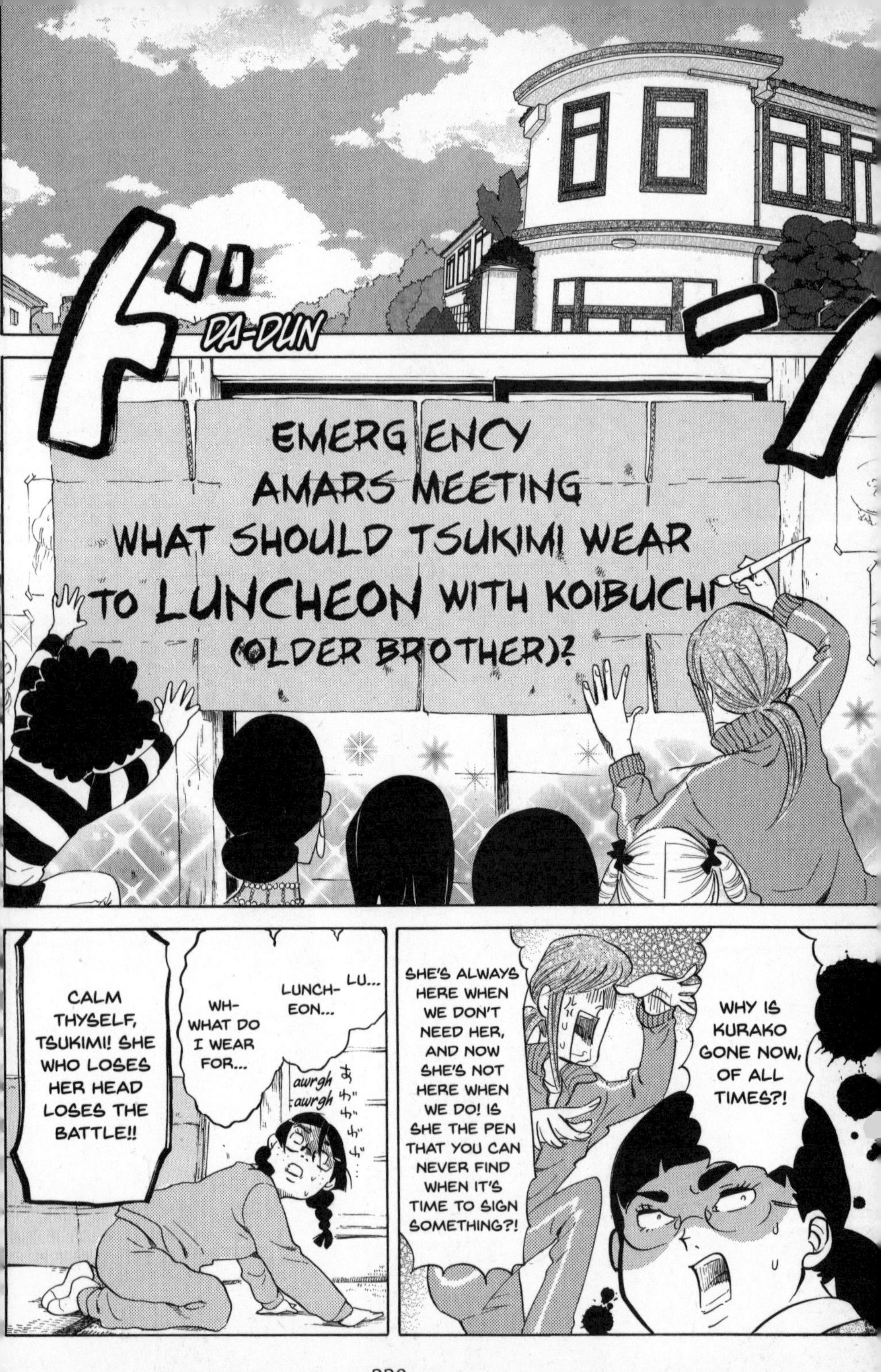
DA-DUN
EMERGENCY
AMARS MEETING
WHAT SHOULD TSUKIMI WEAR
TO LUNCHEON WITH KOIBUCHI
(OLDER BROTHER)?
WHY IS KURAKO GONE NOW, OF ALL TIMES?!
SHE'S ALWAYS HERE WHEN WE DON'T NEED HER, AND NOW SHE'S NOT HERE WHEN WE DO! IS SHE THE PEN THAT YOU CAN NEVER FIND WHEN IT'S TIME TO SIGN SOMETHING?!
LU...
LUNCH-EON...
WH-WHAT DO I WEAR FOR...
awrgh awrgh
CALM THYSELF, TSUKIMI! SHE WHO LOSES HER HEAD LOSES THE BATTLE!!

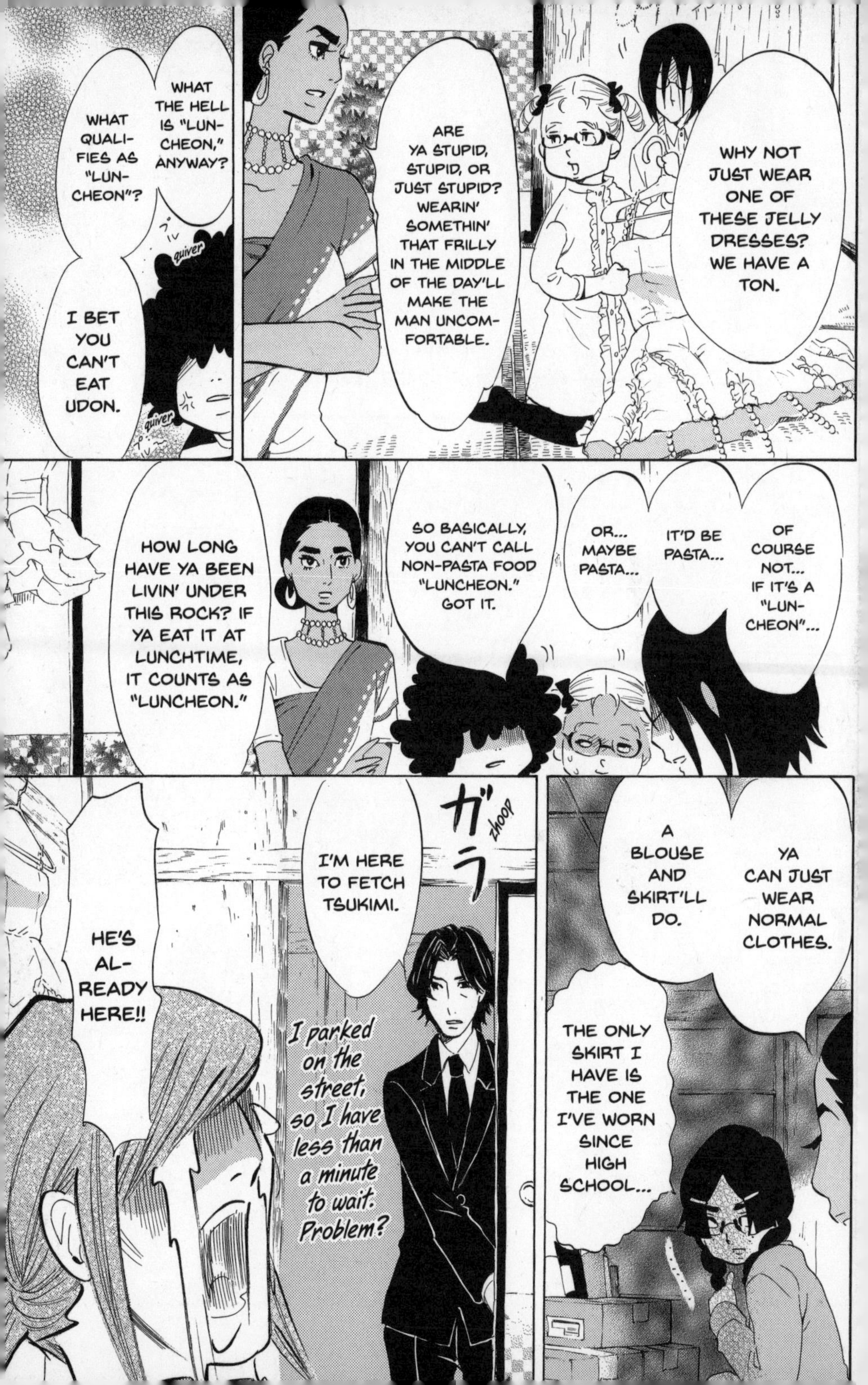
WHY NOT JUST WEAR ONE OF THESE JELLY DRESSES? WE HAVE A TON.
ARE YA STUPID, STUPID, OR JUST STUPID? WEARIN' SOMETHIN' THAT FRILLY IN THE MIDDLE OF THE DAY'LL MAKE THE MAN UNCOMFORTABLE.
WHAT THE HELL IS "LUNCHEON," ANYWAY?
WHAT QUALIFIES AS "LUNCHEON"?
quiver
I BET YOU CAN'T EAT UDON.
quiver
OF COURSE NOT... IF IT'S A "LUNCHEON"...
IT'D BE PASTA...
OR... MAYBE PASTA...
SO BASICALLY, YOU CAN'T CALL NON-PASTA FOOD "LUNCHEON." GOT IT.
HOW LONG HAVE YA BEEN LIVIN' UNDER THIS ROCK? IF YA EAT IT AT LUNCHTIME, IT COUNTS AS "LUNCHEON."
YA CAN JUST WEAR NORMAL CLOTHES.
A BLOUSE AND SKIRT'LL DO.
THE ONLY SKIRT I HAVE IS THE ONE I'VE WORN SINCE HIGH SCHOOL...
ガラ
zhoop
I'M HERE TO FETCH TSUKIMI.
I parked on the street, so I have less than a minute to wait. Problem?
HE'S ALREADY HERE!!

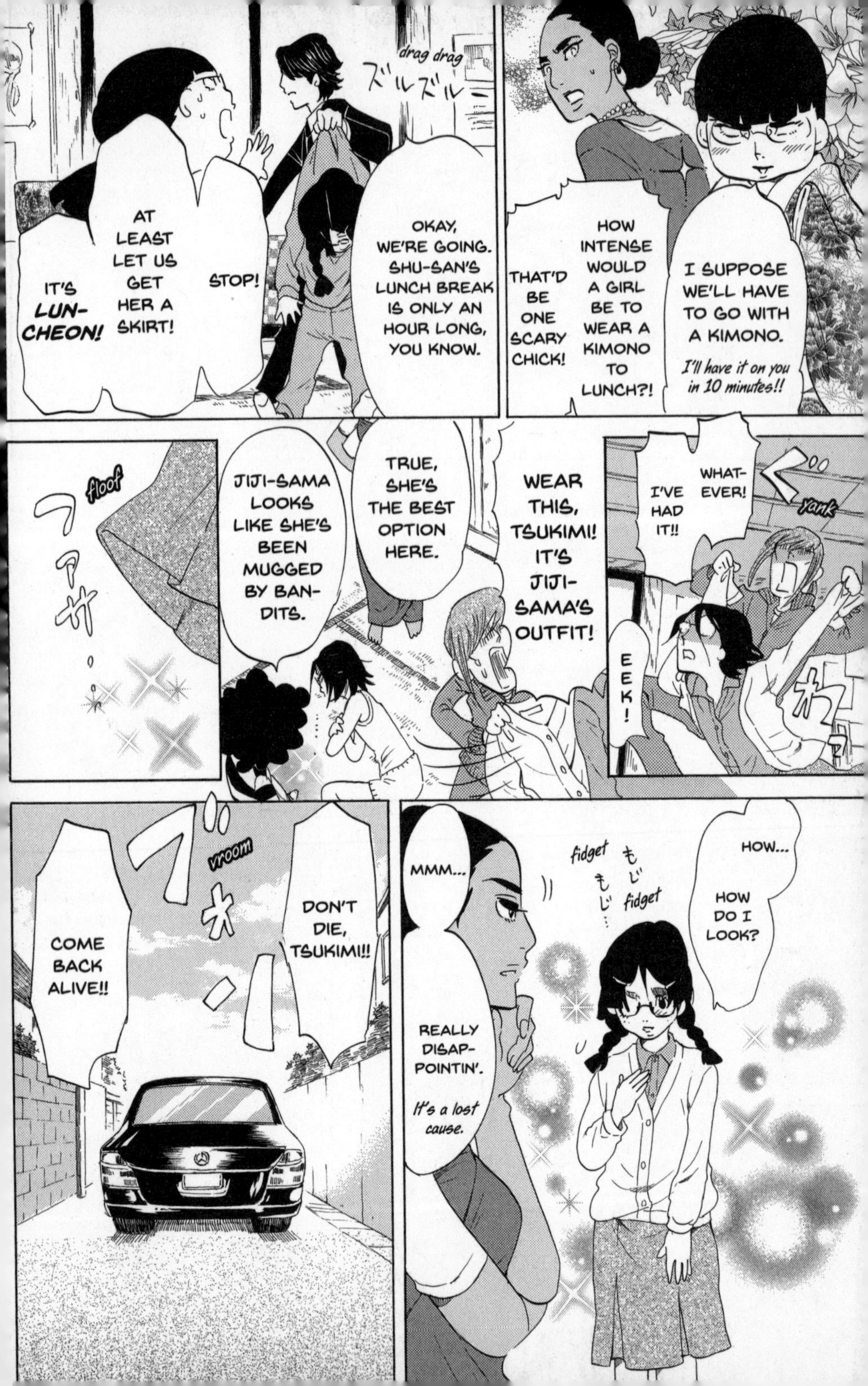
I SUPPOSE WE'LL HAVE TO GO WITH A KIMONO.
I'll have it on you in 10 minutes!!
HOW INTENSE WOULD A GIRL BE TO WEAR A KIMONO TO LUNCH?!
THAT'D BE ONE SCARY CHICK!
OKAY, WE'RE GOING. SHU-SAN'S LUNCH BREAK IS ONLY AN HOUR LONG, YOU KNOW.
drag drag
ズルズル
STOP!
AT LEAST LET US GET HER A SKIRT!
IT'S LUN-CHEON!
yank
WHAT-EVER!
I'VE HAD IT!!
EEK!
WEAR THIS, TSUKIMI! IT'S JIJI-SAMA'S OUTFIT!
TRUE, SHE'S THE BEST OPTION HERE.
JIJI-SAMA LOOKS LIKE SHE'S BEEN MUGGED BY BAN-DITS.
floof
HOW...
HOW DO I LOOK?
fidget
もじもじ
fidget
MMM...
REALLY DISAP-POINTIN'.
It's a lost cause.
vroom
DON'T DIE, TSUKIMI!!
COME BACK ALIVE!!

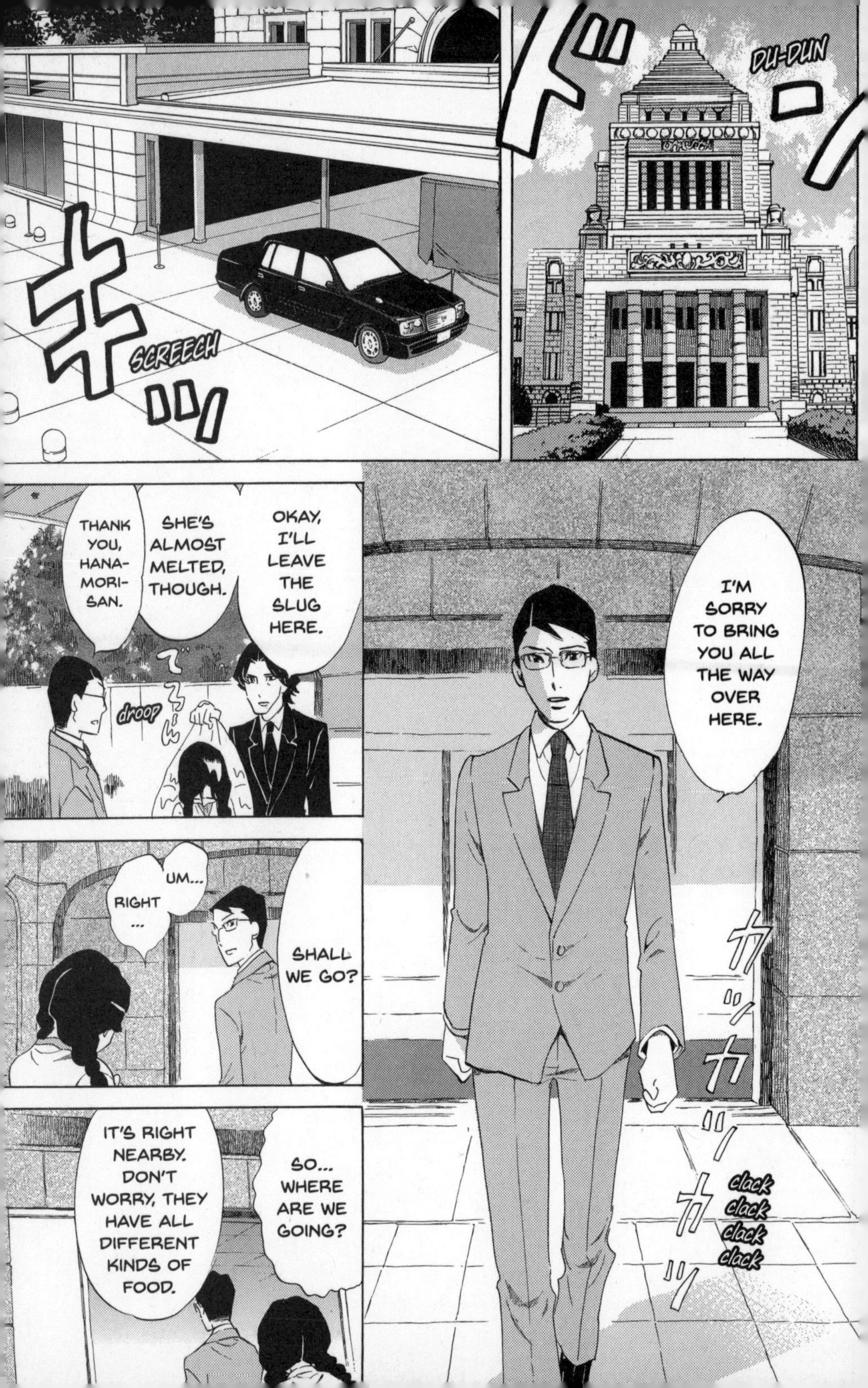
DU-DUN
SCREECH
I'M SORRY TO BRING YOU ALL THE WAY OVER HERE.
clack clack clack clack
OKAY, I'LL LEAVE THE SLUG HERE.
SHE'S ALMOST MELTED, THOUGH.
THANK YOU, HANAMORI-SAN.
droop
SHALL WE GO?
UM... RIGHT ...
SO... WHERE ARE WE GOING?
IT'S RIGHT NEARBY. DON'T WORRY, THEY HAVE ALL DIFFERENT KINDS OF FOOD.

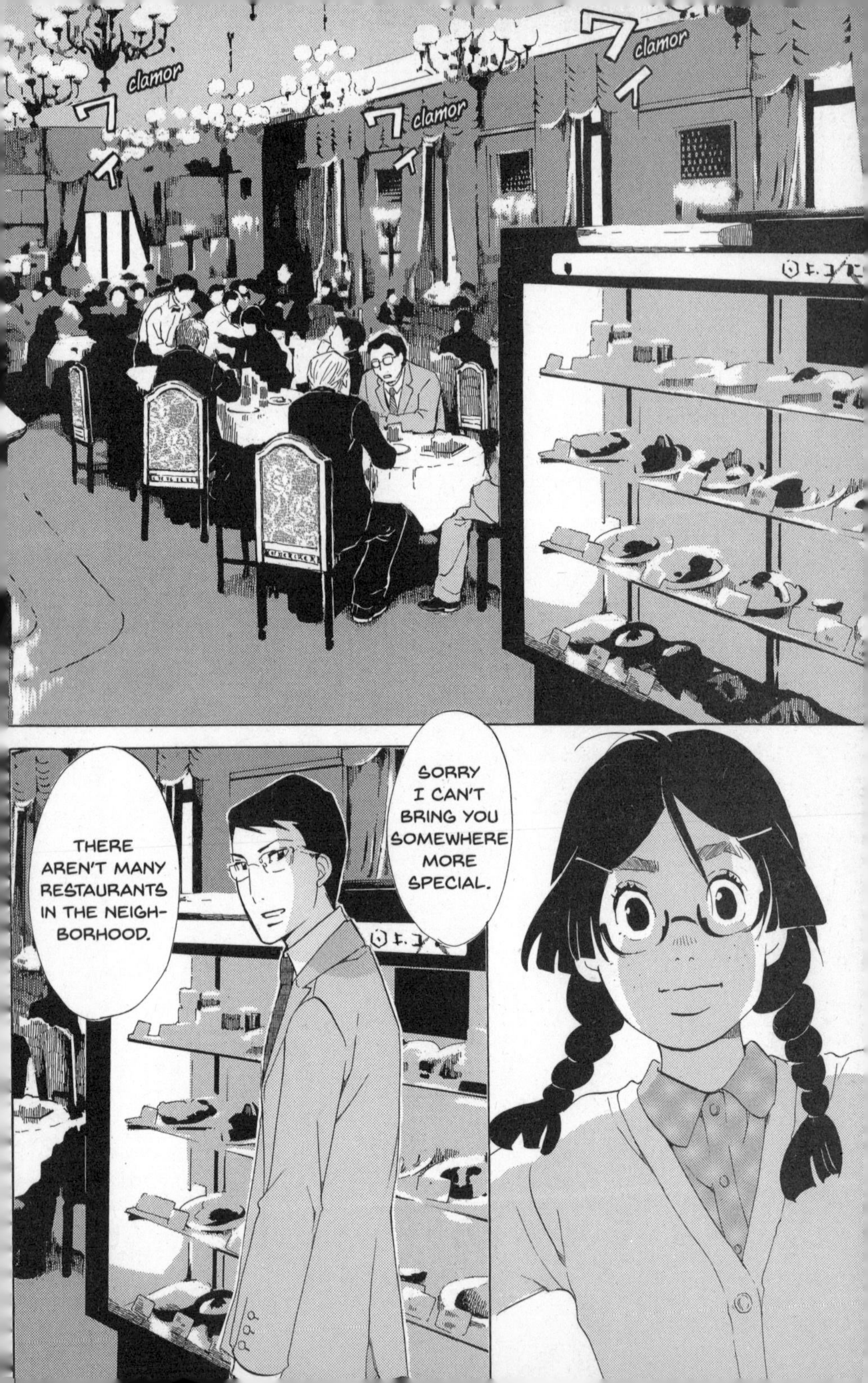
ワイ clamor
ワイ clamor
ワイ clamor
SORRY I CAN'T BRING YOU SOMEWHERE MORE SPECIAL.
THERE AREN'T MANY RESTAURANTS IN THE NEIGH-BORHOOD.

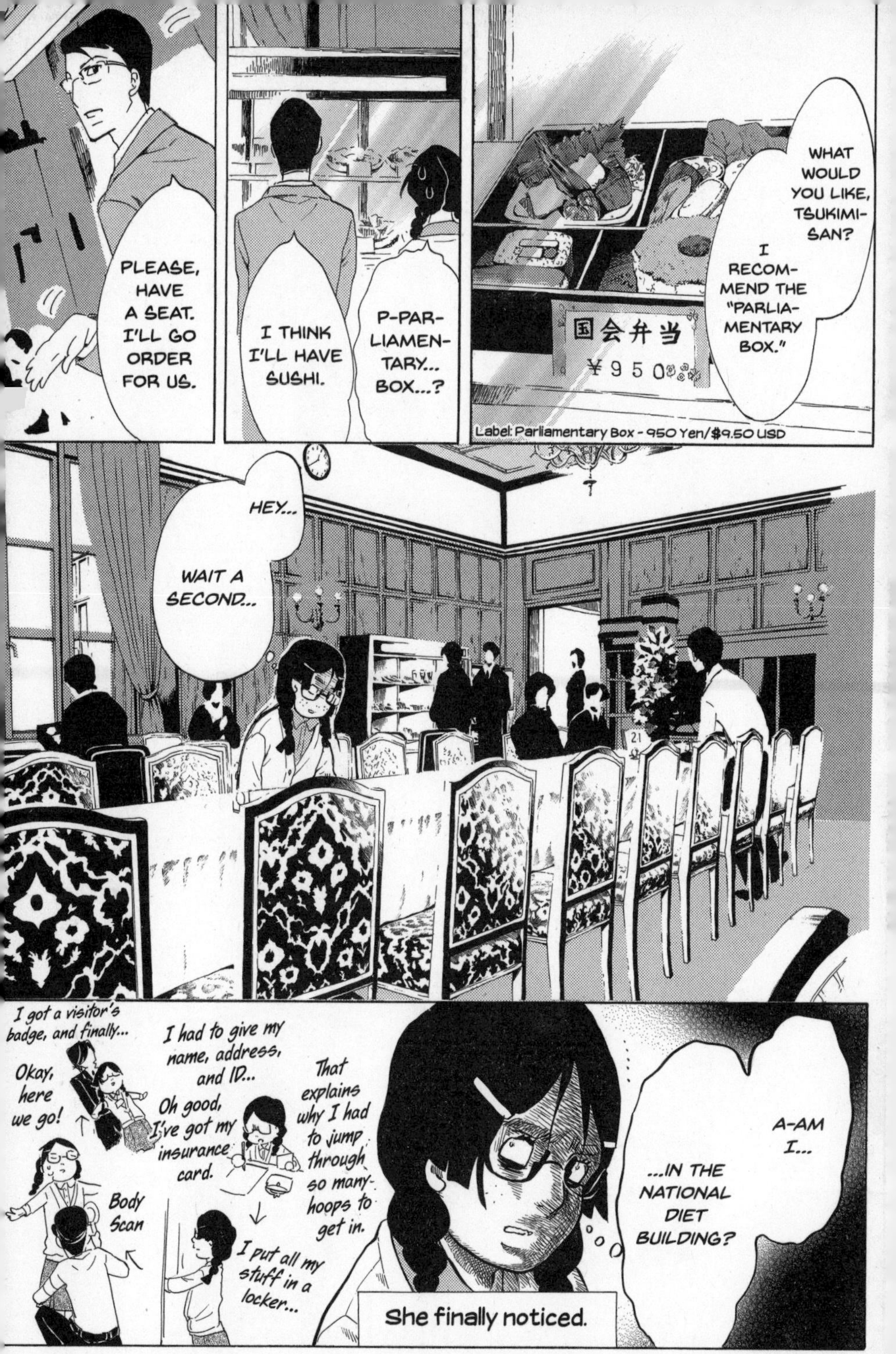
WHAT WOULD YOU LIKE, TSUKIMI-SAN?
I RECOMMEND THE "PARLIAMENTARY BOX."
国会弁当
¥950
Label: Parliamentary Box - 950 Yen/$9.50 USD
P-PARLIAMENTARY... BOX...?
I THINK I'LL HAVE SUSHI.
PLEASE, HAVE A SEAT. I'LL GO ORDER FOR US.
HEY...
WAIT A SECOND...
A-AM I...
...IN THE NATIONAL DIET BUILDING?
She finally noticed.
That explains why I had to jump through so many hoops to get in.
I had to give my name, address, and ID...
Oh good, I've got my insurance card.
I got a visitor's badge, and finally...
Okay, here we go!
Body Scan
I put all my stuff in a locker...

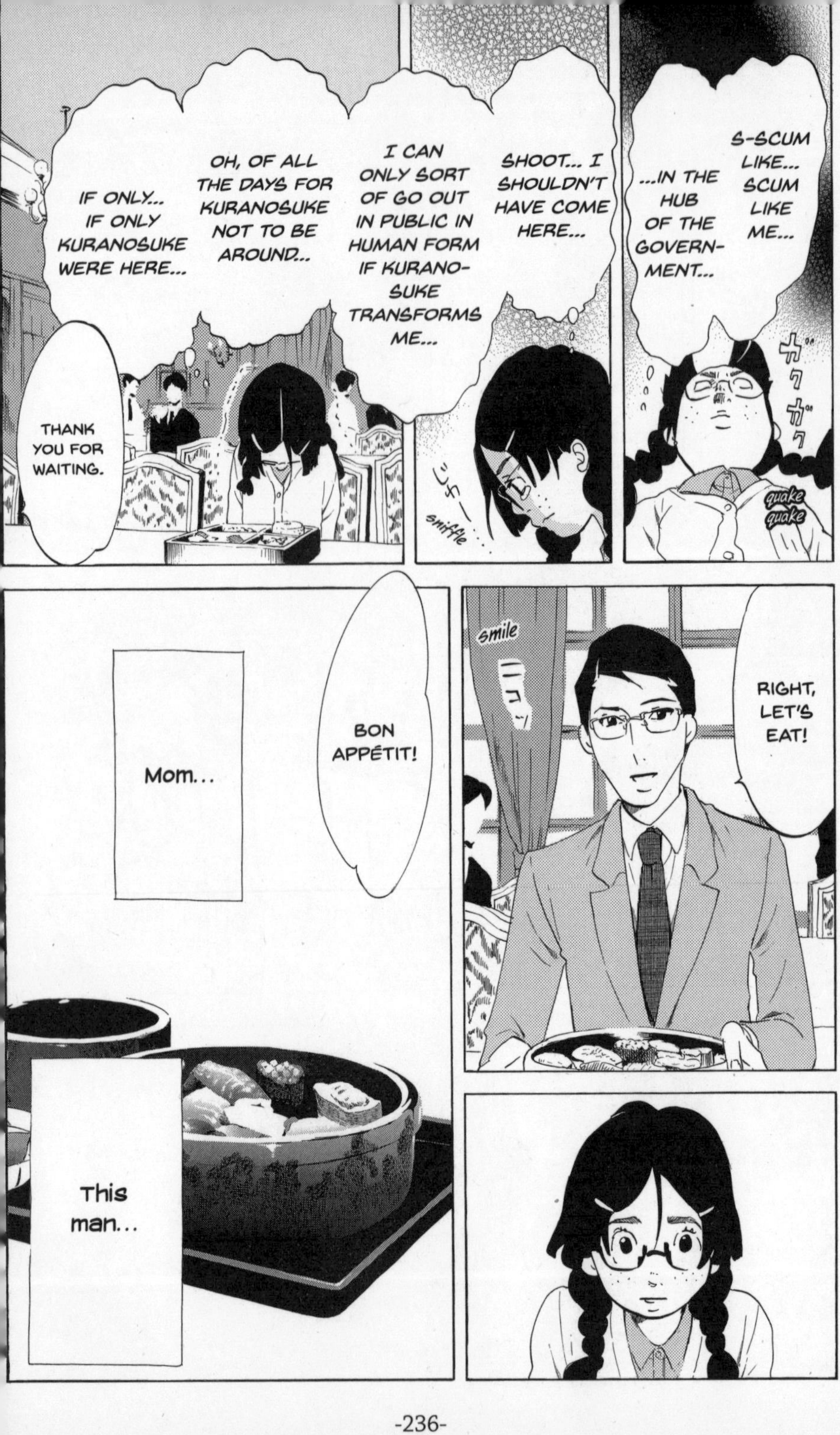
S-SCUM LIKE... SCUM LIKE ME...
...IN THE HUB OF THE GOVERNMENT...
quake quake
SHOOT... I SHOULDN'T HAVE COME HERE...
sniffle
I CAN ONLY SORT OF GO OUT IN PUBLIC IN HUMAN FORM IF KURANOSUKE TRANSFORMS ME...
OH, OF ALL THE DAYS FOR KURANOSUKE NOT TO BE AROUND...
IF ONLY... IF ONLY KURANOSUKE WERE HERE...
THANK YOU FOR WAITING.
RIGHT, LET'S EAT!
smile
BON APPÉTIT!
Mom...
This man...

...in this place that's just like a castle...
...in this glittery, chandelier-filled room...
He's here with my shabby, untrans-formed self...
He's willing to eat lunch here with a girl like me.
Mom, I...
I really think I...

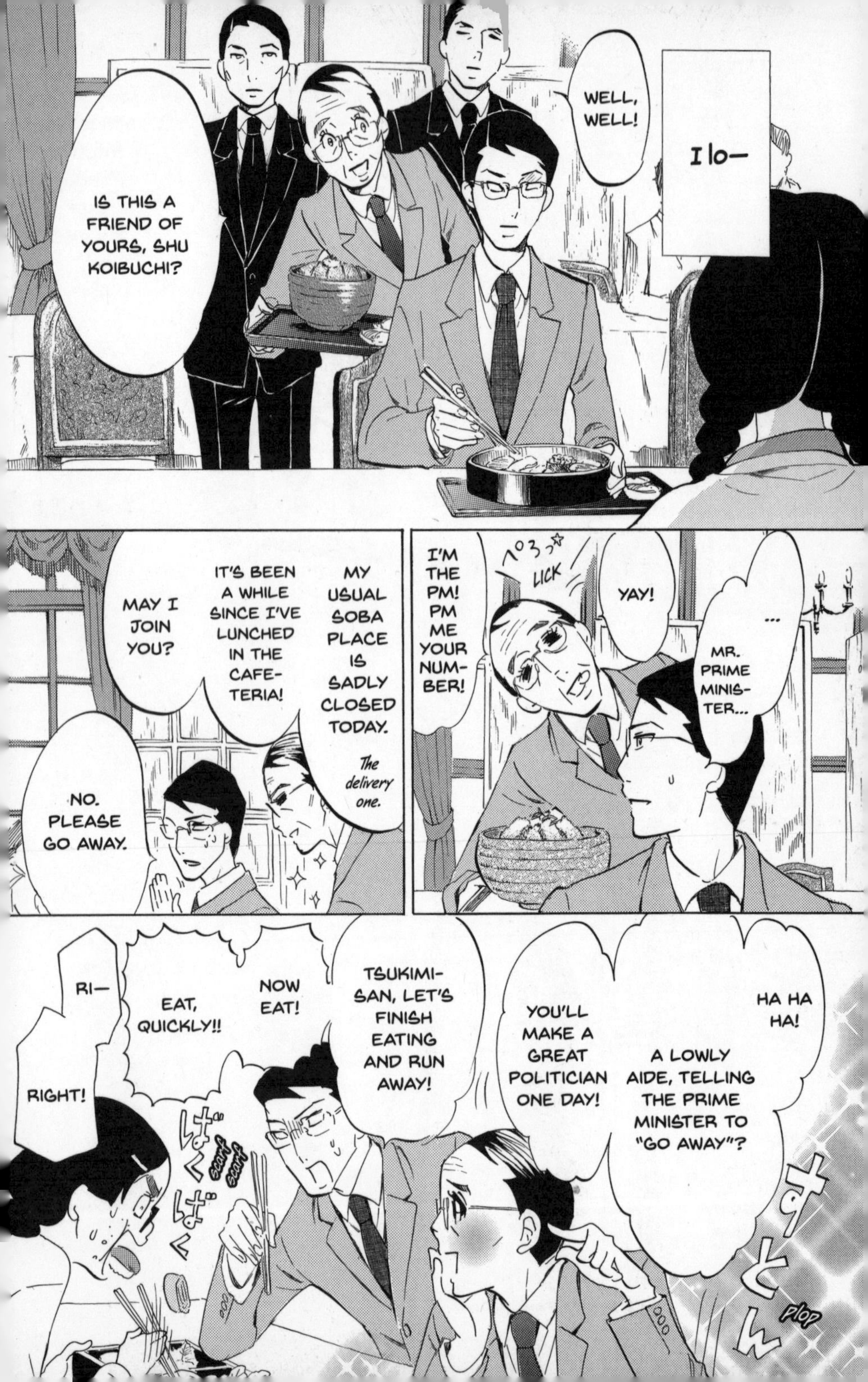
I lo—
WELL, WELL!
IS THIS A FRIEND OF YOURS, SHU KOIBUCHI?
... MR. PRIME MINISTER...
YAY!
ぺろっ☆
LICK
I'M THE PM! PM ME YOUR NUMBER!
MY USUAL SOBA PLACE IS SADLY CLOSED TODAY.
The delivery one.
IT'S BEEN A WHILE SINCE I'VE LUNCHED IN THE CAFETERIA!
MAY I JOIN YOU?
NO. PLEASE GO AWAY.
HA HA HA!
A LOWLY AIDE, TELLING THE PRIME MINISTER TO "GO AWAY"?
YOU'LL MAKE A GREAT POLITICIAN ONE DAY!
すとん
plop
TSUKIMI-SAN, LET'S FINISH EATING AND RUN AWAY!
NOW EAT!
EAT, QUICKLY!!
ばくばく
scarf scarf
RI— RIGHT!

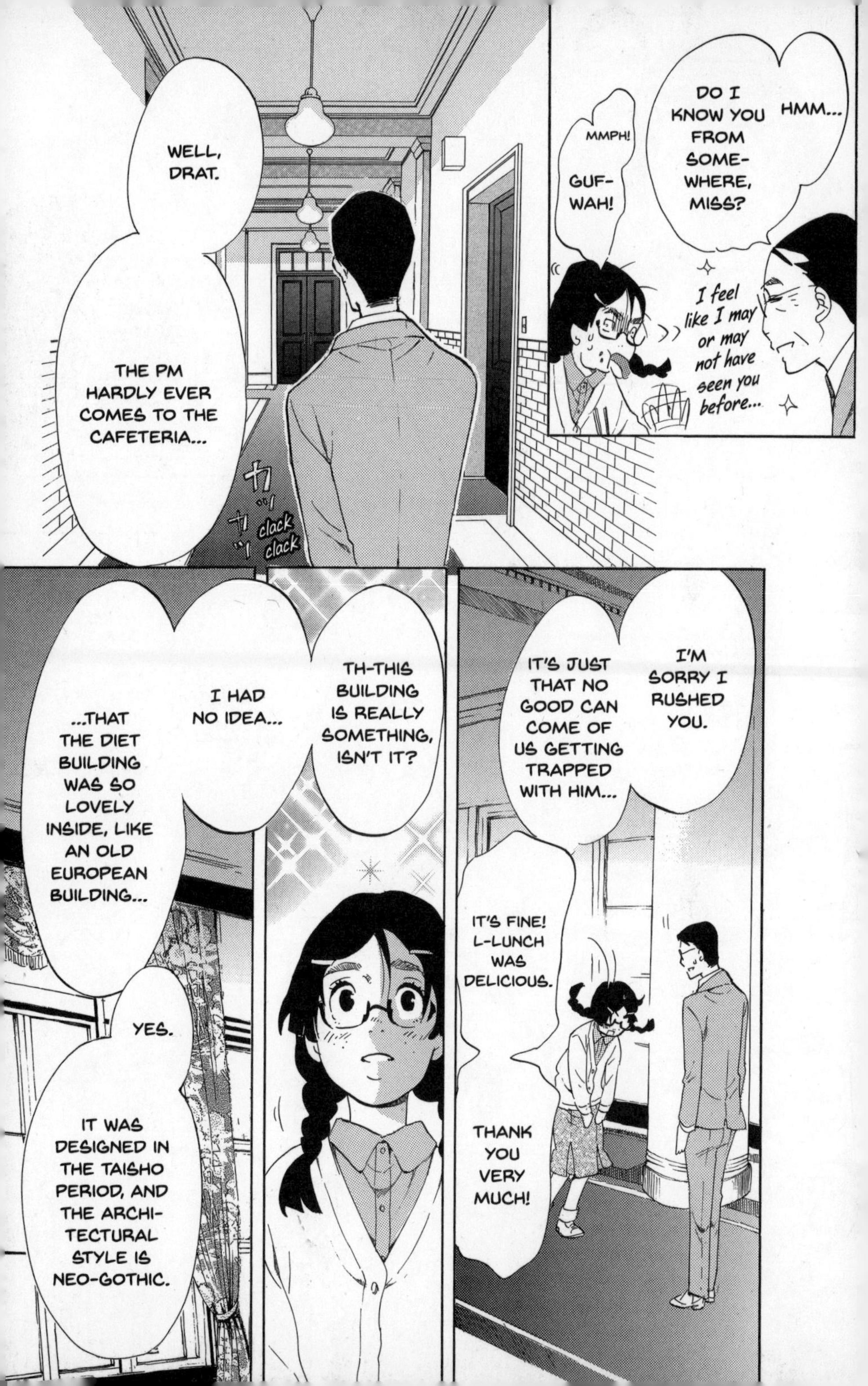
HMM...
DO I KNOW YOU FROM SOME-WHERE, MISS?
MMPH!
GUF-WAH!
I feel like I may or may not have seen you before...
WELL, DRAT.
THE PM HARDLY EVER COMES TO THE CAFETERIA...
clack clack
I'M SORRY I RUSHED YOU.
IT'S JUST THAT NO GOOD CAN COME OF US GETTING TRAPPED WITH HIM...
IT'S FINE! L-LUNCH WAS DELICIOUS.
THANK YOU VERY MUCH!
TH-THIS BUILDING IS REALLY SOMETHING, ISN'T IT?
I HAD NO IDEA...
...THAT THE DIET BUILDING WAS SO LOVELY INSIDE, LIKE AN OLD EUROPEAN BUILDING...
YES.
IT WAS DESIGNED IN THE TAISHO PERIOD, AND THE ARCHI-TECTURAL STYLE IS NEO-GOTHIC.

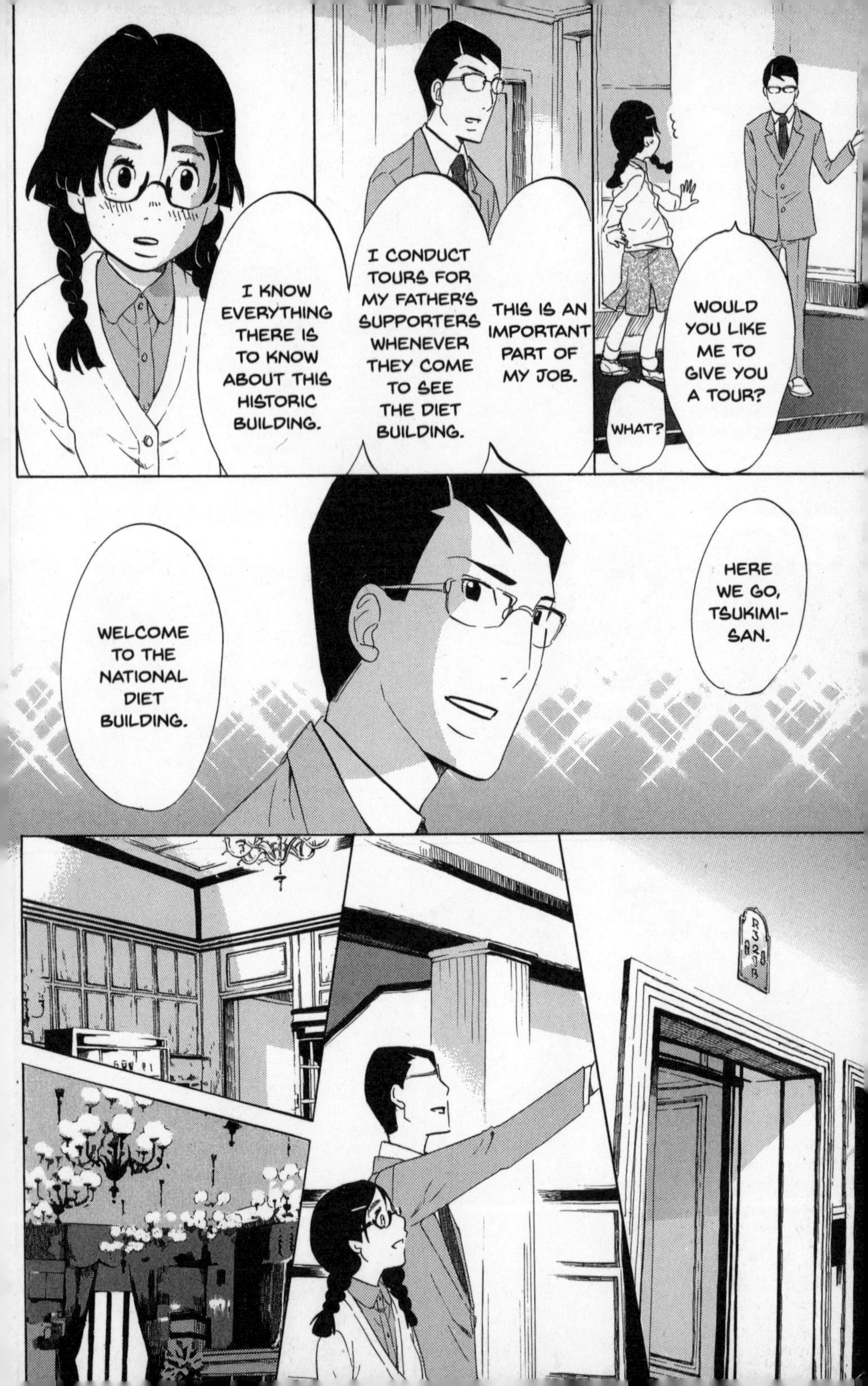
WOULD YOU LIKE ME TO GIVE YOU A TOUR?
WHAT?
THIS IS AN IMPORTANT PART OF MY JOB.
I CONDUCT TOURS FOR MY FATHER'S SUPPORTERS WHENEVER THEY COME TO SEE THE DIET BUILDING.
I KNOW EVERYTHING THERE IS TO KNOW ABOUT THIS HISTORIC BUILDING.
HERE WE GO, TSUKIMI-SAN.
WELCOME TO THE NATIONAL DIET BUILDING.

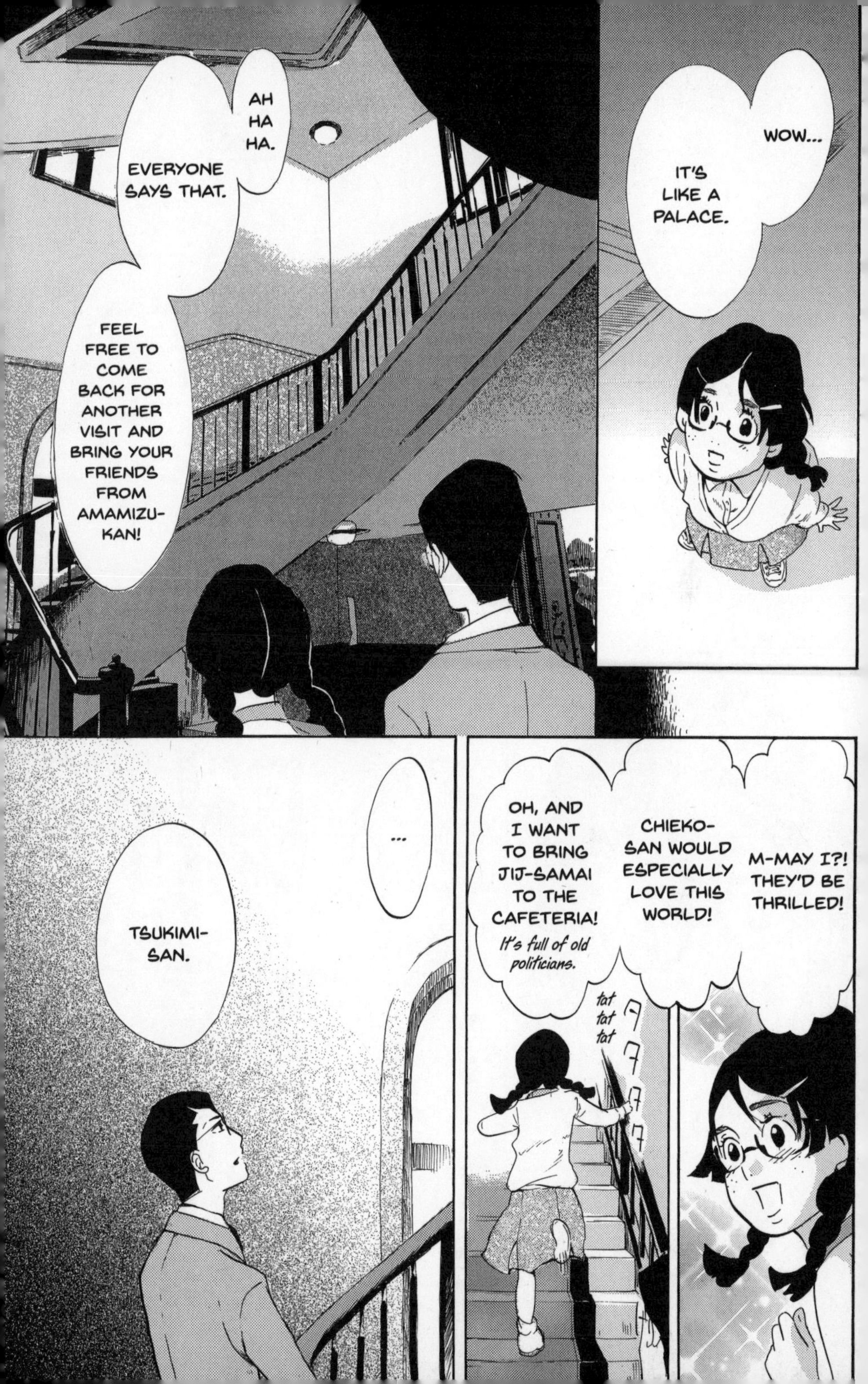
WOW...
IT'S LIKE A PALACE.
AH HA HA.
EVERYONE SAYS THAT.
FEEL FREE TO COME BACK FOR ANOTHER VISIT AND BRING YOUR FRIENDS FROM AMAMIZU-KAN!
M-MAY I?! THEY'D BE THRILLED!
CHIEKO-SAN WOULD ESPECIALLY LOVE THIS WORLD!
OH, AND I WANT TO BRING JIJ-SAMAI TO THE CAFETERIA!
It's full of old politicians.
tat tat tat
...
TSUKIMI-SAN.

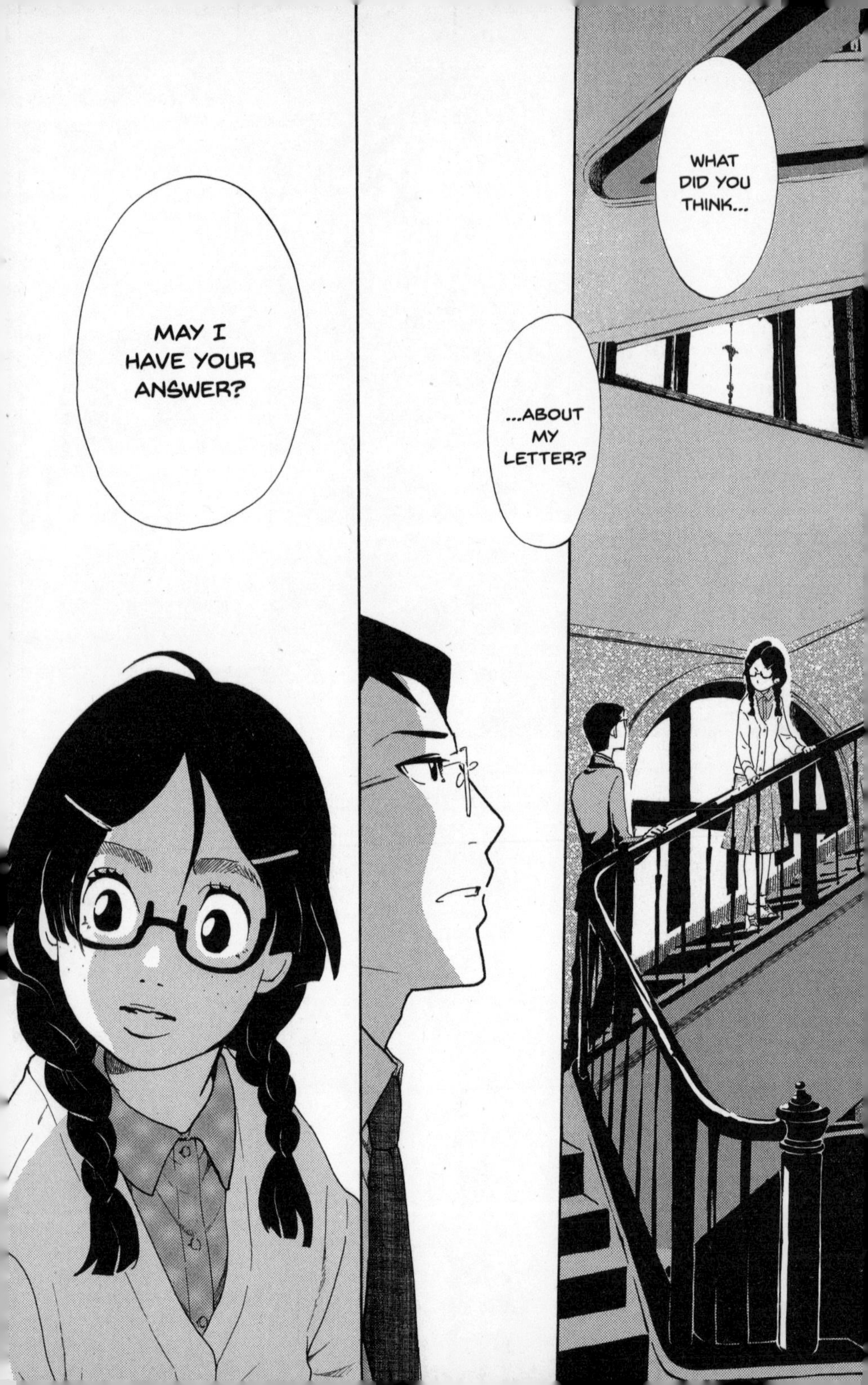
WHAT DID YOU THINK...
...ABOUT MY LETTER?
MAY I HAVE YOUR ANSWER?

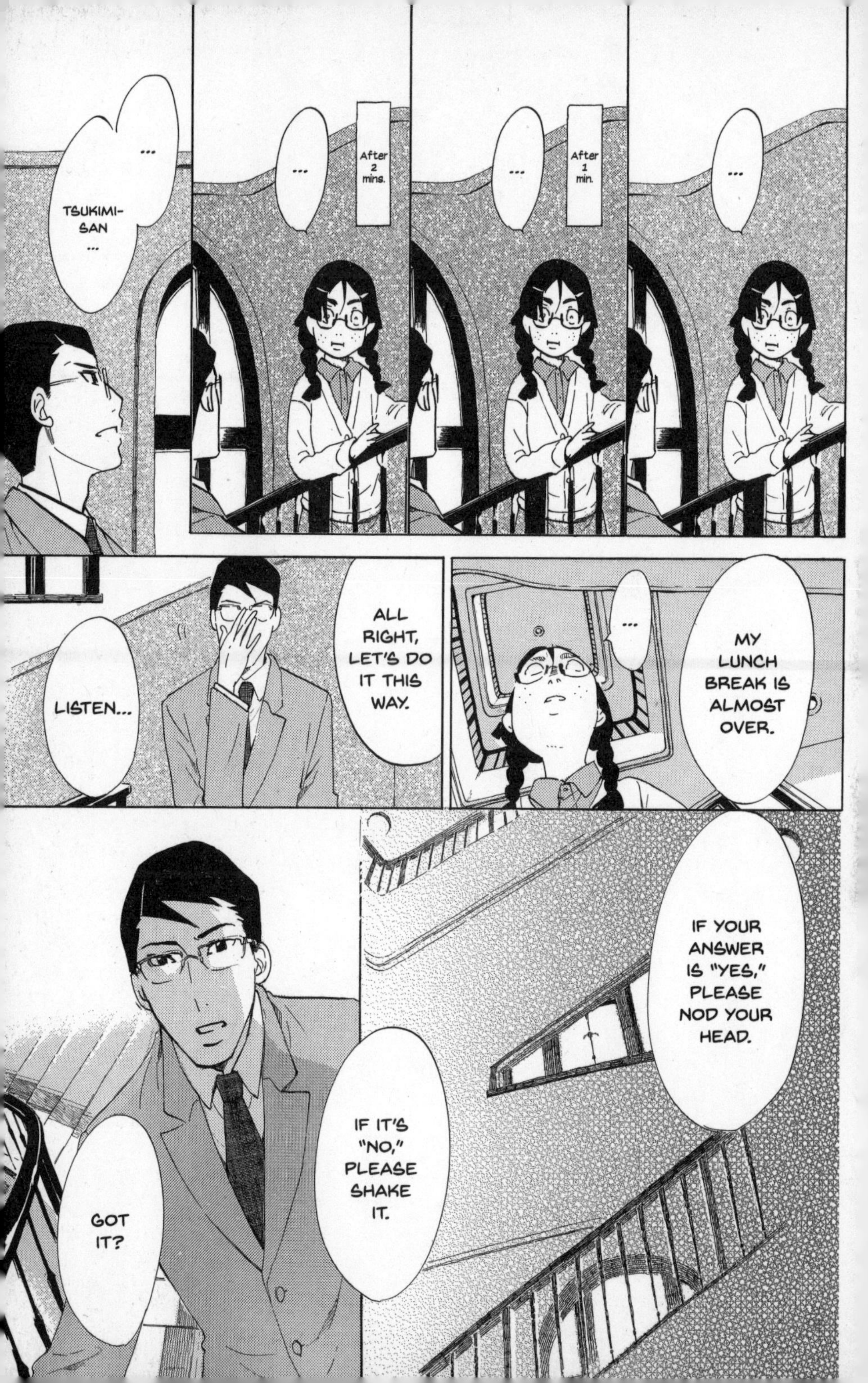
...
After 1 min.
...
After 2 mins.
...
...
TSUKIMI-SAN ...
MY LUNCH BREAK IS ALMOST OVER.
...
ALL RIGHT, LET'S DO IT THIS WAY.
LISTEN...
IF YOUR ANSWER IS "YES," PLEASE NOD YOUR HEAD.
IF IT'S "NO," PLEASE SHAKE IT.
GOT IT?

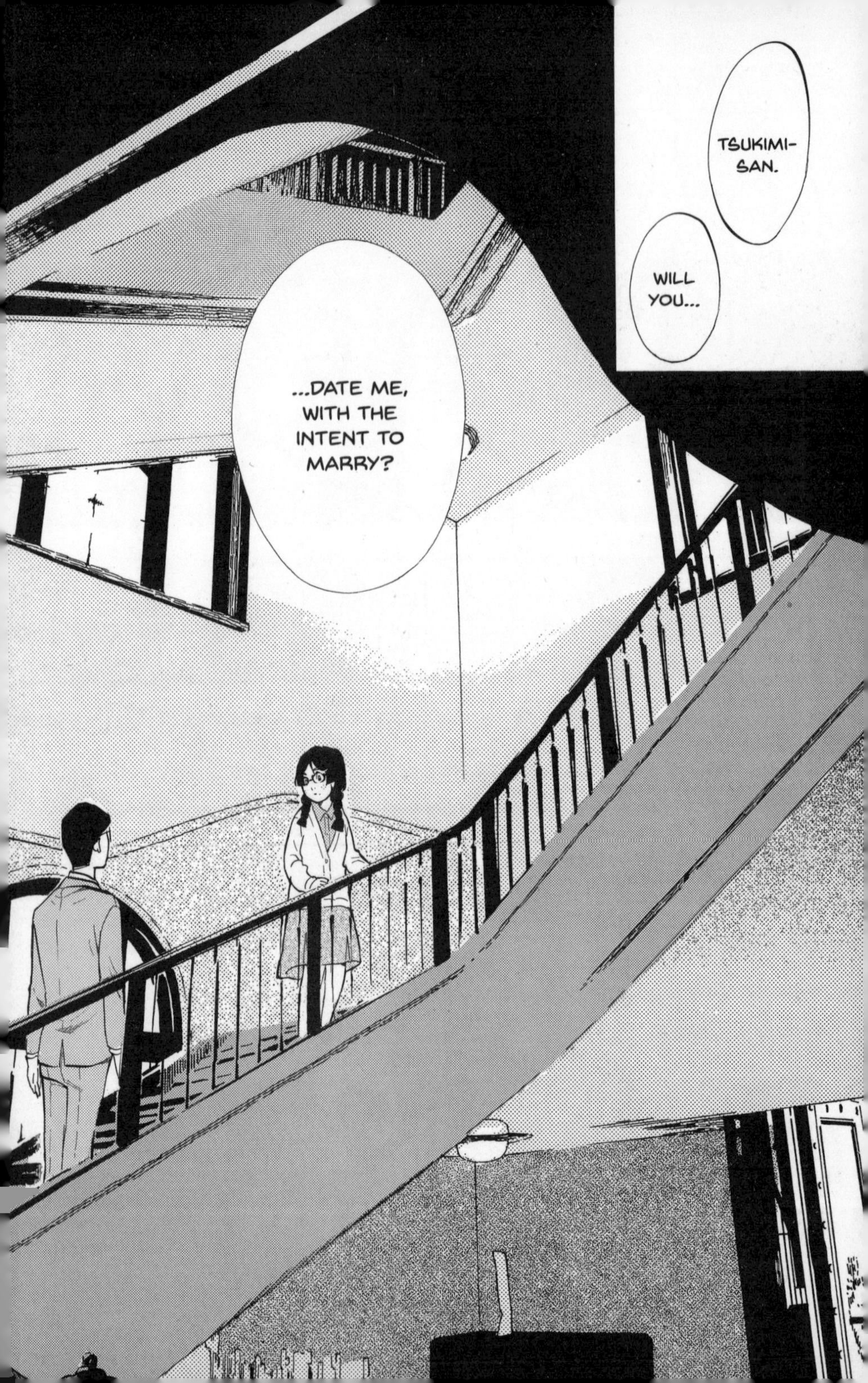
TSUKIMI-SAN.
WILL YOU...
...DATE ME, WITH THE INTENT TO MARRY?

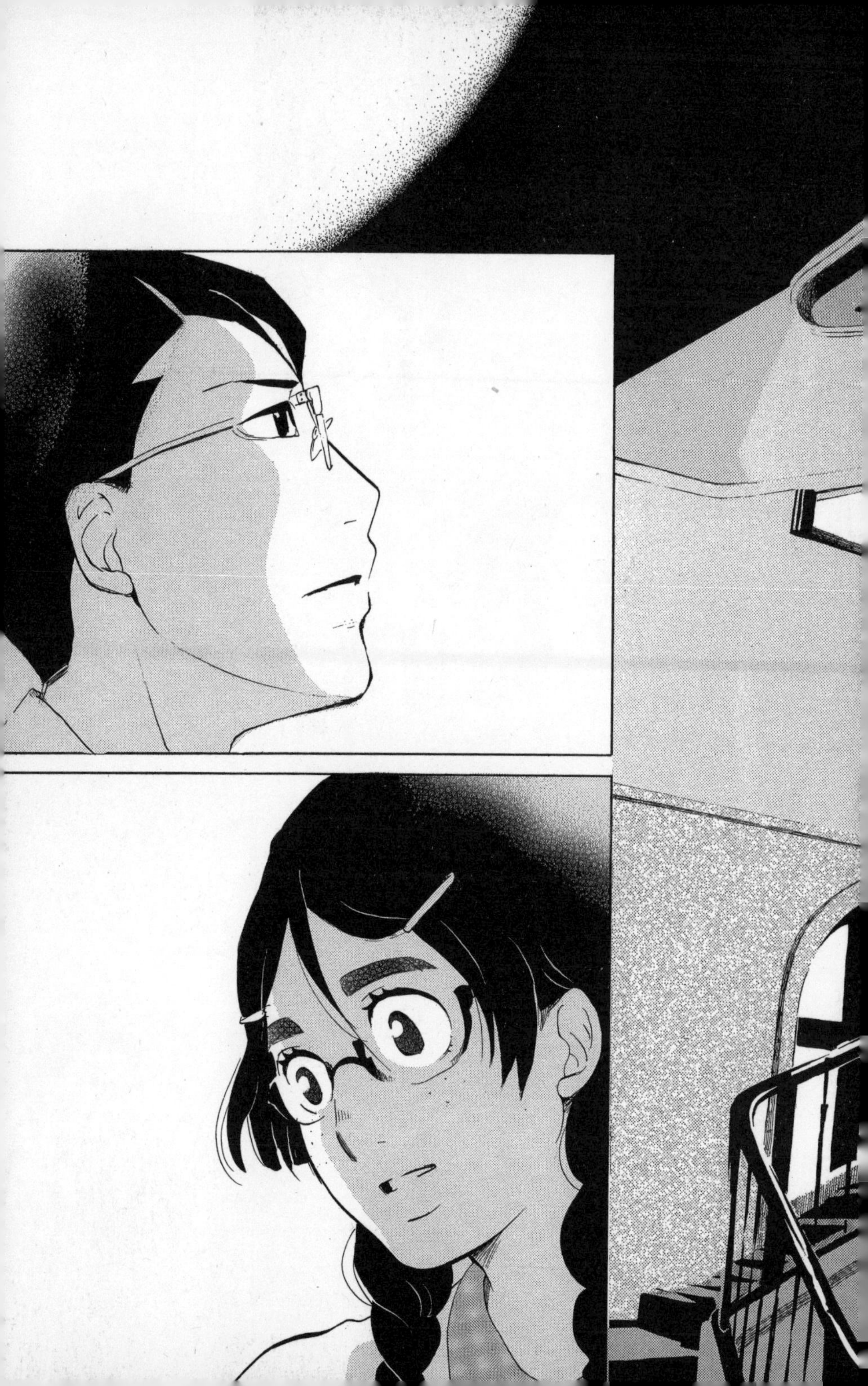

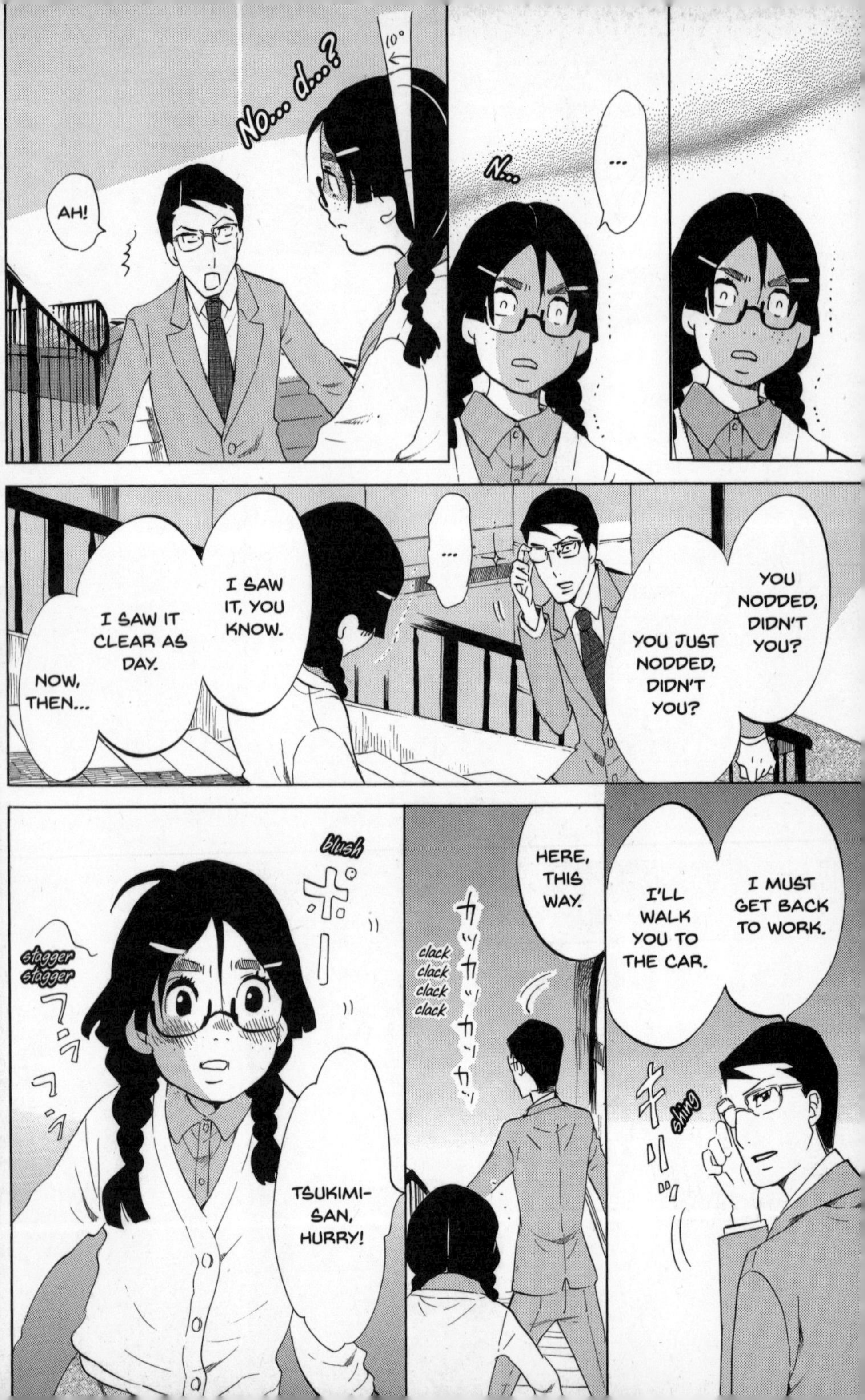

...
N...
10°
No... d...?
AH!
YOU NODDED, DIDN'T YOU?
YOU JUST NODDED, DIDN'T YOU?
...
I SAW IT, YOU KNOW.
I SAW IT CLEAR AS DAY.
NOW, THEN...
I MUST GET BACK TO WORK.
I'LL WALK YOU TO THE CAR.
shing
HERE, THIS WAY.
clack clack clack clack
blush
TSUKIMI-SAN, HURRY!
stagger stagger

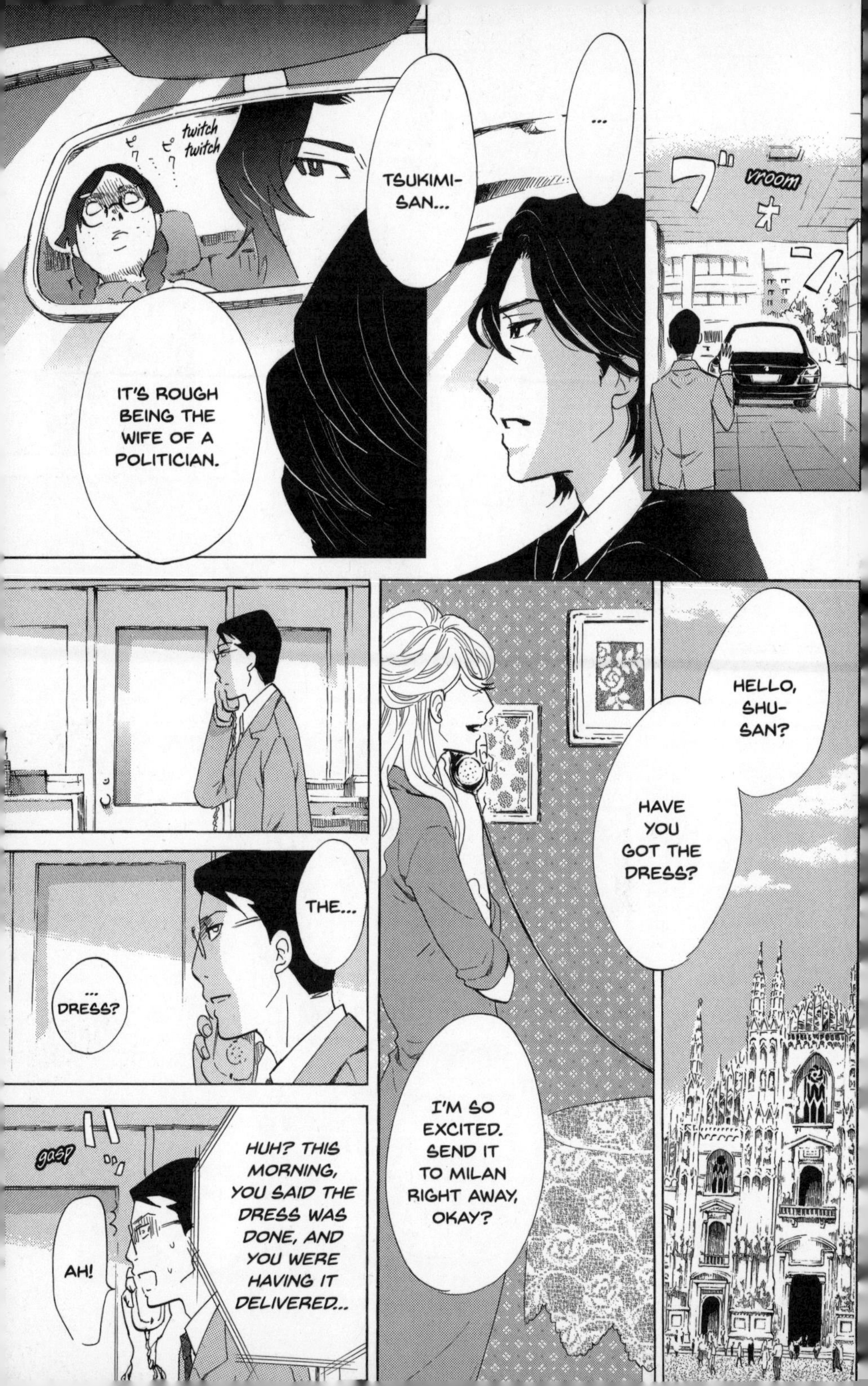
vroom
...
TSUKIMI-SAN...
twitch twitch
IT'S ROUGH BEING THE WIFE OF A POLITICIAN.
HELLO, SHU-SAN?
HAVE YOU GOT THE DRESS?
I'M SO EXCITED. SEND IT TO MILAN RIGHT AWAY, OKAY?
THE...
... DRESS?
gasp
HUH? THIS MORNING, YOU SAID THE DRESS WAS DONE, AND YOU WERE HAVING IT DELIVERED...
AH!

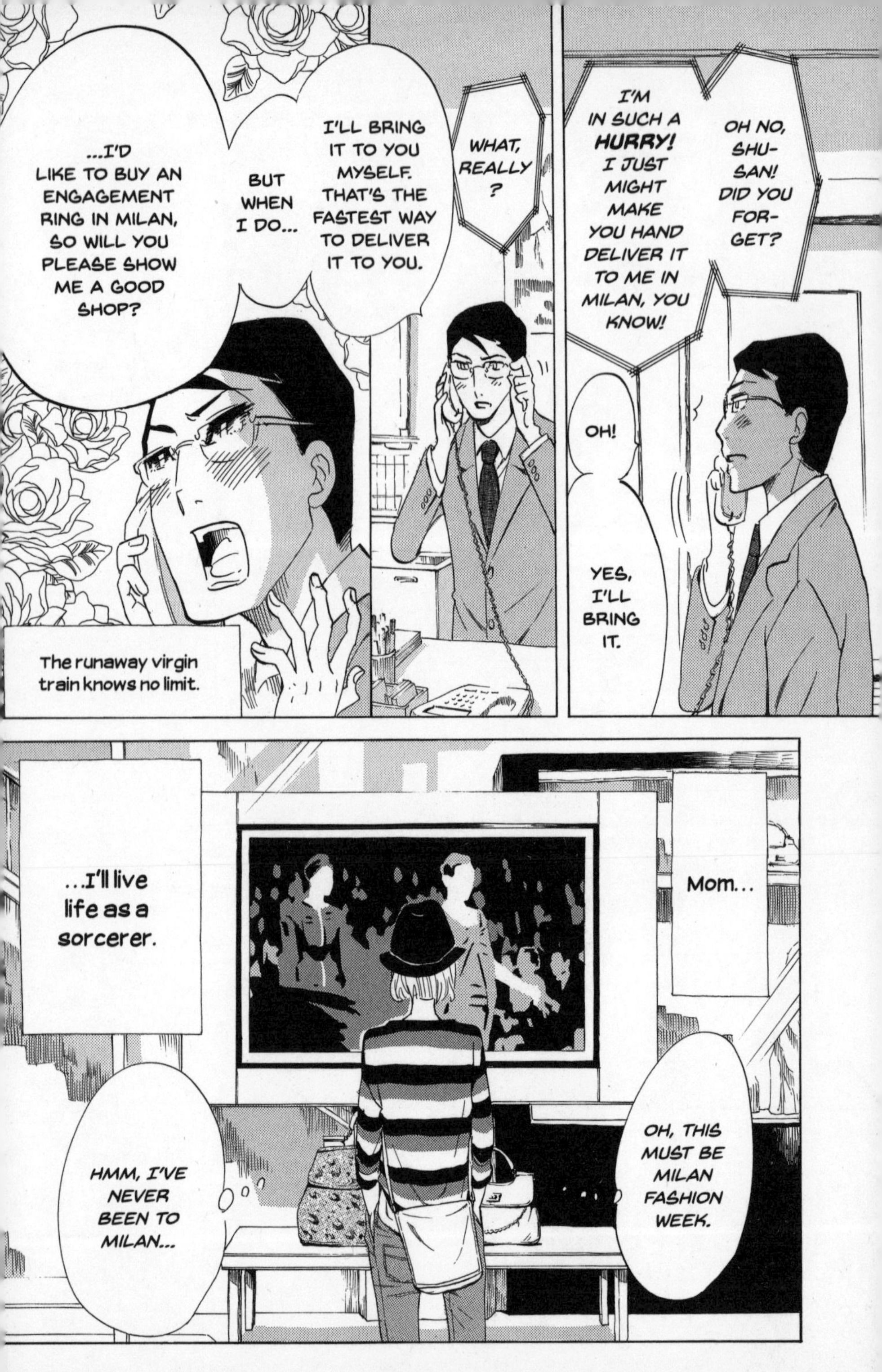
OH NO, SHU-SAN! DID YOU FOR-GET?
I'M IN SUCH A **HURRY!** I JUST MIGHT MAKE YOU HAND DELIVER IT TO ME IN MILAN, YOU KNOW!
OH!
YES, I'LL BRING IT.
WHAT, REALLY?
I'LL BRING IT TO YOU MYSELF. THAT'S THE FASTEST WAY TO DELIVER IT TO YOU.
BUT WHEN I DO...
...I'D LIKE TO BUY AN ENGAGEMENT RING IN MILAN, SO WILL YOU PLEASE SHOW ME A GOOD SHOP?
The runaway virgin train knows no limit.
Mom...
...I'll live life as a sorcerer.
OH, THIS MUST BE MILAN FASHION WEEK.
HMM, I'VE NEVER BEEN TO MILAN...

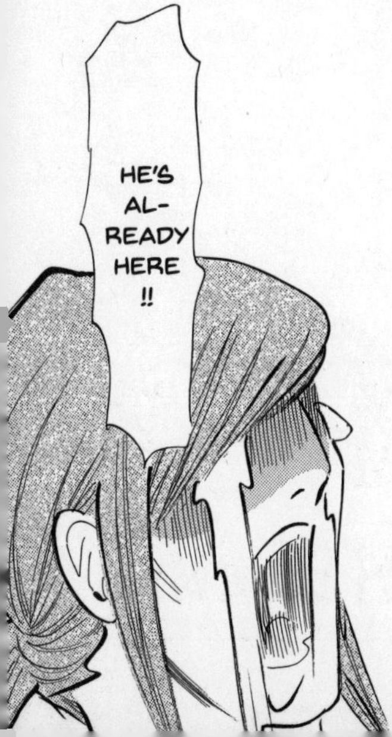
HE'S AL-READY HERE !!

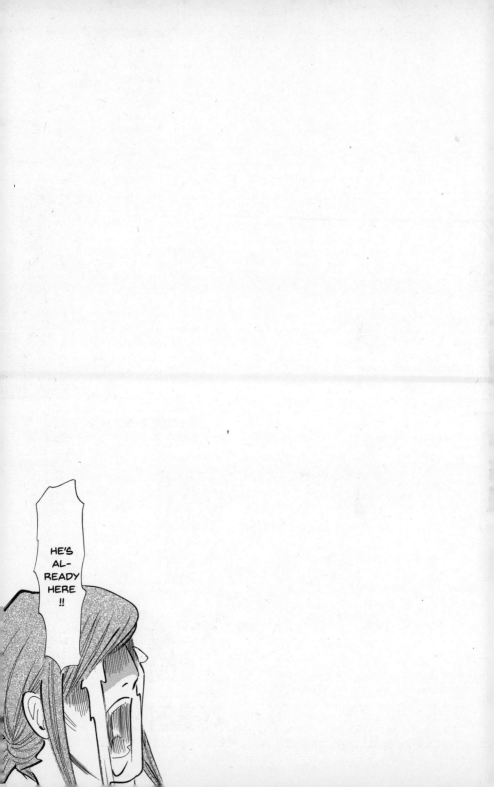

Episode 52
Casual Line?

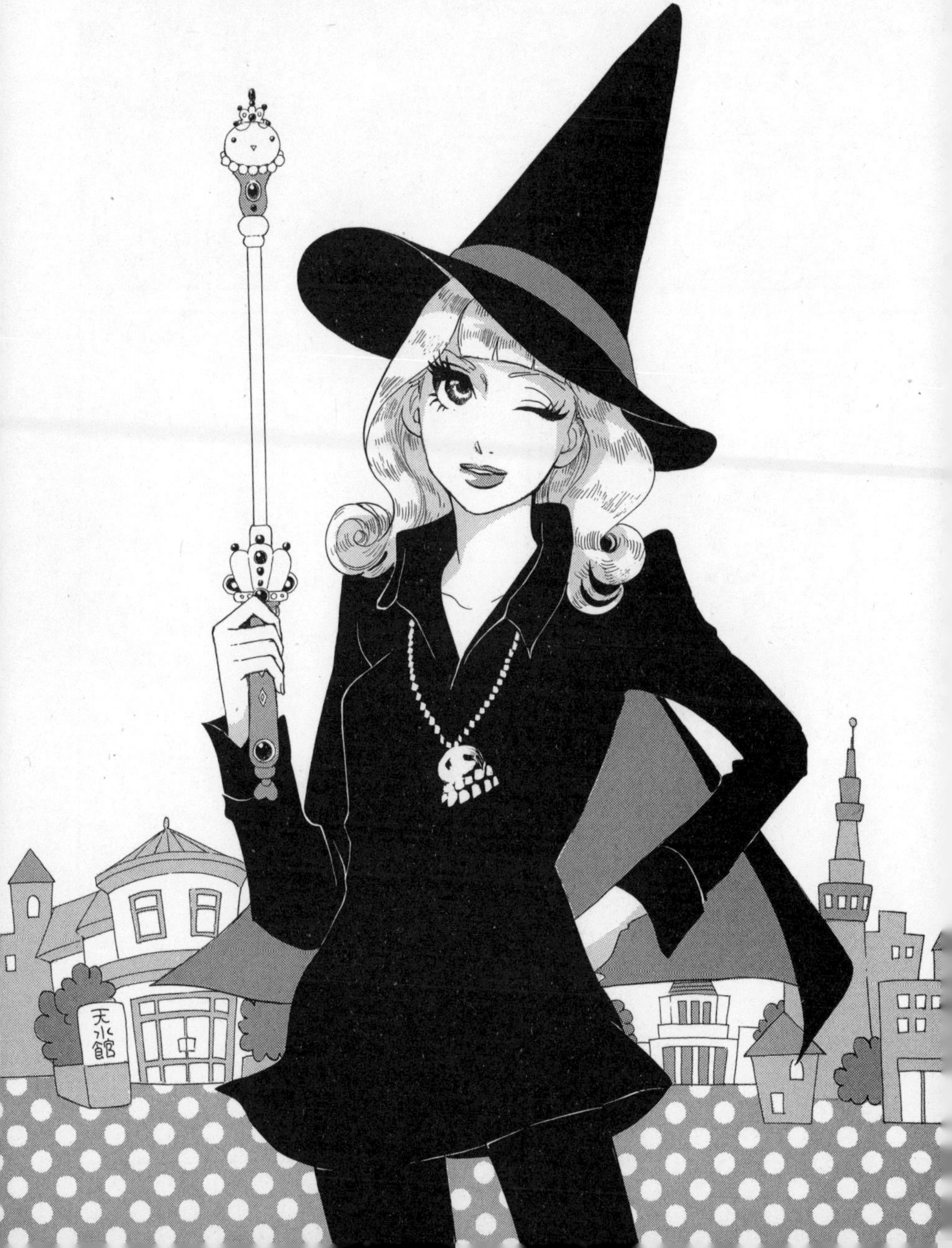
天水館

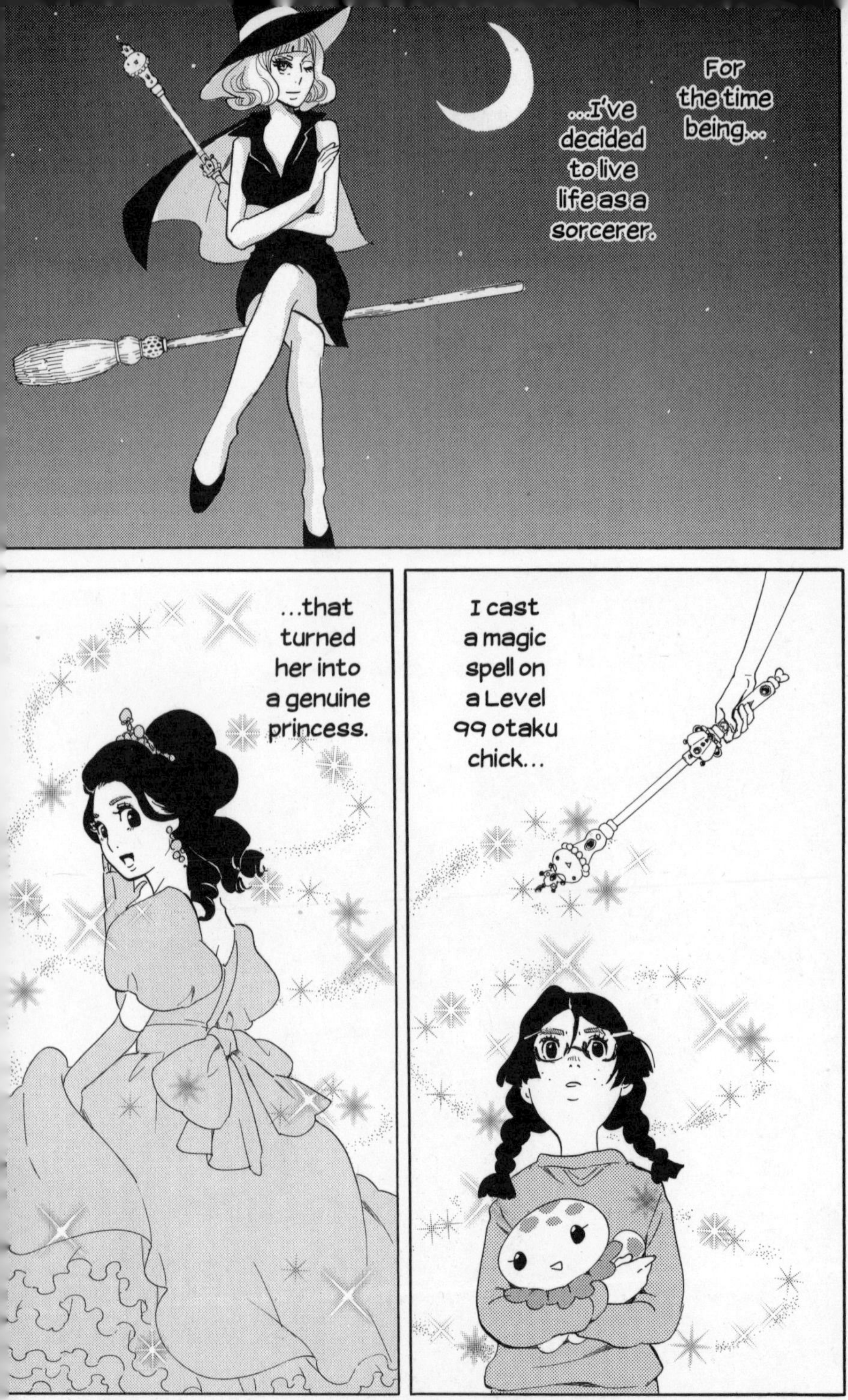
For the time being...
...I've decided to live life as a sorcerer.
I cast a magic spell on a Level 99 otaku chick...
...that turned her into a genuine princess.

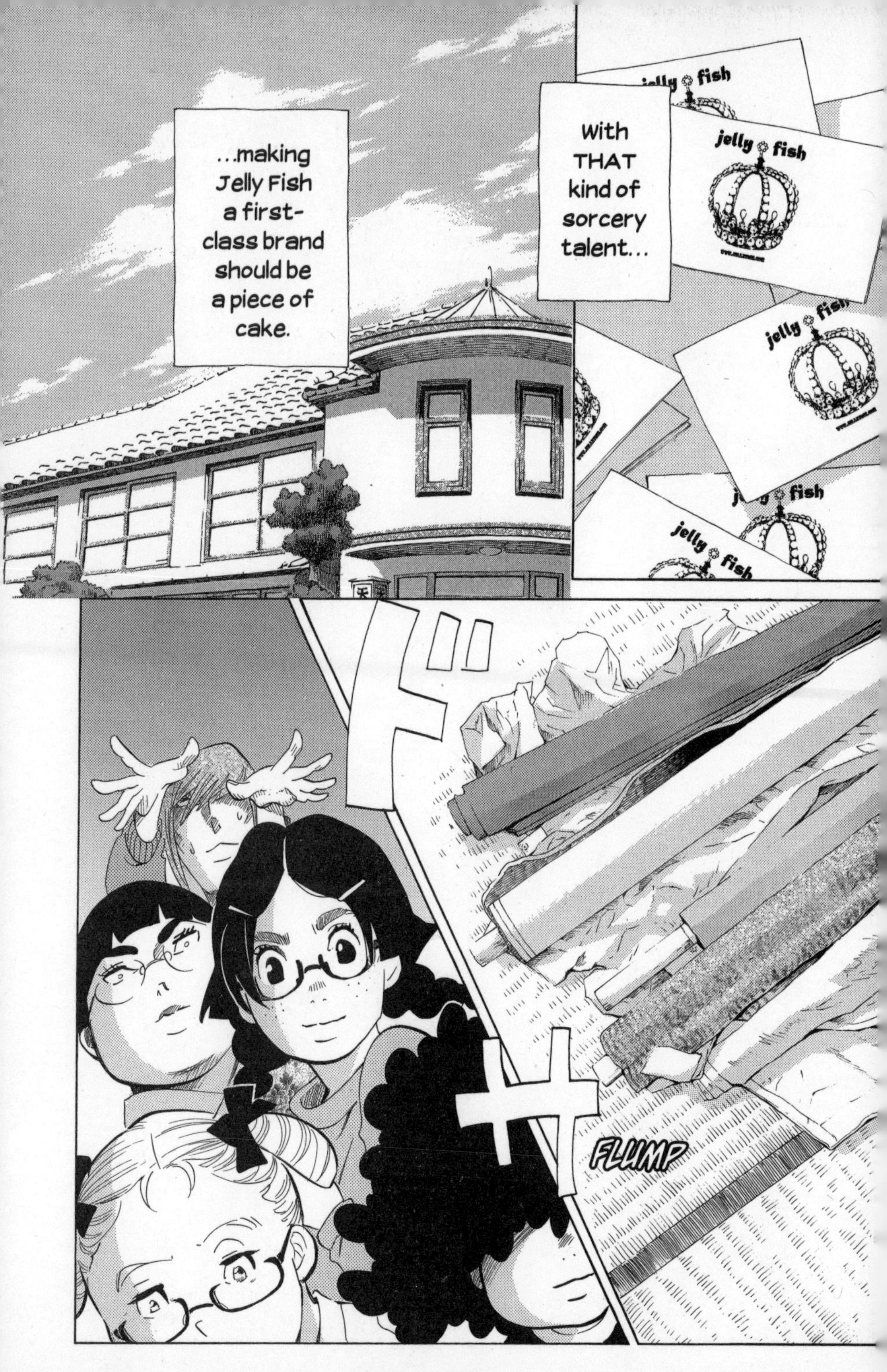
jelly fish
With THAT kind of sorcery talent...
...making Jelly Fish a first-class brand should be a piece of cake.
ド
FLUMP

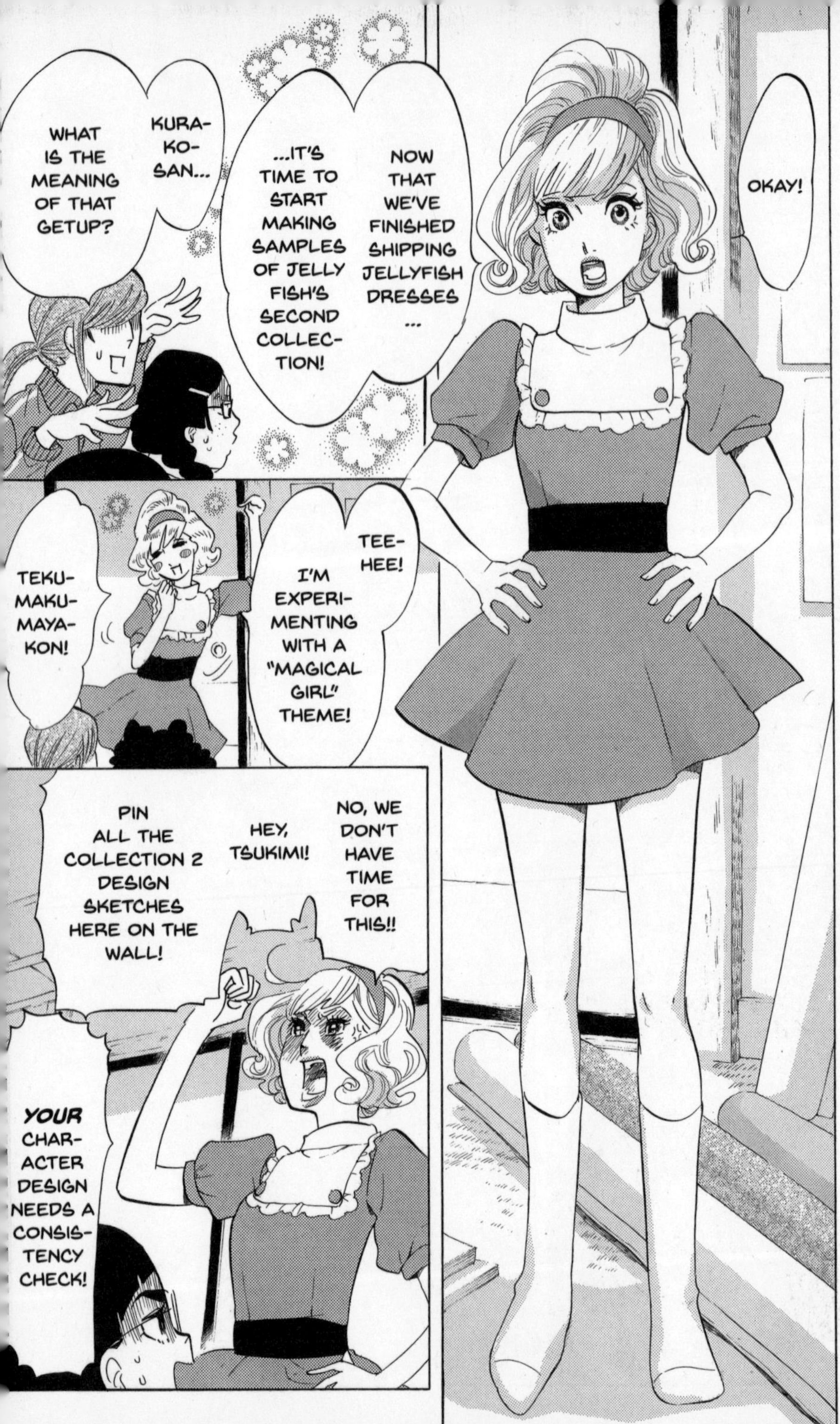
OKAY!
NOW THAT WE'VE FINISHED SHIPPING JELLYFISH DRESSES ...
...IT'S TIME TO START MAKING SAMPLES OF JELLY FISH'S SECOND COLLECTION!
KURA-KO-SAN...
WHAT IS THE MEANING OF THAT GETUP?
TEE-HEE!
I'M EXPERIMENTING WITH A "MAGICAL GIRL" THEME!
TEKU-MAKU-MAYA-KON!
NO, WE DON'T HAVE TIME FOR THIS!!
HEY, TSUKIMI!
PIN ALL THE COLLECTION 2 DESIGN SKETCHES HERE ON THE WALL!
YOUR CHARACTER DESIGN NEEDS A CONSISTENCY CHECK!

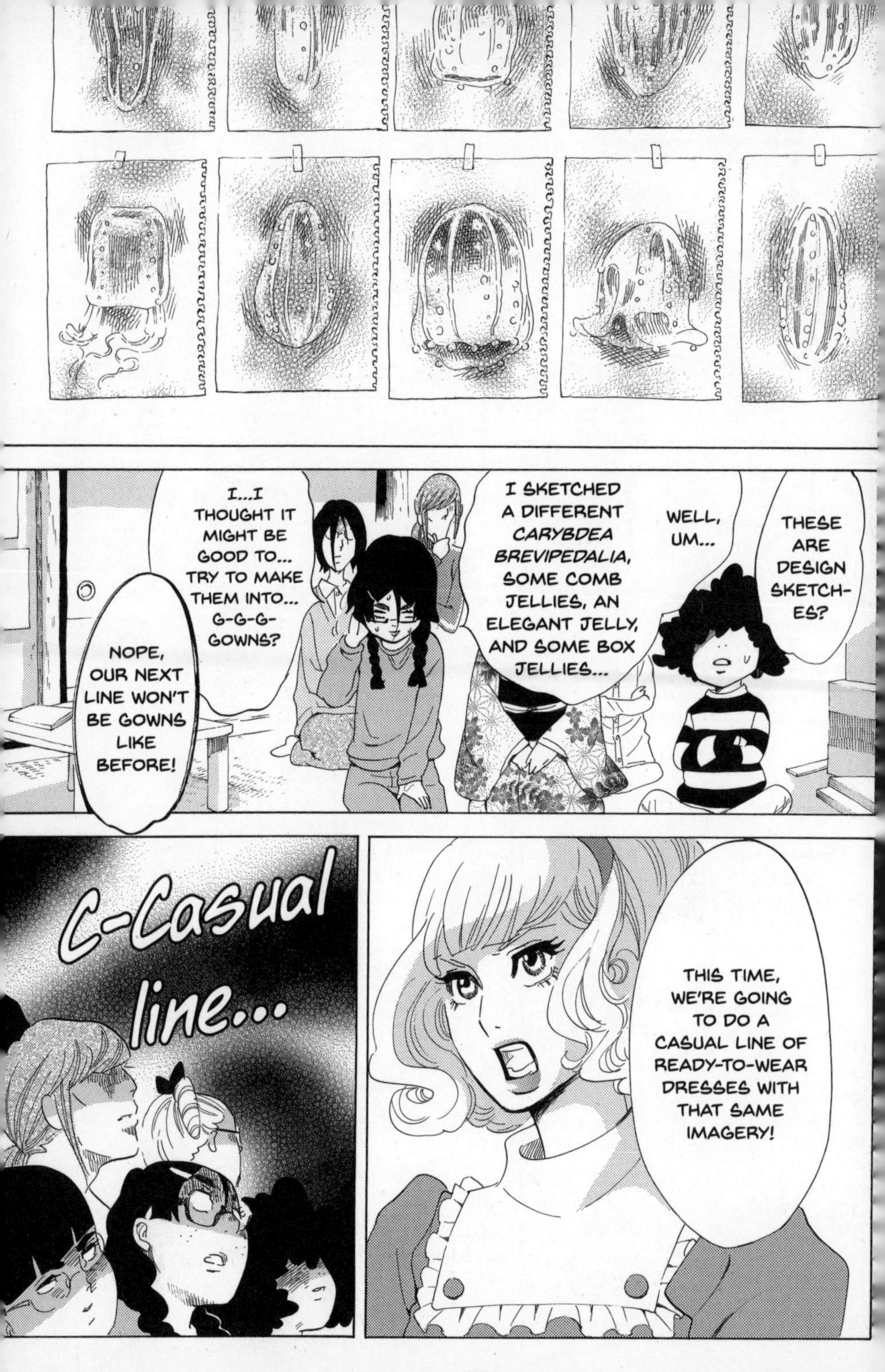
THESE ARE DESIGN SKETCH-ES?
WELL, UM...
I SKETCHED A DIFFERENT CARYBDEA BREVIPEDALIA, SOME COMB JELLIES, AN ELEGANT JELLY, AND SOME BOX JELLIES...
I...I THOUGHT IT MIGHT BE GOOD TO... TRY TO MAKE THEM INTO... G-G-G-GOWNS?
NOPE, OUR NEXT LINE WON'T BE GOWNS LIKE BEFORE!
THIS TIME, WE'RE GOING TO DO A CASUAL LINE OF READY-TO-WEAR DRESSES WITH THAT SAME IMAGERY!
C-Casual line...

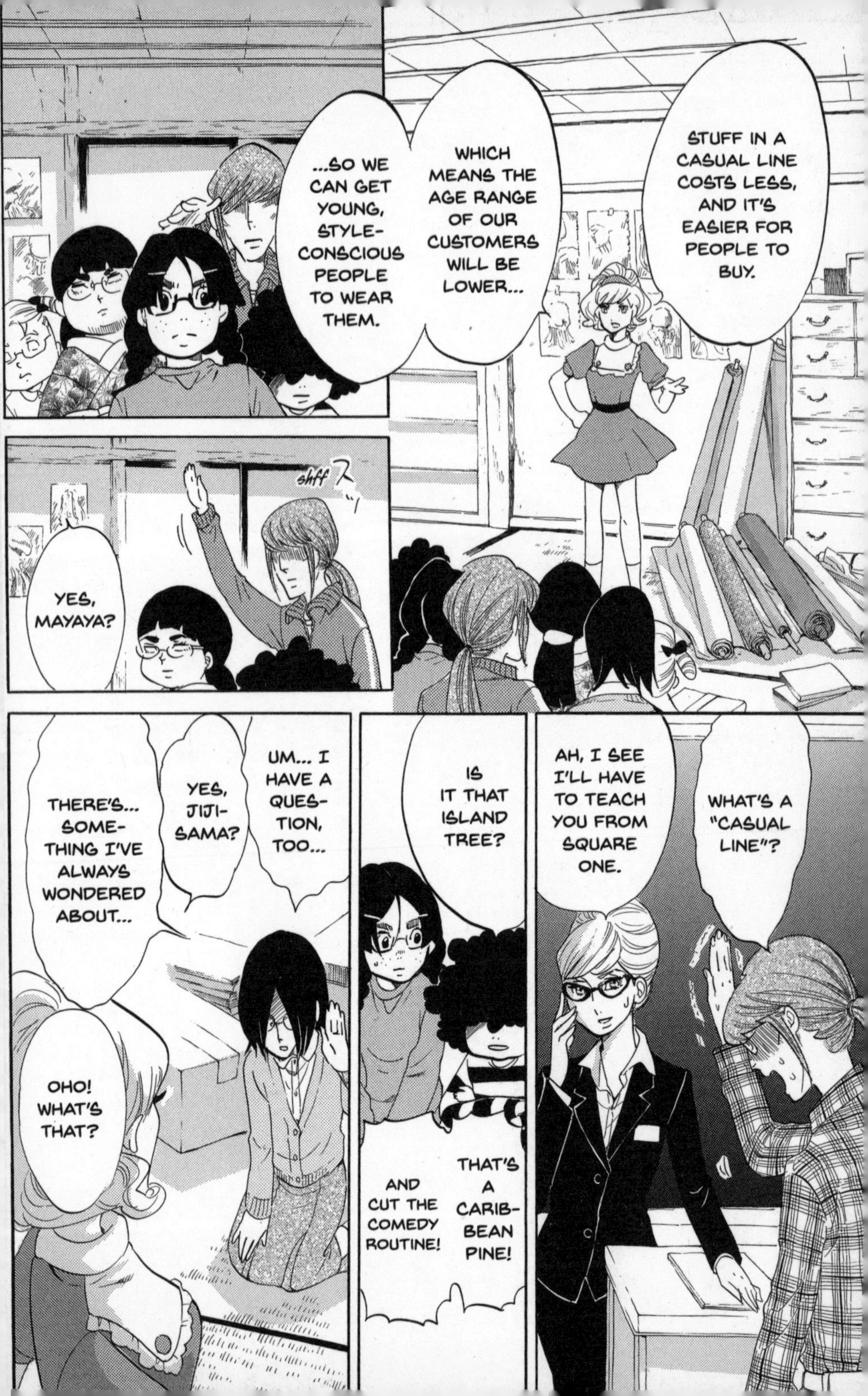
STUFF IN A CASUAL LINE COSTS LESS, AND IT'S EASIER FOR PEOPLE TO BUY.
WHICH MEANS THE AGE RANGE OF OUR CUSTOMERS WILL BE LOWER...
...SO WE CAN GET YOUNG, STYLE-CONSCIOUS PEOPLE TO WEAR THEM.
shff ス
YES, MAYAYA?
WHAT'S A "CASUAL LINE"?
AH, I SEE I'LL HAVE TO TEACH YOU FROM SQUARE ONE.
IS IT THAT ISLAND TREE?
THAT'S A CARIB-BEAN PINE!
AND CUT THE COMEDY ROUTINE!
UM... I HAVE A QUES-TION, TOO...
YES, JIJI-SAMA?
THERE'S... SOME-THING I'VE ALWAYS WONDERED ABOUT...
OHO! WHAT'S THAT?

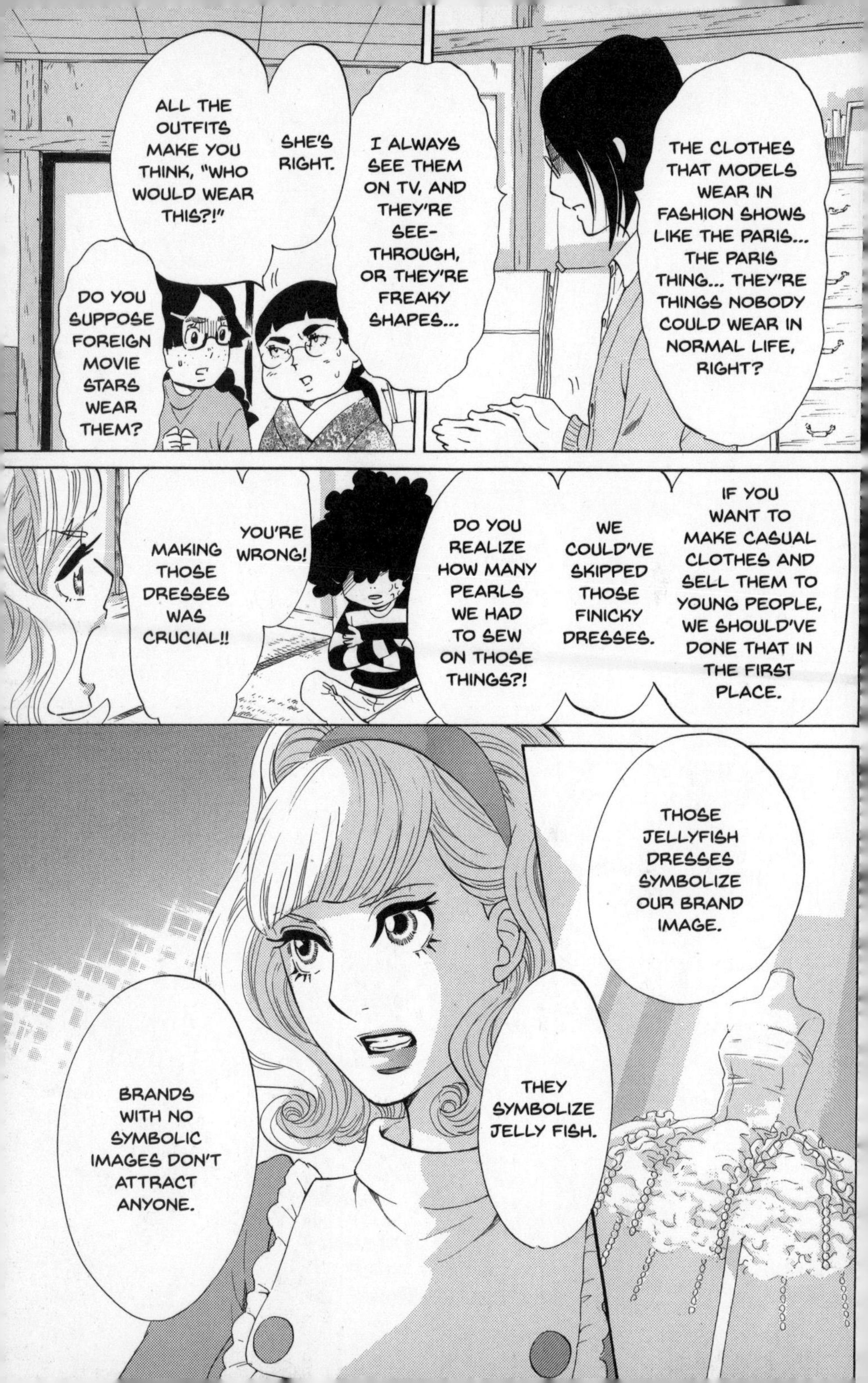
THE CLOTHES THAT MODELS WEAR IN FASHION SHOWS LIKE THE PARIS... THE PARIS THING... THEY'RE THINGS NOBODY COULD WEAR IN NORMAL LIFE, RIGHT?
I ALWAYS SEE THEM ON TV, AND THEY'RE SEE-THROUGH, OR THEY'RE FREAKY SHAPES...
SHE'S RIGHT.
ALL THE OUTFITS MAKE YOU THINK, "WHO WOULD WEAR THIS?!"
DO YOU SUPPOSE FOREIGN MOVIE STARS WEAR THEM?
IF YOU WANT TO MAKE CASUAL CLOTHES AND SELL THEM TO YOUNG PEOPLE, WE SHOULD'VE DONE THAT IN THE FIRST PLACE.
WE COULD'VE SKIPPED THOSE FINICKY DRESSES.
DO YOU REALIZE HOW MANY PEARLS WE HAD TO SEW ON THOSE THINGS?!
YOU'RE WRONG!
MAKING THOSE DRESSES WAS CRUCIAL!!
THOSE JELLYFISH DRESSES SYMBOLIZE OUR BRAND IMAGE.
THEY SYMBOLIZE JELLY FISH.
BRANDS WITH NO SYMBOLIC IMAGES DON'T ATTRACT ANYONE.

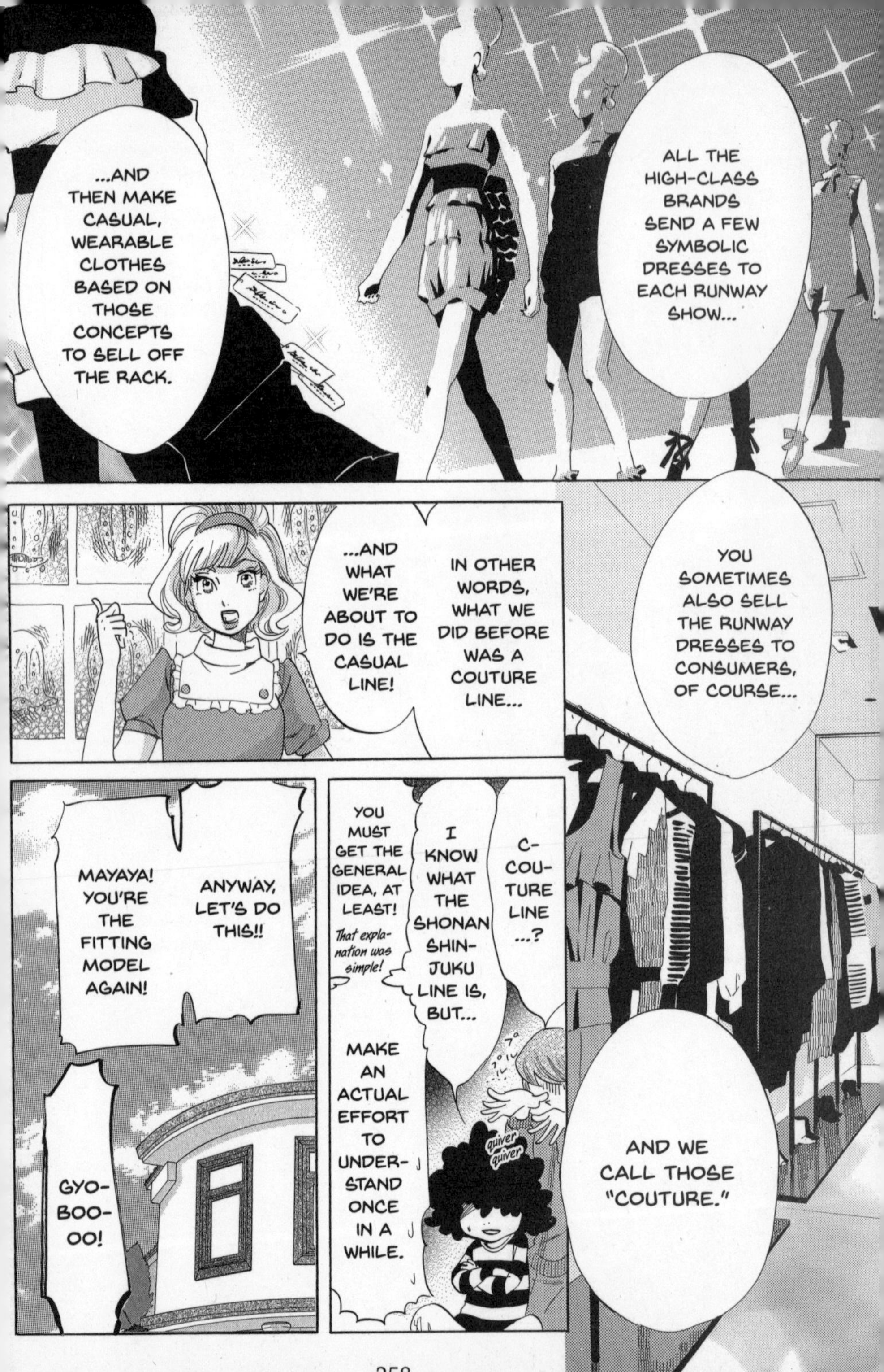
ALL THE HIGH-CLASS BRANDS SEND A FEW SYMBOLIC DRESSES TO EACH RUNWAY SHOW...
...AND THEN MAKE CASUAL, WEARABLE CLOTHES BASED ON THOSE CONCEPTS TO SELL OFF THE RACK.
YOU SOMETIMES ALSO SELL THE RUNWAY DRESSES TO CONSUMERS, OF COURSE...
AND WE CALL THOSE "COUTURE."
IN OTHER WORDS, WHAT WE DID BEFORE WAS A COUTURE LINE...
...AND WHAT WE'RE ABOUT TO DO IS THE CASUAL LINE!
C-COUTURE LINE...?
I KNOW WHAT THE SHONAN SHINJUKU LINE IS, BUT...
YOU MUST GET THE GENERAL IDEA, AT LEAST!
That explanation was simple!
MAKE AN ACTUAL EFFORT TO UNDERSTAND ONCE IN A WHILE.
quiver quiver
ANYWAY, LET'S DO THIS!!
MAYAYA! YOU'RE THE FITTING MODEL AGAIN!
GYO-BOO-OO!

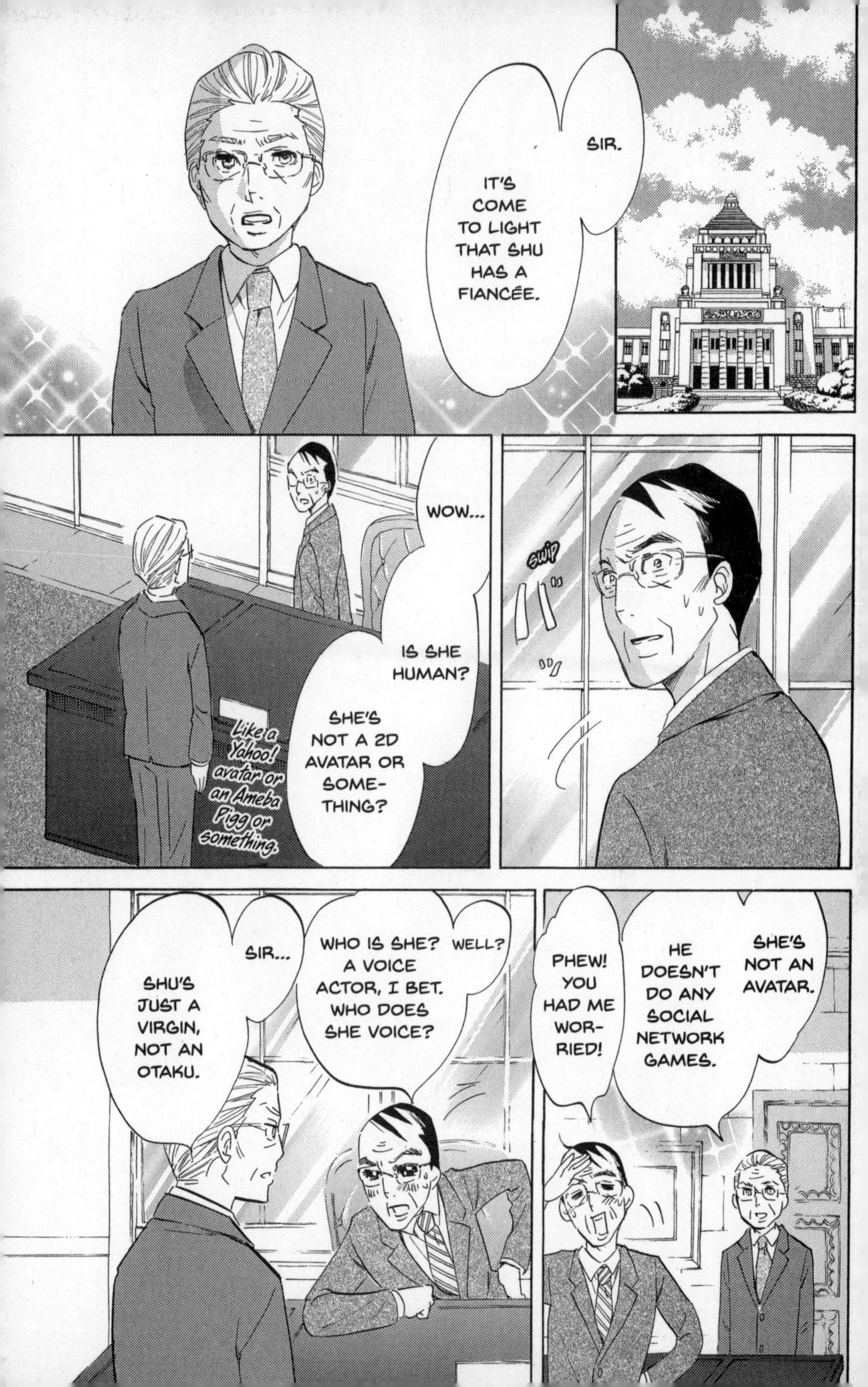
SIR.
IT'S COME TO LIGHT THAT SHU HAS A FIANCÉE.
swip
WOW...
IS SHE HUMAN?
SHE'S NOT A 2D AVATAR OR SOME-THING?
Like a Yahoo! avatar or an Ameba Pigg or something.
SHE'S NOT AN AVATAR.
HE DOESN'T DO ANY SOCIAL NETWORK GAMES.
PHEW! YOU HAD ME WOR-RIED!
WELL?
WHO IS SHE? A VOICE ACTOR, I BET. WHO DOES SHE VOICE?
SIR...
SHU'S JUST A VIRGIN, NOT AN OTAKU.

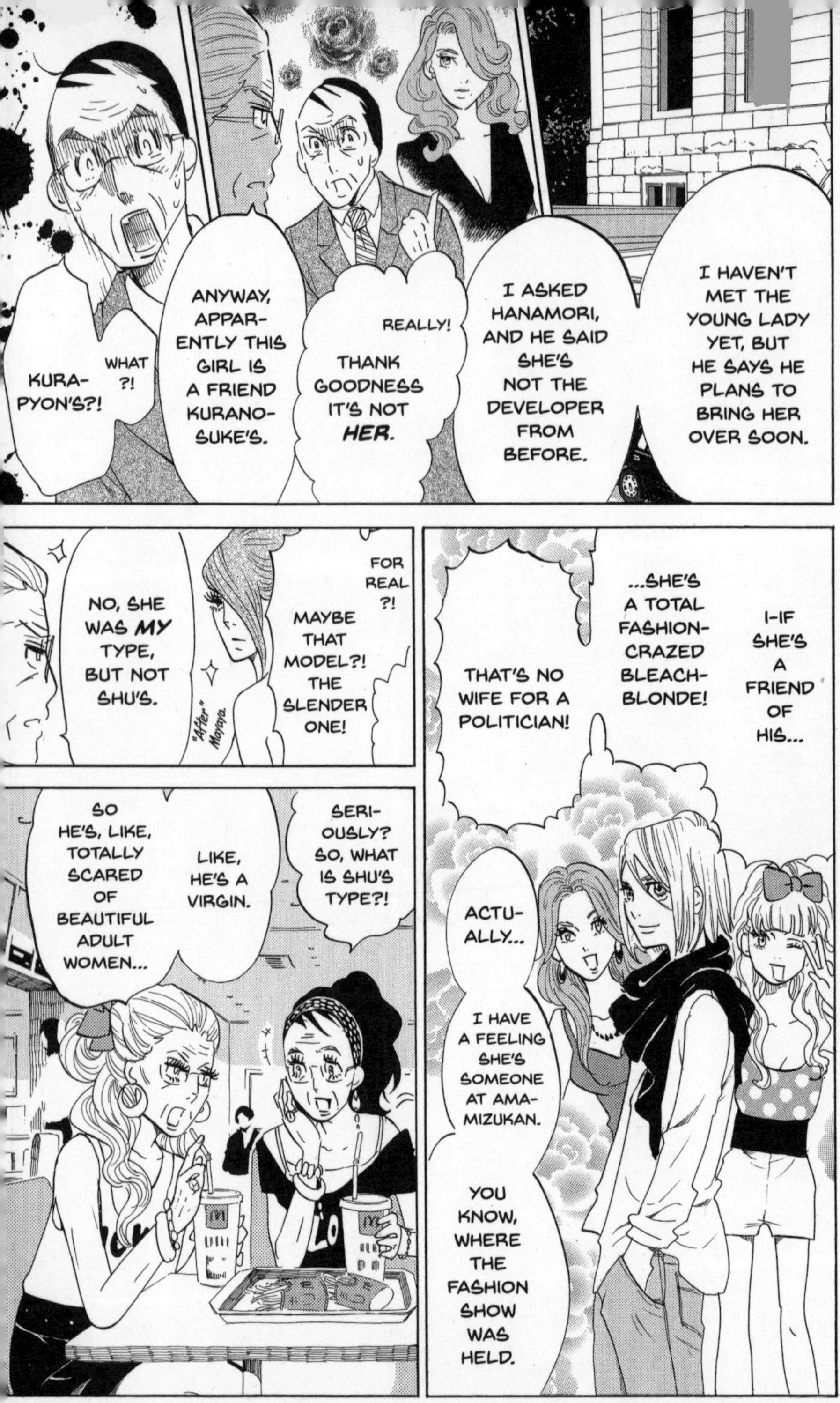
I HAVEN'T MET THE YOUNG LADY YET, BUT HE SAYS HE PLANS TO BRING HER OVER SOON.
I ASKED HANAMORI, AND HE SAID SHE'S NOT THE DEVELOPER FROM BEFORE.
REALLY!
THANK GOODNESS IT'S NOT HER.
ANYWAY, APPARENTLY THIS GIRL IS A FRIEND KURANOSUKE'S.
WHAT?!
KURA-PYON'S?!
I-IF SHE'S A FRIEND OF HIS...
...SHE'S A TOTAL FASHION-CRAZED BLEACH-BLONDE!
THAT'S NO WIFE FOR A POLITICIAN!
ACTUALLY...
I HAVE A FEELING SHE'S SOMEONE AT AMAMIZUKAN.
YOU KNOW, WHERE THE FASHION SHOW WAS HELD.
FOR REAL?!
MAYBE THAT MODEL?! THE SLENDER ONE!
"After" Mayaya.
NO, SHE WAS MY TYPE, BUT NOT SHU'S.
SERIOUSLY? SO, WHAT IS SHU'S TYPE?!
LIKE, HE'S A VIRGIN.
SO HE'S, LIKE, TOTALLY SCARED OF BEAUTIFUL ADULT WOMEN...

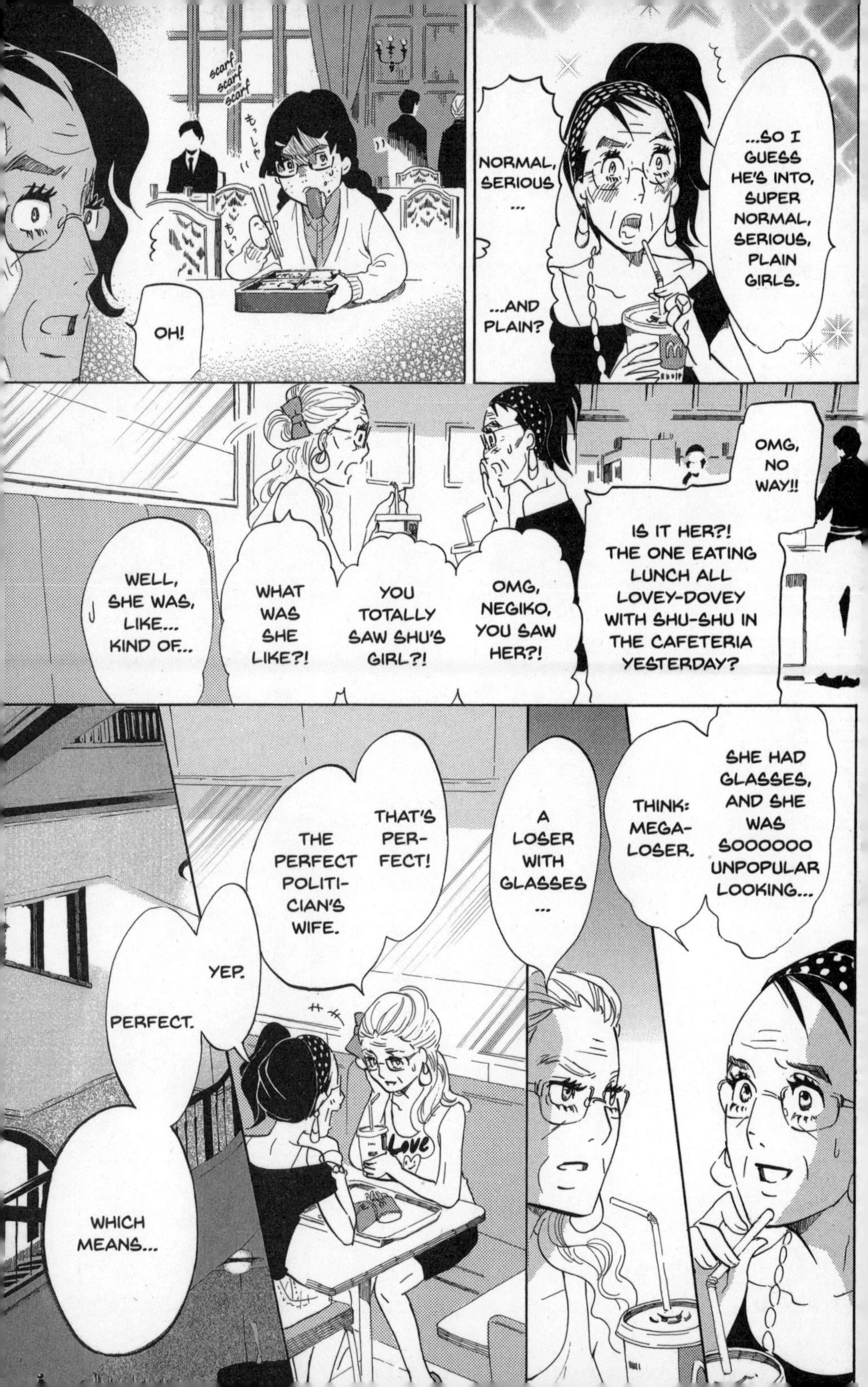
...SO I GUESS HE'S INTO, SUPER NORMAL, SERIOUS, PLAIN GIRLS.
NORMAL, SERIOUS ...
...AND PLAIN?
scarf
scarf
scarf
もっしゃ
OH!
OMG, NO WAY!!
IS IT HER?! THE ONE EATING LUNCH ALL LOVEY-DOVEY WITH SHU-SHU IN THE CAFETERIA YESTERDAY?
OMG, NEGIKO, YOU SAW HER?!
YOU TOTALLY SAW SHU'S GIRL?!
WHAT WAS SHE LIKE?!
WELL, SHE WAS, LIKE... KIND OF...
SHE HAD GLASSES, AND SHE WAS SOOOOOO UNPOPULAR LOOKING...
THINK: MEGA-LOSER.
A LOSER WITH GLASSES ...
THAT'S PER-FECT!
THE PERFECT POLITI-CIAN'S WIFE.
YEP.
PERFECT.
WHICH MEANS...

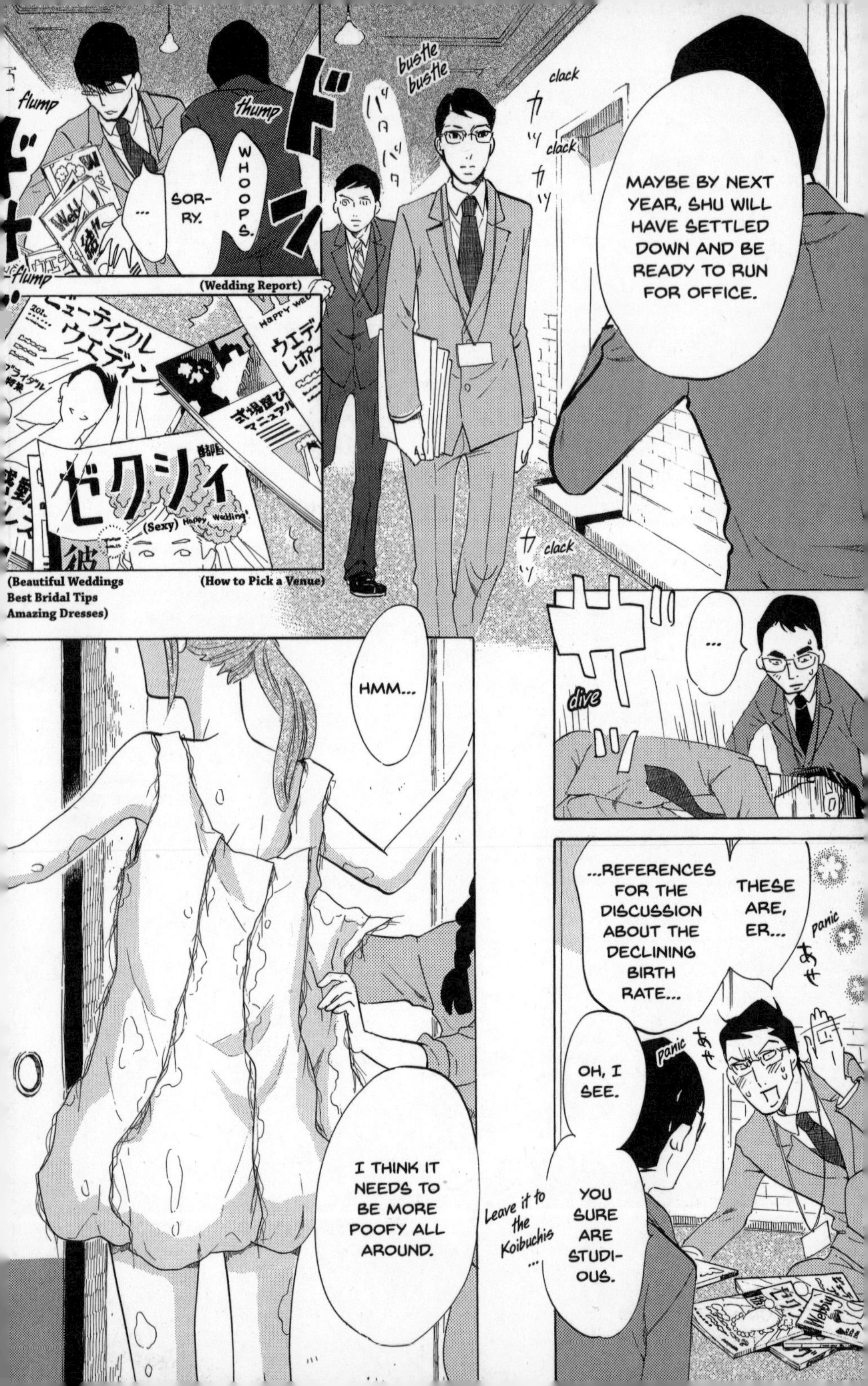
clack
clack
MAYBE BY NEXT YEAR, SHU WILL HAVE SETTLED DOWN AND BE READY TO RUN FOR OFFICE.
clack
bustle bustle
thump
WHOOPS.
SORRY.
...
flump
flump
(Wedding Report)
(Sexy) Happy Wedding
(Beautiful Weddings
Best Bridal Tips
Amazing Dresses)
(How to Pick a Venue)
...
dive
THESE ARE, ER...
...REFERENCES FOR THE DISCUSSION ABOUT THE DECLINING BIRTH RATE...
panic
panic
OH, I SEE.
YOU SURE ARE STUDIOUS.
Leave it to the Koibuchis...
HMM...
I THINK IT NEEDS TO BE MORE POOFY ALL AROUND.

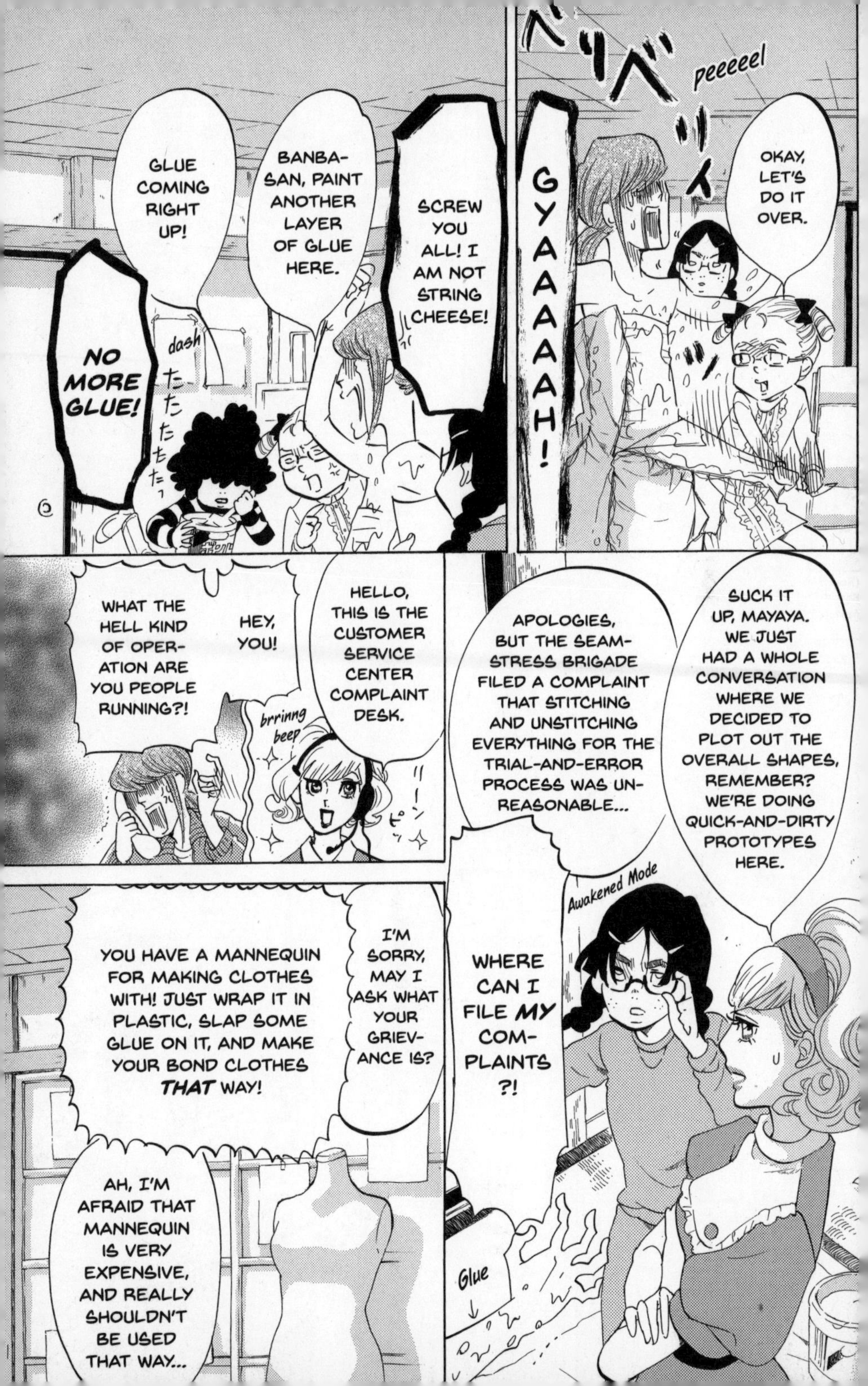

ベリベリィ
peeeeel
GYAAAAAH!
OKAY, LET'S DO IT OVER.
SCREW YOU ALL! I AM NOT STRING CHEESE!
BANBA-SAN, PAINT ANOTHER LAYER OF GLUE HERE.
GLUE COMING RIGHT UP!
NO MORE GLUE!
dash
SUCK IT UP, MAYAYA. WE JUST HAD A WHOLE CONVERSATION WHERE WE DECIDED TO PLOT OUT THE OVERALL SHAPES, REMEMBER? WE'RE DOING QUICK-AND-DIRTY PROTOTYPES HERE.
APOLOGIES, BUT THE SEAM-STRESS BRIGADE FILED A COMPLAINT THAT STITCHING AND UNSTITCHING EVERYTHING FOR THE TRIAL-AND-ERROR PROCESS WAS UN-REASONABLE...
Awakened Mode
WHERE CAN I FILE *MY* COM-PLAINTS ?!
Glue
HELLO, THIS IS THE CUSTOMER SERVICE CENTER COMPLAINT DESK.
brrinng beep
HEY, YOU!
WHAT THE HELL KIND OF OPER-ATION ARE YOU PEOPLE RUNNING?!
I'M SORRY, MAY I ASK WHAT YOUR GRIEV-ANCE IS?
YOU HAVE A MANNEQUIN FOR MAKING CLOTHES WITH! JUST WRAP IT IN PLASTIC, SLAP SOME GLUE ON IT, AND MAKE YOUR BOND CLOTHES ***THAT*** WAY!
AH, I'M AFRAID THAT MANNEQUIN IS VERY EXPENSIVE, AND REALLY SHOULDN'T BE USED THAT WAY...

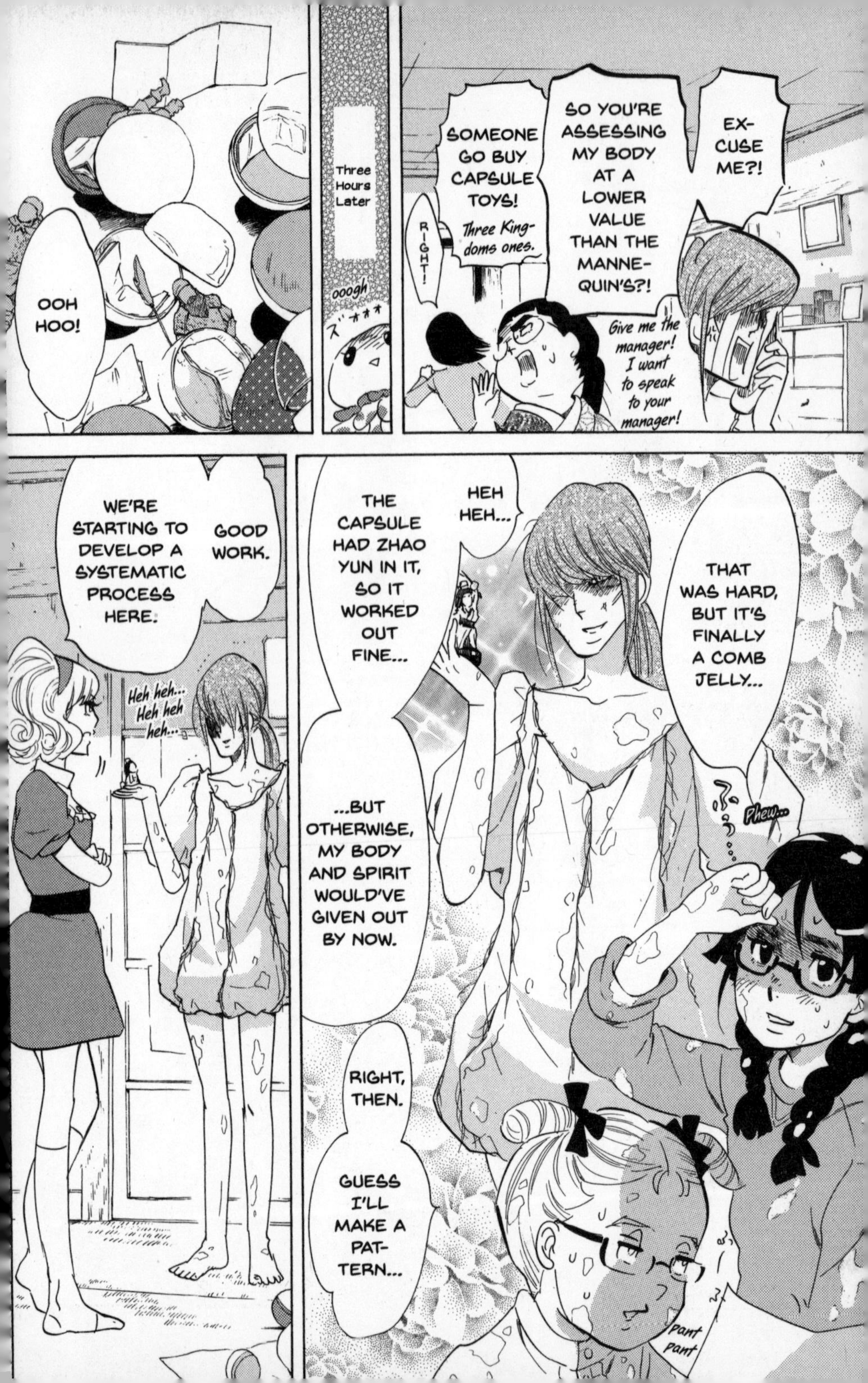
EX-CUSE ME?!
SO YOU'RE ASSESSING MY BODY AT A LOWER VALUE THAN THE MANNE-QUIN'S?!
SOMEONE GO BUY CAPSULE TOYS!
Three King-doms ones.
RIGHT!
Give me the manager! I want to speak to your manager!
Three Hours Later
ズオオオ
ooogh
OOH HOO!
THAT WAS HARD, BUT IT'S FINALLY A COMB JELLY...
Phew...
HEH HEH...
THE CAPSULE HAD ZHAO YUN IN IT, SO IT WORKED OUT FINE...
...BUT OTHERWISE, MY BODY AND SPIRIT WOULD'VE GIVEN OUT BY NOW.
RIGHT, THEN.
GUESS I'LL MAKE A PAT-TERN...
Pant pant
GOOD WORK.
WE'RE STARTING TO DEVELOP A SYSTEMATIC PROCESS HERE.
Heh heh... Heh heh heh...

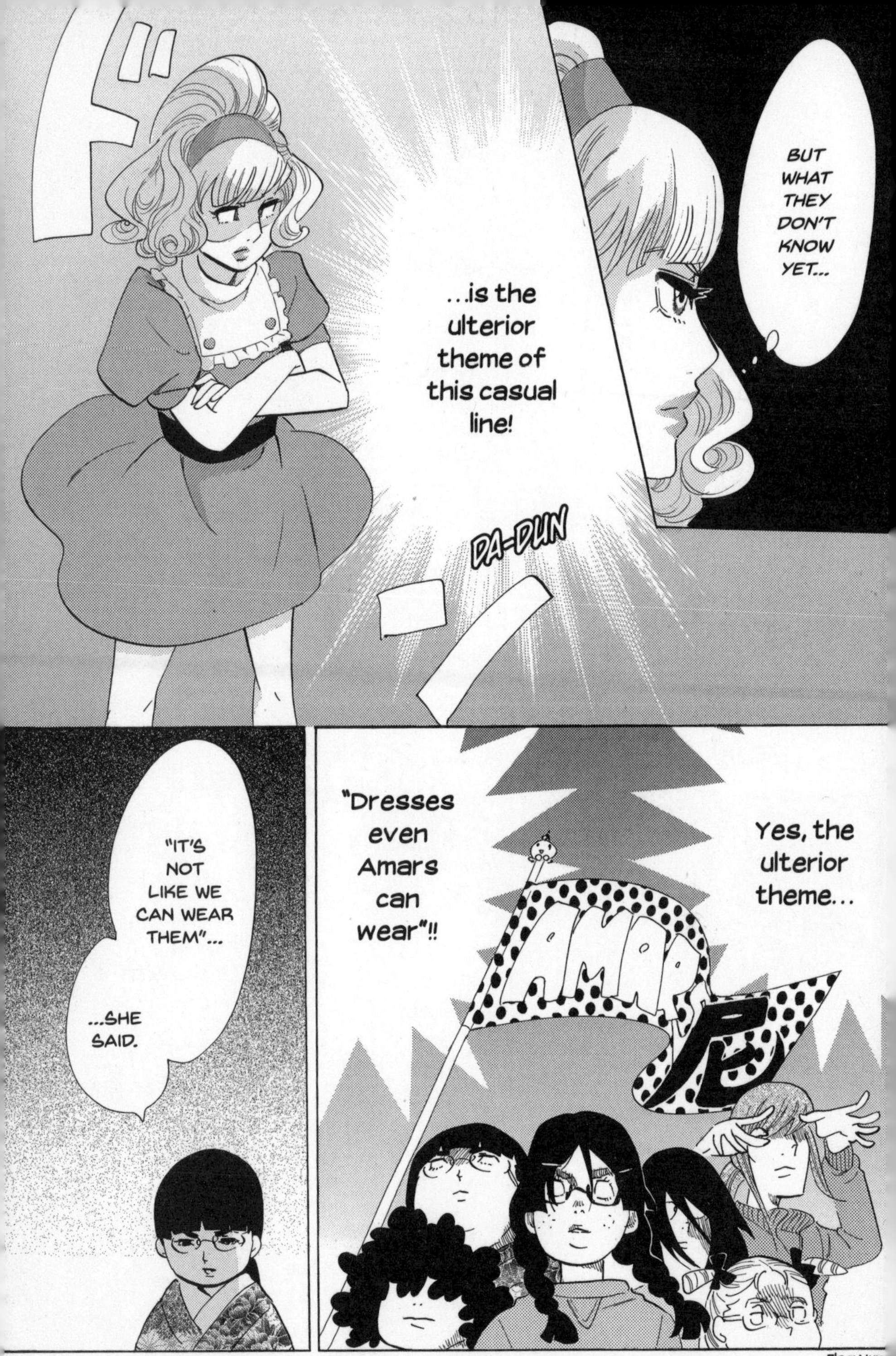
BUT WHAT THEY DON'T KNOW YET...
...is the ulterior theme of this casual line!
DA-DUN
Yes, the ulterior theme...
"Dresses even Amars can wear"!!
"IT'S NOT LIKE WE CAN WEAR THEM"...
...SHE SAID.

Flag: Nun

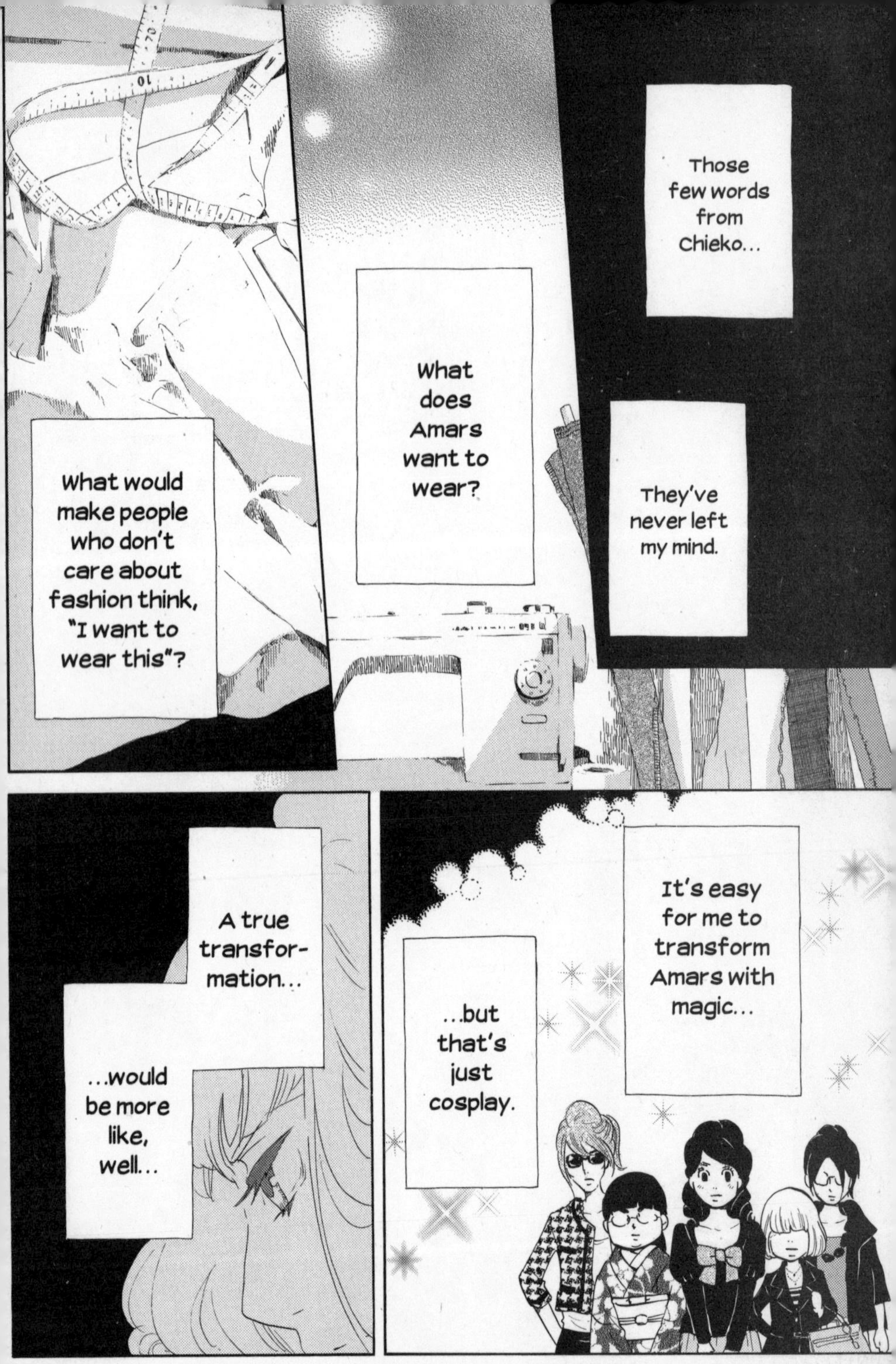
Those few words from Chieko...
They've never left my mind.
What does Amars want to wear?
What would make people who don't care about fashion think, "I want to wear this"?
It's easy for me to transform Amars with magic...
...but that's just cosplay.
A true transfor-mation...
...would be more like, well...

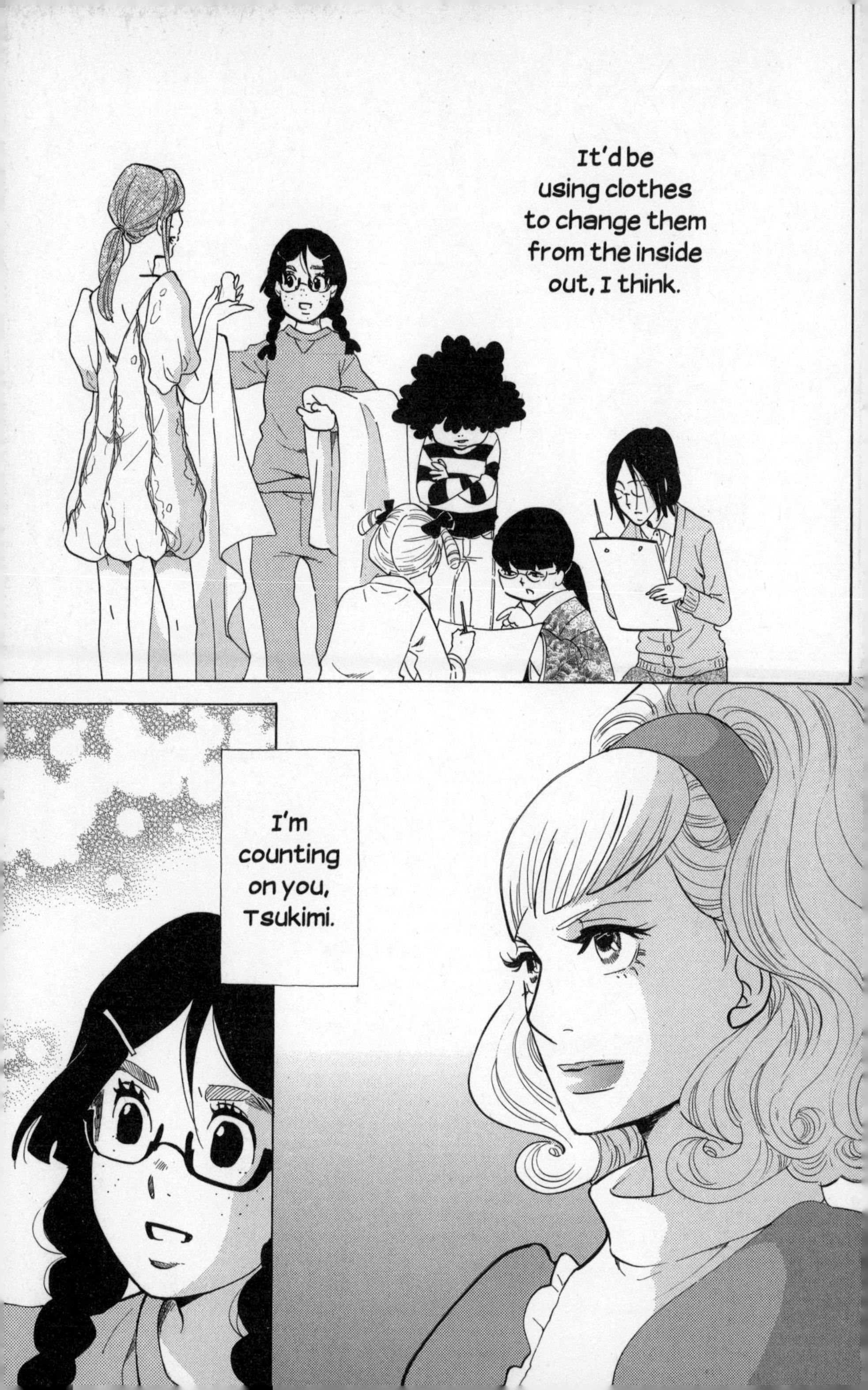
It'd be using clothes to change them from the inside out, I think.
I'm counting on you, Tsukimi.

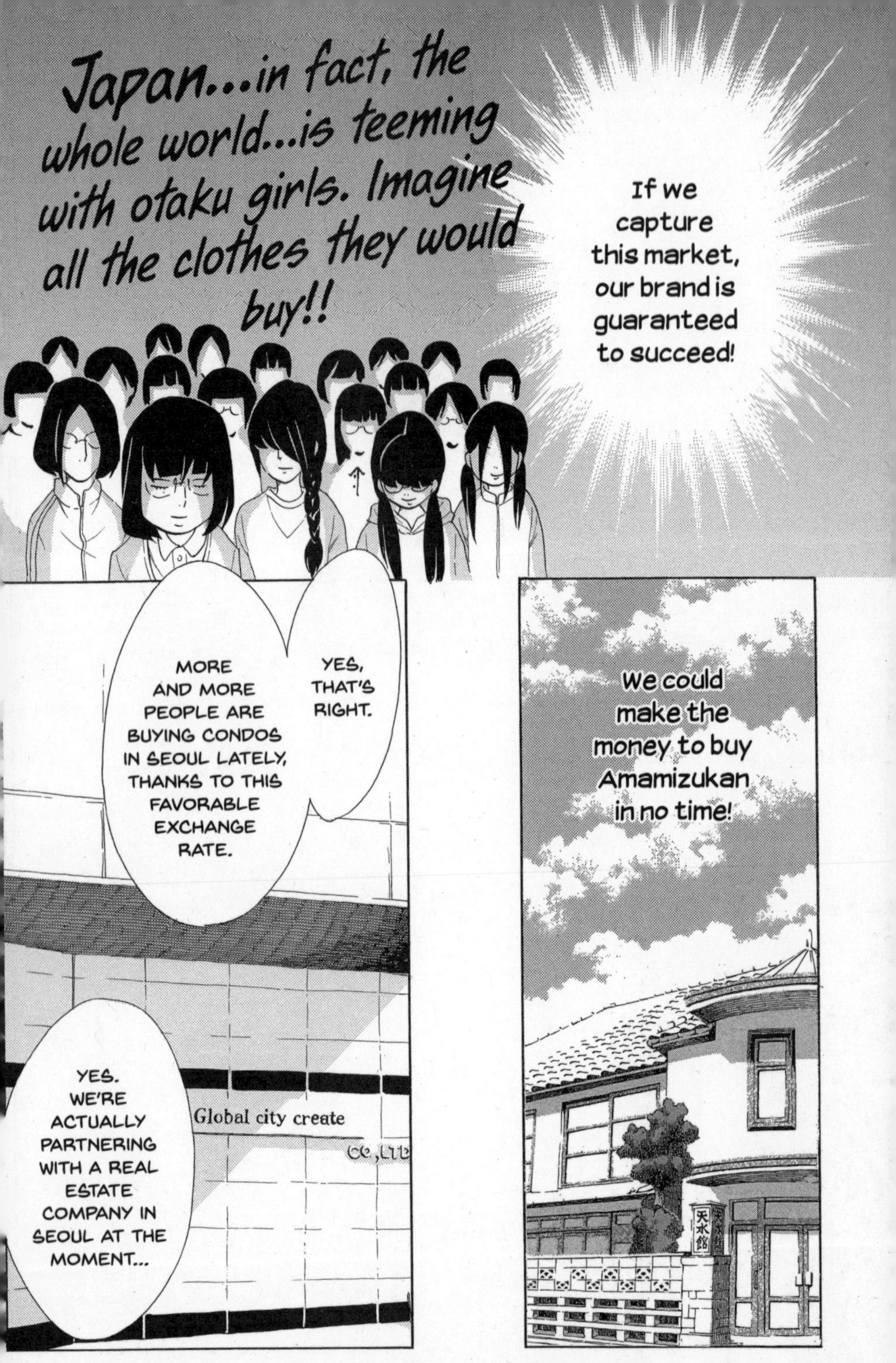
Japan...in fact, the whole world...is teeming with otaku girls. Imagine all the clothes they would buy!!
If we capture this market, our brand is guaranteed to succeed!
We could make the money to buy Amamizukan in no time!
YES, THAT'S RIGHT.
MORE AND MORE PEOPLE ARE BUYING CONDOS IN SEOUL LATELY, THANKS TO THIS FAVORABLE EXCHANGE RATE.
Global city create
YES. WE'RE ACTUALLY PARTNERING WITH A REAL ESTATE COMPANY IN SEOUL AT THE MOMENT...

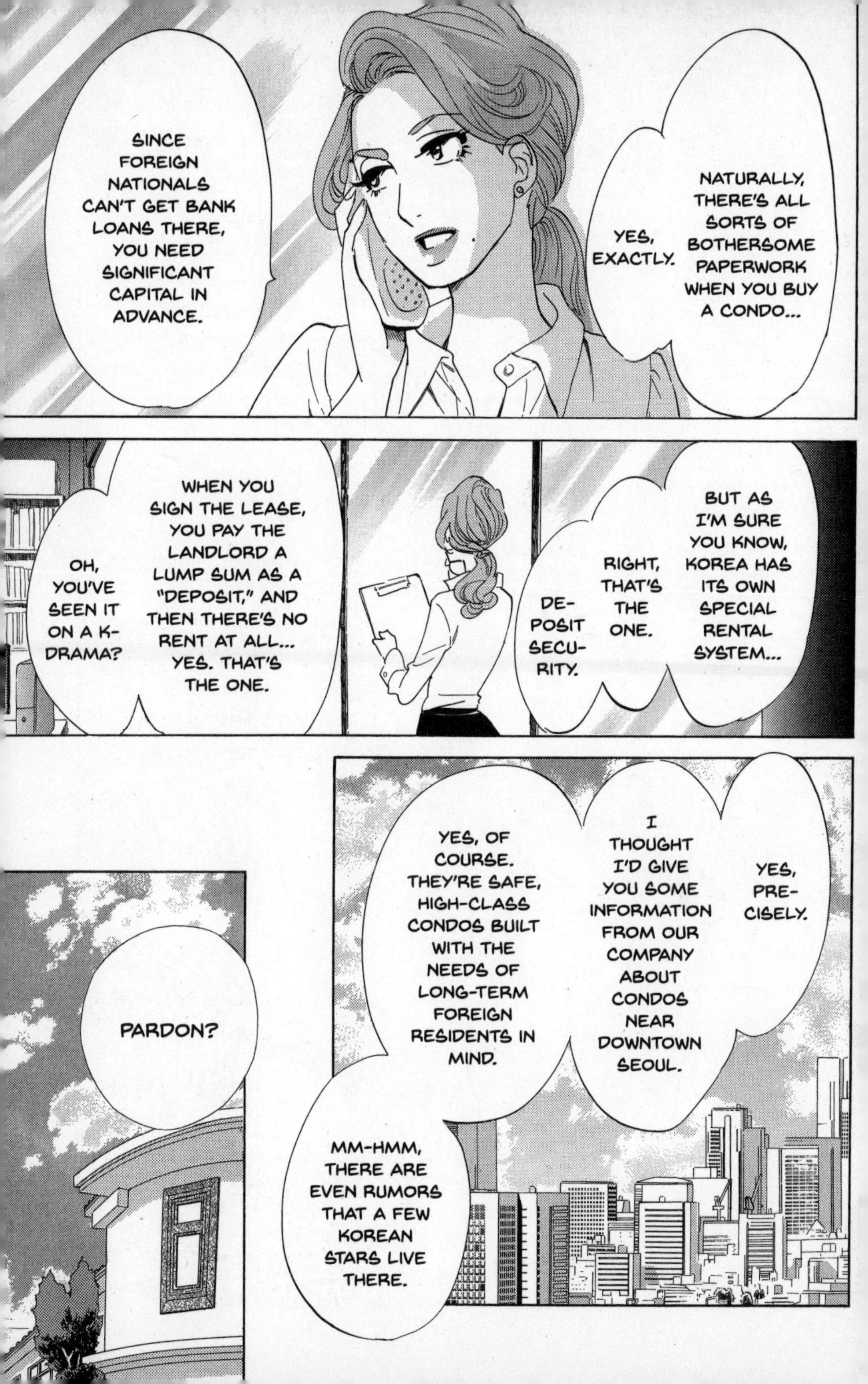
NATURALLY, THERE'S ALL SORTS OF BOTHERSOME PAPERWORK WHEN YOU BUY A CONDO...
YES, EXACTLY.
SINCE FOREIGN NATIONALS CAN'T GET BANK LOANS THERE, YOU NEED SIGNIFICANT CAPITAL IN ADVANCE.
BUT AS I'M SURE YOU KNOW, KOREA HAS ITS OWN SPECIAL RENTAL SYSTEM...
RIGHT, THAT'S THE ONE.
DE-POSIT SECU-RITY.
WHEN YOU SIGN THE LEASE, YOU PAY THE LANDLORD A LUMP SUM AS A "DEPOSIT," AND THEN THERE'S NO RENT AT ALL... YES. THAT'S THE ONE.
OH, YOU'VE SEEN IT ON A K-DRAMA?
YES, PRE-CISELY.
I THOUGHT I'D GIVE YOU SOME INFORMATION FROM OUR COMPANY ABOUT CONDOS NEAR DOWNTOWN SEOUL.
YES, OF COURSE. THEY'RE SAFE, HIGH-CLASS CONDOS BUILT WITH THE NEEDS OF LONG-TERM FOREIGN RESIDENTS IN MIND.
MM-HMM, THERE ARE EVEN RUMORS THAT A FEW KOREAN STARS LIVE THERE.
PARDON?

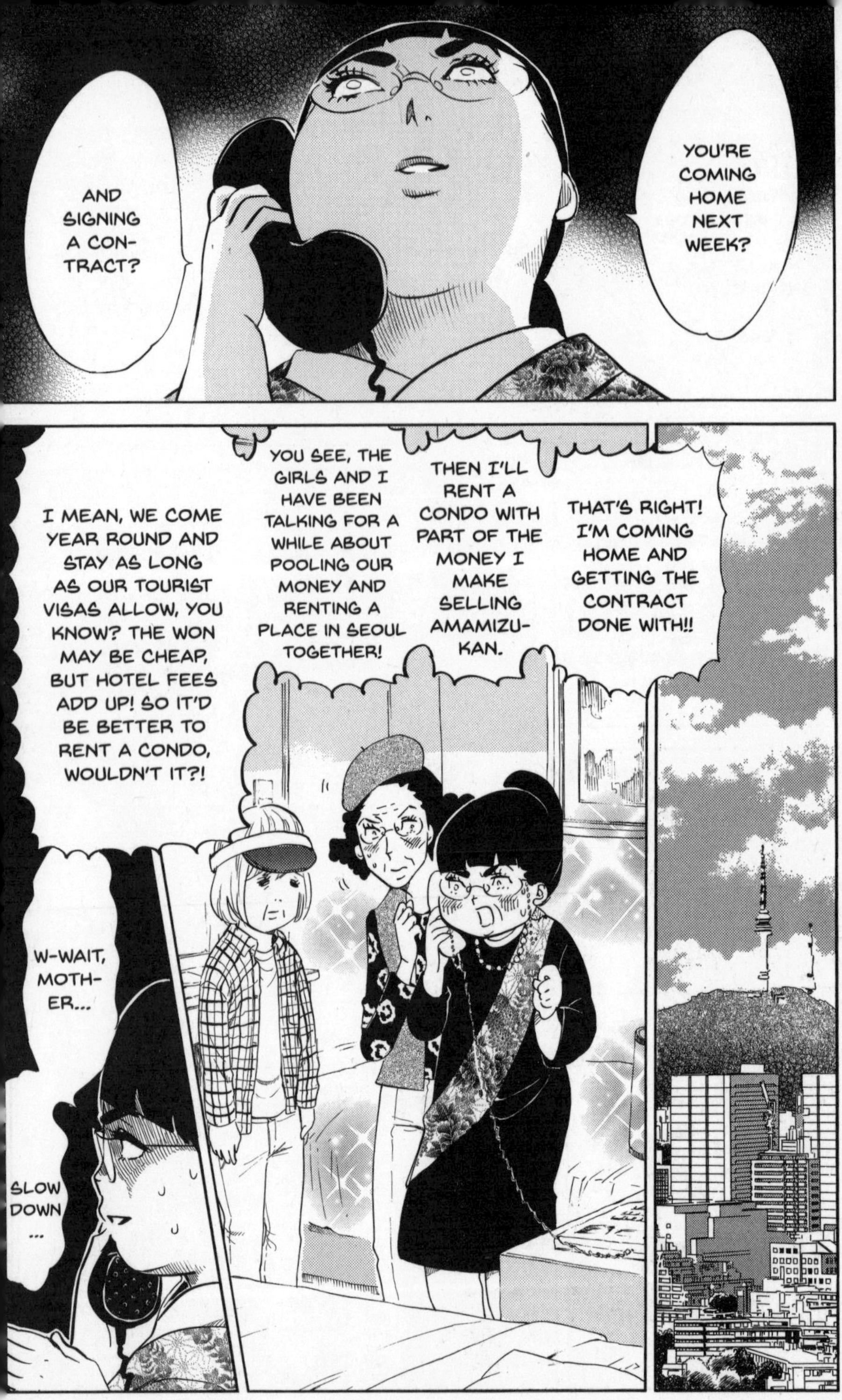

YOU'RE COMING HOME NEXT WEEK?
AND SIGNING A CON-TRACT?
THAT'S RIGHT! I'M COMING HOME AND GETTING THE CONTRACT DONE WITH!!
THEN I'LL RENT A CONDO WITH PART OF THE MONEY I MAKE SELLING AMAMIZU-KAN.
YOU SEE, THE GIRLS AND I HAVE BEEN TALKING FOR A WHILE ABOUT POOLING OUR MONEY AND RENTING A PLACE IN SEOUL TOGETHER!
I MEAN, WE COME YEAR ROUND AND STAY AS LONG AS OUR TOURIST VISAS ALLOW, YOU KNOW? THE WON MAY BE CHEAP, BUT HOTEL FEES ADD UP! SO IT'D BE BETTER TO RENT A CONDO, WOULDN'T IT?!
W-WAIT, MOTH-ER...
SLOW DOWN...

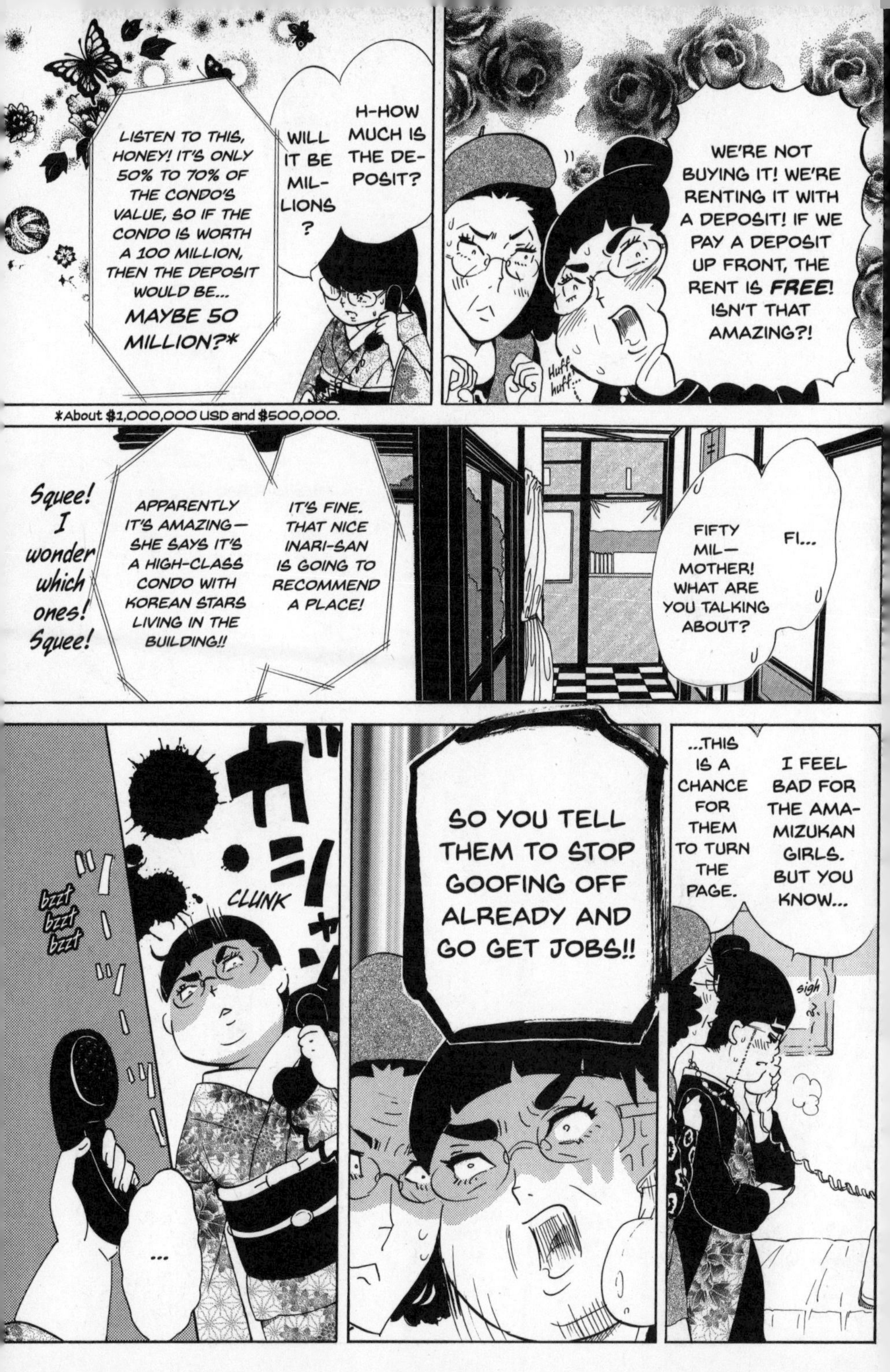
WE'RE NOT BUYING IT! WE'RE RENTING IT WITH A DEPOSIT! IF WE PAY A DEPOSIT UP FRONT, THE RENT IS **FREE**! ISN'T THAT AMAZING?!
Huff huff...
H-HOW MUCH IS THE DEPOSIT?
WILL IT BE MILLIONS?
LISTEN TO THIS, HONEY! IT'S ONLY 50% TO 70% OF THE CONDO'S VALUE, SO IF THE CONDO IS WORTH A 100 MILLION, THEN THE DEPOSIT WOULD BE... **MAYBE 50 MILLION?***
*About $1,000,000 USD and $500,000.
FI...
FIFTY MIL— MOTHER! WHAT ARE YOU TALKING ABOUT?
IT'S FINE. THAT NICE INARI-SAN IS GOING TO RECOMMEND A PLACE!
APPARENTLY IT'S AMAZING—SHE SAYS IT'S A HIGH-CLASS CONDO WITH KOREAN STARS LIVING IN THE BUILDING!!
Squee! I wonder which ones! Squee!
I FEEL BAD FOR THE AMAMIZUKAN GIRLS. BUT YOU KNOW...
...THIS IS A CHANCE FOR THEM TO TURN THE PAGE.
sigh
SO YOU TELL THEM TO STOP GOOFING OFF ALREADY AND GO GET JOBS!!
CLUNK
bzzt bzzt bzzt
...

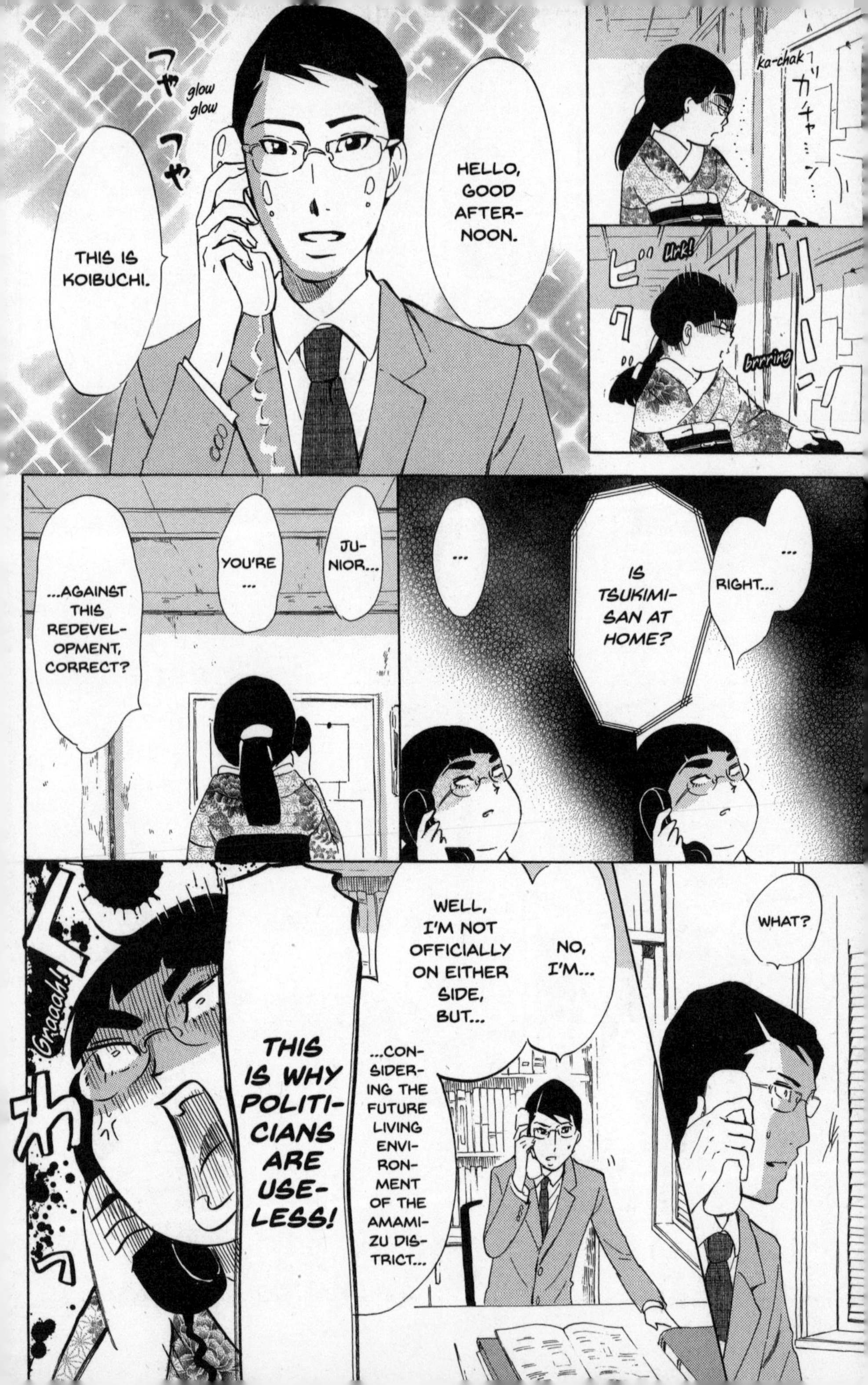

ka-chak
Urk!
brrring
glow glow
HELLO, GOOD AFTER-NOON.
THIS IS KOIBUCHI.
...
RIGHT...
IS TSUKIMI-SAN AT HOME?
...
JU-NIOR...
YOU'RE ...
...AGAINST THIS REDEVEL-OPMENT, CORRECT?
WHAT?
NO, I'M...
WELL, I'M NOT OFFICIALLY ON EITHER SIDE, BUT...
...CON-SIDER-ING THE FUTURE LIVING ENVI-RON-MENT OF THE AMAMI-ZU DIS-TRICT...
THIS IS WHY POLITI-CIANS ARE USE-LESS!
Gnaaah!

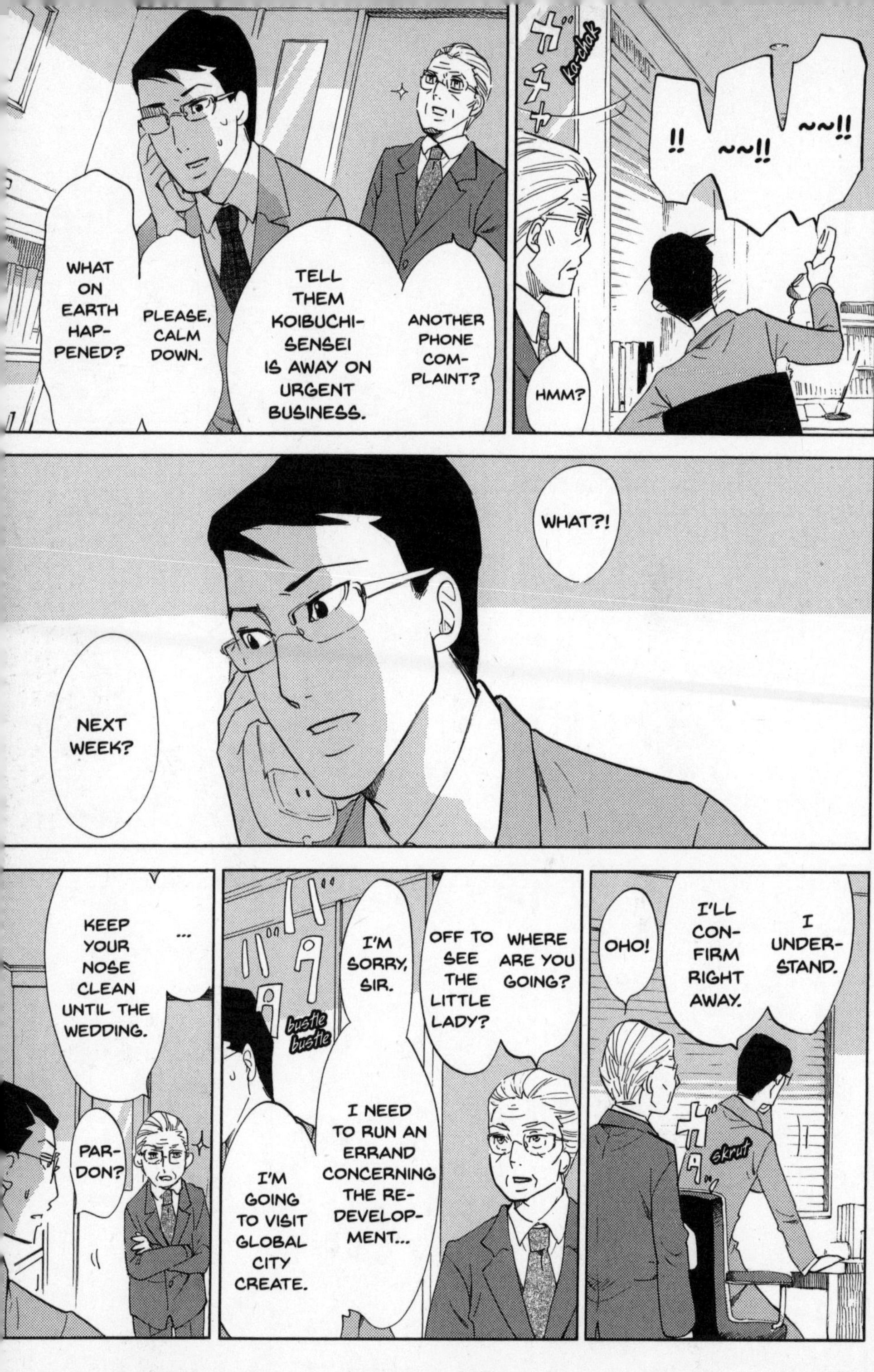
ka-chak
!! ~~!! ~~!!
HMM?
ANOTHER PHONE COMPLAINT?
TELL THEM KOIBUCHI-SENSEI IS AWAY ON URGENT BUSINESS.
PLEASE, CALM DOWN.
WHAT ON EARTH HAPPENED?
WHAT?!
NEXT WEEK?
I UNDERSTAND.
I'LL CONFIRM RIGHT AWAY.
OHO!
skrut
WHERE ARE YOU GOING?
OFF TO SEE THE LITTLE LADY?
I'M SORRY, SIR.
bustle bustle
I NEED TO RUN AN ERRAND CONCERNING THE REDEVELOPMENT...
I'M GOING TO VISIT GLOBAL CITY CREATE.
...
KEEP YOUR NOSE CLEAN UNTIL THE WEDDING.
PARDON?

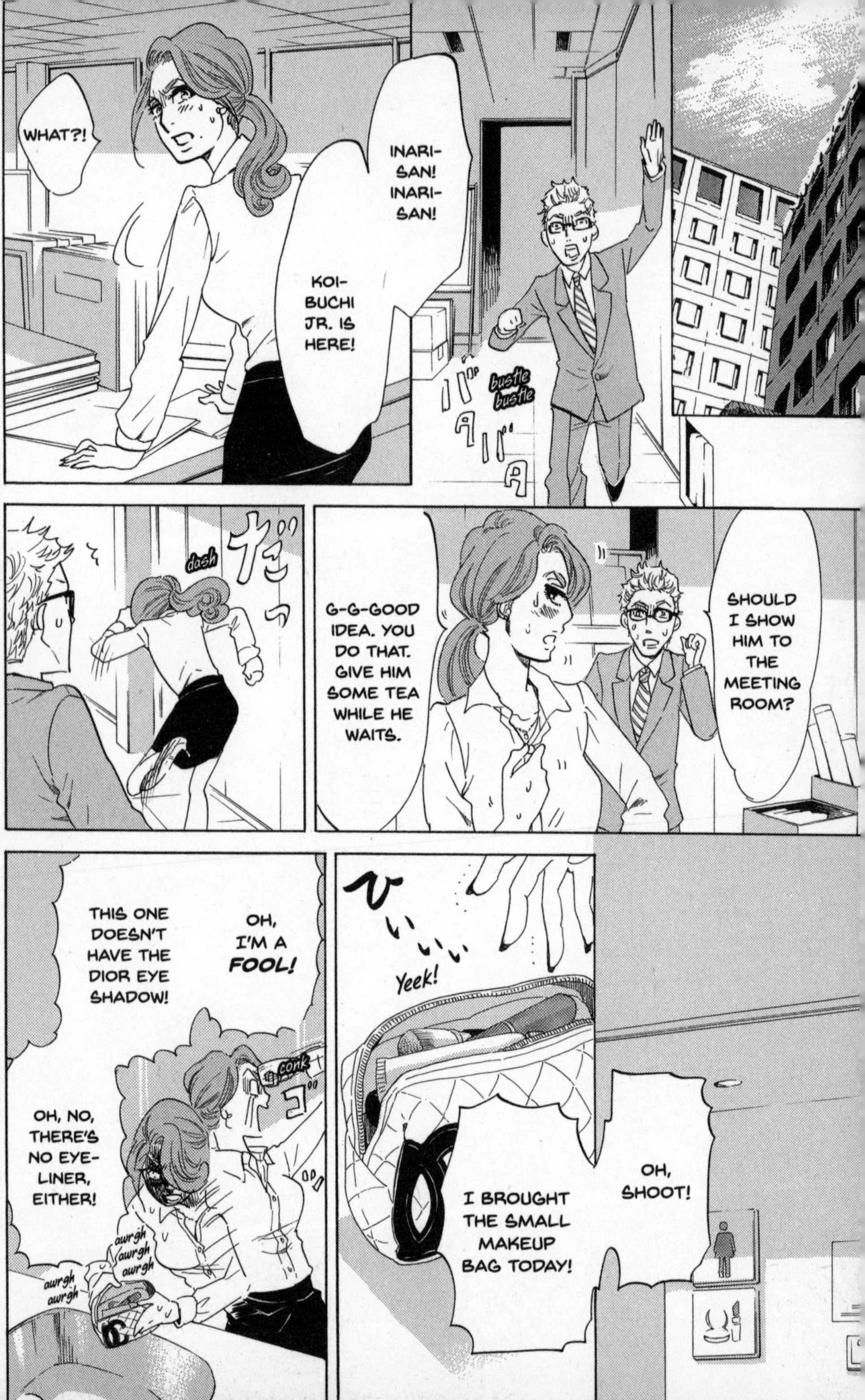
INARI-SAN! INARI-SAN!
KOI-BUCHI JR. IS HERE!
bustle bustle
WHAT?!
SHOULD I SHOW HIM TO THE MEETING ROOM?
G-G-GOOD IDEA. YOU DO THAT. GIVE HIM SOME TEA WHILE HE WAITS.
dash
Yeek!
OH, SHOOT!
I BROUGHT THE SMALL MAKEUP BAG TODAY!
OH, I'M A FOOL!
THIS ONE DOESN'T HAVE THE DIOR EYE SHADOW!
conk
OH, NO, THERE'S NO EYE-LINER, EITHER!
awrgh awrgh awrgh
awrgh awrgh

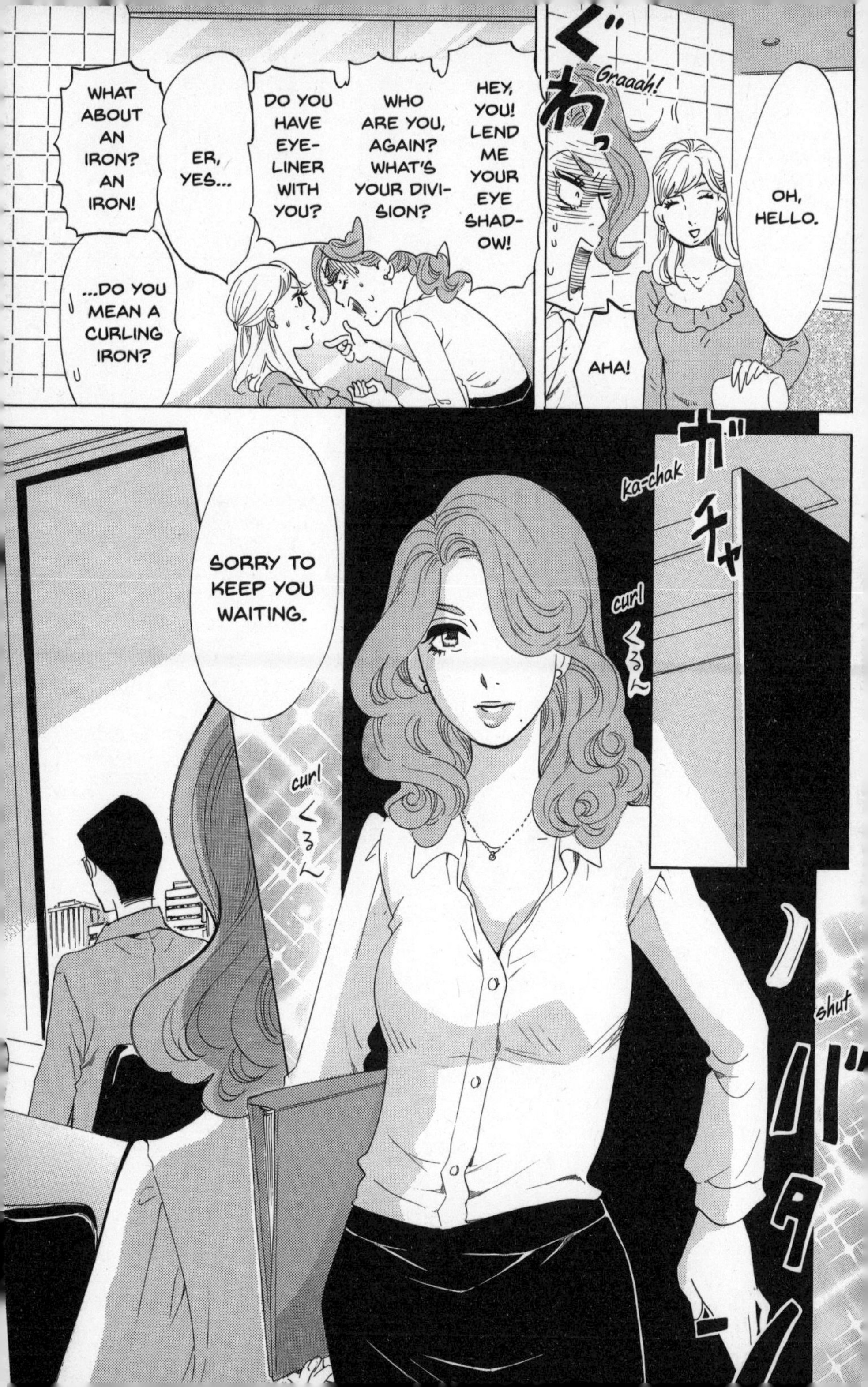
ぐわっ
Graaah!
OH, HELLO.
AHA!
HEY, YOU! LEND ME YOUR EYE SHADOW!
WHO ARE YOU, AGAIN? WHAT'S YOUR DIVISION?
DO YOU HAVE EYE-LINER WITH YOU?
ER, YES...
WHAT ABOUT AN IRON? AN IRON!
...DO YOU MEAN A CURLING IRON?
ガチャ
ka-chak
curl
くるん
SORRY TO KEEP YOU WAITING.
curl
くるん
shut
バタ

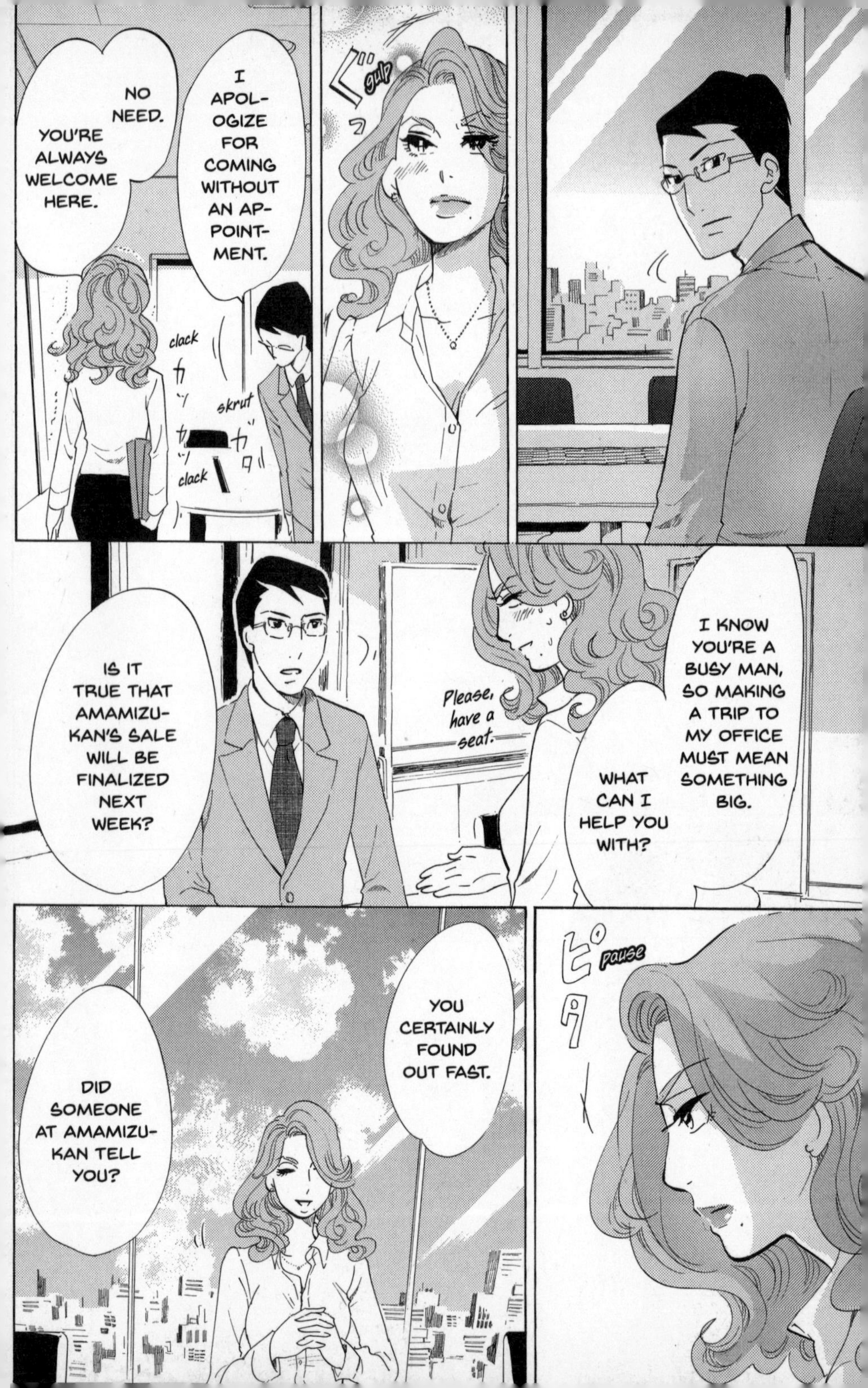
gulp
I APOLOGIZE FOR COMING WITHOUT AN APPOINTMENT.
NO NEED. YOU'RE ALWAYS WELCOME HERE.
clack
skrut
clack
I KNOW YOU'RE A BUSY MAN, SO MAKING A TRIP TO MY OFFICE MUST MEAN SOMETHING BIG.
WHAT CAN I HELP YOU WITH?
Please, have a seat.
IS IT TRUE THAT AMAMIZUKAN'S SALE WILL BE FINALIZED NEXT WEEK?
pause
YOU CERTAINLY FOUND OUT FAST.
DID SOMEONE AT AMAMIZUKAN TELL YOU?

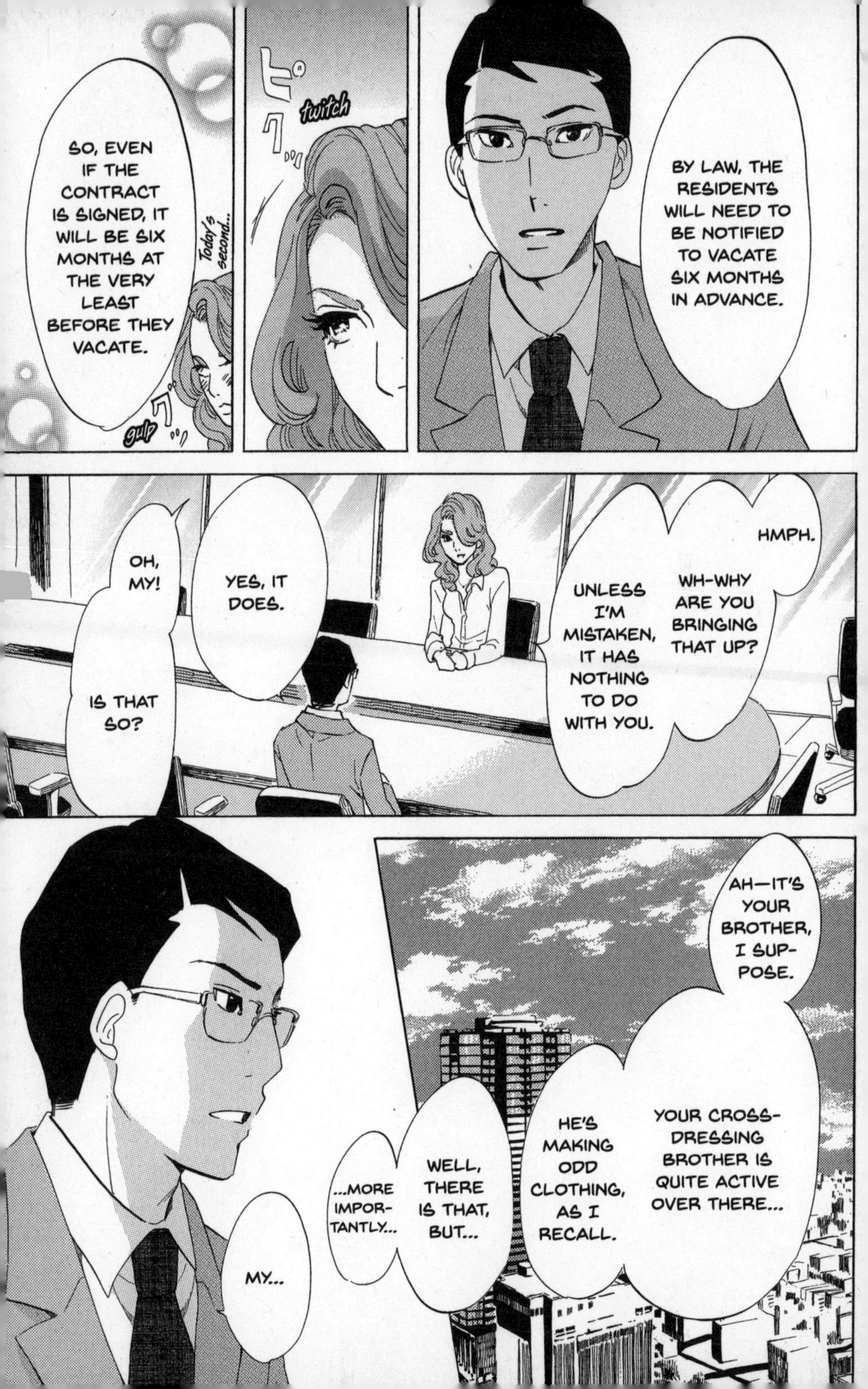
BY LAW, THE RESIDENTS WILL NEED TO BE NOTIFIED TO VACATE SIX MONTHS IN ADVANCE.
twitch
SO, EVEN IF THE CONTRACT IS SIGNED, IT WILL BE SIX MONTHS AT THE VERY LEAST BEFORE THEY VACATE.
Today's second...
gulp
HMPH.
WH-WHY ARE YOU BRINGING THAT UP?
UNLESS I'M MISTAKEN, IT HAS NOTHING TO DO WITH YOU.
YES, IT DOES.
OH, MY!
IS THAT SO?
AH—IT'S YOUR BROTHER, I SUPPOSE.
YOUR CROSS-DRESSING BROTHER IS QUITE ACTIVE OVER THERE...
HE'S MAKING ODD CLOTHING, AS I RECALL.
WELL, THERE IS THAT, BUT...
...MORE IMPORTANTLY...
MY...

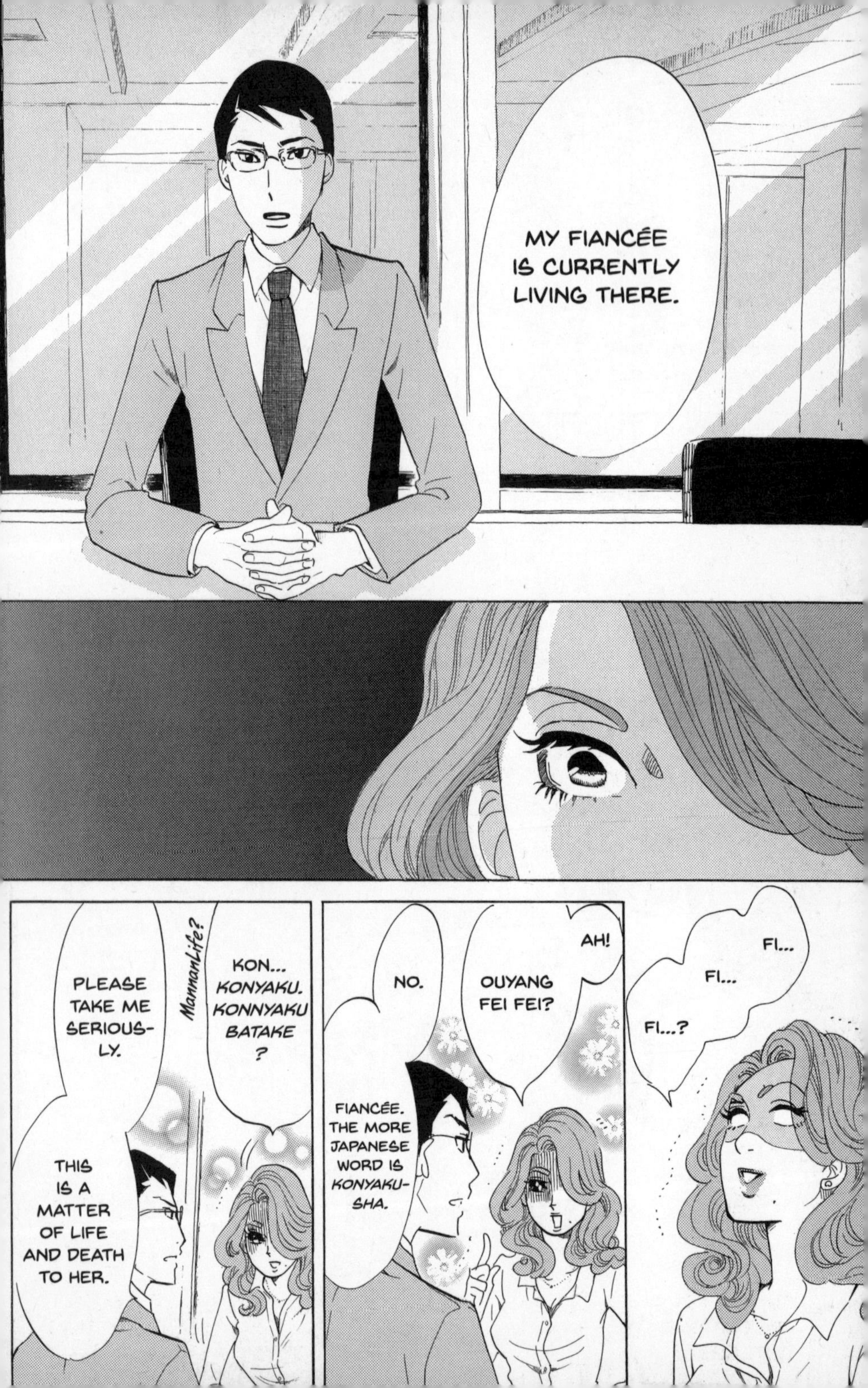
MY FIANCÉE IS CURRENTLY LIVING THERE.
FI... FI... FI...?
AH! OUYANG FEI FEI?
NO.
FIANCÉE. THE MORE JAPANESE WORD IS KONYAKU-SHA.
KON... KONYAKU. KONNYAKU BATAKE?
MannanLife?
PLEASE TAKE ME SERIOUS-LY.
THIS IS A MATTER OF LIFE AND DEATH TO HER.

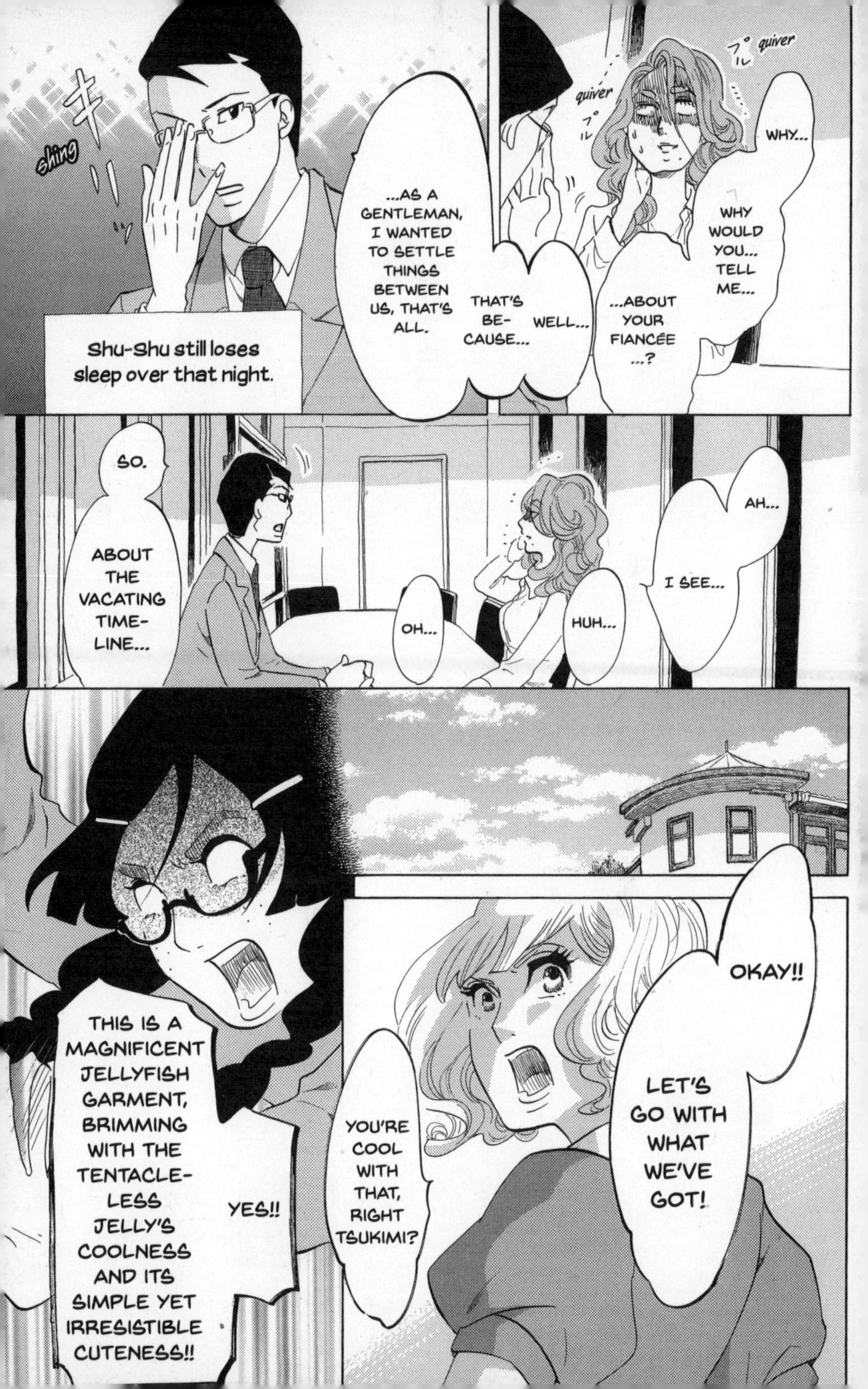
quiver
quiver
WHY...
WHY WOULD YOU... TELL ME...
...ABOUT YOUR FIANCÉE ...?
WELL...
THAT'S BE-CAUSE...
...AS A GENTLEMAN, I WANTED TO SETTLE THINGS BETWEEN US, THAT'S ALL.
shing
Shu-Shu still loses sleep over that night.
AH...
I SEE...
HUH...
OH...
SO.
ABOUT THE VACATING TIME-LINE...
OKAY!!
LET'S GO WITH WHAT WE'VE GOT!
YOU'RE COOL WITH THAT, RIGHT TSUKIMI?
YES!!
THIS IS A MAGNIFICENT JELLYFISH GARMENT, BRIMMING WITH THE TENTACLE-LESS JELLY'S COOLNESS AND ITS SIMPLE YET IRRESISTIBLE CUTENESS!!

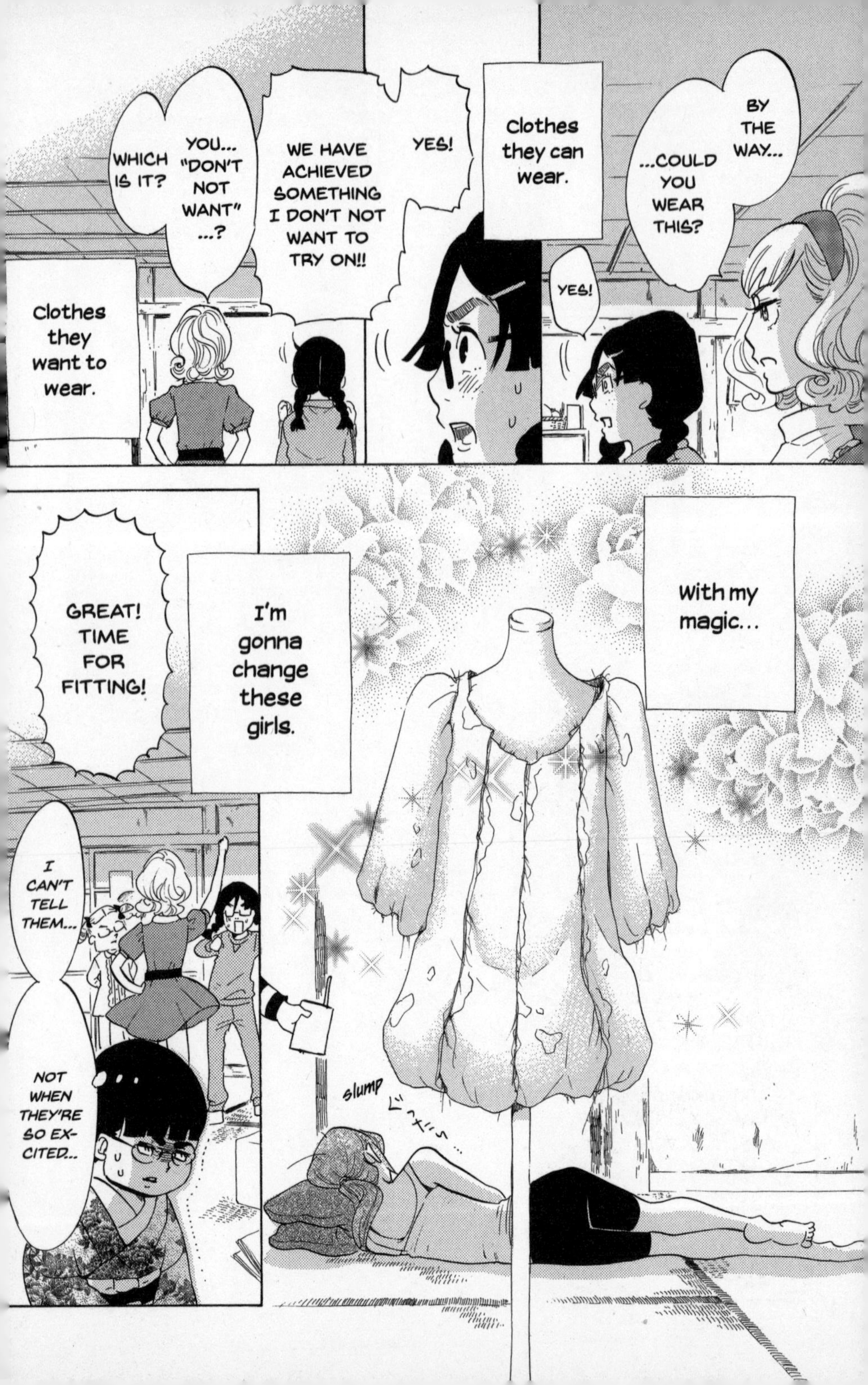

BY THE WAY...
...COULD YOU WEAR THIS?
YES!
Clothes they can wear.
YES!
WE HAVE ACHIEVED SOMETHING I DON'T NOT WANT TO TRY ON!!
YOU... "DON'T NOT WANT" ...?
WHICH IS IT?
Clothes they want to wear.
With my magic...
slump
I'm gonna change these girls.
GREAT! TIME FOR FITTING!
I CAN'T TELL THEM...
NOT WHEN THEY'RE SO EX-CITED...

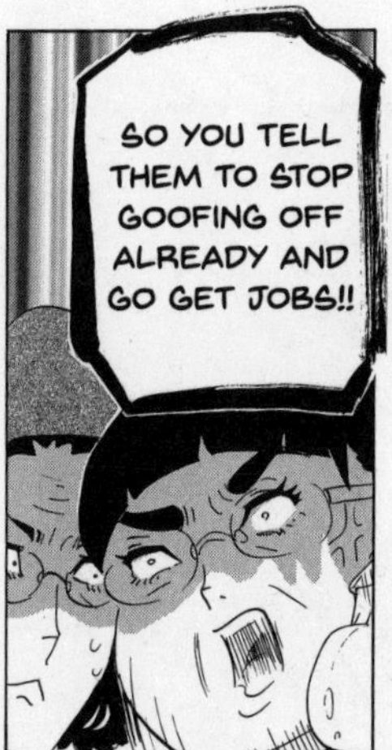
SO YOU TELL THEM TO STOP GOOFING OFF ALREADY AND GO GET JOBS!!

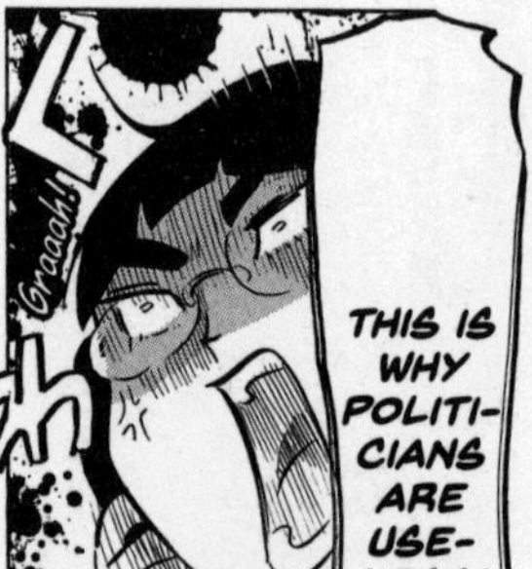
Graaah!
THIS IS WHY POLITICIANS ARE USELESS!

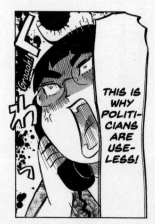

Episode 53
Children of Men

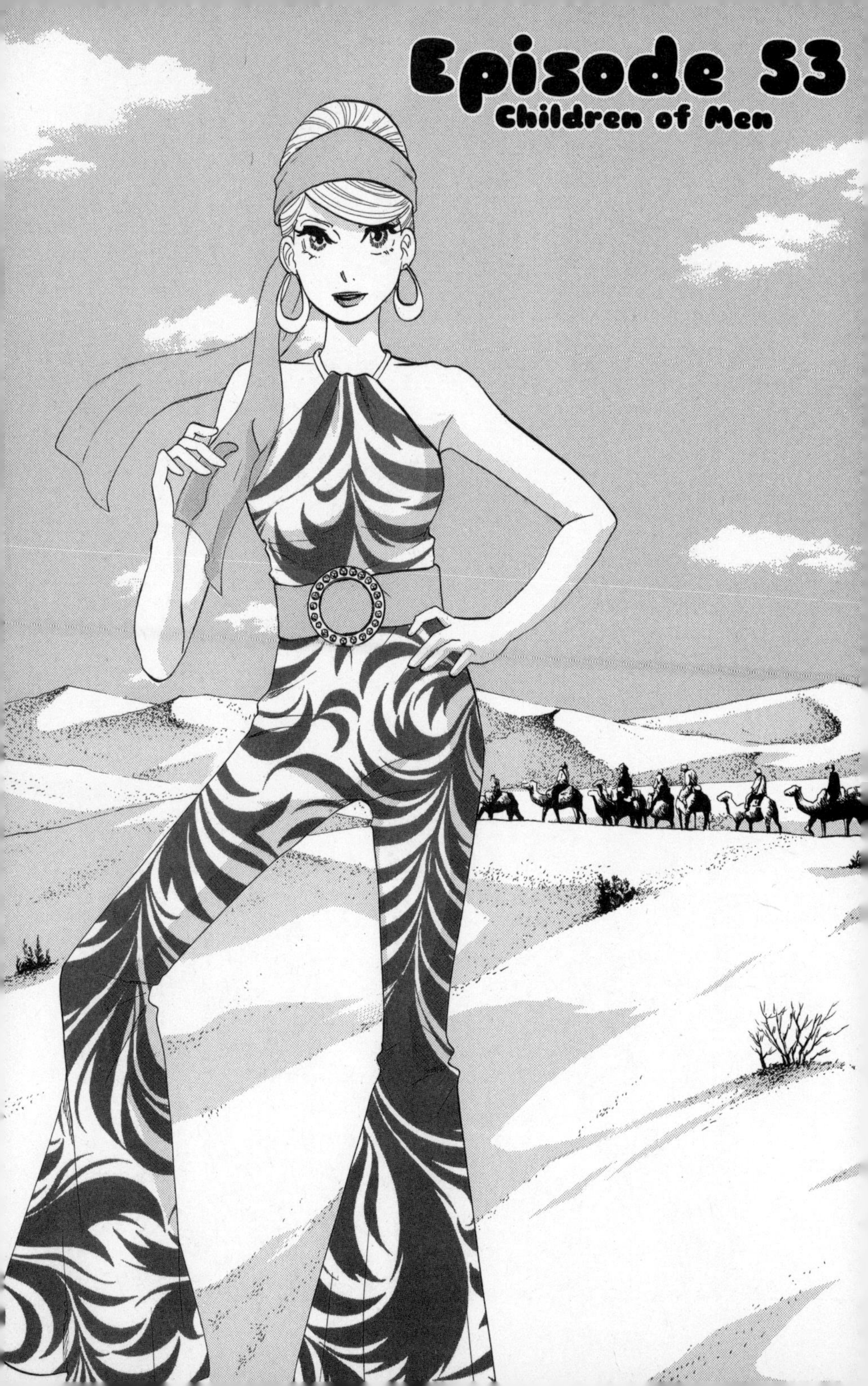

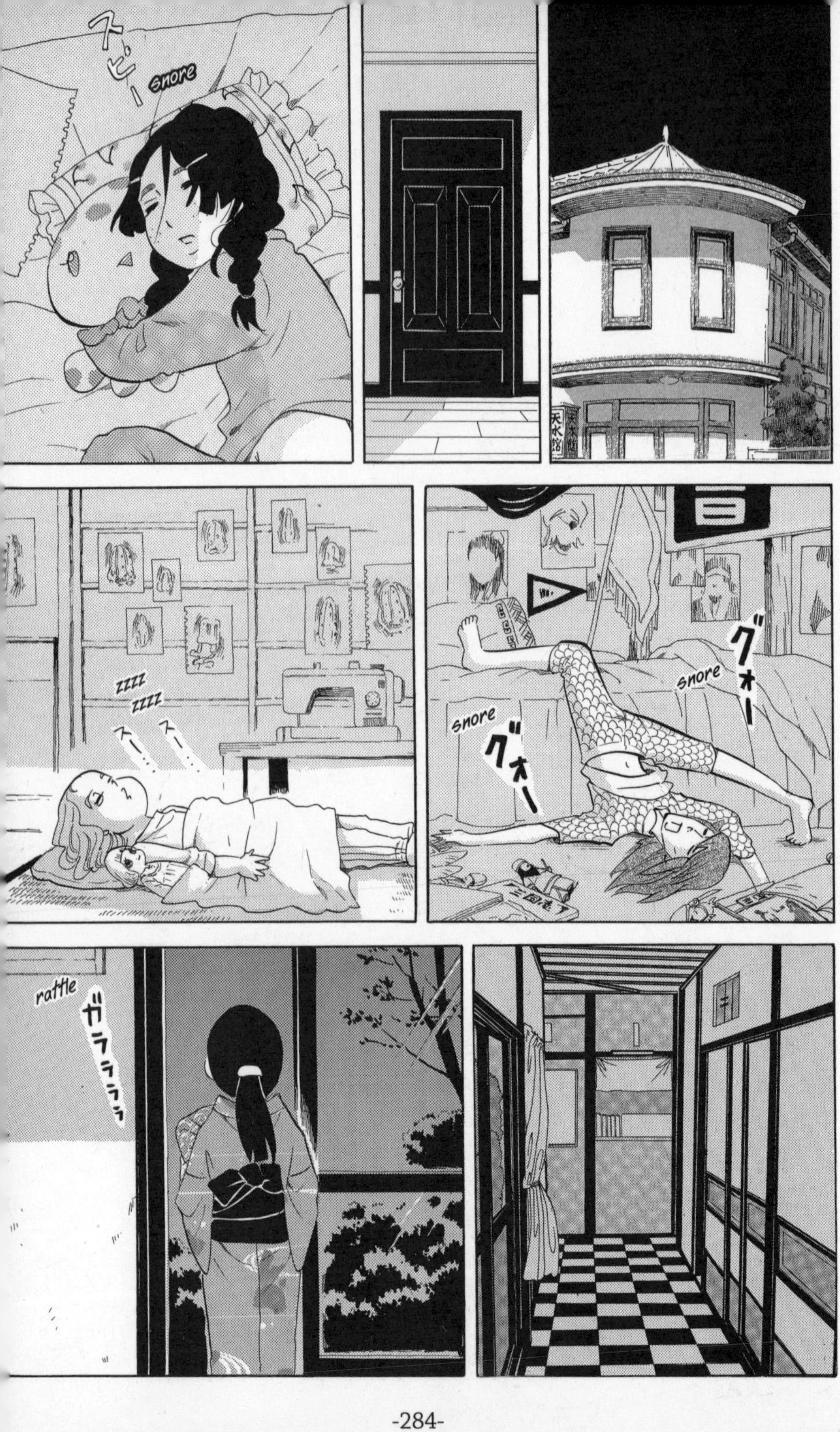
スピー
snore
グオー
snore
snore
グオー
zzzz
zzzz
スー…
スー…
rattle
ガラララ

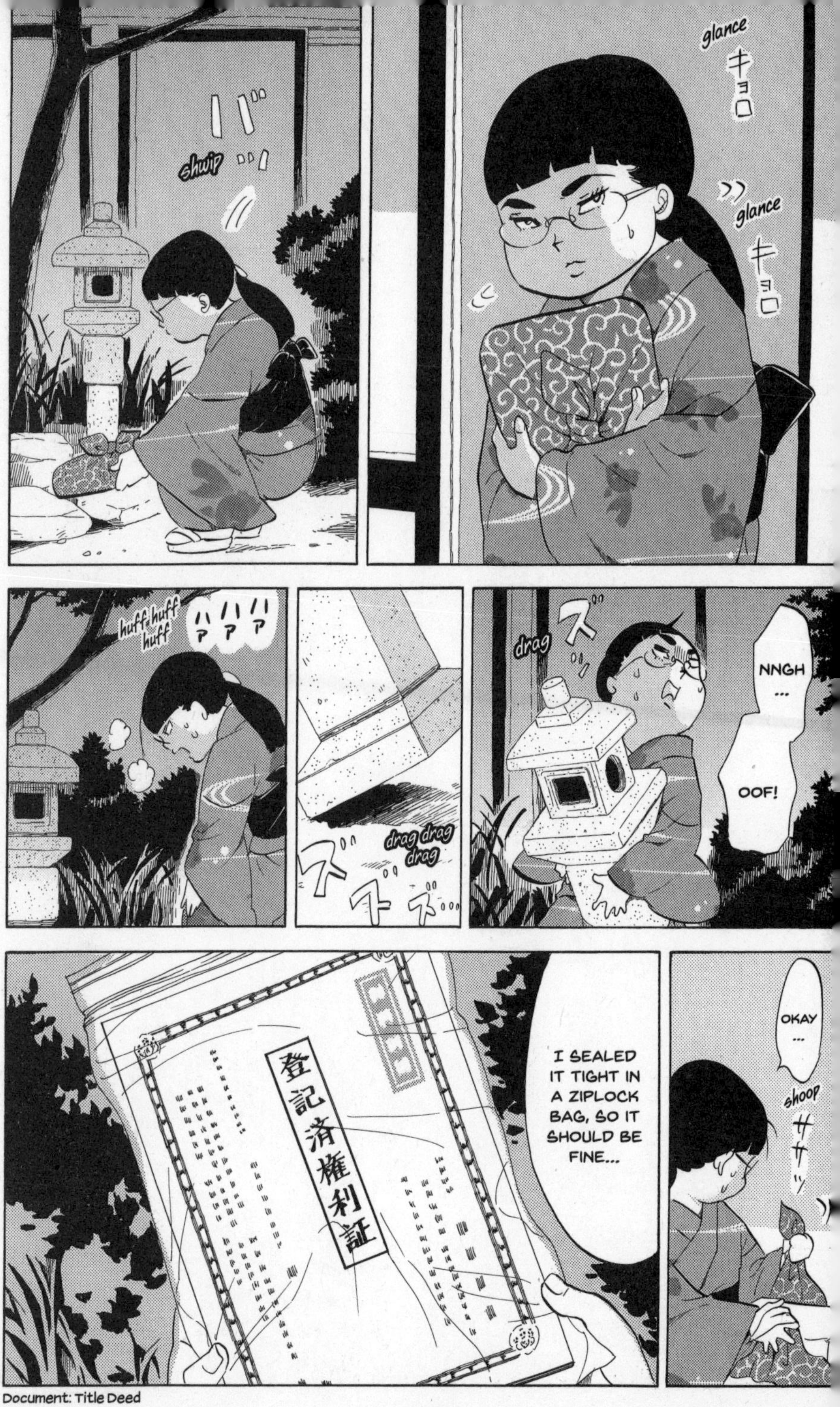
glance
キョロ
glance
キョロ
バッ
shwip
drag
ズ
NNGH...
OOF!
drag drag drag
ズズズ
huff huff huff
ハァハァ
OKAY...
shoop
ササッ
I SEALED IT TIGHT IN A ZIPLOCK BAG, SO IT SHOULD BE FINE...
登記済権利証

Document: Title Deed

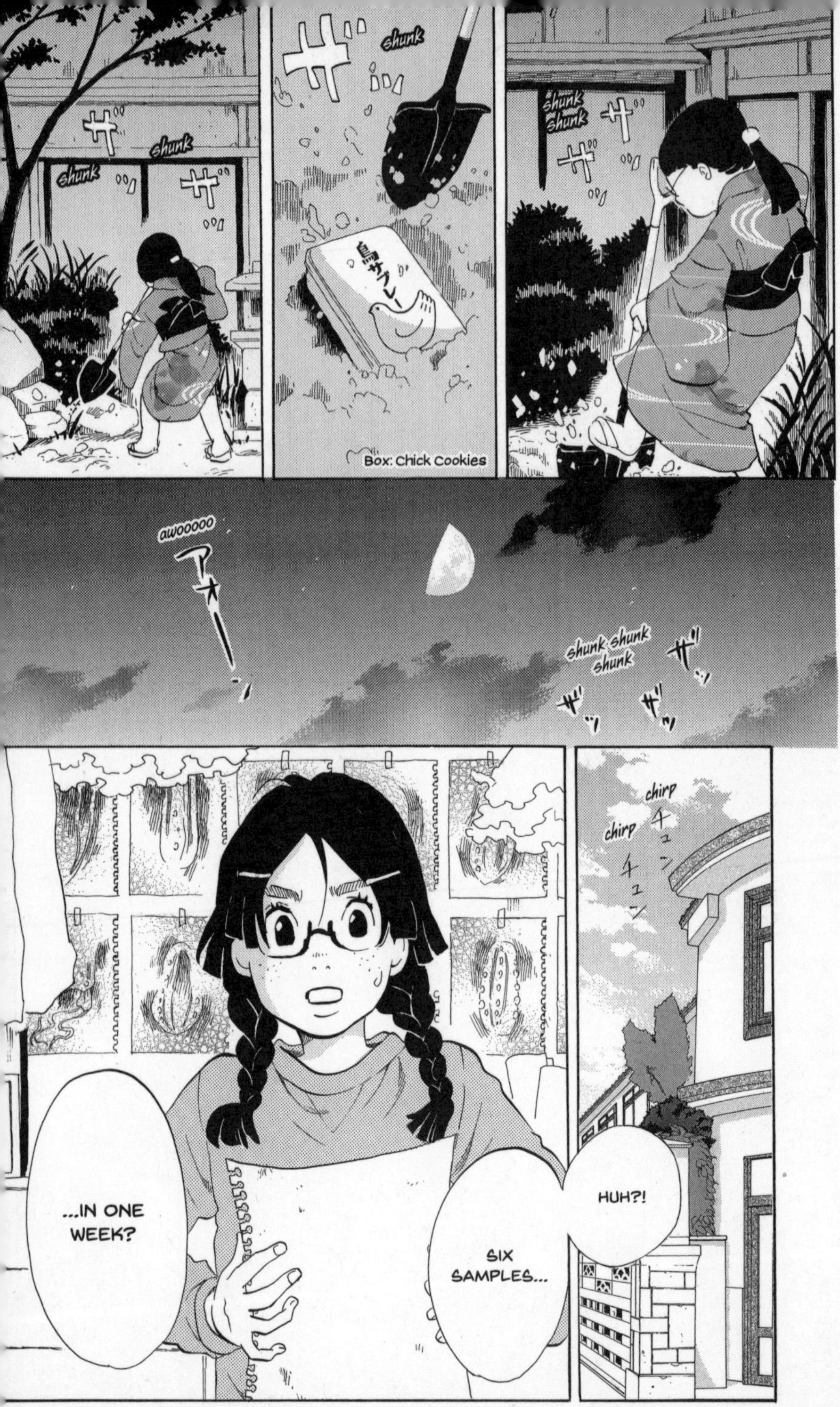
shunk
shunk
shunk
鳥サブレー
Box: Chick Cookies
shunk
shunk
shunk shunk
shunk
awoooo
chirp
chirp
HUH?!
SIX SAMPLES...
...IN ONE WEEK?

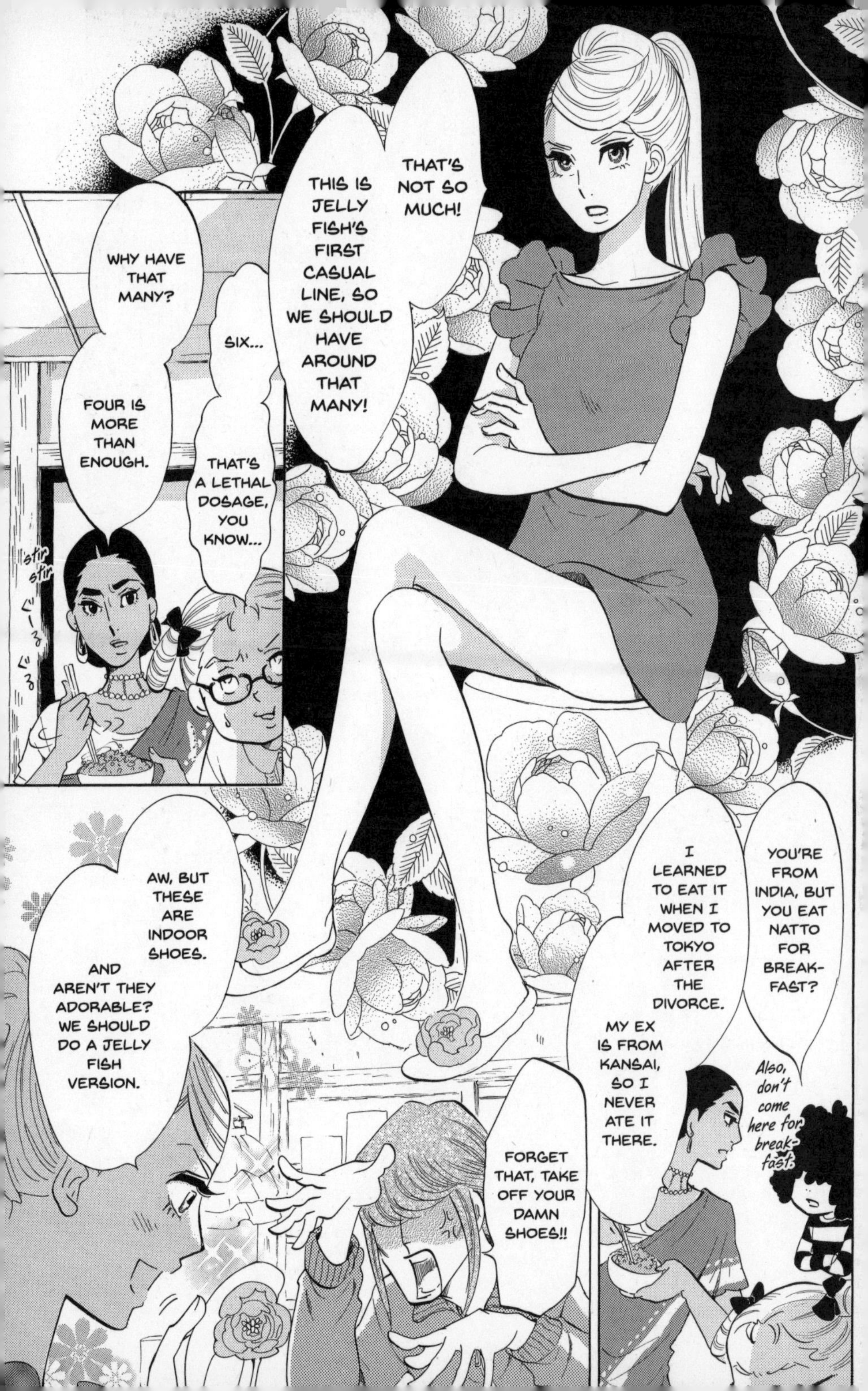
THAT'S NOT SO MUCH!
THIS IS JELLY FISH'S FIRST CASUAL LINE, SO WE SHOULD HAVE AROUND THAT MANY!
SIX...
THAT'S A LETHAL DOSAGE, YOU KNOW...
WHY HAVE THAT MANY?
FOUR IS MORE THAN ENOUGH.
stir stir
ぐーるぐーる
YOU'RE FROM INDIA, BUT YOU EAT NATTO FOR BREAK-FAST?
I LEARNED TO EAT IT WHEN I MOVED TO TOKYO AFTER THE DIVORCE.
MY EX IS FROM KANSAI, SO I NEVER ATE IT THERE.
Also, don't come here for break-fast.
FORGET THAT, TAKE OFF YOUR DAMN SHOES!!
AW, BUT THESE ARE INDOOR SHOES.
AND AREN'T THEY ADORABLE? WE SHOULD DO A JELLY FISH VERSION.

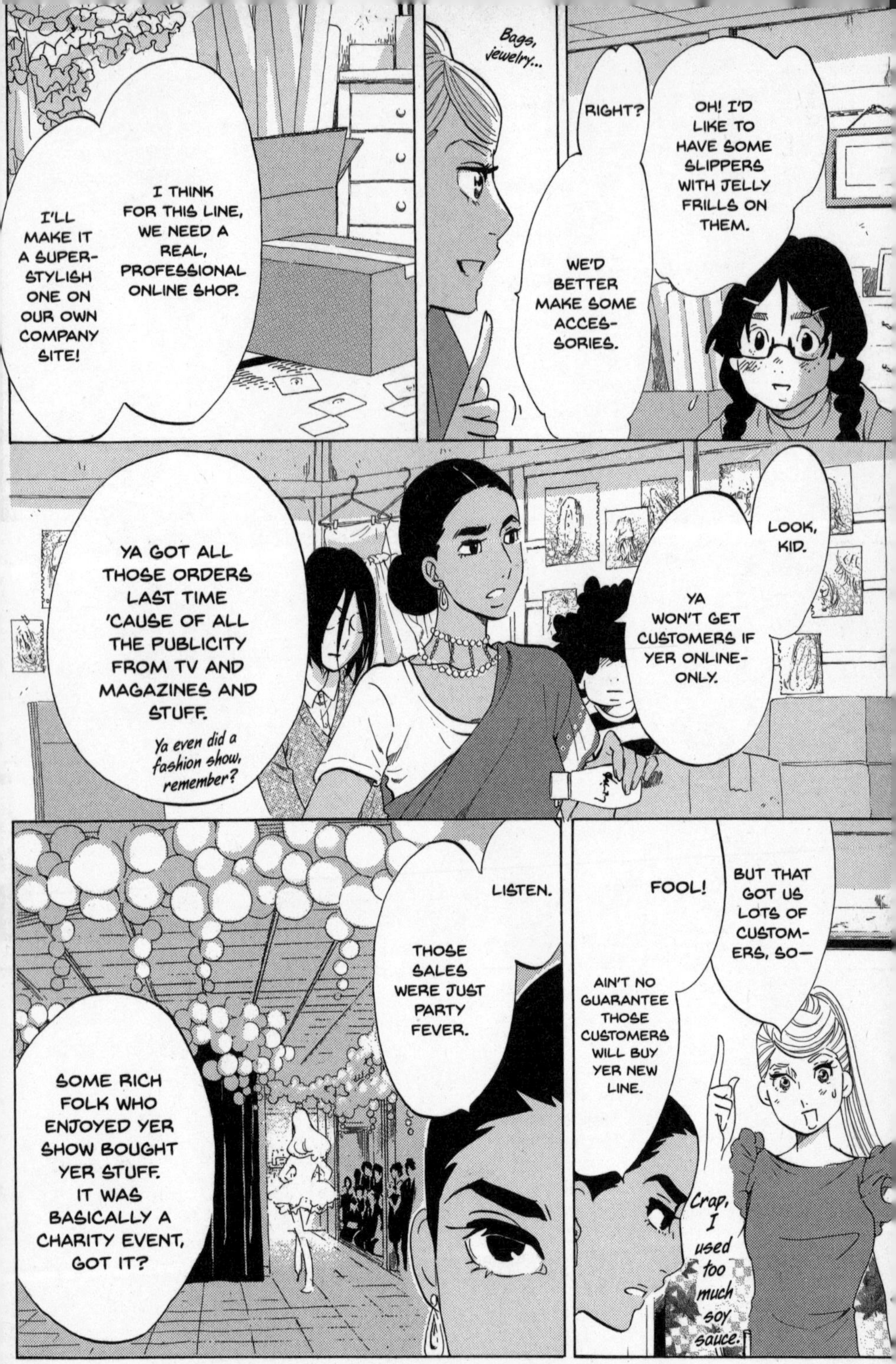
Bags, jewelry...
RIGHT?
WE'D BETTER MAKE SOME ACCES-SORIES.
OH! I'D LIKE TO HAVE SOME SLIPPERS WITH JELLY FRILLS ON THEM.
I THINK FOR THIS LINE, WE NEED A REAL, PROFESSIONAL ONLINE SHOP.
I'LL MAKE IT A SUPER-STYLISH ONE ON OUR OWN COMPANY SITE!
LOOK, KID.
YA WON'T GET CUSTOMERS IF YER ONLINE-ONLY.
YA GOT ALL THOSE ORDERS LAST TIME 'CAUSE OF ALL THE PUBLICITY FROM TV AND MAGAZINES AND STUFF.
Ya even did a fashion show, remember?
BUT THAT GOT US LOTS OF CUSTOM-ERS, SO—
FOOL!
AIN'T NO GUARANTEE THOSE CUSTOMERS WILL BUY YER NEW LINE.
Crap, I used too much soy sauce.
LISTEN.
THOSE SALES WERE JUST PARTY FEVER.
SOME RICH FOLK WHO ENJOYED YER SHOW BOUGHT YER STUFF. IT WAS BASICALLY A CHARITY EVENT, GOT IT?

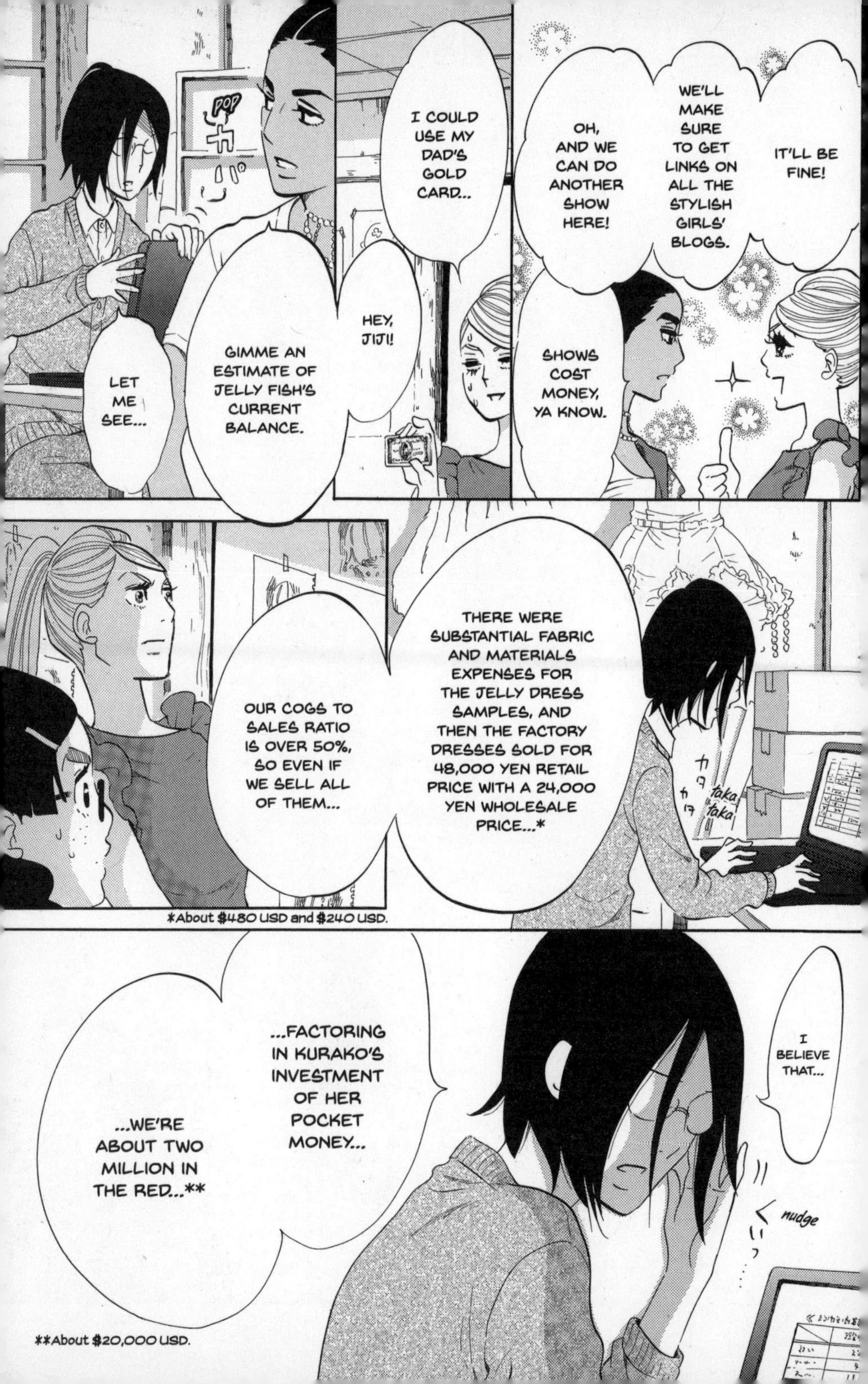
IT'LL BE FINE!
WE'LL MAKE SURE TO GET LINKS ON ALL THE STYLISH GIRLS' BLOGS.
OH, AND WE CAN DO ANOTHER SHOW HERE!
SHOWS COST MONEY, YA KNOW.
I COULD USE MY DAD'S GOLD CARD...
HEY, JIJI!
GIMME AN ESTIMATE OF JELLY FISH'S CURRENT BALANCE.
POP
LET ME SEE...
taka taka
THERE WERE SUBSTANTIAL FABRIC AND MATERIALS EXPENSES FOR THE JELLY DRESS SAMPLES, AND THEN THE FACTORY DRESSES SOLD FOR 48,000 YEN RETAIL PRICE WITH A 24,000 YEN WHOLESALE PRICE...*
OUR COGS TO SALES RATIO IS OVER 50%, SO EVEN IF WE SELL ALL OF THEM...
I BELIEVE THAT...
nudge
...FACTORING IN KURAKO'S INVESTMENT OF HER POCKET MONEY...
...WE'RE ABOUT TWO MILLION IN THE RED...**

*About $480 USD and $240 USD.

**About $20,000 USD.

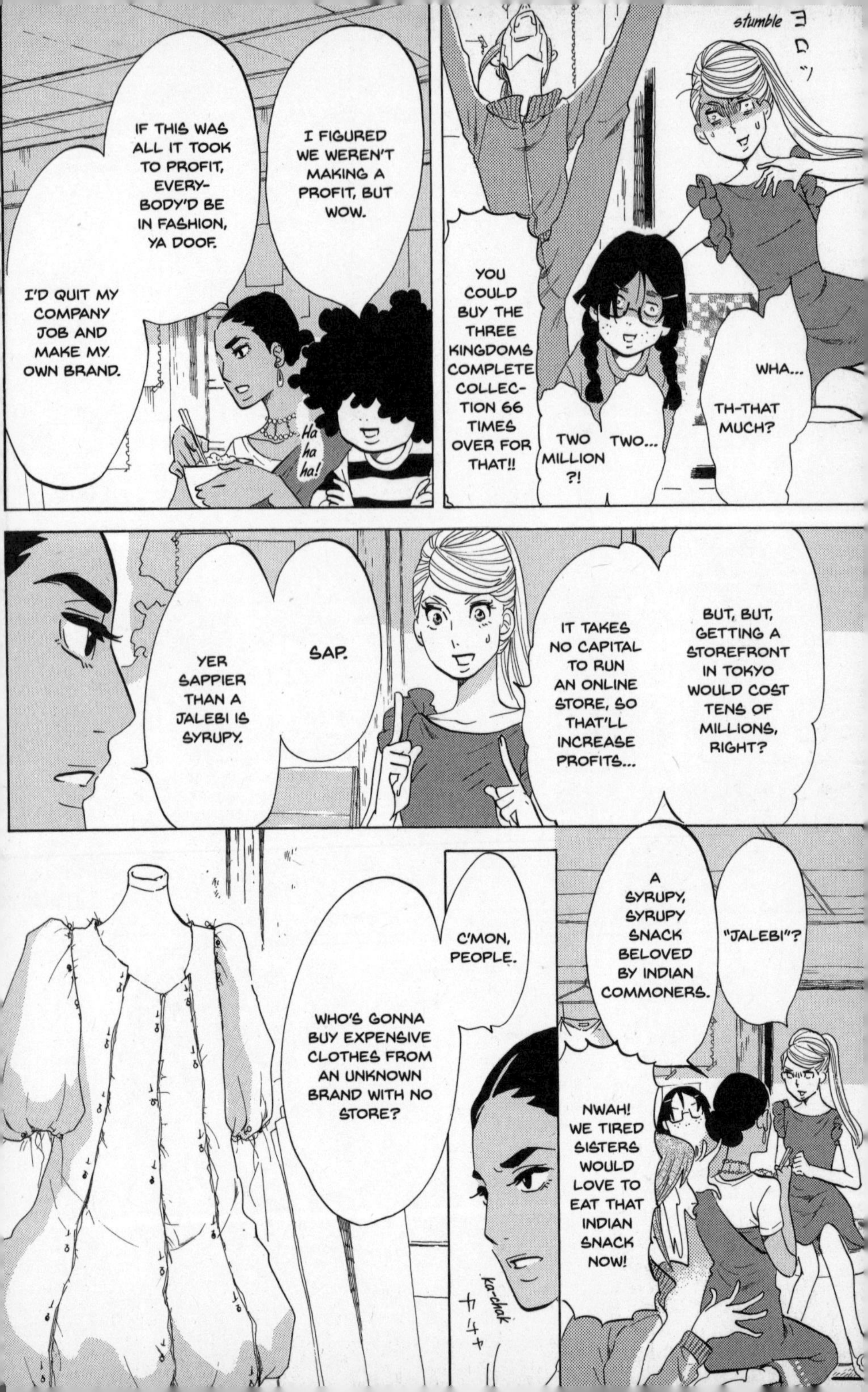
stumble
WHA...
TH-THAT MUCH?
TWO...
TWO MILLION ?!
YOU COULD BUY THE THREE KINGDOMS COMPLETE COLLECTION 66 TIMES OVER FOR THAT!!
I FIGURED WE WEREN'T MAKING A PROFIT, BUT WOW.
IF THIS WAS ALL IT TOOK TO PROFIT, EVERYBODY'D BE IN FASHION, YA DOOF.
I'D QUIT MY COMPANY JOB AND MAKE MY OWN BRAND.
Ha ha ha!
BUT, BUT, GETTING A STOREFRONT IN TOKYO WOULD COST TENS OF MILLIONS, RIGHT?
IT TAKES NO CAPITAL TO RUN AN ONLINE STORE, SO THAT'LL INCREASE PROFITS...
SAP.
YER SAPPIER THAN A JALEBI IS SYRUPY.
"JALEBI"?
A SYRUPY, SYRUPY SNACK BELOVED BY INDIAN COMMONERS.
NWAH! WE TIRED SISTERS WOULD LOVE TO EAT THAT INDIAN SNACK NOW!
C'MON, PEOPLE.
WHO'S GONNA BUY EXPENSIVE CLOTHES FROM AN UNKNOWN BRAND WITH NO STORE?
ka-chak

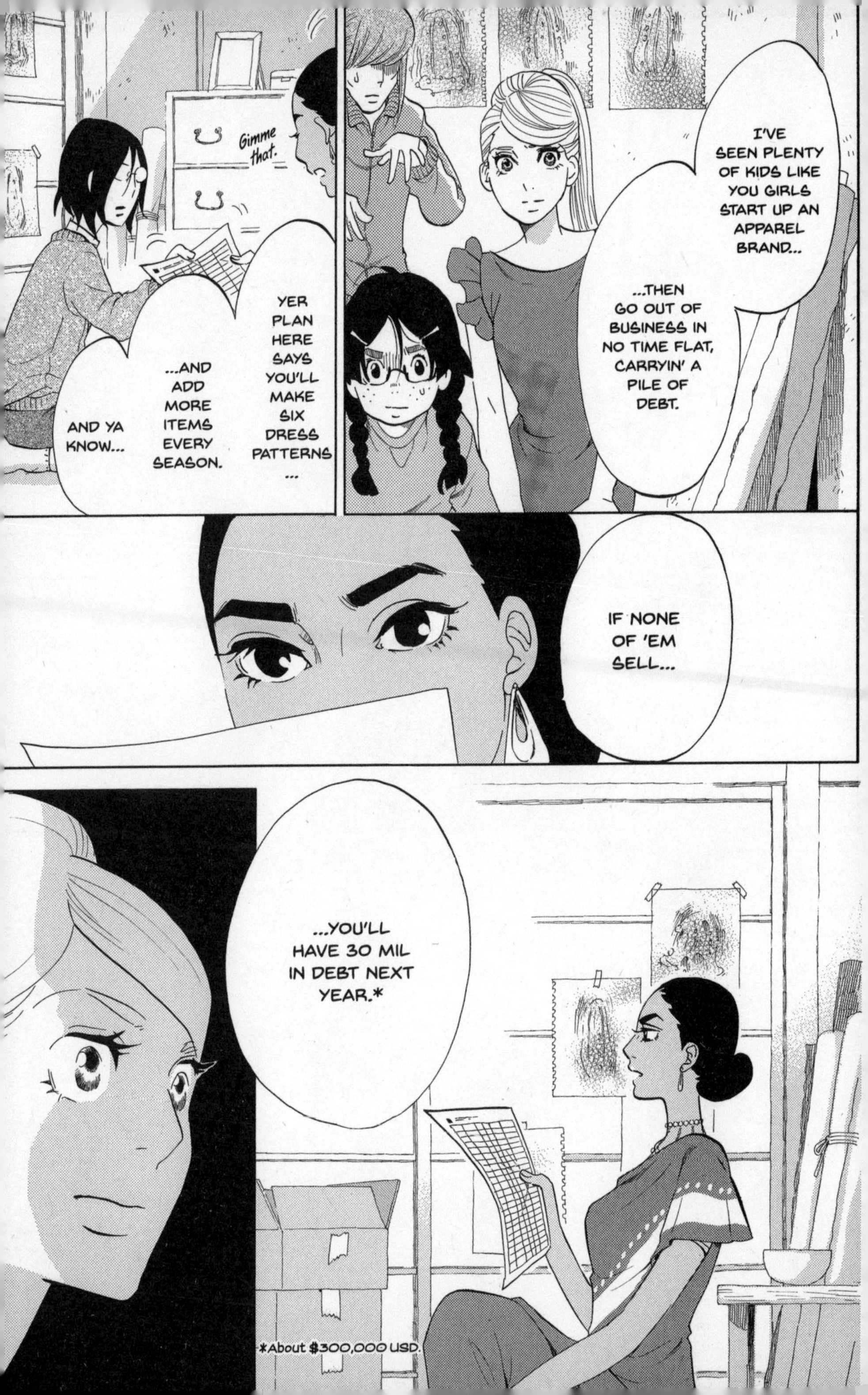
I'VE SEEN PLENTY OF KIDS LIKE YOU GIRLS START UP AN APPAREL BRAND...
...THEN GO OUT OF BUSINESS IN NO TIME FLAT, CARRYIN' A PILE OF DEBT.
Gimme that.
YER PLAN HERE SAYS YOU'LL MAKE SIX DRESS PATTERNS...
...AND ADD MORE ITEMS EVERY SEASON.
AND YA KNOW...
IF NONE OF 'EM SELL...
...YOU'LL HAVE 30 MIL IN DEBT NEXT YEAR.*

*About $300,000 USD.

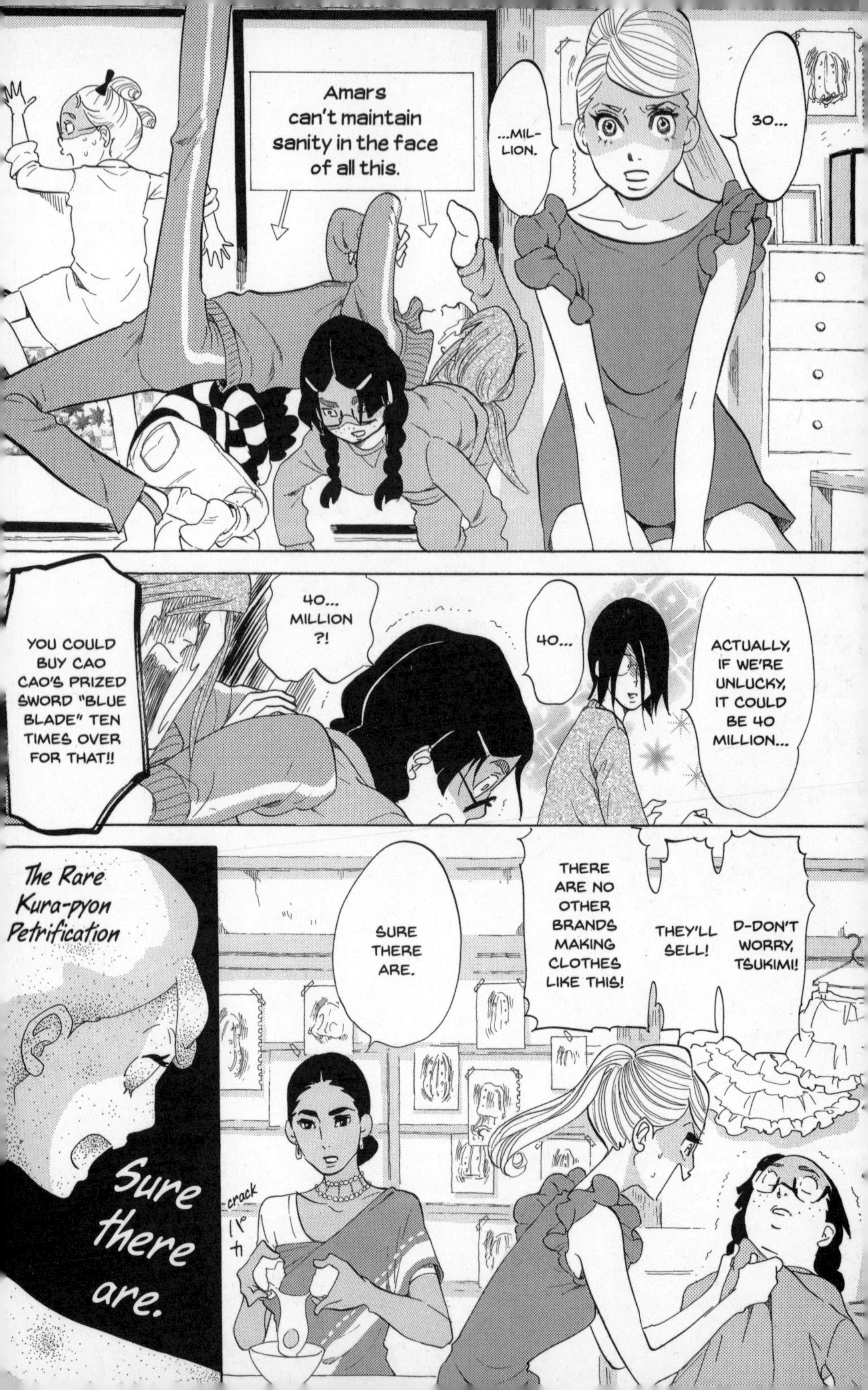
30...
...MIL- LION.
Amars can't maintain sanity in the face of all this.
ACTUALLY, IF WE'RE UNLUCKY, IT COULD BE 40 MILLION...
40...
40... MILLION ?!
YOU COULD BUY CAO CAO'S PRIZED SWORD "BLUE BLADE" TEN TIMES OVER FOR THAT!!
D-DON'T WORRY, TSUKIMI!
THEY'LL SELL!
THERE ARE NO OTHER BRANDS MAKING CLOTHES LIKE THIS!
SURE THERE ARE.
crack
パカ
The Rare Kura-pyon Petrification
Sure there are.

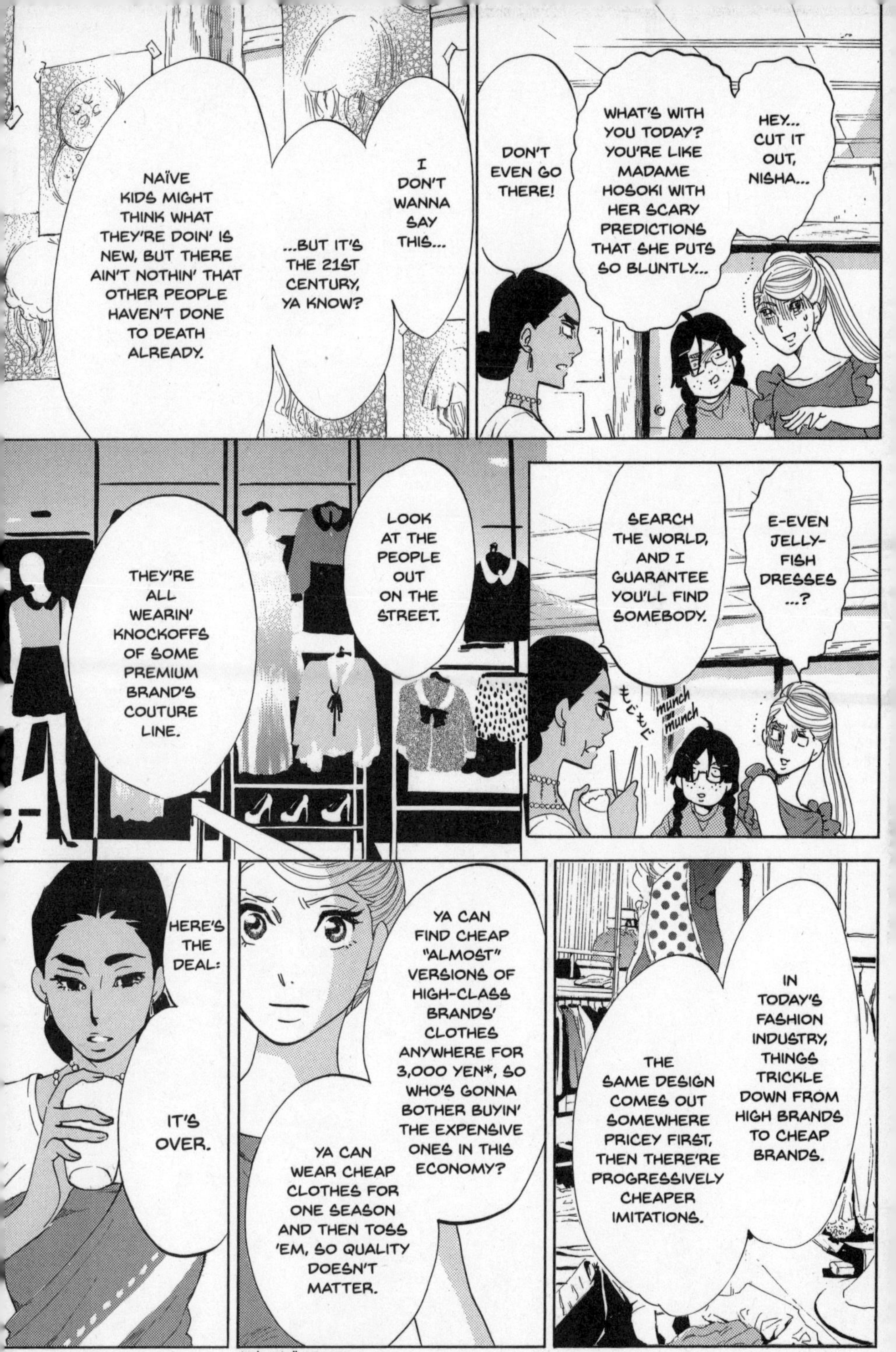
HEY... CUT IT OUT, NISHA...
WHAT'S WITH YOU TODAY? YOU'RE LIKE MADAME HOSOKI WITH HER SCARY PREDICTIONS THAT SHE PUTS SO BLUNTLY...
DON'T EVEN GO THERE!
I DON'T WANNA SAY THIS...
...BUT IT'S THE 21ST CENTURY, YA KNOW?
NAÏVE KIDS MIGHT THINK WHAT THEY'RE DOIN' IS NEW, BUT THERE AIN'T NOTHIN' THAT OTHER PEOPLE HAVEN'T DONE TO DEATH ALREADY.
E-EVEN JELLY-FISH DRESSES ...?
SEARCH THE WORLD, AND I GUARANTEE YOU'LL FIND SOMEBODY.
もぐもぐ munch munch
LOOK AT THE PEOPLE OUT ON THE STREET.
THEY'RE ALL WEARIN' KNOCKOFFS OF SOME PREMIUM BRAND'S COUTURE LINE.
IN TODAY'S FASHION INDUSTRY, THINGS TRICKLE DOWN FROM HIGH BRANDS TO CHEAP BRANDS.
THE SAME DESIGN COMES OUT SOMEWHERE PRICEY FIRST, THEN THERE'RE PROGRESSIVELY CHEAPER IMITATIONS.
YA CAN FIND CHEAP "ALMOST" VERSIONS OF HIGH-CLASS BRANDS' CLOTHES ANYWHERE FOR 3,000 YEN*, SO WHO'S GONNA BOTHER BUYIN' THE EXPENSIVE ONES IN THIS ECONOMY?
YA CAN WEAR CHEAP CLOTHES FOR ONE SEASON AND THEN TOSS 'EM, SO QUALITY DOESN'T MATTER.
HERE'S THE DEAL:
IT'S OVER.

*About $30 USD.

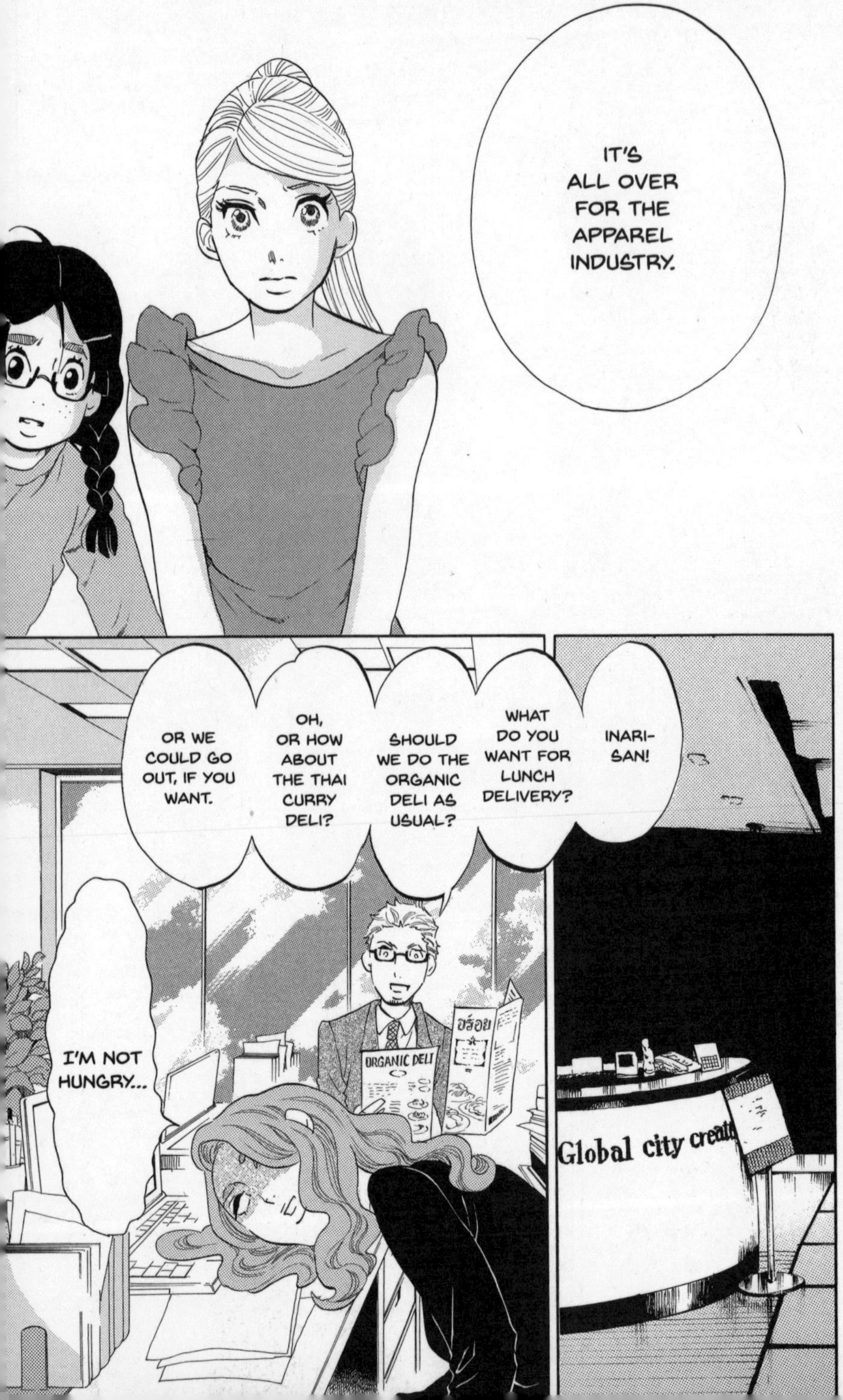
IT'S ALL OVER FOR THE APPAREL INDUSTRY.
INARI-SAN!
WHAT DO YOU WANT FOR LUNCH DELIVERY?
SHOULD WE DO THE ORGANIC DELI AS USUAL?
OH, OR HOW ABOUT THE THAI CURRY DELI?
OR WE COULD GO OUT, IF YOU WANT.
Global city creat
อร่อย
ORGANIC DELI
I'M NOT HUNGRY...

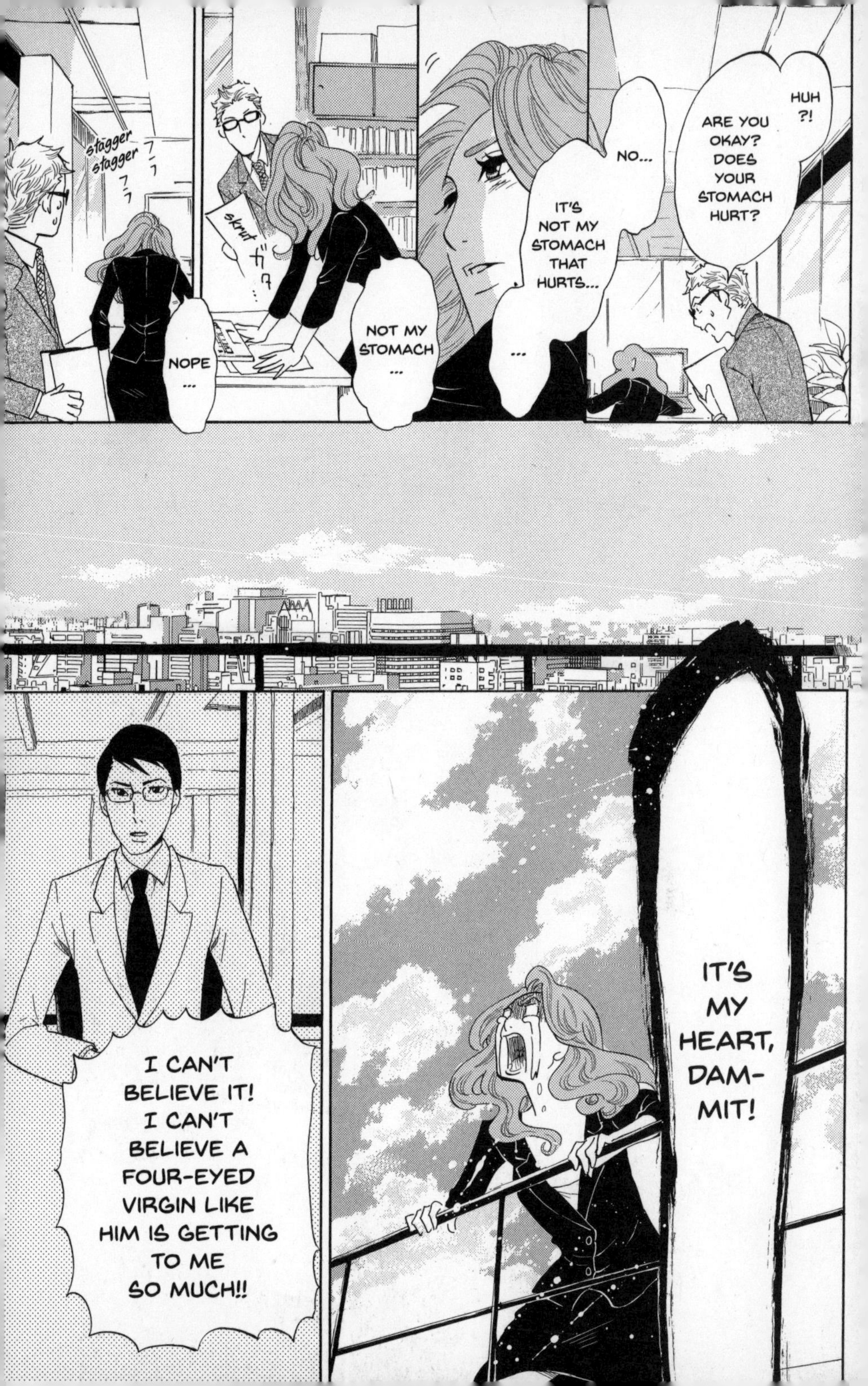
HUH ?!
ARE YOU OKAY? DOES YOUR STOMACH HURT?
NO...
IT'S NOT MY STOMACH THAT HURTS...
...
NOT MY STOMACH ...
stagger stagger
NOPE ...
IT'S MY HEART, DAM-MIT!
I CAN'T BELIEVE IT! I CAN'T BELIEVE A FOUR-EYED VIRGIN LIKE HIM IS GETTING TO ME SO MUCH!!

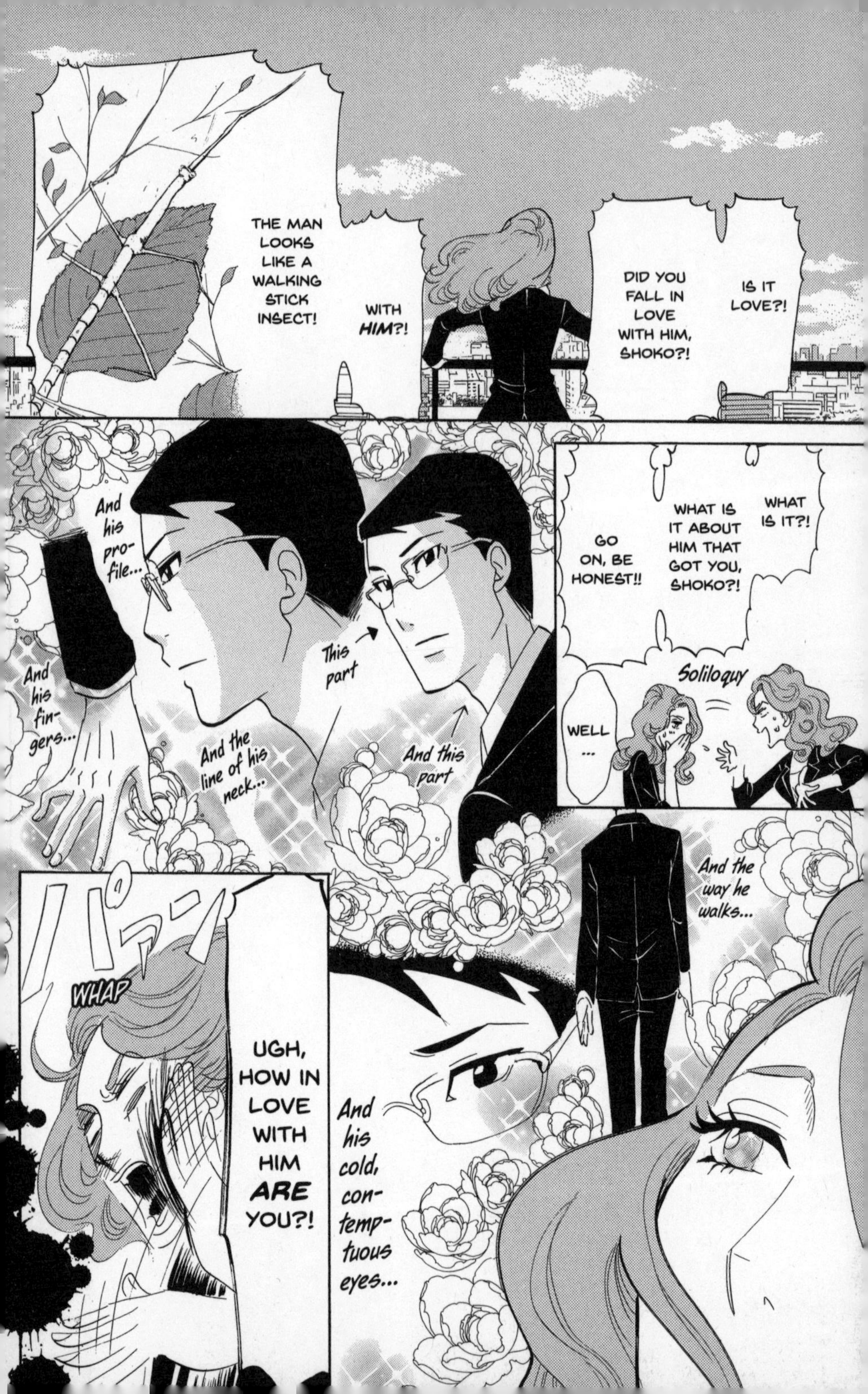

IS IT LOVE?!
DID YOU FALL IN LOVE WITH HIM, SHOKO?!
WITH **HIM**?!
THE MAN LOOKS LIKE A WALKING STICK INSECT!
WHAT IS IT?!
WHAT IS IT ABOUT HIM THAT GOT YOU, SHOKO?!
GO ON, BE HONEST!!
Soliloquy
WELL ...
And this part
This part
And the line of his neck...
And his profile...
And his fingers...
And the way he walks...
And his cold, contemptuous eyes...
WHAP
UGH, HOW IN LOVE WITH HIM **ARE** YOU?!

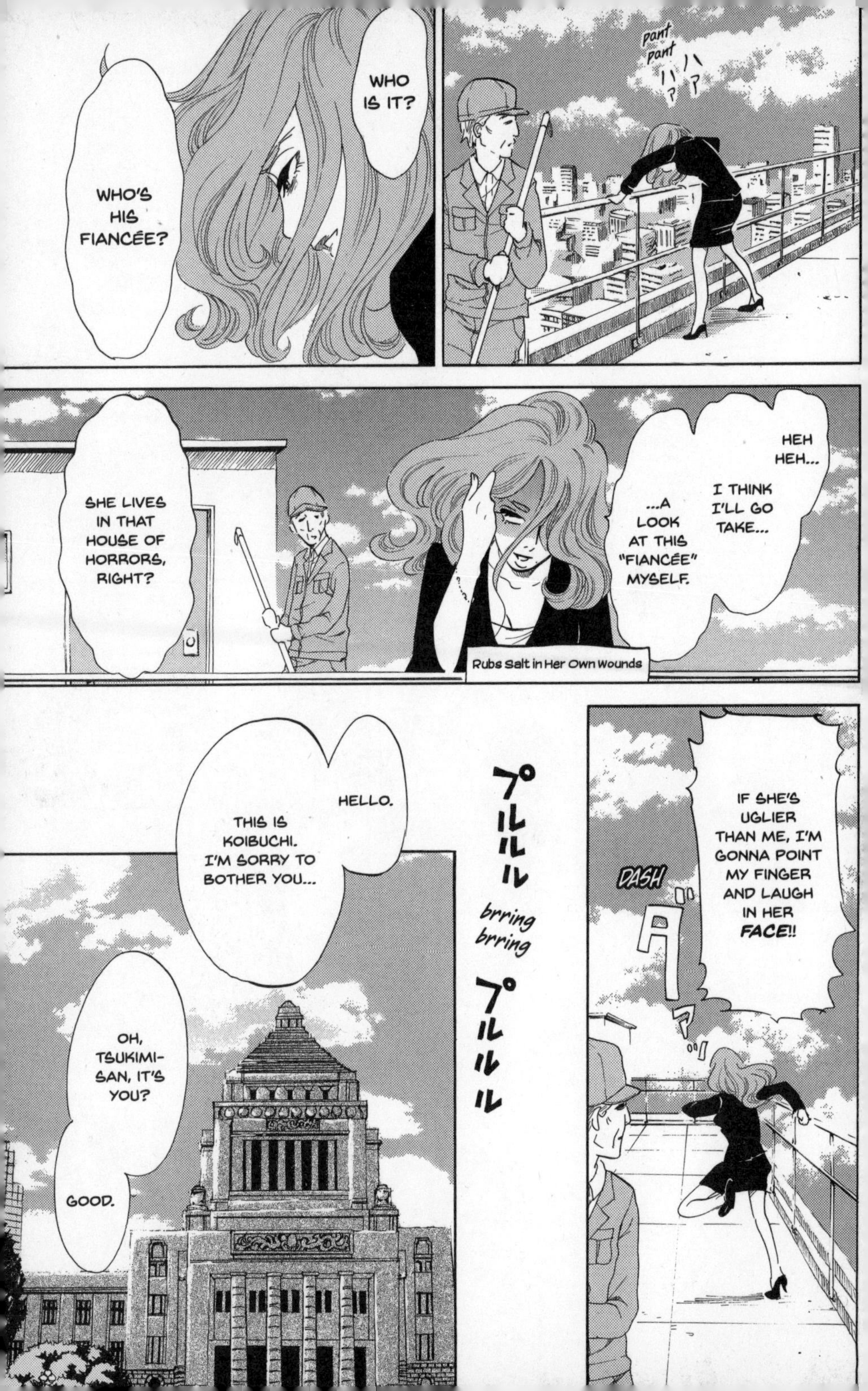
pant pant
ハァハァ
WHO IS IT?
WHO'S HIS FIANCÉE?
HEH HEH...
I THINK I'LL GO TAKE...
...A LOOK AT THIS "FIANCÉE" MYSELF.
Rubs Salt in Her Own Wounds
SHE LIVES IN THAT HOUSE OF HORRORS, RIGHT?
IF SHE'S UGLIER THAN ME, I'M GONNA POINT MY FINGER AND LAUGH IN HER FACE!!
DASH
ダァッ
プルルル brring brring プルルル
HELLO.
THIS IS KOIBUCHI. I'M SORRY TO BOTHER YOU...
OH, TSUKIMI-SAN, IT'S YOU?
GOOD.

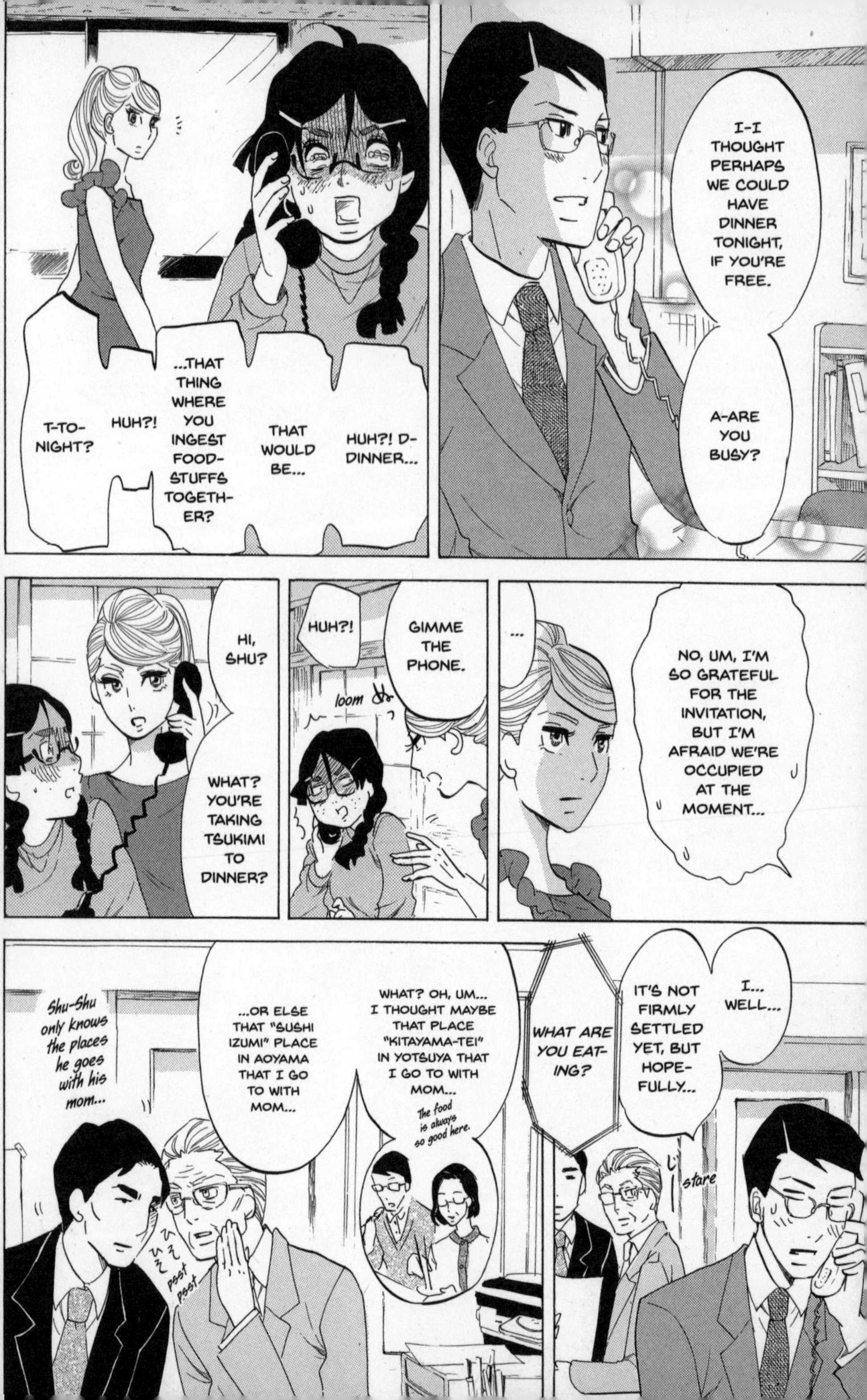
I-I THOUGHT PERHAPS WE COULD HAVE DINNER TONIGHT, IF YOU'RE FREE.
A-ARE YOU BUSY?
HUH?! D-DINNER...
THAT WOULD BE...
...THAT THING WHERE YOU INGEST FOOD-STUFFS TOGETH-ER?
HUH?!
T-TO-NIGHT?
NO, UM, I'M SO GRATEFUL FOR THE INVITATION, BUT I'M AFRAID WE'RE OCCUPIED AT THE MOMENT...
...
GIMME THE PHONE.
loom
HUH?!
HI, SHU?
WHAT? YOU'RE TAKING TSUKIMI TO DINNER?
I... WELL...
IT'S NOT FIRMLY SETTLED YET, BUT HOPE-FULLY...
stare
WHAT ARE YOU EAT-ING?
WHAT? OH, UM... I THOUGHT MAYBE THAT PLACE "KITAYAMA-TEI" IN YOTSUYA THAT I GO TO WITH MOM...
The food is always so good here.
...OR ELSE THAT "SUSHI IZUMI" PLACE IN AOYAMA THAT I GO TO WITH MOM...
Shu-Shu only knows the places he goes with his mom...
psst psst

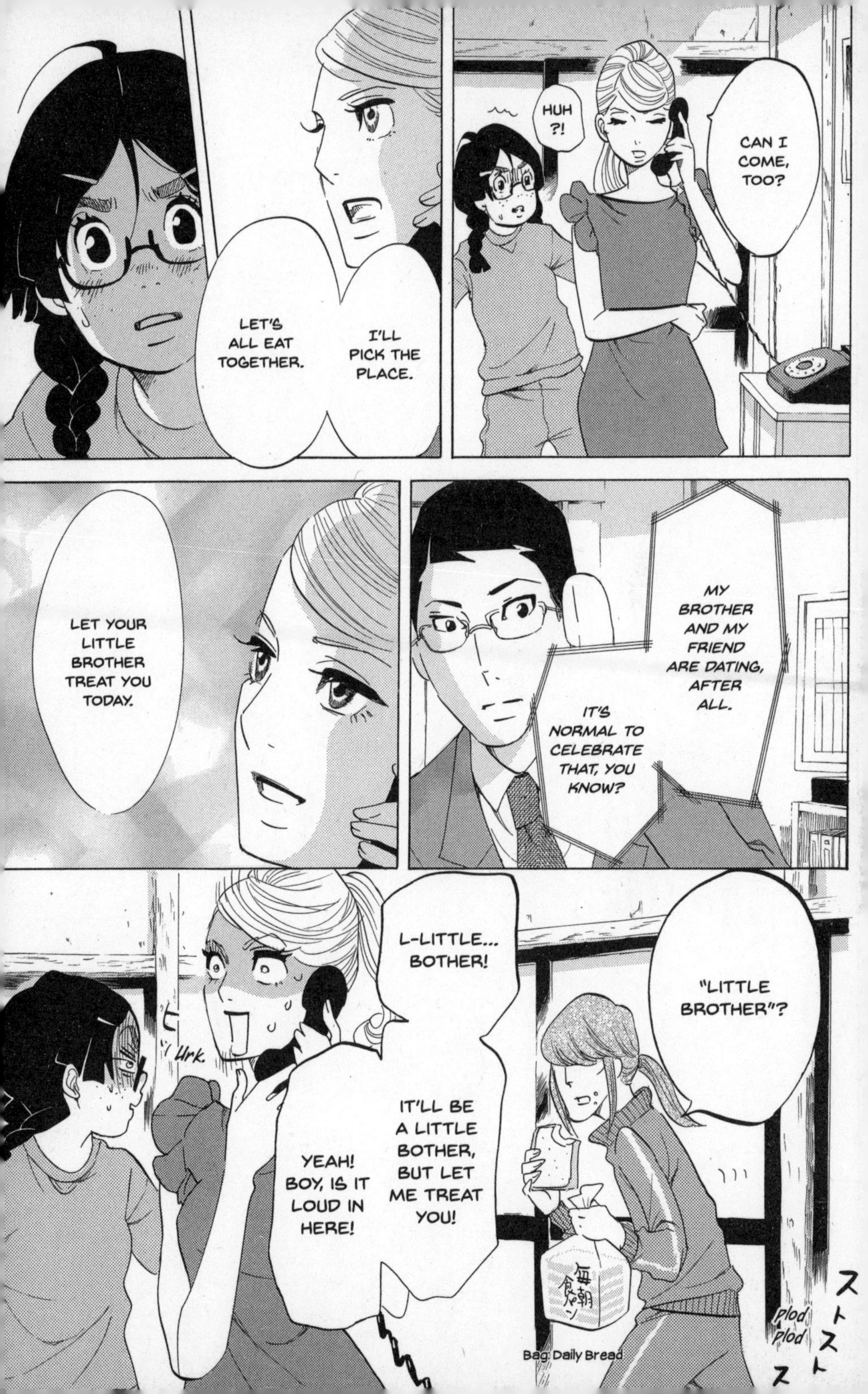
CAN I COME, TOO?
HUH ?!
I'LL PICK THE PLACE.
LET'S ALL EAT TOGETHER.
MY BROTHER AND MY FRIEND ARE DATING, AFTER ALL.
IT'S NORMAL TO CELEBRATE THAT, YOU KNOW?
LET YOUR LITTLE BROTHER TREAT YOU TODAY.
"LITTLE BROTHER"?
ストストス
plod plod
L-LITTLE... BOTHER!
IT'LL BE A LITTLE BOTHER, BUT LET ME TREAT YOU!
YEAH! BOY, IS IT LOUD IN HERE!
Urk.
Bag: Daily Bread

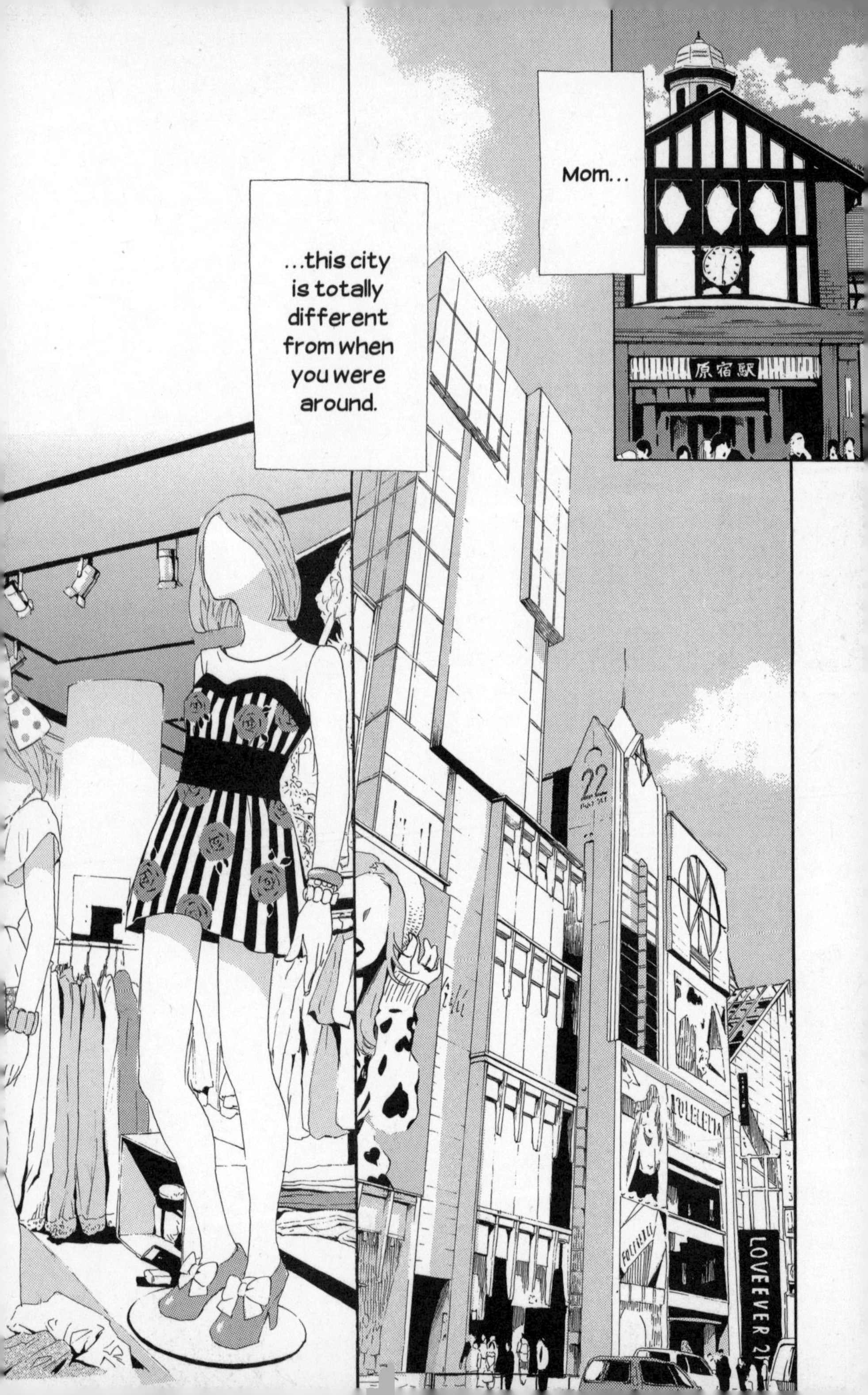
Mom...
原宿駅
...this city is totally different from when you were around.

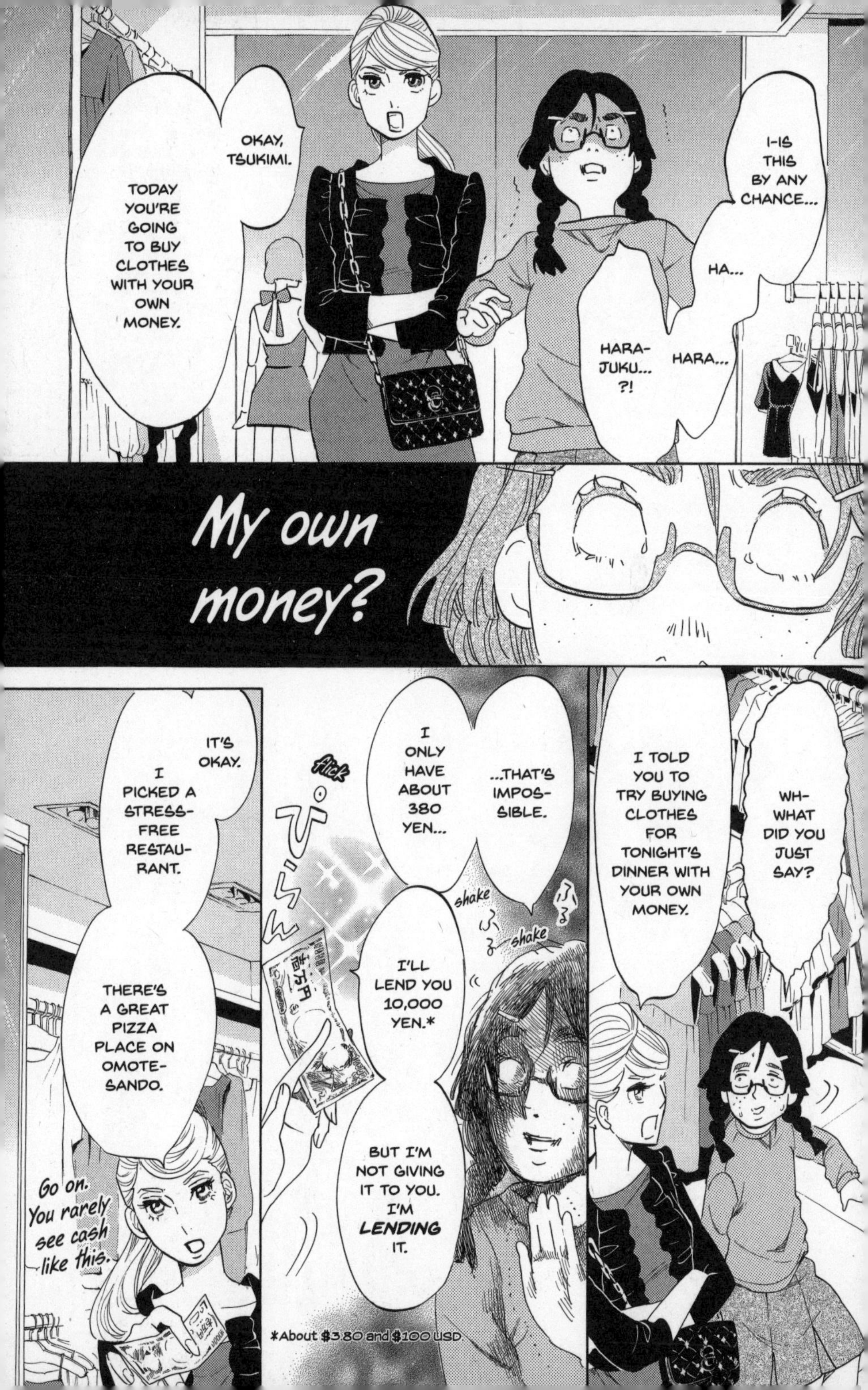
I-IS THIS BY ANY CHANCE...
HA...
HARA...
HARA-JUKU...?!
OKAY, TSUKIMI.
TODAY YOU'RE GOING TO BUY CLOTHES WITH YOUR OWN MONEY.
My own money?
WH-WHAT DID YOU JUST SAY?
I TOLD YOU TO TRY BUYING CLOTHES FOR TONIGHT'S DINNER WITH YOUR OWN MONEY.
...THAT'S IMPOS-SIBLE.
I ONLY HAVE ABOUT 380 YEN...
shake
shake
flick
I'LL LEND YOU 10,000 YEN.*
BUT I'M NOT GIVING IT TO YOU. I'M *LENDING* IT.
IT'S OKAY.
I PICKED A STRESS-FREE RESTAU-RANT.
THERE'S A GREAT PIZZA PLACE ON OMOTE-SANDO.
Go on. You rarely see cash like this.
*About $3.80 and $100 USD

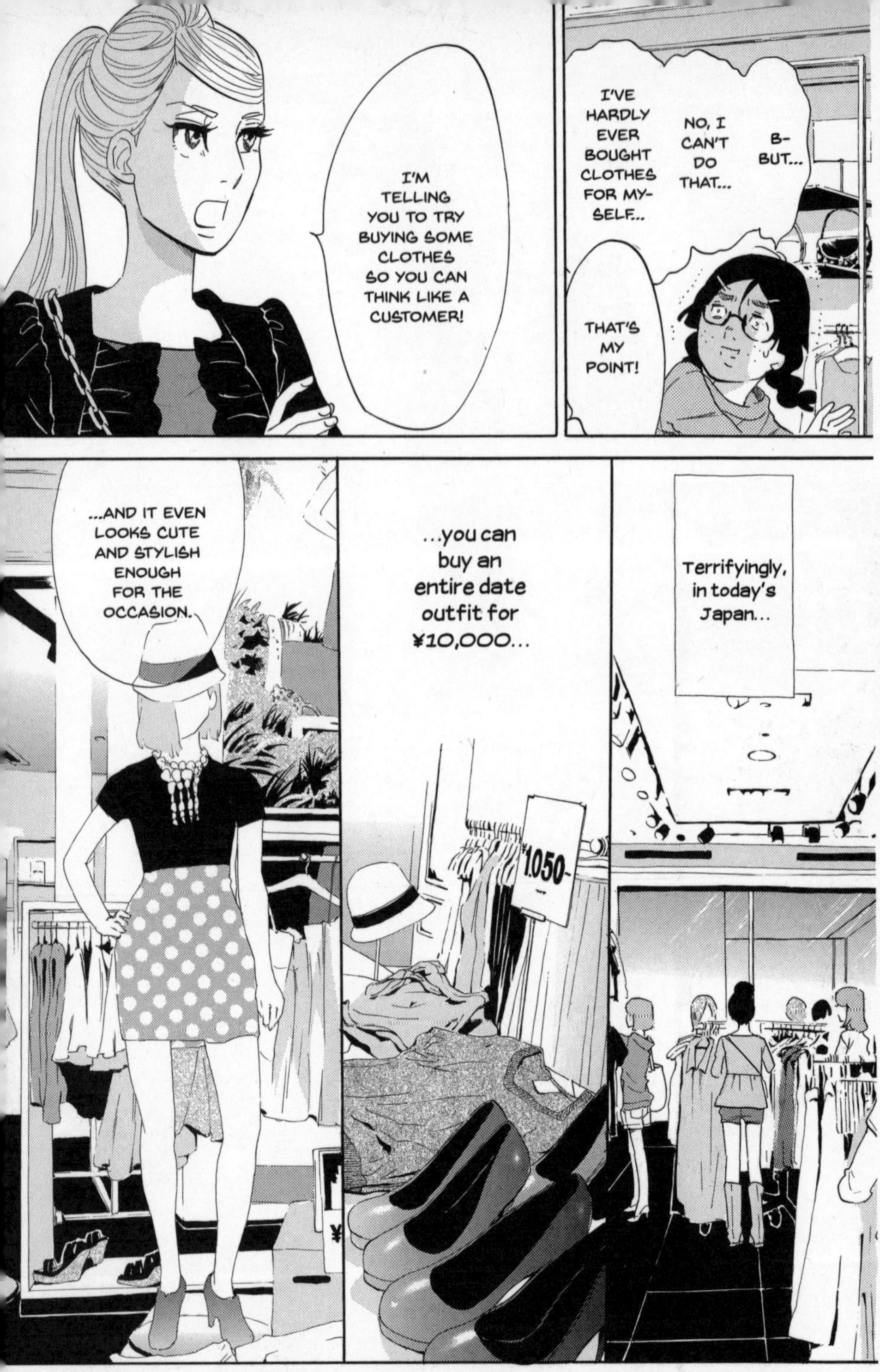
B-BUT...
NO, I CAN'T DO THAT...
I'VE HARDLY EVER BOUGHT CLOTHES FOR MY-SELF...
THAT'S MY POINT!
I'M TELLING YOU TO TRY BUYING SOME CLOTHES SO YOU CAN THINK LIKE A CUSTOMER!
Terrifyingly, in today's Japan...
...you can buy an entire date outfit for ¥10,000...
¥1,050-
...AND IT EVEN LOOKS CUTE AND STYLISH ENOUGH FOR THE OCCASION.

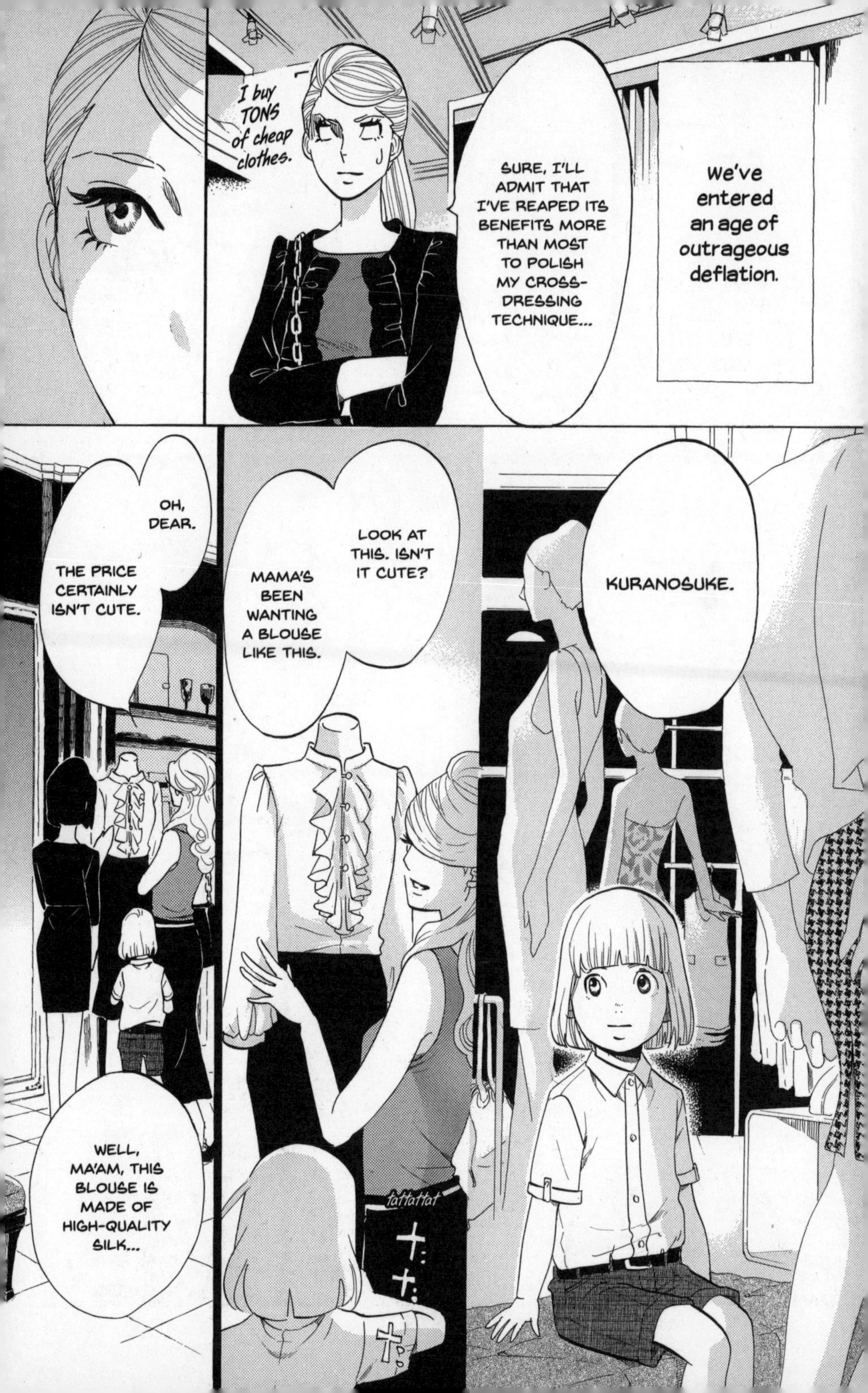

We've entered an age of outrageous deflation.
SURE, I'LL ADMIT THAT I'VE REAPED ITS BENEFITS MORE THAN MOST TO POLISH MY CROSS-DRESSING TECHNIQUE...
I buy TONS of cheap clothes.
KURANOSUKE.
LOOK AT THIS. ISN'T IT CUTE?
MAMA'S BEEN WANTING A BLOUSE LIKE THIS.
tattattat
OH, DEAR.
THE PRICE CERTAINLY ISN'T CUTE.
WELL, MA'AM, THIS BLOUSE IS MADE OF HIGH-QUALITY SILK...

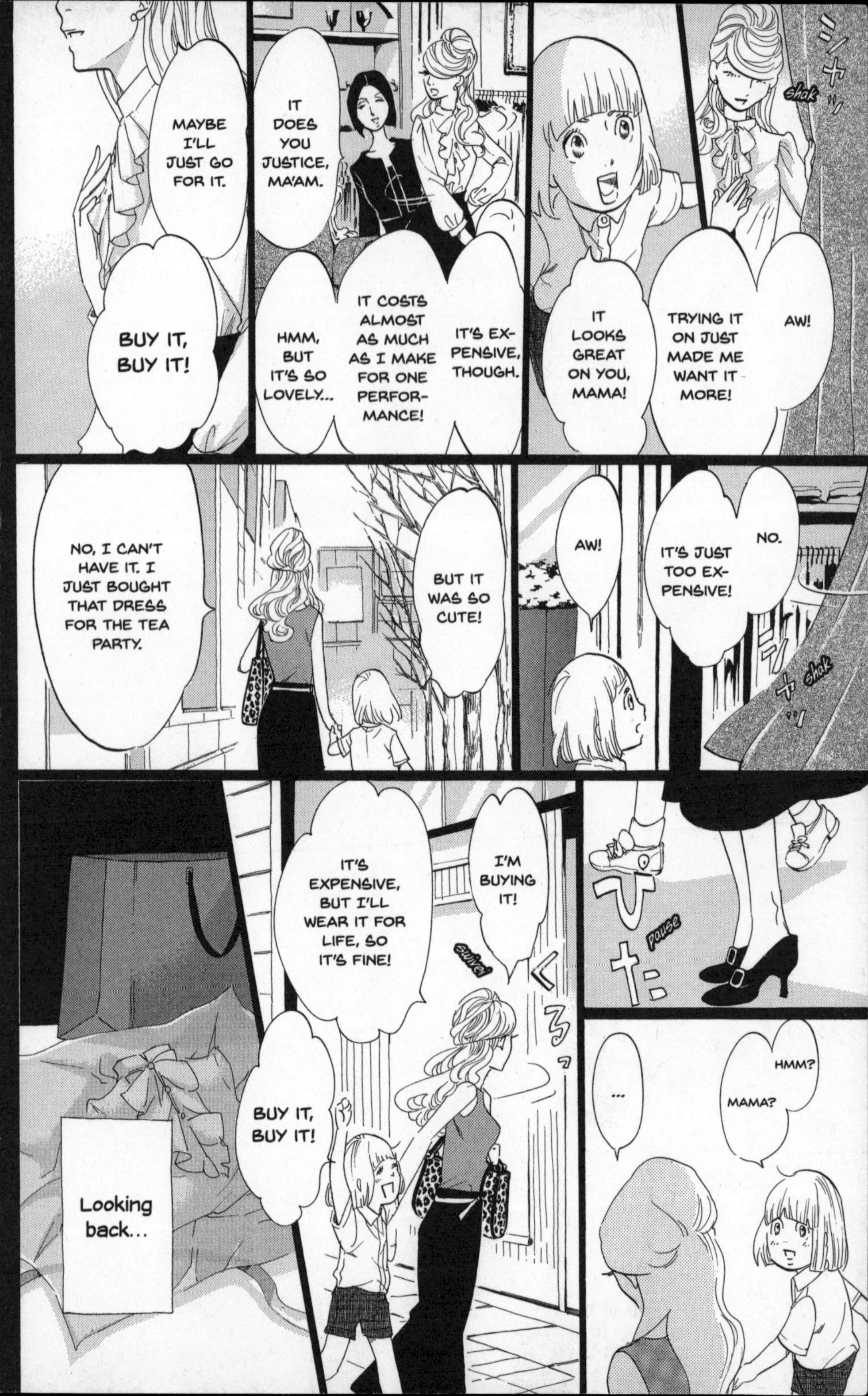
shak
AW!
TRYING IT ON JUST MADE ME WANT IT MORE!
IT LOOKS GREAT ON YOU, MAMA!
IT DOES YOU JUSTICE, MA'AM.
IT'S EXPENSIVE, THOUGH.
IT COSTS ALMOST AS MUCH AS I MAKE FOR ONE PERFORMANCE!
HMM, BUT IT'S SO LOVELY...
MAYBE I'LL JUST GO FOR IT.
BUY IT, BUY IT!
NO.
IT'S JUST TOO EXPENSIVE!
AW!
shak
BUT IT WAS SO CUTE!
NO, I CAN'T HAVE IT. I JUST BOUGHT THAT DRESS FOR THE TEA PARTY.
pause
HMM?
MAMA?
...
I'M BUYING IT!
IT'S EXPENSIVE, BUT I'LL WEAR IT FOR LIFE, SO IT'S FINE!
swivel
BUY IT, BUY IT!
Looking back...

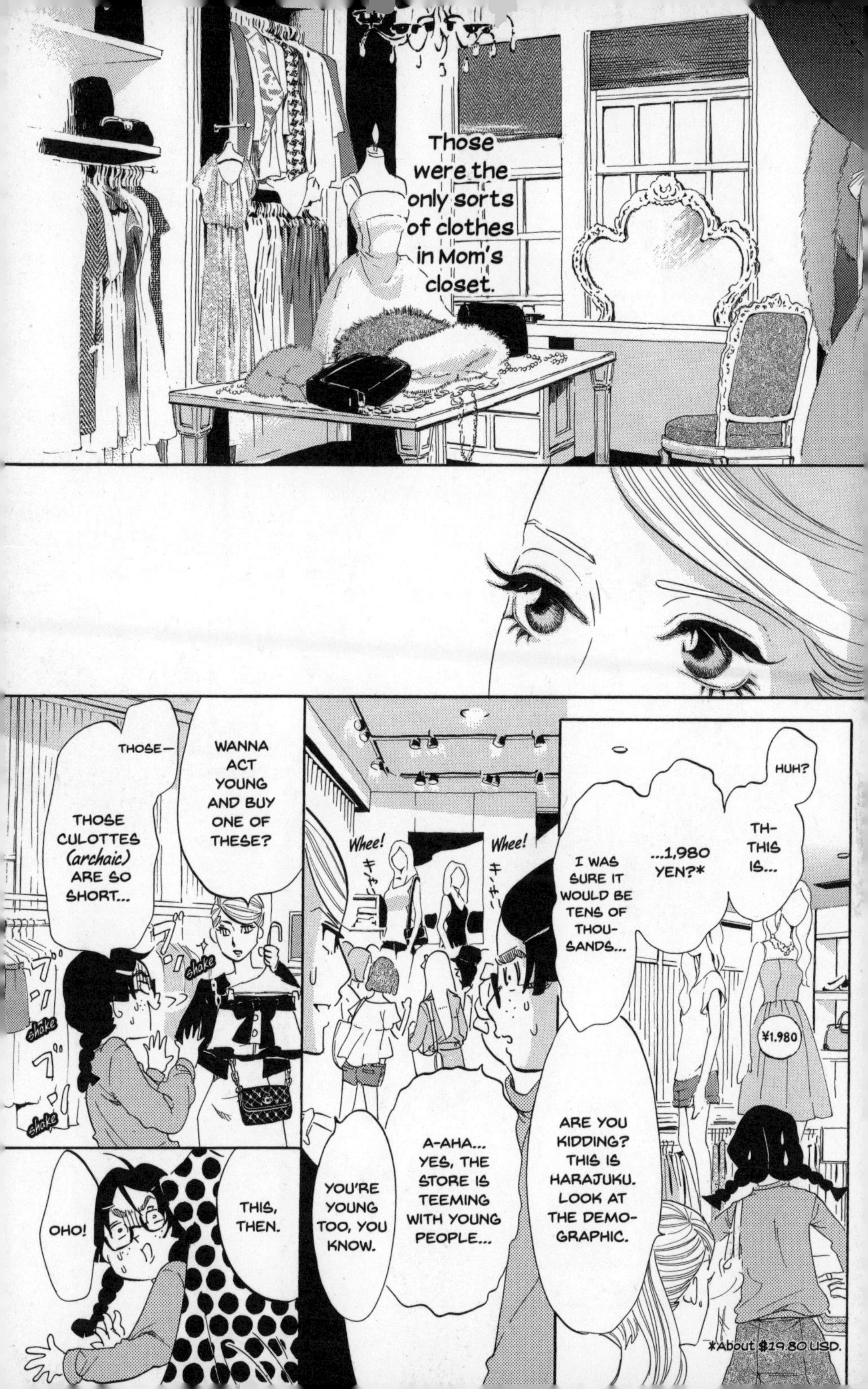
Those were the only sorts of clothes in Mom's closet.
HUH?
TH- THIS IS...
...1,980 YEN?*
I WAS SURE IT WOULD BE TENS OF THOUSANDS...
¥1,980
Whee!
Whee!
ARE YOU KIDDING? THIS IS HARAJUKU. LOOK AT THE DEMOGRAPHIC.
A-AHA... YES, THE STORE IS TEEMING WITH YOUNG PEOPLE...
YOU'RE YOUNG TOO, YOU KNOW.
WANNA ACT YOUNG AND BUY ONE OF THESE?
THOSE—
THOSE CULOTTES (archaic) ARE SO SHORT...
shake
shake
shake
THIS, THEN.
OHO!
*About $19.80 USD.

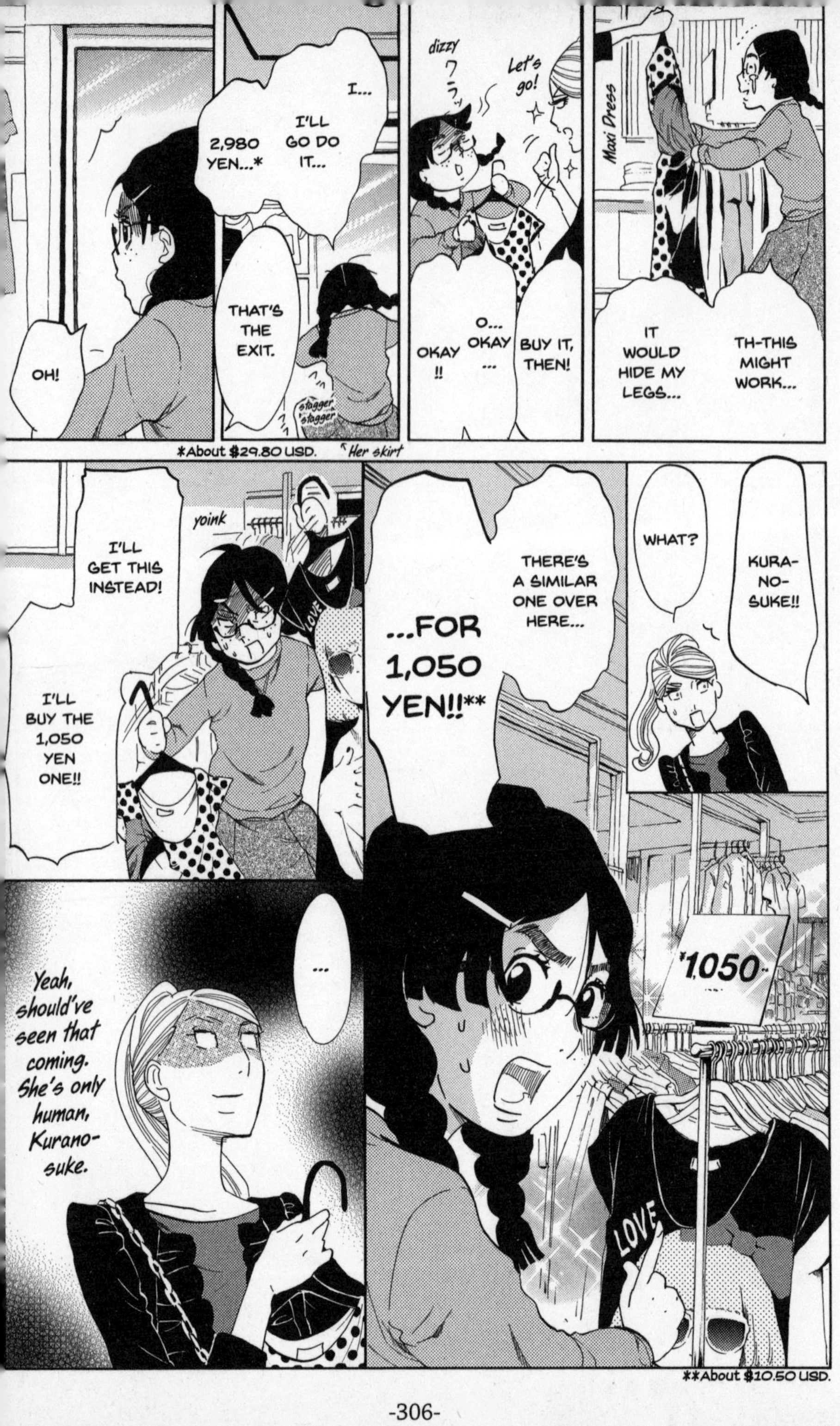
TH-THIS MIGHT WORK...
IT WOULD HIDE MY LEGS...
Maxi Dress
Let's go!
BUY IT, THEN!
dizzy
フラッ
O... OKAY ...
OKAY !!
I...
I'LL GO DO IT...
2,980 YEN...*
THAT'S THE EXIT.
stagger stagger
OH!
*About $29.80 USD.
Her skirt
KURA-NO-SUKE!!
WHAT?
THERE'S A SIMILAR ONE OVER HERE...
...FOR 1,050 YEN!!**
¥1,050
yoink
I'LL GET THIS INSTEAD!
I'LL BUY THE 1,050 YEN ONE!!
LOVE
...
Yeah, should've seen that coming. She's only human, Kuranosuke.
LOVE
**About $10.50 USD.

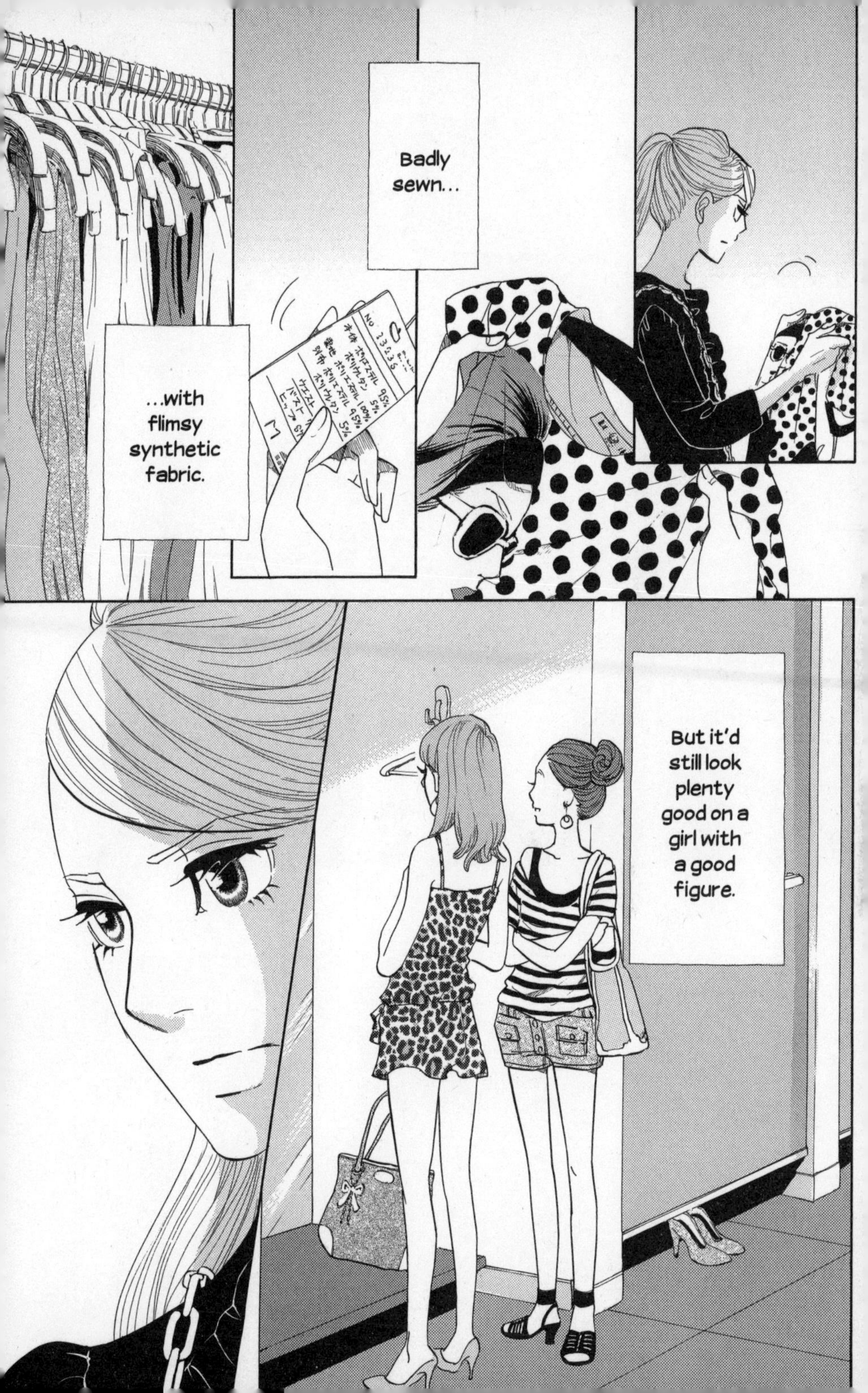
Badly sewn...
...with flimsy synthetic fabric.
But it'd still look plenty good on a girl with a good figure.

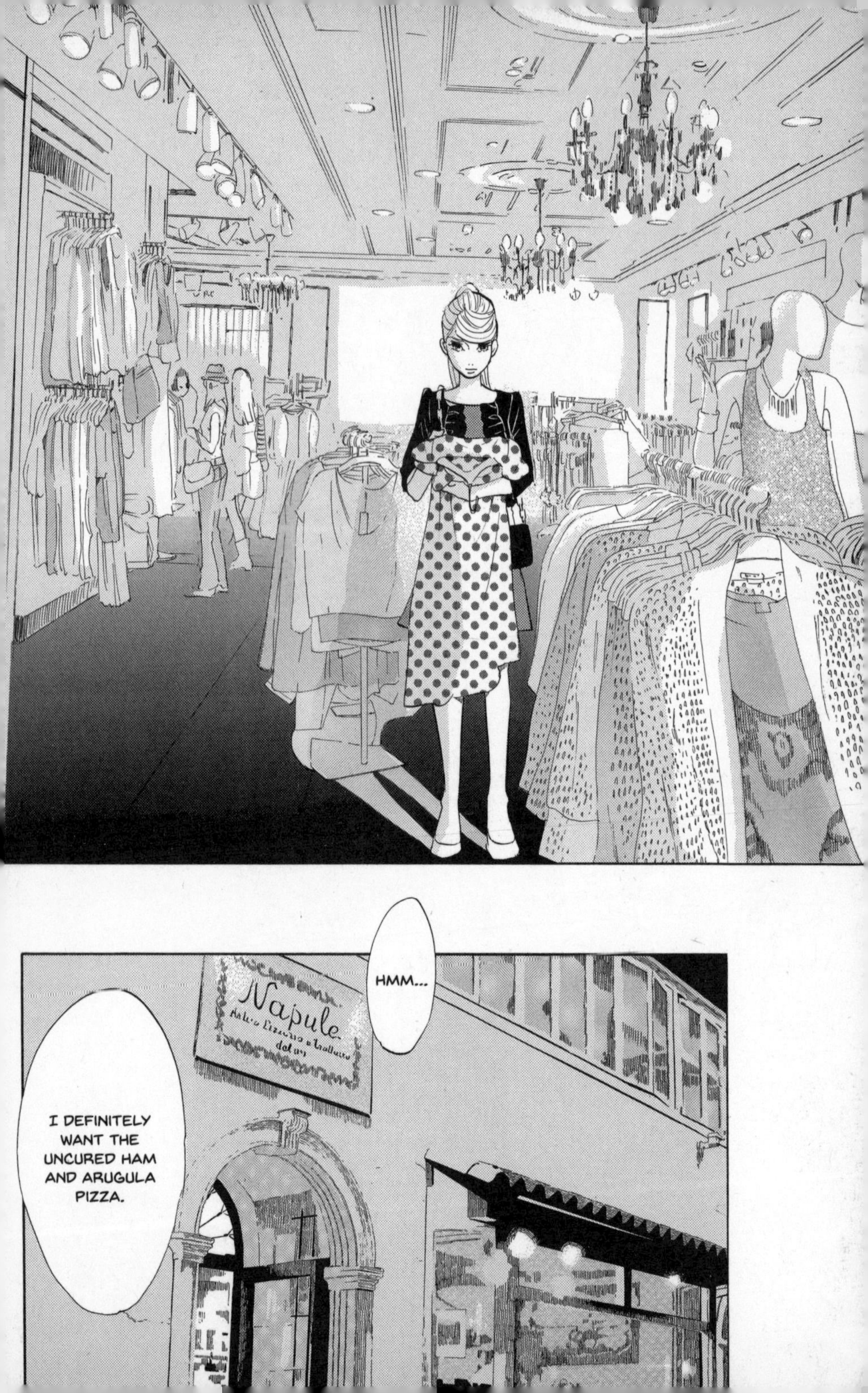
HMM...
Napule
I DEFINITELY WANT THE UNCURED HAM AND ARUGULA PIZZA.

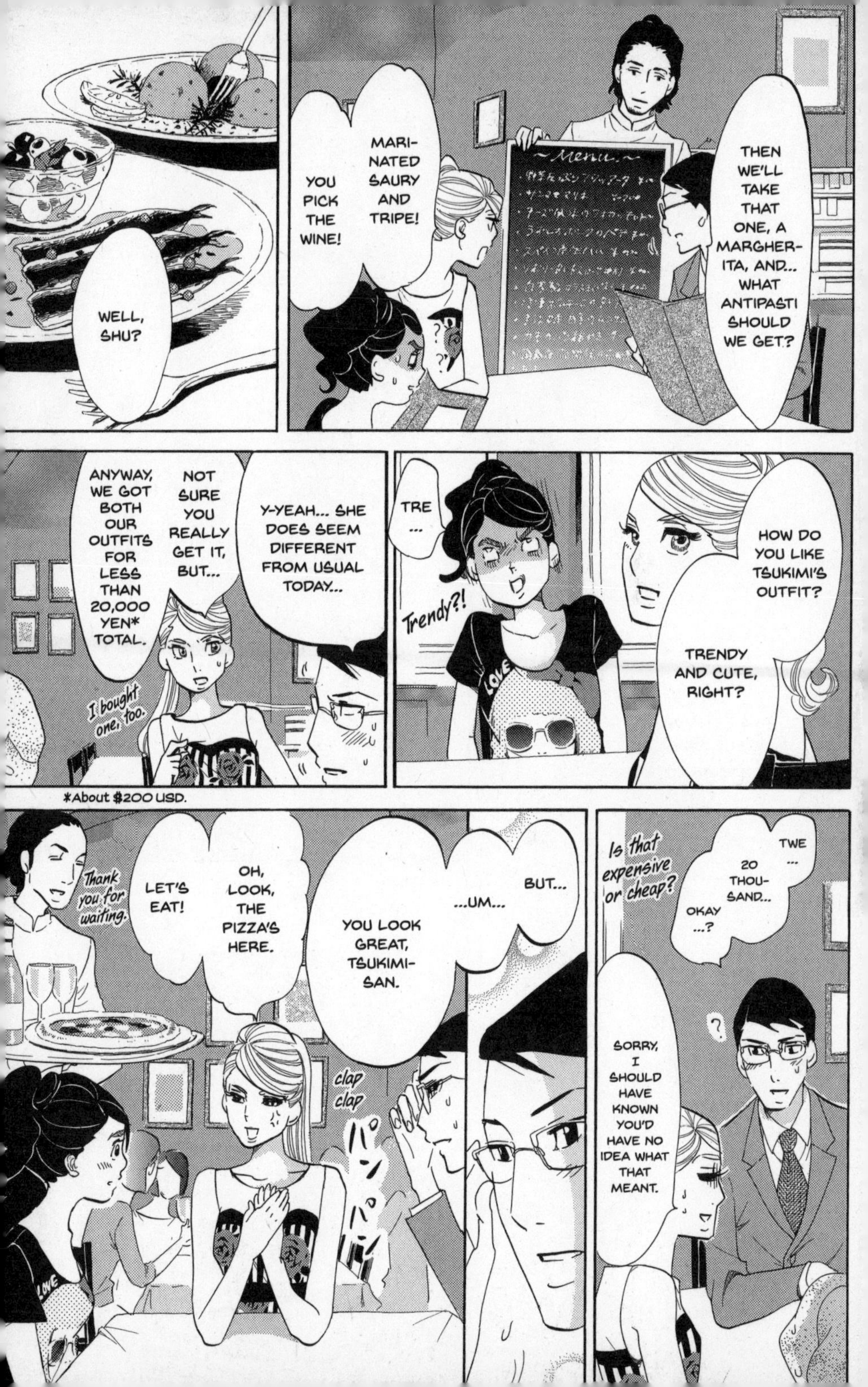
THEN WE'LL TAKE THAT ONE, A MARGHERITA, AND... WHAT ANTIPASTI SHOULD WE GET?
MARINATED SAURY AND TRIPE!
YOU PICK THE WINE!
WELL, SHU?
HOW DO YOU LIKE TSUKIMI'S OUTFIT?
TRENDY AND CUTE, RIGHT?
TRE...
Trendy?!
Y-YEAH... SHE DOES SEEM DIFFERENT FROM USUAL TODAY...
NOT SURE YOU REALLY GET IT, BUT...
ANYWAY, WE GOT BOTH OUR OUTFITS FOR LESS THAN 20,000 YEN* TOTAL.
I bought one, too.
TWE...
20 THOUSAND... OKAY...?
Is that expensive or cheap?
SORRY, I SHOULD HAVE KNOWN YOU'D HAVE NO IDEA WHAT THAT MEANT.
BUT...
...UM...
YOU LOOK GREAT, TSUKIMI-SAN.
clap clap
OH, LOOK, THE PIZZA'S HERE.
LET'S EAT!
Thank you for waiting.

*About $200 USD.

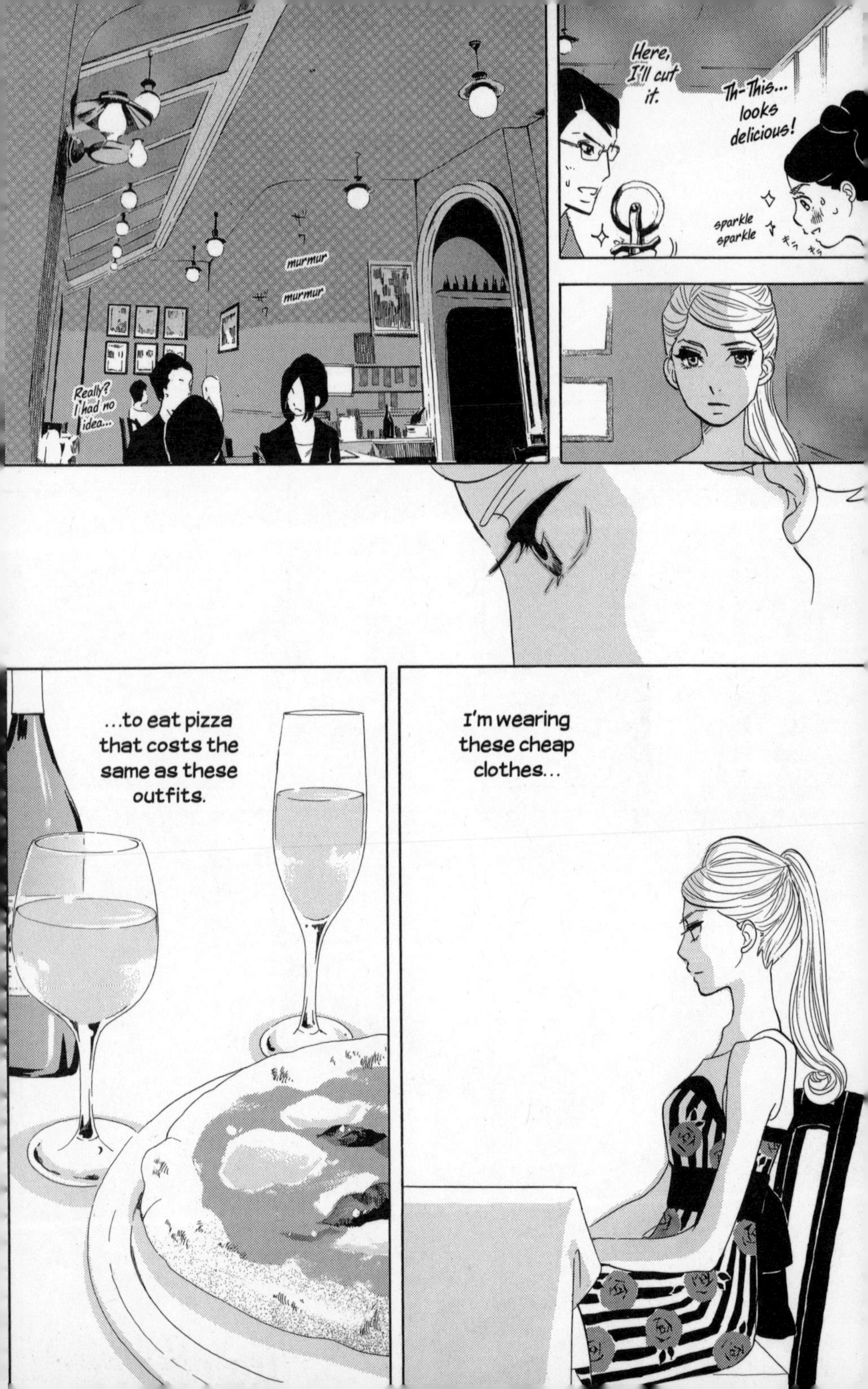

Th-This... looks delicious!
Here, I'll cut it.
sparkle sparkle
murmur
murmur
Really? I had no idea...
I'm wearing these cheap clothes...
...to eat pizza that costs the same as these outfits.

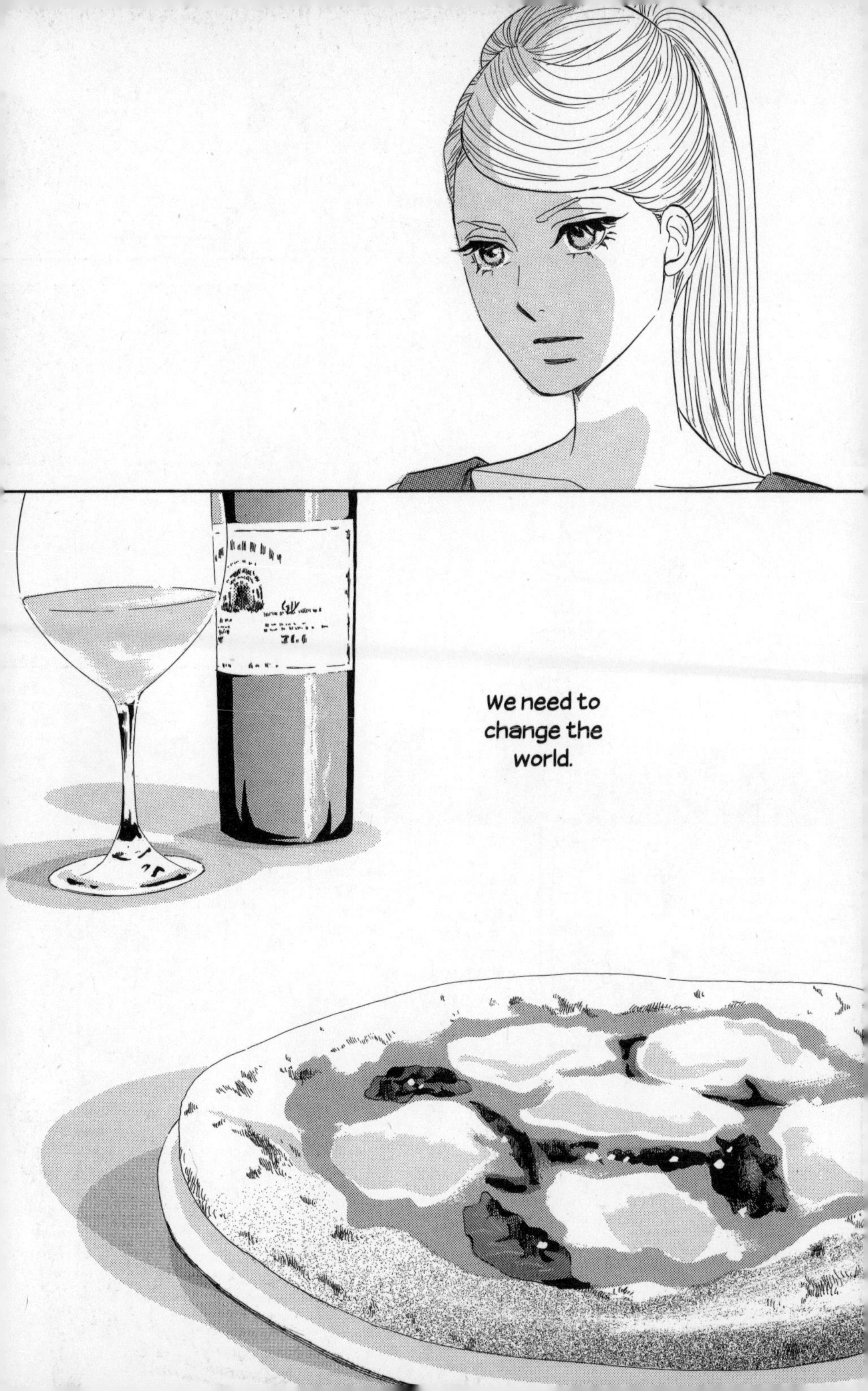
We need to change the world.

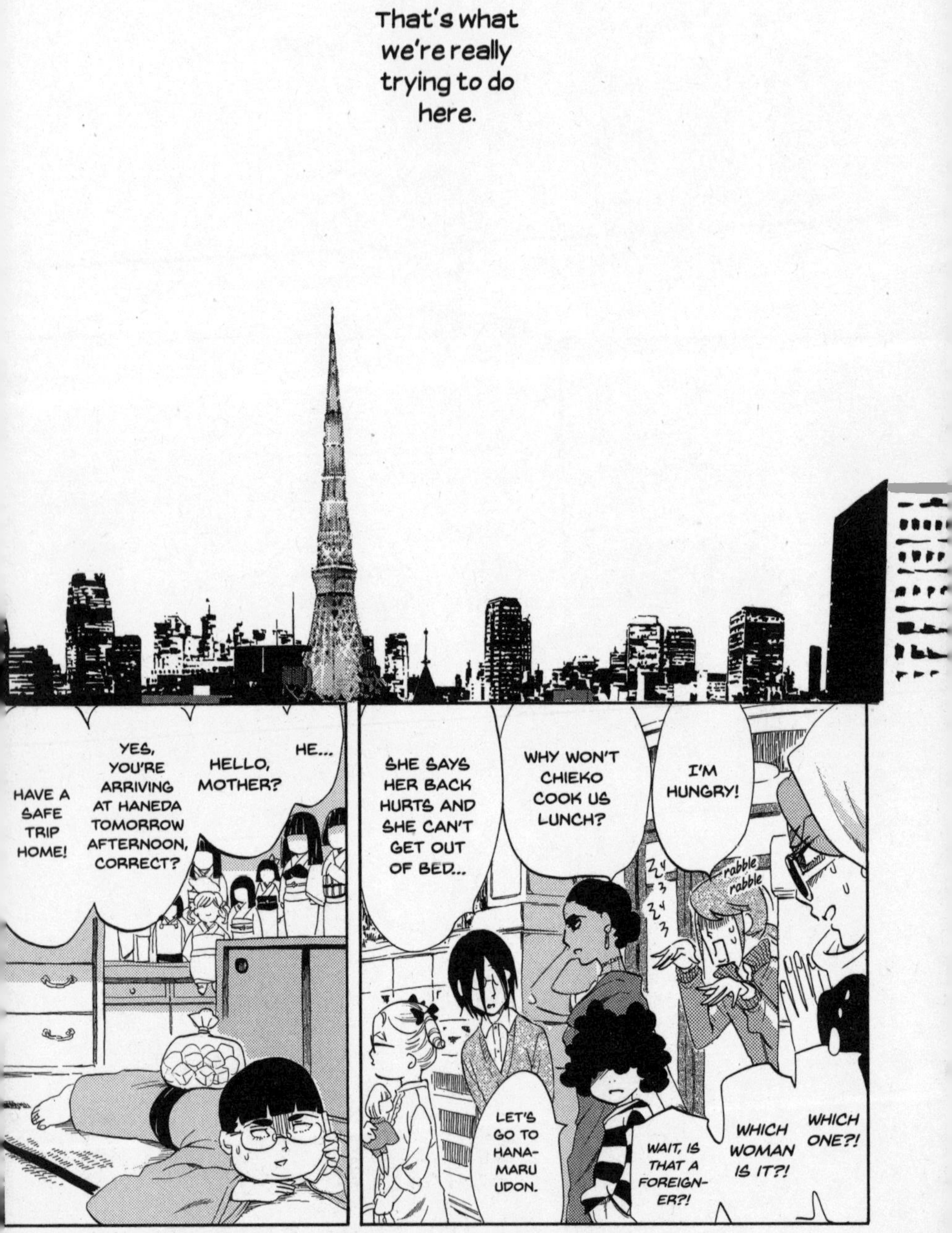
That's what we're really trying to do here.
I'M HUNGRY!
WHY WON'T CHIEKO COOK US LUNCH?
SHE SAYS HER BACK HURTS AND SHE CAN'T GET OUT OF BED...
rabble rabble
WHICH ONE?!
WHICH WOMAN IS IT?!
WAIT, IS THAT A FOREIGN-ER?!
LET'S GO TO HANA-MARU UDON.
HE...
HELLO, MOTHER?
YES, YOU'RE ARRIVING AT HANEDA TOMORROW AFTERNOON, CORRECT?
HAVE A SAFE TRIP HOME!

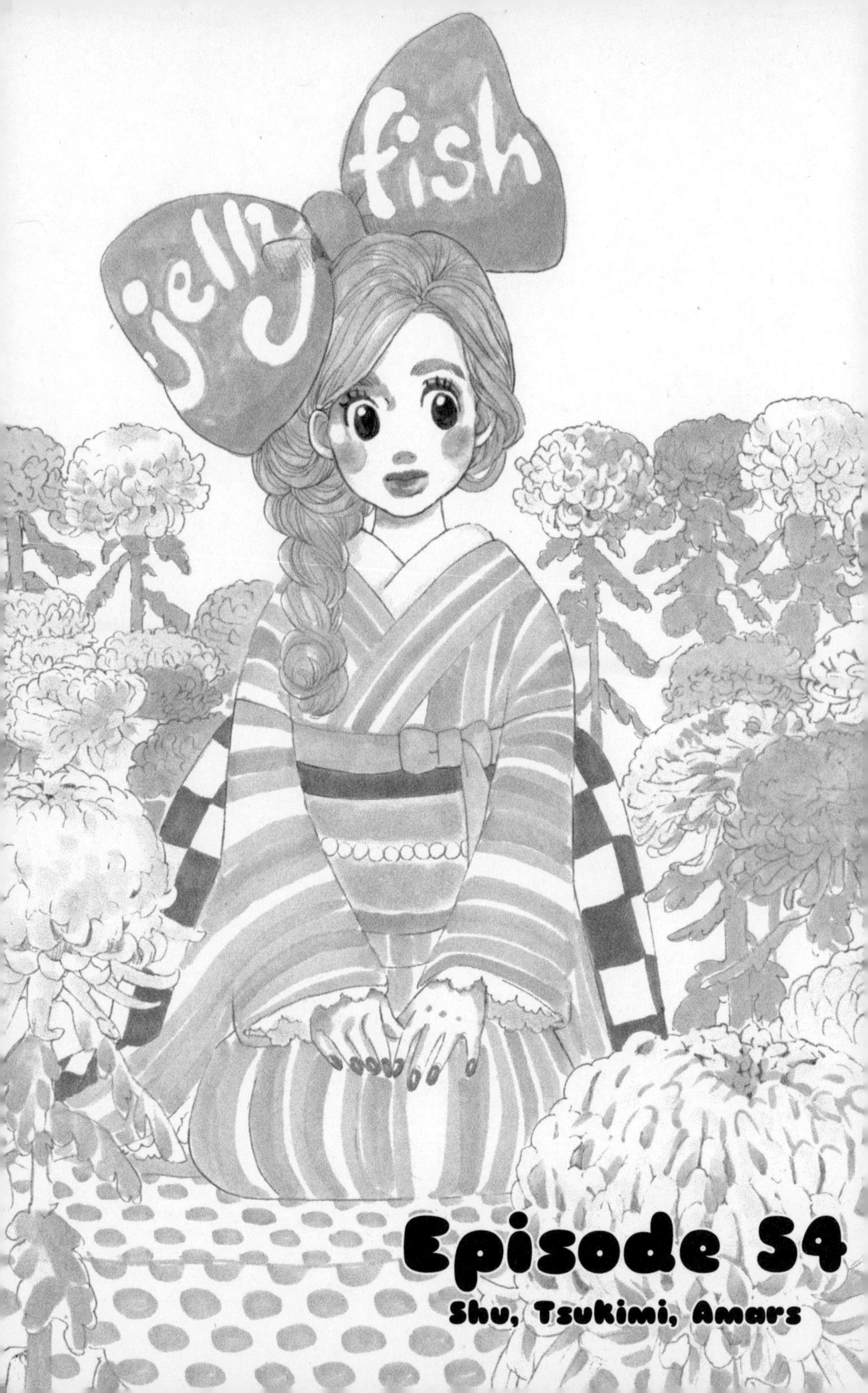
jelly fish

Episode 54

Shu, Tsukimi, Amars

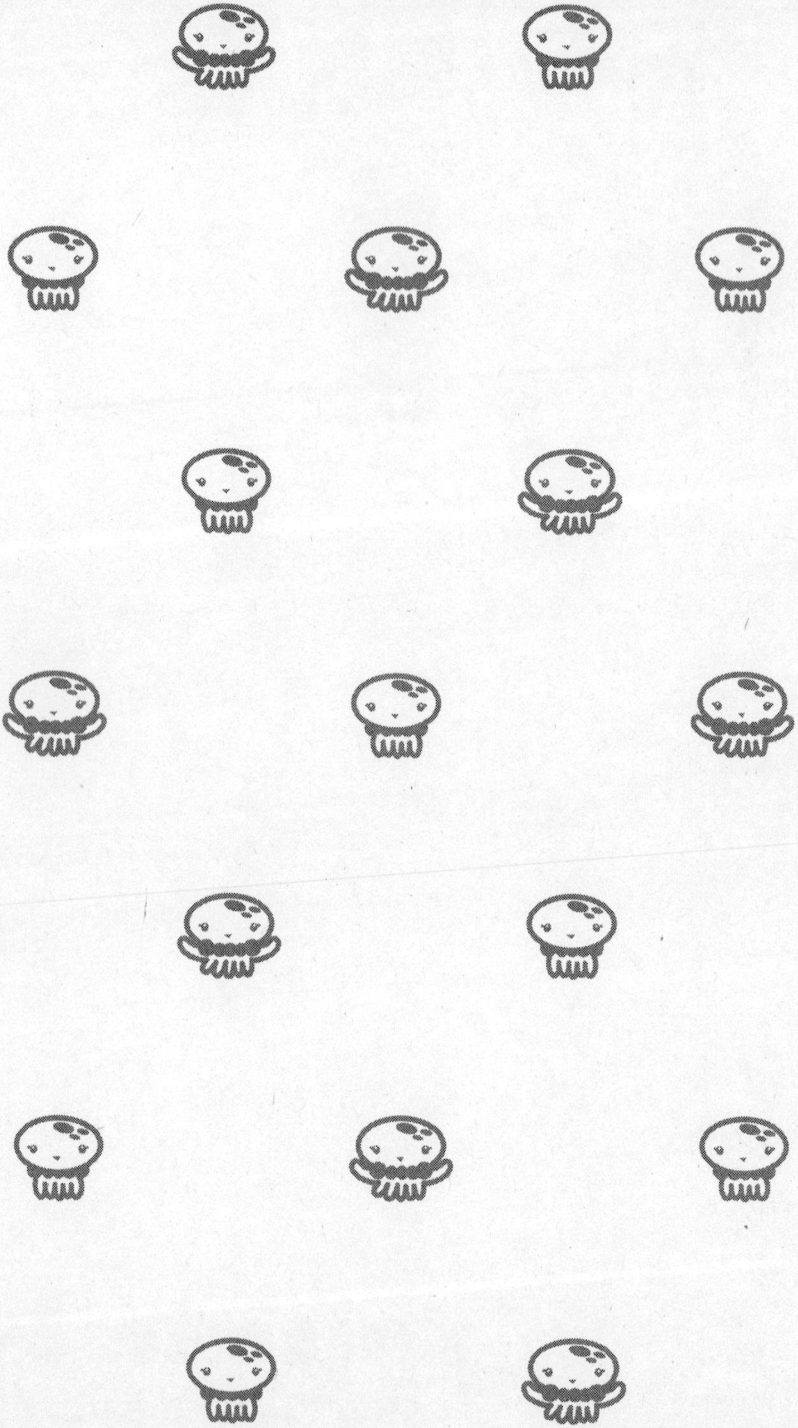

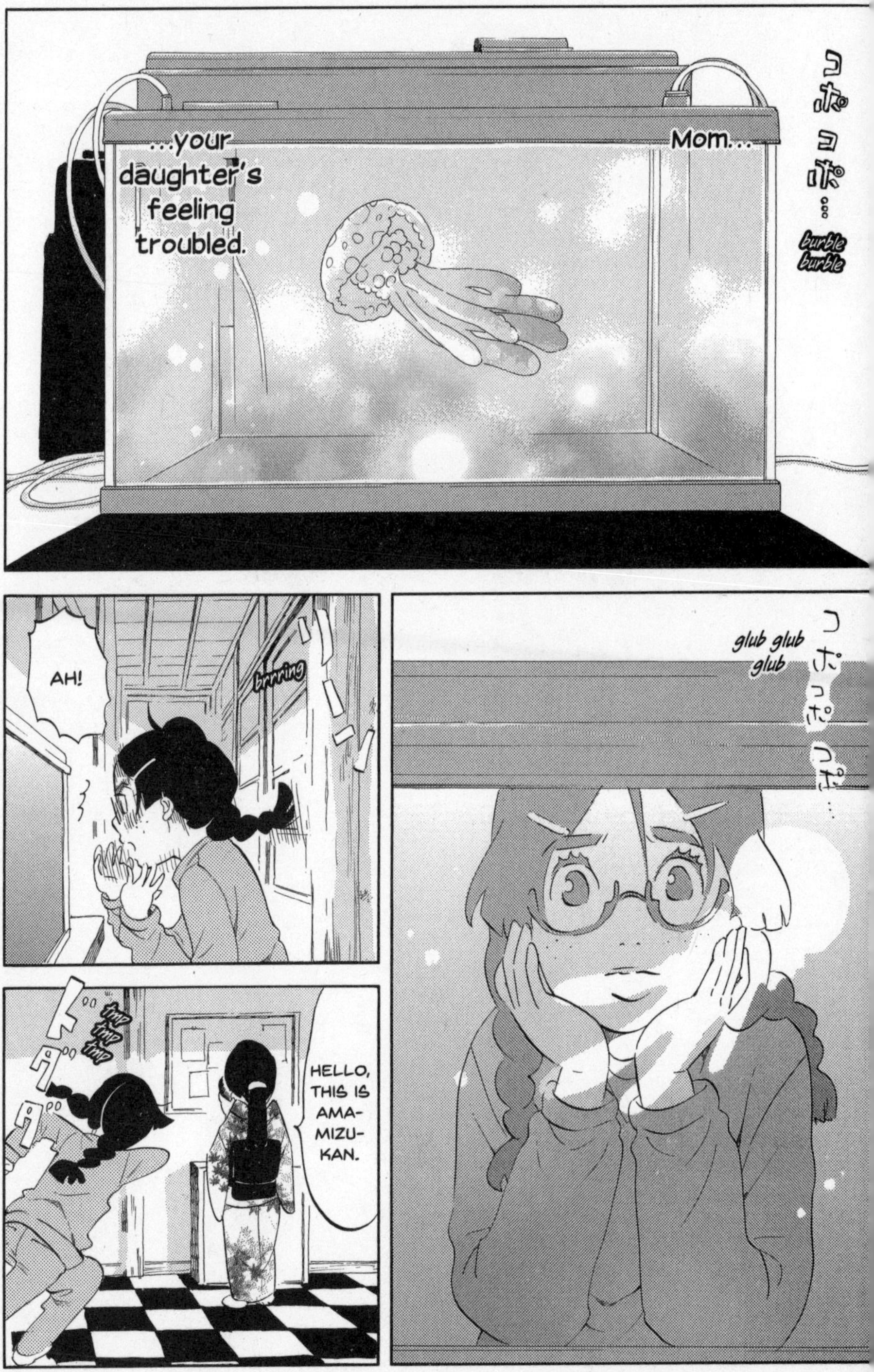

Mom...
...your daughter's feeling troubled.
コポコポ…
burble burble
コポッコポッコポ…
glub glub glub
AH!
brrring
HELLO, THIS IS AMA-MIZU-KAN.
tmp tmp tmp
ドタタ

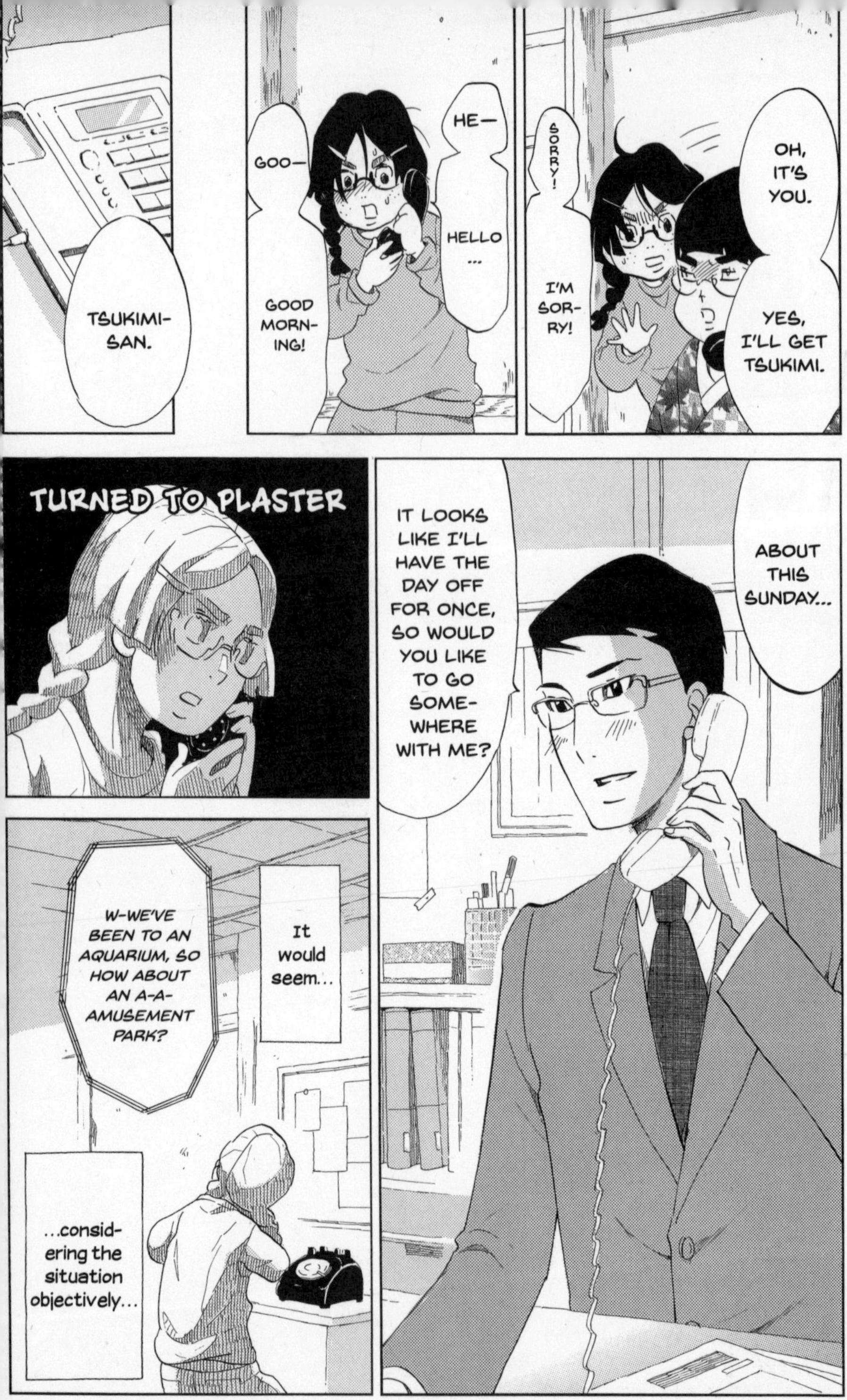
OH, IT'S YOU.
YES, I'LL GET TSUKIMI.
SORRY!
I'M SORRY!
HE—
HELLO ...
GOO—
GOOD MORNING!
TSUKIMI-SAN.
ABOUT THIS SUNDAY...
IT LOOKS LIKE I'LL HAVE THE DAY OFF FOR ONCE, SO WOULD YOU LIKE TO GO SOMEWHERE WITH ME?
TURNED TO PLASTER
It would seem...
W-WE'VE BEEN TO AN AQUARIUM, SO HOW ABOUT AN A-A-AMUSEMENT PARK?
...considering the situation objectively...

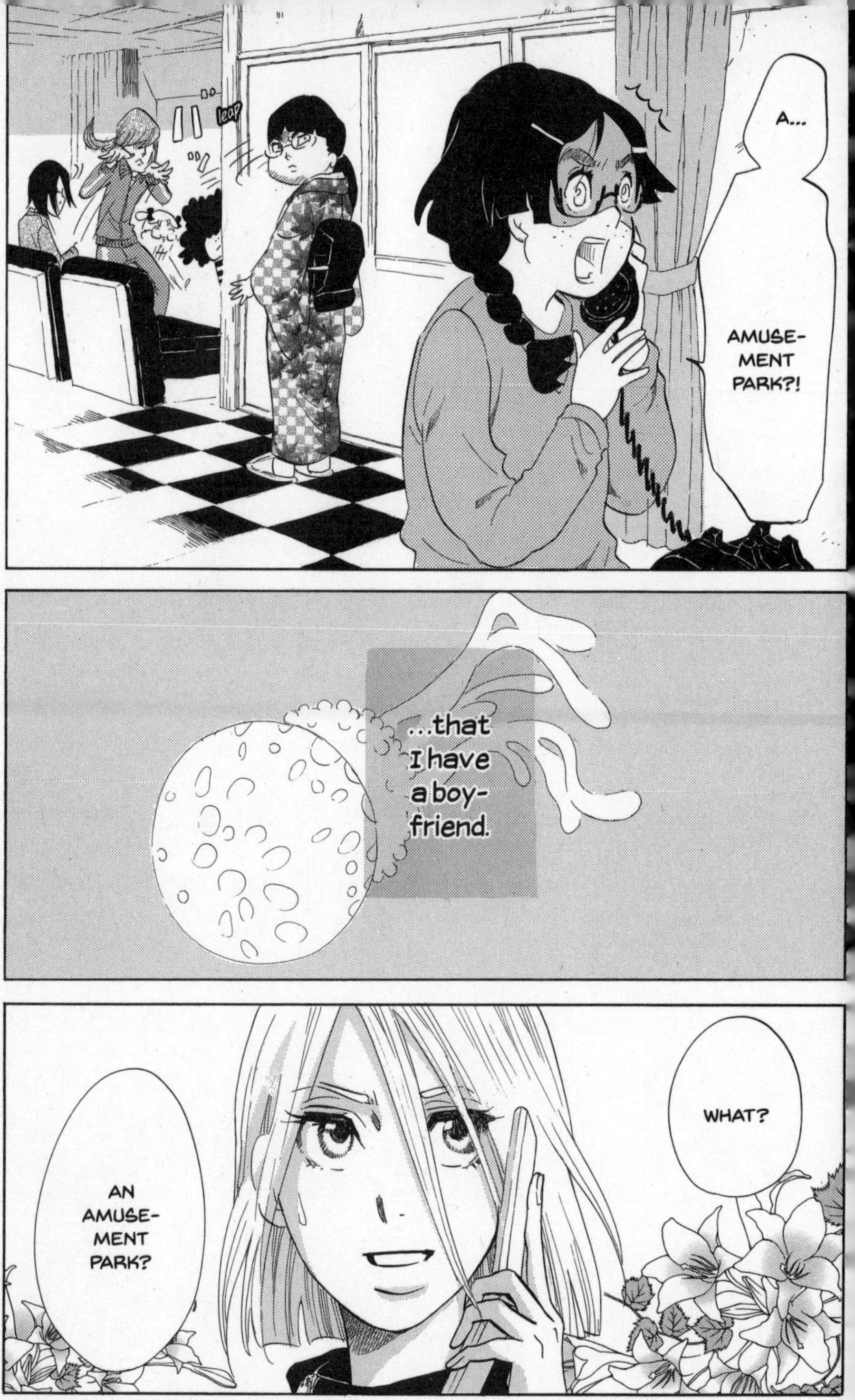
leap
A...
AMUSE-MENT PARK?!
...that I have a boy-friend.
WHAT?
AN AMUSE-MENT PARK?

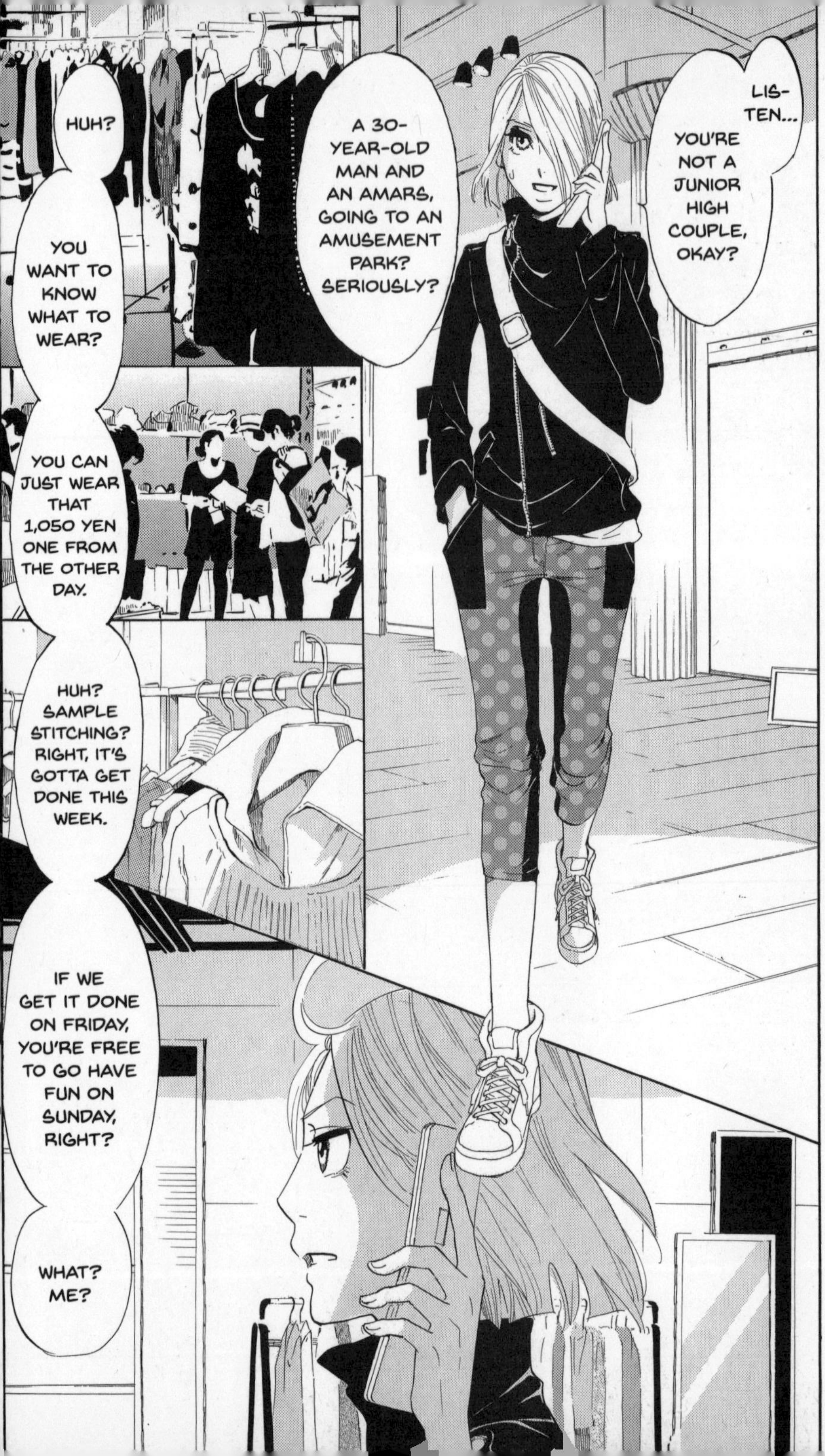
LIS-TEN... YOU'RE NOT A JUNIOR HIGH COUPLE, OKAY?
A 30-YEAR-OLD MAN AND AN AMARS, GOING TO AN AMUSEMENT PARK? SERIOUSLY?
HUH?
YOU WANT TO KNOW WHAT TO WEAR?
YOU CAN JUST WEAR THAT 1,050 YEN ONE FROM THE OTHER DAY.
HUH? SAMPLE STITCHING? RIGHT, IT'S GOTTA GET DONE THIS WEEK.
IF WE GET IT DONE ON FRIDAY, YOU'RE FREE TO GO HAVE FUN ON SUNDAY, RIGHT?
WHAT? ME?

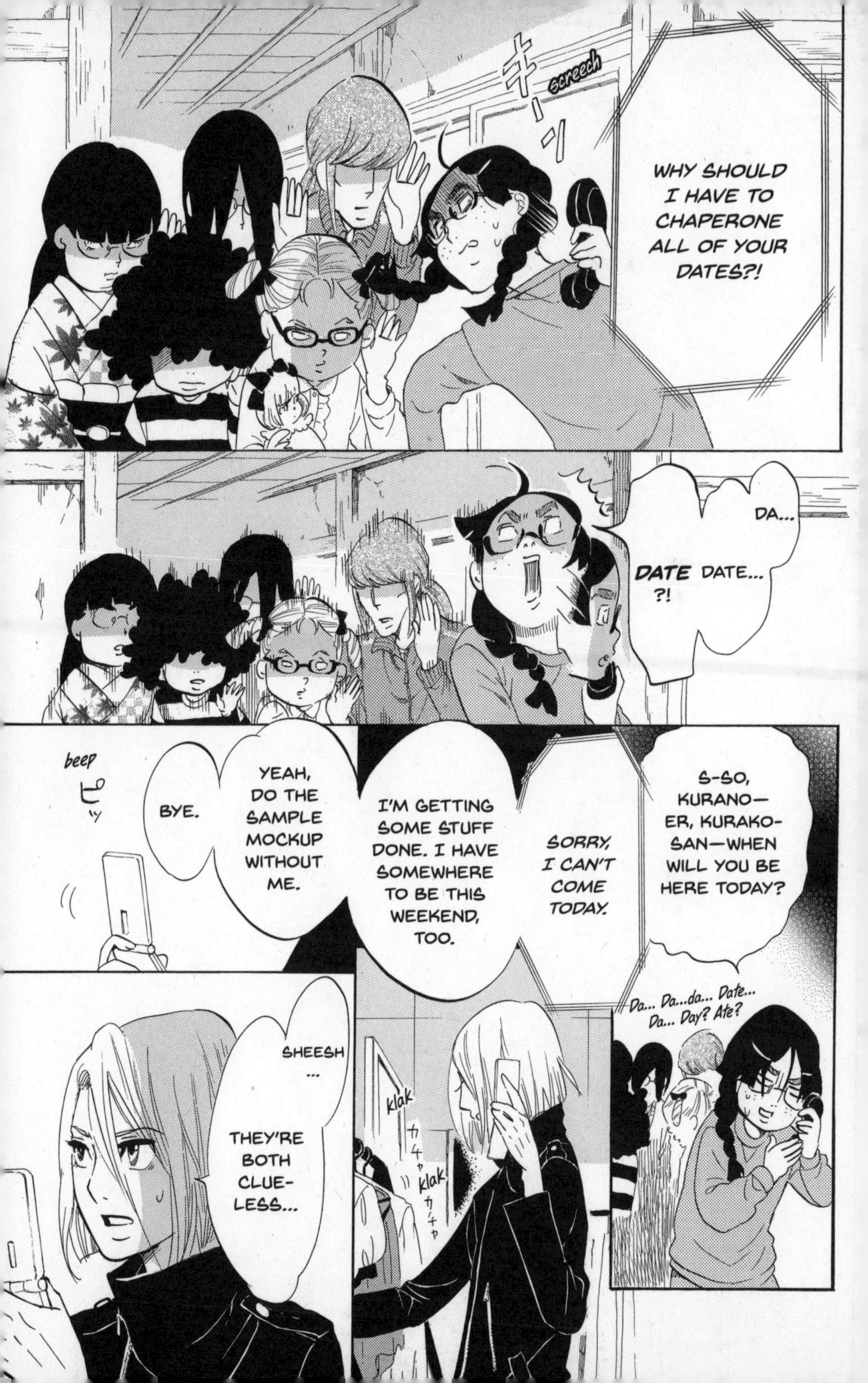
キーッ
screech
WHY SHOULD I HAVE TO CHAPERONE ALL OF YOUR DATES?!
DA...
DATE DATE... ?!
S-SO, KURANO—ER, KURAKO-SAN—WHEN WILL YOU BE HERE TODAY?
SORRY, I CAN'T COME TODAY.
I'M GETTING SOME STUFF DONE. I HAVE SOMEWHERE TO BE THIS WEEKEND, TOO.
YEAH, DO THE SAMPLE MOCKUP WITHOUT ME.
BYE.
beep
ピッ
Da... Da...da... Date... Da... Day? Ate?
klak
カチャ
klak
カチャ
SHEESH...
THEY'RE BOTH CLUELESS...

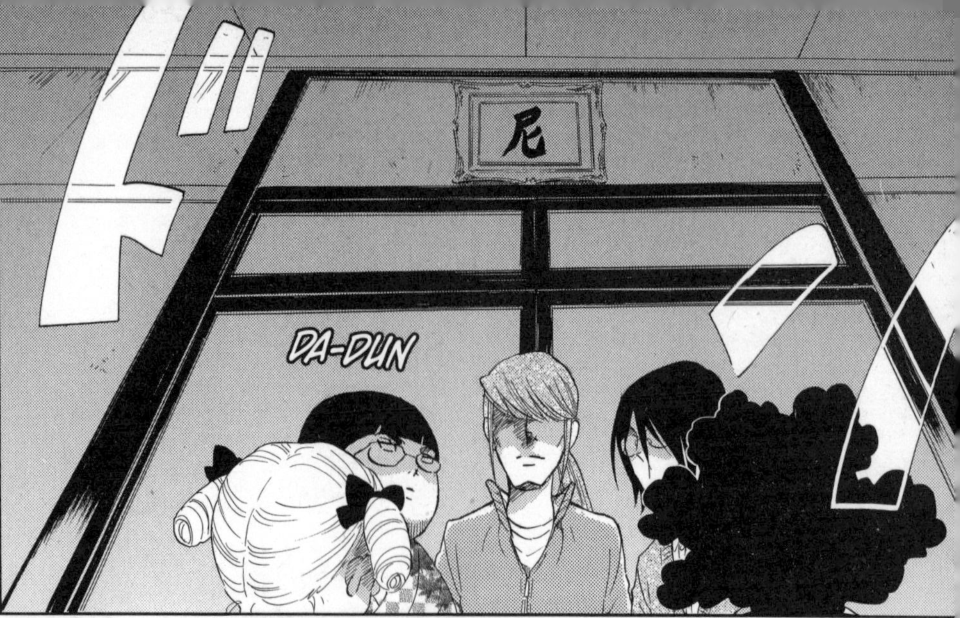
尼
DA-DUN

Painting: "Nun"

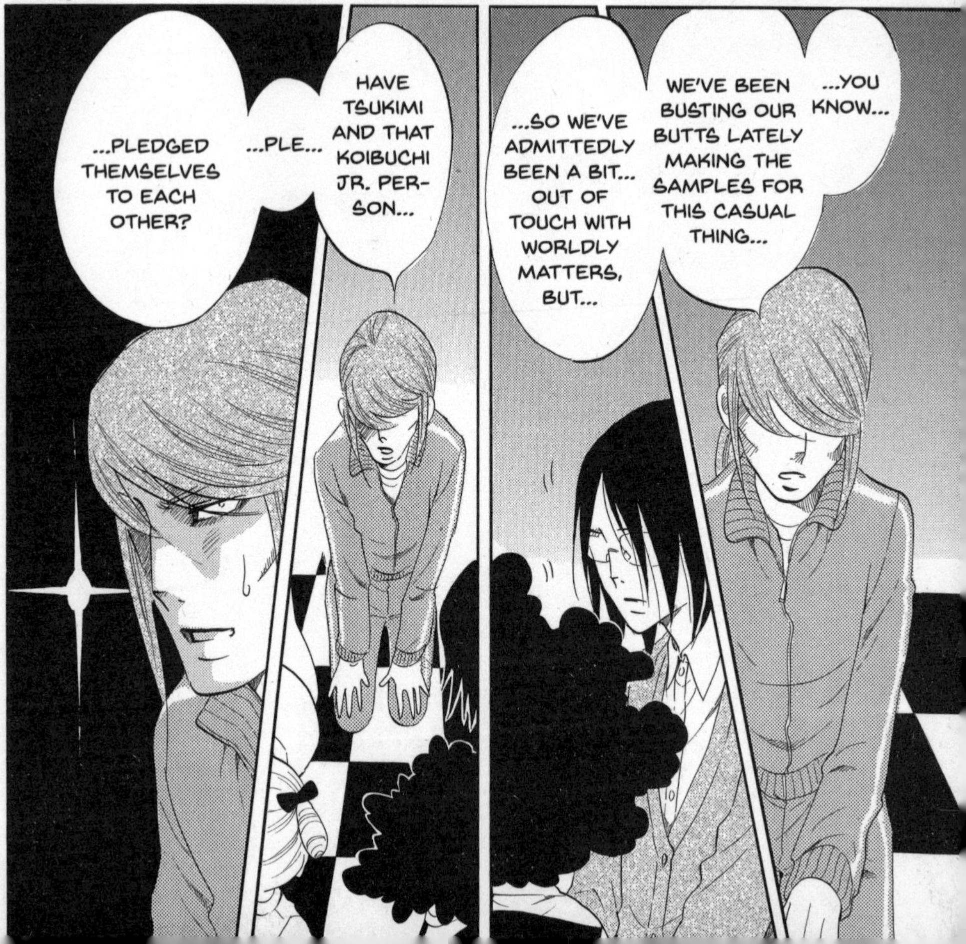
...YOU KNOW...
WE'VE BEEN BUSTING OUR BUTTS LATELY MAKING THE SAMPLES FOR THIS CASUAL THING...
...SO WE'VE ADMITTEDLY BEEN A BIT... OUT OF TOUCH WITH WORLDLY MATTERS, BUT...
HAVE TSUKIMI AND THAT KOIBUCHI JR. PERSON...
...PLE...
...PLEDGED THEMSELVES TO EACH OTHER?

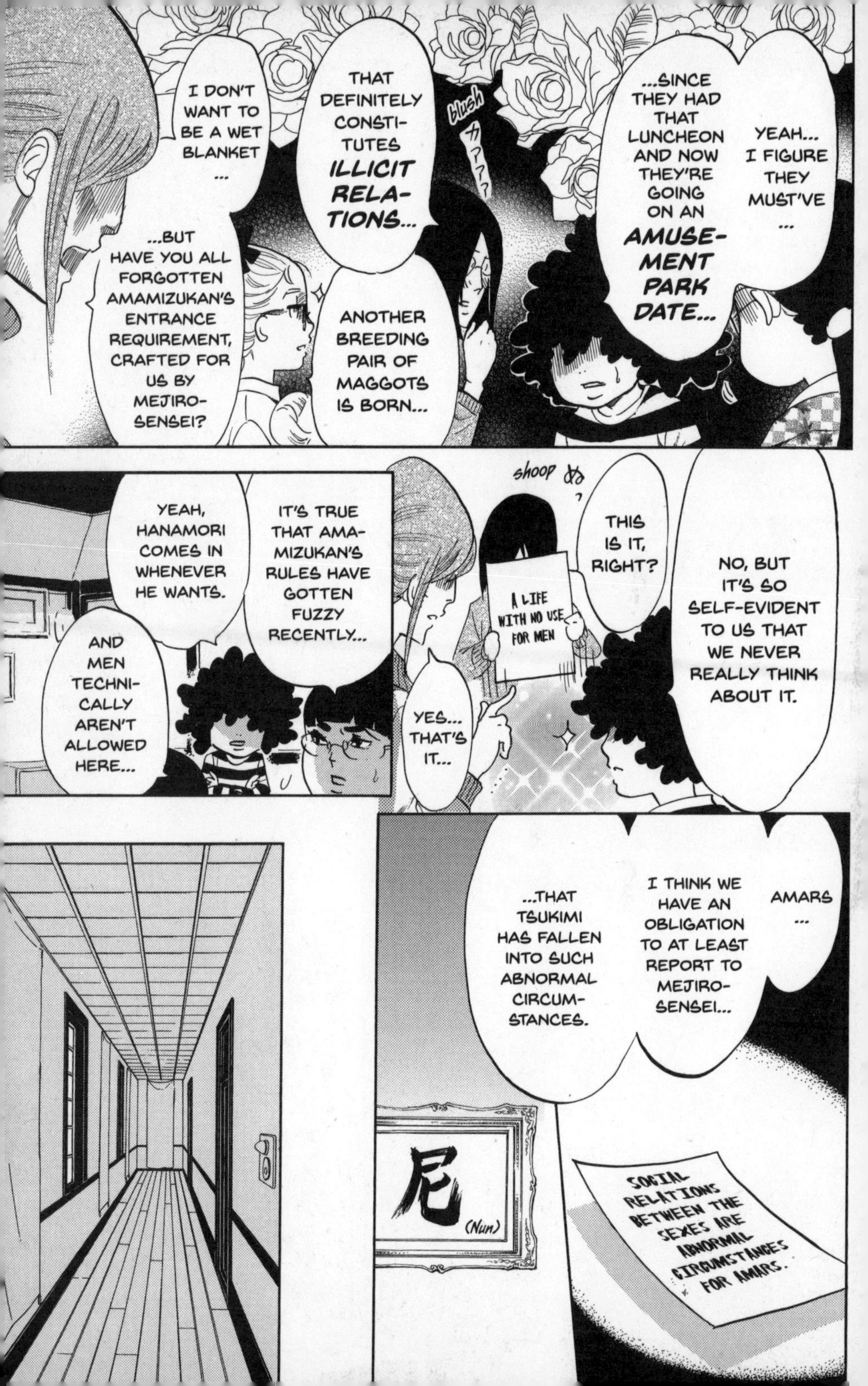
YEAH... I FIGURE THEY MUST'VE ...
...SINCE THEY HAD THAT LUNCHEON AND NOW THEY'RE GOING ON AN AMUSEMENT PARK DATE...
blush
THAT DEFINITELY CONSTITUTES ILLICIT RELATIONS...
ANOTHER BREEDING PAIR OF MAGGOTS IS BORN...
I DON'T WANT TO BE A WET BLANKET ...
...BUT HAVE YOU ALL FORGOTTEN AMAMIZUKAN'S ENTRANCE REQUIREMENT, CRAFTED FOR US BY MEJIRO-SENSEI?
shoop
NO, BUT IT'S SO SELF-EVIDENT TO US THAT WE NEVER REALLY THINK ABOUT IT.
THIS IS IT, RIGHT?
A LIFE WITH NO USE FOR MEN
YES... THAT'S IT...
IT'S TRUE THAT AMAMIZUKAN'S RULES HAVE GOTTEN FUZZY RECENTLY...
YEAH, HANAMORI COMES IN WHENEVER HE WANTS.
AND MEN TECHNICALLY AREN'T ALLOWED HERE...
AMARS ...
I THINK WE HAVE AN OBLIGATION TO AT LEAST REPORT TO MEJIRO-SENSEI...
...THAT TSUKIMI HAS FALLEN INTO SUCH ABNORMAL CIRCUMSTANCES.
尼 (Nun)
SOCIAL RELATIONS BETWEEN THE SEXES ARE ABNORMAL CIRCUMSTANCES FOR AMARS.

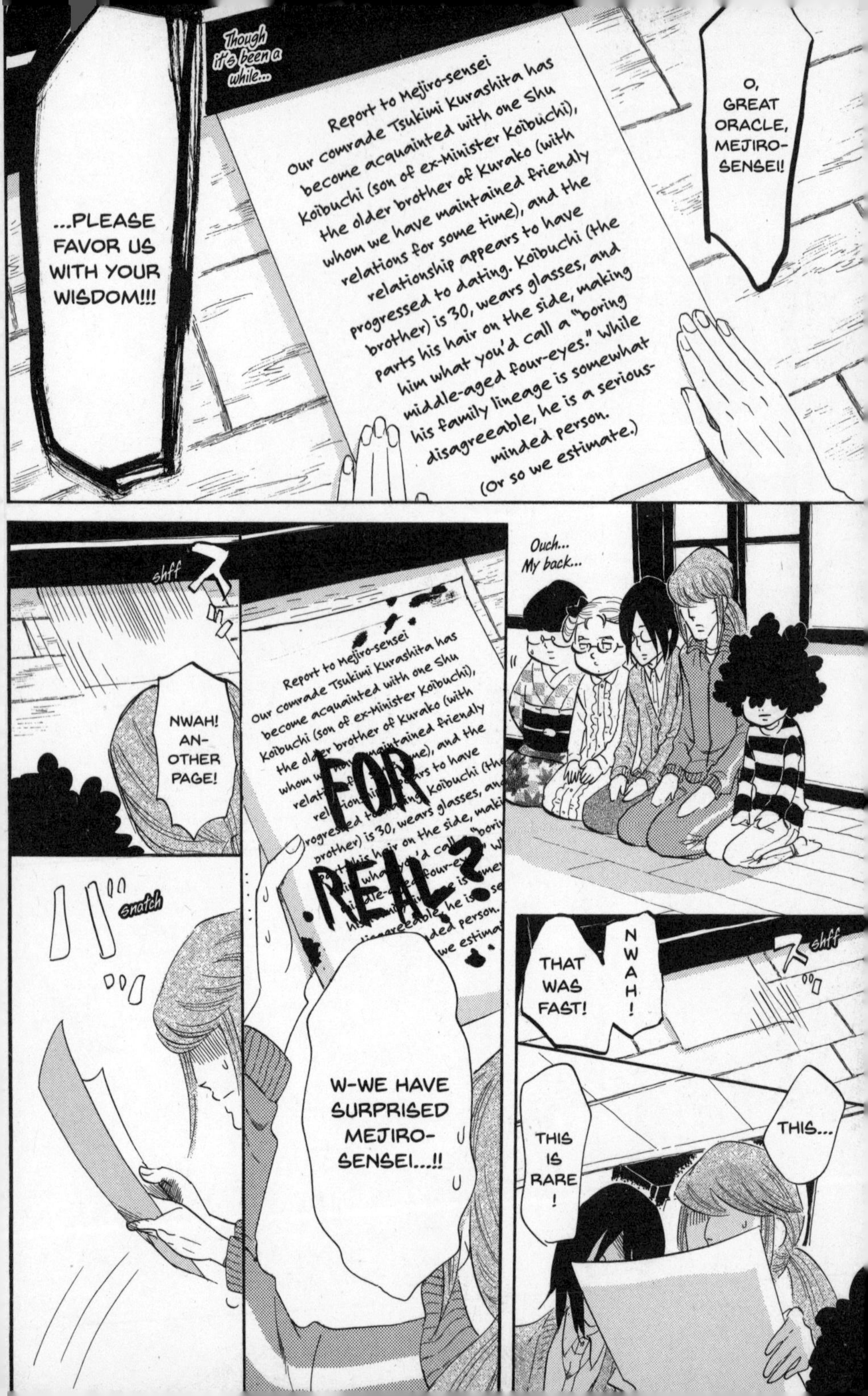
O, GREAT ORACLE, MEJIRO-SENSEI!
Though it's been a while...
Report to Mejiro-sensei
Our comrade Tsukimi Kurashita has become acquainted with one Shu Koibuchi (son of ex-Minister Koibuchi), the older brother of Kurako (with whom we have maintained friendly relations for some time), and the relationship appears to have progressed to dating. Koibuchi (the brother) is 30, wears glasses, and parts his hair on the side, making him what you'd call a "boring middle-aged four-eyes." While his family lineage is somewhat disagreeable, he is a serious-minded person.
(Or so we estimate.)
...PLEASE FAVOR US WITH YOUR WISDOM!!!
Ouch... My back...
shff
NWAH!
THAT WAS FAST!
THIS...
THIS IS RARE!
Report to Mejiro-sensei
Our comrade Tsukimi Kurashita has become acquainted with one Shu Koibuchi (son of ex-Minister Koibuchi), the older brother of Kurako (with
FOR REAL?
W-WE HAVE SURPRISED MEJIRO-SENSEI...!!
shff
NWAH! AN-OTHER PAGE!
snatch

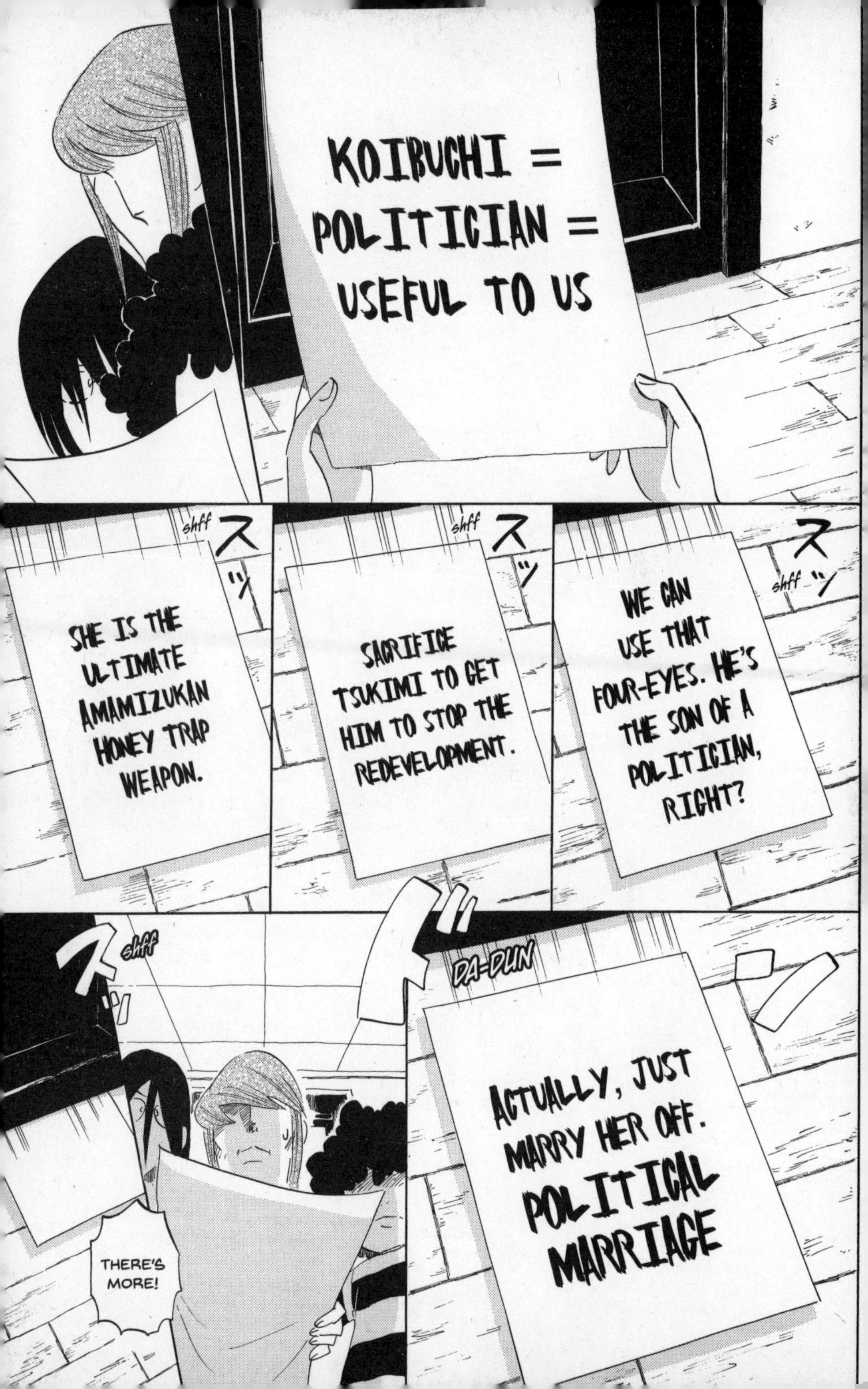
KOIBUCHI = POLITICIAN = USEFUL TO US
スッ
shff
WE CAN USE THAT FOUR-EYES. HE'S THE SON OF A POLITICIAN, RIGHT?
スッ
shff
SACRIFICE TSUKIMI TO GET HIM TO STOP THE REDEVELOPMENT.
スッ
shff
SHE IS THE ULTIMATE AMAMIZUKAN HONEY TRAP WEAPON.
DA-DUN
ACTUALLY, JUST MARRY HER OFF. POLITICAL MARRIAGE
スッ
shff
THERE'S MORE!

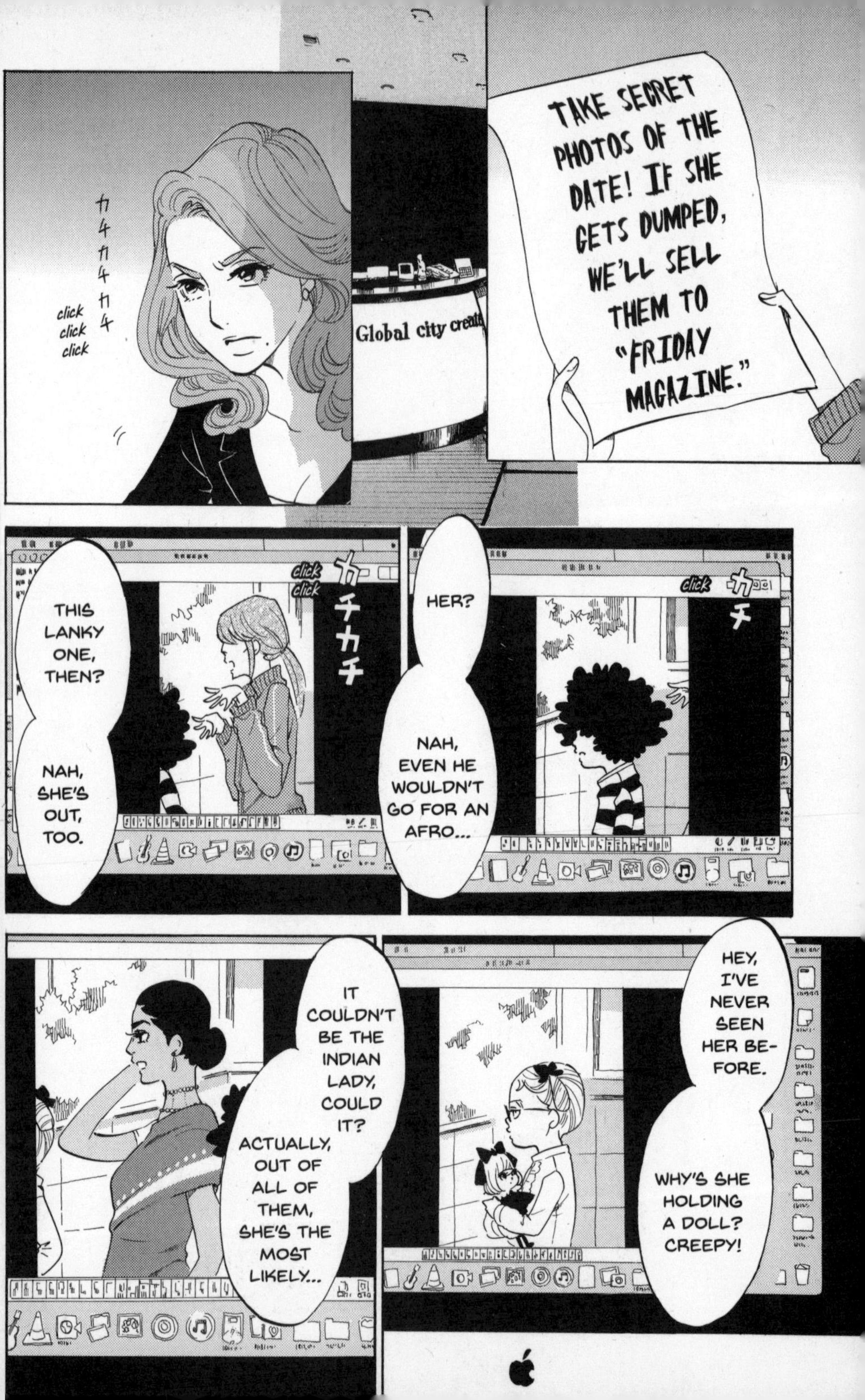
TAKE SECRET PHOTOS OF THE DATE! IF SHE GETS DUMPED, WE'LL SELL THEM TO "FRIDAY MAGAZINE."
Global city creat
カチカチカチ
click click click
HER?
click
カチ
NAH, EVEN HE WOULDN'T GO FOR AN AFRO...
click click
カチカチ
THIS LANKY ONE, THEN?
NAH, SHE'S OUT, TOO.
HEY, I'VE NEVER SEEN HER BE- FORE.
WHY'S SHE HOLDING A DOLL? CREEPY!
IT COULDN'T BE THE INDIAN LADY, COULD IT?
ACTUALLY, OUT OF ALL OF THEM, SHE'S THE MOST LIKELY...

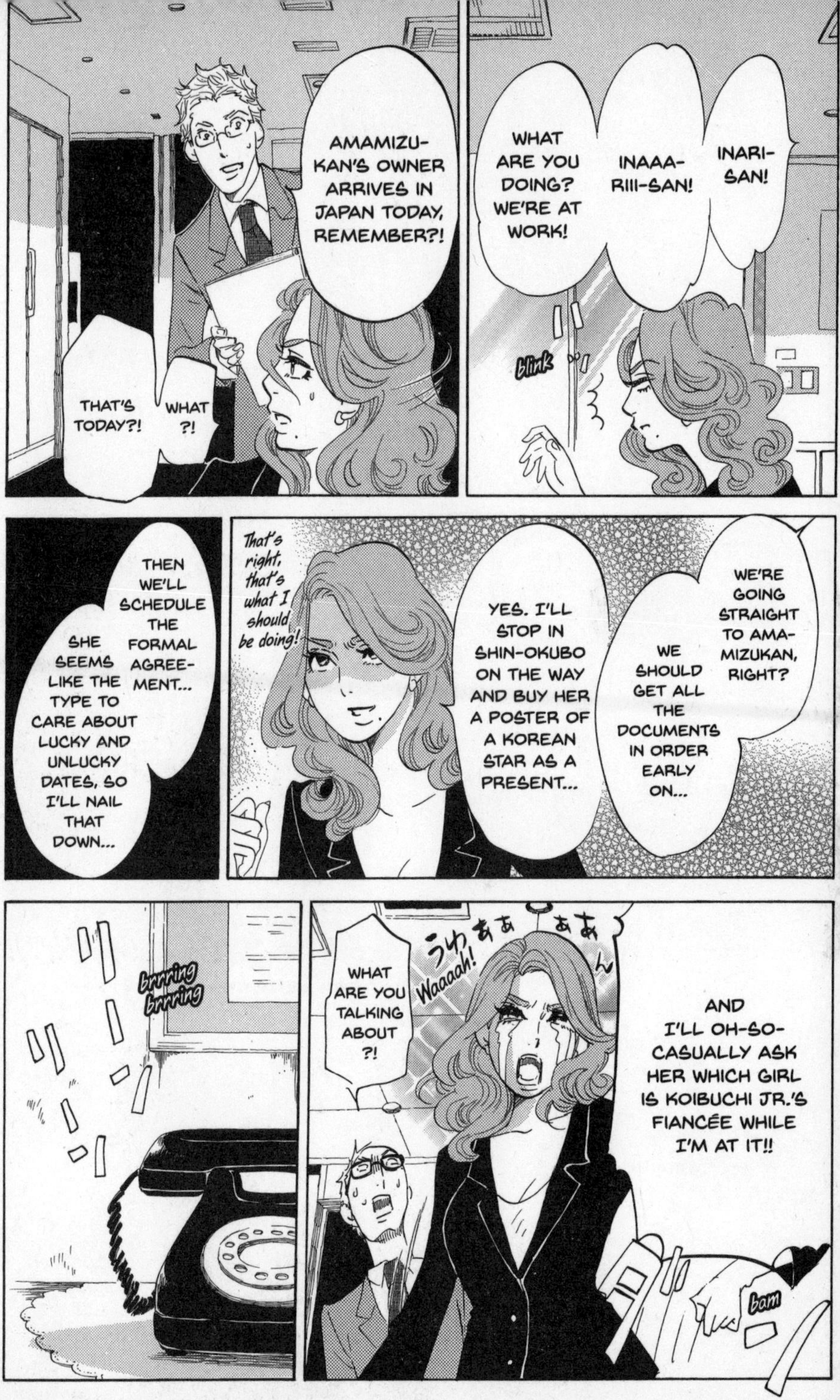
INARI-SAN!
INAAA-RIII-SAN!
WHAT ARE YOU DOING? WE'RE AT WORK!
blink
AMAMIZU-KAN'S OWNER ARRIVES IN JAPAN TODAY, REMEMBER?!
WHAT ?!
THAT'S TODAY?!
WE'RE GOING STRAIGHT TO AMA-MIZUKAN, RIGHT?
WE SHOULD GET ALL THE DOCUMENTS IN ORDER EARLY ON...
YES. I'LL STOP IN SHIN-OKUBO ON THE WAY AND BUY HER A POSTER OF A KOREAN STAR AS A PRESENT...
That's right, that's what I should be doing!
THEN WE'LL SCHEDULE THE FORMAL AGREE-MENT...
SHE SEEMS LIKE THE TYPE TO CARE ABOUT LUCKY AND UNLUCKY DATES, SO I'LL NAIL THAT DOWN...
AND I'LL OH-SO-CASUALLY ASK HER WHICH GIRL IS KOIBUCHI JR.'S FIANCÉE WHILE I'M AT IT!!
bam
うわああああん
Waaaah!
WHAT ARE YOU TALKING ABOUT?!
brrring brrring

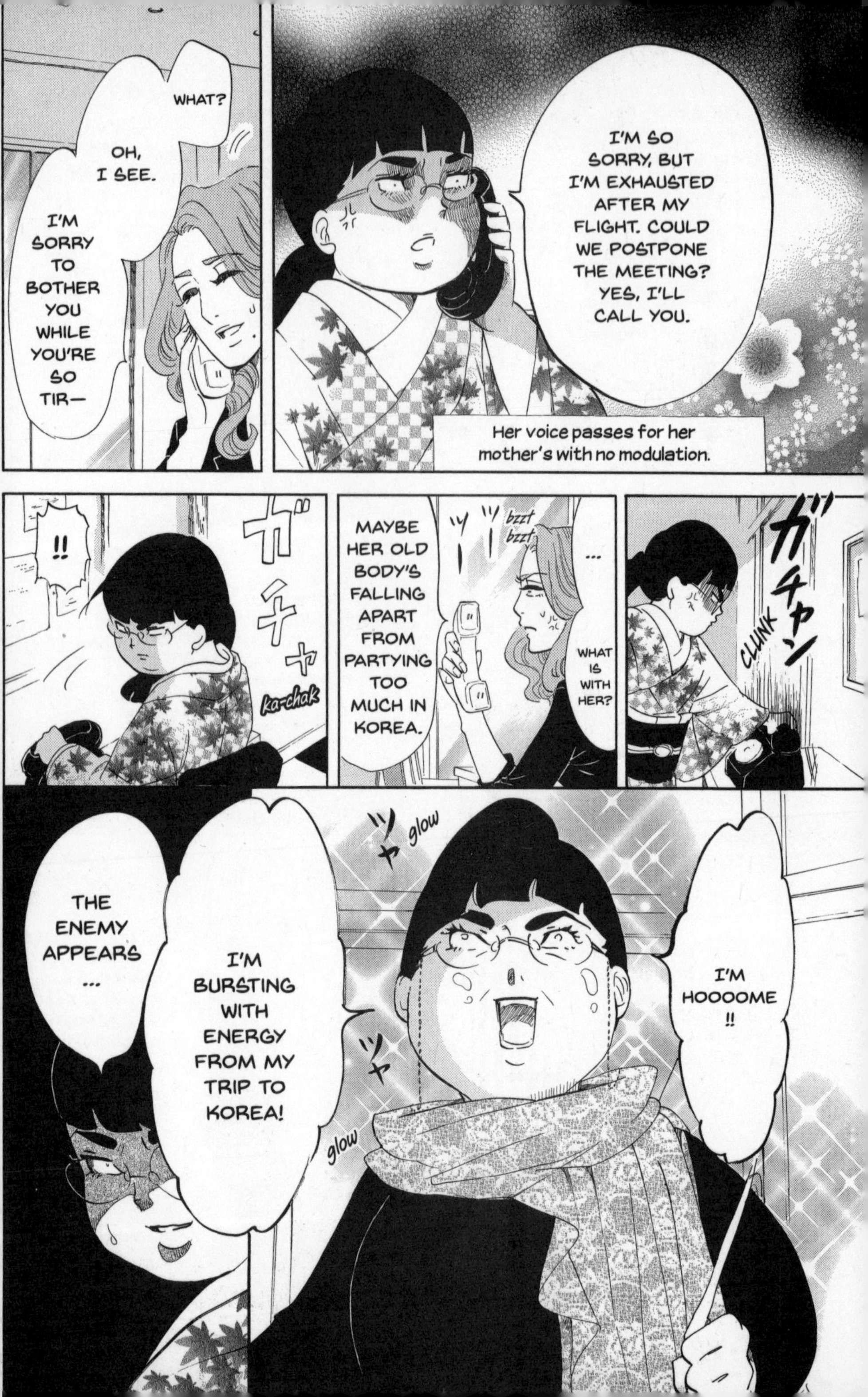
I'M SO SORRY, BUT I'M EXHAUSTED AFTER MY FLIGHT. COULD WE POSTPONE THE MEETING? YES, I'LL CALL YOU.
Her voice passes for her mother's with no modulation.
WHAT?
OH, I SEE.
I'M SORRY TO BOTHER YOU WHILE YOU'RE SO TIR—
ガチャン
CLUNK
ツツ
bzzt bzzt
...
WHAT IS WITH HER?
MAYBE HER OLD BODY'S FALLING APART FROM PARTYING TOO MUCH IN KOREA.
ガチャ
ka-chak
!!
I'M HOOOOME!!
ツヤ
glow
I'M BURSTING WITH ENERGY FROM MY TRIP TO KOREA!
ツヤ
glow
THE ENEMY APPEARS...

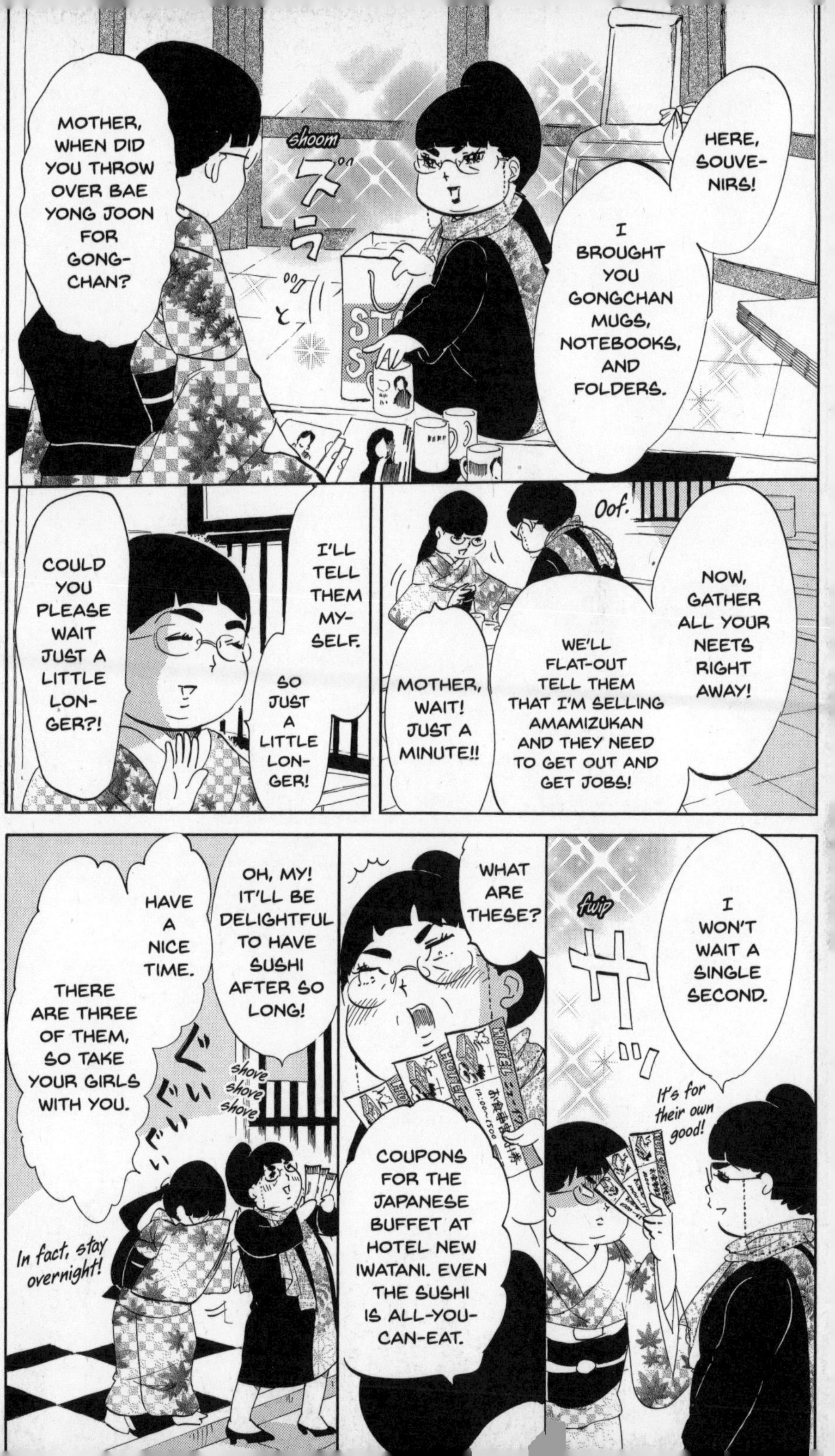
HERE, SOUVENIRS!
I BROUGHT YOU GONGCHAN MUGS, NOTEBOOKS, AND FOLDERS.
shoom
MOTHER, WHEN DID YOU THROW OVER BAE YONG JOON FOR GONG-CHAN?
Oof.
NOW, GATHER ALL YOUR NEETS RIGHT AWAY!
WE'LL FLAT-OUT TELL THEM THAT I'M SELLING AMAMIZUKAN AND THEY NEED TO GET OUT AND GET JOBS!
MOTHER, WAIT! JUST A MINUTE!!
I'LL TELL THEM MYSELF.
SO JUST A LITTLE LONGER!
COULD YOU PLEASE WAIT JUST A LITTLE LONGER?!
I WON'T WAIT A SINGLE SECOND.
fwip
It's for their own good!
WHAT ARE THESE?
COUPONS FOR THE JAPANESE BUFFET AT HOTEL NEW IWATANI. EVEN THE SUSHI IS ALL-YOU-CAN-EAT.
OH, MY! IT'LL BE DELIGHTFUL TO HAVE SUSHI AFTER SO LONG!
HAVE A NICE TIME.
THERE ARE THREE OF THEM, SO TAKE YOUR GIRLS WITH YOU.
shove shove shove
In fact, stay overnight!

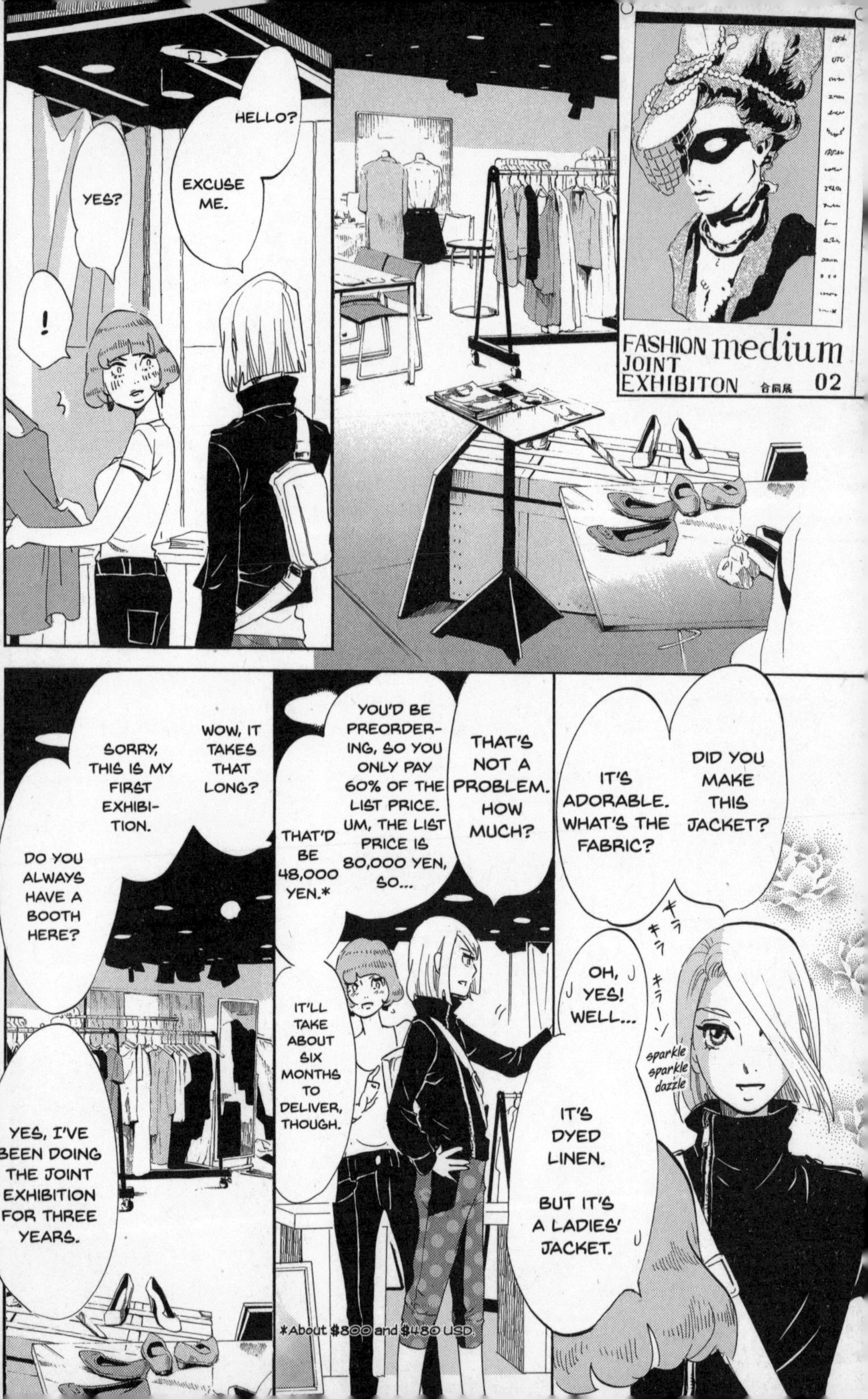
FASHION medium
JOINT EXHIBITON 合同展 02
HELLO?
EXCUSE ME.
YES?
!
DID YOU MAKE THIS JACKET?
IT'S ADORABLE. WHAT'S THE FABRIC?
キラ キラ キラーン
sparkle sparkle dazzle
OH, YES! WELL...
IT'S DYED LINEN.
BUT IT'S A LADIES' JACKET.
THAT'S NOT A PROBLEM. HOW MUCH?
YOU'D BE PREORDERING, SO YOU ONLY PAY 60% OF THE LIST PRICE. UM, THE LIST PRICE IS 80,000 YEN, SO...
THAT'D BE 48,000 YEN.*
IT'LL TAKE ABOUT SIX MONTHS TO DELIVER, THOUGH.
*About $800 and $480 USD.
WOW, IT TAKES THAT LONG?
SORRY, THIS IS MY FIRST EXHIBITION.
DO YOU ALWAYS HAVE A BOOTH HERE?
YES, I'VE BEEN DOING THE JOINT EXHIBITION FOR THREE YEARS.

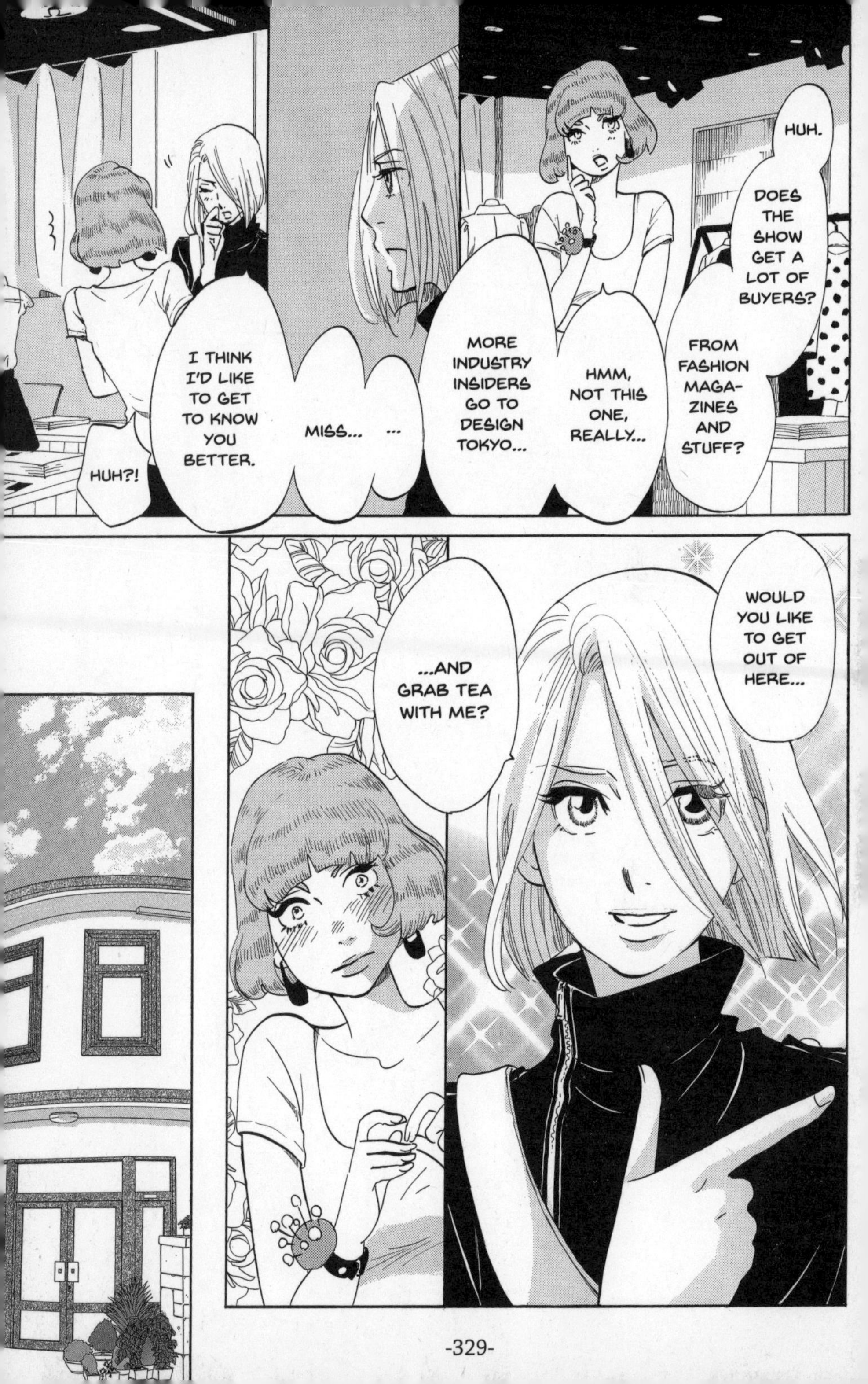
HUH.
DOES THE SHOW GET A LOT OF BUYERS?
FROM FASHION MAGAZINES AND STUFF?
HMM, NOT THIS ONE, REALLY...
MORE INDUSTRY INSIDERS GO TO DESIGN TOKYO...
...
MISS...
I THINK I'D LIKE TO GET TO KNOW YOU BETTER.
HUH?!
WOULD YOU LIKE TO GET OUT OF HERE...
...AND GRAB TEA WITH ME?

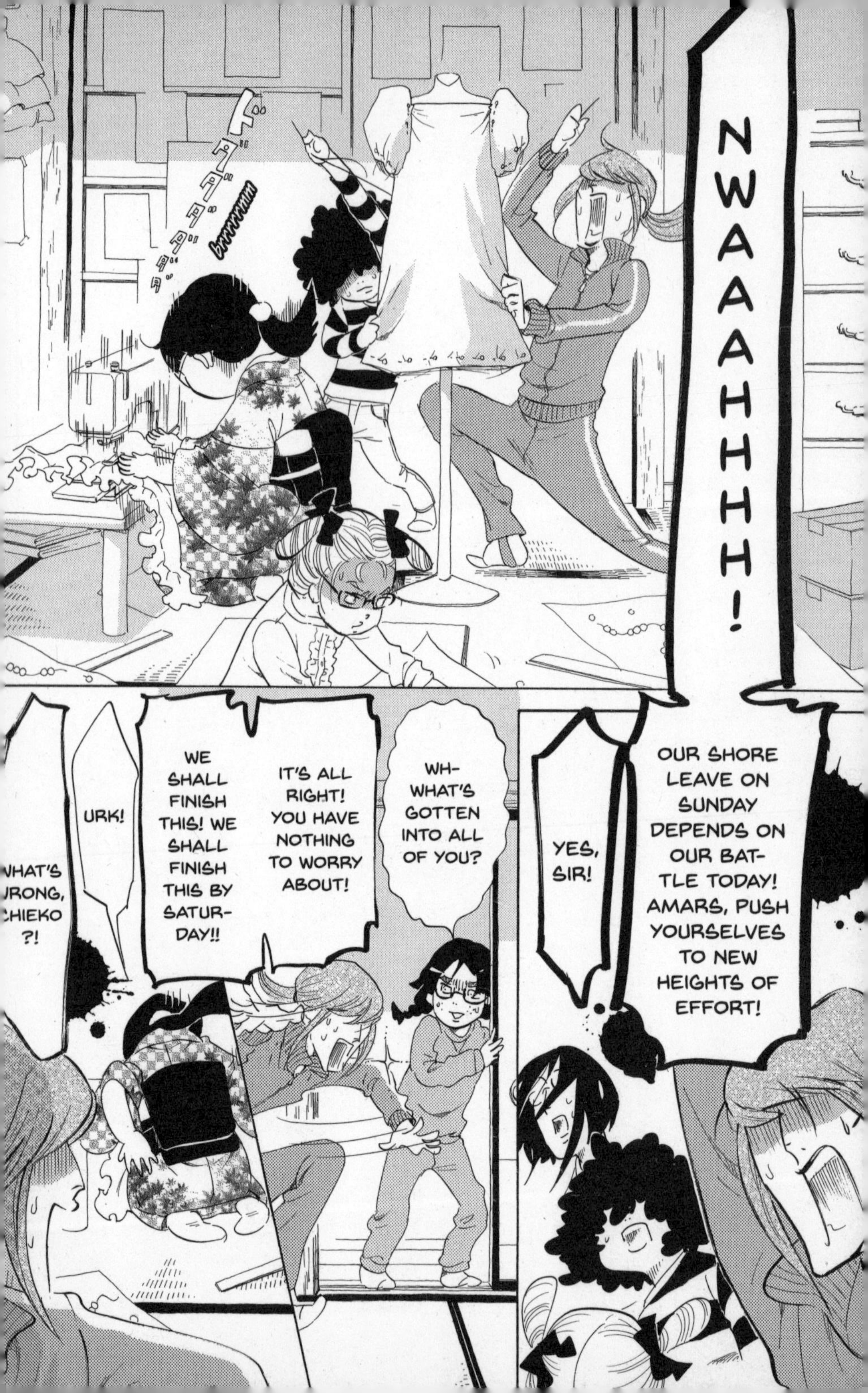
NWAAAHHHH!
brrrrrrmm
OUR SHORE LEAVE ON SUNDAY DEPENDS ON OUR BAT-TLE TODAY! AMARS, PUSH YOURSELVES TO NEW HEIGHTS OF EFFORT!
YES, SIR!
WH-WHAT'S GOTTEN INTO ALL OF YOU?
IT'S ALL RIGHT! YOU HAVE NOTHING TO WORRY ABOUT!
WE SHALL FINISH THIS! WE SHALL FINISH THIS BY SATUR-DAY!!
URK!
WHAT'S WRONG, CHIEKO ?!

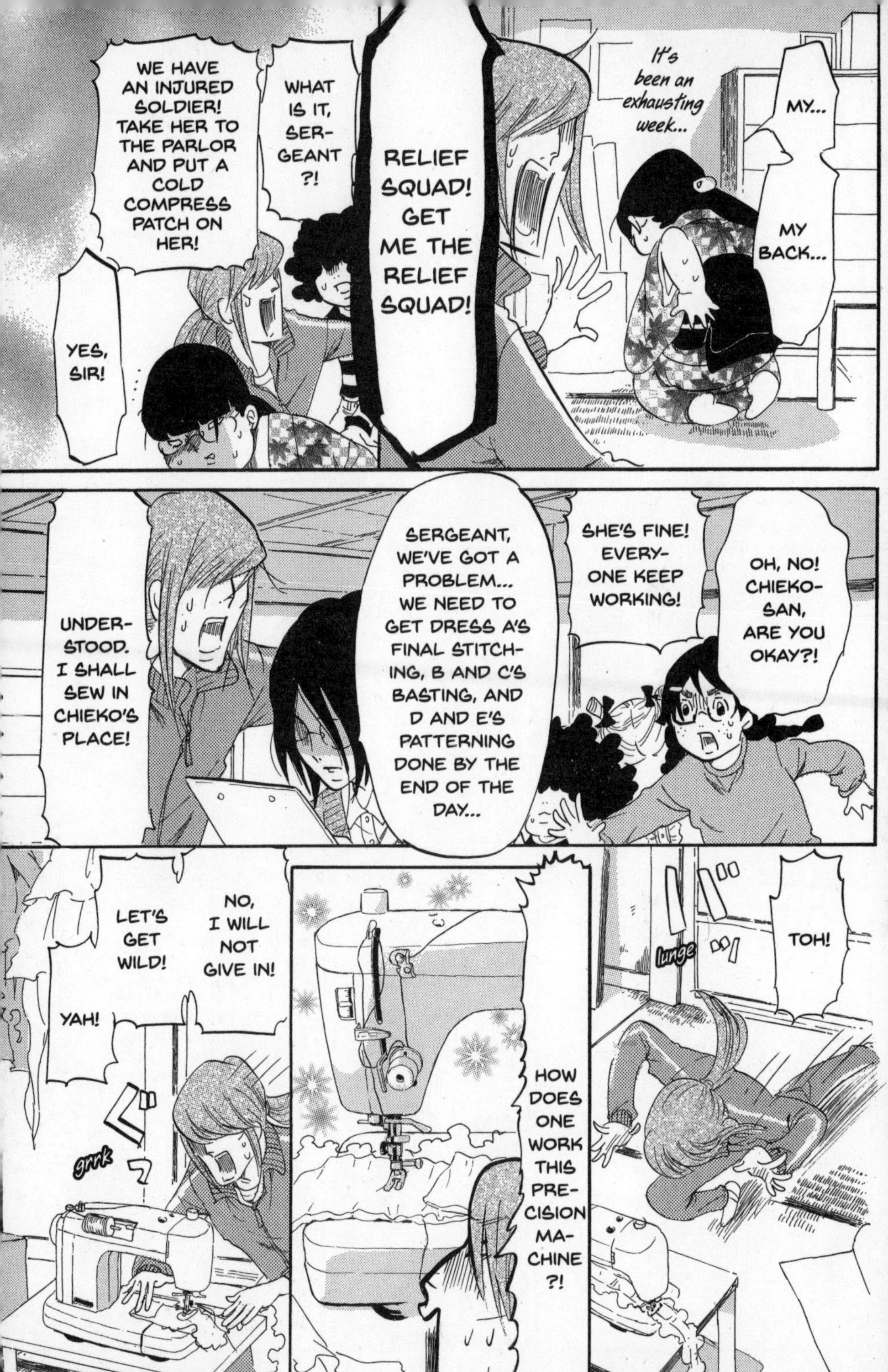
MY...
It's been an exhausting week...
MY BACK...
RELIEF SQUAD! GET ME THE RELIEF SQUAD!
WHAT IS IT, SER-GEANT?!
WE HAVE AN INJURED SOLDIER! TAKE HER TO THE PARLOR AND PUT A COLD COMPRESS PATCH ON HER!
YES, SIR!
OH, NO! CHIEKO-SAN, ARE YOU OKAY?!
SHE'S FINE! EVERY-ONE KEEP WORKING!
SERGEANT, WE'VE GOT A PROBLEM... WE NEED TO GET DRESS A'S FINAL STITCH-ING, B AND C'S BASTING, AND D AND E'S PATTERNING DONE BY THE END OF THE DAY...
UNDER-STOOD. I SHALL SEW IN CHIEKO'S PLACE!
TOH!
lunge
HOW DOES ONE WORK THIS PRE-CISION MA-CHINE?!
NO, I WILL NOT GIVE IN!
LET'S GET WILD!
YAH!
grrk

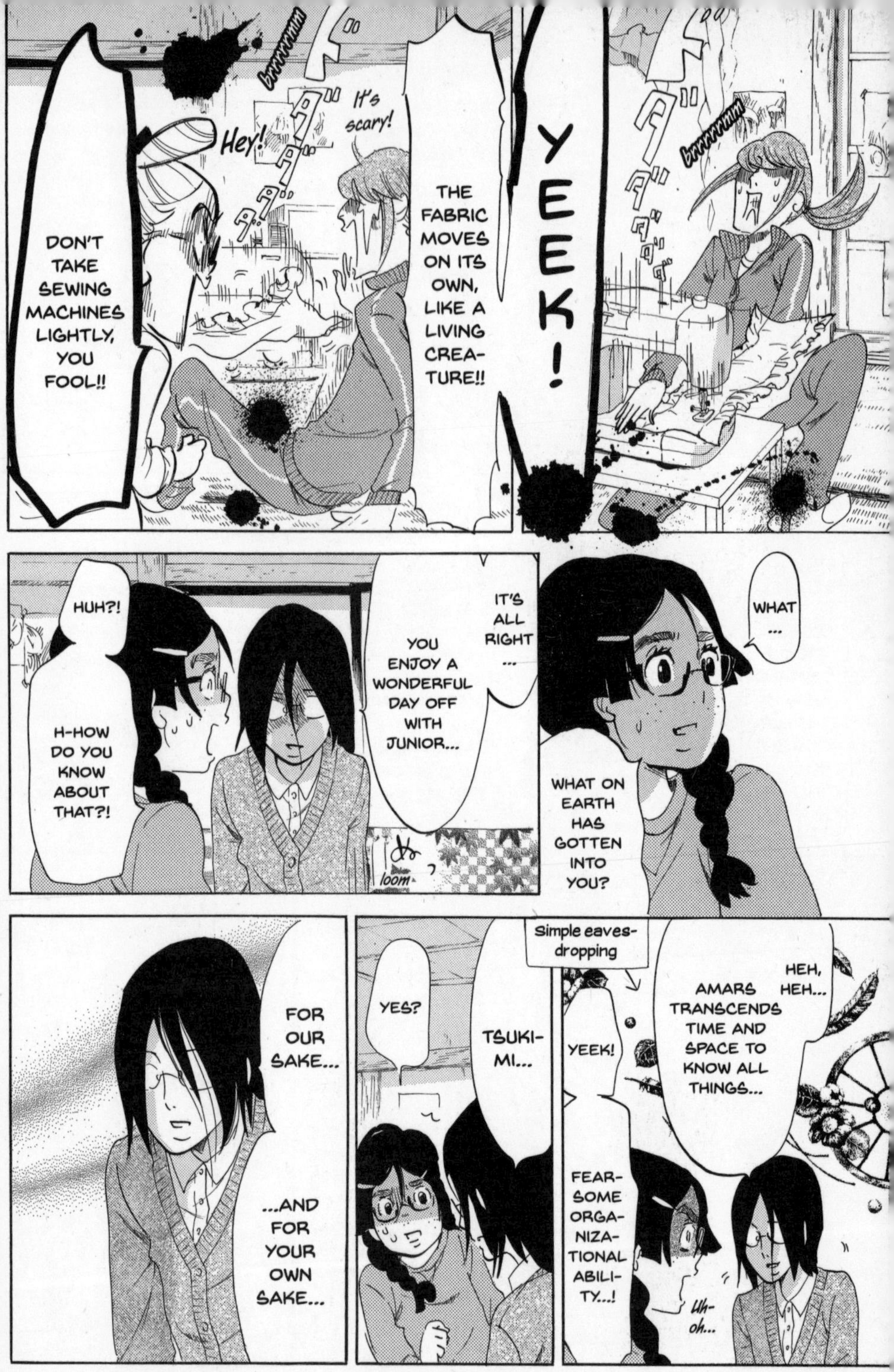
brrrrrrmm
YEEK!
THE FABRIC MOVES ON ITS OWN, LIKE A LIVING CREATURE!!
It's scary!
brrrrrrmm
Hey!
DON'T TAKE SEWING MACHINES LIGHTLY, YOU FOOL!!
WHAT ...
WHAT ON EARTH HAS GOTTEN INTO YOU?
IT'S ALL RIGHT ...
YOU ENJOY A WONDERFUL DAY OFF WITH JUNIOR...
loom
HUH?!
H-HOW DO YOU KNOW ABOUT THAT?!
Simple eaves-dropping
HEH, HEH...
AMARS TRANSCENDS TIME AND SPACE TO KNOW ALL THINGS...
YEEK!
FEAR-SOME ORGA-NIZA-TIONAL ABILI-TY...!
Uh-oh...
TSUKI-MI...
YES?
FOR OUR SAKE...
...AND FOR YOUR OWN SAKE...

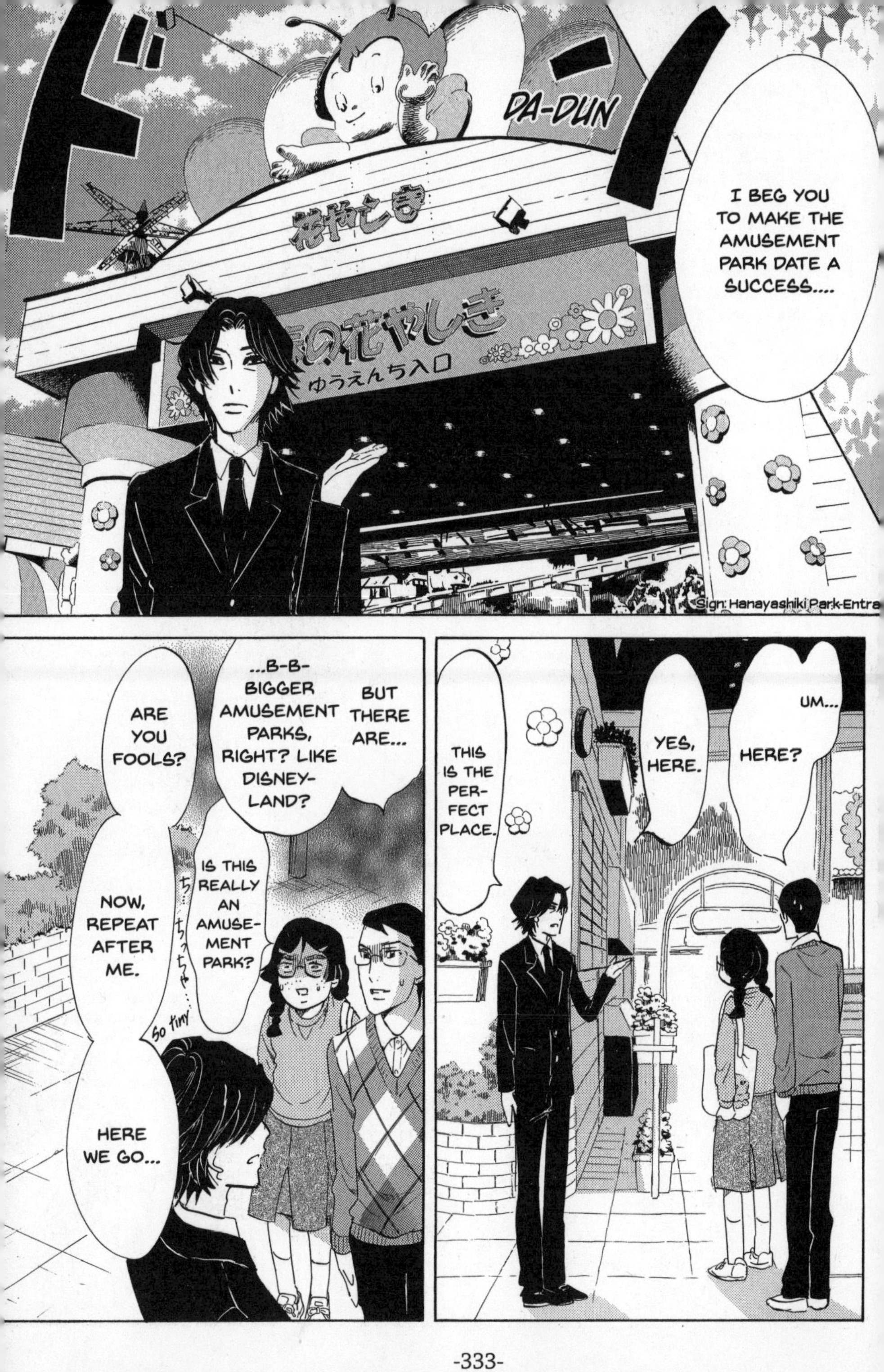
ドドーン
DA-DUN
I BEG YOU TO MAKE THE AMUSEMENT PARK DATE A SUCCESS....
花やしき
ゆうえんち入口
Sign: Hanayashiki Park-Entra
UM... HERE?
YES, HERE.
THIS IS THE PERFECT PLACE.
BUT THERE ARE...
...B-B-BIGGER AMUSEMENT PARKS, RIGHT? LIKE DISNEY-LAND?
ARE YOU FOOLS?
IS THIS REALLY AN AMUSEMENT PARK?
ちっちゃ…
So tiny
NOW, REPEAT AFTER ME.
HERE WE GO...

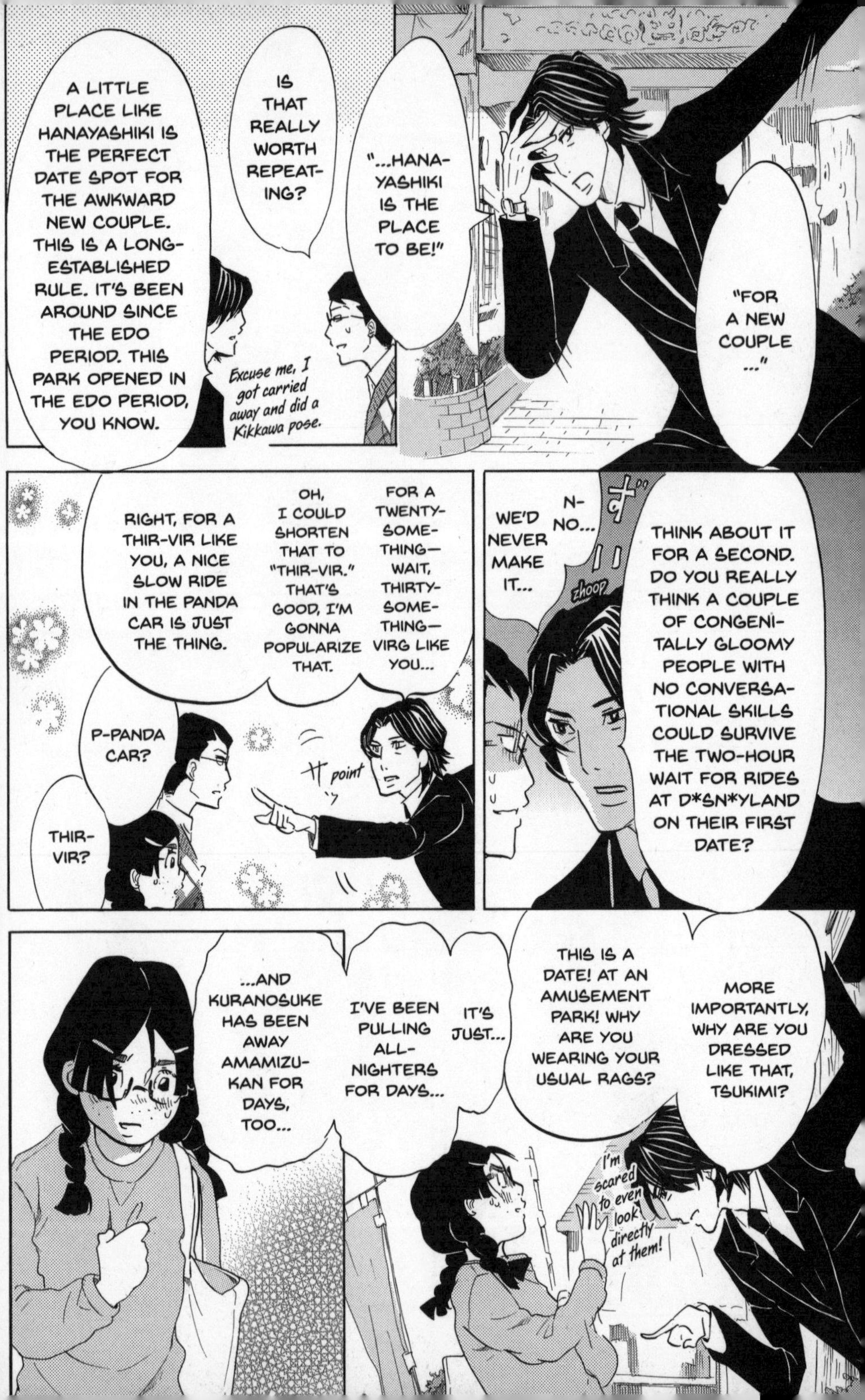
"FOR A NEW COUPLE ..."
"...HANAYASHIKI IS THE PLACE TO BE!"
IS THAT REALLY WORTH REPEATING?
A LITTLE PLACE LIKE HANAYASHIKI IS THE PERFECT DATE SPOT FOR THE AWKWARD NEW COUPLE. THIS IS A LONG-ESTABLISHED RULE. IT'S BEEN AROUND SINCE THE EDO PERIOD. THIS PARK OPENED IN THE EDO PERIOD, YOU KNOW.
Excuse me, I got carried away and did a Kikkawa pose.
THINK ABOUT IT FOR A SECOND. DO YOU REALLY THINK A COUPLE OF CONGENITALLY GLOOMY PEOPLE WITH NO CONVERSATIONAL SKILLS COULD SURVIVE THE TWO-HOUR WAIT FOR RIDES AT D*SN*YLAND ON THEIR FIRST DATE?
N-NO...
WE'D NEVER MAKE IT...
zhoop
FOR A TWENTY-SOMETHING—WAIT, THIRTY-SOMETHING—VIRG LIKE YOU...
OH, I COULD SHORTEN THAT TO "THIR-VIR." THAT'S GOOD, I'M GONNA POPULARIZE THAT.
RIGHT, FOR A THIR-VIR LIKE YOU, A NICE SLOW RIDE IN THE PANDA CAR IS JUST THE THING.
point
P-PANDA CAR?
THIR-VIR?
MORE IMPORTANTLY, WHY ARE YOU DRESSED LIKE THAT, TSUKIMI?
THIS IS A DATE! AT AN AMUSEMENT PARK! WHY ARE YOU WEARING YOUR USUAL RAGS?
IT'S JUST...
I'VE BEEN PULLING ALL-NIGHTERS FOR DAYS...
I'm scared to even look directly at them!
...AND KURANOSUKE HAS BEEN AWAY AMAMIZUKAN FOR DAYS, TOO...

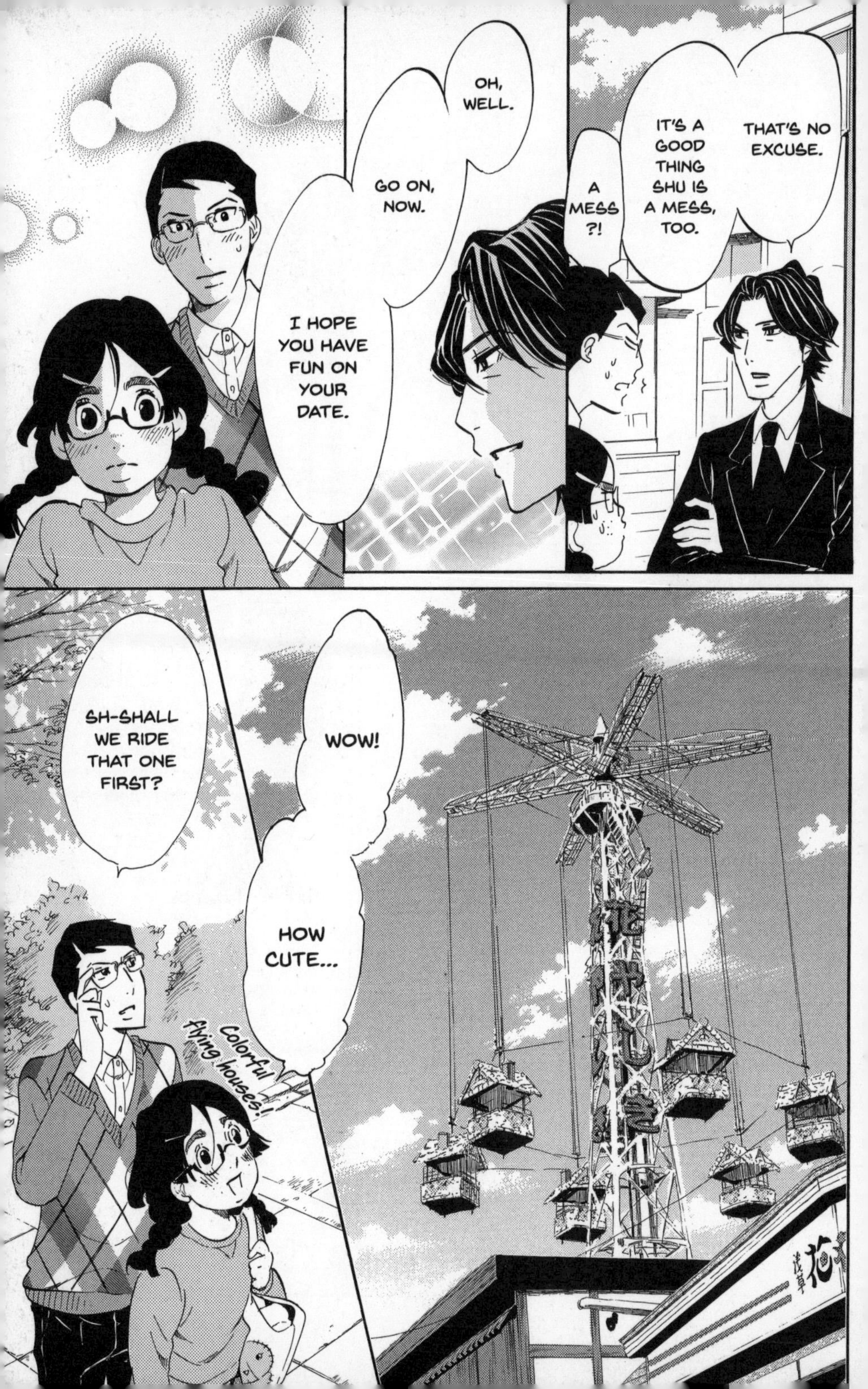
THAT'S NO EXCUSE.
IT'S A GOOD THING SHU IS A MESS, TOO.
A MESS?!
OH, WELL.
GO ON, NOW.
I HOPE YOU HAVE FUN ON YOUR DATE.
WOW!
HOW CUTE...
Colorful flying houses!
SH-SHALL WE RIDE THAT ONE FIRST?

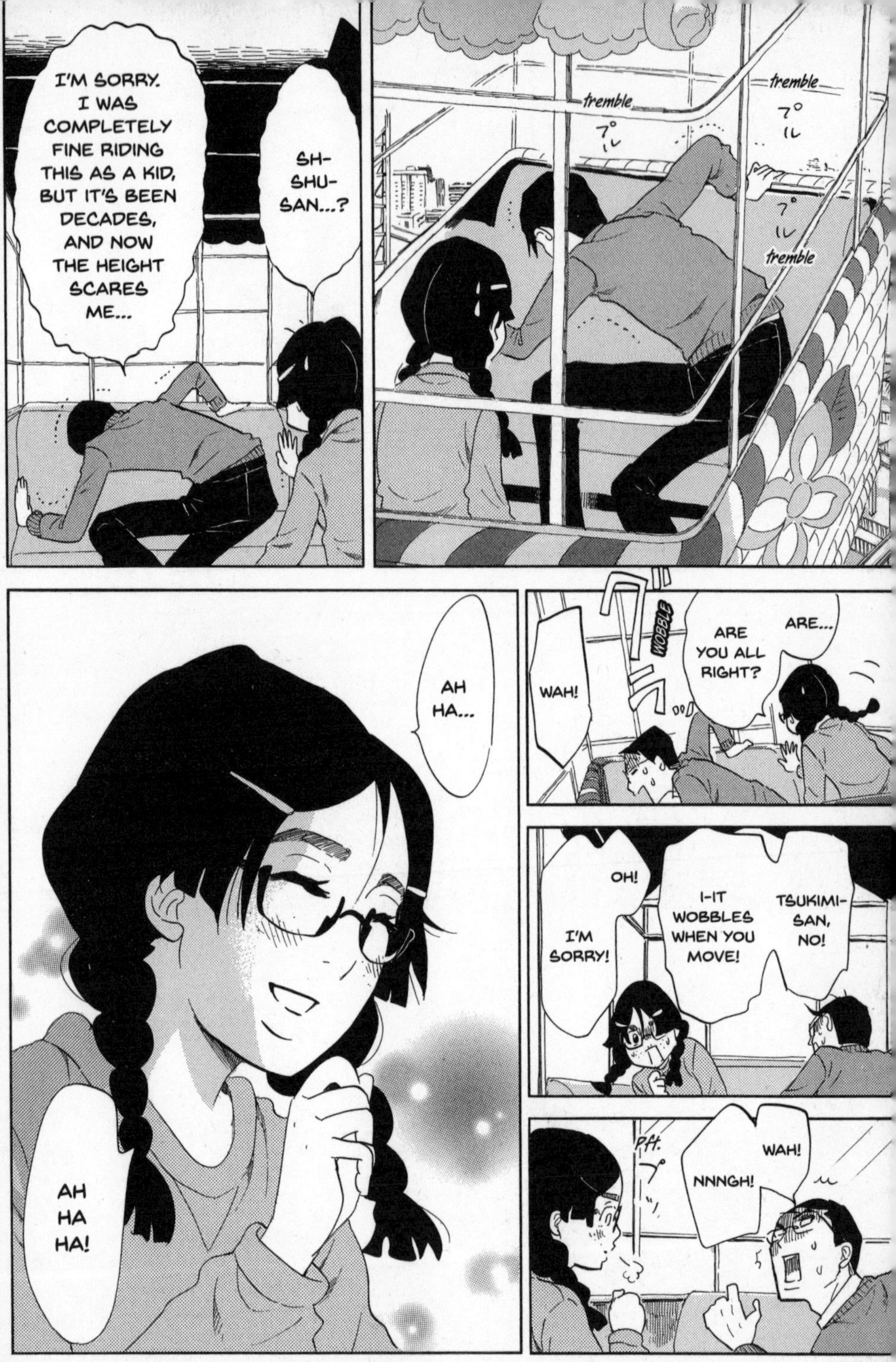
tremble
プル
tremble
プル
tremble
SH-SHU-SAN...?
I'M SORRY. I WAS COMPLETELY FINE RIDING THIS AS A KID, BUT IT'S BEEN DECADES, AND NOW THE HEIGHT SCARES ME...
ARE...
ARE YOU ALL RIGHT?
WOBBLE
WAH!
TSUKIMI-SAN, NO!
I-IT WOBBLES WHEN YOU MOVE!
OH!
I'M SORRY!
WAH!
NNNGH!
Pft.
AH HA...
AH HA HA!

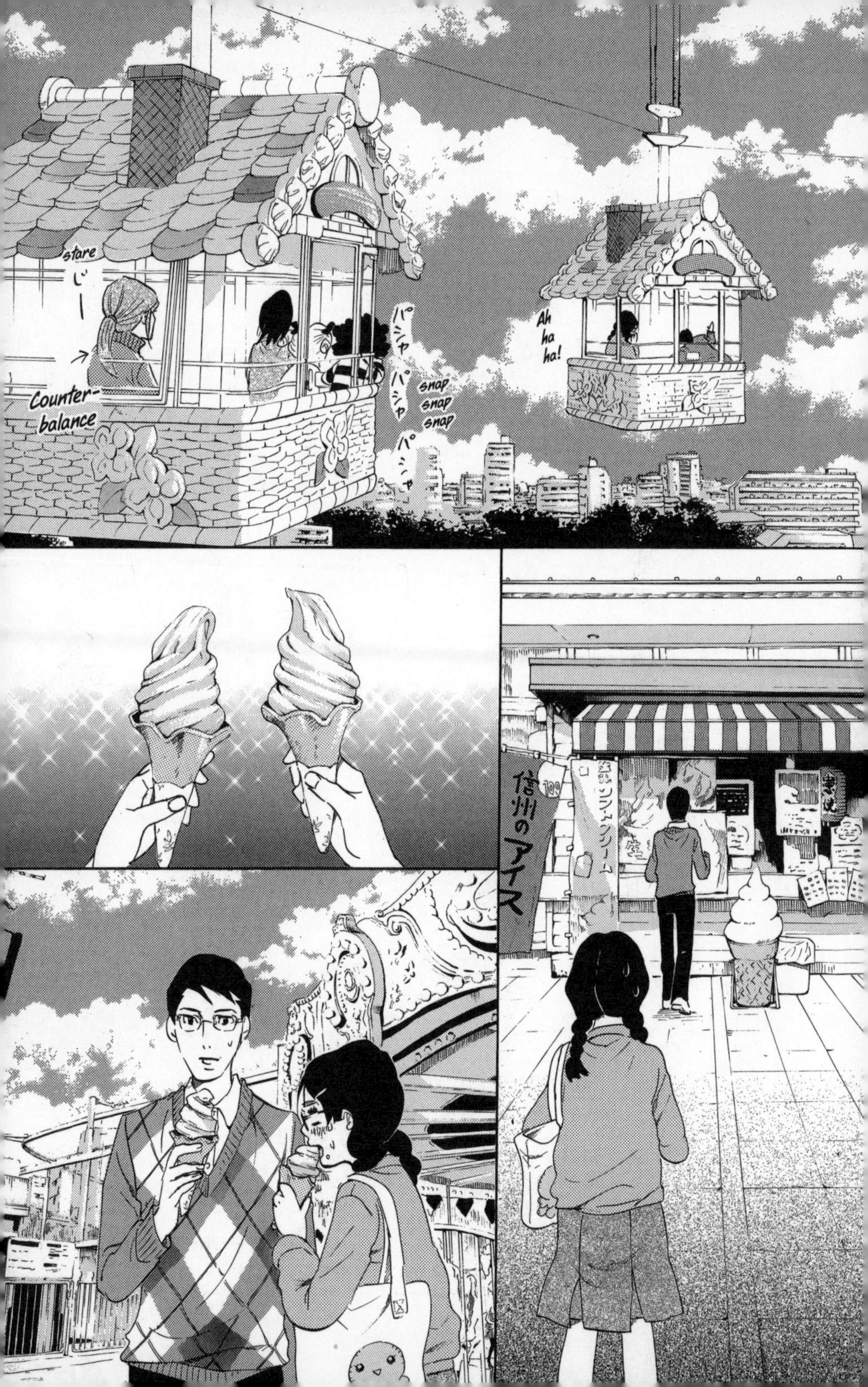
Ah ha ha!
snap snap snap
パシャ パシャ パシャ
stare
じー
Counter-balance
信州のアイス
100

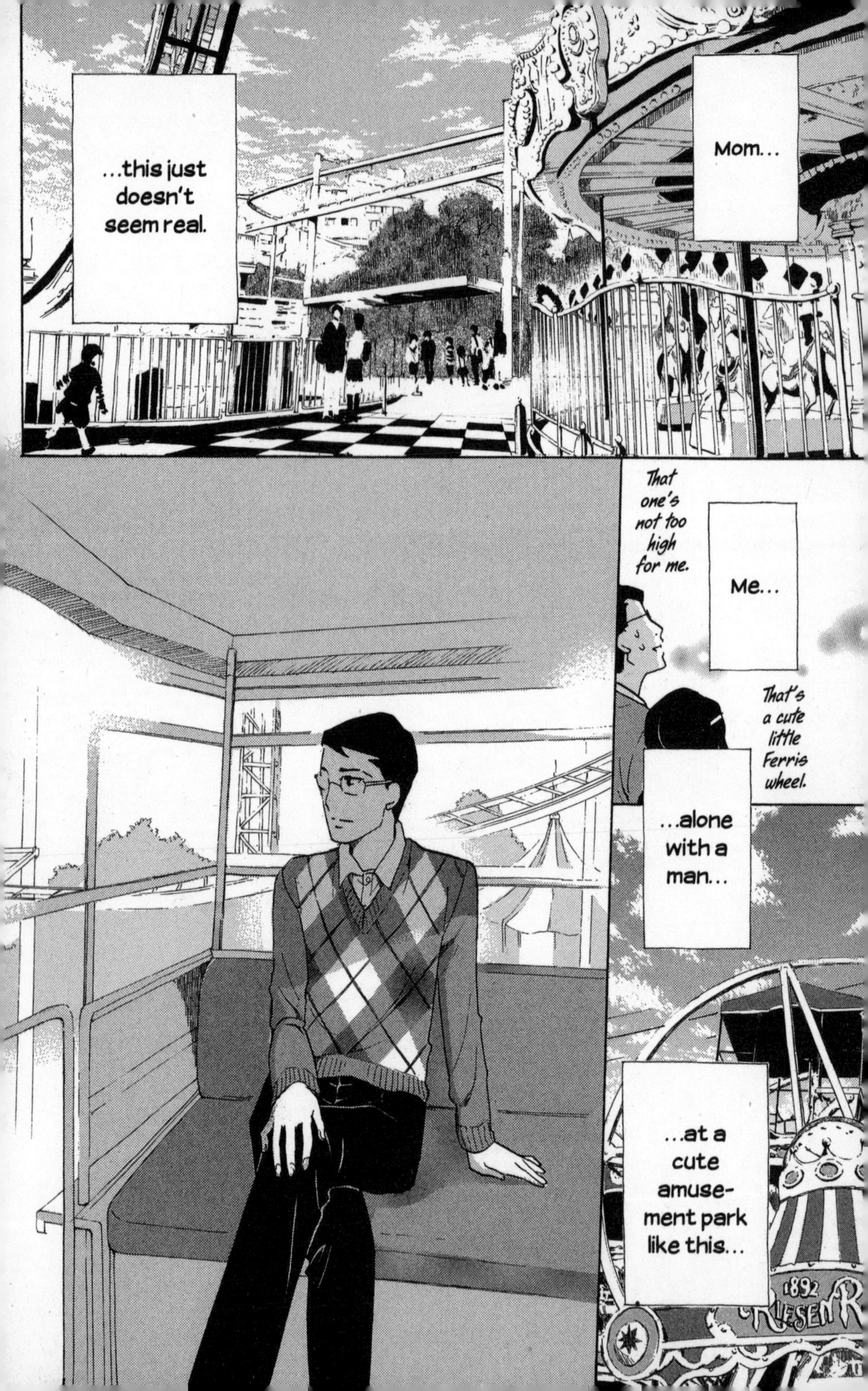
Mom...
...this just doesn't seem real.
Me...
That one's not too high for me.
That's a cute little Ferris wheel.
...alone with a man...
...at a cute amusement-ment park like this...
1892

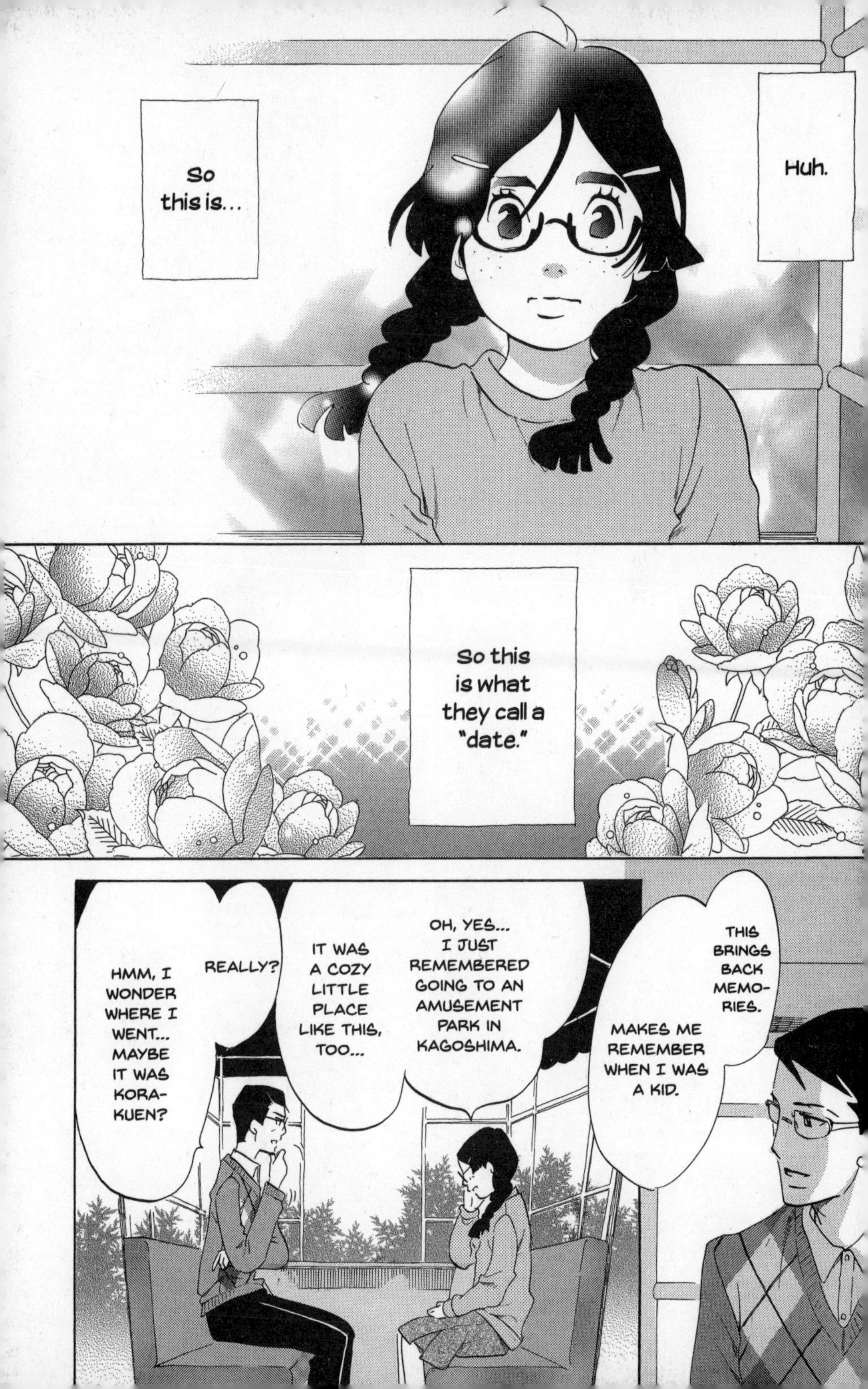
Huh.
So this is...
So this is what they call a "date."
THIS BRINGS BACK MEMORIES.
MAKES ME REMEMBER WHEN I WAS A KID.
OH, YES... I JUST REMEMBERED GOING TO AN AMUSEMENT PARK IN KAGOSHIMA.
IT WAS A COZY LITTLE PLACE LIKE THIS, TOO...
REALLY?
HMM, I WONDER WHERE I WENT... MAYBE IT WAS KORAKUEN?

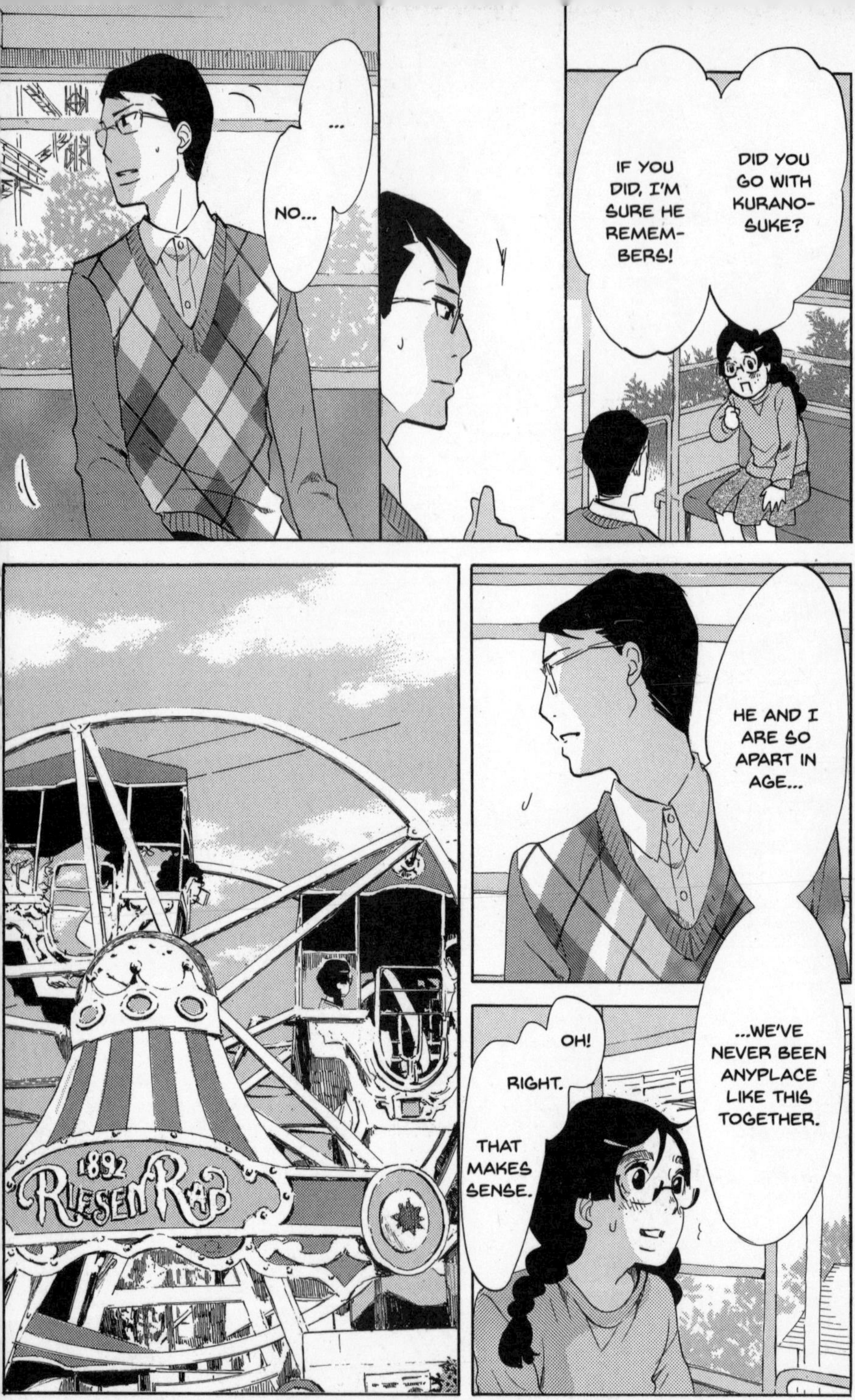
DID YOU GO WITH KURANO-SUKE?
IF YOU DID, I'M SURE HE REMEMBERS!
...
NO...
HE AND I ARE SO APART IN AGE...
...WE'VE NEVER BEEN ANYPLACE LIKE THIS TOGETHER.
OH!
RIGHT.
THAT MAKES SENSE.
1892
RIESEN RAD

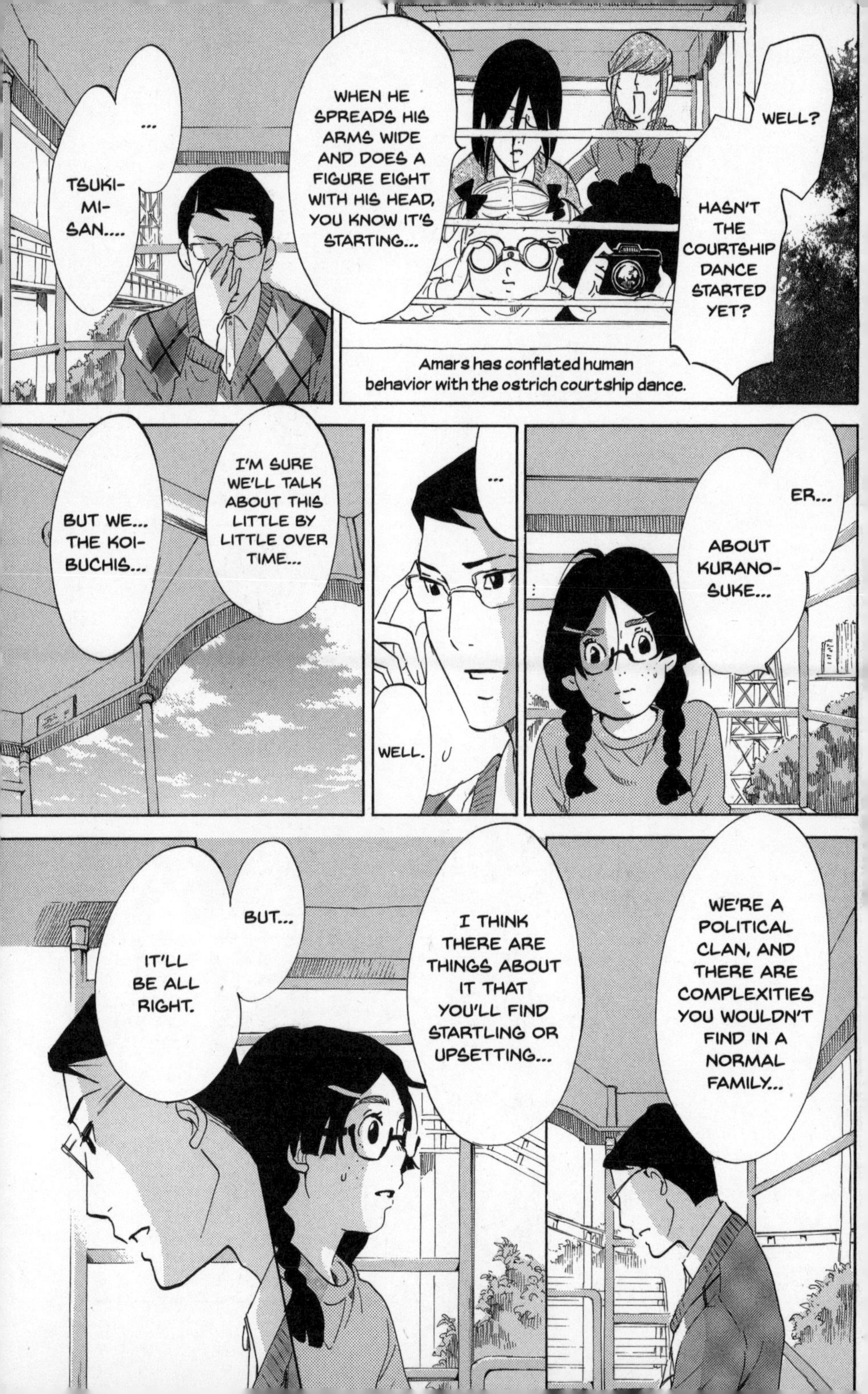
WELL?
HASN'T THE COURTSHIP DANCE STARTED YET?
WHEN HE SPREADS HIS ARMS WIDE AND DOES A FIGURE EIGHT WITH HIS HEAD, YOU KNOW IT'S STARTING...
Amars has conflated human behavior with the ostrich courtship dance.
...
TSUKIMI-SAN....
ER...
ABOUT KURANOSUKE...
...
WELL.
I'M SURE WE'LL TALK ABOUT THIS LITTLE BY LITTLE OVER TIME...
BUT WE... THE KOIBUCHIS...
WE'RE A POLITICAL CLAN, AND THERE ARE COMPLEXITIES YOU WOULDN'T FIND IN A NORMAL FAMILY...
I THINK THERE ARE THINGS ABOUT IT THAT YOU'LL FIND STARTLING OR UPSETTING...
BUT...
IT'LL BE ALL RIGHT.

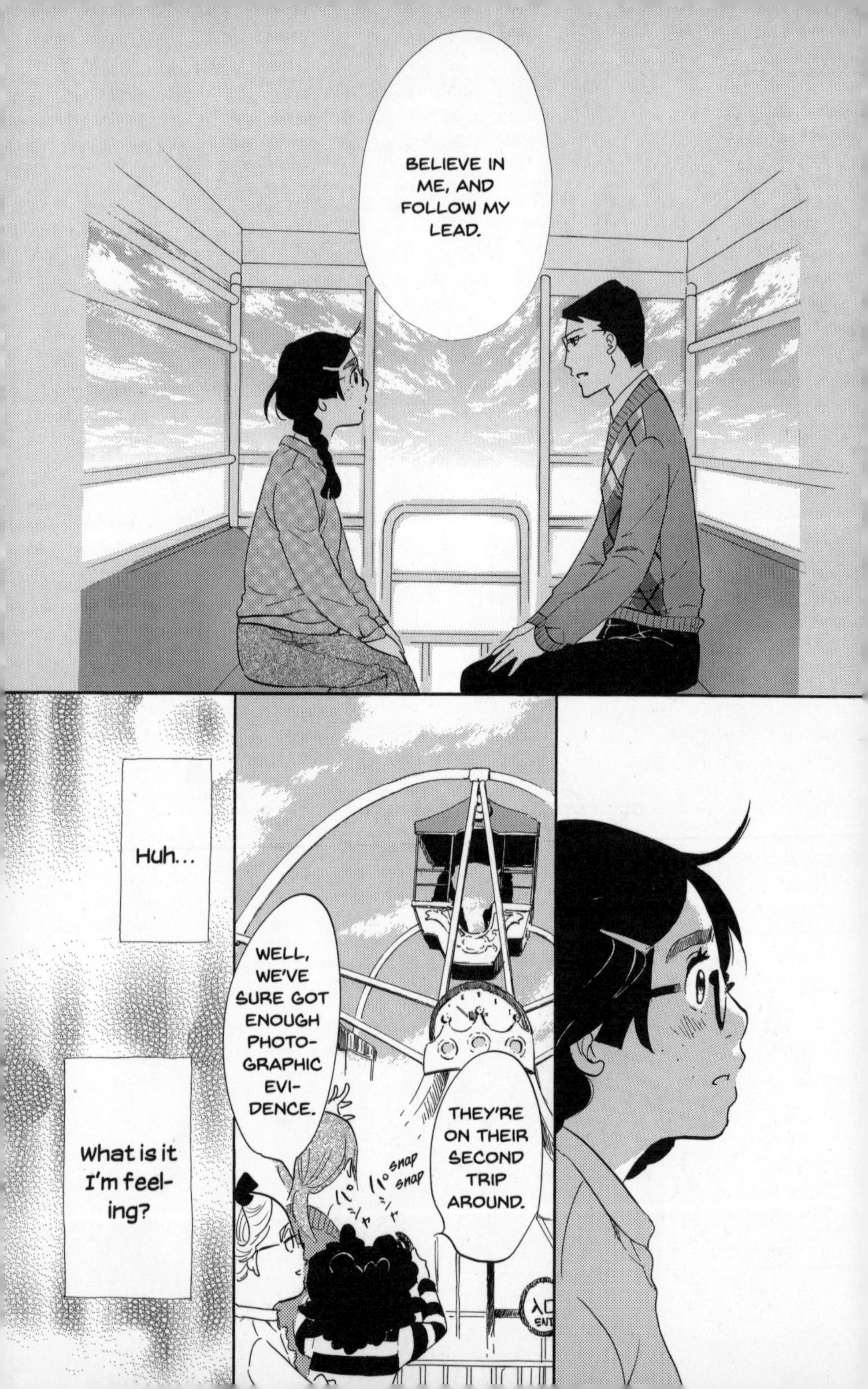
BELIEVE IN ME, AND FOLLOW MY LEAD.
THEY'RE ON THEIR SECOND TRIP AROUND.
WELL, WE'VE SURE GOT ENOUGH PHOTO-GRAPHIC EVI-DENCE.
snap snap
Huh...
What is it I'm feel-ing?

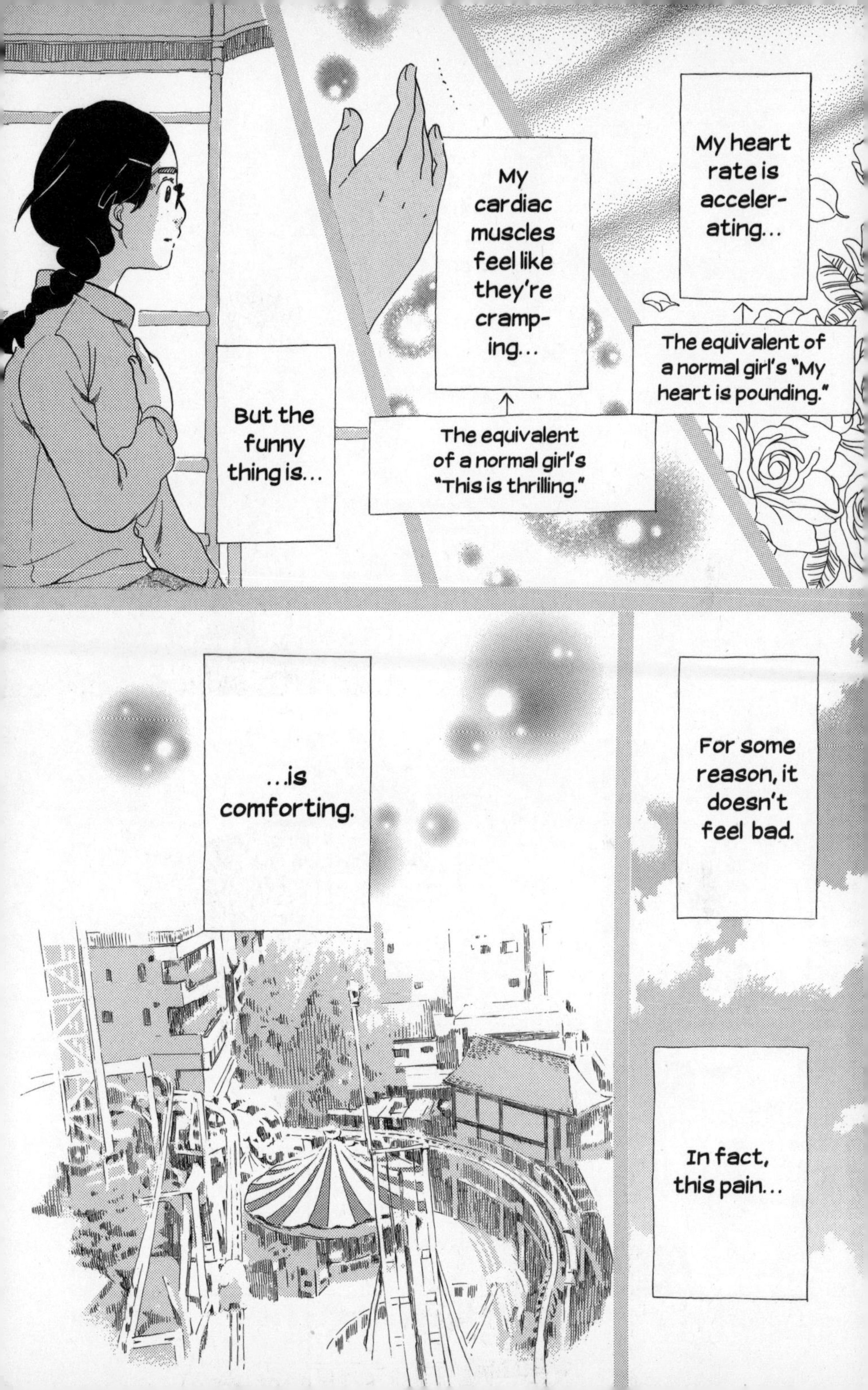

My heart rate is acceler-ating...
The equivalent of a normal girl's "My heart is pounding."
My cardiac muscles feel like they're cramp-ing...
The equivalent of a normal girl's "This is thrilling."
But the funny thing is...
For some reason, it doesn't feel bad.
In fact, this pain...
...is comforting.

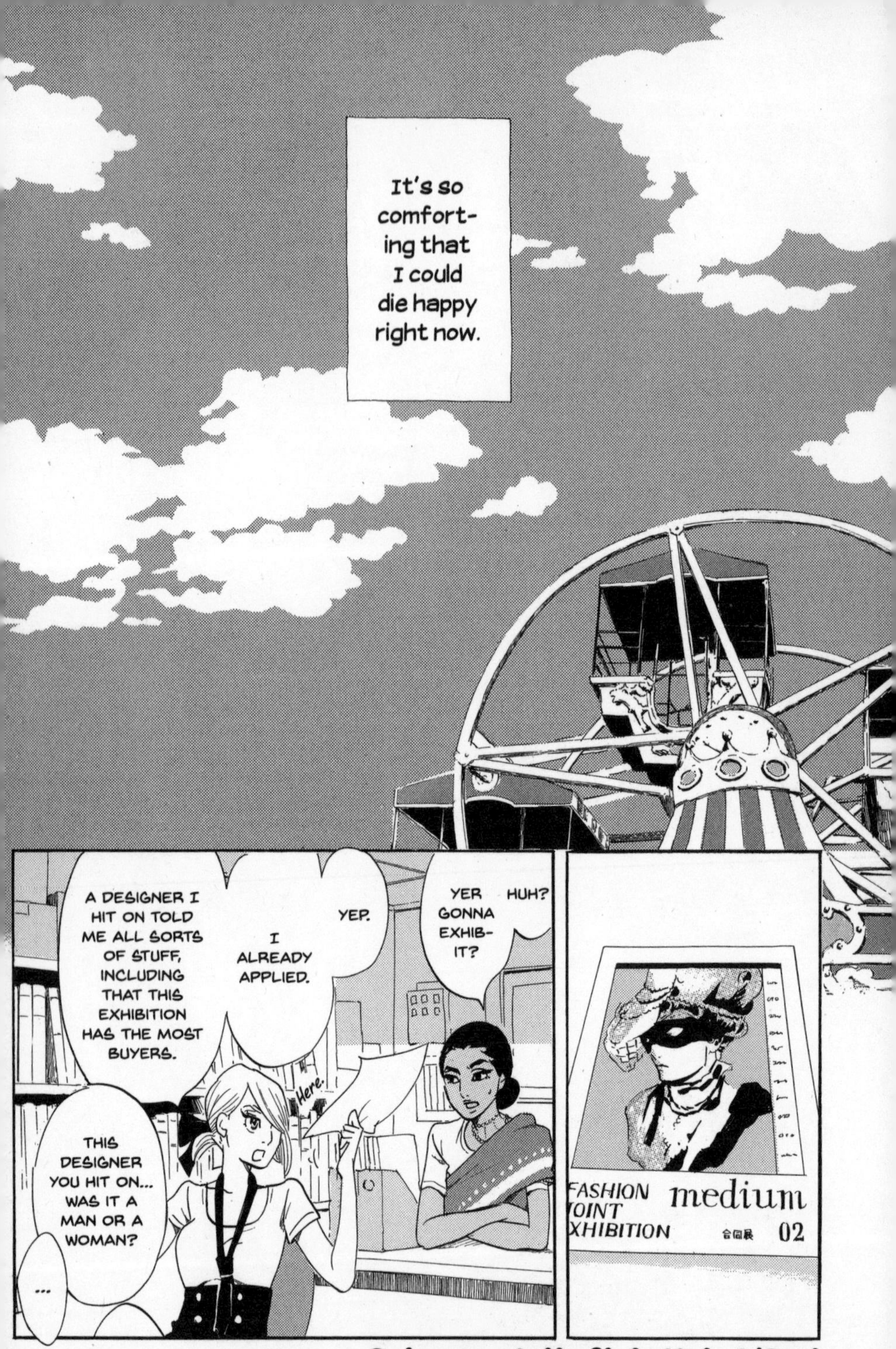
It's so comforting that I could die happy right now.
FASHION JOINT EXHIBITION
medium
合同展
02
HUH?
YER GONNA EXHIB-IT?
YEP.
I ALREADY APPLIED.
A DESIGNER I HIT ON TOLD ME ALL SORTS OF STUFF, INCLUDING THAT THIS EXHIBITION HAS THE MOST BUYERS.
Here.
THIS DESIGNER YOU HIT ON... WAS IT A MAN OR A WOMAN?
...

Princess Jellyfish Vol. 5/End

グオー
snore
snore
グオー

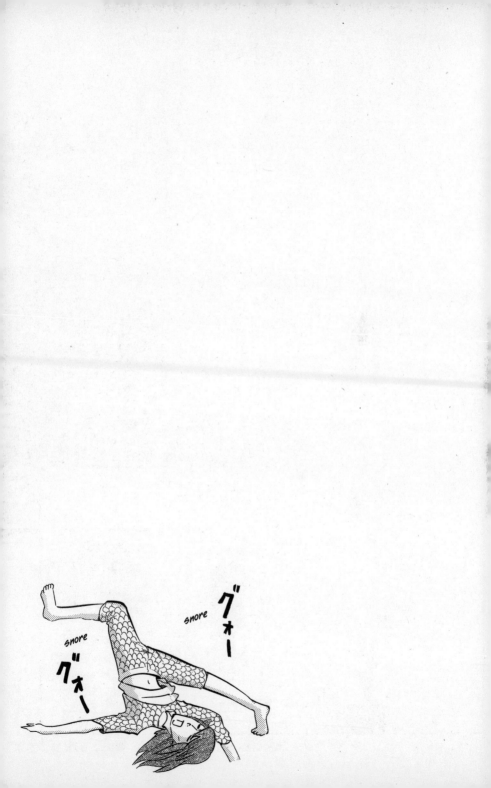

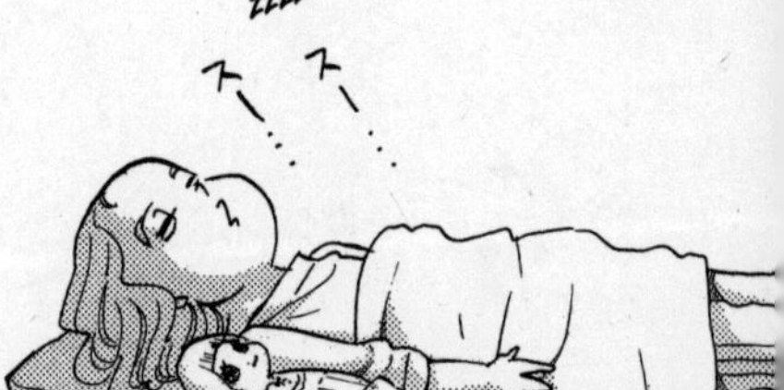
zzzz
zzzz
スー…
スー…

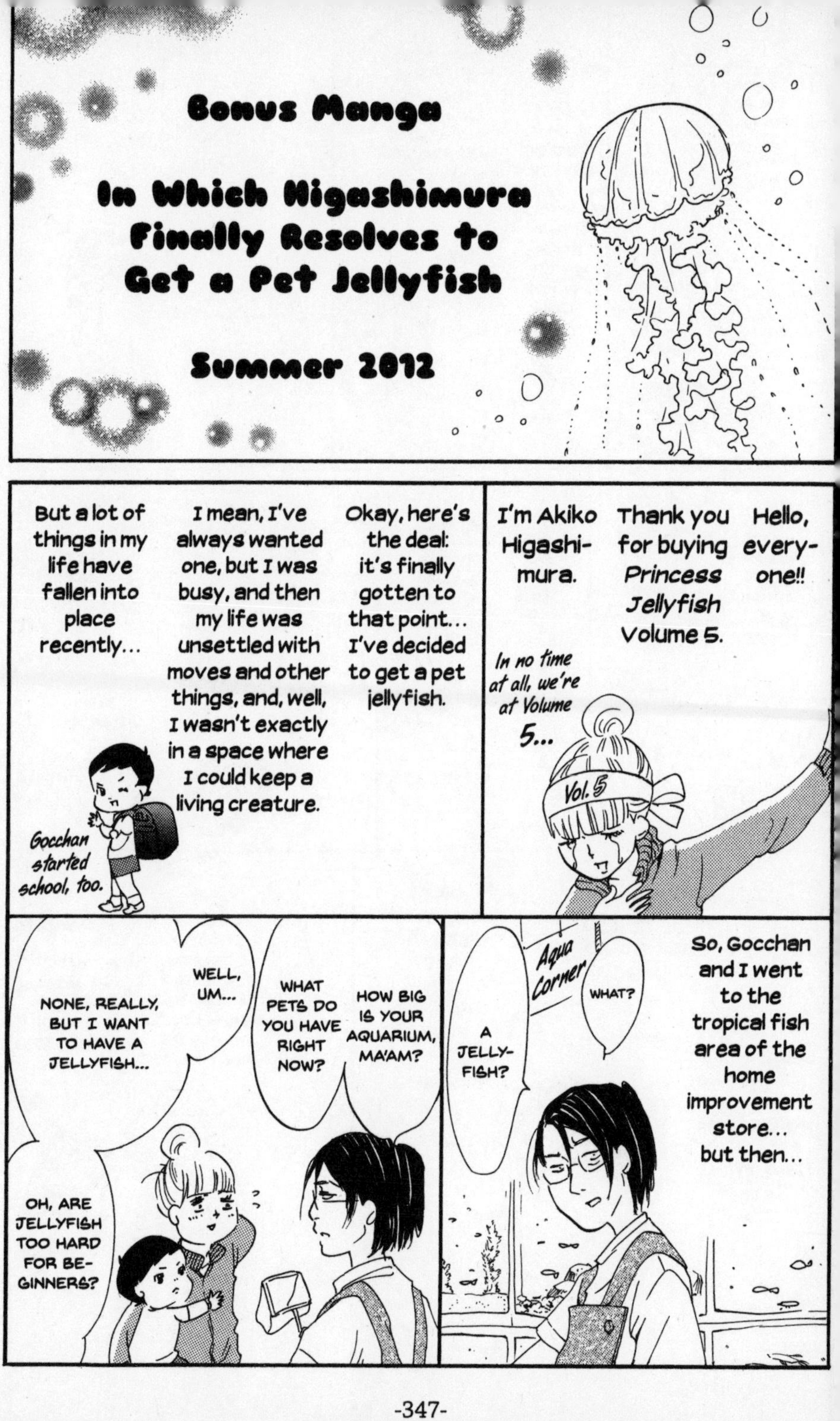
Bonus Manga
In Which Higashimura Finally Resolves to Get a Pet Jellyfish
Summer 2012
Hello, everyone!!
Thank you for buying *Princess Jellyfish* Volume 5.
I'm Akiko Higashimura.
In no time at all, we're at Volume 5...
Vol. 5
Okay, here's the deal: it's finally gotten to that point... I've decided to get a pet jellyfish.
I mean, I've always wanted one, but I was busy, and then my life was unsettled with moves and other things, and, well, I wasn't exactly in a space where I could keep a living creature.
But a lot of things in my life have fallen into place recently...
Gocchan started school, too.
So, Gocchan and I went to the tropical fish area of the home improvement store... but then...
Aqua Corner
WHAT?
A JELLY-FISH?
HOW BIG IS YOUR AQUARIUM, MA'AM?
WHAT PETS DO YOU HAVE RIGHT NOW?
WELL, UM...
NONE, REALLY, BUT I WANT TO HAVE A JELLYFISH...
OH, ARE JELLYFISH TOO HARD FOR BE-GINNERS?

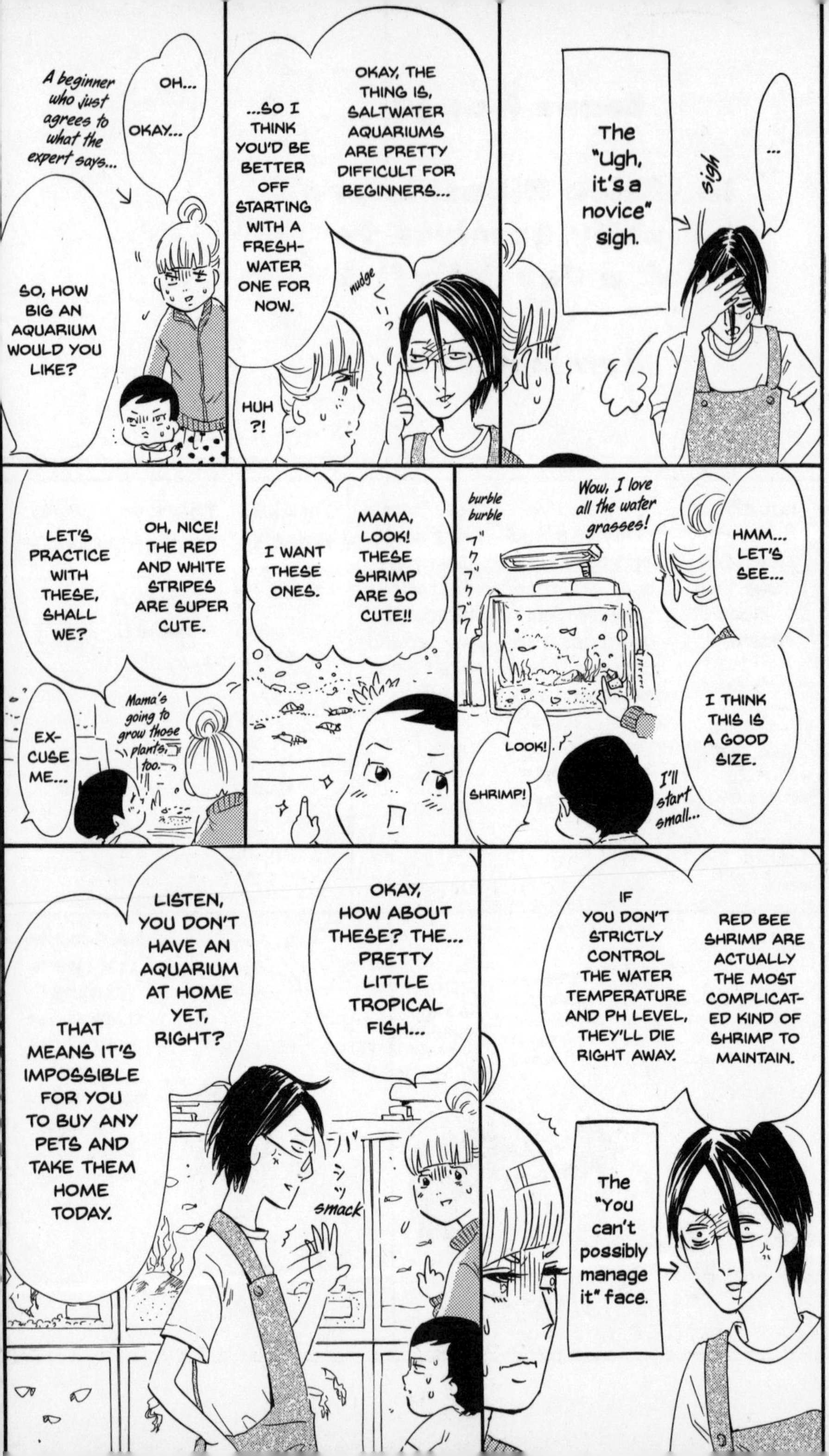
...
sigh
The "Ugh, it's a novice" sigh.
OKAY, THE THING IS, SALTWATER AQUARIUMS ARE PRETTY DIFFICULT FOR BEGINNERS...
...SO I THINK YOU'D BE BETTER OFF STARTING WITH A FRESH-WATER ONE FOR NOW.
nudge
HUH ?!
OH... OKAY...
A beginner who just agrees to what the expert says...
SO, HOW BIG AN AQUARIUM WOULD YOU LIKE?
HMM... LET'S SEE...
Wow, I love all the water grasses!
burble burble
I THINK THIS IS A GOOD SIZE.
LOOK! SHRIMP!
I'll start small...
MAMA, LOOK! THESE SHRIMP ARE SO CUTE!!
I WANT THESE ONES.
OH, NICE! THE RED AND WHITE STRIPES ARE SUPER CUTE.
LET'S PRACTICE WITH THESE, SHALL WE?
Mama's going to grow those plants, too.
EX-CUSE ME...
RED BEE SHRIMP ARE ACTUALLY THE MOST COMPLICAT-ED KIND OF SHRIMP TO MAINTAIN.
IF YOU DON'T STRICTLY CONTROL THE WATER TEMPERATURE AND PH LEVEL, THEY'LL DIE RIGHT AWAY.
The "You can't possibly manage it" face.
OKAY, HOW ABOUT THESE? THE... PRETTY LITTLE TROPICAL FISH...
smack
LISTEN, YOU DON'T HAVE AN AQUARIUM AT HOME YET, RIGHT?
THAT MEANS IT'S IMPOSSIBLE FOR YOU TO BUY ANY PETS AND TAKE THEM HOME TODAY.

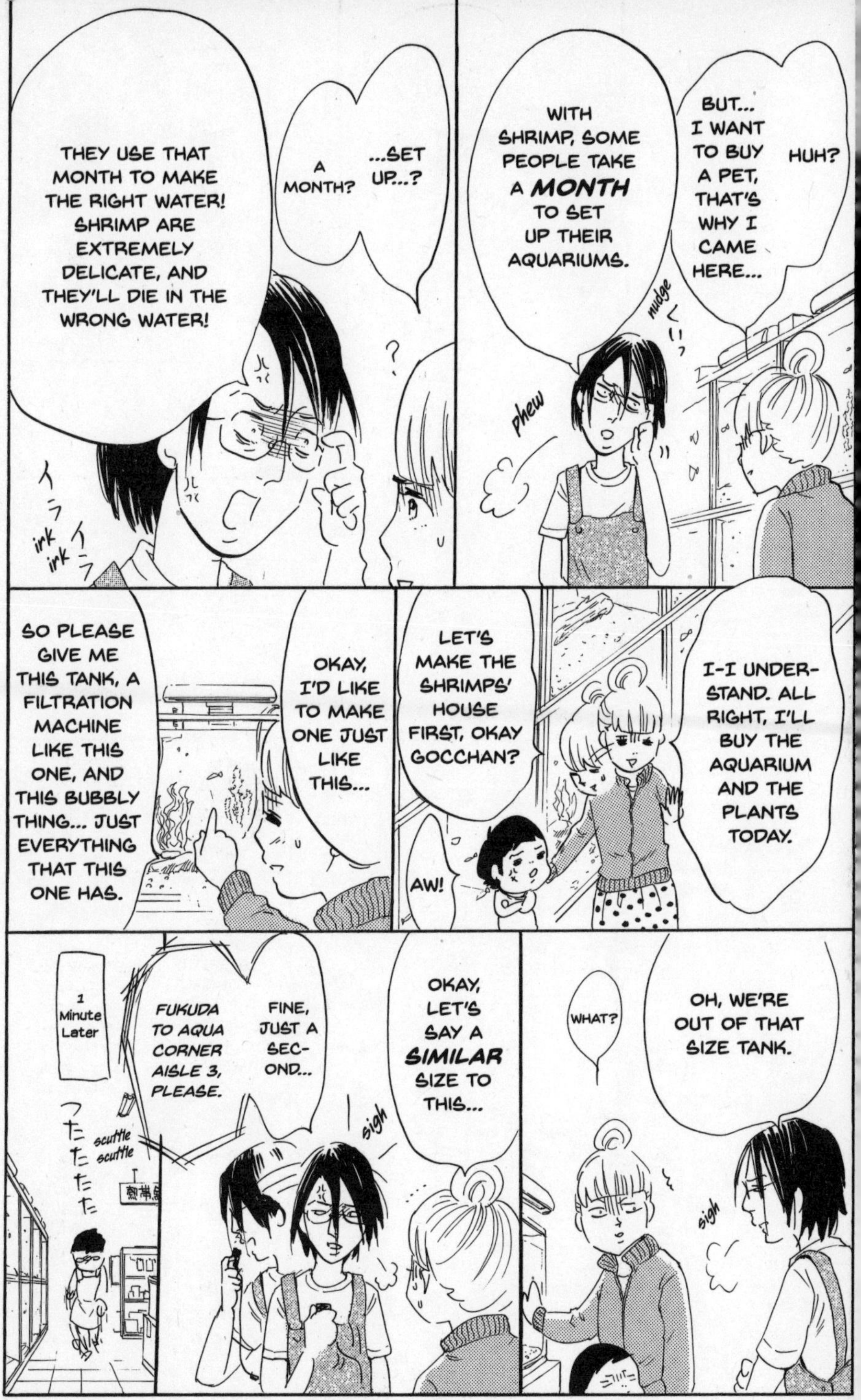
HUH?
BUT... I WANT TO BUY A PET, THAT'S WHY I CAME HERE...
WITH SHRIMP, SOME PEOPLE TAKE A **MONTH** TO SET UP THEIR AQUARIUMS.
nudge
phew
...SET UP...?
A MONTH?
THEY USE THAT MONTH TO MAKE THE RIGHT WATER! SHRIMP ARE EXTREMELY DELICATE, AND THEY'LL DIE IN THE WRONG WATER!
irk irk
I-I UNDERSTAND. ALL RIGHT, I'LL BUY THE AQUARIUM AND THE PLANTS TODAY.
LET'S MAKE THE SHRIMPS' HOUSE FIRST, OKAY GOCCHAN?
AW!
OKAY, I'D LIKE TO MAKE ONE JUST LIKE THIS...
SO PLEASE GIVE ME THIS TANK, A FILTRATION MACHINE LIKE THIS ONE, AND THIS BUBBLY THING... JUST EVERYTHING THAT THIS ONE HAS.
OH, WE'RE OUT OF THAT SIZE TANK.
WHAT?
sigh
OKAY, LET'S SAY A **SIMILAR** SIZE TO THIS...
sigh
FINE, JUST A SEC-OND...
FUKUDA TO AQUA CORNER AISLE 3, PLEASE.
1 Minute Later
scuttle scuttle

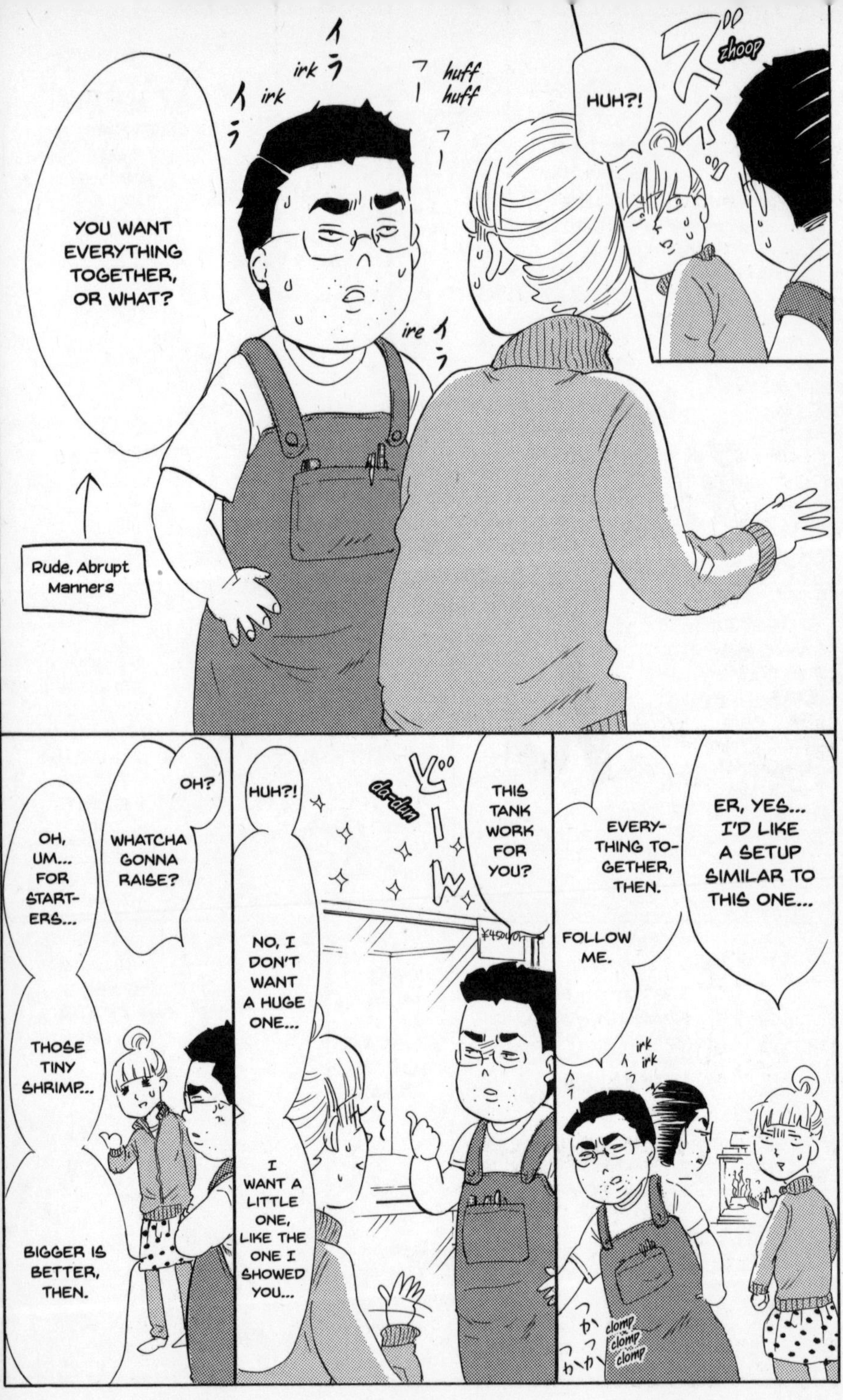
zhoop
HUH?!
huff huff
irk
irk
ire
YOU WANT EVERYTHING TOGETHER, OR WHAT?
Rude, Abrupt Manners
ER, YES... I'D LIKE A SETUP SIMILAR TO THIS ONE...
EVERY-THING TO-GETHER, THEN.
FOLLOW ME.
irk irk
clomp clomp clomp
THIS TANK WORK FOR YOU?
da-dun
HUH?!
NO, I DON'T WANT A HUGE ONE...
I WANT A LITTLE ONE, LIKE THE ONE I SHOWED YOU...
OH?
WHATCHA GONNA RAISE?
OH, UM... FOR START-ERS...
THOSE TINY SHRIMP...
BIGGER IS BETTER, THEN.

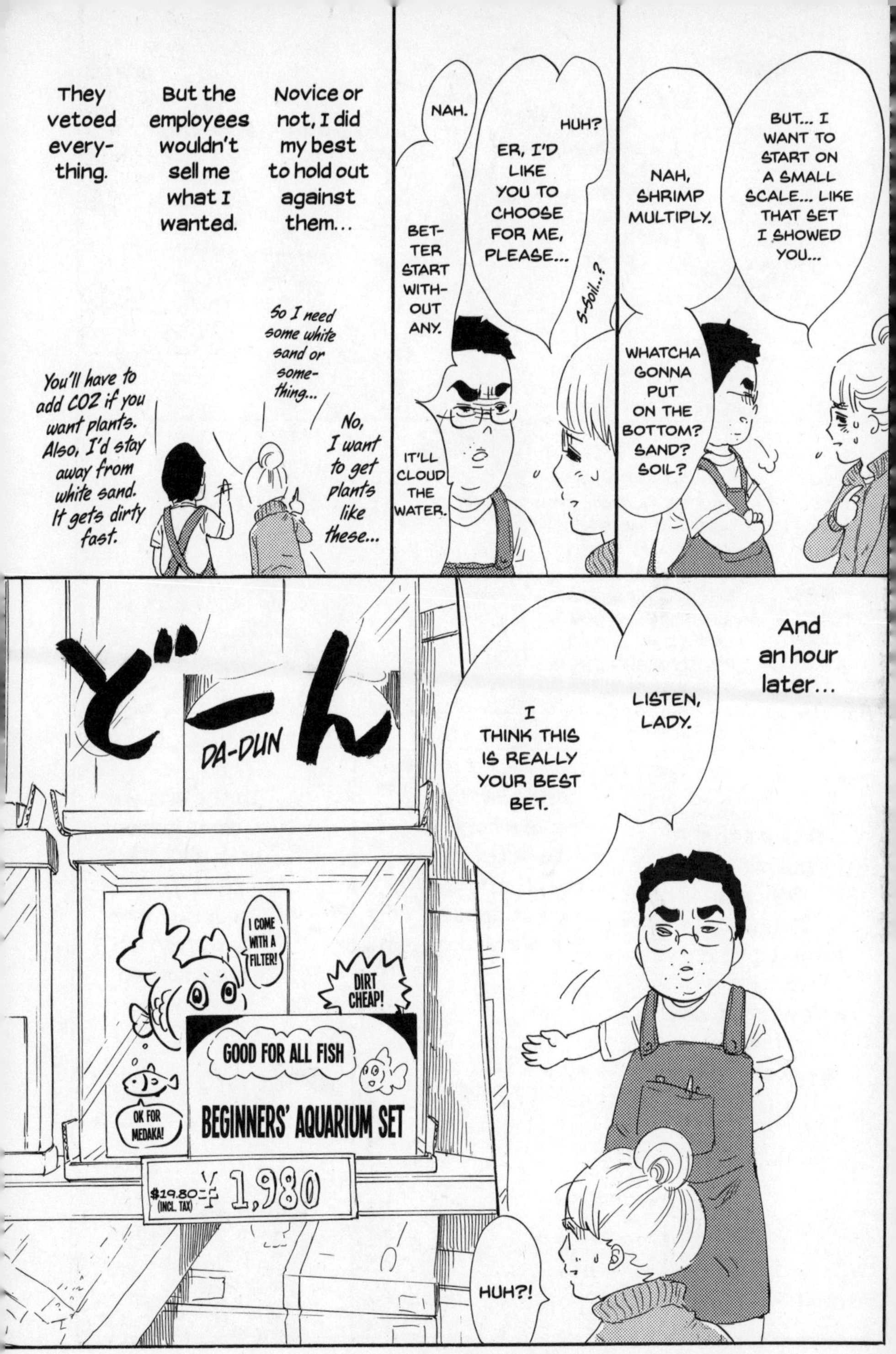
BUT... I WANT TO START ON A SMALL SCALE... LIKE THAT SET I SHOWED YOU...
NAH, SHRIMP MULTIPLY.
WHATCHA GONNA PUT ON THE BOTTOM? SAND? SOIL?
HUH?
ER, I'D LIKE YOU TO CHOOSE FOR ME, PLEASE...
NAH.
S-Soil...?
BET-TER START WITH-OUT ANY.
IT'LL CLOUD THE WATER.
Novice or not, I did my best to hold out against them...
But the employees wouldn't sell me what I wanted.
They vetoed every-thing.
So I need some white sand or some-thing...
No, I want to get plants like these...
You'll have to add CO2 if you want plants. Also, I'd stay away from white sand. It gets dirty fast.
And an hour later...
LISTEN, LADY.
I THINK THIS IS REALLY YOUR BEST BET.
HUH?!
どーん
DA-DUN
I COME WITH A FILTER!
DIRT CHEAP!
GOOD FOR ALL FISH
OK FOR MEDAKA!
BEGINNERS' AQUARIUM SET
$19.80 (INCL. TAX)
¥1,980

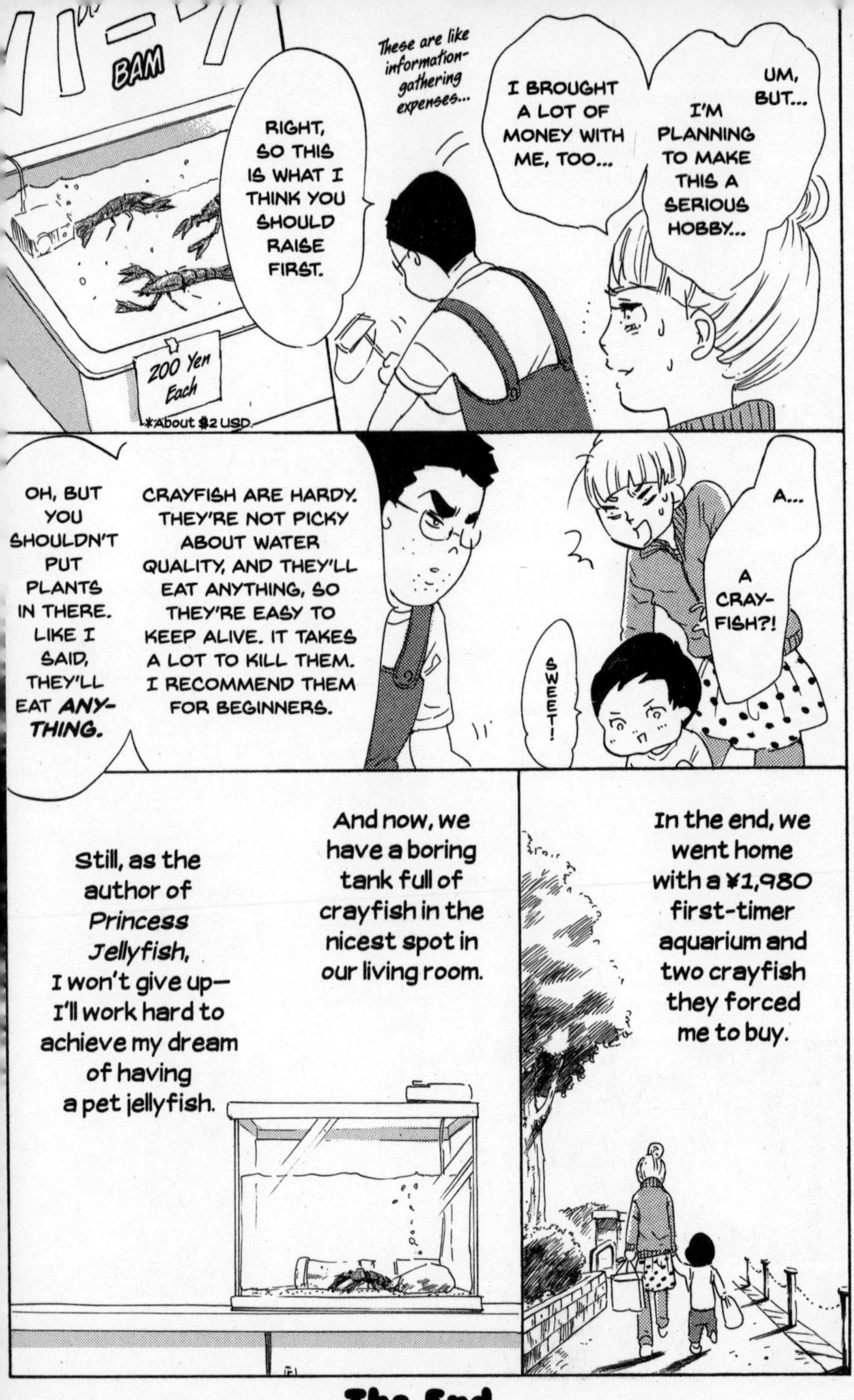
UM, BUT... I'M PLANNING TO MAKE THIS A SERIOUS HOBBY...
I BROUGHT A LOT OF MONEY WITH ME, TOO...
These are like information-gathering expenses...
RIGHT, SO THIS IS WHAT I THINK YOU SHOULD RAISE FIRST.
BAM
200 Yen Each
*About $2 USD.
A... A CRAYFISH?!
SWEET!
CRAYFISH ARE HARDY. THEY'RE NOT PICKY ABOUT WATER QUALITY, AND THEY'LL EAT ANYTHING, SO THEY'RE EASY TO KEEP ALIVE. IT TAKES A LOT TO KILL THEM. I RECOMMEND THEM FOR BEGINNERS.
OH, BUT YOU SHOULDN'T PUT PLANTS IN THERE. LIKE I SAID, THEY'LL EAT *ANYTHING.*
In the end, we went home with a ¥1,980 first-timer aquarium and two crayfish they forced me to buy.
And now, we have a boring tank full of crayfish in the nicest spot in our living room.
Still, as the author of *Princess Jellyfish*, I won't give up—I'll work hard to achieve my dream of having a pet jellyfish.

The End

drag
NNGH ...
OOF!

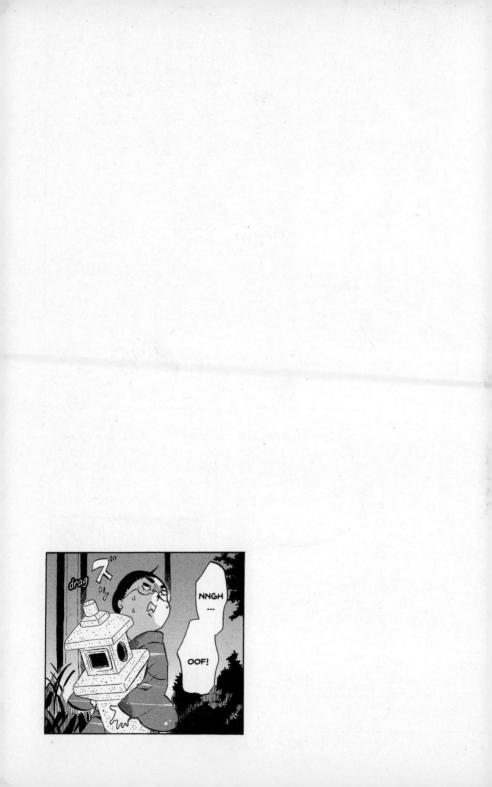

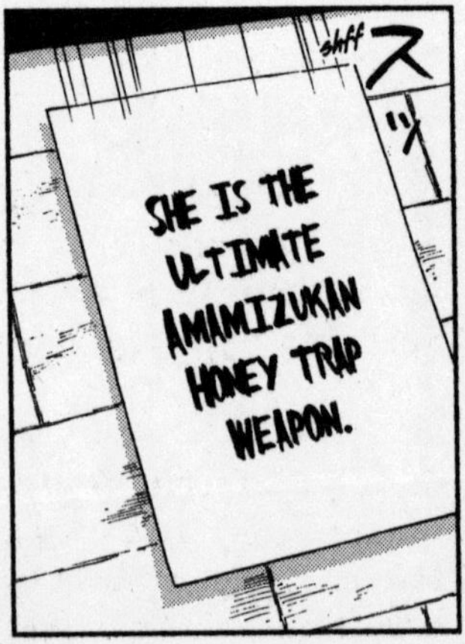shff
スッ
SHE IS THE ULTIMATE AMAMIZUKAN HONEY TRAP WEAPON.

Translation Notes

The Three Sacred Regalia of the Stylish People, page 189
This is a riff on the Three Sacred Regalia of Japan, also called the Imperial Regalia. These three sacred treasures are a sword, a mirror, and a jewel; the jewel is comma-shaped and known as a *magatama*. The Regalia are presented to each new Japanese emperor.

Sannen Netaro, page 192
Sannen Netaro is the title character of a Japanese folk tale. There are many different variations, but the point here is that this character slept for three years and was considered lazy by his village.

Nwaaahhh! Run 1,000 li with our boxes, Black Cat Y----o!!, page 205
The Kuroneko Yamato shipping service is overlapping with Red Hare, the horse, in Mayaya's mind, because "Kuroneko" means "Black Cat."

The Sorcerer's Younger Brother, page 219
While this title comes from *The Sorcerer's Apprentice* in Japanese, the same phrase can be interpreted to mean "the sorcerer's younger brother" or "the younger brother, who is a sorcerer."

Shimizu no Jirocho, page 223
Shimizu no Jirocho isn't a place like Nagatacho. Rather, he's a historical figure—a highly successful 1800s outlaw who has been romanticized into a folk hero in the years since.

Magical Girl Theme, page 254
Kuranosuke is dressed and coiffed very much in the *Himitsu no Akko*-chan style, and "*teku-maku-mayakon*" is Akko-chan's famous spell chant. Akko-chan isn't a well-known magical girl in the U.S., but she's so famous in Japan that even Mayaya recognizes the cosplay.

Ameba Pigg, page 259
Ameba Pigg is a Japanese virtual world platform which at one time had an equivalent English-language Facebook app called Pico World. Pico World shut down in 2012.

Ouyang Fei Fei and Konnyaku Batake, page 278
Ouyang Fei Fei is the vocalist who performed "Love Is Over," one of the songs on Hanamori's "Mood Music to Bring You Closer" mix in Volume 4. The company called MannanLife sells the jelly snack called Konnyaku Batake.

Children of Men, page 283
This 2006 film was released as *Tomorrow World* in Japan, underlining the "changing times" theme of this chapter.

You're like Madame Hosoki with her scary predictions that she puts so bluntly., page 293
Kazuko Hosoki is a celebrity fortune-teller who was also parodied in the anime *Nerima Daikon Brothers*, where she was the basis for the character Gokutsubushi. She's famous for starting dramatic proclamations with *zubari iu*, or "I'll tell it to you straight."

Ultimate Weapon Tsukimi, page 323
"She, the Ultimate Amamizukan Honey Trap Weapon" is a riff on the manga *Saikano*, aka *She, The Ultimate Weapon*.

Mother, when did you throw over Bae Yong Joon for Gongchan?, page 327
Gong Chansik, aka Gongchan, is a member of the Korean boy band B1A4. They've released a number of their songs in Japanese as well, including separately-filmed Japanese versions of their music videos, and have a large following in Japan.

I got carried away and did a Kikkawa pose., page 334
Singer-songwriter Koji Kikkawa is the king of the dramatic pose. Like Elvis, his singing is smooth, and his onstage movements and hand gestures are striking.

KC
KODANSHA
COMICS

"I'm pleasantly surprised to find modern shojo using cross-dressing as a dramatic device to deliver social commentary... Recommended."

-Otaku USA Magazine

The prince in his dark days

By Hico Yamanaka

A drunkard for a father, a household of poverty... For 17-year-old Atsuko, misfortune is all she knows and believes in. Until one day, a chance encounter with Itaru–the wealthy heir of a huge corporation–changes everything. The two look identical, uncannily so. When Itaru curiously goes missing, Atsuko is roped into being his stand-in. There, in his shoes, Atsuko must parade like a prince in a palace. She encounters many new experiences, but at what cost...?

© Hico Yamanaka/Kodansha Ltd. All rights reserved

KC

KODANSHA
COMICS

Japan's most powerful spirit medium delves into the ghost world's greatest mysteries!

Story by Kyo Shirodaira, famed author of mystery fiction and creator of *Spiral*, *Blast of Tempest*, and *The Record of a Fallen Vampire*.

Both touched by spirits called yôkai, Kotoko and Kurô have gained unique superhuman powers. But to gain her powers Kotoko has given up an eye and a leg, and Kurô's personal life is in shambles. So when Kotoko suggests they team up to deal with renegades from the spirit world, Kurô doesn't have many other choices, but Kotoko might just have a few ulterior motives...

IN/SPECTRE

STORY BY **KYO SHIRODAIRA**
ART BY **CHASHIBA KATASE**

© Kyo Shirodaira/Kodansha Ltd. All rights reserved.

"Parasyte fans should get a kick out of the chance to revisit Iwaaki's weird, violent, strangely affecting universe. Recommended." -Otaku USA Magazine

"A great anthology containing an excellent variety of genres and styles." -Manga Bookshelf

Based on the critically acclaimed classic horror manga

The first new *Parasyte* manga in over 20 years!

NEO PARASYTE f

BY ASUMIKO NAKAMURA, EMA TOYAMA, MIKI RINNO, LALAKO KOJIMA, KAORI YUKI, BANKO KUZE, YUUKI OBATA, KASHIO, YUI KUROE, ASIA WATANABE, MIKIMAKI, HIKARU SURUGA, HAJIME SHINJO, RENJURO KINDAICHI, AND YURI NARUSHIMA

A collection of chilling new *Parasyte* stories from Japan's top shojo artists!

Parasites: shape-shifting aliens whose only purpose is to assimilate with and consume the human race... but do these monsters have a different side? A parasite becomes a prince to save his romance-obsessed female host from a dangerous stalker. Another hosts a cooking show, in which the real monsters are revealed. These and 13 more stories, from some of the greatest shojo manga artists alive today, together make up a chilling, funny, and entertaining tribute to one of manga's horror classics!

© Hitoshi Iwaaki, Asumiko Nakamura, Ema Toyama, Miki Rinno, Lalako Kojima, Kaori Yuki, Banko Kuze, Yuuki Obata, Kashio, Yui Kuroe, Asia Watanabe, Mikimaki, Hikaru Suruga, Hajime Shinjo, Renjuro Kindaichi, Yuri Narushima/Kodansha Ltd. All rights reserved.

KC
KODANSHA
COMICS

The award-winning manga about what happens inside you!

"Far more entertaining than it ought to be... what kid doesn't want to think that every time they sneeze a torpedo shoots out their nose?"
—Anime News Network

Strep throat! Hay fever! Influenza! The world is a dangerous place for a red blood cell just trying to get her deliveries finished. Fortunately, she's not alone...she's got a whole human body's worth of cells ready to help out! The mysterious white blood cells, the buff and brash killer T cells, even the cute little platelets— everyone's got to come together if they want to keep you healthy!

Cells at Work!

はたらく細胞

By Akane Shimizu

© Akane Shimizu/Kodansha Ltd. All rights reserved.

Having lost his wife, high school teacher Kōhei Inuzuka is doing his best to raise his young daughter Tsumugi as a single father. He's pretty bad at cooking and doesn't have a huge appetite to begin with, but chance brings his little family together with one of his students, the lonely Kotori. The three of them are anything but comfortable in the kitchen, but the healing power of home cooking might just work on their grieving hearts.

"This season's number-one feel-good anime!" —Anime News Network

"A beautifully-drawn story about comfort food and family and grief. Recommended." —Otaku USA Magazine

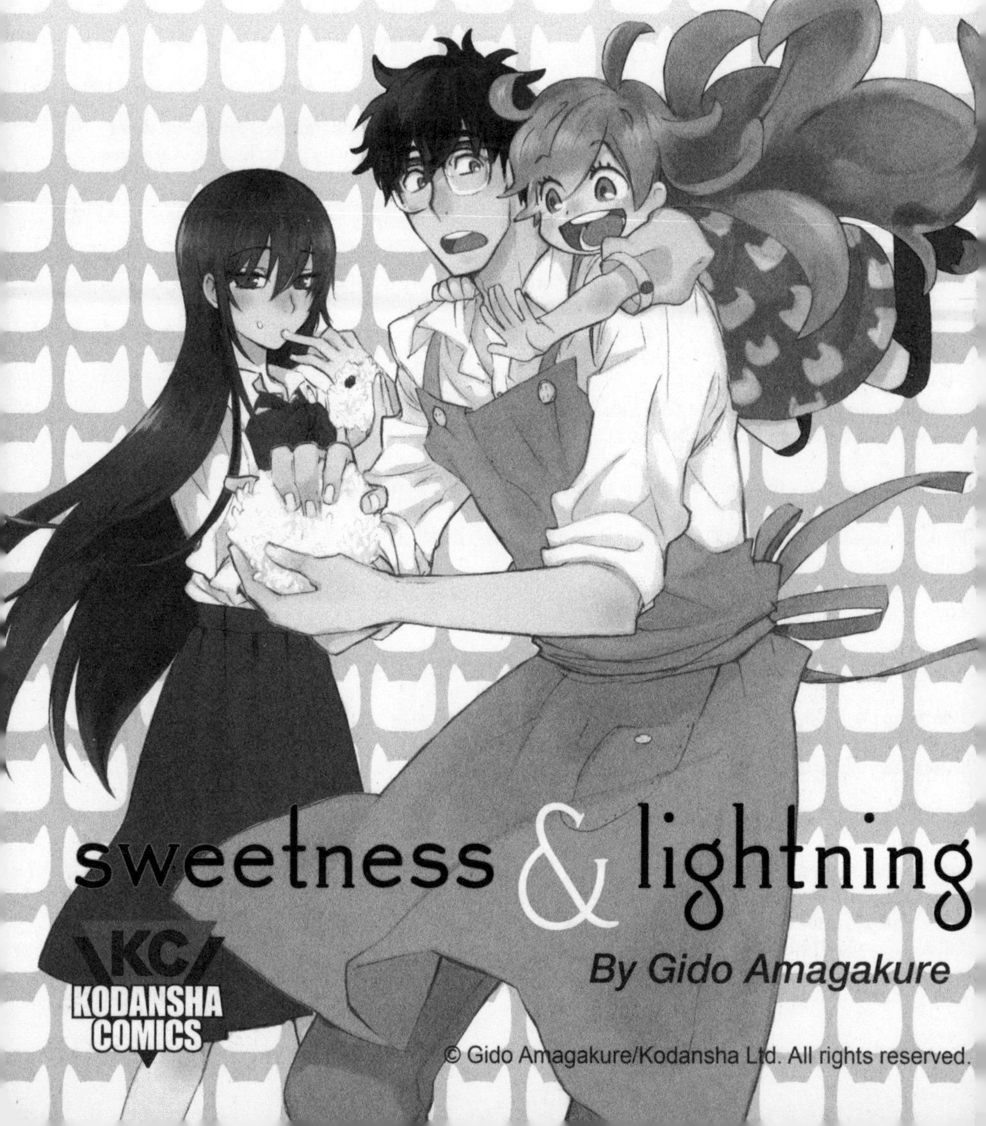

sweetness & lightning

By Gido Amagakure

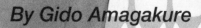
© Gido Amagakure/Kodansha Ltd. All rights reserved.

KC
KODANSHA COMICS

Princess Jellyfish volume 5 is a work of fiction. Names, characters, places, and incidents are the products of the author's imagination or are used fictitiously. Any resemblance to actual events, locales, or persons, living or dead, is entirely coincidental.

A Kodansha Comics Trade Paperback Original.

Princess Jellyfish volume 5 copyright © 2012 Akiko Higashimura
English translation copyright © 2017 Akiko Higashimura

All rights reserved.

Published in the United States by Kodansha Comics,
an imprint of Kodansha USA Publishing, LLC, New York.

Publication rights for this English edition arranged through Kodansha Ltd., Tokyo.

First published in Japan in 2012 by Kodansha Ltd., Tokyo,
as *Kuragehime* volumes 9 & 10.

ISBN 978-1-63236-233-9

Icon design by UCHIKOGA tomoyuki & RAITA ryoko (CHProduction Inc.)

Printed in the United States of America.

www.kodanshacomics.com

9 8 7 6 5 4 3 2 1

Translation: Sarah Alys Lindholm
Lettering: Carl Vanstiphout
Additional Layout: Belynda Ungurath
Editing: Haruko Hashimoto
Kodansha Comics Edition Cover Design: Phil Balsman